ACING THE SECURITY+ CERTIFICATION EXAM

Patrick Regan

PEARSON
Prentice
Hall

Upper Saddle River, New Jersey
Columbus, Ohio

Library of Congress Cataloging in Publication Data

Regan, Patrick E.
  Acing the security+ certification exam/Patrick Regan. — 1st ed.
      p.cm.
Includes index.
ISBN 0-13-112164-2 (pbk.)
    1. Electronic data processing personnel—Certification. 2. Computer networks—
    Examinations—Study guides. 3. Computer security—Examinations—Study guides.
I. Title.

QA76.3.R455 2005
005.8—dc20

2003066395

Editor in Chief: Stephen Helba
Assistant Vice President and Publisher: Charles E. Stewart, Jr.
Assistant Editor: Mayda Bosco
Production Editor: Alexandrina Benedicto Wolf
Production Coordination: Carlisle Publishers Services
Design Coordinator: Diane Ernsberger
Cover Designer: Kristina Holmes
Cover art: PhotoDisc
Production Manager: Matt Ottenweller
Marketing Manager: Ben Leonard

This book was set in Times by Carlisle Communications, Ltd. It was printed and bound by
Courier Kendallville, Inc. The cover was printed by Phoenix Color Corp.

Pearson Education Ltd.
Pearson Education Singapore Pte. Ltd.
Pearson Education Canada, Ltd.
Pearson Education—Japan

Pearson Education Australia Pty. Limited
Pearson Education North Asia Ltd.
Pearson Educación de Mexico, S.A. de C.V.
Pearson Education Malaysia Pte. Ltd.

10 9 8 7 6 5 4 3 2 1
ISBN 0-13-112164-2

This book is dedicated to Charles Stewart, Mayda Bosco,
and Alex Wolf for their great support of this and other books.

Brief Contents

Contents

Preface

In the last 15 years, the networking of computers has grown at an exponential rate. While it was then common for people to carry data on disks back and forth between computers, data transfer can now be done within seconds across the world. It wasn't long before one network was connected to another network, which was then connected to another network. Eventually the Internet that we know today connected millions of computers around the world.

Unfortunately, connecting all of these together also brings other issues with which everyone needs to be concerned. You often see and hear of security issues that can plague a company. Therefore, it is important that you take the extra steps in securing your computers, network resources, and data.

This book is intended to prepare someone for CompTIA's Security+ certification exam. This book will not only prepare you for the exam, but will also make you a better administrator. Therefore, this book does go beyond the scope of the Security+ exam.

This book already assumes that you know about PCs, how they work, and how to configure and troubleshoot them. It also assumes that you already know about network operating systems and networks. This book teaches you how to secure your network from unauthorized access by using routers and firewalls. It discusses how to secure major network operating systems, including Microsoft Windows, Linux, and Novell NetWare. It also discusses how to secure your major network applications/ services. Most of all, it discusses the plans, procedures, and policies you need to have in place and the training you will need to help keep your network secure.

I would like to thank the following reviewers for their valuable input: Phillip Davis, Del Mar College, TX; Gary Kessler, Champlain College, VT; Jeffrey L. Rankinen, Pennsylvania College of Technology; and Rob Robertson, Southern Utah University.

CompTIA Security+ Certification Exam Objectives

1. General Security Concepts

1.1.	Access Control 1.1.1. MAC/DAC/RBAC	Section 2.4 Section 2.4.4

1.2.	Authentication
	    1.2.1. Kerberos
	    1.2.2. CHAP
	    1.2.3. Certificates
	    1.2.4. Username/Password
	    1.2.5. Tokens
	    1.2.6. Multi-Factor
	    1.2.7. Mutual Authentication
	    1.2.8. Biometrics
		Section 2.4 and Section 5.4
		Section 5.6.4
		Section 7.3.3
		Section 5.4.5
		Section 5.4.1
		Section 5.4.6
		Section 5.4
		Section 5.4
		Section 5.4.7

1.3.	Nonessential Services and Protocols—Disabling unnecessary systems / process / programs.	Section 2.4.7, 12.6 and 12.6.2

1.4.	Attacks
	    1.4.1. DOS/DDOS
	    1.4.2. Back Door
	    1.4.3. Spoofing
	    1.4.4. Man in the Middle
	    1.4.5. Replay
	    1.4.6. TCP/IP Hijacking
	    1.4.7. Weak Keys
	    1.4.8. Mathematical
	    1.4.9. Social Engineering
	    1.4.10. Birthday
	    1.4.11. Password Guessing
	           1.4.11.1 Brute Force
	           1.4.11.2 Dictionary
	    1.4.12. Software Exploitation
		Section 5.8, 12.1, 12.2
		Section 12.1
		Section 12.2.8
		Section 12.1.2
		Section 12.1.3
		Section 12.1.3
		Section 12.1.3
		Section 5.8.1
		Section 5.8.1
		Section 2.4.6
		Section 5.8.1
		Section 5.8
		Section 5.8.1
		Section 5.8.1
		Section 12.2.8

1.5.	Malicious Code
	    1.5.1. Viruses
	    1.5.2. Trojan Horses
	    1.5.3. Logic Bombs
	    1.5.4. Worms
		Section 12.2
		Section 12.2.1, 12.2.5, 12.2.6 and 12.2.7
		Section 12.2.2
		Section 12.2.8
		Section 12.2.3

1.6.	Social Engineering	Section 2.4.6
1.7.	Auditing—Logging, system scanning	Section 12.4 and 12.5

4. Basics of Cryptography

5. Operational/Organizational Security

5.1.	Physical Security	Section 6.1
	5.1.1. Access Control	Section 6.1
	5.1.1.1. Physical Barriers	Section 6.1
	5.1.1.2. Biometrics	Section 6.1
	5.1.2. Social Engineering	Section 2.4.6
	5.1.3. Environment	Section 2.4.1
	5.1.3.1. Wireless Cells	Section 8.1 and 8.4.7
	5.1.3.2. Location	Section 8.4.7
	5.1.3.3. Shielding	Section 8.4.7
	5.1.3.4. Fire Suppression	Section 13.10
5.2.	Disaster Recovery	Chapter 13
	5.2.1. Backups	Section 13.9
	5.2.1.1 Offsite Storage	Section 13.9
	5.2.2. Secure Recovery	Section 13.2
	5.2.2.1 Alternate Sites	Section 13.2
	5.2.3. Disaster Recovery Plan	Section 13.3
5.3.	Business Continuity	Chapter 13
	5.3.1. Utilities	Section 13.6
	5.3.2. High Availability/Fault Tolerance	Chapter 13
	5.3.3. Backups	Section 13.9
5.4.	Policy and Procedures	Section 2.5.4
	5.4.1. Security Policy	Section 2.5.4
	5.4.1.1 Acceptable Use	Section 2.5.4
	5.4.1.2 Due Care	Section 2.5.4
	5.4.1.3 Privacy	Section 2.5.4
	5.4.1.4 Separation of Duties	Section 2.1
	5.4.1.5 Need to Know	Section 2.1
	5.4.1.6 Password Management	Section 2.5.4
	5.4.1.7 SLA	Section 2.5.4
	5.4.1.8 Disposal/Destruction	Section 2.5.4
	5.4.1.9 HR Policy	Section 2.5.4
	5.4.1.9.1 Termination—Adding/revoking passwords, privileges, etc.	Section 2.5.4
	5.4.1.9.2 Hiring—Adding/revoking passwords, privileges, etc.	Section 2.5.4
	5.4.1.9.3 Code of Ethics	Section 2.5
	5.4.2. Incident Response Policy	Section 2.5.4 and 12.7
5.5.	Privilege Management	Section 4.1.4
	5.5.1. User/Group/Role Management	Section 2.1.3
	5.5.2. Single Sign-on	Section 2.1.4 and 4.5.1
	5.5.3. Centralized vs. Decentralized	Section 2.1.4 and 4.1.6
	5.5.4. Auditing (Privilege, Usage, Escalation)	Section 2.4.3 and 12.4
	5.5.5. MAC/DAC/RBAC	Section 2.4.4
5.6.	Forensics (Awareness, Conceptual Knowledge and Understanding—Know What Your Role Is)	Section 12.7
	5.6.1. Chain of Custody	Section 12.7
	5.6.2. Preservation of Evidence	Section 12.7
	5.6.3. Collection of Evidence	Section 12.7

## CHAPTER 1

CompTIA and the Security+ Certification Exam

Topics Covered in this Chapter

Introduction

Before we start covering the material that is on the Security+ exam, you should take a look at who is CompTIA and what is the Security+ exam. Understanding how the Security+ fits into the IT scheme will let you see the "big picture." In addition, this chapter will also take a quick look on how to study for the Security+ exam and how to overcome test anxiety.

Objectives

1. Describe who is CompTIA.
2. Describe the Security+ exam and how it relates to IT jobs and careers.
3. Describe how to study for the Security+ exam.
4. Describe how to overcome test anxiety.

1.1   THE VALUE OF CERTIFICATION

It is an established fact that computers and networking are fast-paced environments. Therefore, employees who work in Information Technology (IT) must learn to keep up with ever-changing technology and have the ability to learn new technology. It is said that a person in IT must be able to learn or retrain him or herself every 1 to 1½ years.

According to *Certification Magazine* (http://www.certmag.com), the successful IT worker must:

- Be proficient in two or more technical specialties.
- Be able to wear multiple hats.
- Be more business-oriented because hiring managers will be looking for employees who see the big picture of profit, loss, competitive advantage, and customer retention, and who understand that IT fits into this picture.
- Able to work easily with nontechnical personnel.
- Must have soft skills of good listening, problem solving, and effective written and verbal communication.

In addition, there is a demand for those who can demonstrate expertise in IT project management. Those moving from a mid- to high-level position will have a mix of academic credentials and industry certifications, as well as increasing levels of responsibility.

Today, technical certifications are highly valuable. Depending on which certification or certifications an individual has, they can allow a user to begin as an entry-level technician or administrator or it demonstrates the knowledge and capabilities of a current technician or administrator. Technical companies see some technical certifications are as valuable as a college degree, and nontechnical companies see them just as a little less than a college degree.

In 2001, researchers from Gartner Consulting surveyed nearly 18,000 IT managers, certified professionals, and certification candidates. They reported that:

- IT professionals seek certification to increase compensation, find employment, or boost productivity.
- Of those certified, 66 percent of certified professionals received an increase in salary after becoming certified, and 83 percent reported that certification helped them gain a new position.
- Although most certification candidates combine several study methods, printed materials designed for self-study and instructor-led training were reported as the most useful preparation methods.

From the employer's perspective, although many managers (42 percent) feared that certified employees would move on to another organization, 71 percent of IT professionals gaining certification stay put. IT managers cited a higher level of service, competitive advantage, and increased productivity as key benefits of having certified staff. Of course, the drawbacks include cost of training and testing.

So, as you can see, many people in IT view certification as a valuable tool. Certification is:

- A demonstration of specific areas of competence with particular technologies.
- A credential desired or required by an increasing number of employers.
- A tool people use successfully to challenge themselves.
- A road map for continuing education.
- A potential bridge to a new specialty.
- Evidence that you are self-motivated and actively working to stay current.

On the other hand, certification is not a substitute for extensive hands-on experience, and it is not a career cure-all. Finally, usually a little bit of work and discipline is needed to pass these exams.

1.2   CompTIA

The Computing Technology Industry Association (CompTIA) is a nonprofit organization that represents more than 8,000 computing and communications companies. CompTIA's main goal is to develop vendor-neutral certifications to provide credibility, recognition of achievement, and quality assurance.

Employers and recruiters benefit from the widespread acceptance of certification credentials. First, CompTIA certifications simplify recruiting and hiring because an appropriate vendor-neutral certification assures a minimum knowledge level in applicants thus gaining higher-quality candidates while minimizing the initial applicant screening process. In addition, since it is not tied to a particular vendor's product, this means greater flexibility in a fast-changing technology marketplace. Finally, it reduces the redundancy of being similarly certified as people move from one organization to another. Of course, for the certified individuals, the benefits would include enhanced job opportunities, career enhancement, and recognized proof of professional achievement.

CompTIA currently offers several certifications (and this is still expanding) that identify the necessary skills for individuals to perform their job competently and successfully. They include:

- **A+**—Entry-level personal computer technology.
- **Certified Document Imaging Architech (CDIA+)**—Mastery-level document-imaging technology.
- **i-Net+**—Base-level Internet technologies.
- **Network+**—Networking technologies.
- **Server+**—Industry Standard Server Architecture Technologies.
- **Linux+**—Vendor-neutral Linux knowledge.
- **IT Project+**—Project management for IT.
- **e-Biz+**—Electronic Business.
- **CTT+**—Technical Trainer.
- **Security+**—Network Security.

1.3   SECURITY+ EXAM

Anyone who has been working with networks already knows the importance of security. Over the last couple of years as the Internet grew and connected to most networks, security has become even more important. Today, you have to protect the network against someone breaking in or hacking your network, viruses, and denial-of-service attacks. So it is easy to see the importance of having qualified people to protect your network.

The CompTIA Security+ certification exam is targeted at professionals with at least 2 years of networking experience who possess a thorough knowledge of TCP/IP. Those holding the Security+ certification have demonstrated the aptitude and ability to master such knowledge areas as:

- General security concepts.
- Communications security.
- Infrastructure security.
- Basics of cryptography.
- Operational/organizational security.

The CompTIA Security+ certification is a strong foundation that can be applied to a wide variety of careers in many industries. While some jobs are security-specific, there is no one who works with networks who would not benefit from being Security+ certified.

The Security+ test contains situational, traditional, and identification types of questions. There is either one answer for each question or the question identifies how many answers you should select. While the test covers a broad range of hardware and software technologies, it is not bound to any vendor-specific or distribution-specific product.

The exam code for the Server+ test is currently SY0-101. The CompTIA Security+ exam consists of one hundred questions to be completed in 90 minutes. You must score a 764 out of 900 (85%) correctly to pass the exam.

The Security+ certification is open to anyone who wants to take the test. No specific requirements are necessary, except the payment of the fee. However, it is highly recommended that you have A+ and Network+ certifications or equivalent knowledge.

In the event that a candidate fails his or her first attempt to pass any CompTIA certification test, CompTIA does not require any waiting period between the first and second attempt to pass that same CompTIA certification test. However, before any candidate's third attempt or any subsequent attempt to pass any CompTIA certification test, such candidate shall be required to wait for a period of at least 30 calendar days from the date of such candidate's last attempt to pass such test.

You may register by selecting one of the following test vendors:

NCS/VUE

http://www.vue.com/comptia/

Prometric

http://www.2test.com/index.jsp

When you take the test, try to arrive at the testing center at least 15 minutes before the test is scheduled to begin. The administrator of the testing center can demonstrate how to use the computer-based testing system before the actual test begins. Two forms of identification must be presented to the test-center administrator. One form should be a photo ID, such as a valid driver's license. The other can be a major credit card or a passport. Please be aware that both forms of identification must have a signature. Books, calculators, laptop computers, or other reference materials are not allowed during the test. Because the test is computer-based, pens, pencils, or paper will not be needed. It is CompTIA's policy to make reasonable accommodations for individuals with disabilities.

As soon as you finish the test, you receive the final score. You will see the results immediately on the computer screen. In addition, a hard copy of the score report is provided at the testing center. The score report shows whether or not you passed the certification. It will also show all objectives related to every item not answered correctly. It can be used to verify your certification until your certificate arrives.

For more information, please refer to the following websites:

COMPTIA Home Page

http://www.comptia.org

Security+ Certification

http://www.comptia.org/certification/Security/default.asp

NOTE: Since the Security+ exam may change in content or format, you should refer to the above web addresses before you take the exam.

1.4 CAREERS IN IT

Everyone will agree that computers and the Internet are here to stay. In addition, the need to connect computers to form a network and to connect computers at home and in businesses to the Internet is still great. Even if you don't choose a career in computers and technology, the reality of today's workplace is that you're going to be using computers, whatever your job.

There are education, sales, training, managerial, and customer service jobs in the computer and technology industries. For these jobs, you don't have to know programming or electronic design. Liberal arts graduates, business majors, and many others find careers in computers and technology. Of course, it does help if you've been bitten by the "computer bug" and find technology fascinating.

Most workers in the field of computers and technology make considerably more than the average wage for all workers in the United States. Salaries vary with the job performed, the experience, the location, the amount of responsibility, and other factors, but many computer and technology jobs start in the $20,000 to $40,000 range and go much higher with experience. Note: While money is important to many people, you should always choose a career that you know you will enjoy.

Most jobs require a combination of technical and people skills. Today, being able to speak well, write well, and relate to other people (frequently people less technically savvy than you are) is very important. Every day brings something new in the field of computers and technology. If you want to be part of that process, if you're up to the challenge of constantly pushing the boundaries of new technology and harnessing it for useful work, there's a place for you in computers and technology.

While the economy may have hiccupped in 2001 and 2002, the need for technical-trained people is still as important as ever, and the number of these jobs is still growing. Job growth is projected to be above average for nearly all careers in computers and technology. In addition, while new studies find that employers will attempt to fill many new IT jobs, many of these positions will go unfilled because of a lack of applicants with the requisite technical and nontechnical skills.

A recent study by the Information Technology Association of America (ITAA) reports that IT companies view IT certifications as at least as important as a bachelor's degree; non-IT companies placed certifications slightly below a bachelor's degree in importance.

Finally, if you choose technology as your career, you should be prepared to retrain or reeducate yourself approximately every 1 to 1½ years. This is, of course, needed to stay current with today's ever-changing technology.

1.5   LOOKING FOR A JOB

Now after you have earned yourself one or more certificates and you feel comfortable with computers, you are finally going to have to look for a job. A while ago, if you had a network engineer certification, it was thought to be a guarantee of a job. Unfortunately, many people looking to change jobs would purchase practice tests, study the practice tests, pass the certification tests without ever installing a network operating system, and then look for a job. At this time, this has devalued the certification because these people do not have hands-on experience. Today, if you get a certification, many jobs are still looking for 1 year of experience. But after you get that 1 year of experience, your job opportunities increase greatly.

So what do you need to do? First, you will have to prepare at least two resumes. The resume is a document that describes your knowledge, skills, and experiences. The reason for at least two resumes is you will need one that is formatted with fonts, and styles such as boldface, italics, and underlines, while the other one will be a plain-text document with no formatting. The formatted resume is what you will give when you go on interviews and what you can send using email. The unformatted document is what you will use to post on job websites.

Of course, in either case, you want the resume to be readable and well organized. In addition, you should make sure that you are using correct English and spelling. Remember, that the resume represents you, and if the resume is not organized well, then the reader may also assume that you are not well organized. Note: Being organized is a valuable trait when working in IT. In addition, the English and spelling will show some of your communication ability and attention to detail.

When you apply for a job via the mail or email, you should also create a cover letter. While the resume tells the reader your qualifications for a job, the cover letter should tell the reader why you are a good fit for the specific job for which you are applying. I would even recommend listing each of the requirements that the company posted for the job and explaining why you are qualified for this job.

Eventually, you will get someone's attention, and you will have to go for an interview. First, you should dress well. That does not necessarily mean dressing in a business suit. But you should consider a nice shirt (and possibly a tie for males). While many IT jobs have a relaxed dress code, you should dress a little bit better than the job for which you are applying because it shows your professionalism. Of course, make sure that your clothes are neat and in good repair. Finally, make sure that you are clean-cut and well-scrubbed.

When you go for the interview, make sure that you are friendly and very attentive. It also doesn't hurt to smile. If the interviewer asks you a question and you really don't know the answer, say that you don't know the answer. When the interview is done, you should immediately send a thank-you letter thanking the interviewer for his or her time. In addition, if questions were asked and you did not know the answer, you should research them and include your response in the letter. This shows that you really want the job and that you can find the answers when you need them. Note: Of course, in IT jobs, you will not know all of the answers, but how quickly you find the answers will make or break a network administrator.

So the next question is, where do you find a job? Well, first, you would check the newspaper. Of course, when an IT job is posted in a newspaper, it could mean that many people will apply for the job, many of whom are not qualified. So you need to make sure that your cover letter and resume show that you are more than qualified.

The next place to go is to job agencies, specifically job agencies that handle technical jobs. These job agencies will have some permanent jobs and will most likely have more temporary jobs. A temporary job allows you to try out a company, but it also allows the company to try you out before permanently hiring you. It is also the role of the job agency to find and screen qualified applicants, especially since many jobs remain open for long periods of time because the company cannot find qualified applicants.

Next, you want to use the Internet. First, if there is a particular company that you want to work for, go to its website and find what jobs are available and where you can send your resume.

In addition, go to job websites, particular those that focus on technology. When looking for a job, this is where you can get the most job leads. Of course, how you fill out your profile on the web page is just as important as your resume. In addition, this is where you can post your resume, most likely the unformatted resume.

Some good job websites include:

Dice

> http://www.dice.com/

Monster

> http://www.monster.com/
> http://technology.monster.com/

Hot Jobs

> http://www.hotjobs.com/index.html
> http://www.hotjobs.com/htdocs/channels/tech/

Tech-Engine

> http://www.tech-engine.com/

Computer Jobs

> http://www.computerjobs.com

Careerbuilder.com

> http://www.careerbuilder.com/
> http://informationtechnology.careerbuilder.com

Techies.com

> http://www.techies.com/

Career Mag

> http://www.careermag.com/

ManPower Inc.

> http://www.manpower.com
> http://www.manpower.com/mpcom/JobSearch.jsp

Another important source of jobs is not through any advertisement, but through networking. In this case, networking is meeting people and making contacts with other people. From these people, when a company needs to hire someone, you will get the job because of who you know. Of course, in most of these cases, you will still need to show that you have the necessary skills and experience for the new position, but you will get opportunities that would not be open to the general public.

1.6   STUDYING FOR YOUR EXAM

While many websites offer information on *what* to study for a particular exam, few sites offer information on *how* you should study for an exam. The study process can be broken down into various stages. However, key to all of these stages is the ability to concentrate. Concentration, or the lack thereof, plays a big part in the study process.

To be able to concentrate, you must remove all distractions. While you should plan for study breaks, it is the unplanned breaks caused by distractions that do not allow you to concentrate on what you need to learn. Therefore, first, you need to create an environment that's conducive to studying or seek out an existing environment that meets these criteria, like a library.

First, do not study with the TV on, and do not have other people in the room. It is easy for the TV to break your concentration and grab your attention. In addition, if you have people in the room, you have to pretend that you are not there and that they are not causing distractions, including talking with other people. Finally, there are varying opinions on whether it is better to study with or without music playing. While some people need to have a little white noise in the background to study, if you do choose to have music, you should keep the volume on a low level, and you should listen to music without vocals in it.

After you find a place to study, you must schedule the time to study. This should take into consideration not to study on an empty stomach. You should also not study on a full stomach, since it tends to make people drowsy. You may also consider having a glass of water nearby to sip on.

In addition, make sure you are well rested so that you don't start dozing off when you start. Next, make sure that you find a position that is comfortable and that the furniture that you are using is also comfortable. Finally, make sure that your study area is well lit. Natural light is best for fighting fatigue.

The first thing that you should do when you study is to clear your mind of distractions. So take a minute or two, close your eyes, and empty your mind.

When you prepare for an exam, the best place to start is to take the list of exam objectives and study them carefully for their scope. During this time, you then organize your study keeping these objectives in mind. This will narrow down your focus area to an individual topic or subtopic. In addition, you need to understand and visualize the process as a whole. This will help address practical problems in a real environment, as well as some unsuspecting questions.

In a multiple-choice-type exam, you do have one advantage: The answer or answers are already there, and you simply choose the correct ones. Since the answers are already there, you can start eliminating the incorrect answers using your knowledge and some logical thinking. One common mistake is to select the first obvious-looking answers without checking the other options, so always examine all the options, think, and choose the right answer. Of course, with multiple-choice questions, you have to be exact and should be able to differentiate between very similar answers. This is where a peaceful place of study without distractions helps so that you can read between the lines and so that you don't miss key points.

1.7   DEALING WITH TEST ANXIETY

Since a certification exam costs money to take and time to prepare for, and failing an exam can be a blow to your self-confidence, most people feel a certain amount of anxiety when they are about to take a certification exam. It is no wonder that most of us are a little sweaty in the palms when taking the exam. However, certain levels of stress can actually help you raise your level of performance when taking an exam. This anxiety usually serves to help you focus your concentration and think clearly through a problem.

But for some individuals, exam anxiety is more than just a nuisance. For these people, exam anxiety is a debilitating condition that affects their performance resulting in a negative impact on the exam results.

Exam anxiety reduction begins with the preparation process. The first thing that you should think of is that if you know the material, there should not be anything that you should be nervous over. It goes without saying that the better prepared you are for an exam, the less stress you will experience when taking it. Always give yourself plenty of time to prepare for an exam; don't place yourself under unreasonable deadlines. But again, make goals and make every effort to meet those goals. Procrastination and making excuses will only add to exam anxiety.

There is not a hard-and-fast rule for how long it takes to prepare for an exam. The time required will vary from student to student and depends on a number of different factors, including reading speed, access to study materials, personal commitments, and so on. In addition, don't compare yourself to peers, especially if doing so has a negative effect on your confidence.

For many students, practice exams are a great way to shed some of the fears that arise in the test center. Practice exams are best used near the end of the exam preparation, and be sure to use them as an assessment of your current knowledge, not as a method for memorizing key concepts. When reviewing these questions, be sure you understand the question and understand all answers (right and wrong). Finally, set time limits on the practice exams.

If you know the material, don't plan on studying the day of your exam. You should end your studying the evening before the exam. In addition, don't make it a late night so that you can get a full good night's rest. Of course, you should be studying on a regular basis for at least a few weeks prior to the evening of the exam so that you should not need last-minute cramming.

Before you take an exam, eat something light, even if you have no appetite. If your stomach is actively upset, try mild foods like toast or crackers. Plain saltine crackers are great for settling a cranky stomach. Keep your caffeine and nicotine consumption to a minimum; excessive stimulants aren't exactly conducive to reducing stress. Plan to take a bottle of water or lozenges or hard candies with you to combat dry mouth.

Arrive at the testing center early and dress comfortably. If you have never been to the testing center before, make sure that you know where it is at. You may even consider taking a test drive. If you arrive between 15 and 30 minutes early for any certification exam, it gives you:

- Ample time for prayer, meditation, and/or breathing.
- Time to scan glossary terms and quick access tables before taking the exam so that you can get the intellectual juices flowing and to build a little confidence.
- Time to practice physical relaxation techniques.
- Time to visit the washroom.

But don't arrive too early.

When you are escorted into the testing chamber, you will usually be given two sheets of paper (or laminated paper) with pen or pencil (or wet-erase pen). As soon as you hear the door close behind you, immediately unload bits of exam information that you need to quickly recall onto the paper. Then throughout the exam, you can refer to this information easily without thinking about it. This way, you can focus on answering the questions and use this information as reference. Then before you actually start the exam, close your eyes and take a deep breath to clear your mind of distractions.

WHAT YOU NEED TO KNOW

1. The Computing Technology Industry Association (CompTIA) is a nonprofit organization that represents more than 8,000 computing and communications companies.
2. CompTIA's main goal is to develop vendor-neutral certifications to provide credibility, recognition of achievement, and quality assurance.
3. Security is very important.
4. The CompTIA Security+ certification exam is targeted at professionals with at least 2 years of networking experience who possess a thorough knowledge of TCP/IP.
5. The CompTIA Security+ certification is a strong foundation that can be applied to a wide variety of careers in many industries.
6. No matter what networking job that you have, you will always benefit from being Security+ certified.
7. After you have earned yourself one or more certificates and you feel comfortable with computers, you are finally going to have to look for a job.
8. When you prepare for an exam, the best place to start is to take the list of exam objectives and study the objectives carefully for their scope.
9. Since a certification exam costs money to take and time to prepare for, and failing an exam can be a blow to their self-confidence, most people feel a certain amount of anxiety when they are about to take a certification exam.

HANDS-ON EXERCISES

1. Go to www.dice.com and search for networking jobs. Specifically look for jobs looking for security specialists and jobs that require or recommend the CompTIA Sercurity+ certification.
2. Go to two other jobs sites and perform the same type of search.
3. Go to the website of your local newspaper and perform the same type of search.
4. Choose a company that you might want to work for. Then go to its website and find out what jobs are available and what you would need to apply for those jobs.

CHAPTER 2

Introduction to Security

Topics Covered in this Chapter

Introduction

Before you implement security, you need to first look at what you are trying to protect and what you are trying to protect it from. After you understand those two things, you can then come up with a security plan and policy to protect those resources. While planning a security plan and policy, you must remember that while you are securing your network resources, your network resources must be available to the users who need them so that they can do their jobs.

Objectives

1. Security+ Objective 1.1—Access Control
2. Security+ Objective 1.1.1—MAC/DAC/RBAC
3. Security+ Objective 1.2—Authentication
4. Security+ Objective 1.3—Non-essential Services and Protocols—Disabling unnecessary systems/process/programs
5. Security+ Objective 1.4.9—Social Engineering
6. Security+ Objective 1.6—Social Engineering
7. Security+ Objective 3.1.1—Firewalls
8. Security+ Objective 5.1.2—Social Engineering
9. Security+ Objective 5.1.3—Environment
10. Security+ Objective 5.4—Policy and Procedures
11. Security+ Objective 5.4.1—Security Policy
12. Security+ Objective 5.4.1.1—Acceptable Use
13. Security+ Objective 5.4.1.2—Due Care
14. Security+ Objective 5.4.1.3—Privacy
15. Security+ Objective 5.4.1.4—Separation of Duties
16. Security+ Objective 5.4.1.5—Need to Know
17. Security+ Objective 5.4.1.6—Password Management
18. Security+ Objective 5.4.1.7—SLA
19. Security+ Objective 5.4.1.8—Disposal/Destruction
20. Security+ Objective 5.4.1.9—HR Policy
21. Security+ Objective 5.4.1.9.1—Termination—Adding/revoking passwords, privileges, etc.
22. Security+ Objective 5.4.1.9.2—Hiring—Adding/revoking passwords, privileges, etc.
23. Security+ Objective 5.4.1.9.3—Code of Ethics
24. Security+ Objective 5.4.2—Incident Response Policy
25. Security+ Objective 5.5.2—Single Sign-on
26. Security+ Objective 5.5.3—Centralized vs. Decentralized
27. Security+ Objective 5.5.4—Auditing (Privilege, Usage, Escalation)
28. Security+ Objective 5.5.5—MAC/DAC/RBAC
29. Security+ Objective 5.7—Risk Identification
30. Security+ Objective 5.7.1—Asset Identification
31. Security+ Objective 5.7.2—Risk Assessment
32. Security+ Objective 5.7.3—Threat Identification
33. Security+ Objective 5.7.4—Vulnerabilities
34. Security+ Objective 5.8—Education—Training of end users, executives, and HR
35. Security+ Objective 5.8.1—Communication
36. Security+ Objective 5.8.2—User Awareness
37. Security+ Objective 5.8.3—Education
38. Security+ Objective 5.8.4—Online Resources
39. Security+ Objective 5.9—Documentation
40. Security+ Objective 5.9.1—Standards and Guidelines
41. Security+ Objective 5.9.2—Systems Architecture
42. Security+ Objective 5.9.3—Change Documentation
43. Security+ Objective 5.9.4—Logs and Inventories
44. Security+ Objective 5.9.5—Classification
45. Security+ Objective 5.9.5.1—Notification
46. Security+ Objective 5.9.6—Retention/Storage
47. Security+ Objective 5.9.7—Destruction

2.1   WHAT ARE YOU TRYING TO SECURE?

Data is the raw facts, numbers, letters, or symbols that the computer processes into meaningful information. Examples of data include a letter to a company or a client, a report for your boss, a budget proposal of a large project or an address book of your friends and business associates. Whatever the data is, it can be saved (or written to disk) so that it can be retrieved at any time, it can be printed on paper, or it can be sent to someone else over the telephone lines.

Data stored on a computer or stored on the network is vital to the users and probably the company. The data represents hours of work, and data is sometimes irreplaceable. Data loss can be caused by many things including hardware failure, viruses, user error, and malicious users. While equipment can always be replaced, the data may not always be replaced, and you don't always have the time to recreate the data.

Security, at least network security, refers to the process and techniques by which digital information assets are protected. The goals of network security are to:

■ maintain integrity.
■ protect confidentiality.
■ assure availability.

Confidentiality, integrity, and availability are sometimes referred to as the C-I-A triad.

Integrity refers to the assurance that data is not altered or destroyed in an unauthorized manner. If you sent a message from one user to another, you want to make sure that the message sent is identical to the message received. If you have files on a server, you want to make sure that they are not tampered with or deleted. Although the security that you put in place does not improve the accuracy of data that is put into the system by users, it can help ensure that any changes are intended and correctly applied.

The basic principles used to establish integrity controls are:

1. Granting access on a need-to-know basis (rule of least privilege).
2. Separation of duties.

Users should be granted access only to those network resources that they need in order to perform their assigned job functions.

Need to know is a basic security concept that holds that information should be limited to only those individuals who require it. When planning out the rights and permissions to the network resources, you should follow two main rules:

■ Give the rights and permissions for the user to do his or her job.
■ Don't give any additional rights and permissions that a user does not need.

While you want to keep these resources secure, you want to make sure that users can easily get what they need. For example, give users access to the necessary files, and only give them the rights that they need. If they need to read a document but don't need to make changes to the document, they only need to have read rights. When you give a person or group only the required amount of access and nothing more, this is known as the **rule of least privilege.**

To ensure that no single user has control of a task or transaction from beginning to end, two or more people should be responsible for performing it. For example, anyone allowed to create a transaction should not be allowed to execute it. Since it takes two people to perform the transaction from start to end, this reduces the risk that someone will perform a transaction for personal gain. Of course, there is a risk that multiple people can perform a transaction for personal gain, but its risk is less than a single person performing transactions for personal gain.

Confidentiality is the protection of data from unauthorized disclosure to a third party. Whether it is customer information or company secrets, a business is responsible for protecting the privacy of its data. Along with confidentiality, the company must also be concerned with privacy.

Availability is defined as the continuous operation of computers systems. When your system is a target of a denial-of-service attack, your system may become very slow or may be totally disabled.

In reality, you will find that it is a balance between these three goals. See figure 2.1. You don't want to add so much security that it becomes a heavy burden on your users. If it is a heavy burden, you will find that users will be reluctant to use it and then may try to circumvent or bypass the security. For example, if you set up the network so that the users have to change their passwords too frequently or that they have to remember passwords that are too long, then people may tend to write them down on a piece of paper or sticky note, which is kept near their computer. As a result, by making the network so secure, you have just opened up a major security hole, which makes the network security less effective. In addition, if you make your network so secure that the users who need to access the network resources cannot, then those people cannot do their jobs.

2.1.1   Networks

A **network** is two or more computers connected together to share resources such as files or a printer. For a network to function, it requires a network service to share or access a common media or pathway to connect the computers. To bring it all together, protocols give the entire system common communication rules. See figure 2.2)

After you have something to share as a file or a printer, you must then have a pathway to access the network resource. Computers connect to the network by using a special expansion card (or it can be built into the motherboard) called a network interface card (NIC). The network card will then communicate by sending signals through a cable (twisted-pair, coaxial, and fiber optics) or by using wireless technology (infrared or radio waves). The role of the network card is to prepare and send data to another computer, receive data from another computer, and control the flow of data between the computer and the cabling system.

Figure 2.1   Security is Balance between Confidentiality, Integrity and Availability (Also Known as the C-I-A Triad)

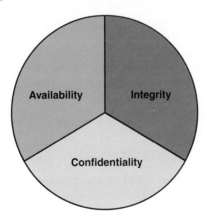

Figure 2.2   Computers Networked Together

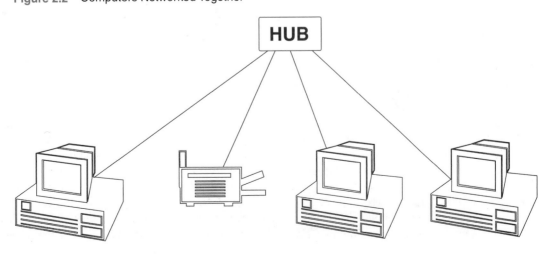

Protocols (TCP/IP and IPX) are the rules or standards that allow the computers to connect to one another and enable computers and peripheral devices to exchange information with as little error as possible. Common protocol suites (also referred to as stack) are TCP/IP and IPX. A suite is a set of protocols that work together.

Today, networks are broken into three main categories: a **local area network (LAN), metropolitan area network (MAN)** or a **wide area network (WAN).** A LAN has computers that are connected within a geographically close network, such as a room, a building, or a group of adjacent buildings. A MAN is a network designed for a town or city, usually using high-speed connections such as fiber optics. A WAN is a network that uses long-range telecommunication links to connect the network computers over long distances and often consists of two or more smaller LANs. Typically, the LANs are connected through public networks, such as the public telephone system.

The WAN can be broken down into either an enterprise WAN or a global WAN. An **enterprise WAN** is a WAN that is owned by one company or organization. A **global WAN** is not owned by any one company and could cross national boundaries. The best-known example of a global WAN is the Internet, which connects millions of computers. As of February, 2002, there are over 544.2 million users on the Internet, and the number is growing rapidly. See figure 2.3.

Internetworking is the art and science of connecting individual local area networks (LANs) to create wide area networks (WANs), and connecting WANs to form even larger WANs by using routers, bridges, and gateways. The smaller LANs are known as **subnetworks** or **subnets.** Internetworking can be extremely complex because it generally involves connecting networks that use different protocols.

Today, when dealing with networks, you will often hear two more terms: intranet and extranet. An **intranet** is a network based on TCP/IP protocols (an internet) belonging to an organization, usually a corporation, accessible only by the organization's members, employees, or others with authorization. An intranet's websites look and act just like any other websites, but the firewall surrounding an intranet fends off unauthorized access. Like the Internet itself, intranets are used to share information. Secure intranets are now the fastest-growing segment of the Internet because they are much less expensive to build and manage than private networks based on proprietary protocols. Note: An intranet could have access to the Internet, but does not require it.

The **extranet** refers to an intranet that is partially accessible to authorized outsiders. Whereas an intranet resides behind a firewall and is accessible only to people who are members of the same company or organization, an extranet provides various levels of accessibility to outsiders. You can access an extranet only if you have a valid username and password, and your identity determines which parts of the extranet you can view. Extranets are becoming a very popular means for business partners to exchange information.

A **private network** is a network that belongs to a particular person or group. Of course when you own the network, a private WAN network is one where you have exclusive access to dedicated links. Of course, a private network is much more expensive than public networks.

Figure 2.3   WAN

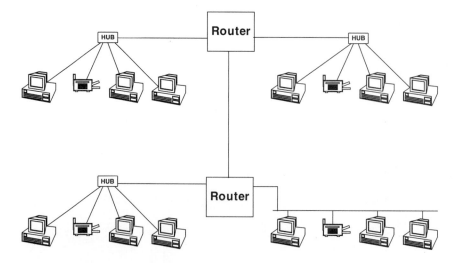

While a majority of LANs connect to the WAN through a public interface, an increasing number of WAN connections are privately owned. Private network operators typically lease lines from public network providers while maintaining control and management of the network from their own facilities. Most private WANs also include a separate connection to the public WAN. Government regulation of private WAN operations is relatively limited. Because many corporations and universities base their internal networks on leased lines, they may be making interstate and intrastate calls from one site to another.

If leasing a physical WAN connection does not make economic sense, a private WAN operator has several other options to consider. Wireless WAN connections, such as satellite or laser line-of-sight between buildings, are one common solution, but they are subject to potential environmental interference and breaches of security.

Another non-lease WAN option is a virtual private network (VPN). A **virtual private network (VPN)** is a network that is constructed by using public wires to connect nodes. For example, there are a number of systems that enable you to create networks using the Internet as the medium for transporting data. These systems use encryption and other security mechanisms to ensure that only authorized users can access the network and that the data cannot be intercepted.

The best example of a public WAN designed for voice is the **Public Switched Telephone Network (PSTN),** while the Internet is the largest public WAN designed for data. In North America, telephone services across PSTN are provided by a telephone company, commonly referred to as Telco. Telco may be used to refer to the local telephone companies only, or it may represent the telephone industry in general, including both local and long distance carriers. In many European countries, a governmental agency known as the **Postal, Telegraph and Telephone (PTT)** is responsible for providing combined postal, telegraph, and telephone services. A similar centrally controlled system is used in China.

So why is it important to have security on a network? Since a network is two or more computers connected together with the ability to share resources such as files or a printer, you make it possible for multiple people to access the computer and its network resources. If the proper steps are not taken to protect that computer and its network resources, someone could read confidential files, delete or corrupt important data files, steal trade secrets, prevent people from accessing the computer and its network resources, and so on.

2.1.2 Network Services

The most common two services provided by a network is file sharing and print sharing. **File sharing** allows you to access files, which are on another computer, without using a floppy disk or other forms of removable media. To ensure that the files are secure, most networks can limit the access to a directory or file and what kind of access (permissions or rights) that a person or a group of people have. For example, if you have full access to your home directory (personal directory on the network to store files), you can list, read, execute, create, change, and delete files in your home directory.

Depending on the contents of a directory or file, you could specify who has access to the directory or file and you can specify what permissions or rights those people have over the directory or file. For example, you could specify a group of people will not be able to see or execute the files, while giving a second group of people the ability to see or execute the file but not make changes to the files and not delete the files. Finally, you could give rights to a third group so that they can see, execute, and change the files.

Print sharing allows several people to send documents to a centrally located printer in the office. Therefore, not everyone requires his or her own personal laser printer. Much like files, networks can limit who has access to the printer. For example, if you have two laser printers (a standard laser printer and an expensive high-resolution color laser printer), you can assign everyone access to the standard laser printer while only assigning a handful of people access to the expensive printer.

Internet services provide important tools to business. Email and World Wide Web access are two popular services. **Electronic mail** or email is a powerful sophisticated tool that allows you to send text messages and file attachments (documents, pictures, sound, and movies) to anyone with an email address.

Much like the mail from the post office, email is delivered to a mailbox (delivery location or holding area for your electronic messages). An Internet mail address will include the user name followed by the @ symbol followed by the name of the mail server. When you connect to the network, you can then access your email messages. Other features may include a return receipt so that you know that the email was read or delivered, replying to the email messages by clicking on the reply button or option, sending the email message to several people at the same time, or forwarding the message to someone else.

Since the Internet is essentially a huge network, it is possible to make your network part of the Internet or to provide a common connection to the Internet for many users. You can create your own web page on the Internet to provide products and services to the public, or you can perform research on the Internet.

2.1.3 Users and Groups

When a person logs onto a computer or accesses a network resource, that person is known as a **user.** To keep track of the user, a **user account** is created, which is identified by a username. It is the user account which is usually assigned a password so that the **password** can be used to validate the person's identity when that person logs on. When the user account is created, the person is added to a security database, which then allows the administrator to assign access to network resources to the user account.

To simplify the tasks of assigning access to network resources, users are often assigned to groups. A **group** is no more than a list of users. But instead of assigning access to a network resource to each user individually, you can add a bunch of people to the group and assign access to the entire group. As a result, every user listed in the group will get access to the network resource. The intent of a group is to group users together that have the same needs.

While a group can categorize users, a **role** is a special type of group defined by job roles or duties. Some roles an organization might define include customer service rep, accounts payable data entry clerk, and operations supervisor. When users are assigned a specific job duty, you just add them to the role, and those persons get all of the necessary rights and permissions so that they can do their job. When they are no longer assigned those duties, you can remove them from the role. If you have a position that goes through a lot of people, a role is perfect for this.

Novell NetWare actually has both groups and organizational roles. Microsoft Windows and Linux only have groups. So in those cases, you will have to use groups with appropriate names and treat them like roles.

2.1.4 Network Servers

A computer on the network can provide services or request services. A **server** is a service provider that provides access to network resources, and a **client** is a computer that requests services. A network that is made of servers and clients is known as a **client/server network,** which is typically used on medium or large network. A server-based network is the best network for sharing resources and data, while providing centralized network security for those resources and data. In addition, since the data files can be centrally located on a server, it allows for centralized backup of those files. Windows NT Server, Windows 2000 Server, Windows Server 2003 Linux, and Novell NetWare networks are primarily client/server networks.

A **peer-to-peer network,** sometimes referred to as a **workgroup,** has no dedicated servers. Instead, all computers are equal. Therefore, they provide services and request services. Since a person's resources are kept on his or her own machine, a user manages his or her own shared resources. Since each user manages his or her own shared resources, each security database is kept local on each machine. Windows 9X can be used to form a peer-to-peer network.

Security+ Objective 5.5.3—Centralized vs. Decentralized

When network operating systems began, every server maintained its own user accounts, groups, and permissions. When users needed to access to a network resource on a particular server, an administrator had to create an account on that server for the user and assign the appropriate permissions to use that resource. The server would then authenticate and authorize the user using its own security database. If the user needs to access another network resource on another server, the administrator needs to go to that server and create a computer account for the user and assign the appropriate permissions to the second resource. This is known as **decentralized management.** If you have lots of users and/or lots of servers, this can become an administrative nightmare. In addition, if you change a password, you would have to go to every single server and change the password. Of course, decentralized management should only be used on small networks.

Today, most modern network operating systems are used to form a larger network while using a single security database. Using a single security database for all of your network resources is known as **centralized management.** When you create a user, you only have to create the user once and that user is available to all network resources on all servers that use the same security database.

Security+ Objective 5.5.2—Single Sign-on

Best of all, users only have to log on once to be granted access to all the resources that they have access to. This is known as **single sign-on.** In most cases, on private networks, the single sign-on is provided by a directory service such as Microsoft's Active Directory and Novell's Novell Directory Services. In web applications on the Internet, centralized management can be provided by applications, such as Microsoft Passport.

Since different companies have different needs for their networks, that server can assume several different roles. They are:

- **File Server**—A server that manages user access to files stored on a server. When a file is accessed on a file server, the file is downloaded to the client's RAM. For example, if you are working on a report using a word processor, the word processor files will be executed from your client computer and the report will be stored on the server. As the report is accessed from the server, it would be downloaded or copied to the RAM of the client computer. Note: All of the processing done on the report is done by the client's microprocessors. Other advantages of a file server are that it allows easy access to the data files from any computer and allows for easy backup of data files on the server.
- **Print Server**—A server that manages user access to printer resources connected to the network, allowing one printer to be used by many people.
- **Application Server**—A server that is similar to a file and print server except the application server also does some of the processing.
- **Mail Server**—A mail server manages electronic messages (email) between users.
- **Fax Server**—A server that manages fax messages sent into and out of the network through a fax modem.
- **Remote Access Server**—Hosts modems for inbound requests to connect to the network. Remote access servers provide remote users who are working at home or on the road with a connection to the network.
- **Telephony Server**—Functions as an intelligent answering machine for the network. It can also perform call center and call-routing functions.
- **Web Server**—A server that runs WWW and FTP services for access by users of the intranet or the Internet.
- **Proxy Server**—A server that performs a function on behalf of other computers. It is typically used to provide local intranet clients with access to the Internet while keeping the local intranet free from intruders.
- **Directory Services Servers**—A server used to locate information about the network such as domains (logical divisions of the network) and other servers.

NOTE: A single server could have several roles.

2.1.5   Server Rooms

The server room is the work area of the IT department where the servers and most of the communication devices reside. The room should be secure with only a handful of people allowed to have access to it by using keys or security cards. In addition, you should use cameras to help monitor the access to the server room.

In addition, the server should also be secure. Therefore, you should consider the following:

- The computer should be locked when not in use.
- You should always require user names and passwords.
- You should always log out when the server is not being used.
- You should restrict accounts so that they cannot log on directly (interactive) to the server.
- You should enable security monitoring such as auditing.

Besides securing the servers in the server room, you should also consider the following criteria. Since the computers and telecommunication systems can generate a lot of heat, and a dry room is more susceptible to electrostatic discharge that can damage electronic components, you should consider separate environment controls for the server room. **Electrostatic discharge (ESD)** is electricity generated by friction such as when your arm slides on a tabletop or when you walk across a carpet. To reduce ESD, you should:

■ Consider an electrostatic discharge prevention program, which would include using ESD wrist straps when opening computers and handling computer components, installing antistatic flooring, and/or placing the servers on an antistatic mat.
■ Keep humidity low (less than 50 percent).

In addition, you should:

■ Install an uninterruptible power supply (UPS) to protect your system against power fluctuations including outages.
■ Keep your system cool (room temperature or less).
■ Always have a tape backup system or some other method to back up all important data files.

For the best results and longevity of the system, ensure that the server room is a clean environment. It is important that the server room have clean air. Most office environments are clean enough that the computer equipment only needs to be cleaned out annually or biannually as part of a regular preventive maintenance program.

However, if the server room is in an industrial environment or the air is dusty or full of pollutants, you should move the server to a better location. If that is not an option, at least maintain a regular cleaning schedule to keep it and the server room clear of air problems. One easy preventive measure is to use an air cleaner in the server room. You can also buy special cases and enclosures for server hardware designed for industrial environments to prevent damage from dirt and pollutants.

If you find that dust bunnies are continually causing the server to heat up and shut down, you should perform a weekly or at least monthly preventive maintenance schedule that includes cleaning the cooling system elements and the interior of the system case.

If you have several servers, you should also consider a **server rack** or **rackmount cabinet** to hold the servers. In addition, you can also purchase a switch box to connect a single keyboard, mouse, and monitor to several servers. This will allow for less equipment and allow for a more organized work environment.

As you can imagine when you stack these servers on top of one another, you can easily put a large number of servers in a small area. Of course, you must remember that when having this many servers in a small area, all of these servers require special electrical and cooling requirements. The cabinet should have exhaust fans over each bay to pull the heat up and away from the servers and other devices, helping to maximize the cooling systems of this equipment. Of course, you must make sure that the ventilation fans are operating properly.

Rackmount cabinets can also be equipped with surge suppressor power strips, but in most situations, you are much better off to install a UPS (uninterruptible power supply) in the bottom of the rack and use it to power the devices mounted in the rack.

Finally, when buying a server cabinet, you should buy a cabinet that has locking doors. These doors are a vital part of the server's security. In addition, you should avoid cabinets that use the same keys for the doors on every bay. And of course, for the lock to work, you must keep the cabinet locked.

2.1.6   The Individual PC and Security

So you might say to yourself, "If I don't connect the computer to the network, then I should be secure." This is not necessarily true. Again, if you don't take the proper steps, your computer is still vulnerable. For example, if you don't have a secure operating system that uses secure passwords and that is physically secured when you are not using it, someone could sit down at your computer when you are not using it and access the information. In addition, if your PC is not connected to the network, you will not be able to access other network resources such as email or shared printers.

2.2   SECURITY RISKS

Security+ Objective 5.7—Risk Identification

Security+ Objective 5.7.1—Asset Identification

Security+ Objective 5.7.2—Risk Assessment

Security+ Objective 5.7.3—Threat Identification

Security+ Objective 5.7.4—Vulnerabilities

A **risk** is simply a potential for loss or harm. However, the definition of a risk varies from person to person. Some organizations are more comfortable with some risks, whereas others are not. Some persons might go to greater lengths to try to reduce or eliminate the risk, whereas others will not care whether something happens.

Everyone should agree that for a network, security is a high concern and a major responsibility for administrators. Of course, when you examine your environment, you will need to assess the risks you currently face, determine an acceptable level of risk, and maintain risk at or below that level. Risks are reduced by increasing the security of your environment.

As a general rule, the higher the level of security in an organization, the more costly it is to implement. Unfortunately, at a higher level of security, you may reduce the functionality of the network. Sometimes, extra levels of security will result in more complex systems for users. However, if the authentication process is made too complex, some customers will not bother to use the system, which could potentially cost more than the attacks the network suffers.

A **threat** is a person, place, or thing that has the potential to cause harm. The threats can be divided into three categories:

- Natural and Physical—includes fire, flooding, storms, earthquakes, and power failures.
- Unintentional—includes uninformed employees and customers.
- Intentional—includes attackers, terrorists, spies, and malicious code.

A **hacker,** also known as a cracker, is someone who breaks security on an automated information system or a network. The hacker typically does something mischievous or malicious by first breaking into a system.

When identifying the source of a threat, several questions can help you identify the type of threat. Some of these questions are:

Is the threat from a disaster of some sort, or is it from an attack?
If it is an attack, is the threat coming from someone who works for your company or from someone outside your company?
If it is an attack, is the attack a well-known attack?
If it is an attack, can the attack be tracked or identified by performing auditing or looking at logs?

After you understand the types of threats, you can then plan to minimize the risk.

Disaster is defined as sudden or great misfortune, such as those found in natural disasters such as fire, flooding, or earthquakes. While most people may think that it is a natural disaster, some of these can be manmade such as arson or a terrorist attack.

An attack is an attempt to bypass security controls on a computer. The attack could alter, release, or deny data. Threats from attack are more common and are typically harder to plan for than disasters. This is because these types of threat are constantly changing as new security holes are found and security holes are closed.

Other forms of threats include malicious code. Malicious code is software or firmware that is intentionally placed in a system for an unauthorized purpose. They include:

- **Viruses**—A program designed to replicate and spread, generally without the knowledge or permission of the user. A virus often has destructive tendencies.
- **Worms**—A program or algorithm that replicates itself over a computer network and usually performs malicious actions, such as using up the computer's resources and possibly shutting the system down.

Typically, a worm enters the computer because of vulnerabilities available in the computer's operating system.

■ **Trojan horse**—A piece of software that appears to be legitimate software such as game or useful utility but may be a destructive program or a program used to bypass security.

Every security system and network has vulnerability. A **vulnerability** is a point where a resource is susceptible to attack. It can be thought of as a weakness. Vulnerabilities are often categorized as:

■ **Physical**—such as an unlocked door.
■ **Natural**—such as a broken fire suppression system or no UPS.
■ **Hardware and Software**—such as out-of-date antivirus software.
■ **Media**—such as electrical interference.
■ **Communication**—such as unencrypted protocols.
■ **Human**—such as insecure help-desk procedures.

An **exploit** is a type of attack on a resource that is accessed by a threat that makes use of a vulnerability in your environment. The exploitation of resources can be performed in many ways. Some of the more common are given in the following table. When a threat uses a vulnerability to attack a resource, some severe consequences can result.

Countermeasures are deployed to counteract threats and vulnerabilities, therefore reducing the risk in your environment. For example, an organization producing fragile electronics may deploy physical security countermeasures such as securing equipment to the building's foundation or adding buffering mechanisms. These countermeasures reduce the likelihood that an earthquake could cause physical damage to their assets. Residual risk is what remains after all countermeasures have been applied to reduce threats and vulnerabilities.

Risk management is the complete process used to identify, control, and mitigate the impact of uncertain events. Because it is impossible to eliminate risk completely, the goal of risk management is to reduce the risk and manage the CIA triad. You do this by determining what the risks are, identifying threats and vulnerabilities, and then reducing them. See figure 2.4.

Risk analysis or **risk assessment** is the process of reviewing all the aspects of the resource that you are trying to protect, and determining the possible risks. This process also involves developing any countermeasures to eliminate or reduce the risks.

To determine the amount of the risk, you must first look at the value *of the damage that the threat can cause.* The more valuable the information or assets you are trying to protect, the higher the impact of the risk. The risk of an exploit on a web server that is used only to display static web pages may not be as high as an exploit to a web server that is used for e-commerce. If a vulnerability is exploited on a web server that is used for e-commerce, the impact of such an exploit could be catastrophic to the company, since the vulnerability renders the website inoperable causing the company to lose money every hour during which the site is inoperable. The damage is not necessarily limited to financial damages. There is also the loss of customer confidence, loss of new clients, or damage to the company's reputation.

Figure 2.4   Risk Management Cycle

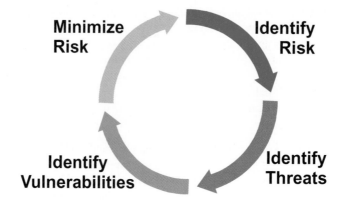

Then you must look at the threat and the type of damage that the threat can cause and the likelihood of the threat actually occurring. If the risk occurs, the damage could be anything from a nuisance to catastrophic. If you are in a region that gets violent thunderstorms two or three times a year, that risk is greater than your site being hit by a meteor shower or a satellite falling and striking your site. The chances are there for all three, but the last two are very unlikely, while the thunderstorm will cause power outages and power spikes eventually.

There are four options for handling risks:

- **Eliminate the risk**—The best solution in handling a risk is to eliminate it by getting rid of the cause of that risk. Unfortunately, this is not always possible because you cannot eliminate the risk completely or it is not in your control.
- **Minimize the risk**—In most cases, the best you can do is to minimize the risk. This means reducing the risk to an acceptable level that you can live with. In other words, you minimize the risk by reducing it to a level that is acceptable but also allows for the continuation of business operations.
- **Accept the risk**—In some cases, you just need to accept the risk. Sometimes, threats are unavoidable, and you can live with their consequences.
- **Transfer the risk**—The last option is to transfer the risk to someone else.

2.3   GOALS OF NETWORK SECURITY

So how do you make a network secure? First, you must have the following goals in security:

- Prevention
- Detection
- Response

Of course, the best goal is to prevent a security violation from occurring. This includes locking down the computer so that when someone tries to break into a computer or a network, he or she is not allowed to enter. In addition, since everyone does not need access to every file or document on a server, you can group files into folders and assign rights and permissions to the folders that a person truly needs. Users should be trusted with information on a least-privilege basis (rule of least privilege). This means that an individual should have enough permissions to carry out his or her job function and no more. If a person has too many privileges, there is more risk to your company. Lastly, you need to test your security controls and keep testing your security controls to keep them from being vulnerable.

Of course, while you try to prevent all attacks, eventually attacks do occur. Therefore, when they do, it is best to detect those attacks as soon as possible so you can put a stop to the attack. Since most hackers typically need to try many things before they break into a system, if you detect that someone is trying to break in, you can identify the hacker and stop him or her from moving forward with the attacks. In addition, if you detect that an attack has occurred, you then need to look at how the attack occurred so that you can figure out how to stop the same type of attack in the future.

To detect intrusions, you will need to use accounting or auditing. This will include using a wide range of tools, and you will have to examine system log files on a regular basis. The reason that you have to look at the logs on a regular basis is so that you know what is normal and what is abnormal. You can then take a closer look at the abnormal entries and more easily identify intrusions when they occur.

Finally, when an intrusion occurs and is detected, you need to quickly respond to the attack, stopping the attack and preventing the attack in the future. You need to also restore operations as soon as possible. You should also have a review procedure so that if you need to change a procedure, the procedure can be changed to prevent the same or similar type of problem in the future.

When building a defense, you should use a layered approach that includes securing the network infrastructure, the communication protocols, servers, applications that run on the server, and the file system. In addition, you should require some form of user authentication. When you configure a strong layered defense, an intruder has to break through several layers to reach his or her objective. See figure 2.5.

Figure 2.5   When you configure a strong layered defense, an intruder has to break through several layers to reach his or her objective.

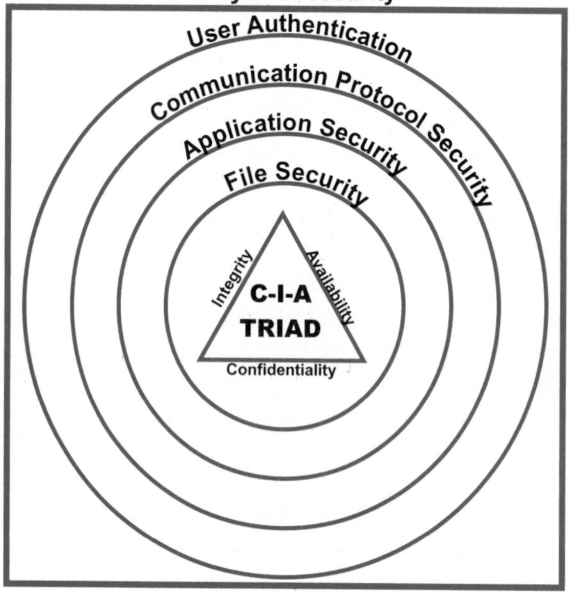

2.4   DEVELOPING A SECURITY PLAN

To establish a security program, you must define a foundation that should be documented. While this documentation may be influenced by government regulations, industry standards, or other guidelines, the standards and guidelines that your company documents should explain how your business is governed and how it conducts business. Standards must be complied with, whereas guidelines are generally recommendations and best practices.

The document that specifies how you are going to protect your systems is your security plan. When developing a security plan, you must evaluate the risks to your network and network resources and develop strategies to make everything secure. Protecting your network and network resources can be divided into three areas:

- Physical security.
- Operational security.
- Policies and procedures.

2.4.1   Physical Security

Security+ Objective 5.1.3—Environment

When securing a network, it is essential that you physically secure all equipment including computers, routers, hubs, switches, cables, and other network and storage devices. If someone can take a computer, a hacker can easily bypass all security put on that computer and access the information on the computer. In addition, if a hacker can physically access a server, with a little knowledge, a person can bypass the security and access the information on the server. In addition, it is always easier to destroy, disable, or degrade a network if someone can physically access a computer or any network device. Some simple examples might be to disconnect a cable, unplug a computer or network device, or format a hard drive.

To physically secure a site would most likely involve using locks and cameras to restrict access to a server room or an office. In addition, you can use special locking devices to secure computers, including notebook computers, that are in an open area.

The environment refers to the physical surroundings in which your network operates. Along with the physical security, you need to look at the environment where the site is so that you can plan for disaster prevention and recovery. For example, you will need to determine that the type of fire detection and suppression system that you use will put out the fire without damaging the computer any further. You also need to look at where you are going to place your servers and network devices so that they are not excessively vulnerable to harm. In addition, since your data is the most important thing on your network, how are you going to back it up so that if the worst does happen, you have an extra copy or two of your data so that you can at least put everything back to the way it was?

2.4.2 Operational Security

Operational security is security as it relates to how an organization operates or does things. Operational issues include the daily operations of the network and the connections to other networks. Operational security issues include authentication, access control, and security topologies after network installation is complete. It should also include backup and recovery procedures.

2.4.3 Authentication, Authorization, and Accounting

One commonly used model to intelligently control access to a network and its resources is **authentication, authorization, and accounting (AAA).** These combined processes are considered important for effective network management and security. Authentication, authorization, and accounting services are often provided by a dedicated AAA server, a program that performs these functions.

Security+ Objective 1.2—Authentication

In networks, **authentication** is the ability to verify the identity of a user, system, or system element. A system element can be an internal process or program or packets sent from one computer to another. Authentication can be based on something you know, something you have, or something you are. The most common method of authentication for users is by using a username and password. After you supply a username and password, the server compares a user's authentication credentials with other user credentials stored in a database. If the credentials match, the user is granted access to the network. If the credentials do not, authentication fails and network access is denied.

Authorization is the process of giving someone permission to do or have something. In multiuser computer systems, a system administrator defines for the system which users are allowed access to the system and what privileges of use they shall have (such as access to which files and directories, hours of access and so forth).

Security+ Objective 5.5.4—Auditing (Privilege, Usage, Escalation)

Finally, when a user accesses a network resource, **accounting** (sometimes known as auditing) records each resource a user uses or accesses while using a PC or network. This can include the amount of system time or the amount of data a user has sent and/or received during a session. Accounting is carried out by logging of session statistics and usage information and is used for authorization control, billing, trend analysis, resource utilization, and capacity planning activities.

Nonrepudiation is the ability of a system to verify that data was either sent or received by the sender or receiver. In other words, it makes sure that they received the data and it cannot be repudiated or disputed that it arrived.

2.4.4 Access Control

Security+ Objective 1.1—Access Control

Access control is the process by which you restrict access to computing resources. It is a combination of authentication (proving who you claim to be) and authorization (what are you allowed to see, presuming you are whom you claim you are). It defines how users and systems communicate and in what manner. Access control allows you to enforce the security principle of least privilege, which states that individuals should be assigned the minimum privilege level required to carry out their assigned tasks. Only those individuals authorized to access resources are permitted access to them. In other words, access control protects information from unauthorized access.

Security+ Objective 1.1.1—MAC/DAC/RBAC

Security+ Objective 5.5.5—MAC/DAC/RBAC

Three basic models for access control are:

- Discretionary access control (DAC)—The owner of an object (such as a program or process, file, or folder) manages access control at his or her own discretion.
- Mandatory access control (MAC)—Access to an object is restricted based on the sensitivity of the object (defined by the label or level that is assigned), and granted through authorization (clearance) to access that level of data.
- Role-based access control (RBAC)—Access is based on the role a user plays in the organization.

In a **discretionary access control (DAC)** environment, resource owners and administrators jointly control access to resources. With this model, it allows the owners of a resource to establish privileges to the information they own. This model allows for much greater flexibility and drastically reduces the administrative burdens of security implementation. With DAC, an access control list (ACL) is maintained that lists the user with access and what type of access the user has. The ACL can be stored as part of the file, in a file, or in a database.

There are solid arguments both for and against DAC systems. DAC grants administrative control of resources to the people responsible for their everyday use. Theoretically, these individuals would be best suited to assess a user's "need to know." In addition, since DAC allows the owner to grant or revoke access to individuals or groups of individuals based on the situation, it allows information to be shared easily between users.

On the other hand, DAC systems widen the circle of users with administrative powers over those resources and there is a lack of centralized administration. In addition, as each file owner controls the access level to his or her personal file, some owners may not know how to properly secure a file or a network resource. In addition, this system depends on the owner being security-conscious. Finally, it may be difficult to establish auditing.

An example of using a DAC model is when you use Windows 2000 Server, Windows Server 2003, Linux or Novell NetWare to make available a folder to other users. With these operating systems, the owner of a directory can share the directory and specify who has access to that directory and what type of access.

The **mandatory access control (MAC)** model is based on nondiscretionary control based on multilevel security. In the MAC model, you classify all users and resources to a security label or level. If the user has the same level or higher as the resource that the user is trying to access, the user is granted access. If not, the user is denied access. In the MAC model, the system administrators establish these parameters and associate them with an account, file, or network resource. Administrators are the only people who can change the security label or level of a person or network resource. The MAC model can be very restrictive. In general, MAC access control mechanisms are more secure than DAC yet have trade-offs in performance and convenience to users. MAC is usually appropriate for extremely secure systems including multilevel secure military applications or mission-critical data applications.

Controlling the import of information from other systems and export to other systems (including printers) is a critical function of MAC-based systems, which must ensure that sensitivity labels are properly maintained and implemented so that sensitive information is appropriately protected at all times.

Rule-based access control is one method of applying mandatory access control. Actually, all MAC-based systems implement a simple form of rule-based access control by matching an object's sensitivity label and a subject sensitivity label to determine whether it should be granted or denied. Additional rules can be applied using rule-based access control to further define specific conditions for access to a requested object.

Lattice-based access controls are another method for implementing mandatory access controls. A lattice model is mathematical structure that combines multilevel and multilateral security and applies a need-to-know condition. For example, the military uses four levels, unclassified, confidential, secret, and top secret, and each project and parts of each project are given labels. For example, technical information for the Air Force B2 stealth bomber is assigned the highest level of top secret and the project label B2 stealth bomber. Technical information for the Navy stealth submarine would also be assigned highest of top secret, but it would be given a project label of stealth submarine. While a person may be given a top-secret security clearance, that person would also have to be assigned the B2 stealth bomber label to have access to the technical information of the Air Force B2 stealth bomber. Since one person who fixes the B2 stealth bomber may be given the top-secret security clearance for the B2 stealth bomber, that person does not have a top-secret clearance for the stealth submarine. This is also based on the technician for the bomber having no "need to know" for the technical information of the submarine.

The Bell-LaPadula model was the first formal confidentiality model of a mandatory access control system. The Bell-LaPadula model states that a subject cannot read information from an object with a higher sensitivity label (no read up), and a subject cannot write information to an object with a lower sensitivity label (no write down). The first rule makes sure that only authorized people will read the information, and the second rule makes sure that the subject cannot accidentally or intentionally share confidential information by writing to an object at a lower security level.

While the Bell-LaPadula model provided confidentiality, the Biba and Clark-Wilson model provides integrity. The Biba model states that a subject cannot read information from an object with a lower integrity level (no read down), and a subject cannot write information to an object with a higher integrity level (no write up). The first rule makes sure that only authorized people will read the data, and the second rule makes sure that only authorized people can make changes to the data.

The Clark-Wilson integrity model establishes a security framework for use in commercial activities, such as the banking industry. It divides data into:

- **Unconstrained Data Item (UDI)**—Data outside the control area, such as input data.
- **Constrained Data Item (CDI)**—Data inside the control area, where integrity must be preserved.

It then uses integrity verification procedures (IVP) to check the validity of CDIs and transformation procedures (TP) to maintain integrity of CDIs.

Role-based access control (RBAC) is another method of implementing discretionary access controls. In role-based access control, access decisions are based on an individual's roles and responsibilities within the organization or user base. Roles are assigned by the administrator based on relative relationships within the organization or user base. It allows a user to be assigned to a role and access is granted to the role. The user can perform certain functions or duties based on the role he or she is assigned. In other words, access rights and permissions are assigned to groups (or role) rather than to individuals, which greatly simplifies the management of access rights and permissions. The role will determine what actions the user can perform, when, from where, and in what order. For instance, a manager would have certain authorized transactions over his or her employees. An administrator would have certain authorized transactions over his or her specific realm of duties (backup, account creation, etc.)

The process of defining roles is usually based on analyzing the fundamental goals and structure of an organization and is usually linked to the security policy. For example, in a medical organization, the different roles of users may include those such as doctor, nurse, attendant, patients or office administrator. Obviously, these members require different levels of access in order to perform their functions, but also the types of transactions and their allowed context vary greatly depending on the security policy and any relevant regulations.

An example of using a DAC model is when you use Windows 2000 Server or Windows Server 2003 and assigning a user to a predefined group such as the backup operator. Anyone who is a member of the backup operator can back up files to a tape drive even if they don't own the file or have permissions to use the file.

2.4.5   Policies and Procedures

A **policy** is a document that makes a specific statement requiring that a rule must be met. They are usually point-specific, covering a single area. Policies should be general in nature and not have to be updated on a regular basis. A policy often includes procedures, which outline methods for achieving or maintaining the stated goals of the policy. A policy is a statement of what to do, and a procedure is a statement of how to do it.

For your organization, you should have policies and procedures to define how your organizational assets should be acquired, utilized, maintained, and discarded. Of course, for policies to be effective, they must have the full support of the management team. If you don't, while you can recommend policies, if you don't have management support, you will not be able to enforce them.

A **security policy** is a document that states in writing how a company plans to protect the company's physical and information technology (IT) assets. A security policy is often considered to be a "living document," meaning that the document is never finished but is continuously updated as technology and employee requirements change.

A company's security policy may include an acceptable-use policy, a description of how the company plans to educate its employees about protecting the company's assets, an explanation of how security measurements will be carried out and enforced, and a procedure for evaluating the effectiveness of the security policy to ensure that necessary corrections will be made.

A number of key policies that needed to be created and documented for a secure network include:

- **Acceptable-use policy**—Defines the way personnel can use the organization's equipment. It should include if they can or cannot use email for personal use, what websites persons can visit or what material they can store or display using company resources. An acceptable-use policy signed by an employee can be interpreted as an employee's written consent for allowing an employer to search an employee's workstation.
- **Access policy**—Specifies rights, privileges, and restrictions for using the organization's technology and information assets.
- **Accountability policy**—Specifies the responsibilities of people in the organization including how audits of information assets are done and what happens when an intrusion occurs.
- **Antivirus policy**—Specifies the procedures to minimize the exposure and damage from malicious software.
- **Authentication policy**—Specifies the acceptable methods, equipment, and parameters for allowing access to resources.
- **Availability statement**—Specifies the hours of operation, scheduled maintenance, recovery procedures, and availability of redundant resources.
- **Change and configuration management policy**—Specifies who is allowed to make changes to systems architecture.
- **Computer technology purchasing guidelines**—Specifies security features of equipment purchased that are required or preferred by the organization.
- **Disaster recovery policies**—Covers every type of failure so that you can minimize its occurrence and effect.
- **Disposal and destruction**—Specifies how data and documents are disposed of or destroyed.
- **Firewall policy**—Describes the type of network traffic and data that is and is not allowed to go through the firewall.
- **Human resource policy**—Describes the procedures to add and remove employees and the training of employees on the above policies. The HR department creates the handbook that each employee gets with the policies defined. They must also ensure that paperwork is in place acknowledging that the employee has read the book and understands the provisions. Many policies recommend that the employee's computer access be disabled before the employee is notified of termination. When you hire a new employee, be sure to remember the principle of least privilege when adding accounts.
- **Incident response policy**—Defines an incident, which employees are primarily responsible for handling the incidents and the reporting procedure for an incident.
- **Password policy**—Specifies how passwords are managed, including password length, password complexity, expiration, and lockout parameters.
- **Privacy policy**—Explains the expectations of privacy for clients, customers, and partners.
- **Retention and storage policy**—Describes how information is stored and protected.
- **Service-level agreement (SLA)**—A contract that defines business and technical support parameters that an IT outsourcing firm agrees to provide to its clients. Hosting SLA ensures availability of server based resources.
- **System architecture documentation**—Consists of network layout, connections, and system configuration (including operating systems, hardware, and applications) so that you can identify suspicious change to that structure.
- **Violation reporting policy**—Defines violations and how they should be reported.

If you don't already have a security policy in place, you need to convince upper management of its importance. Of course, a good management team should not take much convincing. After winning their support, you need to put together a team from major departments to help compose the policy. As you can imagine, building a security policy can take quite some time. Creating a security policy follows the formal life-cycle model consisting of the three phases:

- **Development**—Start with a risk assessment so that you can identify potential sources of risk, and then determine ways to eliminate, reduce, or transfer such risks. When creating, writing, or modifying security policies, you should first determine whether your company already has security policies in any form. If it has security policies in place, review them and make changes as necessary to update them to meet current needs and to reflect any new principles or additional security measures that you have developed.
- **Deployment**—After a security policy has been defined, it must be deployed. This requires not only implementing the security policy but also communicating clearly that it is desirable for all employees to follow the security policy.
- **Monitoring and maintenance**—After the security policy has been implemented, the IT and security professionals must make sure that security policies are monitored and updated to remain relevant to today's activities and concerns, manage today's risk, and anticipate future potential risks.

This is an ongoing process that must be updated as the security in your organization changes.

To help you establish security for your organization, to ensure that your security policies and practices are applied in a consistent manner, and that nothing is missed about the security of a system or network, you should create security checklists. It might include the steps for installing and configuring an operating system and which service packs, patches, and security fixes you need to load. You can also use these checklists to recheck the security status of a system.

When developing the security policy, you should perform separation of duties to act as a form of checks and balances to make sure that no one entity becomes too powerful. This also includes having checks and balances for the administrator. While the administrator has system-wide rights and permissions, you can often establish an auditor, which the administrator cannot overwrite. It would be the job of the auditor to check on the administrator so that the administrator is not overstepping his or her bounds.

In addition, you need to establish due care. **Due care** means that reasonable precautions are being taken that indicate an organization is being responsible. If you don't exercise due care and a major security incident occurs because of a lack of countermeasures or incident response, you and your company may be held responsible for any damage caused by your lack of action. By establishing a solid security policy and adhering to it, a company can show that it has exercised due care, which will help protect itself from unnecessary lawsuits.

Security+ Objective 5.9.3—Change Documentation

As it was stated above, some of these documents are "living documents." Therefore, these documents need to be changed from time to time. In addition, even your semipermanent documents also need to be changed from time to time. Therefore, you need to have some type of change management to change these documents. Change management defines a systematic way to control how changes are introduced and handled. This way, all departments that have a stake in the changes can give input into the changes to be made.

To find more information about establishing and implementing a security policy, visit the following websites:

The SANS Security Policy Project with Templates
http://www.sans.org/resources/policies/

RFC 2196 Site Security Handbook
http://www.faqs.org/rfcs/rfc2196.html
ftp://ftp.rfc-editor.org/in-notes/rfc2196.txt

NIST Special Publication 800-12 An Introduction to Computer Security: The NIST Handbook (Chapter 5, Communications Security, discusses security policy)
http://cs-www.ncsl.nist.gov/publications/nistpubs/800-12/

Guidelines on Firewall and Firewall Policy
http://cs-www.ncsl.nist.gov/publications/nistpubs/800-41/sp800-41.pdf

Common Criteria Documentation (used to evaluate the security of computer and network devices)
http://www.commoncriteria.org/cc/cc.html

Common Criteria for Information Technology Security Evaluation
http://www.commoncriteria.org/introductory_overviews/CCUsersGuide.pdf

2.4.6   Human Factor

Security+ Objective 5.8—Education—Training of end users, executives, and HR

Security+ Objective 5.8.1—Communication

Security+ Objective 5.8.2—User Awareness

Security+ Objective 5.8.3—Education

Security+ Objective 5.8.4—Online Resources

When it comes to your organization, you will find that people and knowledge are the organization's greatest assets. However, they can also be the greatest risks, often making them the weakest link when it comes to security. Even at their best, people make mistakes. They fail to see the issues or do not appreciate the consequences. Sometimes, bad judgment or failure to communicate clearly can be the root of the problem.

To minimize the problems caused by people, establish systems procedures and rules that can be accepted by the user without causing too much hindrance. You must establish a security awareness program that consists of a security website on the company intranet, newsletters, posters, login banners, and emails. Security must be sold to your users; they must understand and accept the need for security. In addition, you have to train your users about security and give them constant reminders.

Many security procedures fail because the designers do not consider the user. Remember that if you make a network or system too difficult for the users to utilize, the users may try to bypass the security or perform steps that would circumvent the security such as writing down long passwords. Other times, users do not know any better or are not disciplined to following security procedures such as locking their computer when they are away from their desk.

Security+ Objective 1.4.9—Social Engineering

Security+ Objective 1.6—Social Engineering

Security+ Objective 5.1.2—Social Engineering

One of the simplest, yet often the most effective, attacks is social engineering. **Social engineering** is the process whereby an attacker attempts to acquire information about your network and system by talking to people in the organization. A social engineering attack may occur over the phone, by email, or by a visit. The intent is to acquire access information, such as user IDs and passwords. These types of attacks are relatively low-tech, very similar to a con done by a con artist, and the hardest attacks to defend against.

I have heard stories in which a small group of people have been able to gain access to the entire corporate network just by doing their homework, performing some social engineering, and by being friendly. The first part would involve researching the company, and learning key employee names by calling the HR department. By pretending to lose their key and/or identity badges, and with a smile, someone had let them in. Then by digging through the corporate trash (dumpster diving), they found useful documents. Then by having enough information, they then called the company's help desk by pretending to be someone who forgot his or her password. After the password was reset, they were able to gain access to the entire network.

The only preventative measure in dealing with social engineering attacks is to educate your users and staff to never give out user IDs or passwords over the phone or email to anyone who is not positively verified as being who they say they are. In addition, you should have procedures established for destroying confidential documents such as organizational charts, phone numbers, and addresses so that they cannot be retrieved by dumpster diving.

2.4.7   Operating Systems and Network Operating Systems

So what tools do you have to protect your network and the network resources? First, every PC must have an operating system. While some operating systems are more secure than others, you must also configure the operating system properly to allow authorized access and stop unauthorized access. This may also include installing additional components or software such as antivirus software and intruder detection systems.

Related to the operating system is the network operating system. A **network operating system (NOS)** is an operating system that includes special functions for connecting computers and devices to a local area network (LAN), to manage the resources and services of the network, and to provide network security for multiple users. The most common client/server network operating systems are Windows NT Server, Windows 2000 Server, Windows Server 2003, Novell NetWare, UNIX, and Linux. Note: Some operating systems such as Windows 9X, Windows NT Workstation, Windows 2000 Professional, and Windows XP can provide network resources as file and printer access although they are not servers.

Microsoft's early attempt at a network operating system began as a combined effort between Microsoft and IBM as OS/2. After some disagreement, Microsoft abandoned OS/2 to develop Windows NT. Windows NT (NT stands for New Technology) was an advanced, high-performance network operating system, which is robust in features and services, security, performance, and upgradeability. While Windows NT provides a good file and print server, it makes an excellent application server.

The early versions of Windows NT (such as Windows NT 3.51) used the Windows 3.XX Program Manager Interface. Newer versions of Windows NT use the popular Windows 95 or the Internet Explorer Active Desktop interface.

The next version of Windows NT is Windows 2000 (NT 5.0). There are four versions of Windows 2000, Windows 2000 Professional (workstation version), Windows 2000 Server, Windows 2000 Advanced Server and Windows 2000 DataCenter Server. Windows 2000 servers provide the following:

- **File and Print Sharing**—All Microsoft operating systems since Windows 95 support file and print sharing through File and Print Sharing for Microsoft Networks and Client for Microsoft Networks services.
- **Internet Information Server (IIS)**—Provides Web services (HTTP and FTP)
- **SQL Server**—Provides database services.
- **Microsoft Exchange**—Provides email services.
- **NTFS**—Provides a robust, flexible file system with file security.
- **Active Directory (AD)**—Similar to NDS in Netware, AD uses the "tree" concept for managing resources on a network. Its benefits will especially be realized in Enterprise applications where network administration and management will be almost painless. Everything is treated as an object that can be moved or edited across servers and domains.
- **Internet Connection Sharing (ICS)**—Microsoft Windows since Windows 98SE will allow a single dial-up connection to be shared across the network. This has great implications for SOHO's and home users with multiple machines that will no longer need to purchase an application to provide this feature for them.
- **Kerberos Security**—A security protocol that is used for distributed security within a domain tree/forest. This allows for transitive trusts and a single logon to provide access to all domain resources.
- **Clustering**—Windows 2000 Advanced Server and Windows 2000 Datacenter Server support clustering. Clustering enables two or more servers to work together to keep server-based applications available.

More recently, Microsoft released an updated family of Windows servers, Windows Server 2003 (Web Server, Standard Server, Enterprise Server and Datacenter Server). Note: Windows XP is the client version of Windows Server 2003. The Windows Server 2003 is still based on much of the same code used in Windows 2000, especially to the deployment and administration of Active Directory. In addition, IIS version 6.0 is said to be up to 30 percent faster than IIS version 5.0. In addition, all Windows Server 2003 include the .NET Framework, a run-time environment for XML-based Web services.

Microsoft Security and Privacy

http://www.microsoft.com/security/default.asp

HotFix and Security Bulletin Service

http://www.microsoft.com/technet/security/current.asp

Security

http://www.microsoft.com/technet/treeview/default.asp?url=/technet/security/Default.asp

Windows Security

http://www.microsoft.com/technet/treeview/default.asp?url=/technet/security/prodtech/windows/windows2000/default.asp

UNIX, a multiuser, multitasking operating system, the grandfather of network operating systems, was developed at Bell Labs in the early 1970s. Although UNIX is a mature, powerful, reliable operating system, it has been traditionally known for its cryptic commands and its general lack of user-friendliness. It is designed to handle high-usage loads while having support for common Internet services such as web server, FTP server, Terminal Emulation (Telnet), and database access. In addition, it can use the Network File System (NFS), which allows various network clients running different operating systems to access shared files stored on a UNIX machine.

Different from the other network operating systems, UNIX is produced by many manufacturers. The two main dialects of UNIX are AT&T's System V, and Berkeley University's BSD4.x. Popular manufacturer versions include Digital Equipment Corporation UNIX, Hewlett-Packard HP-UX, SCO OpenServer, Sun Microsystems Solaris. Another popular NOS, known as Banyan Vines, was based on a highly modified UNIX System V core. The "official" trademarked UNIX is now owned by "The Open Group," an industry standards organization, which certifies and brands UNIX implementations.

Linux (pronounced LIH-nuhks with a short "I") is a UNIX-like operating system that was designed to provide personal computer users a free or very low-cost operating system comparable to traditional and usually more expensive UNIX systems. Linux comes in versions for all the major microprocessor platforms including the Intel, PowerPC, SPARC, and Alpha platforms. Because it conforms to the POSIX standard user and programming interfaces, developers can write programs that can be ported to other platforms running Linux (or UNIX that also conforms to the POSIX standard).

The Linux kernel acts as a mediator for your programs and your hardware. Like the UNIX kernel, the Linux kernel is designed to do one thing well. It handles low-level things like managing memory, files, programs that are running, networking, and various hardware devices. For example, it arranges for the memory management for all of the running programs (processes), and makes sure that they all get a fair share of the processor clock cycles. In addition, it provides a nice, fairly portable interface for programs to talk to your hardware. Therefore, you can often think of the kernel as a cop directing traffic. Unlike Windows, it does not include a windowing system or GUI. Instead, Linux users can choose among a number of X servers and Window Managers.

By the time Linux version 1.0 was released, several Linux distributors had begun packaging the Linux kernel with basic support programs, the GNU utilities and compilers, the X Window System, and other useful programs. In 1995, the Linux 1.2 kernel was released, which supported kernel modules, the PCI bus, kernel-level firewalls, and non-TCP/IP networking protocols. By this time, Linux had become as stable as any commercial version of UNIX on the Intel x86 platforms.

Since Linux is often used as a server, it has a complete implementation of TCP/IP networking software, including drivers for the popular Ethernet cards, and the ability to use serial line protocols, such as SLIP and PPP to provide access to a TCP/IP network via a modem. With Linux, TCP/IP, and a connection to the network, you can communicate with users and machines across the Internet via electronic mail, USENET news, file transfers, and more.

In fact, Linux owes its versatility to the wide availability of software that runs on it. Understanding what software to use to solve what problem is key to maximizing the utility of Linux.

- **Web server**—Apache (http://www.apache.org) is the most popular web server.
- **Web proxy**—To better control web usage and to allow for caching of frequently accessed pages, Squid (http://www.squid-cache.org) is used.
- **File sharing**—Linux can be made to look like an NT server with respect to file and print sharing. Samba (http://www.samba.org) is the software that does this.
- **Email**—Linux excels at handling email. Sendmail (http://www.sendmail.org) is the most widely used Mail Transfer Agent (MTA). Qmail (http://www.qmail.org) and PostFix (http://www.postfix.org) are alternatives.
- **DNS**—The Domain Name Service provides mappings between names and IP addresses, along with distributing network information (i.e., mail servers). BIND (http://www.isc.org/products/BIND/) is the most widely used name server.

Several years ago, Novell NetWare was the standard LAN-based NOS. Since it was one of the primary players that brought networking to the PC arena, it helped replace the dumb terminals with a PC allowing a much easier way to share data files, applications, and printers. Novell NetWare is known as a strong file and print server. Unlike the other primary network operating systems, Novell NetWare runs as a dedicated stand-alone server.

Novell NetWare dominance was lost because the popularity of the popular Windows GUI interface versus NetWare's command/menu interface. In addition, you could not perform common administration tasks, such as creating users and giving a user access to a network resource, at the server, only at a client computer. Finally, Novell initially missed key opportunities during the development of the Internet.

Early versions of NetWare (NetWare 3.11, 3.12, and 3.2) use the NetWare Bindery for security. The Bindery is a flat-based database that resides on a single server and contains profiles of the network users for that server.

Newer versions of NetWare use NetWare Directory Services (NDS), a global, distributed, replicated database that keeps track of users and resources and provides controlled access to network resources. It is global because it spans an enterprise or multiple-server network. It is a distributed database because the database is kept close to the users rather than in a single central location, and it is replicated to several servers for fault-tolerance. Since the database exists for multiple servers, a user has to be only created once and the user only has to login to access all of the servers. Within the NDS design, the network objects such as users, printers, and storage units are grouped into containers (used to organize the network objects), much like files are divided into subdirectories or folders on your hard drive.

The latest versions of NetWare, NetWare 5 and 6, come with support for both Novell's own IPX network protocol and for the Internet's TCP/IP protocol. NetWare has integrated its own Novell Directory Services (NDS) with the TCP/IP's Domain Name System (DNS), Dynamic Host Configuration Protocol (DHCP), and application-level support for a Web server. In addition, NetWare 5 and 6 supports Java applications and includes an enhanced file system, enhanced printing services and advanced security.

Security+ Objective 1.3—Non-essential Services and Protocols—Disabling unnecessary systems/process/programs

After a network operating system (or an operating system) is installed, you must secure the system. To correct and close security holes within the operating system, you need to check for and load any service packs, patches, and security fixes. You will then need to disable any network services that are not required so that those network services cannot be exploited. On many network operating systems, there is one major user account that has full privileges to the system. If possible, you should rename this account. If the account has no password, you should add a password, and if it has a default password, you should change the password. Lastly, if the system has a guest account, you need to make sure that is disabled.

2.4.8   Routers and Firewalls

Another step in protecting your network and network resources is perimeter security. **Perimeter security** is controlling access to critical network applications, data, and services. The services offered include secure web and file servers, gateways, remote access, and naming services. Each organization should be prepared to select perimeter security tools based on their network requirements and budget.

Perimeter security is often controlled with routers and firewalls. A router, which works at the network OSI layer, is a device that connects two or more LANs. As multiple LANs are connected together, multiple routes are created to get from one LAN to another. Note: Since a router needs to know which network to route to, each port must have a unique network address. The primary role of a router is to transmit similar types of data packets from one local area network or wide area communications link (such as a T-1 or Fiber links) to another. The second role of a router is to select the best path between the source and destination.

When you send a packet from one computer to another computer, it first determines if the packet is sent locally to another computer on the same LAN or if the packet is sent to the router so that it can be routed to the destination LAN. If the packet is meant to go to a computer on another LAN, it is sent to the router (or gateway). The router will then determine what is the best route to take and forward the packets to that route. The packet will then go to the next router, and the entire process will repeat itself until it gets to the destination LAN. The destination router will then forward the packets to the destination computer.

To determine the best route, the routes use complex routing algorithms, which take into account a variety of factors, including the speed of transmission media, the number of network segments, and the network segment that carries the least amount of traffic. Routers then share status and routing information to other routers so that they can provide better traffic management and bypass slow connections. In addition, routers provide additional functionality, such as the ability to filter messages and forward them to different places based on various criteria. Most routers are multiprotocol routers because they can route data packets using many different protocols.

To keep track of the various routes in a network, the routers will create and maintain routing tables based on both network and node addresses (Layer 3—Network Layer of the OSI model). The routers communicate with one another to maintain their routing tables through a routing update message. The routing update message can consist of all or a portion of a routing table. By analyzing routing updates from all other routers, a router can build a detailed picture of network topology.

In addition to performing these basic functions, routers may perform any of the following options:

- Filter out broadcast transmissions to alleviate network congestion.
- Prevent certain types of traffic from getting to a network, enabling customized segregation and security.
- Monitor network traffic and report statistics to a Management Information Base (MIB).
- Diagnose internal or other connectivity problems and trigger alarms.

A **firewall** is a system designed to prevent unauthorized access to or from a private network. Firewalls can be implemented in both hardware and software, or a combination of both. It could be a router or a server. Firewalls are frequently used to prevent unauthorized Internet users from accessing private networks connected to the Internet, especially intranets. All messages entering or leaving the intranet pass through the firewall, which examines each message and blocks those that do not meet the specified security criteria. A firewall is considered a first line of defense in protecting private information. For greater security, data can be encrypted.

2.4.9   Documentation

Security+ Objective 5.9—Documentation

Security+ Objective 5.9.1—Standards and Guidelines

Security+ Objective 5.9.2—Systems Architecture

Security+ Objective 5.9.4—Logs and Inventories

Security+ Objective 5.9.5—Classification

Security+ Objective 5.9.5.1—Notification

Security+ Objective 5.9.6—Retention/Storage

Security+ Objective 5.9.7—Destruction

As a network administrator, you should know that your network needs to be documented. Besides how the computers are configured, your entire network infrastructure needs to be documented, including how the subnets and sites are connected, how IP addresses are assigned, how your remote access services are connected, and the addresses and configuration of all of your servers. It would also include details on how a system is installed and configured. The importance of documentation cannot be emphasized enough. It is essential for troubleshooting problems on the network, and it allows you to determine the best way to make changes to the network. It also reduces the learning curve of any new network technicians or administrators.

With the documentation listed above, you should also have logs and inventory documents that show you what systems you have, where they are placed, what work has been done on them, and what problems you have had with them. This will help you with warranties and service contracts, scheduled maintenance, and diagnosis of problems. It might also show when backups have occurred, which can also show proof of due care.

Now that you understand the importance of the documentation, you should also figure out that it is also a guide for someone else in how to hack into or infiltrate your network. Therefore, it is important to protect this documentation by keeping it under lock and key and never handing out documentation to people who don't need it.

You will usually classify any internal documents into groups. While the military has confidential, secret, and top secret, business may label them as public, confidential, private, and trade secret. Even when you send out notifications on any unexpected events, such as an intrusion or a planned change, such as an upgrade to a piece of equipment that is critical to operations, you need to treat these documents with care.

Since these documents are important, you should also have proper procedures when deleting them. This may involve shredding of paper-based data or maybe even burning for higher-security items. For electronic media, you may need to format them or overwrite them many times so that the information cannot be retrieved. Other security measures may involve using a strong electromagnet such as a bulk tape eraser. Higher security (for example some DoD requirements) may demand the opening of a hard drive and filing the metal on the platters.

2.5   CODE OF CONDUCT

While there is no industry-wide code of ethics to which all computer security professionals must subscribe, several associations have created their own codes of ethics for members, with the aim of promoting certain standards of behavior. The Information System Security Association is a nonprofit organization for security professionals. The association has a code of ethics for its members, and these appear to be good guidelines for anyone working in the computer industry. The code of ethics from ISSA includes:

- Perform all professional activities and duties in accordance with the law and the highest ethical principles.
- Promote good information security concepts and practices.
- Maintain the confidentiality of all proprietary or otherwise sensitive information encountered in the course of professional activities.
- Discharge professional responsibilities with diligence and honesty.
- Refrain from any activities which might constitute a conflict of interest or otherwise damage the reputation of employers, the information security profession, or the Association.
- Do not intentionally injure or impugn the professional reputation or practice of colleagues, clients, or employers.

2.6   DOD SECURITY STANDARDS

The U.S. Department of Defense (DoD) gave responsibility for computer security to the National Security Agency (NSA) in 1981, and the National Computing Security Center (NCSC) was formed. The DoD published a series of books dealing with computer and network security issues known as the Rainbow Series.

The NCSC first released *A Trusted Computer System Evaluation Criteria (TCSEC)* in 1983 for stand-alone, non-networked computers, which is unofficially referred to as the Orange Book. The Orange Book defines the standard parameters of a trusted computer in several classes, indicated by a letter and a number. The higher the letter, the higher the certification. For example, class A is the highest class, and class D is the lowest class. Note: Recently, the U.S. government has discontinued the TCSEC in favor of the Common Criteria, which is explained in the next section.

According to TCSEC, system security is evaluated at one of four broad levels, ranging from class D to class A1, each level building on the previous one, with added security measures at each level and partial level.

- Class D is defined as Minimum Security; systems evaluated at this level have failed to meet higher-level criteria.
- Class C1 is defined as Discretionary Security Protection; systems evaluated at this level meet security requirements by controlling user access to data. Note: C1 has been discontinued as a certification.

- Class C2, defined as Controlled Access Protection adds to C1 requirements additional user accountability features, such as login procedures.
- Class B1 is defined as Labeled Security Protection; systems evaluated at this level also have a stated policy model and specifically labeled data.
- Class B2, defined as Structured Protection, adds to B1 requirements a more explicit and formal security policy.
- Class B3, defined as Security Domains, adds stringent engineering and monitoring requirements and is highly secure.
- Class A1 is defined as Verified Design; systems evaluated at this level are functionally equivalent to B3 systems but include more formal analysis of function to assure security.

In 1987, the NCSC released enhanced testing criteria based on the Orange Book standard. The new standard, often referred to as the Red Book, is the Trusted Network Interpretation Environment Guidelines. They also use the D through A levels. As with the C2 class in the Trusted Computer implantation, the C2 class is the highest class for generic network operating systems. Higher-level classes require that operating systems be specifically written to incorporate security-level information as the data is input.

The most publicized class is C2, Controlled Access Protection, which must provide a unique user account for each person on the network and provide accountability for the information the user uses. Additionally, the network communications must be secure. Higher-level classes require that operating systems be specifically written to incorporate security-level information as the data is input.

Currently, several network operating systems are under evaluation for C2 Trusted Network certification. The following operating systems are C2-level certified for Trusted Computer (Orange Book):

- Windows NT Workstation and Windows NT Server Version 3.5 with Service Pack 3.
- Windows NT Workstation and Windows NT Server Version 4.0 with Service Pack 6a and C2 Update.

If the computer on which Windows NT Server is installed is connected to a network, it loses the C2 Trusted Computer certification. The only currently available network operating system that has achieved C2 Trusted Network certification is:

- Novell IntranetWare [NetWare 4.11 Server] with IntranetWare Support Pack 3A and Directory Services Update DS.NLM v5.90, DSREPAIR.NLM v4.48 and ROLLCALL.NLM v4.10.

Information Technology Security Evaluation Criteria (ITSEC) is a European criteria similar to the TCSEC, but with some important differences. ITSEC emphasizes the integrity and availability of products and systems and introduces the distinctions of effectiveness and correctness. The TCSEC is primarily concerned with security policy, accountability, and assurance. Various European certification bodies grant ratings based upon the ITSEC. Examples of ITSEC ratings are Level E2, which is a measure of effectiveness, and Class F-C2, which is a measure of functionality. A combined E2/F-C2 evaluation is similar in scope to the Class C2 TCSEC evaluation.

> **To Verify Security Certification or Check out Officially Released Documents, go to the following Website:**
>
> http://www.radium.ncsc.mil/tpep/epl/index.html

2.7   COMMON CRITERIA

A standard that is gaining popularity and importance is the **Common Criteria (CC),** which is a standard for evaluating the security of computer and network devices. This standard was developed as a joint effort between organizations in the United States, Canada, France, the Netherlands, and the United Kingdom. The International Organization for Standardization (ISO) also recognizes the CC as ISO 15408. Prior to the implementation of the CC, the U.S. government used the Trusted Computer System Evaluation Criteria (TSEC). The website for the Common Criteria is http://www.commoncriteria.org.

The CC is available at http://www.commoncriteria.org/cc/cc.html. The Common Criteria (CC) is presented as a set of three distinct but related parts:

1. **Introduction and general model**—The introduction to the CC. It defines general concepts and principles of IT security evaluation and presents a general model of evaluation. Part 1 also presents constructs for expressing IT security objectives, for selecting and defining IT security requirements, and for writing high-level specifications for products and systems. In addition, the usefulness of each part of the CC is described in terms of each of the target audiences.
2. **Security functional requirements**—It establishes a set of security functional components as a standard way of expressing the security functional requirements for Targets of Evaluation (TOEs). Part 2 catalogues the set of functional components, families, and classes.
3. **Security assurance requirements**—It establishes a set of assurance components as a standard way of expressing the assurance requirements for TOEs. Part 3 catalogues the set of assurance components, families, and classes. Part 3 also defines evaluation criteria for Protection Profiles (PPs) and Security Targets (STs) and presents evaluation assurance levels that define the predefined CC scale for rating assurance for TOEs, which is called the Evaluation Assurance Levels (EALs).

The version 2.1 standard outlines a comprehensive set of evaluation criteria. These criteria are broken down into seven Evaluation Assurance levels (EAL). EAL 0 to EAL 7 are shown in table 2.1.

Table 2.1   EAL Levels

Level	Definition
EAL 0	Inadequate Assurance.
EAL 1	Functionally Tested. Provides analysis of the security functions, using a functional and interface specification of the TOE, to understand the security behavior. The analysis is supported by independent testing of the security functions.
EAL 2	Structurally Tested. Analysis of the security functions using a functional and interface specification and the high-level design of the subsystems of the TOE. Independent testing of the security functions, evidence of developer "black box" testing, and evidence of a development search for obvious vulnerabilities.
EAL 3	Methodically Tested and Checked. The analysis is supported by "grey box" testing, selective independent confirmation of the developer test results, and evidence of a developer search for obvious vulnerabilities. Development environment controls and TOE configuration management are also required.
EAL 4	Methodically Designed, Tested, and Reviewed. Analysis is supported by the low-level design of the modules of the TOE, and a subset of the implementation. Testing is supported by an independent search for obvious vulnerabilities. Development controls are supported by a life-cycle model, identification of tools, and automated configuration management.
EAL 5	Semiformally Designed and Tested. Analysis includes all of the implementation. Assurance is supplemented by a formal model and a semiformal presentation of the functional specification and high-level design, and a semiformal demonstration of correspondence. The search for vulnerabilities must ensure relative resistance to penetration attack. Covert channel analysis and modular design are also required.
EAL 6	Semiformally Verified Design and Tested. Analysis is supported by a modular and layered approach to design, and a structured presentation of the implementation. The independent search for vulnerabilities must ensure high resistance to penetration attack. The search for covert channels must be systematic. Development environment and configuration management controls are further strengthened.
EAL 7	Formally Verified Design and Tested. The formal model is supplemented by a formal presentation of the functional specification and high-level design showing correspondence. Evidence of developer "white box" testing and complete independent confirmation of developer test results are required. Complexity of the design must be minimized.

More information about the Evaluation Assurance Level can be found at:

http://www.commoncriteria.org/docs/EALs.html

The recommended level of certification for commercial systems is EAL 4. Currently, only a very few operating systems have been approved at the EAL 4 level. As of September 2002, Sun Microsystems has Sun Solaris 8 Operating Environment and Sun Trusted Solaris Version 8 4/01. Windows 2000 family achieved a rating of EAL 4 + Flaw Remediation under the Common Criteria. To meet the Flaw Remediation requirement over and above EAL 4, as Windows 2000 did, the developer/vendor must establish flaw remediation procedures that describe the tracking of security flaws, the identification of corrective actions, and the distribution of corrective action information to customers. The Microsoft Security Response Center fulfills these roles for Windows 2000. For more information, see the following website:

http://www.microsoft.com/technet /security/issues/w2kccwp.asp

WHAT YOU NEED TO KNOW

Introduction

1. Data stored on a computer or stored on the network is vital to the users and probably the company.
2. Security, at least network security, refers to the process and techniques by which digital information assets are protected.
3. The goals of network security are to maintain integrity, protect confidentiality, and assure availability.

Security+ Objective 1.1—Access Control

1. Access Control involves the process by which you restrict access to computing resources. It is a combination of Authentication (proving who you claim to be) and Authorization (what are you allowed to see, presuming you are whom you claim you are).
2. Users should be granted access only to those network resources that they need in order to perform their assigned job functions.
3. Need to know is a basic security concept that holds that information should be limited to only those individuals who require it.
4. When you give a person or group only the required amount of access and nothing more, this is known as the rule of least privilege.

Security+ Objective 1.1.1—MAC/DAC/RBAC

Security+ Objective 5.5.5—MAC/DAC/RBAC

1. In a discretionary access control (DAC) environment, resource owners and administrators jointly control access to resources.
2. The mandatory access control (MAC) model is based on nondiscretionary control based on multilevel security. In the MAC model, you classify all users and resources to a security label or level. If users have the same level or higher as the resource that they are trying to access, they are granted access.
3. In role-based access control (RBAC), access decisions are based on an individual's roles and responsibilities within the organization or user base. It allows a user to be assigned to a role, and access is granted to the role.
4. When a person logs onto a computer or accesses a network resource, that person is known as a user.
5. A group is no more than a list of users.
6. Instead of assigning access to a network resource to each user individually, you can add a bunch of people to the group and assign access to the entire group.
7. While a group can categorize users, a role is a special type of group defined by job roles or duties.

Security+ Objective 1.2—Authentication

Security+ Objective 5.5.4—Auditing (Privilege, Usage, Escalation)

1. One commonly used model to intelligently control access to a network and its resources is authentication, authorization, and accounting (AAA).
2. In networks, authentication is the ability to verify the identity of a user, system, or system element.
3. Authorization is the process of giving someone permission to do or have something.
4. When a user accesses a network resource, accounting (sometimes known as auditing) records each resource a user uses or accesses while using a PC or network.
5. To detect intrusions, you will need to use auditing, you will have to use a wide range of tools, and you will have to examine system log files.
6. Confidentiality is the protection of data from unauthorized disclosure to a third party.
7. Availability is defined as the continuous operation of computers systems.

8. Nonrepudiation is the ability of a system to verify that data was either sent or received by the sender or receiver.

Security+ Objective 1.3—Nonessential Services and Protocols—Disabling unnecessary systems/process/programs

1. You will then need to disable any network services that are not required so that those network services can be exploited.

Security+ Objective 1.4.9—Social Engineering

Security+ Objective 1.6—Social Engineering

Security+ Objective 5.1.2—Social Engineering

1. Social engineering is the process whereby an attacker attempts to acquire information about your network and system by talking to people in the organization.
2. The only preventative measure in dealing with social engineering attacks is to educate your users and staff to never give out user IDs or password over the phone or email to anyone who is not positively verified as being who they say they are.

Security+ Objective 3.1.1—Firewalls

1. Perimeter security is controlling access to critical network applications, data, and services.
2. A firewall is a system designed to prevent unauthorized access to or from a private network.

Security+ Objective 5.1.3—Environment

1. When securing a network, it is essential that you physically secure all equipment including computers, routers, hubs, switches, cables, and other network and storage devices.
2. Operational security is security as it relates to how an organization operates or does things.

Security+ Objective 5.5.2—Single Sign-on

1. Single sign-on is when users only have to log on once to be granted access to all the resources that they have access to.

Security+ Objective 5.5.3—Centralized vs. Decentralized

1. Using a single security database for all of your network resources is known as centralized management.
2. Using a multiple security database for all of your network resources is known as decentralized management.

Security+ Objective 5.4—Policy and Procedures

Security+ Objective 5.4.1—Security Policy

Security+ Objective 5.4.1.1—Acceptable Use

Security+ Objective 5.4.1.2—Due Care

Security+ Objective 5.4.1.3—Privacy

Security+ Objective 5.4.1.4—Separation of Duties

Security+ Objective 5.4.1.5—Need to Know

Security+ Objective 5.4.1.6—Password Management

Security+ Objective 5.4.1.7—SLA

Security+ Objective 5.4.1.8—Disposal/Destruction

Security+ Objective 5.4.1.9—HR Policy

Security+ Objective 5.4.1.9.1—Termination—Adding/revoking passwords, privileges, etc.

Security+ Objective 5.4.1.9.2—Hiring—Adding/revoking passwords, privileges, etc.

Security+ Objective 5.4.1.9.3—Code of Ethics

Security+ Objective 5.4.2—Incident Response Policy

1. A policy is a document that states the goals of an organization with regard to certain areas of operation.
2. A policy often includes procedures, which outline methods for achieving or maintaining the stated goals of the policy.
3. A policy is a statement of what to do and a procedure is a statement of how to do it.
4. Policies and procedures are created and used to define how organizational assets should be acquired, utilized, maintained, and discarded.
5. A security policy is a single document or a set of related documents that describes the security controls that govern an organization's systems, behavior, and activities.
6. When developing a security policy, you need to establish due care. Due care means that reasonable precautions are being taken that indicate an organization is being responsible.
7. A standard that is gaining popularity and importance is the Common Criteria (CC), which is a standard for evaluating the security of computer and network devices.

Security+ Objective 5.7—Risk Identification

Security+ Objective 5.7.1—Asset Identification

Security+ Objective 5.7.2—Risk Assessment

Security+ Objective 5.7.3—Threat Identification

Security+ Objective 5.7.4—Vulnerabilities

1. A risk is simply a potential for loss or harm.
2. A threat is a person, place, or thing that has the potential to access resources and cause harm.
3. A hacker, also known as a cracker, is someone who breaks security on an automated information system or a network. The hacker typically does something mischievous or malicious by first breaking into a system.
4. Every security system and network has vulnerability.

5. A vulnerability is a point where a resource is susceptible to attack. It can be thought of as a weakness.

6. An exploit is a type of attack on a resource that is accessed by a threat that makes use of a vulnerability in your environment.

7. Countermeasures are deployed to counteract threats and vulnerabilities, therefore reducing the risk in your environment.

8. Risk analysis or risk assessment is the process of reviewing all the aspects of the resource that you are trying to protect, and determining the possible risks. This process also involves developing any countermeasures to eliminate or reduce the risks.

9. The best goal is to prevent a security violation from occurring.

10. When developing a security plan, you must evaluate the risks to your network and network resources and develop strategies to make everything secure.

11. Integrity refers to the assurance that data is not altered or destroyed in an unauthorized manner.

Security+ Objective 5.8—Education—Training of end users, executives, and HR

Security+ Objective 5.8.1—Communication

Security+ Objective 5.8.2—User Awareness

Security+ Objective 5.8.3—Education

Security+ Objective 5.8.4—Online Resources

1. When it comes to your organization, you will find that people and knowledge are the organization's greatest asset. However, they can also be the greatest risks, often making them the weakest link when it comes to security.

2. To minimize the problems caused by people, establish systems, procedures, and rules that can be accepted by users without causing too much hindrance.

3. You must establish a security awareness program that consists of a security website on the company intranet, newsletters, posters, login banners, and emails.

4. Security must be sold to your users; they must understand and accept the need for security.

5. You have to train your users about security and give them constant reminders.

Security+ Objective 5.9—Documentation

Security+ Objective 5.9.1—Standards and Guidelines

Security+ Objective 5.9.2—Systems Architecture

Security+ Objective 5.9.3—Change Documentation

Security+ Objective 5.9.4—Logs and Inventories

Security+ Objective 5.9.5—Classification

Security+ Objective 5.9.5.1—Notification

Security+ Objective 5.9.6—Retention/Storage

Security+ Objective 5.9.7—Destruction

1. To establish a security program, you must define a foundation that usually comes in the form of documentation.

2. Some of these documents are "living documents." Therefore, these documents need to be changed from time to time. In addition, even your semipermanent documents need to be changed from time to time.

3. You need to have some type of change management to change these documents. Change management defines a systematic way to explain how changes are introduced and handled. This way, all departments that have a stake in the changes can give input into the changes to be made.

4. As a network administrator, you should know that your network needs to be documented.

5. Any internal documents are often classified into groups. While the military has confidential, secret, and top secret, business may label them as public, confidential, private, and trade secret.

6. Since the network documentation is important, you should also figure out that it is also a guide for someone else in how to hack into or infiltrate your network. Therefore, it is important to protect this documentation by keeping it under lock and key and never handing out documentation to people who don't need it.

7. Since these documents are important, you should also have proper procedures when deleting them.

QUESTIONS

1. You have identified a number of risks to which your company's assets are exposed and want to implement policies, procedures, and various security measures. In doing so, what will be your objective?
   a. Eliminate every threat that may affect the business.
   b. Manage the risks so that the problems resulting from them will be minimized.
   c. Implement as many security measures as possible to address every risk that an asset may be exposed to.
   d. Ignore as many risks as possible to keep costs down.

2. DAC (Discretionary Access Control) systems operate under which following statements?
   a. Files that don't have an owner CAN NOT be modified.

b. The administrator of the system is an owner of each object.

c. The operating system is an owner of each object.

d. Each object has an owner, which has full control over the object.

3. The term "due care" best relates to:

a. Policies and procedures intended to reduce the likelihood of damage or injury.

b. Scheduled activity in a comprehensive preventative maintenance program.

c. Techniques and methods for secure shipment of equipment and supplies.

d. User responsibilities involved when sharing passwords in a secure environment.

4. What are access decisions based on in a MAC (mandatory access control) environment?

a. Access control lists

b. Ownership

c. Group membership

d. Sensitivity labels

5. The de facto IT (Information Technology) security evaluation criteria for the international community is called:

a. Common Criteria.

b. Global Criteria.

c. TCSEC (Trusted Computer System Evaluation Criteria).

d. ITSEC (Information Technology Security Evaluation Criteria).

6. Access control decisions are based on responsibilities that an individual user or process has in an organization. This best describes:

a. MAC (mandatory access control).

b. RBAC (role-based access control).

c. DAC (discretionary access control).

d. None of the above.

7. Of the following services, which one determines what a user can change or view?

a. Data integrity

b. Data confidentiality

c. Data authentication

d. Access control

8. While performing a routing site audit of your wireless network, you discover an unauthorized Access Point placed on your network under the desk of accounting department security. When questioned, the security person denies any knowledge of it but informs you that her new boyfriend has been to visit her several times, including taking her to lunch one time. What type of attack have you just become a victim of?

a. SYN flood

b. Distributed denial of service

c. Man in the middle attack

d. TCP flood

e. IP spoofing

f. Social engineering

g. Replay attack

h. Phone tag

i. Halloween attack

9. Giving each user or group of users only the access they need to do their job is an example of which security principle?

a. Least privilege

b. Defense in depth

c. Separation of duties

d. Access control

10. Access controls that are created and administered by the data owner are considered:

a. MACs (mandatory access control).

b. RBACs (role-based access control).

c. LBACs (list-based access control).

d. DACs (discretionary access control).

11. In a decentralized privilege management environment, user accounts and passwords are stored on:

a. One central authentication server.

b. Each individual server.

c. No more than two servers.

d. One server configured for decentralized management.

12. User A needs to send a private email to User B. User A does not want anyone to have the ability to read the email except for User B, thus retaining privacy. Which tenet of information security is User A concerned about?

a. Authentication   b. Integrity

c. Confidentiality   d. Nonrepudiation

13. Controlling access to information systems and associated networks is necessary for the preservation of their:

a. Authenticity, confidentiality, integrity, and availability.

b. Integrity and availability.

c. Confidentiality, integrity, and availability.

d. Authenticity, confidentiality, and availability.

14. You are assessing risks and determining which asset protection policies to create first. Another member of the IT staff has provided you with a list of assets, which have importance weighted on a scale of 1 to 10. Internet connectivity has an importance of 8, data has an importance of 9, personnel has an importance of 7, and software has an importance of 5. Based on the weights, what is the order in which you will generate new policies?

a. Internet policy, data security, personnel safety policy, software policy.

b. Data security policy, Internet policy, software policy, personnel safety policy.

c. Software policy, personnel safety policy, Internet policy, data security policy.

d. Data security policy, Internet policy, personnel safety policy, software policy.

15. The protection of data against unauthorized access or disclosure is an example of what?

a. Confidentiality   b. Integrity

c. Signing   d. Hashing

16. You need the ability to ensure that a party to a contract or a communication cannot deny the authenticity of his or her signature on a document

or the sending of a message that this party originated. This is a form of what?

a. Hoaxing   b. Cracking

c. Nonrepudiation   d. Smurfing

17. The servers in your network are all kept in a secure server vault that has a locked door and a guard. If an intruder were able to gain physical access to your server vault without physically breaking in, what form of attack would you have been a victim of?

a. Halloween attack

b. SYN flood

c. Man in the middle attack

d. TCP flood

e. IP spoofing

f. Phone tag

g. Distributed denial of service

h. Social engineering

i. Replay attack

18. The company that Joe works for has three departments: Accounting, Sales, and Management. The CIO has directed Joe to design an access control method that revolves around specific jobs, such as Administrator, Print Operator, and User. What access control method should be used to accomplish this goal?

a. Role-based access control

b. Discretionary access control

c. Blocking access control

d. Mandatory access control

e. Closed access control

f. Permission-based access control

19. Pat is one of the help-desk assistants in your organization. If you call Pat on the phone and get privileged network information from him, such as server names or account passwords, you have performed what type of attack?

a. Halloween attack

b. SYN flood

c. Man in the middle attack

d. TCP flood

e. IP spoofing

f. Phone tag

g. Distributed denial of service

h. Social engineering

i. Replay attack

20. What type of access control by default blocks all access to resources unless you specifically have permission to access them?

a. Role-based access control

b. Discretionary access control

c. Blocking access control

d. Mandatory access control

e. Closed access control

f. Permission-based access control

21. _____ is the type of access control commonly associated with Windows NT and Windows 2000 networks. (Select the correct answer for the blank.)

a. Role-based access control

b. Discretionary access control

c. Blocking access control

d. Mandatory access control

e. Closed access control

f. Permission-based access control

22. Your help-desk has been caught handing out passwords and other authentication data that has caused many security breaches. The help-desk technicians, when asked, told you that they were tricked into giving this information away. What kind of attack would this be considered?

a. Buffer overflow

b. Smurf

c. Spoof

d. Social engineering

23. An extranet is considered to be _____ . (Select the correct answer for the blank.)

a. Inside the company's network

b. Outside the company's network

c. Bordering the company's gateway

d. Connected to the company's network via the BGP protocol

24. What is the name for the portion of a network that is contained within an organization?

a. Internet   b. Extranet

c. Intranet   d. Gateway

e. Demilitarized Zone

25. _____ are usually at the highest risk from a security standpoint. (Select the correct answer for the blank.)

a. Firewalls   b. Servers

c. Routers   d. Workstations

e. Switches

26. What principle states that a user be given no more access than is required to perform his or her job?

a. Principle of least privilege

b. Principle of effective privilege

c. Principle of aggregate privilege

d. Principle of most privilege

27. A sound security policy will define:

a. What is considered an organization's assets.

b. What attacks are planned against the organization.

c. How an organization compares to others in security audits.

d. Weaknesses in competitors' systems.

28. Nonrepudiation is generally used to:

a. Protect the system from transmitting various viruses, worms, and Trojan horses to other computers on the same network.

b. Protect the system from DoS (denial of service) attacks.

c. Prevent the sender or the receiver from denying that the communication between them has occurred.

d. Ensure the confidentiality and integrity of the communication.

29. Discouraging employees from misusing company email is best handled by:
    a. Enforcing ACLs (access control lists).
    b. Creating a network security policy.
    c. Implementing strong authentication.
    d. Encrypting company email messages.
30. Which of the following is the best description of "separation of duties"?
    a. Assigning different parts of tasks to different employees.
    b. Employees are granted only the privileges necessary to perform their tasks.
    c. Each employee is granted specific information that is required to carry out a job function.
    d. Screening employees before assigning them to a position.
31. An organization's primary purpose in conducting risk analysis in dealing with computer security is:
    a. To identify vulnerabilities to the computer systems within the organization.
    b. To quantify the impact of potential threats in relation to the cost of lost business functionality.
    c. To identify how much it will cost to implement countermeasures.
    d. To delegate responsibility.
32. A user wants to send an email and ensure that the message is not tampered with while in transit. Which feature of modern cryptographic systems will facilitate this?
    a. Confidentiality   b. Authentication
    c. Integrity   d. Nonrepudiation
33. File encryption using symmetric cryptography satisfies what security requirement?
    a. Confidentiality   b. Access control
    c. Data integrity   d. Authentication
34. When a potential hacker looks through the trash, the most useful items or information that might be found include all except:
    a. An IP address.
    b. System configuration or network map.
    c. Old passwords.
    d. System access requests.
35. Security training should emphasize that the weakest links in the security of an organization are typically:
    a. Firewalls.   b. Policies.
    c. Viruses.   d. People.

36. When a change to user security policy is made, the policy maker should provide appropriate documentation to:
    a. The security administrator.
    b. Auditors.
    c. Users.
    d. All staff.
37. What is generally the most overlooked element of security management?
    a. Security awareness
    b. Intrusion detection
    c. Risk assessment
    d. Vulnerability control
38. Which of the following is most commonly used by an intruder to gain unauthorized access to a system?
    a. Brute force attack
    b. Key logging
    c. Trojan horse
    d. Social engineering
39. Impersonating a dissatisfied customer of a company and requesting a password change on the customer's account is a form of:
    a. Hostile code.
    b. Social engineering.
    c. IP (Internet Protocol) spoofing.
    d. Man in the middle attack.
40. Sensitive material is currently displayed on a user's monitor. What is the best course of action for the user before leaving the area?
    a. The user should leave the area. The monitor is at a personal desk, so there is no risk.
    b. Turn off the monitor.
    c. Wait for the screen saver to start.
    d. Refer to the company's policy on securing sensitive data.
41. Implementation of access control devices and technologies must fully reflect an organization's security position as contained in its:
    a. ACLs.
    b. Access control matrixes.
    c. Information security policies.
    d. Internal control procedures.
42. What is the best method of reducing vulnerability from dumpster diving?
    a. Hiring additional security staff.
    b. Destroying paper and other media.
    c. Installing surveillance equipment.
    d. Emptying the trash can frequently.

HANDS-ON EXERCISES

Exercise 1: Internet Research on Security Policies

1. Open the following website and read its contents:

   http://www.sans.org/resources/policies/

2. Open the NIST Special Publication 800-12 (An Introduction to Computer Security: The NIST Handbook) and read chapter 5.

   http://cs-www.ncsl.nist.gov/publications/nistpubs/800-12/

Exercise 2: Identifying Risks and Developing a Security Policy I

You have been approached by the Acme Corporation, the maker of widgets. The Acme Corporation is designing a new super-magnet, and they are collaborating with Looney Toon University. While the professors and students have developed a new technique in creating magnetic fields, the Acme Corporation will then use this technique to mass produce the super-magnets. The university personnel will provide information on the new technique the Acme Corporation needs to implement. What security implications must you take into consideration?

- Identify the security risks.
- Draft a security policy to cover this research and implementation of this technology and production of the magnets.
- What technology options would you recommend to provide a secure communication between the Acme Corporation and Looney Toon University?
- Provide a detailed list of equipment, costs, and your reasons for selecting the hardware and software you choose.

If you need any additional information, feel free to make it up.

Exercise 3: Identifying Risks and Developing a Security Policy II

If you have a personal network or you are an administrator of a network, identify the risks of your network and develop a security policy to make sure that your network is as secure as possible. Write down what rules you will establish and which technology you will use as a firewall if needed.

Exercise 4: Looking at Hacking Methods

1. Go to the http://www.astalavista.com.
2. Pick a tutorial on hacking and describe an example of hacking.

CHAPTER 3

The OSI Model and Protocol Overview

Topics Covered in this Chapter

Introduction

Before getting deeper into security, it is important that you have a good understanding of the OSI model and the common protocols, including TCP/IP and IPX/SPX. You must know these protocols well enough to troubleshoot and well enough to look at individual packets to determine problems.

Objectives

1. **Security+ Objective 3.1.10**—Network Monitoring/Diagnostic

2. **Security+ Objective 4.4**—Standards and Protocols

3.1   THE NEED FOR STANDARDIZATION

To overcome compatibility issues, hardware and software often follow standards (dictated specifications or most popular). Standards exist for operating systems, data formats, communication protocols, and electrical interfaces. If a product does not follow a widely used standard, the product will usually not be widely accepted in the computer market and will often cause problems with your PC. As far as the user is concerned, standards help you determine what hardware and software to purchase, and they allow you to customize a network made of components from different manufacturers.

As new technology is introduced, manufacturers are usually rushing to get their products out so that their product has a better chance of becoming the standard. Often, competing computer manufacturers introduce similar technology at the same time. Until one is designated as the standard, other companies and customers are sometimes forced to take sides. Since it is sometimes difficult to determine what will emerge as the true standard and the technology sometimes needs time to mature, it is best to wait a little to see what happens.

There are two main types of standards. The first standard is called the de jure standards. The de jure standard or the by law standard is a standard that has been dictated by an appointed committee such as the International Standard Organization (ISO). Some of the more common standard committees are shown in table 3.1.

The other type of standard is the de facto standard. The de facto standard or from the fact standard is a standard that has been accepted by the industry just because it was the most common. These standards are not recognized by a standard committee. For example, the de facto for microprocessors are those produced by Intel, while the de facto standard for the sound cards are those produced by Creative Labs.

When a system or standard has an open architecture, it indicates that the specification of the system or standard is public. This includes approved standards as well as privately designed architecture whose specifications are made public by the designers. The advantage of an open architecture is that anyone can design products based on the architecture and design add-on products for it. Of course, this also allows other manufacturers to duplicate the product.

The opposite of an open architecture is a proprietary system. A proprietary system is privately owned and controlled by a company and has not divulged specifications that would allow other companies to duplicate the product. Proprietary architectures often do not allow mixing and matching products from different manufacturers and may cause hardware and software compatibility problems.

3.2   OSI REFERENCE MODEL

With the goal of standardizing the network world, the **International Organization for Standardization (ISO)** began development of the **Open Systems Interconnection (OSI) reference model.** The key reason that ISO released the OSI model was so that different vendor networks could work with each

Table 3.1   Common Standard Committees or Organizations

American National Standards Institute (ANSI) http://www.ansi.org	ANSI is primarily concerned with software. ANSI has defined standards for a number of programming languages including C Language and the SCSI interface.
Electronics Industry Alliance (EIA) http://www.eia.org	EIA is a trade organization composed of representatives from electronics manufacturing firms across the United States. EIA is divided into several subgroups: the Telecommunications Industry Association (TIA); the Consumer Electronics Manufacturers Association (ECA); the Joint Electron Device Engineering Council (JEDEC); the Solid State Technology Association; the Government Division; and the Electronic Information Group (EIG).
Institute of Electrical and Electronic Engineers (IEEE) http://www.ieee.org	IEEE sets standards for most types of electrical interfaces including RS-232C (serial communication interface) and network communications.
International Standards Organization (ISO) http://www.iso.ch	ISO is an international standard organization for communications and information exchange.
International Telecommunications Union (ITU) http://www.itu.int/	ITU defines international standards, particularly communications protocols. Formerly called the Comité Consultatif Internationale Télégraphique et Téléphonique (CCITT)
Internet Engineering Task Force (IETF) http://www.ietf.org	IETF is responsible for the Internet protocol standards, which include cryptography as used on the Internet.
National Institute of Standards and Technology (NIST) http://www.nist.gov/	NIST is the developer for Federal Information Processing Standards (FIPS) documents. FIPS publications are developed when NIST feels that no existing standards adequately address an area of technology that is useful to the government. Among the FIPS standards related to cryptography are ones for secure hashing, digital signature, and the AES (Advanced Encryption Standard) algorithm.
RSA Data Security, Inc. http://www.rsasecurity.com	RSA Data Security, Inc. provides interoperable solutions for establishing online identities, access rights and privileges for people, applications, and devices. Many of the ANSI X9 standards first appeared in standards documents published by a cryptographic systems vendor, and are known as the RSA Data Security, Inc. Public-Key Cryptography Standards (PKCS) series. Note: RSA is short for Rivest, Shamir, and Adelman, the inventors of public key encryption technique.

other. Since the ISO model separated the various functions, the vendor did not have to write an entire protocol stack. One vendor could write device drivers for their device and not worry about higher layers, and the work can be contained and modularized. This also speeds up the process of bringing a product to market, as it minimizes code that a vendor needs to write. The OSI reference model was completed and released in 1984.

Today, the OSI reference model is the world's prominent networking architecture model. It is a popular tool for learning about networks. The OSI protocols, on the other hand, have had a long "growing up period." While OSI implementations are not unheard of, the OSI protocols have not yet attained the popularity of many proprietary and de facto standards.

The OSI reference model adopts a layered approach in which a communication subsystem is broken down into seven layers, each one of which performs a well-defined function. The OSI reference model defines the functionality that needs to be provided at each layer but does not specify actual services and protocols to be used at each one of these layers. From this reference model, actual protocol architecture can be developed. See figure 3.1 and table 3.2.

Figure 3.1   The OSI Reference Model

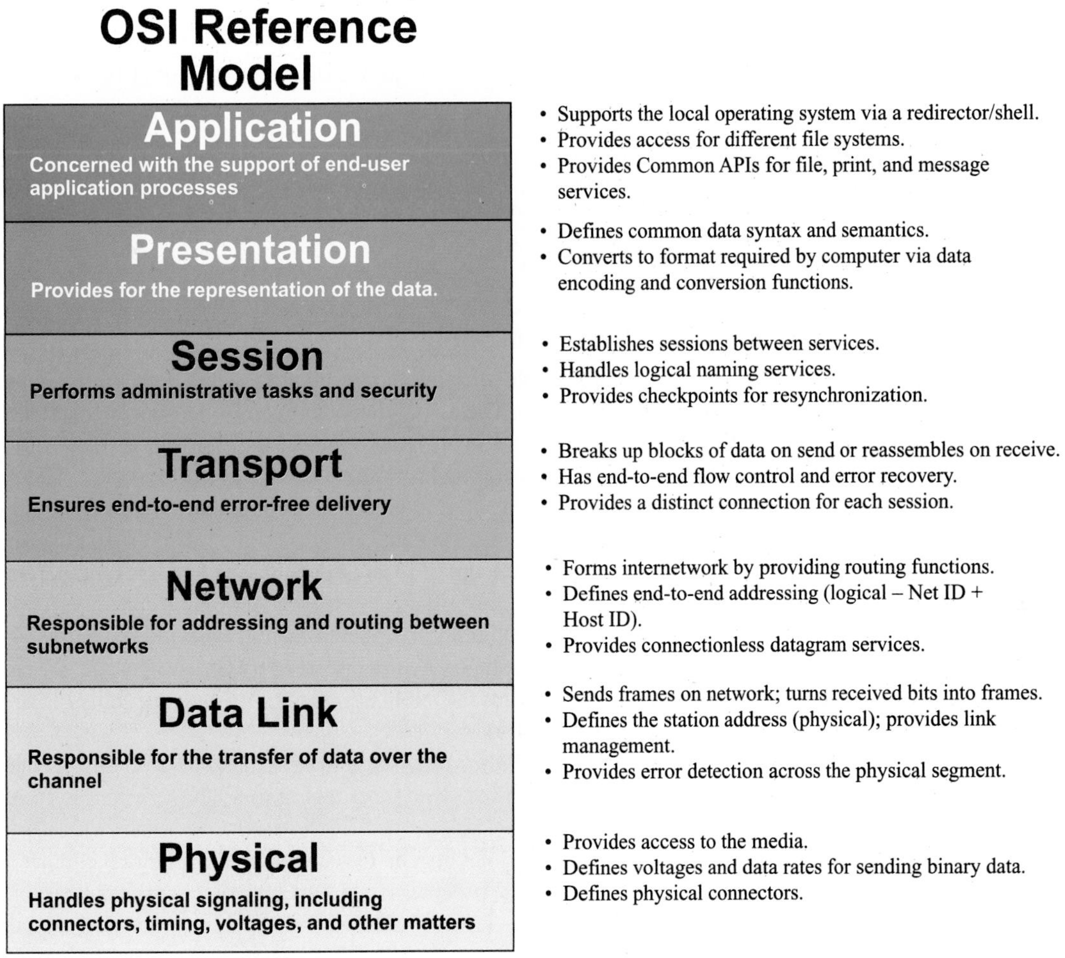

OSI Reference Model

Application Concerned with the support of end-user application processes	• Supports the local operating system via a redirector/shell. • Provides access for different file systems. • Provides Common APIs for file, print, and message services.
Presentation Provides for the representation of the data.	• Defines common data syntax and semantics. • Converts to format required by computer via data encoding and conversion functions.
Session Performs administrative tasks and security	• Establishes sessions between services. • Handles logical naming services. • Provides checkpoints for resynchronization.
Transport Ensures end-to-end error-free delivery	• Breaks up blocks of data on send or reassembles on receive. • Has end-to-end flow control and error recovery. • Provides a distinct connection for each session.
Network Responsible for addressing and routing between subnetworks	• Forms internetwork by providing routing functions. • Defines end-to-end addressing (logical – Net ID + Host ID). • Provides connectionless datagram services.
Data Link Responsible for the transfer of data over the channel	• Sends frames on network; turns received bits into frames. • Defines the station address (physical); provides link management. • Provides error detection across the physical segment.
Physical Handles physical signaling, including connectors, timing, voltages, and other matters	• Provides access to the media. • Defines voltages and data rates for sending binary data. • Defines physical connectors.

Table 3.2   Common Technologies as They Relate to the OSI Model

OSI Model	TCP/IP	Novell NetWare	Microsoft Windows
Application	FTP, SMTP, Telnet	NDS	SMB
Presentation	ACSII, MPEG, GIF, JPEG	NCP	NetBIOS
Session		SAP	NetBEUI
Transport	TCP, UDP	SPX	NetBEUI
Network	IP	IPX	NetBEUI
Data Link	Ethernet, 802.3, 802.5, FDDI, Frame Relay, ISDN	Ethernet, 802.3, 802.5, FDDI, Frame Relay, ISDN	Ethernet, 802.3, 802.5, FDDI, Frame Relay, ISDN
Physical	10Base-T, 100Base-T, UTP 4/16 Unshielded Twisted Pair, SONET	10Base-T, 100Base-T, UTP 4/16 Unshielded Twisted Pair, SONET	10Base-T, 100Base-T, UTP 4/16 Unshielded Twisted Pair, SONET

To facilitate this, ISO has defined internationally standardized protocols for each one of the seven layers. The seven layers are divided into three separate groups: application-oriented (upper layers), an intermediate layer, and the network-oriented (lower) layers.

NOTE: An easy way to remember the order of the OSI Reference Model is to use the following mnemonics:

Please	Do	Not	Take	Sales	Peoples	Advice
Physical	Data-Link	Network	Transport	Session	Presentation	Application

All	People	Seem	To	Need	Data	Processing
Application	Presentation	Session	Transport	Network	Data-Link	Physical

3.2.1   Encapsulation with the OSI Model

When a computer needs to communicate with another computer, it will start with a network service, which is running in the application layer. The actual data that needs to be sent is generated by the software and is sent to the presentation layer. The presentation layer then adds its own control information, called a header, which contains the presentation layer's requests and/or information. The packet then is sent to the session layer where another header is added. It keeps going down the OSI model until it reaches the physical layer, which means that the data is sent on the network media by the network interface card (NIC). See figure 3.2. The concept of placing data behind headers (and before trailers) for each layer is called **encapsulation.**

When the data packet gets to the destination computer, the network interface card sends the data packet to the data link layer. The data link layer then strips the first header off. As it goes up the model, each header is stripped away until it reaches the application layer. At this time, only the original data is left, which is then processed by the network service.

The great thing about this system is that it allows you to communicate with different computer systems. For example, a Windows NT server can send information to a UNIX server or an Apple Macintosh client.

Let's follow the steps of communication between two computers from initial contact to data delivery. A computer wants to request a file. The process would start with a network application on the client computer. Before the request can be made, the client had to first determine the address of the computer. Therefore, it sent a request out to resolve a computer name to a network address.

Figure 3.2   Layer Interaction of the OSI Reference Model

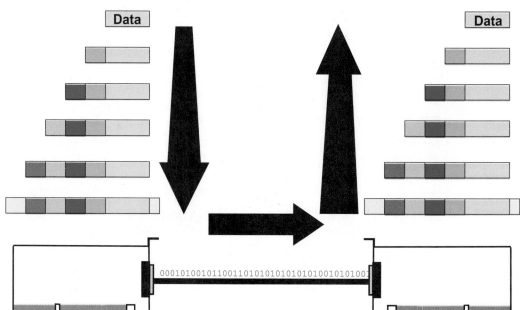

If the client already knows the server's network address, it will make its request in the form of a data packet and send it to a presentation layer protocol. The presentation protocol would encrypt and compress the packet and send it to a session layer protocol, which would establish a connection with the server. During this time the packet would include the type of dialog such as half-duplex connection (discussed later in this chapter) and determine how long the computer can transmit to the server. The session protocol will then send the packet to the transport layer, which will divide the packet to smaller packets so that it can be sent over the physical network. The transport layer protocol will then send the packets to the network layer where the source network and destination network addresses are added. It will then send the packets to a data link layer so that it can add the source and destination address and the port number that identifies the service requested and prepare the packets to be sent over the media. As you can see in figure 3.2, the packet is bigger than when it started. The packet is then converted to electrical or electromagnetic signals that are sent on the network media.

When the packets get to the destination server, the network card sees the signals and interprets the signals as 0s and 1s. It then takes the bits and groups them together into frames. It will then determine the destination address of the packet to see if the packet was meant for the server. After the server has determined that it was, it will then remove the data link header and send the packet up to the network layer. The network layer will remove the network layer header and send the packet to the transport layer. If the data packets have reached the server out of order, the transport layer protocol will put them back into the proper order, merge them into one larger packet and send the packet to the appropriate session layer protocol. The session layer protocol will authenticate the user and send the packet to the presentation layer protocol. The presentation layer protocol will decompress, decrypt, and reformat the packet so that it can be read by the application layer protocol. The application layer protocol will read the request and take the appropriate steps to fulfill the request.

Before the packet is actually sent, it must determine if the packet is to go to another computer within the same network or to a computer in another network. If it is local, the packets are sent to the computer. If it has to go to another network, the packet is sent to a router. The router will then determine the best way to get to its destination and then send the packet from one router to another until it gets to the destination network. If one network route is congested, it can reroute the packet another way and if it detects errors, it can slow down the transmission of the packets in the hopes that the link will become more reliable.

In reality, encapsulation does not occur for all seven layers, Layers 5 through 7 use headers during initialization, but in most flows, there is no specific Layer 5, 6, or 7 header. This is because there is no new information to exchange for every flow of data. Therefore, Layers 5, 6 and 7 can be grouped together and the layers actually used can be simplified into 5 layers: application (equivalent to the application, presentation and session layer), transport, Internet (equivalent to the network layer), Network Interface (equivalent to the data link layer), and physical layer. See figure 3.3.

Figure 3.3 Encapsulation That Actually Occurs on Today's Networks

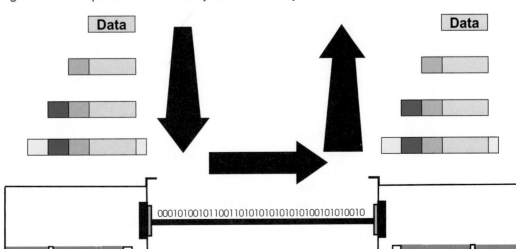

Figure 3.4   Information Blocks Associated with the Simplified OSI Model

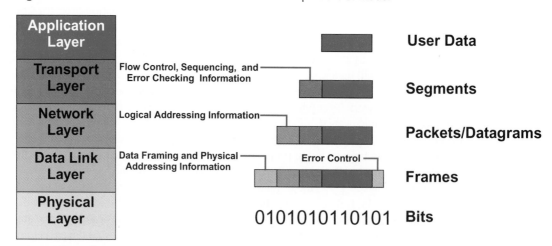

When encapsulation with TCP/IP is used, the order in which information blocks are created is data, segments, packets, frames, and bits. The user application creates the data and a variety of parameters and passes the segment to the network layer. The network layer places the destination network address in a header, puts the data behind it and transmits a packet, or datagram, to the data link layer. The data link layer creates the data link header, which includes the destination MAC address. The datagram is converted to a frame and is passed to the physical layer. The physical layer transmits the bits. (See figure 3.4.)

Many protocols will have the destination computer send back an acknowledgement stating that the packet arrived intact. If the source computer does not receive an acknowledgement after a certain amount of time, it will then resend the packet.

Example 3.1:

Let's say you are a user who is running a word processor, and you decide to access a file that is located on a remote computer's shared directory. A shared directory is a directory on a computer that provides the directory to clients over the network. The user clicks on the open button so that he or she can view the files of the remote computer. The word processor initiates the entire process by generating a network request. The request is sent through a client/redirector, which forwards the request to the network protocol such as TCP/IP. The packet is then forwarded to the NIC driver and sent out through the network card where it is sent through the network to the remote computer. Of course, as the request is being sent down from the word processor to the network card, the request becomes bigger as the packet is encapsulated. See figure 3.5.

When the packets are received at the remote computer, it is processed by the driver on the remote computer. It is then forwarded to the network protocol, which is then forwarded to the server service (file and print sharing). The server service then uses the local file system services to access the file. As the packet goes from the network card to the local file system services, the packet is then stripped back to the original request. The file is then sent back to the requesting computer.

3.2.2   OSI Model and Security

To analyze all of the ways that a network can be attacked or accessed without proper permission, you use the OSI model to categorize the various methods. Most of the attacks that you hear about in the news occur at the application layer, going after Web servers and browsers and the information that they have access to, but application-layer attacks on open file shares are also common. See figure 3.6.

While you can set up an array of defense against specific threats, please keep in mind that a defense could fail the first time that an unanticipated threat shows up. Therefore, you will have to constantly monitor your network.

Figure 3.5   A Network Request Going through the Simplified OSI Model

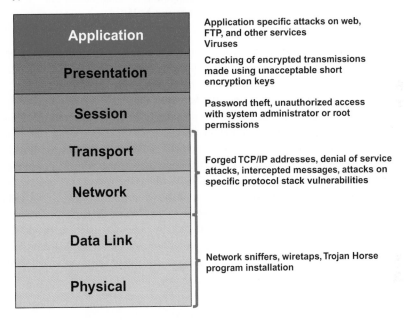

Figure 3.6   Types of Attacks as They Relate to the OSI Model

Application	Application specific attacks on web, FTP, and other services Viruses
Presentation	Cracking of encrypted transmissions made using unacceptable short encryption keys
Session	Password theft, unauthorized access with system administrator or root permissions
Transport	Forged TCP/IP addresses, denial of service attacks, intercepted messages, attacks on specific protocol stack vulnerabilities
Network	
Data Link	Network sniffers, wiretaps, Trojan Horse program installation
Physical	

3.3   TCP/IP AND THE INTERNET

The Internet that you know today began as a U.S. Department of Defense (DoD)–funded experiment to interconnect DoD-funded research sites in the United States. In December 1968, the Advanced Research Projects Agency (ARPA) awarded a grant to design and deploy a packet switching network (messaged divided into packets, transmitted individually, and recompiled into the original message). In September 1969, the first node of the ARPANET was installed at UCLA. By 1971, the ARPANET spanned the continental United States, and by 1973, it had connections to Europe.

Over time, the initial protocols used to connect the hosts together proved incapable of keeping up with the growing network traffic load. Therefore, a new TCP/IP protocol suite was proposed and implemented. By 1983, the popularity of the TCP/IP protocol grew as it was included in the communications kernel for the University of California's UNIX implementation, 4.2BSD (Berkeley Software Distribution) UNIX. Today, the TCP/IP protocol is the primary protocol used on the Internet and is supported by Microsoft Windows, Novell NetWare, UNIX, Linux and Apple Macintoshes.

The standards for TCP/IP are published in a series of documents called **Request for Comments (RFC).** An RFC can be submitted by anyone. Eventually, if it gains enough interest, it may evolve into an Internet standard. Each RFC is designated by an RFC number. Once published, an RFC never changes. Modifications to an original RFC are assigned a new RFC number.

RFCs are classified as one of the following: approved Internet standards, proposed Internet standards (circulated in draft form for review), Internet best practices, or For Your Information (FYI) documents. You should always follow approved Internet standards.

For more information on RFCs, visit the following web sites:

http://www.rfc-editor.org/

http://www.cis.ohio-state.edu/hypertext/information/rfc.html

3.3.1   TCP/IP Protocols

With the TCP/IP protocol suite, TCP/IP does not worry about how the hosts (computers or any other network connection) connect to the network. Instead, TCP/IP was designed to operate over nearly any underlying local or wide area network. See figure 3.7. This would include:

- LAN Protocols: Ethernet, Token Ring, and ARCnet networks.
- WAN Protocols: ATM, Frame Relay and X.25.
- Serial Line Protocols: Serial Line Internet Protocol (SLIP) and Point-to-Point Protocol (PPP)

When you send or receive data, the data is divided into little chunks called packets. Each of these packets contains both the sender's TCP/IP address and the receiver's TCP/IP address. When the packet needs to go to another computer on another network, the packet is then sent to a gateway computer, usually a router. The gateway understands the networks that it is connected to directly.

The gateway computer reads the destination address to determine which direction the packet needs to be forwarded. It then forwards the packet to an adjacent gateway. The packet is then forwarded from gateway to gateway until it gets to the network that the destination host belongs to. The last gateway then forwards the packet directly to the computer whose address is specified. See figure 3.8.

The lowest protocol within the TCP/IP suite is the Internet Protocol (IP). IP is a connectionless protocol, which means that there is no established connection between the end points that are communicating. Each packet (also known as datagrams) that travels through the Internet is treated as an independent unit of data. Therefore, they are not affected by other data packets. In addition, IP does not guarantee any deliveries. Therefore, packets can get lost, delivered out of sequence or delayed. Instead, it must rely on TCP to determine that the data arrived successfully at its destination and to retransmit the data if it did not.

Figure 3.7   TCP/IP Protocol Suite

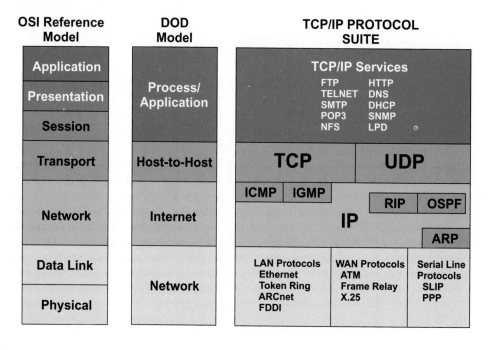

Figure 3.7 Continued

INTERNET PROTOCOLS

Routes data packets between different hosts or networks.

- **Internet Protocol (IP)**—Connectionless protocol primarily responsible for addressing and routing packets between hosts. (RFC 791)
- **Address Resolution Protocol (ARP)**—Used to obtain hardware addresses (MAC addresses) of hosts located on the same physical network. (RFC 826)
- **Internet Control Message Protocol (ICMP)**—Sends messages and reports errors regarding the delivery of a packet. (RFC 792)
- **Internet Group Management Protocol (IGMP)**—Used by IP hosts to report host group membership to local multicast routers. (RFC 1112)
- **Router Information Protocol (RIP)**—Distance Vector Route Discovery Protocol where the entire routing table is periodically sent to the other routers. (RFC 1723)
- **Open Shortest Path First (OSPF)**—Link State Route Discovery Protocol where each router periodically advertises itself to other routers. (RFCs 1245, 1246, 1247 and 1253)

HOST-TO-HOST PROTOCOLS

Maintains data integrity and sets up reliable, end-to-end communication between hosts.

- **Transmission Control Protocol (TCP)**—Provides connection-oriented, reliable communications for applications that typically transfer large amounts of data at one time or that require an acknowledgement for data received. (RFC 793)
- **User Datagram Protocol (UDP)**—Provides connectionless communications and does not guarantee that packets will be delivered. Applications that use UDP typically transfer small amounts of data at one. Reliable delivery is the responsibility of the application. (RFC 768)

PROCESS/APPLICATION PROTOCOLS

Act as the interface for the user. Provides applications that transfer data between hosts.

- **File Transfer Protocol (FTP)**—Allows a user to transfer files between local and remote host computers. (RFC 959)
- **Telecommunication Network (TELNET)**—a Virtual Terminal Protocol (terminal emulation) allowing a user to log on to another TCP/IP host to access network resources. (RFC 854)
- **Simple Mail Transfer Protocol (SMTP)**—The standard protocol for the exchange of electronic mail over the Internet. It is used between email servers on the Internet or to allow an email client to send mail to a server. (RFCs 821 and 822)
- **Post Office Protocol (POP)**—Defines a simple interface between a user's mail client software and email server. It is used to download mail from the server to the client and allows the user to manage their mailboxes. (RFC 1460)
- **Network File System (NFS)**—Provides transparent remote access to shared files across networks. (RFC 1094)
- **Hypertext Transfer Protocol (HTTP)**—The basis for exchange over the World Wide Web (WWW). WWW pages are written in the Hypertext Markup Language (HTML), an ASCII-based, platform-independent formatting language. (RFCs 1945 and 1866)
- **Domain Name System (DNS)**—Defines the structure of Internet names and their association with IP addresses. (RFCs 1034 and 1035)
- **Dynamic Host Configuration Protocol (DHCP)**—Used to automatically assign TCP/IP addresses and other related information to clients. (RFC 2131)
- **Simple Network Management Protocol (SNMP)**—Defines procedures and management information databases for managing TCP/IP-based network devices. (RFCs 1157 and 1441)
- **Line Printer Daemon (LPD)**—Provides printing on a TCP/IP network.
- **Network Time Protocol (NTP)**—An Internet standard protocol that assures accurate synchronization to the millisecond of computer clock times in a network of computers. (RFC 1305)

When a packet is received from the TCP protocol, it inserts its own header in the datagram. The main content of the IP header are the source and destination addresses, the protocol numbers, and a checksum.

The protocol that works on top of the IP protocol is the TCP and UDP protocol. The **Transmission Control Protocol (TCP)** is a reliable, connection-oriented delivery service that breaks the data into manageable packets, wraps them with the information needed to route them to their destination, and then reassembles the pieces at the receiving end of the communication link. It establishes a virtual connection between the two hosts or computers so that they can send messages back and forth for a period of time. A virtual connection appears to be always connected, but in reality it is made of many packets being sent back and forth independently.

The most important information in the header includes the source and destination port numbers, a sequence number for the datagram, and a checksum. The source port number and destination port number

Figure 3.8   TCP/IP Packet

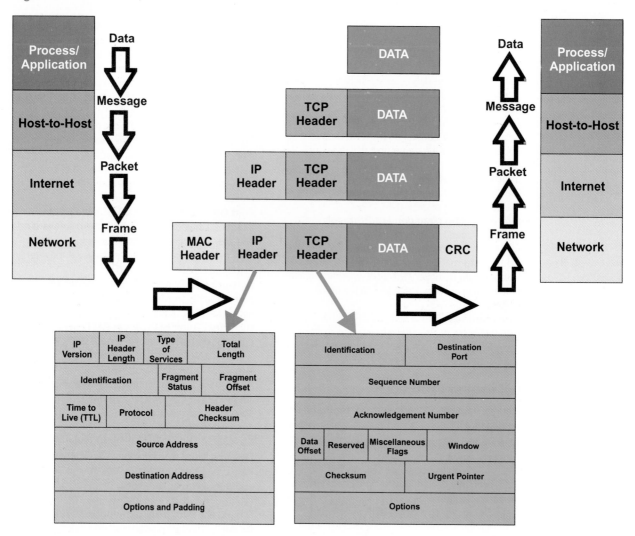

ensure that the data is sent back and forth to the correct process (or program) running on each computer. The sequence number allows the datagram to be rebuilt in the correct order in the receiving computer, and the checksum allows the protocol to check whether the data sent is the same as the data received.

The TCP protocol has two other important functions. First, TCP uses acknowledgements to verify that the data was received by the other host. If an acknowledgement is not sent, the data is resent. In addition, since the data packets can be delivered out of order, the TCP protocol must put the packets back in the correct order.

Before two TCP hosts can exchange data, they must first establish a session with each other. A TCP session is initialized through a process known as a *three-way handshake*. This process synchronizes sequence numbers and provides control information that is needed to establish a virtual connection between both hosts. Once the initial three-way handshake completes, segments are sent and acknowledged in a sequential manner between both the sending and receiving hosts. A similar handshake process is used by TCP before closing a connection to verify that both hosts are finished sending and receiving all data.

The three-way handshake consists of the following steps:

1. The client (or requesting end) performs an active open by activating the SYN flag in the TCP header. The TCP header also contains the desired port number for connection and a sequence number field with the initial sequence number (ISN). The ISN is generated randomly and is used to synchronize the client and server when they transfer data on the byte stream.

Figure 3.9   The Three-way Handshake Used to Make a TCP Connection

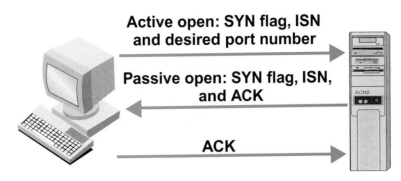

2. The server performs a passive open by sending its own SYN to the client that specifies the server's ISN and an acknowledgment (ACK) of the client's SYN.
3. The client returns an ACK to the server. The client and server can now transfer data using the byte stream, and the connection is established.

See figure 3.9.

Another transport layer protocol is the User Datagram Protocol (UDP). Unlike the TCP protocol, which uses acknowledgements to ensure data delivery, UDP does not. Therefore, the UDP is considered unreliable, "best effort" delivery. Since it is considered unreliable, UDP is used for protocols that transmit small amounts of data at one time or for broadcasts (packets sent to everyone). Note: unreliable doesn't mean that the packets will not get delivered; it is just that there is no guarantee or check to make sure that they get to their destination.

When TCP/IP is used, data is encapsulated in five steps:

1. The user application creates the data, and a variety of parameters is established. The data is then passed to the transport layer.
2. The transport layer adds a TCP or UDP header and establishes the flow control parameters. The data is then passed to the network layer.
3. The network layer places the destination network address in a header, puts the data behind it and passes it to the data link layer.
4. The data is converted to frames. A data link header and a trailer, including a frame sequence check are added.
5. The physical layer transmits the bits.

3.3.2   IP Addressing

Each connection on a TCP/IP address (logical address) is called a host (a computer or other network device that is connected to a TCP/IP network) and is assigned a unique IP address. A host is any network interface, including each network interface card or a network printer that connects directly onto the network. Since the address is used to identify the computer, no two connections can use the same IP address. If there is, one or both of the computers will not be able to communicate.

IP Addresses will be manually assigned and configured (static IP addresses) or dynamically assigned and configured by a DHCP server (dynamic IP addresses). Since the address is used to identify the computer, no two connections can use the same IP address. Otherwise, one or both of the computers would not be able to communicate, and you will usually see a message stating "IP address conflict."

When communication occurs on a TCP/IP network, communications can be classified as unicast, multicast, or anycast. Unicast is when a single sender communicates with a single receiver over the network. The opposite of unicast is multicast, which is communication between a single sender and multiple receivers, and anycast, which is communication between any sender and the nearest of a group of receivers in a network. A broadcast is when packets are sent to every computer on the network or a subnet. Note: Broadcasts are not normally forwarded by routers.

IPv4 is based on 32-bit wide addresses which allow a little over 4 billion hosts. The format of the IP address is four 8-bit numbers (octet) divided by a period (.). Each number can be zero to 255. For example, a TCP/IP address could be 131.107.3.1 or 2.0.0.1.

When configuring a host with an IP address, you must also include its subnet mask. The subnet masks identify which bits of an address identify the network address and which bits identify the host address. Examples of subnet masks may be 255.0.0.0, 255.255.0.0, 255.255.255.0 or 255.255.224.0.

IPv6 uses 128 bits for its addresses, which can have up to 3.4×10^{38} hosts, which can handle all of today's IP-based machines without using Network Address Translation, to allow for future growth and to handle IP addresses for upcoming mobile devices like PDAs and cell phones. They are usually divided into groups of 16 bits written as four hex digits, and the groups are separated by colons. An example is:

```
FE80:0000:0000:0000:02A0:D2FF:FEA5:E9F5
```

Lastly, if you need to communicate with other networks, you just specify the default gateway. The default gateway is usually the address of the nearest router.

When connecting to the Internet, network numbers are assigned to a corporation or business. The number is divided into classes and, therefore, is known as a classful network. If the first number is between 1 and 126, the network is a class A. If the first number is between 128 and 191, the network is a class B. If the number is between 192 and 223, the network is a class C. See table 3.3.

Because Internet addresses must be unique and because address space on the Internet is limited, there is a need for some organization to control and allocate address number blocks. IP number management was formerly a responsibility of the Internet Assigned Numbers Authority (IANA), which contracted with Network Solutions Inc. for the actual services. In December 1997, IANA turned this responsibility over to the following organizations to manage the world's Internet address assignment and allocation:

- **American Registry for Internet Numbers (ARIN)**—North and South America, the Caribbean and sub-Saharan Africa.
- **Réseaux IP Européens Network Coordination Centre (RIPE NCC)**—Europe, the Middle East and parts of Africa and Asia.
- **Asia Pacific Network Information Centre (APNIC)**—Asia Pacific region

Domain name management is still the separate responsibility of Network Solutions and a number of other registrars accredited by the Internet Corporation for Assigned Names and Numbers (ICANN).

Two additional classes should be mentioned. These are used for special functions only and are not commonly assigned to individual hosts. Class D addresses may begin with a value between 224 and 239 and are used for IP multicasting. Multicasting is sending a single data packet to multiple hosts. Class E addresses begin with a value between 240 and 255, and are reserved for experimental use.

Many corporations will connect their corporate network (private network) to the Internet (public network). A **private network** is a network where only authorized users have access to the data, while a **public network** is one where everyone connected has access to the data. In a public network, since the IP hosts are directly accessible from the Internet, the network addresses have to be registered with IANA. In a private network, the IP addresses are assigned by the administrator. Of course, it is recom-

Table 3.3   Standard IP Classes for the IP Address of w.x.y.z

Class Type	First Octet - Decimal Number and Bits	Network Number	Host Number	Default Subnet Mask	Comments
A	1-126 (01xxxxxx)	w	x.y.z	255.0.0.0	Supports 16 million hosts on each of 126 networks.
B	128-191 (10xxxxxx)	w.x	y.z	255.255.0.0	Supports 65,000 hosts on each of 16,000 networks.
C	192-223 (110xxxxx)	w.x.y	z	255.255.255.0	Supports 254 hosts on each of 2 million networks.

mended that you use the addresses reserved for private addresses. If you connect a private network to a public network, you increase the possibility for security break-ins. This is the reason that firewalls are implemented to protect a private network from unauthorized users on a public network.

Since TCP/IP addresses are being used up for the Internet, a series of addresses have been reserved to be used by private networks (networks not connected to the Internet). They are:

Class A—10.x.x.x (1 class A addresses).
Class B—Between 172.16.x.x and 172.31.x.x (16 class B addresses).
Class C—192.168.0.x and 192.168.255.x (256 class C addresses).

If you are not connected to the Internet or are using a proxy server, it is recommended that you use private addresses to prevent a renumbering of your internetwork when you eventually connect to the Internet.

The TCP/IP address is broken down into a network number (sometimes referred to **network prefix**) and a host number. The network number identifies the entire network while the host number identifies the computer or connection on the specified network. If it is a class A network, the first octet describes the network number while the last three octets describe the host address. If it is a class B network, the first two octets describe the network number while the last two octets describe the host address. If it is a class C, the first three octets describe the network number while the last octet describes the host number. See figure 3.10.

Example 3.2:

You have the following network address:

131.107.20.4

The 131 is between 128 and 191, identifying the address as a Class B network. Therefore, the 131.107 identifies the network and the 20.4 identifies the host or computer on the 131.107 network.

Figure 3.10   IP Network with addresses and subnet masks. Notice the Multihomed computer (computer with two network cards connected to two subnets).

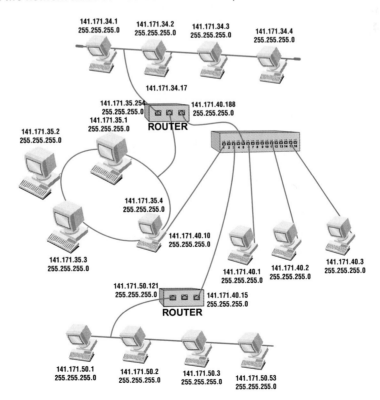

Example 3.3:

You have the following network address:

`208.234.23.4`

The 208 is between 192 and 223, identifying the address as a Class C network. Therefore, the 208.234.23 identifies the network and the 4 identifies the host or computer on the 208.234.23 network.

NOTE: Several address values are reserved and/or have special meaning. The network number 127 is used for loopback testing and the specific host address 127.0.0.1 refers to the localhost or the actual host or computer that you are currently using. Note: the 0.0.0.0 address is reserved for use as the default route.

Usually when you define the TCP/IP for a network connection, you would also specify a subnet mask. The subnet mask is used to define which bits describe the network number and which bits describe the host address. The default subnet mask for a Class A network is 255.0.0.0. If you convert this to a binary equivalent, you would have 11111111.00000000.00000000.00000000, showing that the first 8-bits (1st octet), marked with 1s, is used to define the network address while the last 24 bits, marked with 0s, are used to define the host address. The default subnet mask for a class B network is 255.255.0.0 (11111111.11111111.00000000.00000000) while the default subnet mask for a class C network is 255.255.255.0 (11111111.11111111.11111111.00000000).

If an individual network is connected to another network and you must communicate with any computers on the other network, you must also define the **default gateway,** which specifies the local address of a router. If the default gateway is not specified, you will not be able to communicate with computers on other networks. Note: If the local area network is connected to two or more networks, you only have to specify one gateway. This is because, when a data packet is sent, it will first determine if the data packet needs to go to a local computer or a computer that is on another network. If it is meant to be sent on a computer on another network, it will forward the data packet to the router. The router will then determine the best direction that the data packet must go to get to its destination. Occasionally, it will have to go back through the network to get to another gateway. See figure 3.11.

Broadcasts are used to reach all devices on a network or subnetwork. The broadcast address is used when a machine wants to send the same packet to all devices on the network. They are two types of broadcasts: an all-nets broadcast and a subnet broadcast. Of course, while broadcasts are not forwarded by most routers, broadcasts can take up valuable bandwidth and processing power in the receiving devices. All-nets broadcasts packets are addressed to 255.255.255.255 in the IP header. Literally, the packets are addressed to all networks. Subnet broadcasts contain the subnet address in the broadcast

Figure 3.11   IP Addresses with Default Gateways that Point to the Router

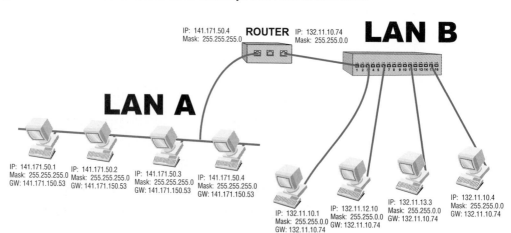

packet and all 1s for the host address, and they are aimed at all computers within the subnet. To get your broadcast address, you set the device or host portion of the IP address to 255. Therefore, if you have the IP address 129.23.123.2 (a class C network address of 129.23.123.0 with a mask of 255.255.255.0), your broadcast address will be 129.23.123.255. Your network address will be 129.23.123.0.

3.3.3 Subnetting

The subnet mask can be changed to take a large network and break it into several small networks called subnets. This allows a corporation or organization to be free to assign a distinct subnetwork number for each of its internal networks. This allows the organization to deploy additional subnets without needing to obtain a new network number from the Internet.

The subnet mask is used to define which bits represent the network prefix (including the subnet number) and which bits represent the host address. The network prefix and the subnet number is sometimes referred to as the **extended network prefix.** For a subnet, the network prefix, subnet number, and the subnet mask must be the same for all computers. See figure 3.12.

3.3.4 Networking Address Translation and Proxy Servers

Because IP addresses are a scarce resource, most Internet Service Providers (ISPs) will only allocate one address to a single customer. In the majority of cases, this address is assigned dynamically, so every time a client connects to the ISP a different address will be provided. Big companies can buy more addresses, but for small businesses and home users the cost of doing so is prohibitive. Because such users are given only one IP address, they can have only one computer connected to the Internet at one time. Network Address Translation (NAT) is a method of connecting multiple computers to the Internet (or any other IP network) using one IP address. With an NAT gateway running on a single computer, it is possible to share that single address between multiple local computers and connect them all at the same time. The outside world is unaware of this division and thinks that only one computer is connected.

To combat certain types of security problems, a number of firewall products are available, which are placed between the user and the Internet to verify all traffic before allowing it to pass through. This means, for example, that no unauthorized user would be allowed to access the company's file or email server. The problem with firewall solutions is that they are expensive and difficult to set up and maintain, putting them out of reach for home and small business users.

NAT automatically provides firewall-style protection without any special set-up. The basic purpose of NAT is to multiplex traffic from the internal network and present it to the Internet as if it was coming from a single computer having only one IP address. The TCP/IP protocols include a multiplexing facility so that any computer can maintain multiple simultaneous connections with a remote computer. For example, an internal client can connect to an outside FTP server, but an outside client will not be able to connect to an internal FTP server because it would have to originate the connection, and NAT will not allow that. It is still possible to make some internal servers available to the outside world via inbound mapping, which maps certain well-known TCP ports (e.g., 21 for FTP) to specific internal addresses, thus making services such as FTP or the web available in a controlled way.

Figure 3.12 The host number can be split into a subnet number and host number.

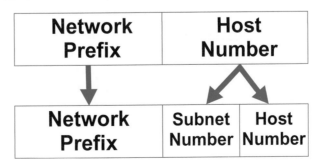

To multiplex several connections to a single destination, client computers label all packets with unique port numbers. Each IP packet starts with a header containing the source and destination addresses and port numbers. This combination of numbers completely defines a single TCP/IP connection. The addresses specify the two machines at each end, and the two port numbers ensure that each connection between this pair of machines can be uniquely identified.

Each separate connection is originated from a unique source port number in the client, and all reply packets from the remote server for this connection contain the same number as their destination port, so that the client can relate them back to their correct connection. In this way, for example, it is possible for a web browser to ask a web server for several images at once and to know how to put all the parts of all the responses back together.

A modern NAT gateway must change the source address on every outgoing packet to be its single public address. It, therefore, also renumbers the source ports to be unique, so that it can keep track of each client connection. The NAT gateway uses a port mapping table to remember how it renumbered the ports for each client's outgoing packets. The port mapping table relates the client's real local IP address and source port plus its translated source port number to a destination address and port. The NAT gateway can therefore reverse the process for returning packets and route them back to the correct clients.

When any remote server responds to a NAT client, incoming packets arriving at the NAT gateway will all have the same destination address, but the destination port number will be the unique source port number that was assigned by the NAT. The NAT gateway looks in its port mapping table to determine which "real" client address and port number a packet is destined for, and replaces these numbers before passing the packet on to the local client.

This process is completely dynamic. When a packet is received from an internal client, NAT looks for the matching source address and port in the port mapping table:

- Incoming packet received on non-NAT port.
- Look for source address, port in the mapping table.
- If found, replace source port with previously allocated mapping port.
- If not found, allocate a new mapping port.
- Replace source address with NAT address, source port with mapping port.

Packets received on the NAT port undergo a reverse translation process:

- Incoming packet received on NAT port.
- Look up destination port number in port mapping table.
- If found, replace destination address and port with entries from the mapping table.
- If not found, the packet is not for us and should be rejected.

Many higher-level TCP/IP protocols embed client addressing information in the packets. For example, during an "active" FTP transfer the client informs the server of its IP address and port number, and then waits for the server to open a connection to that address. NAT has to monitor these packets and modify them on the fly to replace the client's IP address (which is on the internal network) with the NAT address. Since this changes the length of the packet, the TCP sequence/acknowledge numbers must be modified as well.

A proxy is any device that acts on behalf of another. The term is most often used to denote web proxy. A web proxy acts as a "half-way" web server; network clients make requests to the proxy, which then makes requests on their behalf to the appropriate web server. Proxy technology is often seen as an alternative way to provide shared access to a single Internet connection. Note: These proxy servers also use a cache to store recently accessed web pages. Therefore, when the same page is accessed, the proxy server can provide the page without going out to the Internet.

Unlike NAT, web proxying is not a transparent operation. It must be explicitly supported by its clients. Due to early adoption of web proxying, most browsers, including Internet Explorer and Netscape Communicator, have built-in support for proxies, but this must normally be configured on each client machine, and may be changed by the naive or malicious user.

A proxy server operates above the TCP level and uses the machine's built-in protocol stack. For each web request from a client, a TCP connection has to be established between the client and the proxy machine, and another connection between the proxy machine and the remote web server. This puts a lot of strain on the proxy server machine; in fact, since web pages are becoming more and more complicated, the proxy itself may become bottlenecked on the network. This contrasts with a NAT, which operates on packet level and requires much less processing for each connection.

3.3.5   Internet Control Message Protocol (ICMP)

The Internet Control Message Protocol (ICMP) works at the network layer and is used by IP for many different services. ICMP manages IP by reporting on the IP status information. It transmits "destination unreachable" messages to the source device if the target device cannot be located. It can also provide notification that a router's buffer has become full, indicating that the router is congested and it has been forced to drop packets. Additionally, the ICMP protocol notifies a transmitting device that a better route to a destination exists. Both the ping and traceroute utilities use ICMP message to identify whether a destination device is reachable and to track a packet as it is routed from a source to a destination device. As the IP processes the datagrams generated by ICMP, ICMP is not directly apparent to the application user.

3.3.6   TCP/IP Ports and Sockets

Every time a TCP/IP host communicates with another TCP/IP host, it will use the IP address and port number to identify the host and service/program running on the host. A TCP/IP port number is a logical connection place by client programs to specify a particular server program running on a computer on the network defined at the transport layer. The source port number identifies the application that sent the data, and the destination port number identifies the application that receives the data. Port numbers are from 0 to 65536. Additionally, there are two types of ports, TCP and UDP, which are based on their respective protocols.

Today, the very existence of ports and their numbers is typically transparent to the users of the network, as many ports are standardized. Thus, a remote computer will know which port it should connect to for a specific service. Ports 0 to 1023 are reserved for use by certain privileged services and popular higher-level applications. These are known as "well-known ports," which have been assigned by the Internet Assigned Numbers Authority. Some of the well-known protocols are shown in table 3.4. For example, when using your browser to view a web page, the default port to indicate the HTTP service is identified as port 80, and the FTP service is identified as port 21. See figure 3.13. Other application processes are given port numbers dynamically for each connection so that a single computer can run several services. Note: In multiuser systems, a program can define a port on the fly if more than one user requires access to the same service at the same time. Such a port is known as a dynamically allocated port and is assigned only when needed.

When a packet is delivered and processed, the TCP protocol (connection-based services) or UDP protocol (connectionless-based services) will read the port number and forward the request to the appropriate program.

A socket identifies a single network process in terms of the entire Internet. An application creates a socket by specifying three items: the IP address of the host, the type of service, and the port the application is using. Note: For Windows, it is the Windows socket (WinSock) that provides the interface between the network program or service and the Windows environment.

> **For a complete list of registered well-known port numbers, go to the following website:**
>   http://www.isi.edu/in-notes/rfc1700.txt

3.3.7   ARP and MAC Address Resolution

Early IP implementations ran on hosts commonly interconnected by Ethernet local area networks (LAN). Every transmission on these LANs contained the MAC address of the source and destination nodes. Since there is no structure to identify different networks, routing could not be performed.

When a host needs to send a data packet to another host on the same network, the sender application must know both the IP and MAC addresses of the intended receiver. This is because the destination

Table 3.4   Popular TCP/IP Services and Their Default Assigned Port Numbers

Network Program/Service	Default Assigned Port Number
DHCP Client	UDP Port 68
DHCP Server	UDP Port 67
Domain Name Server (DNS)	UDP Port 53
FTP – Data	TCP Port 20
FTP – Control	TCP Port 21
SSH	TCP/UDP Port 22
Telnet	TCP/UDP Port 23
SMTP	TCP/UDP Port 25
DNS	TCP/UDP Port 53
HTTP	TCP/UDP Port 80
NetBIOS Session Service	UDP Port 139
Network News Transport Protocol (NNTP)	TCP Port 119
POP3	TCP Port 110
RPC	UDP Port 111
Secure HTTP	TCP/UDP Port 443
Simple Mail Transfer Protocol	TCP Port 25
Telnet	TCP Port 23
TFTP	UDP Port 69
Radius	TCP/UDP Port 1812

Figure 3.13   Ports Used in TCP/IP

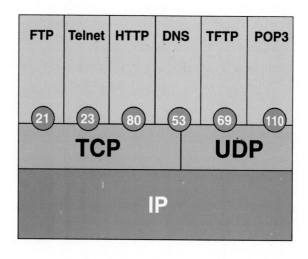

Figure 3.14 Showing the IP addresses (logical address) that are mapped to MAC addresses (physical address).

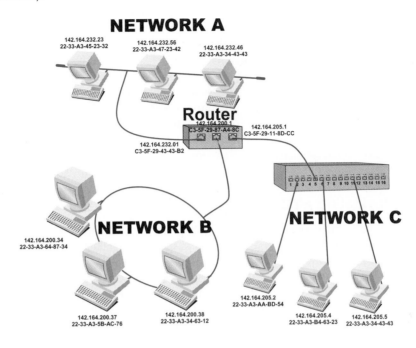

Figure 3.15 Name and Address Resolution Done on an IP Network

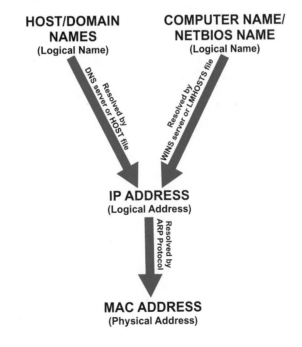

IP address is placed in the IP packet, and the destination MAC address is placed in the LAN's protocol frame (such as Ethernet or Token Ring). If the destination host is on another network, the sender will look instead for the MAC address of the default gateway or router. See figure 3.14.

Unfortunately, the sender's IP process may not know the MAC address of the intended receiver on the same network. Therefore, the Address Resolution Protocol (ARP) protocol (RFC 826) provides a mechanism so that a host can learn a receiver's MAC address when knowing only the IP address. See figure 3.15.

Any time a computer needs to communicate with a local computer, it will first look in the ARP cache in memory to see if it already knows the MAC address of a computer with the specified IP address. If it isn't in the ARP cache, it will try to discover the MAC address by broadcasting an ARP request packet. The station on the LAN recognizes its own IP address, which then sends an ARP response with its own MAC address. Then both the sender of the ARP reply and the original ARP requester record each other's IP address and MAC address as an entry in ARP cache for future reference.

If a computer needs to communicate with another computer that is located on another network, it will do the same, except it will send the packet to the local router. Therefore, it will search for the MAC address of the local port of the router or it will send a broadcast looking for the address of the local port of the router.

When an IP machine happens to be a diskless machine, it has no way of initially knowing its IP address, but it does know its MAC address. The Reverse Address Resolution Protocol (RARP) discovers the identity of the IP address for diskless machines by sending out a packet that includes its MAC address and a request for the IP address assigned to that MAC address. A designated machine, called a RARP server, responds with the answer. RARP uses the information it does know about the machine's MAC address to learn its IP address and complete the machine's ID portrait.

3.3.8   Navigating a TCP/IP Network

Fully Qualified Domain Names (FQDN), sometimes referred to as just domain names, are used to identify computers on a TCP/IP network. Examples include MICROSOFT.COM and EDUCATION. NOVELL.COM.

While IP addresses are 32 bits (or 128 bits for IPv6) in length, most users do not memorize the numeric addresses of the hosts to which they attach. Instead, people are more comfortable with host names. Most IP hosts, then, have both a numeric IP address and a host name. While this is convenient for people, however, the name must be translated back to a numeric address for routing purposes. This is done with either a HOSTS file or by using a DNS server.

The HOSTS file is a text file that lists the IP address followed by the host name. Each entry should be kept on an individual line. In addition, the IP address should be placed in the first column followed by the corresponding host name. A # symbol is used as a comment or REM statement. This means that anything after the # symbol is ignored. See figure 3.16.

If a computer is using the host table shown in figure 3.16, if rhino.acme.com is entered into a browser such as Internet Explorer or Netscape Navigator, it will find the equivalent address of 102.54.94.97 to connect to it. Note: the HOSTS file is kept in the /ETC directory on most UNIX/Linux machines and in the WINDOWS directory in Windows 9X machines and `%systemroot%\SYSTEM32\DRIVERS\ETC` directory in Windows NT, Windows 2000, Windows XP, and Windows Server 2003.

Another way to translate the Fully Qualified Domain Name to the IP address is to use a Domain Name System (DNS) server. DNS is a distributed database (database is contained in multiple servers) containing host name and IP address information for all domains on the Internet. For every domain, there is a single authoritative name server that contains all DNS-related information about the domain.

For example, you type in a web address of Microsoft.com in your browser. Your computer will then communicate with your local area network's DNS server. If the DNS server does not know the address of Microsoft.com, another DNS server will be asked. This will continue until it finds the address of Microsoft.com or it determines that the host name is not listed and reply back with *No DNS Entry.*

When you share a directory, drive, or printer on PCs running Microsoft Windows or Linux machines running Samba, you would access these resources by using the Uniform Naming Convention (UNC), to specify the location of the resources. Uniform Naming Convention is also known as the Universal Naming Convention. UNC uses the following format:

```
\\computer_name\shared-resource-pathname
```

Figure 3.16   Sample Host File

102.54.94.97	rhino.acme.com	# source server
38.25.63.10	x.acme.com	# x client host
127.0.0.1	localhost	

Figure 3.17 Sample LMHOSTS File

```
102.54.94.97    rhino       #PRE  #DOM:networking #File Server

182.102.93.122 MISSERVER    #PRE                  #MIS Server

122.107.9.10    SalesServer                        #Sales Server

131.107.7.29    DBServer                           #Database Server

191.131.54.73   TrainServ                          #Training Server
```

So to access the shared directory called data on the server1 computer, you would type the following:

```
\\server1\data
```

The computer name can actually be the IP address of the PC or the NetBIOS name. Of course, if you use the NetBIOS name, something will be needed to translate the NetBIOS name to the IP address. It could broadcast onto the network asking for the IP address of the computer. Therefore, you would have to connect the TCP/IP address with the computer name (NetBIOS name), Microsoft networks can use a LMHOSTS file (see figure 3.17) or a WINS server.

A **Windows Internet Naming Service (WINS) server** contains a database of IP addresses and NetBIOS (computer names) that update dynamically. For clients to access the WINS server, the clients must know the address of the WINS server. Therefore, the WINS server needs to have a static address that does not change. When the client accesses the WINS server, the client doesn't do a broadcast, the client sends a message directly to the WINS server. When the WINS server gets the requests, it knows whom the computer was that sent the request and can reply directly to the originating IP address. The WINS database stores the information and makes it available to the other WINS clients.

When a WINS client starts up, it registers its name, IP address, and type of services within the WINS server's database. Since WINS was only made for Windows operating systems, other network devices and services (such as a network printer and UNIX machines) can't register with a WINS service. Therefore, these addresses would have to be added manually.

3.3.9 Network Time Protocol

If you have been working with computers for a little while, you are probably aware that a computer has an internal clock to keep track of the time. Therefore, you may wonder why is it important for the computer to have the correct date and time. For starters, when creating or changing a file, it will date and time stamp the file. In addition, when errors occur or when you are investigating security break-ins, PCs, especially servers, will often have logs that will include dates and times of events. Databases can date and time transactions, such as what might occur with banking. Finally, it is used by many security protocols including protocols that provide authentication by dating packets that would give control to the system and its resources.

The **Network Time Protocol (NTP)** is an Internet standard protocol (built on top of TCP/IP) that assures accurate synchronization to the millisecond of computer clock times in a network of computers. Based on the coordinated universal time (abbreviated UTC), NTP synchronizes client workstation clocks to the U.S. Naval Observatory Master Clocks in Washington, D.C. and Colorado Springs, Colorado. Note: UTC was formerly known as Greenwich mean time (GMT). Other terms used to refer to it include "Zulu time," "universal time," and "world time." Running as a continuous background client program on a computer, NTP sends periodic time requests to servers, obtaining server time stamps, and using them to adjust the client's clock. For a list of NTP servers, see the following URL:

A List of the Simple Network Time Protocol Time Servers That Are Available on the Internet

http://support.microsoft.com/default.aspx?scid=kb;EN-US;q262680

3.4 TROUBLESHOOTING A TCP/IP NETWORK

Security+ Objective 3.1.10—Network Monitoring/Diagnostic

For a TCP/IP network, several utilities can be used to test and troubleshoot the network. Yet, when you troubleshoot these types of problems, you should use the following systematic approach:

1. Check configuration.
2. Ping 127.0.0.1 (loopback address).
3. Ping IP address of the computer.
4. Ping IP address of default gateway (router).
5. Ping IP address of remote host.

The first thing that you need to do when troubleshooting an apparent TCP/IP problem is to check your TCP/IP configuration, specifically, your IP address, subnet mask, default gateway, DNS server, and WINS server. If the subnet mask is wrong, you may not be able to communicate with machines on the same subnet or remote subnets. If the default gateway is wrong, you will not be able to connect to any computer on a remote subnet. If the DNS server is wrong, you will not perform name resolution, and you will not be able to surf the Internet. Having the wrong WINS server will stop you using computer BIOS names when using universal name convention (UNC) names.

To verify the TCP/IP configuration in Microsoft Windows, you would use either the IP Configuration program (WINIPCFG.EXE) command (available in Windows 9X) or the IPCONFIG.EXE (available in Windows 98, Windows NT, Windows 2000, Windows XP, and Windows 2003). To verify your TCP/IP in Linux, you can use ifconfig and route commands.

3.4.1 The Ping Command

The ping command sends packets to a host computer and receives a report on their round trip time. See figure 3.18. For example, you can ping an IP address by typing the following command at a command prompt:

```
ping 127.0.0.1
ping 137.23.34.112
```

Figure 3.18 PING Command

```
C:\>ping 132.233.150.4

Pinging 132.233.150.4 with 32 bytes of data:

Reply from 132.233.150.4: bytes=32 time<10ms TTL=128
Reply from 132.233.150.4: bytes=32 time<10ms TTL=128
Reply from 132.233.150.4: bytes=32 time<10ms TTL=128
Reply from 132.233.150.4: bytes=32 time<10ms TTL=128

Ping statistics for 132.233.150.4:
    Packets: Sent = 4, Received = 4, Lost = 0 (0% loss),
Approximate round trip times in milli-seconds:
    Minimum = 0ms, Maximum = 0ms, Average = 0ms
```

Figure 3.19   PING Command Showing Total Failure

```
C:\>ping 132.233.150.2


Pinging 132.233.150.2 with 32 bytes of data:


Request timed out.
Request timed out.
Request timed out.
Request timed out.


Ping statistics for 132.233.150.2:
    Packets: Sent = 4, Received = 0, Lost = 4 (100% loss),
Approximate round trip times in milli-seconds:
    Minimum = 0ms, Maximum = 0ms, Average = 0ms
```

The ping command can also be used to ping a host/computer by NetBIOS (computer) name or host/DNS name. Some examples would include:

```
ping FS1
ping WWW.MICROSOFT.COM
```

If you ping by address but not by name, this tells you that the TCP/IP is running fine but the name resolution is not working properly. Therefore, you must check the LMHOSTS file and the WINS server to resolve computer names, and the HOSTS file and the DNS server to resolve domain names.

If the time takes up to 200 milliseconds, the time is considered very good. If the time is between 200 and 500 milliseconds, the time is considered marginal, and if the time is over 500 milliseconds, the time is unacceptable. A "Request timed out" indicates total failure as shown in figure 3.19.

Viewing the current configuration, pinging the loopback address (ping 127.0.0.1), and pinging the IP address of your computer will verify that the TCP/IP protocol is properly functioning on your PC. By pinging the IP address of the default gateway or router, as well as other local IP computers, you determine if the computer is communicated on the local network. If it cannot connect to the gateway or any other local computer, either you are not connected properly, or the IP protocol is misconfigured (IP address, IP subnet mask, or gateway address). If you cannot connect to the gateway but you can connect to other local computers, check your IP address, IP subnet mask, and gateway address, and check to see if the gateway is functioning by using the ping command at the gateway to connect to your computer and other local computers on your network, as well as pinging the other network connections on the gateway/router or pinging computers on other networks. If you cannot ping another local computer, but you can ping the gateway, most likely the other computer is having problems and you need to restart this procedure at that computer. If you can ping the gateway, but you cannot ping the computer on another gateway, you need to check the routers and pathways between the two computers by using the ping or tracert commands. The tracert command is shown next.

3.4.2   The Tracert Command

Another useful command is the traceroute command (Microsoft uses the tracert command), which sends out a packet of information to each hop (gateway/router) individually. Therefore, the tracert command can help determine where the break is in a network. See figure 3.20 and table 3.5.

Figure 3.20   Tracert Command

```
C:\>tracert www.novell.com


Tracing route to www.novell.com [137.65.2.11]
over a maximum of 30 hops:


  1     97 ms     92 ms    107 ms   tnt3-e1.scrm01.pbi.net [206.171.130.74]
  2     96 ms     98 ms    118 ms   core1-e3-3.scrm01.pbi.net [206.171.130.77]
  3     96 ms     95 ms    120 ms   edge1-fa0-0-0.scrm01.pbi.net [206.13.31.8]
  4     96 ms    102 ms     96 ms   sfra1sr1-5-0.ca.us.ibm.net [165.87.225.10]
  5    105 ms    108 ms    114 ms   f1-0-0.sjc-bb1.cerf.net [134.24.88.55]
  6    107 ms    112 ms    106 ms   atm8-0-155M.sjc-bb3.cerf.net [134.24.29.38]
  7    106 ms    110 ms    120 ms   pos1-1-155M.sfo-bb3.cerf.net [134.24.32.89]
  8    109 ms    108 ms    110 ms   pos3-0-0-155M.sfo-bb1.cerf.net [134.24.29.202]
  9    122 ms    105 ms    115 ms   atm8-0.sac-bb1.cerf.net [134.24.29.86]
 10    121 ms    120 ms    117 ms   atm3-0.slc-bb1.cerf.net [134.24.29.90]
 11    123 ms    131 ms    130 ms   novell-gw.slc-bb1.cerf.net [134.24.116.54]
 12      *          *         *     Request timed out.
 13    133 ms    139 ms    855 ms   www.novell.com [137.65.2.11]


Trace complete.
```

Table 3.5   Tracert Options

-d	In the event a name resolution method is not available for remote hosts, you can specify the -D option to prohibit the utility from trying to resolve host names as it runs. If you don't use this option, tracert will still function, but it will run very slow as it tries to resolve these names.
-h	By specifying the -h option, you can specify the maximum number of hops to trace a route to.
Timeout_value	The timeout value is used to adjust the timeout value; the value determines the amount of time in milliseconds the program will wait for a response before moving on. If you raise this value and the remote devices are responding, whereas they were not responding before, this may indicate a bandwidth problem.
-j	Known as loose source routing, tracert -j <router name> <local computer> allows tracert to follow the path to the router specified and return to your computer.

3.4.3   The ARP Utility

The ARP utility is primarily useful for resolving duplicate IP addresses. For example, your workstation receives its IP address from a DHCP server, but it accidentally receives the same address as another workstation. When you try to ping it, you get no response. Your workstation is trying to determine the MAC address, and it cannot do so because two machines are reporting that they have the same IP ad-

Figure 3.21   Using the ARP Command

```
C:\>arp -a


Interface: 192.168.1.100 --- 0x2
  Internet Address        Physical Address      Type
  192.168.1.254           00-00-89-2d-40-da     dynamic
  192.168.1.223           00-a0-b1-2d-32-45     dynamic
  199.223.164.5           00-a2-c0-c3-c2-14     static
```

dress. To solve this problem, you can use the ARP utility to view your local ARP table and see which TCP/IP address is resolved to which MAC address. To display the entire current ARP table, use the arp command with the -a switch. See figure 3.21. Note: you can also use the IPCONFIG/ALL (Windows) or ifconfig (Linux) commands if you need to identify the MAC address on network interface on your current machine.

In addition to displaying the ARP table, you can use the ARP utility to manipulate it. To add static entries to the ARP table, use the ARP command with the -s switch. These entries stay in the ARP table until the machine is rebooted. A static entry hard-wires a specific IP address to a specific MAC address so that when a packet needs to be sent to that IP address, it is sent automatically to the MAC address. The syntax for this command would:

```
arp -s IP_Address MAC_Address
```

An example of using this command would be:

```
arp -s 199.223.164.5 00-a2-c0-c3-c2-14
```

If you want to delete entries from the ARP table, you can either wait until the dynamic entries time out, or you can use the -d switch with the IP address of the static entry you would like to delete. An example would be:

```
arp -d 199.223.164.5
```

3.4.4   The Netstat Utility

The netstat command is a great way to see the TCP/IP connections, both inbound and outbound on your machine. You can also use it to view the packet statistics, such as how many packets have been sent and received and the number of errors. Novell NetWare uses MONITOR.NLM utility.

When netstat is used without any options, netstat produces output similar to that, which shows all the outbound TCP/IP connections. The netstat utility, used without any options, is particularly useful in determining the status of outbound web connections. Note: If you use -N, addresses, port numbers are converted to names. See figure 3.22.

The NETSTAT –A command displays all connections, and NETSTAT –R displays the route table plus active connections. The NETSTAT –E command displays Ethernet statistics, and NETSTAT –S displays per-protocol statistics. See figure 3.23.

On occasion, you may need to have netstat occur every few seconds. Try placing a number after the netstat–e command, like so:

```
netstat -e 15
```

The command executes, waits the number of seconds specified by the number (in this example, 15), and then repeats until you press the Ctrl+C command.

Figure 3.22 The Netstat Command Without Any Parameters

```
C:\Documents and Settings\Pat>netstat

Active Connections

  Proto  Local Address          Foreign Address          State
  TCP    pregan:3001            pregan:3497              ESTABLISHED
  TCP    pregan:3497            ftp.redhat.com:ftp       ESTABLISHED
  TCP    pregan:3499            ftp.redhat.com:ftp       ESTABLISHED
  TCP    pregan:4275            ftp.redhat.com:ftp-data  ESTABLISHED
  TCP    pregan:4445            200-207-217-21.dsl.telesp.net.br:1214  TIME_WAIT

  TCP    pregan:4446            ads.web.aol.com:http     TIME_WAIT
  TCP    pregan:4447            ads.web.aol.com:http     TIME_WAIT
  TCP    pregan:4448            ads.web.aol.com:http     TIME_WAIT
  TCP    pregan:4449            ads.web.aol.com:http     TIME_WAIT
  TCP    pregan:4450            192.168.124.101:1214     SYN_SENT
  TCP    pregan:4451            192.168.150.102:1214     SYN_SENT
  TCP    pregan:4649            cs34.msg.sc5.yahoo.com:telnet  ESTABLISHED
  TCP    pregan:4669            64.12.29.24:5190         ESTABLISHED
  TCP    pregan:4715            msgr-ns42.msgr.hotmail.com:1863  ESTABLISHED
  TCP    pregan:4889            24.244.138.36:1214       ESTABLISHED
  TCP    pregan:4925            64.12.25.7:5190          ESTABLISHED
  TCP    pregan:4926            64.12.27.196:5190        ESTABLISHED

C:\Documents and Settings\Pat>netstat -n

Active Connections

  Proto  Local Address          Foreign Address          State
  TCP    127.0.0.1:3001         192.168.1.100:3497       ESTABLISHED
  TCP    192.168.1.100:3497     63.240.14.62:21          ESTABLISHED
  TCP    192.168.1.100:3499     63.240.14.62:21          ESTABLISHED
  TCP    192.168.1.100:4275     63.240.14.62:20          ESTABLISHED
  TCP    192.168.1.100:4445     200.207.217.21:1214      TIME_WAIT
  TCP    192.168.1.100:4446     205.188.165.57:80        TIME_WAIT
  TCP    192.168.1.100:4447     205.188.165.57:80        TIME_WAIT
  TCP    192.168.1.100:4448     205.188.165.89:80        TIME_WAIT
  TCP    192.168.1.100:4449     205.188.165.89:80        TIME_WAIT
  TCP    192.168.1.100:4452     192.168.150.102:1214     SYN_SENT
  TCP    192.168.1.100:4453     4.62.189.73:1214         TIME_WAIT
  TCP    192.168.1.100:4454     152.163.226.121:80       TIME_WAIT
  TCP    192.168.1.100:4455     152.163.226.121:80       TIME_WAIT
  TCP    192.168.1.100:4456     152.163.226.153:80       TIME_WAIT
  TCP    192.168.1.100:4457     152.163.226.153:80       TIME_WAIT
  TCP    192.168.1.100:4458     192.168.1.2:1214         SYN_SENT
  TCP    192.168.1.100:4459     4.62.189.73:1214         TIME_WAIT
  TCP    192.168.1.100:4649     216.136.227.168:23       ESTABLISHED
  TCP    192.168.1.100:4669     64.12.29.24:5190         ESTABLISHED
  TCP    192.168.1.100:4715     64.4.13.71:1863          ESTABLISHED
  TCP    192.168.1.100:4889     24.244.138.36:1214       ESTABLISHED
  TCP    192.168.1.100:4925     64.12.25.7:5190          ESTABLISHED
  TCP    192.168.1.100:4926     64.12.27.196:5190        ESTABLISHED
```

3.5 PROTOCOL ANALYZERS

Security+ Objective 3.1.10—Network Monitoring/Diagnostic

Sometimes when you have to troubleshoot some network problems, you need to take a good look at what is being sent through your network to determine the cause. This is where **protocol analyzers** come in. A protocol analyzer, also known as a network analyzer, is software or a hardware/software device that allows you to capture or receive every packet on your media, stores it in a trace buffer, and then shows a breakdown of each of the packets by protocol in the order that they appeared. Therefore, it can help you analyze all levels of the OSI model to determine the cause of the problem. Network analysis is the art of listening in on the network communications to examine how devices communicate and determine the health of that network.

The operation of a protocol analyzer is actually quite simple:

- It receives a copy of every packet on a piece of wire by operating in a promiscuous capture mode (a mode that captures all packets on the wire, not just broadcast packets and packets addressed to the analyzer's adapter).
- It timestamps the packets.
- It filters out the stuff you're not interested in.
- It shows a breakdown of the various layers of protocols, bit by bit.

These packet traces can be saved and retrieved for further analysis. Once a packet is captured from the wire, the analyzer breaks down the headers and describes each bit of every header in detail.

While it is easy to capture and timestamp the packets, often people have the tendency to capture every packet on a segment when trying to troubleshoot a specific problem. The only problem with that

Figure 3.23   The Netstat Command with the -s and -e Options

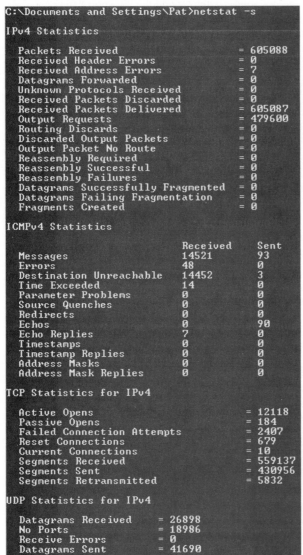

is you will be amazed at how much traffic is sent through a wire. Therefore, when you analyze the packets, you can easily become overwhelmed. By setting up filters to do some basic statistical analysis, you can isolate the problem with more ease and less time.

For example, if the problem only affects users communicating with a certain server, put an analyzer on that segment and filter traffic to and from the server. If the problem only affects users who go through a router, start by putting an analyzer on one of the routed segments and filter traffic to and from the router's MAC addresses. If you are troubleshooting a slow login process, you should start by analyzing from the client's segment and putting a filter on the client's MAC address.

Protocol analyzers can be used for more than just troubleshooting. You can use them to monitor your network performance and head off problems before they occur, and you can determine when your network is becoming too congested. This way, you can update your network hardware or subdivide your network so that your network performance becomes a problem. In addition, you can find out what is using the bandwidth of your network so that you can optimize or tweak your network.

In addition, you can baseline the throughput of a particular application. Therefore, you can determine how much traffic the application is causing. This is particularly important if you can actually test the application before purchasing the application to see if your current network can handle the additional generated traffic. This would include looking at how much traffic is generated when you log onto the new application or server, querying and updating a database and the transfer of files.

Of course, if you analyze your network when everything is working properly, it will be easier to identify packet anomalies and security problems, and you can compare the difference in performance when you update or replace drivers, network interfaces, platform upgrades, and so forth. This will even give you concrete numbers that you can use in reports to management so that you can justify equipment costs and upgrades.

A good analyzer should have some alerts/alarms that notify you of unusual or faulty traffic patterns. Some of the useful alarms should include:

- **Utilization percentage**—Shown as a percentage of the bandwidth that is used up. On Ethernet networks especially, the performance degrades significantly when the utilization gets up above 40 percent. Watch the collision/fragment error count in relationship to utilization.
- **Packets per second**—Shown in number of packets seen per second on the network. This number can give you an idea of how many packets an interconnecting device (such as a router or switch) will need to process per second.
- **Broadcasts per second**—This number tells you how much broadcast (processed by all devices regardless of their operating system or protocol) is on your network. Excessive broadcast will slow your network dramatically.
- **Server/router down**—When the server and/or router goes down.
- **MAC-layer errors**—Shown in "per second" increments. These MAC (media access control) layer errors are defined as Layer 1 and 2 errors that corrupt packet formats or make access to the network impossible.

The analyzer should also be able to build trend graphs to illustrate the current and long-term traffic patterns (such as utilization and packets per second). In order to make the communications information useful to you, the analyzer decodes, or interprets, the actual packet information received.

3.5.1   Placement of Protocol Analyzers

In order for these analyzers to capture all the traffic, you must have a network interface card and driver that supports promiscuous mode operations. A promiscuous mode card is able to capture error packets and packets that are not addressed to the local card. Of course, broadcast and multicast traffic should be visible to the analyzer also.

Most current analyzers require NDIS version 3.0+ drivers to support promiscuous mode operations. In some cases, the analyzer manufacturer offers a specialized driver to enhance the card and provide error reporting. This does not mean that all cards can run in promiscuous mode. Some cards use special functionality to enhance performance at the expense of promiscuous mode operations. For example, some cards support promiscuous mode operation but will not report bad packets so that they will increase network performance.

To analyze multiple LAN and/or WAN segments simultaneously, you have to figure where you want to place your network analyzers. First, you don't necessarily need an analyzer on every network segment. Of course, having multiple analyzers also has its advantages, too. Of course, the network devices that connect your network and the layout of the network will affect where you need to place the routers:

- Since a hub is a multiport repeater, the traffic generated or received by one computer can be seen by all computers connected to the hub. Therefore, if you have a hub, you can connect your protocol analyzer to any port on the hub.
- Since a bridge isolates and localizes traffic, you should consider placing protocol analyzers on both sides of the bridge.
- If you have a switch (a switch is a multiport bridge that isolates and localizes traffic), you will have to either use a hub to connect the switch port, the PC, or host that you want to analyze and the protocol analyzer. This way, you can see all of the traffic being sent or received by the PC or host. Another way is to use analyzer agents or configure your switch for port spanning or mirroring (if your switch supports it). Port spanning or mirroring configures the switch to send a copy of any port's traffic to another port.
- Since routers isolate and direct traffic based on the network address, if you place an analyzer on one side of the router, you would only see traffic that is destined to that network. Therefore, you

should consider placing an analyzer on each side of the router or load analyzer agents on the router. Note: The analyzer agent should be a multisegment agent that can capture packets from both connected networks.

- To test WAN links, you can connect analyzers or agents to both sides of the WAN links, and you can also connect analyzers or agents to the IP router and/or CSU. Of course, you may need assistance from your WAN link provider on how to make the physical connection to your WAN link.

Analyzer agents are typically configuration options or software programs that are loaded on switches or PCs to enable them to capture traffic from the wire and send the data to a management console. This way, you can set up the agents and tap into them as needed without actually being there, and it allows you to analyze all the traffic from a central location.

3.5.2 Looking at a Packet

If you recall from earlier in this chapter, data is encapsulated at the transport layer, which is encapsulated at the network layer, which is encapsulated at the data link layer, converted to bits and sent over some form of media. Of course, when the packet is received at the destination device, the packet is received and processed by the network interface card, and the data is stripped out as you go through the data link layer, the network layer, and the transport layer. The protocol analyzer will typically show the data and the headers that were added by each layer.

Every frame that is captured by a protocol analyzer will have up to four parts. Figure 3.24 shows a capture for a computer trying to ping another computer. As you can see by looking at the packet, the 5th frame is 74 bytes in size. It is an IP packet that is sent on an Ethernet network. The Ethernet (data link layer) header includes the destination and source MAC addresses. The destination MAC address is

Figure 3.24 Looking at a Capture Packet

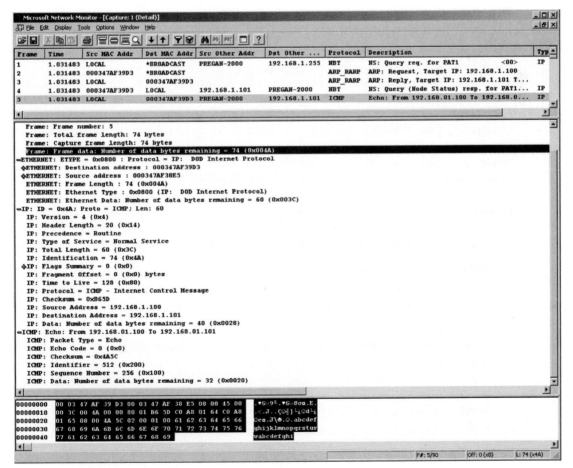

000347AF39D3, and the source MAC address is 000347AF38E5. The Ethernet header also indicates that it is carrying an IP packet.

The IP header shows the packet as an IPv4 packet, which contains an ICMP packet. Its source IP address is 192.168.1.100, and its destination IP address is 192.168.1.101. Of course, ARP was used earlier to determine the MAC addresses for the two IP addresses.

The ICMP packet is an echo packet from 192.168.1.100 to 192.168.1.101. When the packet is received and processed by 192.168.1.101, the host assigned the 192.168.1.101 address will hopefully return an echo reply showing that the two computers have a connection.

By understanding how a workstation creates and transmits a packet, you can identify the step a workstation is performing when an error occurs. For example, the workstation may need to send a DNS query or an ARP broadcast. Knowing when the workstation may need to send a packet and using a network analyzer to track what the workstation actually does is an extremely effective troubleshooting method: You can determine what steps a workstation has completed successfully and identify a relationship between the information contained in the packets sent and the processes that occurred at the workstation.

For example, suppose a workstation sent ARP broadcasts requesting a local device's hardware address, and the requests were unanswered. In this case, you could assume that the workstation had resolved the application port number, obtained the destination IP address, and determined the route (local) to the destination. If you were troubleshooting this problem, you could investigate several possible causes:

- The workstation might not have performed the route resolution process properly, and the destination device might actually be on another network.
- The workstation might have received incorrect DNS information.
- The destination device is not available.

Therefore, to analyze the TCP/IP protocol, you need to know what to expect when everything is working properly. Then you can analyze the packet properly. Of course, many of these transactions will have some things in common.

As mentioned earlier, TCP/IP uses the following resolution process when it needs to communicate with a computer:

1. Resolve the application to the port number.
2. Resolve the host name to the IP address (host file or DNS server). If no answer, go to the secondary DNS server. If there is no response from secondary DNS server, it cannot finish communication.
3. Determine if the destination address indicates that the destination device is local or remote. Upon receipt of the IP address, use the network mask to determine the network portion of your address. In addition, it determines the network portion of your address to the desired target.
   a. If the destination address is local (the network addresses are the same), resolve the MAC address of the local target by first checking the ARP cache for the information. If it does not exist, send an ARP broadcast looking for the target's hardware address.
   b. If the destination address is remote, perform route resolution to identify the appropriate "next-hop" router. Look in the local routing tables to determine if you have a host or network entry for the target. If neither entry is available, check for a default gateway entry. Then resolve the MAC address of the next-hop router. Check your ARP cache first. If the information does not exist in cache, send an ARP broadcast out to get the information.

If a protocol utilizes TCP to establish a logical connection between devices, the procedure uses a three-way handshake. The device that initiates the handshake process is called Device 1, and the destination device, or the target of the connection, is called Device 2.

1. Device 1 sends its TCP sequence number and maximum segment size to Device 2 (Device 1 SYN to device 2).
2. Device 2 responds by sending its synchronize sequence number and maximum segment size to Device 1 (Device 1 SYN ACK to Device 2).
3. Device 1 acknowledges receipt of the sequence number and segment size information (ACK).

By looking inside the handshake packets, you can see what a TCP header actually contains during the handshake process and understand how to troubleshoot this process.

For example, let's look at a DHCP client trying to get an address from a DHCP server. DHCP clients use the following basic startup routine:

1. DHCP Discover
2. DHCP Offer
3. DHCP Request
4. DHCP ACK

Look at your DHCP communications to identify that pattern. What if the discovery process fails? What if more than one address is offered (more than one DHCP server)? Did the client NACK (negative acknowledgement to not accept the address) the second address? What did the client ask for in the Request? Did the server reply with all required information? What if the DHCP Release gets literally "smashed to bits" along the way? ACK is not required for those packets, so the DHCP client just assumes that if it sent the packet, it got there. The DHCP server won't release this address until the lease time has expired.

3.5.3   Using ICMP Packets to Troubleshoot

The TCP/IP protocol suite includes Internet Control Message Protocol (ICMP), a message protocol that can help you identify network problems, such as incorrect gateway settings, unavailable applications or processes, and fragmentation problems. If your job responsibilities include troubleshooting or testing TCP/IP networks, you should know ICMP.

ICMP messages provide feedback on communication problems such as the following:

- A client has been configured with the wrong IP address for its Domain Naming System (DNS) server. The destination device sends an ICMP message, indicating that this device does not support the DNS port (port 53).
- An application does not permit fragmentation of its communications, but fragmentation is required to communicate with the destination device. The router that would normally fragment the packet sends the source device an ICMP message, indicating that the packet could not be forwarded because the packet's "don't fragment" bit was set.
- A client sends all communications to a default router although another router offers the best route. The default router sends an ICMP message that includes the IP address of the router that provides the best route.
- A packet arrives at a router with a Time To Live (TTL) value of 1. The IP TTL value decrements as the IP packet is forwarded through each router. If an IP packet has a TTL value of 1, the router cannot decrement the TTL value by one and then forward the packet. Instead, the router discards the packet and sends an ICMP message, indicating that the packet's TTL expired in transit.

See table 3.6. In addition, certain utilities use ICMP for testing and diagnostics, including ping and traceroute.

ICMP packets are a little different from other packets. For example, ICMP packets do not rely on User Datagram Protocol (UDP) or Transmission Control Protocol (TCP). Instead, ICMP packets sit directly on the IP header. The structure of the ICMP packet depends on the type of information being exchanged and the function of the packet.

Before you can use ICMP to troubleshoot your company's network, you must capture the ICMP traffic on that network. You can set up a network analyzer to capture all TCP/IP traffic and filter just the ICMP traffic (post-filtering), or you can set up a prefilter to capture just ICMP traffic (if the network analyzer you are using provides prefiltering capabilities).

After setting up the network analyzer to filter ICMP traffic, you should take a good look at the ICMP traffic that crosses the network. How many ICMP redirect messages do you see? It is typical to have some redirect messages (especially during start-up hours in the morning), but if one device is constantly being redirected before communicating with other devices on the network, you may need to assign that device a different default gateway.

Network and host unreachable messages may indicate a route or routing failure. For example, if a router cannot forward a packet addressed to a certain device or network because that device or network is considered "down," the router will send a network unreachable or host unreachable message to the source device. This problem could be caused by a faulty IP stack on the destination device or by routing failures that have made a network unreachable.

Table 3.6   ICMP Programs

ICMP Type	Name	Description
3 (Destination Unreachable Codes)	Net Unreachable	The sending device knows about the network but believes it is not available at this time. Perhaps the network is too far away through the known route.
	Host Unreachable	The sending device knows about host but doesn't get ARP reply, indicating the host is not available at this time.
	Protocol Unreachable	The protocol defined in IP header cannot be forwarded.
	Port Unreachable	The sending device does not support the port number you are trying to reach.
	Fragmentation Needed and Don't Fragment was Set	The router needs to fragment the packet to forward it across a link that supports a smaller maximum transmission unit (MTU) size. However, application set the Don't Fragment bit.
	Source Route Failed	ICMP sender can't use the strict or loose source routing path specified in the original packet.
	Destination Network Unknown	ICMP sender does not have a route entry for the destination network, indicating this network may never have been available.
	Destination Host Unknown	ICMP sender does not have a host entry, indicating the host may never have been available on connected network.
	Source Host Isolated	ICMP sender (router) has been configured to not forward packets from source (the old electronic pink slip).
	Communication with Destination Network is Administratively Prohibited	ICMP sender (router) has been configured to block access to the desired destination network.
	Communication with Destination Host is Administratively Prohibited	ICMP sender (router) has been configured to block access to the desired destination host.
	Destination Network Unreachable for Type of Service	The sender is using a Type of Service (TOS) that is not available through this router for that specific network.
	Destination Host Unreachable for Type of Service	The sender is using a Type of Service (TOS) that is not available through this router for that specific host.
	Communication Administratively Prohibited	ICMP sender is not available for communications at this time.
	Host Precedence Violation	Precedence value defined in sender's original IP header is not allowed (for example, using Flash Override precedence).
5 (Redirect Codes)	Redirect Datagram for the Network (or subnet)	ICMP sender (router) is not the best way to get to the desired network. Reply contains IP address of best router to destination. Dynamically adds a network entry in original sender's routing tables.
	Redirect Datagram for the Host	ICMP sender (router) is not the best way to get to the desired host. Reply contains IP address of best router to destination. Dynamically adds a host entry in original sender's route tables.
	Redirect Datagram for Type of the Service and Network	ICMP sender (router) does not offer a path to the destination network using the TOS requested. Dynamically adds a network entry in original sender's route tables.

Table 3.6   Continued

	Redirect Datagram for the Type of Service and Host	ICMP sender (router) does not offer a path to the destination host using the TOS requested. Dynamically adds a host entry in original sender's route tables.
6 (Alternate Host Address Codes)	Alternate Address for Host	Reply indicates another host address should be used for the desired service. Should redirect application to another host.
11 (Time Exceeded Codes)	Time to Live exceeded in Transit	ICMP sender (router) indicates that originator's packet arrived with a Time To Live (TTL) of 1. Routers cannot decrement the TTL value to 0 and forward the packet.
	Fragment Reassembly Time Exceeded	ICMP sender (destination host) did not receive all fragment parts before the expiration (in seconds of holding time) of the TTL value of the first fragment received.
12 (Parameter Problem Codes)	Pointer indicates the error	Error is defined in greater detail within the ICMP packet.
	Missing a Required Option	ICMP sender expected some additional information in the Option field of the original packet.
	Bad Length	Original packet structure had an invalid length.

Port unreachable messages, on the other hand, may indicate that a device is configured incorrectly. For example, if a device continually sends DNS queries to a specific IP address and receives port unreachable messages, the IP address for the DNS server may not be valid.

Although ICMP messages are invaluable for troubleshooting TCP/IP networks, you should be aware that hackers find ICMP messages equally useful. For example, excessive port unreachable messages may be the first sign that a hacker is trying to discover what network services are running on a network. Port scanning utilities often use the simplistic approach of sending packets to a device and incrementing the destination port number by 1 in each packet. Port unreachable messages help determine which ports are not active, thereby identifying the ports or processes that are available on a system. Because hackers sometimes use port unreachable messages in this way, you should carefully examine these types of messages on your company's network.

You should also examine the echo request and echo reply messages being transmitted on the network. Hackers sometimes use echo requests to "discover" IP addresses of live devices on the network. If echo requests are being used in this way, the destination IP address is typically incremented by one in each message. For example, you will see an echo request sent to 10.0.0.1, an echo request sent to 10.0.0.2, an echo request sent to 10.0.0.3, and so on.

These types of requests may also be sent by a management product that is building a map of your company's network (and, therefore, has a legitimate reason for discovering devices). However, if an unknown or suspect device is performing this type of discovery, it can be the first sign that a hacker is attempting to get information about your company's network.

In addition, hackers use ICMP messages to cripple network devices. For example, if you find an excessive number of ICMP echo packets on a network, you may have cause for concern. An excessive number of ICMP echo packets may indicate a denial of service attack. A denial of service attack focuses on overloading or crippling a device to the point where it cannot provide services to other devices.

Because hackers can use ICMP messages to gain information about a network or to actually harm a network, many companies restrict devices from transmitting specific ICMP messages across their connection to the Internet. If your company's security policy doesn't cover ICMP messages, you may want to revise it to include such a restriction.

3.5.4   Analyzing Security Issues

Denials-of-service (DoS) attacks are far too common these days. A Denial-of-Service attack is based on the theory that if you hog up all the CPU of a device, that device must deny services to anyone else. There are two primary types of DoS attacks:

- Brute force attacks
- Stealthy attacks

Brute force attacks are typically easy to spot with an analyzer. We'd think of a brute force attack if a device were sending out 10,000 pings in rapid succession to another device. Stealthy attacks typically only require one or two packets to kill the target. For example, a TCP SYN packet that uses the target's IP address in both the source and destination address field of the IP header can kill some implementations of IP. If you use a protocol analyzer, you can see the 10,000 pings (ICMP packets) or see that TCP SYN packets.

Lastly, a protocol analyzer can be used to capture packets that include passwords. This is particularly dangerous when passwords are sent in clear text in which the password can be read without being cracked.

WHAT YOU NEED TO KNOW

Security + Objective 3.1.10—Network Monitoring/ Diagnostic

1. For a TCP/IP network, several utilities can be used to test and troubleshoot the network. The first thing that you need to do when troubleshooting an apparent TCP/IP problem is to check your TCP/IP configuration, specifically, your IP address, subnet mask, default gateway, DNS server, and WINS server.
    a. If the subnet mask is wrong, you may not be able to communicate with machines on the same subnet or remote subnets.
    b. If the default gateway is wrong, you will not be able to connect to any computer on a remote subnet.
    c. If the DNS server is wrong, you will not perform name resolution, and you will not be able to surf the Internet.
    d. Having the wrong WINS server will stop you from using computer BIOS names when using UNC names.
2. To verify the TCP/IP configuration in Microsoft Windows, you would use either the IP Configuration program (WINIPCFG.EXE) command (available in Windows 9X) or the IPCONFIG.EXE (available in Windows 98, Windows NT, Windows 2000, Windows XP, and Windows 2003).
3. To verify your TCP/IP in Linux, you can use ifconfig and route commands.
4. The ping command sends packets to a host computer and receives a report on their round-trip time.
5. Viewing the current configuration, pinging the loopback address (ping 127.0.0.1) and pinging the IP address of your computer will verify that the TCP/IP protocol is properly functioning on your PC.

6. By pinging the IP address of the default gateway or router, as well as other local IP computers, you determine if the computer is communicating on the local network. If it cannot connect to the gateway or any other local computer, either you are not connected properly or the IP protocol is misconfigured (IP address, IP subnet mask, or gateway address).
7. If you cannot connect to the gateway but you can connect to other local computers, check your IP address, IP subnet mask, and gateway address. Check to see if the gateway is functioning by using the ping command at the gateway to connect to your computer and other local computers on your network, as well as pinging the other network connections on the gateway/router or pinging computers on other networks.
8. If you cannot ping another local computer, but you can ping the gateway, most likely the other computer is having problems and you need to restart this procedure at that computer. If you can ping the gateway, but you cannot ping computer on another gateway, you need to check the routers and pathways between the two computers by using the ping or tracert commands.
9. Another useful command is the traceroute command (Microsoft uses the tracert command), which sends out a packet of information to each hop (gateway/router) individually. Therefore, the tracert command can help determine where the break is in a network.
10. The ARP utility is primarily useful for resolving duplicate IP addresses.
11. Sometimes when you have to troubleshoot some network problems, you need to take a good look on what is being sent through your network to determine the cause.

12. A protocol analyzer, also known as a network analyzer, is software or a hardware/software device that allows you to capture or receive every packet on your media, stores it in a trace buffer, and then shows a breakdown of each of the packets by protocol in the order that they appeared.

13. Therefore, it can help you analyze all levels of the OSI model to determine the cause of the problem. Network analysis is the art of listening in on the network communications to examine how devices communicate and to determine the health of that network.

14. Protocol analyzers can be used to diagnose security attacks such as a denial-of-service attack, and they can also be used to capture packets with passwords.

Security + Objective 4.4—Standards and Protocols

1. To overcome compatibility issues, hardware and software often follow standards (dictated specifications or most popular).

2. Standards exist for operating systems, data formats, communication protocols, and electrical interfaces.

3. The first standard is called the de jure standard. The de jure standard or the by law standard is a standard that has been dictated by an appointed committee.

4. The de facto standard or from the fact standard is a standard that has been accepted by the industry just because it was the most common.

5. When a system or standard has an open architecture, it indicates that the specification of the system or standard is public.

6. A proprietary system is privately owned and controlled by a company and has not divulged specifications that would allow other companies to duplicate the product.

7. With the goal of standardizing the network world, the International Organization for Standardization (ISO) began developing the Open Systems Interconnection (OSI) reference model.

8. The key reason that ISO released the OSI model was so that different vendor networks could work with each other.

9. Today, the OSI reference model is the world's prominent networking architecture model.

10. To analyze all of the ways that a network can be attacked or accessed without proper permission, you use the OSI model to categorize the various methods.

11. Most of the attacks that you hear about in the news occur at the application layer, going after Web servers and browsers and the information that they have access to, but application-layer attacks on open file shares are also common.

12. Today, the TCP/IP protocol is the primary protocol used on the Internet and is supported by Microsoft Windows, Novell NetWare, UNIX, Linux, and Apple Macintoshes.

13. The standards for TCP/IP are published in a series of documents called Request for Comments (RFC).

14. Each connection on a TCP/IP address (logical address) is called a host (a computer or other network device that is connected to a TCP/IP network) and is assigned a unique IP address.

15. IP Addresses will be manually assigned and configured (static IP addresses) or dynamically assigned and configured by a DHCP server (dynamic IP addresses).

16. Since the address is used to identify the computer, no two connections can use the same IP address.

17. If an individual network is connected to another network and you must communicate with any computers on the other network, you must also define the default gateway, which specifies the local address of a router.

18. The subnet mask can be changed to take a large network and break it into several small networks called subnets.

19. Network Address Translation (NAT) is a method of connecting multiple computers to the Internet (or any other IP network) using one IP address.

20. With an NAT gateway running on this single computer, it is possible to share that single address between multiple local computers and connect them all at the same time. The outside world is unaware of this division and thinks that only one computer is connected.

21. NAT automatically provides firewall-style protection without any special set-up.

22. The Internet Control Message Protocol (ICMP) works at the network layer and is used by IP for many different services. ICMP manages IP by reporting on the IP status information.

23. Both the ping and traceroute utilities use ICMP message to identify whether a destination device is reachable and to track a packet as it is routed from a source to a destination device.

24. Every time a TCP/IP host communicates with another TCP/IP host, it will use the IP address and port number to identify the host and service/program running on the host.

25. A TCP/IP port number is a logical connection place by client programs to specify a particular server program running on a computer on the network defined at the transport layer.

26. Therefore, the Address Resolution Protocol (ARP) protocol provides a mechanism so that a host can learn a receiver's MAC address when knowing only the IP address.

27. Fully Qualified Domain Names (FQDN), sometimes just referred to as domain names, are used to identify computers on a TCP/IP network.

28. To translate the Fully Qualified Domain Name to the IP address, you would use a HOST files and Domain Name System (DNS) server.

29. When you share a directory, drive, or printer on PCs running Microsoft Windows or Linux machines running Samba, you would access these resources by using the Uniform Naming Convention (UNC), to specify the location of the resources.

30. Uniform Naming Convention is also known as the Universal Naming Convention. UNC uses the `\computer_name\shared-resource-pathname` format.

31. To translate NetBIOS names to IP addresses, you would use the LMHOST files or a WINS server.

QUESTIONS

1. Which model is the most well-known model for networking architecture and technologies?
   a. OSI model
   b. Peer-to-peer model
   c. Client/server model
   d. IEEE model

2. Which is the 4th layer of the OSI model?
   a. Datalink
   b. Presentation
   c. Session
   d. Transport

3. Which layer of the OSI model is between the Session layer and the Application layer?
   a. Presentation   b. Datalink
   c. Network   d. Transport

4. Which layer of the OSI model determines route from source to destination computer?
   a. The transport layer
   b. The network layer
   c. The session layer
   d. The physical layer

5. What OSI layer is the window for application processes to access network services?
   a. Presentation   b. Session
   c. Network   d. Application

6. The protocol used by the Internet is _____.
   a. TCP/IP   b. NetBEUI
   c. IPX   d. Appletalk

7. To connect to a TCP/IP network, you must configure which of the following? (Choose two answers)
   a. TCP/IP address
   b. The IPX address
   c. The DNS server address
   d. The gateway
   e. The subnet mask

8. To connect to a TCP/IP network that contains several subnets, which of the following must be configured? (Select all that apply)
   a. TCP/IP address
   b. The IPX address
   c. The DNS server address
   d. The gateway
   e. The subnet mask

9. What does the 127.0.0.1 address represent?
   a. A broadcast address
   b. A loopback address
   c. A network address
   d. A subnet address

10. _____ is when you take a large network and divide it into smaller networks.
   a. Subnetting   b. Gatewaying
   c. Broadcasting   d. Hosting

11. What is the default assigned ports for a web server browser?
   a. 21   b. 119
   c. 80   d. 139

12. What protocol provides reliable, connection-based delivery?
   a. TCP   b. IP
   c. UDP   d. ARP

13. Several users are complaining that they cannot access one of your Windows NT file servers, which has an IP address that is accessible from the Internet. When you get paged, you are not in the server room but at another company in a friend's office that only has a UNIX workstation available, which also has Internet access. What can you do to see if the file server is still functioning on the network?
   a. Use PING from the UNIX workstation
   b. Use ARP from the UNIX workstation
   c. Use WINS from the UNIX workstation
   d. Use DNS from the UNIX workstation

14. Which TCP port does SMTP use?
   a. 21   b. 25
   c. 23   d. 53

15. Which TCP port does Telnet use?
   a. 25   b. 23
   c. 119   d. 21

16. You administer a local area network (LAN) that uses TCP/IP as its network communications protocol. You want to view the number of User Datagram Protocol (UDP) packets that have been sent to SERVER_1 from CLIENT_A. Which tool should you use to view this information?
   a. A hardware loopback
   b. Performance monitor
   c. Monitor.nlm
   d. A protocol analyzer

17. Your network has been slow lately, and after looking into various possible causes and installing both client and server patches and upgrades, you decide to look at packet traffic. You want to be able to capture a packet stream and decode it to determine each packet's origination and destination, as well as its contents. What device will allow you to do this?

a. Protocol analyzer   b. Tone locator
c. Tone generator   d. TDR

18. In order to ensure packet-switching networks function properly, what MUST be included in every packet? (Choose all correct answers)
    a. The MAC address of the proxy server
    b. The IP address of the source computer
    c. The MAC address of the RRAS server
    d. The IP address of the RRAS server
    e. The IP address of the destination server
    f. The metric of the route

19. At what layer of the seven-layer OSI model do routers operate?
    a. Physical   b. Network
    c. Session   d. Application
    e. Data link   f. Transport
    g. Presentation

20. The process by which an attack can capture and view packets flowing across the network is known as what?
    a. Spoofing   b. Smelling
    c. Sniffing   d. Sloughing
    e. Stealing   f. Flagging
    g. Fragging   h. Filing
    i. Finding

21. At what layer of the seven-layer OSI model do switches operate?
    a. Physical   b. Network
    c. Session   d. Application
    e. Data link   f. Transport
    g. Presentation

22. What network mapping tool uses ICMP (Internet Control Message Protocol)?
    a. Port scanner   b. Map scanner
    c. Ping scanner   d. Share scanner

EXERCISES

Exercise 1: Installing Windows 2000 Server

NOTE: You can also install Windows Server 2003.

1. Reboot the computer with the proper DOS CD-ROM drivers. Note: You can also boot with a bootable network disk and connect to a network drive to load the Windows 2000 files.
2. Load the Windows 2000 Server CD or go to the network drive/directory where the Windows 2000 installation files are.
3. Change into the I386 directory by using the `CD I386` command.
4. Type in `WINNT` and press the Enter key.
5. When Windows 2000 Setup needs to know where the Windows 2000 files are located, press the Enter key. Windows 2000 will copy the installation files over the C drive. Be patient, this will take a few minutes.
6. When the MS-DOS based portion of Setup is complete, remove any floppy disks from the A drive and press the Enter key to restart the computer.
7. Windows 2000 will welcome you to Setup. To setup up Windows now, press the enter key.
8. When the license agreement appears, press the F8 key to continue.
9. When Windows shows the partitions, select the C drive (2047 MB partition). This way, the system partition will be the C drive, and the boot partition for Windows 2000 Server will be the C drive. Press the Enter key to install.
10. If needed, Convert or Format the partition to NTFS option and press the Enter key. Windows 2000 will copy some more files. The system will reboot again.
11. When the system reboots and starts a graphical interface, it will then automatically detect and install the hardware devices. Next it will ask for the Regional Settings. Select the appropriate regional settings and click on the Next button.
12. To personalize your software, enter the name and the company that you work for. Click on the Next button.
13. In the next screen, select the Per Server licensing mode and enter 50 connections. Click on the Next button.

    NOTE: To get the most out of this book, you will need to be working with a partner or a second computer. The computer on the left will be designated as computer A and the computer on the right will be designated as computer B.

14. The next screen shows a random computer name. Change the computer name to Server2000-xxy where xx represent your two-digit partner number in the class and y represents A if you are computer A or B if you are computer B. If you are not doing this in class, use 01. Therefore, if you are the first set of partners and you are using the computer on the left, you would use Server2000-01A. If you are the first set of partners and you are using the computer on the right, you would use Server2000-01B. Lastly, enter the password in the Administrator password and confirm password text boxes. Click on the Next button.

15. The installation wizard will ask you to add or remove components of Windows 2000. Since there is nothing that we want to add at this time, click on the OK button.
16. If your computer has a modem, a modem dialing information box will appear. Enter your area code and type in the appropriate options for your computer. Click on the Next button.
17. For the Date and Time Settings, enter the proper information and click on the Next button.
18. Windows 2000 will configure the Networking Settings. Select Custom settings and click on the Next button.
19. The network components chosen by default are client for Microsoft networks, file and printer sharing for Microsoft networks, and Internet Protocol (TCP/IP). Click on the Internet Protocol and click on the Properties button.
20. In the Internet Protocol (TCP/IP) properties dialog box, click on the Use the following IP address option and input the following:
    IP Address: 192.168.XXX.1YY
    Subnet mask: 255.255.255.0
    where XXX (1-255) is your room number, and YY is the computer number assigned. If you are working at home, use 1 and 01. Therefore, the address would be 192.168.1.101. In addition, if your network has a gateway and a DNS server, specify them. Click on the OK button and click on the next button. Note: If the card is not recognized, you need to finish the installation and install the appropriate driver and configure the network card.
21. The next window asks if you want to be a member of a workgroup or a computer domain. For now, select No and click on the Next button. It will then copy some files and perform final tasks.
22. When the Windows 2000 setup wizard is complete, click on the Finish button and the computer will reboot.
23. If the boot menu appears, select the Windows 2000 Server.
24. Logon as the administrator.
25. Open the Device Manager. Either right-click the My Computer or click the Start button, select settings, select Control Panel and double-click the System applet, then click on the Hardware tab and the Device Manager button. Make sure that all drivers loaded properly. If not, load the appropriate drivers.
26. Right-click on the desktop and create a DATA folder.
27. Open the Data folder. Right-click the empty space of the Data folder and select New to create a Text file. In the Text file, type your name in the document.
28. Right-click the Data folder and select Sharing. Click the Share this folder, and click on the OK button.
29. Open the My Network Places and browse to your computer to see the Data share. You may need to click on Computers Near Me or Entire Network.
30. Browse to your partner's computer to see the Data share.

Exercise 2: Troubleshooting TCP/IP Networks in Windows

1. Start a DOS prompt by clicking on the Start button, selecting the Programs option, selecting the Accessories option and selecting the Command prompt option.
2. Execute the IPCONFIG command and record the following settings:

   IP Address
   Subnet mask
   Default Gateway

3. Use the IPCONFIG /ALL command and record the following settings:

   MAC address
   Wins server (if any)
   DNS server (if any)
   If it is DHCP enabled or not

4. Ping the loopback address of 127.0.0.1.
5. Ping your IP address.
6. Ping your instructor's computer.
7. Ping your partner's computer.
8. Use the tracert command to your instructor's computer.
9. If you are connected to the Internet, use the tracert command to Novell.com.
10. If you have router on your network, ping your gateway or local router connection.
11. Your network has a DHCP network; right-click My Network Places and select the Properties option.
12. Click on the Internet Protocol (TCP/IP), and then click on the Properties button.
13. In the Internet Protocol (TCP/IP) Properties dialog box, select Obtain an IP address automatically. Click on the OK button.

14. Execute the IPCONFIG command at the command prompt and record the following settings:

      IP Address
      Subnet mask
      Default Gateway
      WINS server (if any)
      DNS server (if any)
      If it is DHCP enabled or not

15. Ping the loopback address of 127.0.0.1.
16. Ping your IP address.
17. Ping your instructor's computer.
18. Ping your partner's computer.
19. If you have a router on your network, ping your gateway or local router connection.
20. At the command prompt execute the IPCONFIG /RELEASE to remove your values specified by a DHCP server.
21. At the command prompt, execute the IPCONFIG command and compare the recorded values from number 2.
22. At the command prompt, execute the IPCONFIG /RENEW command.
23. At the command prompt, execute the IPCONFIG command and compare the recorded values from number 2.
24. Have your instructor stop the DHCP server (or DHCP service).
25. At the command prompt, execute the IPCONFIG /RELEASE command followed by the IPCONFIG/RENEW. Note: There will be a pause while Windows 2000 attempts to locate a DHCP server.
26. At the command prompt, execute the IPCONFIG prompt. Record the address and try to determine where this address came from.
27. Try to ping your instructor's computer and the local gateway. You should not be able to ping the IP addresses (and subnet mask) since the two computers are on two different networks.
28. After your partner has acquired an Automatic Private IP address, try to ping each other. Since these addresses are on the same network (physically and logically), it should work.
29. Go back into the TCP/IP dialog box and enter the static addresses that you recorded in question 2 and question 3.
30. Test your network by pinging your partner, instructor computer, and gateway.
31. Disconnect the network cable from the back of the computer.
32. Look at the taskbar in the notification area (near the clock) and notice the Red X.
33. From the command prompt, type in IPCONFIG.
34. Go into the Network and Dial-up Connection dialog box by right-clicking My Network Places and selecting properties. Notice the Red X.
35. Connect the cable back into the network card. Notice that the red X in both places goes away. In addition, notice that the icon disappears altogether from the notification area.
36. Right-click Local Area Connection and select properties.
37. Select the Show icon in taskbar when connected. Click on the OK button. Close the Local Area Connection dialog box.
38. Go to the notification area and notice the new icon representing the network connection.
39. Without clicking on the new icon, move the mouse pointer onto the icon. Without moving the mouse, notice the information given.
40. Double-click the icon to bring up the Local Area Connection dialog box.
41. From the command prompt, execute the ARP −A.
42. Close all windows.

Exercise 3: Using Network Monitoring in Windows

1. On the Windows server, click the Start button, select settings, select Control Panel, then select Add/Remove Programs.
2. In Add/Remove Programs, click Add/Remove Windows Components.
3. In the Windows Component Wizard, highlight Management and Monitoring Tools, then click the Details button.
4. In the Management and Monitoring Tools window, select the Network Monitor Tools check box, then click OK.
5. Click the Next button in the Windows Components wizard to continue. If you are prompted for additional files, insert your Windows 2000 Server disk or type a path to the location of the files on the network.
6. Click Finish to complete the installation.
7. Reboot the computer to clear the caches.

8. Click the Start button, select programs, select administrative tools, and choose Network Monitor. If you are prompted for a default network on which to capture frames, select the local network from which you want to capture data by default.
9. On the Capture menu, click Start.
10. Open a DOS Window and ping your partner's computer by computer name.
11. Change back to Network Monitor and click on the Stop button (4th from the right on the toolbar).
12. Look at the statistics, specifically, how many frames, how many broadcast, how many frames dropped and the %network utilization.
13. Click on the Display Captured Data button (2nd from the right on the toolbar).
14. Double-click a packet and analyze its parts. Look for Ethernet, IP, TCP, and Upper-layer protocols. Note: Not all packets will have all of these.
15. Look for the packets that resolved the Host address to IP address and the packets that resolved the IP address to MAC address. What type of packets where they?
16. Look for the Ping packets from your computer to your partner's computer. What type of packets were they?
17. Close Network Monitor.

Exercise 4: Installing Red Hat Linux 7.2 or 7.3

Newer versions can also be installed

1. With the Red Hat Linux Boot Disk in drive A and the Red Hat Linux CD #1 in the CD drive, boot the computer. Note: If your system supports a bootable CD, you can insert the CD into the drive and reboot the computer. Note: You may need to enter the CMOS setup program to specify to boot from the A drive or the CD-ROM.
2. At the boot prompt, press the Enter key to install Linux in graphical mode.
3. Select your language and click on the Next button.
4. Select your keyboard, your keyboard layout, and click on the Next button.
5. Select the mouse type and click on the Next button. If the mouse has only two buttons, you can enable the Emulate 3 buttons if you desire.
6. Click on the Next button on the Welcome to Red Hat Linux screen.
7. Select the Custom System and click the Next button.
8. Select the Manually partition with fdisk option and click the Next button.
9. Click the hda button to select the first hard drive.
10. At the Command: prompt, type m⏎.
11. At the Command: prompt, type p⏎. Notice all of the partitions on the drive.
12. At the Command: prompt, type d⏎. To delete the first partition (hda1), type 1⏎. Delete the remaining partitions.
13. To add a new partition, type n⏎. Type p⏎ to add a primary partition. Type 1⏎ for the Partition number. When asked for the First cylinder, type 1⏎. To specify a 4500 MB partition, type +4500M⏎ when it asked for the last cylinder.
14. To add a second partition to be used as a swap partition, type n⏎ to add a new partition. Type p⏎ to specify a primary partition. Type 2⏎ to specify the second partition. For the first cylinder, press the enter key to keep the default. When it asks for the size of the partition, type in the +XXXM⏎ whereas XXX is the amount of your RAM.
15. At the Command prompt, type p⏎ to view the partitions.
16. At the Command: prompt, type l⏎ to view the partition types. Notice that Linux (ext2) is type 83 and the Linux swap type is 82.
17. At the Command: prompt, type t⏎ to change the partition type. To choose the 2nd partition, type 2⏎. When it asks for the hex code, type 82⏎. It should say Changed system type of partition 2 to 82 (Linux swap).
18. Display the partition table again, and notice the two partitions and their types. In addition, notice that no partition is selected as the bootable partition.
19. Display the help menu.
20. To make the first partition bootable, type a⏎ to toggle. When it asks for which partition, type 1⏎.
21. Display the partition. Notice the asterisks (*) under the Boot column.
22. To save all these changes, you must write the table to disk and exit. Therefore, type in w⏎.
23. When you return to the fdisk screen that displays which drive to run fdisk on, click the Next button.
24. If it asks if you would like to format this partition as a swap partition, click on the Yes button.
25. For Red Hat Linux install, you still run Disk Druid to mount the drives. Click on the hda1 partition to select it and click the Edit button. Select the / as the Mount Point, select the EXT2 filesystem and click the Ok button. If a warning appears, click on the Yes button to continue and format these partitions. Click the Next button.
26. To show you how to use Disk Druid, click on the Back button to get back to the Disk Setup screen. Highlight the first partition (hda1) and click the Delete button. When it asks if you are sure you want to delete this partition, click the Yes button. Delete the other partitions.

27. Click the New button. Change the Partition Type to Linux Swap. Enter the size of your RAM (Megs) and click on the OK button.

28. Click the New button. Select the / for the Mount Point, select the EXT2 filesystem and specify 4500 for the Size (Megs). Click on the OK button.

29. Click the New button. Select the /home mount point, select the EXT3 filesystem and specify 500 MB. Then click on the OK button. Click the Next button.

30. When you get to the Boot Loader Configuration screen, select the LILO as the boot loader and click on the Next button.

31. If you have a network card, the Network Configuration box will appear. Uncheck the Configure using DHCP box.

    If you are in a classroom, use the values assigned by your teacher, if not use the following:

    IP Address: 192.168.*XXX*.*1YY*, where *XXX* is your room number and *1YY* is your student number.

    Netmask: 255.255.255.0

    Hostname: host*XX*, where *XX* is your student number.

    If you have the only computer, use 1.101 for *XXX*.*YYY*.

    Enter 192.168.*XXX*.254 for the Primary DNS server.

    If your network is connected to a router, enter the 192.168.*XXX*.254. Click on the Next button.

32. Select no firewall and click on the Next button.

33. Select a default language and select the Next button.

34. Select your time zone and click the Next button.

35. Type in `password` for the root password. Then retype `password` for the Confirm text box. Be sure to use lower case.

36. To create a second account, click on the Add button. Type user1 for the username and type in your full name for the Full Name text box. Then type `password` for your account password and password confirm text boxes. Click the OK button. Click on the Next button.

37. Keep the MD5 passwords and Enable shadow passwords options enabled and click on the Next button.

38. When the Selecting Package Groups screen appears, scroll down to the bottom of the list and enable the Everything option. Click on the Next button.

39. Select your video card and the amount of video memory. Click the Next button.

40. On the About to Install Screen, click the Next button. When it jumps to the next screen, it may appear to freeze. Give it a couple of minutes and it will start moving.

41. When it asks for the second CD, remove the first CD and insert the second CD. Click on the OK button. Note: If you are using Red Hat 7.3, you will also need to insert a third disk.

42. When it gets to the Boot disk Creation screen, remove the Linux Installation boot disk and insert a blank disk. Then click the Next button.

43. Find your monitor and select it. If your monitor is not listed, check the monitor documentation and enter the Horizontal Sync and Vertical Sync values. Click on the Next button.

44. Select an appropriate color depth and screen resolution. Click the Test Setting button. When it asks if you can see this message click the Yes button. If not, when it returns back to the configuration screen, verify which type of video card that you have and the amount of memory.

45. Leave the Gnome desktop environment selected and select the Text login type. Click the Next button.

46. When you get the Congratulations screen, remove the floppy disk and click on the Exit button. Remove the CD Disk and let the computer boot Linux.

Exercise 5: Troubleshooting Network Problems in Linux

1. Run the ifconfig command to verify your IP settings.
2. Run the route command to verify your IP settings.
3. Ping the loopback address of 127.0.0.1.
4. Ping your IP address.
5. Ping the localhost computer.
6. Ping the host*XXX-YY* computer, where *XXX* is your room number and *YY* is your computer number.
7. Ping the host*XXX-YY*.acme.cxm computer.
8. Ping your instructor's computer.
9. Ping your partner's computer.
10. If you have a router on your network, ping your gateway or local router connection.
11. Ping the far end of the router. You may have to get the address from your instructor.
12. Ping another computer on another network. You may have to get an address from your instructor.
13. Run the traceroute command to that other computer.
14. If you are connected to the Internet, ping www.redhat.com.
15. Run the traceroute command to www.redhat.com.

CHAPTER **4**

User Management and Security

Topics Covered in this Chapter

Introduction

The network users are the people who need to access your network resources. The network administrator must manage these users so that they can access the necessary network resources to perform their job yet limit their access to these network resources so that they have less opportunity to access items that they should not be accessing.

Objectives

1. Security+ Objective 2.4—Directory—Recognition not administration
2. Security+ Objective 2.4.1—SSL/TLS
3. Security+ Objective 2.4.2—LDAP
4. Security+ Objective 3.5.3.9.1—Directory Services
5. Security+ Objective 5.5—Privilege Management
6. Security+ Objective 5.5.2—Single Sign-on
7. Security+ Objective 5.5.3—Centralized vs. Decentralized

4.1 ACCOUNT SECURITY

The username and password is the first line of defense since every user needs to have one to access the network and its resources. For the password to be effective, the administrator should set guidelines and policies on how the user should use the network, provide training of these guidelines, and provide frequent reminders.

The purpose of a **password** is a method to ensure that persons who attempt to access computer resources are who they say they are. Therefore, for a secure system, it is important to require passwords for everyone. When a program or service asks for a username and password, you type in the password and you are authenticated as it is compared against a stored password for the user account. If the two passwords match, you are given access to the system.

4.1.1 Username Policy

As you know by now, the username is the name of the account that represents the person or persons who need to access the network, and it is the account that rights and permissions are given to those network resources on the network.

To make it easier to administer, the username should use a consistent naming convention for all users so that it will be easier to find names that follow a consistent pattern. For example, you can use the first initial, middle initial, and last name, or you can use first name and last initial. Of course, if you have hundreds of employees or more, you might need to use something like first name, middle initial, and last name to differentiate all of the users. You should create a document stating the naming scheme of user accounts and provide this document to all administrators who might create accounts.

To identify the type of employee, add additional letters at the beginning or at the end of their name. For example, you can add a T–in front of the name or an X at the end of the name to indicate that the person is under contract or a temporary employee.

While the standard usernames make it easier for the administrator, they do make it easier to hack. Therefore, to make the network a little bit more secure, you should rename the administrator accounts if possible. For Windows NT, Windows 2000, and Windows 2003 servers, the administrator account is administrator. For NetWare, it is admin, and for Linux, it is root. In addition, on any system that has preset passwords, you should change those passwords immediately after the default installation is performed since these passwords are typically well known and can be a vulnerability.

To further help determine if someone is breaking into your system, if you rename the administrator accounts, you should then create dummy accounts with the same name as the original administrator account. Of course, these dummy accounts should have no rights or permissions assigned to them. You should then enable auditing of attempted and successful logins of these dummy accounts to see if someone is trying to break into your system or network.

Lastly, when doing everyday activities, you should not be logged in as the administrator of the server. This will help protect the system from carelessness, and it will restrict the damage that can be caused while logged in as that account. For example, a virus may spread onto the server and then all of the computers on the network if you accessed a virus while logged in as the administrator. If you are not logged in as the administrator, the rights and permissions to many of the files would be read only and, therefore, immune to a virus.

4.1.2   Password Policies

When it comes to security, the password is more important than the username. And there are very important things that can be done to make the password more secure. First, establish some common guidelines for the passwords. Second, educate your users to make sure that they follow those guidelines, and keep giving them reminders on using those passwords. These guidelines should include:

- You should always require usernames and passwords.
- Don't give your password to anyone.
- Change your password frequently.
- Avoid allowing people to see you type in your password.
- Do not write your password down near the computer.
- When you leave your computer unattended, log off from the computer.
- Use password-protected screensaver.
- Do not use obvious passwords, and do not use easy passwords.
- Use strong passwords.
- If you see a security problem or a potential security problem, report it to the network administrator.
- If a system or device has a default password, you need to change that password.

Some of these make common sense. For example, "you should agree not to give your password to anyone" and "avoid allowing people to see you type in your password" are good rules. To prevent people from jumping on your computer while your walk away from your desk, you should get in the habit of logging off. Yet, to help protect your computer when you forget to log off, use a password-protected screensaver. Therefore, when you leave, after a short period of time, the screensaver will start. For someone to get past the screensaver, he or she would have to type in a password. So this will automatically protect your system when you leave your computer.

One of the easiest ways to hack into a network is by exploiting weak passwords. You would be amazed how many people use easy passwords because it is convenient for the user and easy to remember. Unfortunately, any good hacker will try these first. A weak password would include:

- The word *password*
- The person's username
- The person's first name, middle name, or last name
- The person's pet's name
- A name of a family member
- Birthdates or anniversary dates
- Any text or label on the PC or monitor
- The company's name
- The person's occupation
- The person's favorite color
- Typing keys on the keyboard or numeric keypad as they are placed on the keyboard (examples: qwerty, asdfgh, 123 or 147).
- Any derivatives of the above, such as spelling one of the above backwards.

One program that hackers use to break into a server is to use a cracker program that uses a dictionary attack to figure out the password. A dictionary attack initially referred to finding passwords in a specific list, such as an English dictionary. Today, these lists have been expanded to also include combinations of words such as on-the-fly and common words with digits. The program tries by brute force or going through each item in the list until it figures out the password. Depending on the system, the password, and the skills of the attacker, such an attack can be completed in days, hours, or perhaps only a few seconds. With such programs easily available to anyone who wants them, all users should use strong passwords.

Strong passwords are difficult-to-crack passwords. They do not have to be difficult to remember and include a combination of numbers, letters (lowercase and uppercase), and special characters. Special characters are those that cannot be considered letters or numbers such as @#$%^&*.

An example of a strong password is:

tqbf4#jotld

Such a password may look hard to remember, but it is not. This password was actually derived from a common typing phrase that includes every letter in the alphabet:

The quick brown fox jumped over the lazy dog.

By taking the first letter of each word, putting the number 4 and a pound (#) symbol in the middle, you have a strong password.

To make passwords more secure, many network operating systems have password management features either built into the operating system or added by installing an add-on package. One such example would be that some network operating systems will have an option to enforce strong passwords.

Another option is that you can require a minimum number of characters for the password. A strong password should be at least eight characters if not more. They shouldn't be any longer than 15 characters because they would then be too difficult for people to remember and to create. By having a minimum number of characters, this requires a much larger number of combinations for a cracker program to try.

To avoid passwords being randomly guessed, some network operating systems offer an automatic account lockout. For example, you could set up a password where if the wrong password is tried for an account three times within a 30-minute time period, it will disable the account for a minimum amount of time or disable it permanently until a network administrator unlocks the account. In either case, such a failure should also be logged somewhere. As the administrator, you should then check these logs on a regular basis to see if there are patterns showing that someone is trying to hack into a system without the knowledge of the user.

NOTE: If you are the administrator and you accidentally lock yourself out, you will need another administrator to unlock your account. If you are the only administrator, you may not be able to recover.

Another way to avoid passwords being randomly guessed is to set up password expirations where an account will automatically expire on a certain date or after a certain number of days, or it forces the users to change their passwords every so often. This will also help keep the network secure if someone discovers a password and it will be changed from time to time, making the previous password invalid. Most organizations set up passwords to expire every 30 to 45 days. After that, users must reset their passwords immediately or during the allotted grace period. Some systems give the user a few grace logins after the password has expired.

Some systems will require unique passwords. This is when a system will remember so many of the last passwords used by a user and configure the system so that the user cannot use the same password over and over. When implementing a password history policy, be sure to make the password history large enough to contain at least a year's worth of password changes. For a standard 30-day life-span password, a history of 12 or 13 passwords will suffice.

Today, most network operating systems will allow users to reset their own passwords (self-service password resets). If a user feels that their password was compromised or potentially compromised, the person can change his or her own password. It also limits IT staff from exposure to these passwords. Lastly, the ability for users to change their password is especially beneficial.

Before moving on to user management, login troubleshooting should be discussed a little. If a person is having trouble logging in, you should always have the user check to see if his or her keyboard's caps lock is on. Most of the time, this is the problem, since passwords, and sometimes user names, are case-sensitive. If the user is still having problems, it is most likely easier to change the password for the user and have the user try again. If the problem persists after changing the password, you should check your encryption scheme. Sometimes, passwords could be sent in cleartext (unchanged or unencrypted text) when the program is expecting an encrypted password, or the password could be sent encrypted when the program is expecting a cleartext password.

4.1.3   User Management

The next step in securing your network would be user management. For example, if you are hiring a temporary employee, most of the network operating systems allow you to create a temporary account and have it automatically disable itself after a certain amount of days or at a certain date. In addition, when someone leaves the company, you either disable or delete a user account. Note: To make sure that the IT department is aware that a person leaves a company, make sure that the company has an exit processor for the employee that includes recovery of all IT equipment and so that the IT department will disable or delete the account. You should also change other passwords to affected systems that the user may have known.

NOTE: Don't forget to set up a checklist for when people leave the company, and make sure to gather office keys, pagers, cell phones, company software, laptops, badges, and time cards. It is also recommended that if you are going to terminate someone, you should disable their account before informing the person of termination.

Question:

Your company has a safety manager who was just fired. What should you do?

Answer:

Most novice administrators' first reaction would be to immediately delete the account. While this will prevent the person from accessing the network and causing all kinds of problems, it is probably not the best solution.

Before you decide, you should consider how much time and work goes into maintaining a user account. First, you have to create the account and fill in addresses, phone numbers, and titles. In addition, the manager has been assigned to groups and has been given rights/permissions to files, printers, and other network resources. Therefore, it would be a better decision to disable the account. Then, when a person is hired to replace the safety manager, you can rename the user, reset the password, and reactivate the account. This will save you a lot of time and work; and will ensure that you didn't miss anything when assigning rights and permissions, so the person will be able to access all of the old files.

If you decide to use an anonymous account or guest, you need to treat these with extreme care. Typically, it is not recommended to use such a generic account because you cannot audit such an account. But if you decide to use such as account, you must make sure that you only give bare-minimum access to the network resources.

Next, you should limit the amount of concurrent connections or the number of times that a person can log in at one time. For most users, you should only have the user log in once. Therefore, if the user wants to go to another machine to log on, the user must first log out of his or her first machine. This helps avoid the person leaving a machine unattended.

Lastly, if you have the need, some network operating systems allow you to specify which computer a person can log in from and what time the person can log in. Therefore, you can specify that someone cannot log in from 7:00 A.M. to 6:00 P.M. If someone tries to hack in after hours, the hacker will be automatically denied even if he or she has a valid username and password.

4.1.4   Rights and Permissions

Security+ Objective 5.5—Privilege Management

Need to know is a basic security concept that holds that information should be limited to only those individuals who require it. When planning out the rights and permissions to the network resources, you should follow two main rules:

- Give the rights and permissions needed for the user to do his or her job.
- Don't give any additional rights and permissions that a user does not need.

While you want to keep these resources secure, you want to make sure that the user can easily get what he or she needs. For example, give users access to the necessary files, and only give them the rights that they need. If they need to read a document but don't need to make changes to the document, they only need to have read the rights. When you give a person or group only the required amount of access and nothing more, this is known as the **rule of least privilege.**

Lastly, you need to understand how rights and permissions are assigned to a user and a group. For example, you will need to understand that if you assign permission to access a network resource to a group but deny an individual access to the network resource, you need to understand what the resulting rights and permissions are.

You can secure files that are shared over the network in one of two ways:

- Share-level security.
- User-level security.

In a network that uses share-level security, you assign passwords to individual files or other network resources (such as printers) instead of assigning rights to users. You then give these passwords to all users who need access to these resources. All resources are visible from anywhere in the network, any user who knows the password for a particular network resource can make changes to it. With this type of security, the network support staff will have no way of knowing who is manipulating each resource. Share-level security is best used in smaller networks, where resources are more easily tracked. Windows 9X supports share-level security.

In a network that uses user-level security, rights to network resources (such as files, directories, and printers) are assigned to specific users who gain access to the network through individually assigned usernames and passwords. Thus, only users who have a valid username and password and have been assigned the appropriate rights to network resources can see and access those resources. User-level security provides greater control over who is accessing which resources because users are not supposed to share their usernames and passwords with other users. User-level security is, therefore, the preferred method for securing files. Windows NT, Windows 2000, Windows Server 2003, Windows XP, NetWare, UNIX, and Linux support user-level security.

4.1.5   Directory Services

Security+ Objective 2.4—Directory—Recognition not administration

Security+ Objective 2.4.1—SSL/TLS

Security+ Objective 2.4.2—LDAP

Security+ Objective 3.5.3.9.1—Directory Services

Security+ Objective 5.5.2—Single Sign-on

Directory services is a network service that identifies all resources on a network and makes those resources accessible to users and applications. Resources can include e-mail addresses, computers, and peripheral devices (such as printers). Ideally, the directory service should make the physical network including topology and protocols transparent to the users on the network. They should be able to access any resources without knowing where or how they are physically connected. The modern directory services allow you to log on once and access any network service and server that is stored in the directory. If you recall from chapter 2, this is known as **single sign-on.**

NOTE: A user who logs on with a valid user ID and password combination is considered an authenticated user.

Directories are more than a list of network resources. They can be used to distribute public-key information, locate the "closest" server providing a specific network service like electronic mail, and control access to resources. Directory servers can also be set up to communicate among themselves and exchange information so that they know about information managed by other directory servers.

There are a number of directory services that are widely used. The most common is the **X.500,** which uses a hierarchical approach, where objects are organized similar to the files and folders on a hard drive. At the top of the structure, you have the root container with children organized under it. X.500 is part of the OSI model, however it does not translate well into a TCP/IP protocol environment. Therefore, many of the protocols that are based on the X.500 do not fully comply with it.

Lightweight Directory Access Protocol (LDAP) is a set of protocols for accessing information directories. LDAP is based on the standards contained within the X.500 standard, but it is significantly simpler. And unlike X.500, LDAP supports TCP/IP, which is necessary for any type of Internet access. Because it's a simpler version of X.500, LDAP is sometimes called X.500-lite. Microsoft's Active Directory and Novell Directory Services (NDS) use LDAP. Note: LDAP uses TCP port 389 and 636. To receive and respond to LDAP queries made from hosts on the Internet, you will need to open this port on your firewall, in the inbound direction.

Information provided by directory services can include sensitive details about a corporation and its network configuration. Therefore, you want to protect this information so that it cannot be retrieved using a protocol analyzer. Therefore, many directory services make use of encryption when sending data back and forth between directory service client and server. If your directory service supports an encrypted communication path, use it. If you're using pure LDAP, consider moving to LDAP over TLS, which provides such encryption. For more information about SSL and TLS, see Section 10.6.5.

4.1.6   Centralized Versus Decentralized Management

Security+ Objective 5.5.3—Centralized vs. Decentralized

As mentioned earlier in the book, when networking was taking shape, every computer had its own security database which listed its own user accounts, groups, and permissions. When users needed access to the resources on a server, the administrator had to create a user account on that server. When each server has its own security database and each server has its own administrator (technically it could be the same administrator but individual accounts are created on each server), it is known as decentralized management. When users access each server, the server has to perform a separate authentication procedure. Note: In some cases, when a user has the same username and password, the authentication process occurs in the background and is automatic and invisible to the user.

The directory services allowed for a centralized management because you only had to create one user and all servers recognize that one user. When the user logs on, the user is authenticated for the directory service and given access to the resources for which he or she has permission. All users and network resources are administered using a single centralized security database.

In larger networks, as you add more and more users, more and more servers and more and more network resources, the network becomes more than one person can administer. In these cases, the network will typically have multiple administrators.

To administer the network more efficiently, the administrator (or lead administrator) may divide the directory services into sections called containers. A container simply contains objects such as users, servers, and network resources and may be defined by job function or geographical area/site. In these cases, the administrator (or lead administrator) may delegate or give administrative control of a container to an individual or group of individuals. These people will administer the container, yet they don't have rights and permissions to administer the other parts of the directory service.

For example, if you have several sites throughout the United States, you have a corporate administrative team that administers the entire network, and you have site administrators you can create to manage the individual users at an individual site. Therefore, the site administrators handle more of the day-to-day maintenance of the directory service, while the corporate administrative team works on more important things.

4.2   WORKGROUPS AND WINDOWS NT DOMAINS

Windows NT had the ability to work with workgroups and domains. With the release of Windows 2000, domains were combined to form the Active Directory, Microsoft's directory service.

Computers and devices on a peer-to-peer network are usually organized into logical subgroups called **workgroups.** In a workgroup, each computer has a local security database so that it tracks its own user and group account information. The user information is not shared with other workgroup computers. Since the user information is not shared with the other computers, you must create users on each workgroup computer if you want to use the other computer's network resources. A workgroup is used more as a basic grouping of the computers and is only intended to help users find objects such as printers and shared folders within that group.

Workgroup Advantages

- A workgroup does not require a computer running Windows Server to hold centralized security information.
- A workgroup is simple to design and implement.
- A workgroup is convenient for a limited number of computers in close physical proximity and should not be more than 10 computers.
- Each user must manage his or her computer resources.

Workgroup Disadvantages

- A user must have a user account of each computer to which he or she wants to gain access.
- Any changes to user accounts, such as changing a user's password or adding a new user account, must be made on each computer.

Every Windows NT machine has a user database, called **SAM (security accounts manager)**, located at `%systemroot%\system32\config`. The `%systemroot%` directory is the location of the Windows files, which is typically C:\WINNT. SAM is a part of the Registry. If a user wants to access the resources on a Windows NT machine, a user account must be created for him or her.

The Windows **domain** is a logical unit of computers and network resources that define a security boundary. It is typically found on medium- or large-size networks or networks that require a secure environment. Different from a workgroup, a domain uses one database to share its common security and user account information for all computers within the domain. Therefore, it allows centralized network administration of all users, groups, and resources on the network.

DOMAIN BENEFITS:

- A domain provides centralized administration because all user information is stored centrally.
- A domain provides a single log-on process for users to gain access to network resources and only needs to log on once to gain those resources.
- A domain provides scalability so that it can create very large security databases.

In Windows NT, the Security Accounts Manager (SAM) database (also called the domain database) contains information about all the users and groups within a domain. The system of domains and trusts for a Windows NT Server network is known as **Windows NT Directory Service (NTDS).** To manage the users and groups of a domain and to set up trust with other domains (trusts allow users to access resources in other domains), you use the User Manager for Domains program.

In an NTDS network, Windows NT servers can become loaded and configured to have a copy of the domain database (domain controller). However, only one copy of the database can be considered the master copy. The master copy is on the **primary domain controller (PDC),** and the backup copies are located on **backup domain controllers (BDC).** Note: You can promote a BDC to a primary PDC without reinstalling the server. But a member server (a server that is not a domain controller and does not have a copy of the domain database) has to be completely reinstalled if you want to change it to a domain controller.

A trust relationship (or simply trust) is a relationship between domains that makes it possible for users in one domain to access resources in another domain. The domain that grants access to its resources is known as the trusting domain. The domain that accesses the resources is known as the trusted domain. A one-way domain trust relationship is established when domain A allows the users in domain B to access its resources (assuming that the users have the appropriate permissions).

In a one-way trust relationship, the domain with the resources to share trusts the domain with the users who want to access those resources—not the other way around.

If users from domain B should be able to access resources on domain A and users from domain A should be able to access resources from domain B, you need to establish a two-way domain trust relationship. Two-way domain trust relationships are common in WAN situations where two or more locations manage their own domains but need to share information.

Even though trust relationships exist between domains, users and groups within those domains must still be assigned permissions on trusted servers. You assign user and group permissions only after you create trust relationships between servers.

When you establish trust relationships in Windows NT domains, the trust relationships are non-transitive. That means that if domain A trusts domain B, and domain B trusts domain C, domain A does not trust domain C unless you establish a trust between the two.

To configure trust relationships, you need at least two domains. In addition, you must have administrator rights to the domains. To alter the trust relationships for a particular domain, click Start, point to Programs, point to Administrative Tools, and click User Manager for Domains. In the User Manager for Domains dialog box, click Policies on the menu bar, then click Trust Relationships. The Trust Relationship dialog box opens allowing you to add or remove trust relationships between domains.

With Windows NT domains, Microsoft recommends using one of four domain models:

- **Single**—The single domain model is the simplest Windows NT domain model. As its name implies, a single domain model consists of one domain that services every user and resource in an organization. This model works well for small networks.
- **Master**—The master domain model uses a single domain to contain and control user account information. In addition, separate resource domains manage resources such as networked printers and shared files. Each resource domain trusts the master domain. This model suits an environment where each department in an organization controls its files and print sharing and a central department manages the user IDs and groups.
- **Multiple master**—The master domain model uses two or more master domains (domains that contain the users) that are joined in two-way trusts. It also includes many resource domains. A multiple master domain provides the option of centrally managing all user IDs, groups, and account information, or it allows decentralized administration. Because this model lets you manage complex relationships, it's useful for large corporations or when companies merge.
- **Complete Trust**—The complete trust domain model has all domains trust all other domains. To enable domains to communicate with each other, two-way trusts must be established between all domains in the complete trust domain model. Of course, this is the most difficult to establish. Each domain still administers their resources.

The domain model you select will depend on the division of your organization (either by function or geographically), the existing infrastructure, the number of users you support, the site of network administrators, or decisions made by management.

4.3   ACTIVE DIRECTORY

Active Directory was introduced with Windows 2000 and is used in Windows 2000 and Windows Server 2003 domains. **Active Directory** is a directory service that combines domains, X.500 naming services, DNS, X.509 digital certificates, and Kerberos authentication. It stores all information about the network resources and services such as user data, printers, servers, databases, groups, computers, and security policies. In addition, it identifies all resources on a network and makes them accessible to users and applications. Active Directory supports several name formats so that it can be compatible with several standards. They are shown in table 4.1.

Active Directory uses Lightweight Directory Access Protocol (LDAP) to communicate and performs basic read, write, and modify operations. If you query an object in the Active Directory, it allows Windows 2000 and Windows Server 2003 servers to communicate with Windows NT servers.

The Active Directory database uses a data store to hold all of the information about the objects. The data store is sometimes referred to as the directory. It is stored on domain controllers and is accessed by network applications and services. The Active Directory uses the Extensible Storage Engine (ESE), which allows the Active Directory object database to grow to 17 terabytes, giving it the ability to hold up to 10 million objects. It is best, though, to have no more than a million objects.

The Active Directory, similar to a file system found on your hard drive, is a structured hierarchy consisting of domains and organizational units connected together to form a tree of objects (computers,

Table 4.1 Name Format Supported by Windows Active Directory

Format	Description
RFC 822	Internet email addresses that follow a user_name@domain.xxx format.
HTTP Uniform Resource Locators (URL)	Hypertext Transfer Protocol web page addresses use DNS and follows the http://domain.xxx/path_to_page
Universal Naming Convention (UNC)	A NetBIOS address that follows the \\domainname\sharename.
LDAP URL	An address that specifies the server or resource on the Active Directory services tree that follows the LDAP://Domain.xxx/CN=Commonname_of_Resource, OU=Organization_Name, DC=DomainComponentName.

Figure 4.1 Active Directory Structure

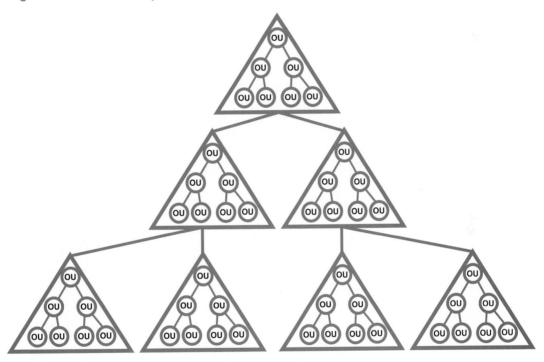

users, and network resources). See figure 4.1. The top of the Active Directory is called the root domain. Domains that are under the root domain are child domains to the root domain, while the root domain is the parent domain to its child domains. In addition, a child domain could have another domain under it. Therefore, the child domain of the root domain is the parent domain to its child domains.

When the Active Directory tree is partitioned into several domains, the Active Directory database is broken up to smaller parts and stored on different domain controllers. Since the parts are smaller and more manageable, there is a lesser load on the individual domain controllers.

One advantage to the administrator and the user is that since all of the computers and network resources are tracked in a single central database (stored in a domain controller), the administrator only has to create one user account and password for each user. Therefore, the user only has to log on once to the domain and is allowed to use any available resource located within the domain, assuming that the user has the necessary permissions to use the resource. When the user logs in, the user is logging onto the domain, not a specific server within the domain. This means that any server that does authentication within the domain can do the authentication for the user.

The domain is not limited to a single network or a specific type of network configuration. For example, they can be the computers located within a single LAN, they can be computers that are part of a LAN, or they can be computers that are spread out over several LANs connected with any number of physical connections, including Ethernet, Token-Ring, dial-up lines, ISDN, fiber optics, and wireless technology.

4.3.1   Organizational Units

To help organize the objects within the Active Directory domain and minimize the number of domains created to organize objects, the domain can contain organizational units. **Organization units** (OU) are used to hold users, groups, computers, and other organization units. See figure 4.2. Note: An organizational unit can only contain objects that are located in the domain that the organizational unit belongs to. There are no restrictions of the depth (layers) of the OU hierarchy. However, a shallow hierarchy performs better than a deep one. Therefore, you should not create an OU hierarchy any deeper than necessary. In addition, you should create organizational units that mirror your organization's function or business structure.

Since domains and organizational units are used to contain objects (users, network resources, and other domains), they are sometimes referred to as containers. Containers can be assigned Group Policy settings or delegate administrative authority. Group policies are a set of configuration settings that control the work environments for users in the domain or organizational unit. Delegate administrative authority allows assigned users to manage objects within the organizational unit.

4.3.2   Objects

An **object** is a distinct, named set of attributes or characteristics that represents a network resource, including computers, people, group, and printers. Attributes have values, which define specific objects. For example, the attributes of a user account might include the user's first and last names, department, and e-mail address, while printers might include the printer name and location. The most common object types include user account, computer, domain controllers, groups, shared folder, and printers. See table 4.2.

Figure 4.2   Active Directory Organization Units and Objects

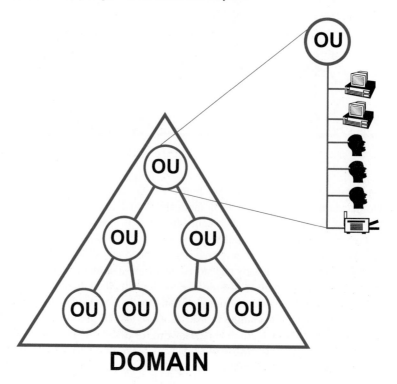

DOMAIN

Table 4.2 Object Classes

Object Type	Description
User Account	The information that allows a user to log on to Windows 2000 including the user logon name.
Computer Account	The information about a computer that is a member of the domain.
Domain Controllers	The information about a domain controller including its DNS name, the version of the OS loaded on the controller, the location, and who is responsible for managing the domain controller.
Groups	A collection of user accounts, groups, or computers that you can create and use to simplify administration.
Organizational Unit (OU)	An OU can contain other objects, including other OUs.
Shared Folders	A pointer to a shared folder on a computer. A pointer contains the address of certain data, not the data itself.
Printers	A pointer to a printer on a computer.

As new objects are created in Active Directory, they are assigned a 128-bit unique number called a globally unique identifier (GUID) [sometimes referred to as a security identifier (SID)]. While objects have several names including a common name, a relative name, or some other identifier and can be moved to another container whenever you want, the GUID stays the same. Therefore, the GUID can be used to locate an object no matter what name it is using or where it has been moved.

The schema of the Active Directory contains a formal definition and set of rules for all objects and attributes of those objects. The default schema contains definitions of commonly used objects, such as user accounts, computers, printers, and groups.

A namespace is a set of unique names for resources or items used in a shared computing environment. A distinguished name (DN) for an object is a name that uniquely identifies an object by using the actual name of the object plus the names of container objects and domains that contain the object. The distinguished name identifies the object as well as its location in a tree.

A DNS distinguished name would have a format that would look like:

CN=<Object Name>,OU=<Orgnazational Unit(s)>,O=<Organization>,C=<CountryCode>

For example:

CN=pregan,OU=users,OU=support,O=Acme.com,C=US

A LDAP distinguished name would have a format that would look like:

/O=<Organization>/DC=<DomainComponent(s)>/CN=<Object Name(s)>

For example:

/O=Internet/DC=Com/DC=Acme/DC=Support/CN=Users/CN=pregan

4.3.3 Forests

A forest is a grouping of one or more trees that are connected by two-way, transitive trust relationships, which allow users to access resources in the other domain/tree. In a forest, each tree in the forest still has its own unique namespace. Therefore, a forest is useful in organizations that need to maintain organization structures, such as a company that needs distinct public identities for its subsidiaries. By default, the name of the root tree, or the first tree that is created in the forest, is used to refer to a given forest.

Active Directory Tree	**Active Directory Forest**
■ A hierarchy of domains	■ One or more sets of trees
■ A contiguous namespace	■ Disjointed namespaces between these trees
■ Transitive Kerberos trust relations between domains	■ Transitive Kerberos trust relationships between the trees
■ A common schema	■ A common schema
■ A common global catalog	■ A common global catalog

A domain controller has a replica (copy) of every object in its own domain. Therefore, when you search for an object or retrieve information about an object within a domain, it can retrieve all of the information from a domain controller. If you need to search for an object or retrieve information about an object in another domain that is part of the forest, you would access a replica of the global catalog within the current domain to find the object.

The global catalog holds a replica of every object in the Active Directory. But instead of storing the entire object, it stores those attributes most frequently used in search operations (such as a user's first and last names). It can even be configured to store additional properties as needed. In addition, the global catalog has sufficient information about each object to locate a full replica of the object at the object's respective domain controller. Of course, since all objects in the forest are listed in the global catalog, all domains within a forest share a single global catalog.

The domain controller that contains the global catalog is known as the global catalog server. By default, a global catalog is created automatically on the initial domain controller in the forest.

Clients must have access to a global catalog to log on. In addition, a global catalog is necessary to determine group memberships during the logon process. Note: If a user is a member of the Domain Admins group, the user is able to log on to the network even when a global catalog is not available. If your network has any slow or unreliable links, you should enable at least one global catalog on each side of the link for maximum availability and fault tolerance.

4.3.4   Domain Controllers and Sites

Forests, domains, and organizational units are considered logical structures because they don't follow any subnet or network boundary. The physical structure of the Active Directory, which uses subnet/network boundaries, consists of domain controllers and sites.

Different from Windows NT, domain database is separate and different from the SAM. When the first domain controller is set up, the user accounts that may be created before are transferred to the domain database, and only the default user accounts are left at the SAM. In two situations, the SAM in the DC is used. They are when you are using the Recovery Console and when you want to restore the system state data from the backup. In these situations, you must log on to the system using the administrator account in the SAM.

The computer that stores a replica (copy) of the account and security information of the domain and defines the domain is known as the domain controller. A Windows 2000 and Windows Server 2003 domain controller is a Windows server with an NTFS partition running Active Directory services. The directory data (account and security information) is stored in the %systemroot%\NTDS.DIT file on an NTFS partition on the domain controller. The %systemroot% will be the directory that holds the Windows files; they are typically C:\WINDOWS or C:\WINNT. Access to domain objects is controlled by access control lists (ACLs). ACLs contain the permissions associated with objects that control which users can gain access to an object and what type of access users can gain to the objects. Lastly, the domain controller manages user-domain interactions including user logon processes, authentication, and directory searches.

Active Directory uses multimaster replication. This means that there is no master domain controller/primary domain controller as there was in Windows NT. Instead, all domain controllers store writable copies of the directory. When a change is made to the one of the domain controllers, it is the job of the domain controller to replicate those changes to other domain controllers within the same domain within a short period of time. By adding a domain controller to a domain, the server is automatically configured for replication.

Another type of server worth mentioning on the domain is a **member server.** A member server does not store copies of the directory database, and therefore does not authenticate accounts or receive synchronized copies of the directory database. These servers are used to run applications dedicated to specific tasks, such as managing print servers, managing file servers, running database applications, or running as a web server.

For each domain, it is recommended to have more than one domain controller. If you only have one domain controller and it goes down for any reason, the users could not use any of the network resources because there is no server to authenticate them and to give the user permission to use the network resources. The extra domain controllers do not provide fault tolerance for the different network services. They only provide fault tolerance for the Active Directory that contains the account and security information. Note: While Windows NT has primary and secondary domain controllers, domain controllers within a Windows 2000 or Windows Server 2003 domain are all equal to one another. Also, additional domain controller would divide the workload of authentication between the different controllers, allowing for faster network response time.

4.3.5 User, Group, and Computer Accounts

As with any modern NOS, Windows uses the concept of users and groups to grant access to the various network resources. Unlike other NOS, Windows also creates computer accounts. Windows NT uses User Manager for Domain while Windows 2000 and Windows Server 2003 servers use Active Directory Users and Computers console. See figure 4.3.

A **user account** enables a user to log onto a computer and domain with an identity that can be authenticated and authorized for access to domain resources. Each user who logs onto the network should have his or her own unique user account and password.

In Windows domain, there are two different types of user accounts. The **domain user account** can log onto a domain to gain access to the network resources. Of course, a domain controller must authenticate the domain user account.

Local user accounts allow users to log on at and gain resources on only the computer where you create the local user account. The local user account is stored in the local security database. When using a local user account, you will not be able to access any of the network resources. In addition, for security reasons, you cannot log on as a local user account on a domain/domain controller.

Windows NT, Windows 2000, and Windows Server 2003 start with two built-in accounts: the administrator and guest accounts. The administrator account is used to manage the overall computer and domain configuration, create and maintain computers, user accounts, groups, manage security policies,

Figure 4.3 Patrick E. Regan User Account and WS1 Computer Account Shown in the Organization Unit Corporate

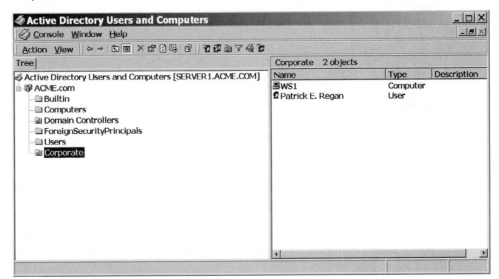

assign rights and permissions, and create and maintain printers. Since the administrator is the most important account within the domain, there are certain precautions and procedures that you should follow.

- Since every Window NT, Windows 2000, and Windows Server 2003 computer begins with having an administrator account, it is a good idea to rename the administrator account. This way, if someone is trying to hack their way in, the hacker will have to guess both the name of the administrator and the password. Note: You can only rename the administrator account, you cannot delete it.
- You should not use the administrator as a general user. Instead, you should create a second account and use it as a general user and use the administrator account for administrative tasks only.

The guest account is supposed to be used for the occasional users who need to log on and to gain access to resources. The guest account, as well as any other account that performs the same function as the administrator account, should only be used in low-security networks. Unlike the administrator account, the guest account is disabled by default. Of course, if you enable it, you should assign it a password. Similar to the administrator account, you cannot delete the account, but you can rename it.

A **group** is a collection of user accounts. By using groups, you can simplify administration by assigning rights and permissions to the group and everyone listed in the group will be assigned these rights and permissions. Users can be members of multiple groups, and groups can be members of groups.

NOTE: Groups are not containers. They list members but they do not contain the members.

In Windows 2000 and Windows Server 2003 domains, there are two group types: security and distribution. The security group is used to assign permissions and to gain access to resources. They can also be used for nonsecurity purposes such as those that you would find in a distribution group. The distribution group is used only for nonsecurity functions such as those used to distribute email messages to many people. Typically, distribution groups are only used for special applications designed to use them such as the Microsoft Exchange Mail Server.

The security group can be divided into group scopes, which define how the permissions and rights are assigned to the group. In Windows 2000 and Windows Server 2003, there are three scopes: global group, domain local group, and universal group. If you have a single domain, it is best to use global and domain local groups to assign permissions to network resources. In a domain tree, it is best to use global and universal groups if you are not using any Windows NT domain controllers.

The **global group** is usually used to group people within its own domain. Therefore, this group can list user accounts and global groups from the same domain. The global group can be assigned access to resources in any domain.

The **domain local group** is usually used to assign rights and permissions to network resources that are in the domain of the local group. Different from a domain local group, it can list user accounts, universal groups, and global groups from any domain and local groups from the same domain. See figure 4.4.

Example 4.1:

Let's say that we have a printer and some files that need to be accessed in the SALES domain. We have users in the FINANCE and SALES domains that need to access these resources.

- First create two global groups called ANALYSTS and MANAGERS in the FINANCE domain and create a global group called SALESPEOPLE in the SALES domain. Then assign the respective users from the FINANCE domain to the ANALYSTS group and MANAGERS group and the users from the SALES domain to the SALESPEOPLE group.
- Next, create a domain local group called SALES_RESOURCES in the SALES domain. Assign rights and permissions to the SALES_RESOURCES group to the printer and directories in the SALES domain.
- You can then assign users from either domain and assign the ANALYSTS group, MANAGER group, and SALESPEOPLE group. Since groups consist of many people, it is best to assign the groups first. Then if you still have certain individuals who need different or special access, you can then assign them as needed.

Figure 4.4 Users are grouped together using global groups. The global groups are assigned to the domain local groups and the domain local groups are assigned permissions to the network resources.

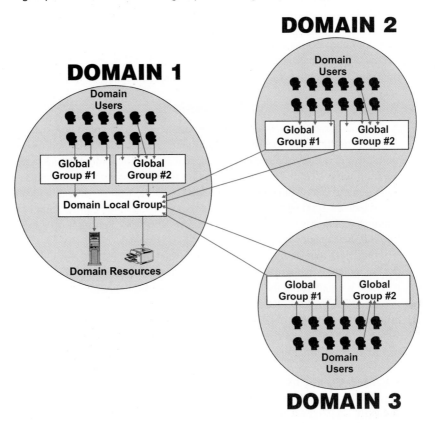

As you can see, the global groups are used to group people with common purposes or who have the need for the same rights and permissions. The advantage of using this scheme is that when you add members to the two global groups, they will automatically get access to the resources.

The universal group was introduced with Windows 2000. The **universal security group** is only available in native mode (not mixed mode, whereas a domain contains both Windows NT and Windows 2000 or Windows Server 2003 domain controllers). Note: In a mixed-mode network, the universal group option will be grayed out. It can contain users, universal groups, and global groups from any domain, and it can be assigned rights and permissions to any network resource in any domain in the domain tree or forest. As you can easily see, the Universal group is much easier to use and more flexible.

NOTE: You can change a global group into a universal group if the global group is not a member of another global group, and you can change a domain local group to a universal group if it doesn't contain any other domain local group.

When choosing a group name, use intuitive names. To help identify groups, groups are assigned unique security identifiers (SID), much like SIDs assigned to domain controllers. If you delete a group and recreate a group with the same name, the second group would have a different SID. Since these are different groups, users, rights, and permissions will have to be reassigned.

Computers that are running Windows NT, Windows 2000, or Windows Server 2003 are, by design, much more secure than Windows 9X. For example, to use the computer, you must log on to the computer with a username and password. If you don't log on, you cannot bypass the logon screen by pressing the escape key and access the computer's files and programs, and you will not able to access any network resources. Note: Windows 2000 and Windows Server 2003 computers are more secure than Windows NT computers.

To use a Windows NT, Windows 2000, or Windows Server 2003 computer that is not a domain controller, you must create a computer account for the computer. The computer account is used to uniquely identify the computer on the domain. By having the computer account, you can then audit the computer to make sure only authorized people access the computer with assigned permissions to gain access to network resources.

A computer account, which matches the name of the computer is an account created by an administrator to uniquely identify the computer on the domain. By being able to identify the computer, a secure communications channel can be created between the client computer and the domain controller. Lastly, the computer account allows the administrator to remotely manage the computer user environment and manage the computer user and group accounts.

4.3.6   Windows Rights and Permissions

A **right** authorizes a user to perform certain actions on a computer, such as logging on to a system interactively/logging on locally to the computer, backing up files and directories, performing a system shutdown, or adding/removing a device driver. Administrators can assign specific rights to individual user accounts or group accounts. Rights are managed with the User Rights policy. For Windows NT 4.0, you open the User Manager for Domains, open the Policies menu, and select the User Rights Policy. For Windows 2000 and Windows Server 2003 user rights can be found by opening the group policy, opening Computer Configuration, opening Windows Settings, opening Security Settings, opening Local Policies, and opening User Rights Assignment.

One right that should be pointed out is the logon locally right. This right allows a user to log on at the computer's keyboard. Since most protection can be bypassed by being able to log on directly to a machine without going though the network, this right should only be given to a few people.

Permission defines the type of access granted to an object or object attribute. The permissions available for an object depend on the type of object. For example, a user has different permissions from a printer. When a user or service tries to access an object, its access will be granted or denied by an Object Manager. Common Object Managers are shown in table 4.3.

When a computer, user, or group is assigned rights or permissions, the computer, user, or group is assigned a Security Identifier (SID). Similar to the SID that is assigned to a domain, a SID assigned to a computer, user, or group is a unique alphanumeric structure. The first part of the SID identifies the domain in which the SID was issued, and the second part identifies an account object within the domain. Therefore, when a computer, user, or group accesses an object, they are identified by their SID and not their username.

Each object uses an Access Control List (ACL) to list users and groups. The ACL is divided into Discretionary Access Control Lists (DACLs) and System Access Control Lists (SACLs). The DACL contains the access control permissions for an object and its attributes, and the SIDs, which can use the object. The permissions and rights that a user has are referred to as Access Control Entries (ACEs). The SACL contains a list of events that can be audited for an object. The ACE entries include Deny Access and Grant Access.

Every object in Active Directory has an owner, which controls how permissions are set on an object and to whom permissions are assigned. The person who creates the object automatically becomes the owner and, by default, has full control over the object, even if the ACL does not grant that person access. If the member of the Administrators group creates an object or takes ownership of an object, the

Table 4.3   Common Object Types

Object Type	Object Manager	Management Tool
Files and Folders	NTFS	Windows Explorer
Shares	Server service	Windows Explorer
Active Directory Objects	Active Directory	Active Directory Users and Computers Console or Snap-in
Registry Keys	The registry	Registry editor (REGEDT32.EXE)
Services	Service controllers	Security Templates, Security Configuration and Analysis
Printer	Print spooler	Printer folder

Administrators group becomes the object group. A member of the domain administrator group has the ability to take ownership of any object in the domain and then change permissions.

Standard permissions are the most commonly used assigned permissions that apply to the entire object. Assigning standard permissions are sufficient for most administrative tasks. The standard permissions are made of special permissions. Special permissions provide a finer degree of control. See table 4.4.

Explicit permissions are those that are specifically given to the object when the object is created or assigned by another user. See figure 4.5. Inherited permissions are those rights that are given to a container and apply to all of the child objects under the container. By using inherited permissions, you can manage permissions more easily, and you can ensure consistency of permission among all objects within a given container.

The permissions can be allowed or denied for each user or group. To explicitly allow or deny the permission, click the appropriate check box. If a check box is shaded, the permission was granted to the user or group for a container that the object is in and the permission was inherited. If the allow or the deny box is not checked for a permission, the permission may be still granted from a group. You would then have to check the groups that the user or group is a member of to determine if the rights are granted or denied.

Every object, whether it is in the Active Directory or it is an NTFS volume, has an owner. The owner controls how permissions are set on the object and to whom permissions are granted. When an object is

Table 4.4 Standard Permissions

Object Permission	Description
Full Control	Contains all permissions for the object including take ownership
Read	View objects and object attributes including the object owner and the Active Directory permissions
Write	Able to change all object attributes
Create All Child Objects	Able to add any child object to an OU
Delete All Child Objects	Able to delete any child object from an OU

Figure 4.5 Permissions for the User Account

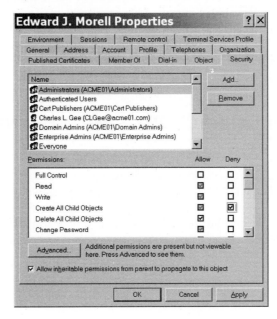

Figure 4.6   Delegation of Control Wizard

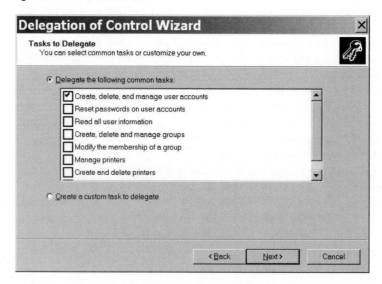

created, the person creating the object automatically becomes the owner. Administrators will create and own most objects in Active Directory and on network servers (when installing programs on the server). Users will create and own data files in their home directories and some data files on network servers.

Ownership can be transferred in the following ways:

- The current owner can grant the Take Ownership permission to other users, allowing those users to take ownership at any time.
- An administrator can take ownership of any object under his or her administrative control. For example, if an employee leaves the company suddenly, the administrator can take control of the employee's files.

Although an administrator can take ownership, the administrator cannot transfer ownership to others. This restriction keeps administrators accountable for their actions.

The best way to give sufficient permissions to an organizational unit is to delegate administrative control to the container (decentralized administration), so that the user or group will have administrative control for the organizational unit and the objects in the organizational unit. To delegate control to an organizational unit is to run the Delegation of Control wizard. To start the Delegation of Control wizard, right-click the organizational unit and select the Delegate Control. You can then select the user or group to which you want to delegate control, the organizational units and objects you want to grant those users the right to control, and the permissions to access and modify objects. For example, a user can be given the right to modify the Owner Of Accounts property, without being granted the right to delete accounts in that organizational unit. See figure 4.6.

4.4   NOVELL DIRECTORY SERVICES (NDS)

With the **Novell Directory Services** (NDS), which is based primarily on the X.500 Internet directory standard, all of the network resources are represented as objects and placed into a hierarchical structure, called an NDS Tree. This tree is a logical representation of a network and includes all network resources including users, groups, printers, and servers. Since the tree can have multiple servers, you only have to create one user on the tree, and you can give access to the server and its resources to that one user without creating multiple users for the various servers. Therefore, NDS provides central management of network information, resources, and servers. In addition, it gives a standard method of managing, viewing, and accessing network information, resources, and servers. Lastly, like the Active Directory, the NDS directory follows the X.500 standard and the Domain Name System. To change the directory database, a NetWare network administrator uses a program called NetWare

Administrator (32-bit Windows version - NWADMIN32) and Novell ConsoleOne. NetWare Administrator is considered as the legacy software, and ConsoleOne is the utility that is available on the NetWare server. See figure 4.7 and figure 4.8.

The NDS can be partitioned and replicated on multiple servers. A server could contain the entire NDS, pieces of it, or none at all. This way, if the directory becomes too large, you can divide it up into smaller pieces and put them on several servers. When planning the tree structure, you should make sure that the part of the tree that has the resources needed by a group of users has a server with the needed information near to them. This way, when a user needs to access a network resource, he or she does not have to connect to a computer that is far away to get authenticated.

NOTE: NDS for Solaris 2.0 implements the NDS service on SPARC Solaris servers and workstations so that the Solaris server or workstation acts as a directory server. The product allows you to place replicas of the NDS database on a Solaris server. These replicas utilize the same directory services provided on NetWare server. The ability to add replicas provides access to the NDS database on local Solaris servers, enabling accessibility on remote networks.

Figure 4.7   Novell ConsoleOne Is to Administer and Network Users and Resources

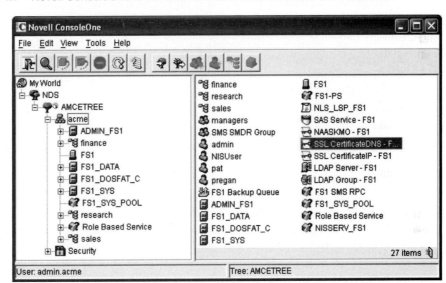

Figure 4.8   Administering an Organizational Unit Using ConsoleOne

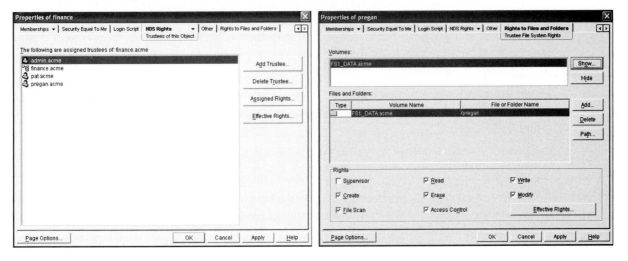

4.4.1   The NDS Tree Structure

The NDS consists of objects. An object is a unit of information about a resource, comparable to a record in a conventional database. NDS represents each network resource as an object in the directory. Different types or categories of objects exist.

Much like the root directory found on your C: drive in DOS, the top of the NDS tree is the [Root] object. The objects that are your network resources are called leaf objects. To organize your leafs, you use containers, which are analogous to the directories. As a network administrator, you can make trustee assignments and grant rights to the entire NDS tree from the [Root] object. Country, Organization, and Alias objects can be created directly under the [Root] object.

Container objects contain Leaf or other container objects. They are used to logically group and organize the objects of your Directory. They can represent countries, locations within countries, companies, departments, responsibility centers, workgroups, and shared resources.

- The Country container organizes the NDS tree by countries. It is identified by a predetermined 2-character country abbreviation.
- An Organization container organizes objects by organization groups, such as company, university, or department.
- The Organizational Unit organizes objects by subunit groups such as division, business unit, project team, or department. It can exist in organization and organization unit objects only.

NDS version 8 also included locality and domain containers. The domain container can be contained by all the other containers in the operational schema including the Tree Root and it can contain all the other operational container objects, except Tree Root.

The Leaf objects represent network resources, such as users, servers, and NetWare volumes. Common Leaf objects include:

- **NetWare Server**—Represents a NetWare server, which is used by many objects, such as volume objects, to identify the server that provides a service.
- **User**—Represents a person who uses the network. It contains the password and other login restriction properties.
- **Alias**—Points to another object at a different location in the NDS tree so that it allows a user to access an object outside of the user's normal working context.
- **Volume**—Represents a physical volume. Note: A volume is not a container although the NetWare Administrator gives you this impression since when you open it, it shows the files on the volume. When you are managing the files, the files are not part of the NDS tree.
- **Groups**—a Leaf object that allows you to group users together. By having people grouped together, you can give permissions for an object to the group and all users in the group get access to the object. Note: A group is not a container; it is just a list of users.

4.4.2   Naming of Objects

A Leaf object's common name (CN) is the name shown to the Leaf object in the NDS tree. When users need to access a resource such as a server in the NDS tree, the common name for the server object must be included in the request. To use a resource outside the user's parent container, the user must change his or her location, or context, in the NDS tree.

Context is represented as either of the following:

- An object's position in the NDS tree.
- A position you navigate to in the NDS tree after logging in (similar to your current directory when using DOS).

Contexts may be expressed in two ways: typeful and typeless. The typeful notation is a relatively lengthy way of expressing context that includes identifiers for the organization (O=) and organization unit (OU=). Typeless notation eliminates the "O" and "OU" designations.

When used to define an object's position in the NDS tree, context is a list of container objects leading from the object to the [Root]. Locating an object through context is similar to locating a file using the directory path.

For example, if you have the ACME organization located under the [Root] container, a NY under the ACME organization and an OU under CORP, the context or location on the NDS tree of the CORP object would be represented by

Typeful:
OU=CORP.OU=NY.O=ACME
Typeless:
CORP.NY.ACME

An object's distinguished name is a combination of its common name and its context. To make it easily seen as a distinguished name, it always starts with a leading period (.). For example, if you have a user called PRegan located in the CORP organization unit, the distinguished named of the PRegan object would be:

Typeful:
.CN=PRegan.OU=CORP.OU=NY.O=ACME
Typeless:
.PRegan.CORP.NY.ACME

Since a distinguished name must be unique, you cannot have two Leaf objects with the same name in the same container. However, an NDS tree can have two Leaf objects with the same name in different containers.

A relative distinguished name lists the path of objects leading from the object being named to the container representing the object's current context, or current location, in the NDS tree. It does not start with a leading period. When you use a relative distinguished name, NDS builds a distinguished name from:

current context + relative distinguished name = distinguished name

4.4.3   The Admin

The admin object is the only default user account. It is created automatically when the NetWare is installed. It has the authority to manage all aspects of the network and is the primary user object in initial network setup. The admin account/object is a user object; it can be deleted or modified, and it can have its security access revoked. Never delete or modify the Admin account/object unless you know that additional user objects have the same rights. If you delete the Admin object and no other user object has the same rights, you won't be able to change security access to any object in the tree. You are not limited to one object with supervisory authority; you can create additional user objects with the same rights as the Admin object.

4.4.4   Trustees

Every object in the NDS and every directory and file has an Access Control List (ACL) that shows who has what rights to the object, directory, and file. The list of users that have been given access is known as a trustee list. A trustee can be a user, a group (a list of users), or a container. A container actually acts as a natural group, which contains groups and users. When a container is made a trustee, any user or group also acquires those rights to the object, directory, or file. Any of the following NDS objects can be made a trustee of an object:

- User object
- Group object
- Organizational role object
- Containers and parent containers
- [Root]
- [Public] trustee

Assigning any of these objects, except the user object, as object trustees of other objects allows access to be granted to multiple users at once. With exception of the user object, all users who are members of the objects listed above receive rights simultaneously when assigned as a trustee. NDS security is easier to implement and manage when you grant rights to objects, such as group objects and container objects that pass their rights to multiple users. In addition, a user object can receive rights by being granted security equivalence to another user object.

NDS security has two distinct sets of rights: object (or entry) and property (or attribute). Rights, in all but one case, do not flow from NDS into the file system. One important note is that both the Supervisor object right and the Supervisor property right can be blocked by an Inherited Rights Filter (IRF).

Because NDS security and file system security are separate, file system administration and administration of NDS objects can be handled by one network administrator or divided among various network administrators.

Object rights are rights granted to a trustee of an object. They control what a trustee can do with the object, such as browsing, renaming, or deleting the object and control access to the object as a whole but not to the object's property values. See table 4.5.

An object contains information about its associated network resource. This information makes up the object's attributes and is stored in the properties of the object. For example, the user object contains information such as the person's address and phone number. Property rights are rights that grant access to the attributes of an object. See table 4.6. They control access to the attribute values stored within an NDS object's properties, allowing users to see, search for, or change the attribute values, and it controls a user's ability to use a network resource represented by an NDS object.

NDS, like the file system, uses rights inheritance. Inheritance minimizes the individual rights assignments needed to administer the network. Because NDS is a hierarchical structure, rights flow downward from a container to subcontainers. To keep objects from having some or all of the NDS rights they inherit, you can stop rights from inheriting by either making a new object trustee assignment at a lower level in the NDS tree and assign new rights (which overwrite the inherited rights) or by blocking rights with an Inherited Rights Filter (IRF). The IRF of an NDS object does not block rights that are granted to an object trustee of the same object. Only those rights inherited from object trustee assignments made higher in the tree are affected.

The Inherited Rights Filter (IRF) filters rights inheritance in the NDS tree. An IRF can be placed to block the inheritance of either object rights or property rights. An IRF placed on an object can block property rights granted through either the All Properties option or the Selected Properties option. Property rights granted through the Selected Properties option will only be filtered if the Inheritable property right is granted to a selected property.

Table 4.5   Object Rights

Right	Description
Supervisor (S)	Grants all access privileges. A trustee with the Supervisor right also has complete access to all the object's property rights.
Browse (B)	Enables an object trustee to see the object in the NDS tree.
Create (C)	Enables an object trustee to create objects below this object in the NDS tree. This right is available only on container objects.
Delete (D)	Enables an object trustee to delete the object from the NDS tree.
Rename (R)	Enables an object trustee to change the name of the object.
Inheritable (I)	Enables an object trustee of a container to inherit the assigned object rights to objects and subcontainers within a container. This right is granted by default to facilitate inheritance of rights to container objects and subcontainers. Revoking this right limits trustees to the rights assigned for the trustee to the container object only. No rights to the container's objects and subcontainers are inherited. This right is available only for container objects.

Table 4.6   Properties Rights

Right	Description
Supervisor (S)	Grants all rights to the object's properties.
Compare (C)	Enables the comparison of any value to a value of the property, returning a True or False response. The value of the property cannot be viewed, only the True or False status of the value submitted for comparison. If the Read write is granted, the Compare right is automatically granted.
Read (R)	Enables the display of the property value. Granting the Read right automatically grants the Compare right.
Write (W)	Enables the object trustee to modify, add, change, and delete a property value. Granting the Write right automatically grants the Add/Remove Self right.
Add/Remove Self (A)	Enables an object trustee to add or remove itself as a value of the object property. If the Write right is granted, the Add/Remove Self right is automatically granted.
Inheritable (I)	Enables an object trustee of a container to inherit the assigned property rights to objects within the container. Without this right, the remaining property rights assigned to the trustee apply only to the container object's properties and not to the properties of the objects in the container. This right is granted by default when the All Properties option is selected, and removed by default when the Selected Properties option is selected. This right is available only on container objects.

If a trustee is not granted the Inheritable property right for a selected property, that right will not be inherited by other objects lower in the NDS tree regardless of IRFs placed on objects lower in the NDS tree. The IRF of an NDS object does not block rights that are granted to an object trustee of the same object. Only those rights inherited from object trustee assignments made higher in the tree are affected.

The default trustees and rights established during installation are:

- Admin (first NDS server in the tree) Supervisor object right to [Root].
- [Public] (first NDS server in the tree) Browse object right to [Root].
- NetWare Server Admin has the Supervisor object right to the NetWare Server object, which means that Admin also has the Supervisor right to the root directory of the file system of any NetWare volumes on the server.
- **Volumes**—[Root] has the Read property right to the Host Server Name and Host Resource properties on all volume objects. This gives all objects access to the physical volume
- **Root directory of the volume**—Admin has the Supervisor right to the root directory of the file systems on the volume. For volume SYS, the container object has Read and File Scan rights to the volume's \PUBLIC directory. This allows user objects under the container to access NetWare utilities in \PUBLIC.
- **Home Directories**—If home directories are automatically created for users, they have the Supervisor right to those directories.

[Public] is not a normal object in NDS. It refers to all objects in the tree and any user that is not authenticated as well. That means that if rights are granted to [Public], users who are not logged in have those rights. Because of this, you must be very careful when granting rights to [Public]. By default, [Public] includes the Read right and the File Scan right. By making [Public] a trustee of an object, directory, or file, you effectively grant all objects in NDS the rights to that object, directory, or file. [Public] is only used in trustee assignments and must always be entered within square brackets. [Public] can be added or deleted like any other trustee.

4.5   USERS AND GROUPS IN LINUX

A **user account** enables a user to log onto a computer with an identity that can be authenticated and authorized for access to computer resources. Users can be either actual people (accounts tied to a particular physical user) or logical users (accounts that exist for applications so that they can do particular things). In Linux, everyone has an owner attached to it. At the very least, it needed one root user; however, most Linux distributions ship with several special users set up.

Any file created is assigned a user and group when it is made, as well as being assigned separate read, write, and execute permissions for the file's owner, the group assigned to the file, and any other users on that host. The user and group of a particular file, as well as the permissions on that file, can be changed by root or, to a lesser extent, by the creator of the file.

Each account is associated with the following:

- **Username**—The username is the name by which the account is known to people. Each user who logs on to the computer must have his or her own unique user ID (UID).
- **Password**—Linux accounts are first protected by a password. A person attempting to log in must provide both a username and password. While the username is generally public knowledge, passwords should be kept secret.
- **Home Directory**—Every account has a home directory associated with it so that a user can store data files. Typically, each user has his or her own home directory, although it is possible to configure a system so that two or more users share a home directory.
- **Default shell**—When using a Linux computer at the command prompt, Linux presents users with a program known as a shell. The default shell (typically bash) specifies which shell the user will use by default.
- **Program-specific files**—Some programs generate files that are associated with a particular user. Many programs create configuration files to remember user settings and options and to remember where the user left off within certain programs.

The user ID (UID) identifies the user behind the scenes. The user creation utilities automatically choose the next available number when adding a new user. The range of UIDs available depends on which distribution is in use. Typically, a certain range of lower numbers are reserved for administrative accounts, and numbers beyond that are available for individual users. The user range is easily determined by looking in /etc/passwd to see which numbers were assigned to the user accounts already created.

4.5.1   User Accounts

Most versions of Linux support usernames consisting of any combination of upper- and lowercase letters, numbers, and most punctuation symbols including periods and spaces. Usernames are case-sensitive although it is recommended to keep them all lowercase for simplicity. You should note that some punctuation symbols, such as spaces, may cause problems for certain Linux utilities. Usernames must begin with a letter and they can be up to 32 characters in length. Some utilities may truncate the user names to 8 characters. Therefore, some administrators try to limit user names to 8 characters.

For a network, especially for a network with lots of users, it is recommended to have a consistent naming convention so that it will be easier to find names that follow a consistent pattern. For example, you can use the first initial, middle initial, and last name or first name and last initial. Of course, if you have hundreds of employees or more, you might need to use something like first name, middle initial and last name to differentiate all of the users. You should create a document stating the naming scheme of user accounts and provide this document to all administrators who might create accounts. To identify the type of employee, add additional letters at the beginning or at the end of the employee's name. For example, you can add a T in front of the name or an X at the end of the name to indicate that the employee is under contract or a temporary employee.

4.5.2   The /etc/password File

When created, user accounts are placed in the /etc/passwd file. Although administrators often use tools to avoid editing this file directly, it is important to be familiar with the file as part of system maintenance.

The syntax of an entry in the /etc/passwd file is:

```
username:password:UID:GUID:name:home:shellUser
```

If the password entry is an "x," it means that shadow passwords are in use, and that the user's password is stored in the /etc/shadow file. If the account does not have a password at all, it will be indicated with an asterisk (*). This is typically used for daemons and system programs such as shutdown. If the password is a series of characters, then the password is encrypted into the /etc/passwd file. Note: Do not edit this password manually. Instead, use the passwd command instead.

The name entry is the real name assigned to the user. Since the username are not always intuitive to others, the name entry is used often by programs to display the user's name.

The shell is a program, which reads and executes commands from the user. You can think of a shell as a command interpreter, much like the command.com does in DOS. A shell uses a command driven interface. Since the shell serves as the primary interface between the operating system and the user, many users identify the shell with Linux. But, in reality, the shell is not part of the kernel; instead, it is the interface. Many shells provide features such as job control (allowing the user to manage several running processes at once), input and output redirection, and a command language for writing shell scripts. A shell script is a file containing a program in the shell command language, analogous to a "batch file" under MS-DOS. The default shell for Linux is the GNU Bourne Again Shell (bash). The shell entry in the /etc/passwd file is the path to the shell used by default for this account.

4.5.3   Shadow Passwords

Traditionally, UNIX and Linux systems have stored passwords and other account information in an encrypted form in a file called /etc/passwd. Various tools need access to this file for non-password information, so it needs to be readable to all users. Shadow passwords takes and removes the encrypted password entries from the password file and place them in a separate file called shadow. This way, the regular password file would continue to be readable by all users on the system, and the actual encrypted password entries would be readable only by the root user (the login prompt is run with root permission). Note: During the installation of Red Hat Linux, shadow password protection for your system is enabled by default, as are MD5 passwords.

Shadow passwords offer a few distinct advantages over the previous standard of storing passwords on UNIX and Linux systems, including:

- Improved system security by moving the encrypted passwords (normally found in /etc/passwd) to /etc/shadow which is readable only by root.
- Information concerning password aging (how long it has been since a password was last changed).
- Control over how long a password can remain unchanged before the user is required to change it.
- The ability to use the /etc/login.defs file to enforce a security policy, especially concerning password aging.

If you did not enable shadow passwords and your version of Linux supports shadow passwords, you can covert your regular passwords to shadow passwords by using the pwconv program.

If shadow passwords are enabled on the system, the /etc/shadow contains the password information. The syntax for the /etc/ shadow file is:

```
username:password:lchange:mchange:change:wchange:disable:expire
:system
```

The lchange is the number of days since January 1, 1970, since the password was last changed. Mchange is the number of days before the password can be changed again. This value is set to zero by default. Change is the number of days until the password must be changed. Wchange is the number of days before the password is set to expire that the system will begin warning the user to change the password.

Once the password reaches the time when it must be changed, the disable value is the count of days before the account is automatically disabled if the password is not changed. Expire is the count of days since January 1, 1970, which equates to the date the account is to expire. System is reserved for the system.

4.5.4   The Root Account

The superuser, which basically is the root account, is the person who has access to everything on the system. Therefore, on the Linux machine, the root account is all powerful. But with that power also comes great responsibility. Many novice system administrators constantly work on the system while logged in as root. This is unwise and dangerous.

Since the root account has ultimate power, if a person logged in as the root account types in the wrong command, that person can wipe out large portions of the file system or accidentally break down the security of a bunch of files or break a number of programs. As a result of mistakes or intentional abuse combined with poor backups and documentation, you could lose days of productivity while repairing the damage. Most systems contain restrictions on root logins, so they can only be done from the console. This helps prevent outsiders from gaining access to a system over network by using a stolen password.

One way to give you temporary superuser privileges or to take on another user's identify is to use the su command. When the su command is executed at the command prompt, you will be prompted for the root password. If you type that password correctly, subsequent commands will be executed as root. To return back to a normal user, you just have to type exit.

To take on another user, you just have to type su followed by the user's name. If you are already logged in as the root, you can take on another user's identify without the user's password. This will allow you to switch to the user to figure out problems with his or her account including problems with accessing computer and network resources (files, printers, and so on).

A safer command is the sudo command, which is similar to the su command except it allows you to execute a single command as root. The /etc/sudoers file contains a list of users who may use sudo, and with what commands.

If you forget the root password, you can follow these steps to setup up a new root password:

1. Power up your PC as usual. At the LILO boot prompt, type the name of the Linux boot partition followed by the word single:

```
linux single
```

This causes Linux to start up as usual, but it will run in a single-user mode that does not require you to log in. After Linux starts, you will see the bash# command-line prompt.

2. Use the passwd command to change the root password and enter the new password. Note: The passwd command will ask you to verify the password. When complete, the passwd command changes the password and displays the message:

```
passwd: all authentication tokens updated successfully
```

3. Reboot the PC by pressing the Ctrl+ Alt+ Del. After Linux starts, it displays the familiar login screen. Log in as normal.

As you can see, it is not difficult to break into a Linux computer. Therefore, you will have to rely on BIOS passwords and physical security to help maintain your system security.

4.5.5   Creating, Modifying, and Deleting Users

Adding users can be accomplished through the useradd utility. Note: This program is called adduser in some distributions. In its simplest form, you may type just useradd *username,* where *username* is the username you want to create. Its basic syntax is:

```
useradd [-c comment] [-d home-dir] [-e expire-date] -f
inactive-time] [-g initial-group] [-G group[,…]]
[-m [-k skeleton-dir] |-M] [-p password] [-s shell]
[-u UID [-o]][-r] [-n] username
```

NOTE: Some of these parameters modify settings that are valid only when the system uses shadow passwords. See table 4.7.

Table 4.7   Useradd Options

Option	Description
-c comment	The comment field for the user. Some administrators store public information like a user's office or telephone number in this field. Others store just the user's real name, or no information at all.
-d home-dir	The account's home directory. The defaults to /home/username on most systems.
-e expire-date	The date on which the account will be disabled, expressed in the form YYY-MM-DD. Many systems will accept alternative forms, such as MM-DD-YYYY, or a single value representing the number of days since January 1, 1970. The default is for an account that does not expire. This option is most useful in environments in which users accounts are inherently time-limited, such as accounts for students taking particular classes or temporary employees.
-f inactive-days	The number of days after a password expires after which the account becomes completely disabled. A value of -1 disables this feature and is the default.
-g default-group	The name or GID of the user's default group. The default for this value varies from one distribution to another.
-G group[,. . .]	The names or GIDs of one or more groups to which the user belongs. These groups need not be the default group, and more than one may be specified by separating them with commas.
-m [-k skeleton-dir]	The system automatically creates the user's home directory if –m is specified. Normally, default configuration files are copied from /etc/skel (such as .Xdefaults, .bash_logout, .bash_profile, .bashrc files) to every new user's home directory when new accounts are created, but you may specify another template directory with the -k option. Many distributions use -m as default when running useradd.
-M	This option forces the system NOT to automatically create a home directory, even if /etc/login.defs specifies that this action is the default. The /etc/login.defs file is explained later in this chapter.
-p encrypted-password	This parameter passes the pre-encrypted password for the user to the system. The encrypted-password value will be added, unchanged, to the /etc/passwd or /etc/shadow file.
-s shell	The name of the user's default login shell. On most systems, this defaults to /bin/bash.
-u UID [-o]	Creates an account with the specified user ID value (UID). This value must be a positive integer, and it is normally above 500 for user accounts. System accounts typically have numbers below 100. The -o option allows the number to be reused so that two usernames are associated with a single UID.
-r	The parameter allows the creation of a system account (an account with a value lower than UID_MIN, as specified in the /etc/login.defs, which is normally 100, 500, or 1000). Note: Useradd also doesn't create a home directory for system accounts.
-n	In some distributions, including Red Hat, the system creates a group with the same name as the specified username. This parameter disables this.

To administer user accounts, you will need to be logged in as root. The example which follows shows how to add a new user account. It is for a user named "jsmith" and home directory of "/home2/jsmith/."

```
useradd jsmith -d /home2/jsmith
```

If you want to create a new user called jsmith, make the new user a member of the audit group and the manager group, and make the manager group as its primary group, you would use the following command:

```
useradd -g manager -G manager,audit jsmith
```

NOTE: Once a user account has been created, a password for the account needs to be set. This is done with the passwd command (shown later in this chapter).

The usermod program is used to modify existing users. It is very similar to the useradd program and has all of the parameters used with the useradd command. In addition, it has the following parameters:

- Usermod allows the addition of a -m parameter when used with -d. Alone -d changes the user's home directory, but it does not move any files. Adding -m causes usermode to move the user's files to the new location.
- Usermod supports a -l parameter, which changes the user's login name to the specified value. For instance, `usermod jsmith johns` changes jsmith to johns. Note: If you change a user's name, you will need to change the owner of all files that the user previously owned including those that are in his or her home directory. This is done with chown command.
- You may lock (disable) or unlock a user's password with the -L and -U options, respectively. When an account is locked, it inserts a encrypted exclamation point (!) making the user not able to log in.

NOTE: When using the -G option to add a user to new groups, if you do not list any groups that were previously a member of, they will be removed.

The chage command allows you to modify account settings relating to account expiration. You can configure Linux to disable the account if the password hasn't been changed in a specified period of time so that it forces users to periodically change their password. You can also have the account expire on a certain date.

The chage utility has the following syntax:

```
chage [-l] [-m mindays] [-M maxdays] [-d lastday] [-I inactive]
[-E expiredate] [-W warndays] username
```

See table 4.8.

To delete a user from the /etc/passwd, you use the `userdel  username` command. To delete a user from the /etc/shadow, `userdel-r  username`. In addition, the -r makes the userdel command to remove all files from the user's home directory and all of the files in the home directory. To delete the jsmith account, use the following command:

```
userdel -r jsmith
```

Of course, users may create files outside of their home directories. To find these files, you would use the find command to search for files that belong to a particular UID. For example, if jsmith has a UID of 623, you could locate all of jsmith's files by using the following command:

```
find / -uid 623
```

You can then decide to delete the files or change the ownership of the files.

Before you consider deleting an account, you should first consider disabling an account rather than deleting it. This can be used when an employee hasn't started yet or someone has left the company and you would like to assign the account to his or her replacement. To disable an account, you can either:

- Open the /etc/passwd or /etc/shadow file and change the password entry to an asterisk (*). To reactive the account, create a new password for them as root with passwd command.
- Disable the account using LinuxConf.

If you hire someone to replace that person, you can then change the username and change the owner with the chown of all the files including those that are in his or her home directory. Again, you would use the chown command.

Table 4.8   The Chage Command Option

Options	Description
-l	This option changes chage to display account expiration and password aging information for a particular user.
-m mindays	This is the minimum number of days between password changes. 0 indicates that a user can change a password multiple times in a day; 1 means that a user can change a password once a day; 2 means a user may change a password once every two days; and so on.
-M maxdays	The maximum number of days during which a password is valid.
-d lastday	This is the last day a password was changed. This value is normally maintained automatically by Linux, but you can use this parameter artificially alter the password change count. lastday is expressed in the format YYYY/MM/DD, or as the number of days since January 1, 1970.
-I inactive	This is the number of days between password expiration and account disablement. An expired account may not be used or may force the user to change the password immediately upon logging in, depending upon the distribution. A disabled account is completely disabled.
-E expiredate	You can set an absolute expiration date with this option. For example, you might use -E 2002/06/01 to have the account expire on June 1, 2002. The date may also be expressed as the number of days since January 1, 1970. The value of -1 represents no expiration date.
-W warndays	This is the number of days before account expiration that the system will warn the user of the impeding expiration. It's generally a good idea to use this feature to alert users of their situation, particularly if you make heavy use of password change expirations.

Table 4.9   Passwd Command Options

Options	Description
-k	This parameter indicates that the system should update an expired account.
-l	This parameter locks an account by prefixing the encrypted password with an exclamation mark (!). The files are still available.
-u [-f]	The -u parameter unlocks an account by removing a leading exclamation mark, user
-d	This parameter removes the password from an account.
-S	The option displays information on the password for an account, whether or not it's set and what type of encryption it uses.

The easiest command to change passwords is the passwd command. The password command has the following syntax:

```
passwd [-k] [-l] [-u [-f]] [-d] [-S] [username]
```

See table 4.9.

Ordinary users may use passwd to change the password, but most parameters may only be used by root. As a security measure, except for when the root account is executing the passwd command, passwd asks for a user's old password before changing the password.

4.5.6   Groups

A group is a collection of user accounts used to organize collections of accounts. A group is not an account. By using groups, you can simplify administration by assigning permissions to the group and everyone listed in the group will be assigned these permissions. Users can be members of multiple groups. Like users, groups also have unique identifiers called group IDs (GIDs). Like the UID, the GID is determined differently among the Linux distributions.

Group membership is controlled through the /etc/group file, which contains a list of groups and the members that belong to the group. In addition to membership defined in the /etc/group file, each user has a default or primary group. The user's primary group is set in the user's configuration in the /etc/passwd file. When users log onto the computer, their group membership is set to their primary groups. When users create files or launch programs, those files and running programs are associated with the person's primary group. A user can still access files that belong to other groups, as long as the user belongs to that group and the group access permissions allow the access.

The group commands are similar to the user commands; however, instead of working on individual users, they work on groups listed in the /etc/group file. Note that changing group information does not cause user information to be automatically changed. For example, if you remove a group whose GID is 100 and a user's default group is specified as 100, the user's default group would not be updated to reflect the fact that the group no longer exists.

The groupadd command adds groups to the /etc/group file. The command options for the group add program are as follows:

```
groupadd [-g gid] [-r] [-f] group
```

See table 4.10.

If you want to add a new group called managers with the GID of 750, you would type in the following command:

```
groupadd -g 750 manager
```

To add users to the group, you would use useradd when you create new users or the usermod for existing users.

The groupmod command allows you to modify the parameters of an existing group. The options for this command are:

```
groupmod -g gid -n group-name group
```

where the -g option allows you to change the GID of the group, and the -n option allows you to specify a new group of a group. Additionally, of course, you need to specify the name of the existing group as the last parameter.

Table 4.10   Groupadd Command Options

Option	Description
-g gid	Specifies the GID for the new group as gid. By default, this value is automatically chosen by finding the first available value.
-r	Tells groupadd that the group being added is a system group and should have first available system group GID.
-f	When adding a new group, Linux will exit without an error if the specified group to add already exists. By using the option, the program will not change the group settings before exiting. This is useful in scripting cases where you want the script to continue if the group already exists.
group	This option is required. It specifies the name of the group you want to add to be group.

For example, if you have the project1 group and you want to change its name to the widget group, you would issue the following command:

```
groupmod -n widget project1
```

To delete a group, you would use the groupdel command. The syntax for this command is:

```
groupdel group
```

For example, if you wanted to remove the widget group, you would type in the following command:

```
groupdel widget
```

Remember that when a user creates a file, the file will be owned by the user and by the user's primary group. If the user wants to assign group ownership of the file to another group that the user is a member of, the user can switch groups by using the newgrp command before he or she creates the file:

```
newgrp group
```

There is an extra level of groups that is often ignored. Within this level exists group administrators, passwords, and more. This comes in handy with workgroups and other project-oriented groupings where the system administrator really does not need to be involved beyond the group creation state. The project manager can be made responsible for the group itself and who belongs to it. Once the group is created, you can assign some group administrator status with the command format:

```
gpasswd -A groupadmin group
```

The system administrator can also add members to the group with

```
gpasswd -M user group
```

After this, the group administrator may choose from a set of commands. To add a group member, use the following command:

```
gpasswd -a user group
```

To remove someone:

```
gpasswd -d user group
```

To add a password to the group to prevent nonmembers from joining it with the newgrp command, you would use the gpasswd group command, which then prompts you for the new password.

4.5.7   Account Restrictions

While passwords are the first line of defense, you can strengthen login security by exercising account restrictions. This includes defining how many characters the password has to be, how often the password has to be changed and what time a person can log in to the Linux computer.

To help you make your computer more secure, you can modify the master configuration file for shadow passwords (/etc/login.defs). See table 4.11 and figure 4.9. It is highly recommended to establish the following rules to make passwords effective:

- They should be at least 6 characters in length, preferably 8 characters.
- They should have an aging period, requiring a new password to be chosen within a specific time frame.
- They should be revoked and reset after a limited number of concurrent incorrect retries.

The minimum acceptable password length by default when you install your Linux system is 5. This means that when a new user is allowed to have access on a Linux machine, his/her password length will be at minimum 5 mixes of character strings, letters, numbers, special characters, etc. This should be increased to 8 characters. To do this, open the /etc/login.defs file with a text editor and change the value of 5 to 8 for the PASS_MIN_LEN option.

Table 4.11 Login.defs File Options

Option	Default	Details
FAIL_DELAY	3	Delay in seconds after a login failure before the system allows another attempt.
DIALUPS_CHECK_ENAB	yes	Enables additional passwords upon dialup lines specified in /etc/dialups.
FAILLOG_ENAB	yes	Enables logging and display of /var/log/faillog login failure info.
LOG_UNKFAIL_ENAB	no	Enables display of unknown usernames when login failures are recorded.
LOG_OK_LOGINS	no	Enables logging of successful logins (the logs are stored in /var/log/wtmp).
LASTLOG_ENAB	yes	Enables logging and display of /var/log/lastlog login time information.
MAIL_CHECK_ENAB	yes	Enables checking and display of mailbox status upon login. Disable this option if the shell startup files already check for mail (mailx -e or equivalent).
OBSCURE_CHECKS_ENAB	yes	Enables additional checks upon password changes.
QUOTAS_ENAB	yes	Enables setting of ulimit, umask, and niceness from passwd gecos field.
SYSLOG_SU_ENAB	yes	If yes and login was compiled with syslog support, then all su activity will be noted through the syslog facility.
SYSLOG_SG_ENAB	yes	Enables syslog logging of su activity in addition to sulog file logging. SYSLOG_SG_ENAB does the same for newgrp and sg.
CONSOLE	/etc/securetty	If specified, this definition provides for a restricted set of lines on which root logins will be allowed.
#CONSOLE	console:tty01:tty02:tty03:tty04	Either full pathname of a file containing device names or a colon-delimited list of device names. Root logins will be allowed only on these devices.
SULOG_FILE	/var/log/sulog	All su activity is logged to the file defined here.
MOTD_FILE	/etc/motd	Colon-delimited list of message-of-the-day files displayed upon login.
ISSUE_FILE	/etc/issue	A file holding a short message displayed before each login prompt.
FTMP_FILE	/var/log/btmp	Login failures are logged here in a utmp format.
NOLOGINS_FILE	/etc/nologin	This file, if present, prevents non-root logins. The contents of the file are displayed when login is denied, so it's a good idea to write in an explanation.
SU_NAME	su	The command name to display when running su.
MAIL_DIR	/var/spool/mail	The command specifies the location of the mail directory.
#MAIL_FILE	.mail	This is the directory (MAIL_DIR) or file (MAIL_FILE) where mail is stored. This is used for the "you have new mail" message displayed upon logging in. If both are defined, MAIL_DIR takes precedence.

Table 4.11   Continued

Option	Default	Details
HUSHLOGIN_FILE	.hushlogin	If this file exists, all the normal messages displayed during the login sequence are suppressed. A full pathname indicates hushed mode will be used if the user's name or shell is in that file; a bare filename indicates hushed mode will be used if a file of that name exists in the user's home directory.
ENV_SUPATH	PATH=/usr/local/sbin: /usr/local/bin: /sbin:/usr/sbin: /bin:/usr/bin	The default PATH settings for superuser.
ENV_PATH	PATH=/usr/local/bin: /bin:/usr/bin	The default PATH settings for normal users.
TTYGROUP	tty	The group ownership of the terminal is initialized to this group name or number.
TTYPERM	0620	Terminal permissions: respectively, the group which owns device tty, and the permissions on the device file. If the write program on your system is setgid to a special group which owns the terminals, then TTYGROUP should be set to the group number and TTYPERM to 0620. Otherwise, leave TTYGROUP commented out and set TTYPERM to either 622 or 600.
ERASECHAR	0177	This is a login configuration initialization. ERASECHAR is the default ERASE character. Terminal ERASE character ('010' = backspace).
KILLCHAR	025	This is a login configuration initialization. KILLCHAR is the default KILL character. Terminal KILL character ('\025' = CTRL/U).
UMASK	022	This is a login configuration initialization. UMASK is the default mask that will be applied to the permissions of all new files created during this login. For example, an umask of 077 means an ordinary file will have default permissions of 600.
#ULIMIT	2097152	This is a login configuration initialization.
ULIMIT	Default ulimit value.	ULIMIT is the maximum file size under this login. Precede the value with 0 to get octal, 0x to get hexadecimal.
PASS_MAX_DAYS	99999	The maximum number of days a password may be used.
PASS_MIN_DAYS	0	The minimum number of days allowed between password changes.
PASS_MIN_LEN	5	The minimum acceptable password length.
PASS_WARN_AGE	7	The number of days' warning given before a password expires.
SU_WHEEL_ONLY	no	If this is set to yes, the user must be listed as a member of the first gid 0 group in /etc/group (called root on most Linux systems) to be able to su to uid 0 accounts. If the group doesn't exist or is empty, no one will be able to su to uid 0.
#CRACKLIB_DICTPATH	/var/cache/cracklib /cracklib_dict	The path to the dictionaries if the suite has been compiled with cracklib support.

Table 4.11 Login.defs File Options—Continued

Option	Default	Details
UID_MIN	1000	The minimum value for automatic uid selection in useradd.
UID_MAX	60000	The maximum value for automatic uid selection in useradd.
GID_MIN	100	The minimum value for automatic gid selection in groupadd.
GID_MAX	60000	The maximum value for automatic gid selection in groupadd.
LOGIN_RETRIES	5	Maximum number of login retries if password fails.
LOGIN_TIMEOUT	60	Maximum time in seconds before a login session expires—in other words, the amount of time allowed between entry of username and entry of password.
PASS_CHANGE_TRIES	5	Maximum number of attempts to change password if initially rejected.
PASS_ALWAYS_WARN	yes	Warns about weak passwords even if you are root. This will not stop root from self-assigning a bad password; it just informs root that the password is weak.
PASS_MAX_LEN	8	Number of significant characters in the password for crypt().
CHFN_AUTH	yes	Require password before chfn/chsh can make any changes.
CHFN_RESTRICT	frwh	Defines which fields may be changed by regular users using chfn. The letters represent full name, room number, work phone, and home phone. If not defined, no changes are allowed.
LOGIN_STRING	%s 's Password:	Determines the password prompt (% will be replaced by username).
MD5_CRYPT_ENAB	no	Only works if compiled with MD5_CRYPT defined: if set to yes, new passwords will be encrypted using the MD5-based algorithm compatible with the algorithm used by recent releases of FreeBSD. It supports passwords of unlimited length and longer salt strings. Set this option to no if you need to copy encrypted passwords to systems that don't understand the new algorithm.
#CONSOLE_GROUPS	floppy:audio:cdrom	List of groups to add to the user's supplementary group set when logging in on the console (as determined by the CONSOLE setting). There is usually no default, though Red Hat creates the above default. Use with caution—it is possible for users to gain permanent access to these groups, even when not logged in on the console. (How to do it is left as an exercise for the reader.)
DEFAULT_HOME	no	Allows or disallows login if you can't cd to the home directory.
ENVIRON_FILE	/etc/environment	If this file exists and is readable, the system will read the login environment from it. Every line should be in the form name=value.
USERDEL_CMD	/usr/sbin/userdel_local	If defined, this command runs when you remove a user. It should remove any at, cron, and print jobs owned by the user (passed as the first argument).

Table 4.11 Continued

Option	Default	Details
NO_PASSWORD_ CONSOLE	tty1:tty2:tty3:tty4:tty5:tty6	If defined, specify either the full pathname of a file containing device names or a colon-delimited list of device names. No password is required to log in on these devices.
TTYTYPE_FILE	/etc/ttytype	Declares terminal types for particular tty lines. A typical file might look like: linux tty1 linux tty2 linux tty3 linux tty4 wyse30 ttyS4 vt100 ttyp0 vt100 ttyp1 vt100 ttyp2 vt100 ttyp3

To force people to change passwords, you can use the PASS_MAX_DAYS. The default is 99999, which means that there is no limit. You should change this to between 30 and 90 days. This way if your password is compromised or people are trying to guess your password, it is changed frequently.

To prevent people from attempting to guess passwords, you can set up account lockout options. The LOGIN_RETRIES option sets the maximum number of login retries if a password fails. The LOGIN_TIMEOUT is the amount of time in seconds which the LOGIN_RETRIES are measured. In other words, if the number of LOGIN_RETRIES occurs within the time specified in the LOGIN_TIMEOUT, the account will be locked out.

Another suggestion would to use a password cracker on a weekly basis to help you find and replace passwords that are easily guessed or weak. Also, a password-checking mechanism should be present to reject a weak password when first choosing a password or changing an old one. One password-checking mechanism could be built using the Pluggable Authentication Modules for Linux (Linux-PAM).

4.5.8   Centralized Authentication Using NIS

If users on your network are working on more than one machine you will need to create a login/ password pair for them on each machine. A more elegant solution is to maintain a centralized database known as **Network Information Service (NIS)** that client machines refer to for authentication. If you are familiar with Microsoft networks, this is similar to Microsoft's domain controller.

NIS makes it possible to share the data of critical files across the local area network. Typically, files, such as /etc/passwd and /etc/group, which ideally would remain uniform across all hosts, are shared via NIS. In this way, every network machine that has a corresponding NIS client can read the data contained in these shared files and use the network versions of these files as extensions to the local versions.

For example, when you need to log onto a machine on your network, you need a login/password pair that is valid on that machine. This can become a problem over a larger network where you may have people using more than one machine. An example of this would be your computer lab where people are going to be working off different machines most of the time. You will then be forced to create logins for each user on every machine that they are likely to use. NIS steps in here to provide centralized authentication. All the logins are created on a single machine, which client machines access to authenticate users.

Once you have centralized your authentication, you should also make the home directory of the users available on the machine that they log on by using the Network File System (NFS). NFS allows you to export a directory for mounting on other machines so that it will appear as a local directory on the client machine. This is completely transparent to the user.

Figure 4.9   Sample login.defs

```
#  *REQUIRED*
#  Directory where mailboxes reside, _or_ name of file, relative to the
#  home directory. If you _do_ define both, MAIL_DIR takes precedence.
#  QMAIL_DIR is for Qmail
#
#QMAIL_DIR Maildir
MAIL_DIR /var/spool/mail
#MAIL_FILE .mail

# Password aging controls:
#
# PASS_MAX_DAYS Maximum number of days a password may be used.
# PASS_MIN_DAYS Minimum number of days allowed between password changes.
# PASS_MIN_LEN Minimum acceptable password length.
# PASS_WARN_AGE Number of days warning given before a password expires.
#
PASS_MAX_DAYS 99999
PASS_MIN_DAYS 10
PASS_MIN_LEN 5
PASS_WARN_AGE 7

#
# Min/max values for automatic uid selection in useradd
#
UID_MIN 500
UID_MAX 60000

#
# Min/max values for automatic gid selection in groupadd
#
GID_MIN 500
GID_MAX 60000

#
# If defined, this command is run when removing a user.
# It should remove any at/cron/print jobs etc. owned by
# the user to be removed (passed as the first argument).
#
#USERDEL_CMD /usr/sbin/userdel_local

#
# If useradd should create home directories for users by default
# On RH systems, we do. This option is ORed with the -m flag on
# useradd command line.
#
CREATE_HOME yes
```

NIS and its associated tools are available across nearly all the distributions. For an NIS client machine, all you need is ypbind and yp-tools. The ypserv package is only required if you're setting up the machine as a server. You will also need the portmap daemon, which is used to manage RPC requests. This is used by NIS as well as NFS and is present in most Linux distributions. Look for a package named portmap on your distribution CD. Fortunately, these are typically installed during the installation of Linux.

WHAT YOU NEED TO KNOW

Security+ Objective 2.4—Directory—Recognition not administration

Security+ Objective 3.5.3.9.1—Directory Services

1. Directory services is a network service that identifies all resources on a network and makes those resources accessible to users and applications.
2. Examples of directory services are the Microsoft's Active Directory and Novell Directory Services (NDS).

Security+ Objective 2.4.1—SSL/TLS

1. Information provided by directory services can include sensitive details about a corporation and its network configuration.
2. Many directory services can make use of encryption when sending data back and forth between directory service client and server.
3. If your directory service supports an encrypted communication path, use it. If you're using pure LDAP, consider moving to LDAP over TLS, which provides such encryption.

Security+ Objective 2.4.2—LDAP

1. The most common directory service is the X.500, which uses a hierarchical approach, where objects are organized similar to the files and folders on a hard drive. At the top of the structure, you have the root container with children organized under it.
2. X.500 is part of the OSI model, however it does not translate well into a TCP/IP protocol environment.
3. Therefore, many of the protocols that are based on the X.500 do not fully comply with it.
4. Lightweight Directory Access Protocol (LDAP) is a set of protocols for accessing information directories.

5. LDAP is based on the standards contained within the X.500 standard, but it is significantly simpler.
6. Because it's a simpler version of X.500, LDAP is sometimes called X.500-lite.
7. Microsoft's Active Directory and Novell Directory Services (NDS) use LDAP.

Security+ Objective 5.5—Privilege Management

Security+ Objective 5.5.2—Single Sign-on

1. The modern directory services allow you to log on once (single sign-on) and access any network service and server that is stored in the directory.
2. A user who logs on with a valid user ID and password combination is considered an authenticated user.

Security+ Objective 5.5.3—Centralized vs. Decentralized

1. When each server has its own security database and each server has its own administrator (technically it could be the same administrator but individual accounts are created on each server), it is known as decentralized management.
2. The directory services allows for a centralized management because you only have to create one user and all servers recognize that one user. When the user logs on, the user is authenticated for the directory service and given access to the resources that he or she has permissions for. All users and network resources are administered using a single centralized security database.

QUESTIONS

1. After installing a new operating system, what configuration changes should be implemented?
   a. Create application user accounts.
   b. Rename the guest account.
   c. Rename the administrator account, disable the guest accounts.
   d. Create a secure administrator account.
2. The start of the LDAP (Lightweight Directory Access Protocol) directory is called the:
   a. Head   b. Top
   c. Root   d. Tree
3. As the security analyst for your company's network, you want to implement Single Signon technology. What benefit can you expect to get when implementing Single Signon?
   a. You will need to log on twice at all times.
   b. You can allow for system-wide permissions with it.

   c. You can install multiple applications.
   d. You can browse multiple directories.
4. The LDAP directory access protocol is based on what larger standard?
   a. X.500   b. X.509
   c. PKCS #7   d. X.400
   e. X.25   f. PKCS #12
5. In a decentralized privilege management environment, user accounts and passwords are stored on:
   a. One central authentication server.
   b. Each individual server.
   c. No more than two servers.
   d. One server configured for decentralized management.
6. When an employee is dismissed, the security administrator should:
   a. Allow the employee to back up computer files then disable network access.

b. Change all network passwords.

c. Disable the employee's network access.

d. Set rules to forward the employee's email to a home address.

7. A user who has accessed an information system with a valid user ID and password combination is considered a(n):

a. Manager

b. User

c. Authenticated user

d. Security officer

8. Why are unique user IDs critical in the review of audit trails?

a. They cannot be easily altered.

b. They establish individual accountability.

c. They show which files were changed.

d. They trigger corrective controls.

9. LDAP (Lightweight Directory Access Protocol) directories are arranged as:

a. Linked lists   b. Trees

c. Stacks   d. Queues

10. The information that governs and associates users and groups to certain rights to use, rad, write, modify, or execute objects on the system is called a(n):

a. Public key ring.

b. ACL (Access Control List).

c. Digital signature.

d. CRL (Certificate Revocation List).

11. LDAP (Lightweight Directory Access Protocol) requires what ports by default?

a. 389 and 636   b. 389 and 139

c. 636 and 137   d. 137 and 139

12. Which of the following is *not* a characteristic of DEN (Directory Enabled Networking)?

a. It is mapped into the directory defined as part of the LDAP (Lightweight Directory Access Protocol).

b. It is inferior to SNMP (Simple Network Management Protocol).

c. It is an object-oriented information model.

d. It is an industry standard indicating how to construct and store information about a network's users, applications, and data.

13. Security requirements for servers *do not* typically include:

a. The absence of vulnerabilities used by known forms of attacks against server hosts.

b. The ability to allow administrative activities to all users.

c. The ability to deny access to information on the server other than that intended to be available.

d. The ability to disable unnecessary network services that may be built into the operating system or server software.

14. What authentication problem is addressed by Single Signon?

a. Authorization through multiple servers

b. Multiple domains

c. Multifactor authentication

d. Multiple usernames and passwords

15. A password management system designed to provide availability for a large number of users includes which of the following?

a. Self-service password resets

b. Locally saved passwords

c. Multiple access methods

d. Synchronized passwords

16. A password security policy can help a system administrator to decrease the probability that a password can be guessed by reducing the password's:

a. Length   b. Lifetime

c. Encryption level   d. Alphabet set

HANDS-ON EXERCISES

Exercise 1: Installing Active Directory in Windows

1. To start the Active Directory Installation Wizard and to make the stand-alone server into a domain controller, you will need to execute the DCPROMO.EXE file. Click on the Start button and select the Run option. Enter DCPROMO in the open text box, and click on the OK button. Click on the Next button.

2. For the Domain Controller Type page, select the Domain controller for a new domain option and click on the Next button.

3. For the Create a Tree or Child Domain page, select the Create a new domain tree option and click on the Next button.

4. For the Create or Join Forest page, select the Create a new forest of domain trees option and click on the Next button.

5. For the New Domain Name page, enter ACMEYY.COM in the Full DNS name for new domain text box. YY is your computer number. Click on the Next button.

6. On the NetBIOS Domain Name page, leave the default Domain NetBIOS name and click on the Next button.

7. On the Database and Log Locations page, leave the default file locations and click on the Next button.

8. On the Shared System Volume page, leave the default location for the SYSVOL folder and click on the Next button.

9. On the Configure DNS page, click on the Yes, install and configure DNS on this computer (recommended) option and click on the Next button.

10. On the Permissions page, select the Permissions compatible only with Windows 2000 servers option and click on the Next button.
11. On the Directory Services Restore Mode Administrator Password page, enter the administrator password and click on the Next button.
12. On the Summary page, click on the Next button.
13. Click on the Finish button. If it asks you to reboot the computer, do so. Note: It may take a few minutes to reboot.
14. Login as administrator.
15. Open your TCP/IP settings and change your DNS address to the address of your computer.

Exercise 2: Creating Organizational Units in Windows

1. Start the Active Directory User and Computers console.
2. To create an organizational unit called Sales, right-click the ACMExx.COM domain, select New option, and select Organizational Unit. In the Name text box, input SALES, and click on the OK button.
3. Using the same method, create the following organization units under ACMExx.COM:
   RESEARCHX
   EDUCATIONX
   MANUFACTURINGX

Exercise 3: Creating Users in Windows

1. To create a user in the ACMExx.COM domain, right-click the ACMExx.COM domain, select New option, and select User. In the New Object—User dialog box, input your first name, middle initial, and last name. For your User Logon Name, use your first initial, middle initial, and last name without spaces. Therefore, if your name is Paul G. Rogers, your login name would be PGRogers. Click on the Next button.
2. Enter the password of PW (upper case) and enable the Password must change password on next logon option. Click on the Finish button.
3. After your account has been created, right-click on your account and select the Properties option. Input your description as domain administrator and your office as the server room. Input your telephone number, email address, and web page URL if you have one. Click on the Address tab, type in your address. Click on the Telephones tab, and input your phone numbers. Click on the Organization tab, and input administrator for the Title, IT for the Department and Acme Corporation for the Company. Click on the OK button.
4. Create the following users in the appropriate Organizational Unit.

First Name	Middle Initial	Last Name	User Logon Name	Title	Department	Organizational Unit
Charles	L	Gee	CLGeeX	Sales Mgr.	Sales	Sales
Frank	J	Biggs	FJBiggsX	Sales Rep.	Sales	Sales
Herold	W	Jones	HWJonesX	Sales Rep.	Sales	Sales
Paul	L	Ray	PLRayX	Sales Rep.	Sales	Sales
Juan	O	Hermes	JOHermesX	Sales Rep.	Sales	Sales
Jill	K	Knight	JKKnightX	Sales Admin. Asst.	Sales	Sales
Jean	A	Mao	JAMaoX	Training Mgr.	Education	Education
Edward	J	Morell	EJMorellX	Trainer	Education	Education
Donna	L	Starr	DLStarrX	Manufact. Mgr.	Manufacturing	Manufacturing
Eric	O	Skow	EOSkowX	Manufact. Technician	Manufacturing	Manufacturing
Victor	N	Sloan	VNSloanX	Manufact. Technician	Manufacturing	Manufacturing
Sonny	K	Wong	SKWongX	Research Engineer	Manufacturing	Research
Gina	J	Smith	GJSmithX	Research Engineer	Manufacturing	Research

5. Right-click on the SALES organizational unit, select the New option, and select the Computer option. Enter computer1 for the name. Click on the OK button.
6. Right-click each of these users and input their appropriate departments.

Exercise 3: Disable, Rename, and Delete an Account

1. Paul Ray just got fired. To disable the account, right-click on the Paul Ray account and select the Disable Account option. Notice the small X that appears.
2. Right-click the Paul L. Ray account and select the Rename option. While the entire name is highlighted, press the delete key, and press the enter key.
3. Change the name to Tom J. Landers.
   Full name: Tom J. Landers
   First name: Tom
   Last Name: Landers
   Display Name: Tom J. Landers
       User logon name: TJLanders
       User logon name: (pre-Windows2000): TJLanders
4. Click on the OK button.
5. Right-click on Tom J. Landers account and select the Reset Password option. Change the password to TEST. Click on the OK button to close the Windows and click on the OK button to close the confirmation dialog box.
6. Right-click on Tom J. Landers account and select the Enable account option.
7. Right-click on Tom J. Landers account and select the Properties option. Select the profile tab and notice the location of the home folder. While the account has been changed, Tom Landers was able to get access to everything that Paul Ray had including his home directory, even though his home directory is still called Paul Ray. Eventually, I would rename the directory and make sure that Tom's profile lab indicates the new name of the home folder.
8. Right-click on Tom Landers folder and select the Delete option. Say Yes to the Are you sure dialog box.
9. Paul Ray got rehired back into his original position. Unfortunately, since his account was deleted, a new one will have to be created. Therefore, in the Sales organizational Unit, create a new Paul Ray account.
10. Using the profile tab located within Paul Ray's properties, recreate his home folder.
11. When the "home directory was not created" warning appears, click on the OK button. Since Paul's old account was created, Paul doesn't automatically get the same rights that he had before because of the account being recreated. All of Paul's previous rights, permissions, and group memberships will have to given again.

Exercise 4: Create and Modify Accounts in Linux

1. To create an account called jsmith, type the following command at the command prompt:
   ```
   useradd jsmith
   ```
2. To change the password for jsmith to pass3Word, type in the following command:
   ```
   passwd jsmith
   ```
3. To create an account called psanchez with a home directory called /home/account, type the following command at the command prompt:
   ```
   useradd psanchez -d /home/account
   ```
4. Change the password for psanchez to test5Town
5. To make it so that jsmith cannot change the password for 7 days is to type in the following command:
   ```
   chage -m 7 jsmith
   ```
6. Change to the 2nd virtual console by pressing Ctrl+ Alt+ F2.
7. Log in as jsmith. Notice the current directory.
8. To change the password to lotus3.Test, type the following command:
   ```
   passwd
   ```
9. In the /home/jsmith directory, create a text1.txt file with your name on it.
10. Log out.
11. Log in as psanchez. Notice the current directory.
12. Create a text file in the /home/account directory called text2.txt file with your name it.
13. Log out.
14. Change back to the 1st virtual console.

15. To delete the jsmith account, type the following command:

    ```
    userdel -r jsmith
    ```

16. To view the contents of the /home directory, change to the /home directory and execute the ls -l command. Notice that the jsmith directory is gone.

17. To move the home directory of psanchez, type in the following command:

    ```
    usermod -d /home/psanchez -m psanchez
    ```

18. Do a ls -l listing of the /home and /home/psanchez directory.

19. To lock psanchez account, type the following command:

    ```
    usermod -L psanchez
    ```

20. Change to the 2nd virtual console.

21. Try to log in as psanchez.

22. Change to the 1st virtual console.

23. To unlock psanchez account, type in the following command:

    ```
    usermod -U psanchez
    ```

24. Change to the 2nd virtual console.

25. Log in as psanchez

26. Log out.

27. Change back to the 1st virtual console.

28. Create a new group called test by using the following command:

    ```
    groupadd test
    ```

29. Add psanchez to the test group by typing in the following command:

    ```
    usermod -G test psanchez
    ```

30. Delete the test group by typing the following command:

    ```
    groupdel test
    ```

Exercise 5: Using the Su Command in Linux

1. Log in as your user1 account, not as root.

2. Try to run the following command:

   ```
   /usr/sbin/useradd user2
   ```

   The path to the useradd command had to be specified because the search path for user2 does not contain the /usr/sbin directory.

3. To temporarily log in as the root account, type the following command:

   ```
   su root
   ```

4. Now run the following command:

   ```
   /usr/sbin/useradd user2
   ```

5. Delete your user2 account with the following command:

   ```
   /usr/sbin/userdel user2
   ```

6. To go back to your user account, type the following command:

   ```
   Exit
   ```

7. Log out.

Exercise 6: Recovering a Lost Root Password

1. Reboot the computer and enter the text mode of LILO.

2. At the command prompt, boot into single mode.

3. At the command prompt, use the passwd command to change the password to testpassword.

4. Reboot the computer and test the new password.

5. Change the password back to password.

CHAPTER 5

Encryption and Authentication

Topics Covered in this Chapter

Introduction

To protect the network resources, you must first limit who can access the network. Then after people connect to the network, you want them to access only what they need to do their jobs and nothing more. To make sure that only allowed people can access the network, you need to use authentication. After people are authenticated, you must then use encryption to protect what is on the network so that unauthorized people cannot access the network and authorized people cannot access items that they are not authorized to access.

Objectives

1. Security+ Objective 1.2—Authentication
2. Security+ Objective 1.2.1—Kerberos
3. Security+ Objective 1.2.3—Certificates
4. Security+ Objective 1.2.5—Tokens
5. Security+ Objective 1.2.6—Multifactor
6. Security+ Objective 1.2.7—Mutual Authentication
7. Security+ Objective 1.2.8—Biometrics
8. Security+ Objective 1.4—Attacks
9. Security+ Objective 1.4.10—Birthday
10. Security+ Objective 1.4.11—Password Guessing
11. Security+ Objective 1.4.11.1—Brute Force
12. Security+ Objective 1.4.11.2—Dictionary
13. Security+ Objective 1.4.7—Weak Keys
14. Security+ Objective 1.4.8—Mathematical
15. Security+ Objective 2.1.7—IPSEC
16. Security+ Objective 3.2.4.6—Smart Cards
17. Security+ Objective 4.1—Algorithms
18. Security+ Objective 4.1.1—Hashing
19. Security+ Objective 4.1.2—Symmetric
20. Security+ Objective 4.1.3—Asymmetric
21. Security+ Objective 4.2—Concepts of Using Cryptography
22. Security+ Objective 4.2.1—Confidentiality
23. Security+ Objective 4.2.2—Integrity
24. Security+ Objective 4.2.2.1—Digital Signatures
25. Security+ Objective 4.2.3—Authentication
26. Security+ Objective 4.2.4—Nonrepudiation
27. Security+ Objective 4.2.4.1—Digital Signatures
28. Security+ Objective 4.2.5—Access Control
29. Security+ Objective 4.3—PKI
30. Security+ Objective 4.3.1—Certificates— Make a distinction between what certificates are used for what purpose. Basics only.
31. Security+ Objective 4.3.1.1—Certificate Policies
32. Security+ Objective 4.3.1.2—Certificate Practice Statements
33. Security+ Objective 4.3.2—Revocation
34. Security+ Objective 4.3.3—Trust Models
35. Security+ Objective 4.5—Key Management/Certificate Lifecycle
36. Security+ Objective 4.5.1—Centralized vs. Decentralized
37. Security+ Objective 4.5.10—Key Usage
38. Security+ Objective 4.5.10.1—Multiple Key Pairs (Single, Dual)
39. Security+ Objective 4.5.2—Storage
40. Security+ Objective 4.5.2.1—Hardware vs. Software
41. Security+ Objective 4.5.2.2—Private Key Protection
42. Security+ Objective 4.5.3—Escrow
43. Security+ Objective 4.5.4—Expiration
44. Security+ Objective 4.5.5—Revocation
45. Security+ Objective 4.5.5.1—Status Checking
46. Security+ Objective 4.5.6—Suspension
47. Security+ Objective 4.5.6.1—Status Checking
48. Security+ Objective 4.5.7—Recovery
49. Security+ Objective 4.5.7.1—M of N Control
50. Security+ Objective 4.5.8—Renewal
51. Security+ Objective 4.5.9—Destruction
52. Security+ Objective 5.4.1—Username/ Password

5.1 ENCRYPTION AND DECRYPTION

Security+ Objective 4.2—Concepts of Using Cryptography

Security+ Objective 4.2.1—Confidentiality

Security+ Objective 4.2.2—Integrity

In networks, sensitive data exist as they are transmitted across the network, sent as email messages and stored on files on the disk. In all cases, the initial unencrypted data is referred to as plaintext or clear text. **Encryption** is the process of disguising a message or data in what appears to be meaningless data (cipher text) to hide and protect the sensitive data from unauthorized access (confidentiality). **Decryption** is the process of converting data from encrypted format back to its original format. **Cryptography** is the art of protecting information by transforming it (encrypting it) into cipher text. In data and telecommunications, cryptography is necessary when communicating over any untrusted medium. Cryptography not only protects data from theft or alteration (integrity), but can also be used for user authentication.

Traffic on a network can be encrypted by using either end-to-end or link encryption:

- **End-to-end encryption**—Packets are encrypted once at the original encryption source and then decrypted only at the final decryption destination. The advantages of end-to-end encryption are its speed and overall security. However, in order for the packets to be properly routed, only the data is encrypted, not the routing information.
- **Link encryption**—Requires that each node (for example, a router) has separate key pairs for its upstream and downstream neighbors. Packets are encrypted and decrypted at every node along the network path.

A cryptosystem is the hardware or software implementation that transforms plaintext into ciphertext and back into plaintext. It will typically be comprised of two elements: cryptographic algorithm (the details of the step-by-step procedures used to produce the produce the ciphertext or the plaintext) and the cryptovariable or key. An effective cryptosystem is efficient for all possible keys within the cryptosystem's keyspace, the cryptosystem is easy to use, and the strength of the cryptosystem depends on the secrecy of the cryptovariables or keys rather than the secrecy of the algorithm.

NOTE: Most cryptographic algorithms are available to the public.

Some of the simpler forms of cryptography use substitution or transposition of characters or words. Another simple form of cryptography is steganography, which is the science of hiding information within other information.

The substitution cipher is a simple method which changes one character or symbol into another. For example, if you have the word:

```
clear text
```

you can substitute g where there is a c, p where there is an e, u where there is a t, and 3 where there is an x. This cipher text for this message would be:

```
glpar ue3u
```

As you can see, this will prevent someone from understanding the message. Unfortunately, these types of codes have been around for many years and are easily decrypted.

A transposition code involves transposing or scrambling the letters in a certain manner. Typically, the message is broken into blocks of equal size, and each block is then scrambled. For example, if you have the following clear text message:

```
This is clear text.
```

You could then break it down into groups of four characters and then jumble the characters within each groups. You would get the following:

```
isThs  ieaclter . xt
```

While this may be a little bit more difficult than the substitution method, it can still be easily decrypted.

Steganography is the process of hiding one message in another. Traditionally, this was achieved with invisible ink, microfilm, or taking the first letter from each word of a message. This is now achieved by hiding the message within a graphics or sound file. For instance in a 256-greyscale image, if the least significant bit of each byte is replaced with a bit from the message, then the result will be indistinguishable to the human eye. An eavesdropper will not even realize a message is being sent. This is not cryptography however, and although it would fool a human, a computer would be able to detect this very quickly and reproduce the original message.

5.2 CRYPTOGRAPHIC SCHEMES

Security+ Objective 4.1—Algorithms

Security+ Objective 4.1.1—Hashing

Security+ Objective 4.1.2—Symmetric

Security+ Objective 4.1.3—Asymmetric

Modern cryptography uses algorithms to encrypt and decrypt data by using a mathematical function. To encrypt and decrypt a file, you must use a key. A **key** is a string of bits used to map text into a code and a code back to text. You can think of the key as a super-decoder ring used to translate text messages to a code and back to text. The security of the data relies on three things: the strength of the algorithm and the secrecy of the key.

There are, in general, three types of cryptographic schemes use on PCs and networks. They are:

- **Symmetric cryptography**—Uses a single key (secret key) for both encryption and decryption
- **Asymmetric cryptography**—Uses one key (shared key) for encryption and another key (secret key) for decryption
- **Hash functions**—Uses a mathematical transformation to irreversibly encrypt information

5.2.1 Symmetric Encryption

Security+ Objective 4.2.5—Access Control

The most basic form of encryption is **symmetric encryption.** This requires that each individual must possess a copy of a private key. Of course, for this to work as intended, you must have a secure way to transport the key to other people. In addition, each pair of senders and receivers must possess a special key, which means that each party maintains multiple keys, which can get very cumbersome. Private-key algorithms are generally very fast and easily implemented in hardware. Therefore, they are commonly used for bulk data encryption. See figure 5.1.

So let's take the following unencrypted message:

```
clear text
```

To convert this to cipher text, you will use a Boolean exclusive-or operator. A Boolean exclusive-or operator compares two bits. If one bit is a 1 or the second bit is a 1, but both bits are not 1, the result is a 1. For anything else, the result is a 0.

A	B	Resultant
0	0	0
0	1	1
1	0	1
1	1	0

Figure 5.1 Symmetric encryption uses the same key to encrypt and decrypt messages.

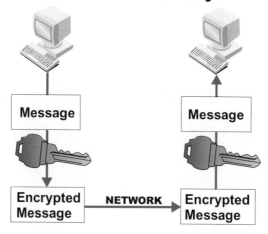

Symmetric encryption uses the same keys

If you take the "clear text" message and you apply the Boolean exclusive-or operation with the key of "password," you get the following:

	c	l	e	a	r	%20	t	e	x	t
	c	l	e	a	r	%20	t	e	x	t
Text	01100011	01101100	01100101	01100001	01110010	00100000	01110100	01100101	01111000	01110100
Key	01110000	01100001	01110011	01110011	01110111	01101111	01110010	01100100	01110000	01100001
	p	a	s	s	w	o	r	d	p	a
Cipher	00010011	00001101	00010110	00010010	00000101	01001111	00000110	00000001	00001000	00010101
	%13	%0d	%16	%12	%05	O	%06	%01	%08	%15

The letters used in the table are the ASCII characters and the numbers that begin with the percentage sign (%), the value is a hexadecimal number. The %20 is the hexadecimal value for a space.

If you use the same key and apply the same algorithm to the cipher text, you convert the message back to the clear text:

	%13	%0d	%16	%12	%05	O	%06	%01	%08	%15
Text	00010011	00001101	00010110	00010010	00000101	01001111	00000110	00000001	00001000	00010101
Key	01110000	01100001	01110011	01110011	01110111	01101111	01110010	01100100	01110000	01100001
	p	a	s	s	w	o	r	d	p	a
Cipher	01100011	01101100	01100101	01100001	01110010	00100000	01110100	01100101	01111000	01110100
	c	l	e	a	r	%20	t	e	x	t

There are two general categories of private key algorithms: block and stream cipher. A block cipher encrypts one block of data at a time. A stream cipher encrypts each byte of the data stream individually. Many symmetric algorithms exist including:

- **Data Encryption Standard (DES)**—A U.S. government standard until 1998, which uses a 56-bit key. It is not considered strong enough for today's standards, and it is relatively slow.
- **Triple DES (3DES)**—Performs 3 DES operations, making it much more secure than DES. Although it is relatively slow, it is widely used.

- **Advanced Encryption Standard (AES)**—The latest standard for the U.S. government to replace DES. It uses variable key lengths (128-, 192-, and 256-bits).
- **International Data Encryption Algorithm (IDEA)**—128-bit key that requires licensing for commercial use. IDEA is used in Pretty Good Privacy (PGP).
- **Blowfish**—A free algorithm, it is extremely fast and uses variable key length.
- **RC4, RC5, and RC6**—A stream cipher that uses variable key length. It is very effective in the public domain.

Since the private-key encryption uses a private key and you share the secret key with someone else, that person would also be able to encrypt and decrypt messages to and from you. The algorithms used with private-key encryption are relatively fast, so they impact system performance less and are good for encrypting large amounts of data such as data on a hard drive or data being transmitted across a network connection. In addition, symmetric algorithms are difficult to decipher without the correct algorithm, which makes them not easy to break. Some of the more secure algorithms such as 3DES and AES are nearly impossible to decipher without the correct key.

A new key would not be sent across the encrypted channel. Keys are sent using an out-of-band method, which means that the key may be sent by letter, courier, or by some other separate method. This may leave the key subject to human error or social engineering exploitation.

A disadvantage of private-key encryption is that it requires the sender and receiver to agree on a key before the transmission of data. In addition, there is no easy way to securely distribute a secret key. If you want a lot of people to access the same message, all of the people have the same key. If you want to communicate with a lot of people in private, you would need to know who uses which key.

When using a shared secret key (symmetric key), all parties need to ensure the key is secured. This can be impractical when working with a large group. In a public/private key arrangement, the private key must remain private. Should a compromise of the private key occur or when a key is no longer needed, it must be destroyed.

5.2.2 Data Encryption Standard

Data Encryption Standard (DES) was developed in 1975 and was standardized by ANSI in 1981 as ANSI X.3.92. It is a popular symmetric-key encryption method that uses block cipher. The key used in DES is based on a 56-bit binary number, which allows for 72,057,594,037,927,936 encryption keys. Of these 72 quadrillion encryption keys, a key is chosen at random. DES applies a 56-bit symmetric key (and 8 parity bits) to each 64-bit block of data. The key actually consists of 64 bits; 8 bits are used in error checking, leaving 56 bits for the key itself.

Since DES is a block cipher, it applies the algorithm to chunks of 64-bit data chunks. Data chunks larger than this are broken into 64-bit blocks; smaller chunks are filled with additional padding bits to create a full 64-bit block. In the first encryption phase, DES shifts the positions of the bits in a block according to its key. This process is called permutation. Next, DES derives an input block from the result and scrambles it by complex mathematical operations. This process is called transformation, the result of which is a pre-output block. Finally, this pre-output block undergoes an additional permutation phase. The result is called encrypted text or encoded text. When given the original key used in the decryption process, DES reconstitutes the original data from DES-encrypted text.

If you want to send an encrypted file from one person (source person) to another person (target person), the source person will encrypt the secret key with the target's persons public key, which was obtained from his or her certificate. Because the target person's key was used to encrypt the secret key, only the target person, using his or her private key, will be the only one able to decrypt the DES secret key and decrypt the DES-encrypted data.

There are four distinct modes of operation that define how the plaintext/ciphertext blocks are processed. They are electronic code book (ECB), cipher block chaining (CBC), cipher feedback (CFB), and output feedback (OFB). Electronic Code Book, which is the default operating mode, and cipher block chaining are the most commonly used.

Although this is considered "good" encryption, it takes quite a bit for a DES-encrypted message to be "broken." Early in 1997, Rivest-Shamir-Adleman, owners of the RSA encryption approach, offered a $10,000 reward for breaking a DES message. A cooperative effort on the Internet of over 14,000 computer users trying out various keys finally deciphered the message, discovering the key after running through only 18 quadrillion of the 72 quadrillion possible keys. Few messages sent today with DES encryption are likely to be subject to this kind of code-breaking effort.

Triple DES (3DES) is a stronger alternative to regular DES, and is used extensively in conjunction with Virtual Private Network implementations. Triple DES encrypts a block of data a DES secret key. The encrypted data is encrypted again using a second DES secret key. Finally, the encrypted data is encrypted a third time using yet another secret key. Triple DES is of particular importance as the DES algorithm keeps being broken in shorter and shorter times.

5.2.3   Advanced Encryption Standard

The **Advanced Encryption Standard (AES)** is an encryption algorithm for securing sensitive but unclassified material by U.S. government agencies and, as a likely consequence, may eventually become the de facto encryption standard for commercial transactions in the private sector. Encryption for the U.S. military and other classified communications is handled by separate, secret algorithms.

In January of 1997, a process was initiated by the National Institute of Standards and Technology (NIST), a unit of the U.S. Commerce Department, to find a stronger encryption algorithm than DES and more efficient than 3DES. Efficiency is measured by how fast the algorithm can encrypt and decrypt information, how fast it can present an encryption key, and how much information it can encrypt.

The specification called for a symmetric algorithm (same key for encryption and decryption) using block encryption (see block cipher) of 128-bits in size, supporting key sizes of 128-, 192-, and 256-bits, as a minimum. The algorithm was required to be royalty-free for use worldwide and offer security of a sufficient level to protect data for the next 20 to 30 years. It was to be easy to implement in hardware and software, as well as in restricted environments (for example, in a smart card) and offered good defenses against various attack techniques.

The entire selection process was fully open to public scrutiny and comment, it being decided that full visibility would ensure the best possible analysis of the designs. In 1998, the NIST selected 15 candidates for the AES, which were then subject to preliminary analysis by the world cryptographic community, including the National Security Agency. On the basis of this, in August 1999, NIST selected five algorithms for more extensive analysis. The end result was that on October 2, 2000, NIST announced that Rijndael had been selected as the proposed standard. On December 6, 2001, the Secretary of Commerce officially approved Federal Information Processing Standard (FIPS) 197, which specifies that all sensitive, unclassified documents will use Rijndael, which was submitted by two Belgian cryptographers, as the Advanced Encryption Standard. FIPS are a set of standards that describe document processing, provide standard algorithms for searching, and provide other information processing standards for use within government agencies.

AES has appeared as an option in several desktop file-encryption programs including Windows XP with service pack 1 and Windows Server 2003. Major AES products will probably appear in network security, where improved security will have the biggest benefit and interfere least with end-user activities.

5.2.4   RC Series

RC2 is a variable key-size block cipher designed by Ronald Rivest for RSA Data Security (now RSA Security). "RC" stands for "Ron's Code" or "Rivest's Cipher." It is faster than DES and is designed as a "drop-in" replacement for DES. It can be made more secure or less secure than DES against exhaustive key search by using appropriate key sizes. It has a block size of 64 bits and is about two to three times faster than DES in software. An additional string (40- to 88-bits long) called a salt can be used to thwart attackers who try to precompute a large look-up table of possible encryptions. The salt is appended to the encryption key, and this lengthened key is used to encrypt the message. The salt is then sent, unencrypted, with the message.

RC4 is a stream cipher designed by Rivest for RSA Data Security (now RSA Security). It is a variable key-size stream cipher with byte-oriented operations. The algorithm is based on the use of a random permutation. Analysis shows that the period of the cipher is overwhelmingly likely to be greater than 10,100. Eight to sixteen machine operations are required per output byte, and the cipher can be expected to run very quickly in software. Independent analysts have scrutinized the algorithm, and it is considered secure. RC4 is used for file encryption in products such as RSA SecurPC. It is also used for secure communications, as in the encryption of traffic to and from secure websites using the SSL protocol

RC5 [Riv95] is a fast block cipher designed by Ronald Rivest for RSA Data Security (now RSA Security) in 1994. It is a parameterized algorithm with a variable block size, a variable key size, and a variable number of rounds. Allowable choices for the block size are 32 bits (for experimentation and evaluation purposes only), 64 bits (for use a drop-in replacement for DES), and 128 bits. The number of rounds can range from 0 to 255, while the key can range from 0 bits to 2040 bits in size. Such built-in variability provides flexibility at all levels of security and efficiency.

There are three routines in RC5: key expansion, encryption, and decryption. In the key-expansion routine, the user-provided secret key is expanded to fill a key table whose size depends on the number of rounds. The key table is then used in both encryption and decryption. The encryption routine consists of three primitive operations: integer addition, bitwise XOR, and variable rotation. The exceptional simplicity of RC5 makes it easy to implement and analyze. Indeed, like the RSA system, the encryption steps of RC5 can be written on the "back of an envelope." The heavy use of data-dependent rotations and the mixture of different operations provide the security of RC5. In particular, the use of data-dependent rotations helps defeat differential and linear cryptanalysis.

RC6 is a block cipher based on RC5 and designed by Rivest, Sidney, and Yin for RSA Security. Like RC5, RC6 is a parameterized algorithm where the block size, the key size, and the number of rounds are variable; again, the upper limit on the key size is 2,040-bits. The main goal for the inventors has been to meet the requirements of the AES.

There are two main new features in RC6 compared to RC5: the inclusion of integer multiplication and the use of four b/4-bit working registers instead of two b/2-bit registers as in RC5 (b is the block size). Integer multiplication is used to increase the diffusion achieved per round so that fewer rounds are needed and the speed of the cipher can be increased. The reason for using four working registers instead of two is technical rather than theoretical. Namely, the default block size of the AES is 128 bits; while RC5 deals with 64-bit operations when using this block size, 32-bit operations are preferable given the intended architecture of the AES

The U.S. patent office granted the RC5 patent to RSA Data Security (now RSA Security) in May 1997. RC6 is proprietary of RSA Security but can be freely used for research and evaluation purposes during the AES evaluation period. We emphasize that if RC6 is selected for the AES, RSA Security will not require any licensing or royalty payments for products using the algorithm; there will be no restrictions beyond those specified for the AES by the U.S. government. However, RC6 may remain a trademark of RSA Security.

5.2.5   Asymmetric Encryption

Asymmetric algorithm, also referred to as public-key encryption, uses two distinct but mathematically related keys: public and private. The public key is the nonsecret key that is available to anyone you choose, or made available to everyone by posting it in a public place. It is often made available through a digital certificate. The private key is kept in a secure location is used only by you. When data needs to be sent, it is protected with a secret key encryption that was encrypted with the public key of the recipient of the data. The encrypted secret key is then transmitted to the recipient along with the encrypted data. The recipient will use the private key to decrypt the secret key. The secret key will then be used to decrypt the message itself. See figure 5.2.

For example, say you want to send data to someone. You would retrieve his or her public key and encrypt the data. You encrypt the data and the secret key, and send both the data and the secret key. Since the recipient's private key is the only thing that can decrypt the secret key, which is the only thing that can decrypt the message, the data can be sent over an insecure communications channel.

Some of the advantages of using public-key encryption is to provide a secure way to communicate with an individual since you can access the public key of the individual to encrypt the message and only that person can decrypt it. The disadvantage is that asymmetric encryption is relatively slower than symmetric algorithms.

Some the popular public-key encryption algorithms include:

■ **Diffie-Hellman**—The oldest public key system in use. This algorithm is not used to encrypt or decrypt messages but is used primarily to send keys across public networks. It is commonly used in IPSec.

Figure 5.2   Asymmetric encryption uses different keys to encrypt and decrypt a message.

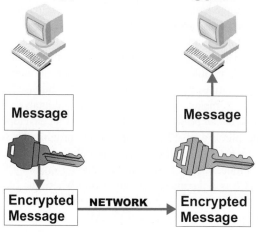

Assymmetric encryption uses different keys for encryption and decryption

- **RSA**—RSA is based on the Diffie-Hellman cipher. It utilizes a public key system with a variable key length and block size. RSA is used in many environments, including SSL.
- **Elliptical curve cryptography (ECC)**—A type of public key system that requires a shorter key length than many other systems and requires less computing power.

5.2.6   RSA Standard

The **RSA standard** (created by Ron **R**ivst, Adi **S**hamir and Leonard **A**dleman) is the most understood, easiest to implement, and most popular asymmetric algorithm. RSA is a worldwide de facto standard, which is used for digital signatures and encryption and is used in many software packages including Microsoft Internet Explorer and Netscape Navigator. It defines the mathematical properties used in public-key encryption and digital signatures. The key length for this algorithm can range from 512 to 2,048, making it a very secure encryption algorithm.

The algorithm involves multiplying two large prime numbers (a prime number is a number divisible only by that number and 1) and through additional operations deriving a set of two numbers that constitutes the public key and another set that is the private key. Once the keys have been developed, the original prime numbers are no longer important and can be discarded. Both the public and the private keys are needed for encryption and decryption but only the owner of a private key ever needs to know it. Using the RSA system, the private key never needs to be sent across the Internet.

The private key is used to decrypt text that has been encrypted with the public key. Thus, if the sender sends a message, the sender can find the public key of the receiver (not the receiver's private key) from a central server and encrypt a message to you using the receiver's public key. When the receiver receives the message, the receiver decrypts it with their private key.

In addition to encrypting messages (which ensures privacy), the sender can authenticate him- or herself to the sender (so that the sender knows who really sent the message) by using the receiver's private key to encrypt a digital certificate. When the receiver gets it, the receiver can use the sender's public key to decrypt it. A table might help us remember this. In addition to encrypting messages (which ensures privacy), the sender can authenticate him- or herself to the receiver (so that the receiver knows who really sent the message) by using the sender's private key to encrypt a digital certificate. Digital certificates are explained later in this chapter. When the message is received, the receiver can use the sender's public key to decrypt it. See table 5.1.

Table 5.1 The Use of Public and Private Keys to Encrypt and Decrypt

To Do This	Use Whose	Kind of Key
Send an encrypted message	Use the receiver's	Public key
Send an encrypted signature	Use the sender's	Private key
Decrypt an encrypted message	Use the receiver's	Private key
Decrypt an encrypted signature (and authenticate the sender)	Use the sender's	Public key

5.2.7 Diffie-Hellman Key Exchange

The Diffie-Hellman algorithm, introduced by Whitfield Diffie and Martin Hellman in 1976, was the first system to utilize public-key or asymmetric cryptographic keys based on the discrete logarithms. Diffie-Hellman key agreement describes a method whereby two parties, without any prior arrangements, can agree upon a secret key that is known only to them (and, in particular, is not known to an eavesdropper listening to the dialogue by which the parties agree on the key). This secret key can be used, for example, to encrypt further communications between the parties using Secret-Key Cryptography.

Diffie-Hellman is not an encryption mechanism as we normally think of them in that we do not typically use it to encrypt data. Instead, it is a method to securely exchange the keys that encrypt data. Diffie-Hellman accomplishes this secure exchange by creating a "shared secret" (sometimes called a "key encryption key") between two devices. The shared secret then encrypts the symmetric key (or "data encryption key," i.e., DES, Triple DES, CAST, IDEA, Blowfish, etc.) for secure transmittal.

The process begins when each side of the communication generates a private key. Each side then generates a public key, which is a derivative of the private key. The two systems then exchange their public keys. Each side of the communication now has its own private key and the other system's public key.

Noting that the public key is a derivative of the private key is important—the two keys are mathematically linked. However, in order to trust this system, you must accept that you cannot discern the private key from the public key. Because the public key is indeed public and ends up on other systems, the ability to figure out the private key from it would render the system useless. This is one area requiring trust in the mathematical experts. The fact that the very best in the world have tried for years to defeat this and failed bolsters my confidence a great deal.

Once the key exchange is complete, the process continues. An important feature of the Diffie-Hellman protocol is its ability to generate "shared secrets"—an identical cryptographic key shared by each side of the communication. By running the mathematical operation against your own private key and the other side's public key, you generate a value. When the distant end runs the same operation against your public key and their own private key, they also generate a value. The important point is that the two values generated are identical.

At this point, the Diffie-Hellman operation could be considered complete. The shared secret is, after all, a cryptographic key that could encrypt traffic. That is very rare however. The reason being that the shared secret is, by its mathematical nature, an asymmetric key. As with all asymmetric key systems, it is inherently slow. If the two sides are passing very little traffic, the shared secret may encrypt actual data. Any attempt at bulk traffic encryption requires a symmetric key system such as DES, Triple DES, IDEA, CAST, Blowfish, etc. In most real applications of the Diffie-Hellman protocol (IPSec in particular), the shared secret encrypts a symmetric key for one of the symmetric algorithms, transmits it securely, and the distant end decrypts it with the shared secret. Because the symmetric key is a relatively short value as compared to bulk data, the shared secret can encrypt and decrypt it very quickly. Speed is not so much of an issue with short values.

5.2.8   Elliptical Curve Cryptography

Elliptical curve cryptography (ECC) is a public-key encryption technique based on elliptic curve theory that can be used to create faster, smaller, and more efficient cryptographic keys. ECC generates keys through the properties of the elliptic curve equation instead of the traditional method of generation as the product of very large prime numbers. The technology can be used in conjunction with most public key encryption methods, such as RSA, and Diffie-Hellman. According to some researchers, ECC can yield a level of security with a 164-bit key that other systems require a 1,024-bit key to achieve. Because ECC helps establish equivalent security with lower computing power and battery resource usage, it is becoming widely used for mobile applications, including cellular phones. ECC was developed by Certicom, a mobile e-business security provider, and was recently licensed by Hifn, a manufacturer of integrated circuitry (IC) and network security products. RSA has been developing its own version of ECC. Many manufacturers, including 3COM, Cylink, Motorola, Pitney Bowes, Siemens, TRW, and VeriFone have included support for ECC in their products.

The properties and functions of elliptic curves have been studied in mathematics for 150 years. Their use within cryptography was first proposed in 1985, by (separately) Neal Koblitz from the University of Washington and Victor Miller at IBM. An elliptic curve is not an ellipse (oval shape), but it is represented as a looping line intersecting two axes (lines on a graph used to indicate the position of a point). ECC is based on properties of a particular type of equation created from the mathematical group (a set of values for which operations can be performed on any two members of the group to produce a third member) derived from points where the line intersects the axes. Multiplying a point on the curve by a number will produce another point on the curve, but it is very difficult to find what number was used, even if you know the original point and the result. Equations based on elliptic curves have a characteristic that is very valuable for cryptography purposes: They are relatively easy to perform and extremely difficult to reverse.

The industry still has some reservations about the use of elliptic curves. Nigel Smart, a Hewlett-Packard researcher, discovered a flaw in which certain curves are extremely vulnerable. However, Philip Deck of Certicom says that, while there are curves that are vulnerable, those implementing ECC would have to know which curves could not be used. He believes that ECC offers a unique potential as a technology that could be implemented worldwide and across all devices. According to Deck (quoted in Wired), "the only way you can achieve that is with elliptic curve."

5.2.9   Hash Encryption

Hash encryption, also called **message digests** and one-way encryption, uses algorithms that don't really use a key. Instead, it converts data from a variable-length to a fixed-length piece of data called a hash value. This shorter hashed key is faster to retrieve and use. Hashing is always a one-way operation. There's no need to "reverse engineer" the hash function by analyzing the hashed values. In fact, the ideal hash function cannot be derived by such analysis. A good hash function also should not produce the same hash value from two different inputs. If it does, this is known as a collision. A hash function that offers an extremely low risk of collision may be considered acceptable.

Users must often utilize hashes, when there is information they never want decrypted or read. Hash algorithms are typically used to provide a digital fingerprint of a file or message contents, often used to ensure that the file has not been altered by an intruder or virus. Hash functions are also commonly employed by many operating systems to encrypt passwords and for digital signatures.

MD5 is an algorithm that is used to verify data integrity through the creation of a 128-bit message digest from data input (which may be a message of any length) that is claimed to be as unique to that specific data as a fingerprint is to the specific individual. MD5, which was developed by Professor Ronald L. Rivest of MIT, is intended for use with digital signature applications, which require that large files must be compressed by a secure method before being encrypted with a secret key, under a public key cryptosystem. MD5 is currently a standard, Internet Engineering Task Force (IETF) Request for Comments (RFC) 1321. According to the standard, it is "computationally infeasible" that any two messages that have been input to the MD5 algorithm could have as the output the same message digest, or that a false message could be created through apprehension of the message digest.

MD5 is the third message digest algorithm created by Rivest. All three (the others are MD2 and MD4) have similar structures, but MD2 was optimized for 8-bit machines, in comparison with the two later formulas, which are optimized for 32-bit machines. The MD5 algorithm is an extension of MD4, which the critical review found to be fast but possibly not absolutely secure. In comparison, MD5 is not quite as fast as the MD4 algorithm but offers much more assurance of data security.

The **Secure Hash Algorithm (SHA),** the algorithm specified in the Secure Hash Standard (SHS, FIPS 180), was developed by NIST. SHA-1 is a revision to SHA that was published in 1994; the revision corrected an unpublished flaw in SHA. Its design is very similar to the MD4 family of hash functions developed by Rivest. SHA-1 is also described in the ANSI X9.30 standard. The algorithm takes a message of less than 2^{64} bits in length and produces a 160-bit message digest. The algorithm is slightly slower than MD5, but the larger message digest makes it more secure against brute-force collision and inversion attacks.

5.2.10 One-Time Pad

In cryptography, a **one-time pad (OTP)** is a system in which a private key generated randomly is used only once to encrypt a message that is then decrypted by the receiver using a matching one-time pad and key. It is considered a perfect encryption scheme because it is unbreakable and each pad is used exactly once.

Messages encrypted with keys based on randomness have the advantage that there is theoretically no way to "break the code" by analyzing a succession of messages. Each encryption is unique and bears no relation to the next encryption so that some pattern can be detected. With a one-time pad, however, the decrypting party must have access to the same key used to encrypt the message and this raises the problem of how to get the key to the decrypting party safely or how to keep both keys secure. One-time pads have sometimes been used when both parties started out at the same physical location and then separated, each with knowledge of the keys in the one-time pad. The key used in a one-time pad is called a secret key because if it is revealed, the messages encrypted with it can easily be deciphered.

Typically, a one-time pad is created by generating a string of characters or numbers that will be at least as long as the longest message that may be sent. This string of values is generated in some random fashion—for example, by someone pulling numbered balls out of a lottery machine or by using a computer program with a random number generator. The values are written down on a pad (or any device that someone can read or use). The pads are given to anyone who may be likely to send or receive a message. Typically, a pad may be issued as a collection of keys, one for each day in a month, for example, with one key expiring at the end of each day or as soon as it has been used once.

When a message is to be sent, the sender uses the secret key to encrypt each character, one at a time. If a computer is used, each bit in the character (which is usually 8 bits in length) is exclusively "OR'ed" with the corresponding bit in the secret key. (With a one-time pad, the encryption algorithm is simply the XOR operation. Where there is some concern about how truly random the key is, it is sometimes combined with another algorithm such as MD5.) One writer describes this kind of encryption as a "100% noise source" used to mask the message. Only the sender and receiver have the means to remove the noise. Once the one-time pad is used, it can't be reused. If it is reused, someone who intercepts multiple messages can begin to compare them for similar coding for words that may possibly occur in both messages.

5.3 ENCRYPTION EXPORT REGULATIONS

Cryptography is export-controlled for several reasons. Strong cryptography can be used for criminal purposes or even as a weapon of war. During wartime, the ability to intercept and decipher enemy communications is crucial. For that reason, cryptographic technologies are subject to export controls.

For many years, the U.S. government did not approve export of cryptographic products unless the key size was strictly limited. For this reason, cryptographic products were divided into two classes: products with "strong" cryptography, and products with "weak" (that is, exportable) cryptography. Weak cryptography generally means a key size of at most 56 bits in symmetric algorithms (such as triple-DES, IDEA, or RC5), an RSA modulus of size at most 512 bits, and an elliptic curve key size of at most 112 bits.

In January 2000, the U.S. Department of Commerce Bureau of Industry and Security (BIS) [formerly the Bureau of Export Administration (BXA)] dramatically relaxed the restrictions on export regulations. Today, any cryptographic product is exportable under a license exception (that is, without a license) unless the end-users are foreign governments or embargoed destinations (Cuba, Iran, Libya, North Korea, Serbia, Sudan, and Syria). Export to government end-users may also be approved but under a license. For the first time, "mass market" encryption commodities and software with symmetric key lengths exceeding 64 bits may be exported and reexported following a 30-day review by the Bureau of Industry and Security. Such "mass market" encryption products will no longer require post-export reporting or additional national security review. For more information about U.S. export control, visit the following websites:

U.S. Department of Commerce Bureau of Industry and Security

http://www.bxa.doc.gov

Commercial Encryption Export Controls

http://www.bxa.doc.gov/Encryption/Default.htm

Commercial Encryption Export Controls Regulations

http://www.bxa.doc.gov/Encryption/regs.htm

Exporting Basics: An Introduction to U.S. Export Controls

http://www.bxa.doc.gov/factsheets/ExportingBasics.htm

For general information about cryptographic policies of other countries, see the following website:
http://www.rsasecurity.com/rsalabs/faq/6-5-1.html

5.4   AUTHENTICATION

Security+ Objective 1.2—Authentication

Security+ Objective 1.2.6—Multifactor

Security+ Objective 1.2.7—Mutual Authentication

Security+ Objective 4.2.3—Authentication

Security+ Objective 4.2.4—Nonrepudiation

Authentication, which is the layer of network security, is the process by which the system validates the user's logon information. Authentication is crucial to secure communication. Users must be able to prove their identity to those with whom they communicate and must be able to verify the identity of others. A user who logs on with a valid user ID and password combination is considered an **authenticated user.**

Users need to authenticate to a server in some manner (username/password, smart card, or biometrics) that is cost-effective and simple. They need to be able to traverse servers without having to reauthenticate. To avoid the user from reauthenticating every time a user tries to access a network server or resource, the user will be given a token when the user first authenticates. You can think of the token as a set of keys which says who the user is and what access the user has. Every time the user moves from server to server to try to access different network resources, the token will be used automatically to prove who the user is and that the user has permission to use the server or network resource. At the end of the user's session, the token is destroyed. Note: Depending on the operating system and situation, if you change a persons rights and/or permissions, the person will not be able to see the changes until they log out and log back in so that a new token can be created.

Authentication requires a user to provide some proof or credential that represents proving what you know, showing what you have, demonstrating who you are or identifying where you are before allowing access to your company's resources. Examples include:

- **Proving what you known**—A password or personal identification number (PIN)
- **Showing what you have**—A smart card or other physical object
- **Demonstrating who you are**—A thumbprint or other biometrics
- **Identifying where you are**—An IP address

When two or more authentication methods are used to authenticate someone, you are implementing a **multifactor authentication** system. Of course, a system that uses two authentication methods such as smart cards and a password can be referred to as a **two-factor authentication.**

The authentication process can be a one-way process, where only the user's credentials are authenticated, or a **mutual authentication** process, in which both the user and resource authenticate to each other. To require strong authentication, you must understand what authentication methods are available, their strengths and weaknesses, and how to combine these methods to provide strong authentication.

5.4.1   Usernames and Passwords

Security+ Objective 5.4.1—Username/Password

One of the common methods used on networks is to use a username and password. A username is used to identify a user account, so that it can keep track of the user. The password is used to validate the person's identity when that person logs on. When the user account is created, the username and password are added to a security database, which then allows the administrator to assign access to network resources to the user account.

A passphrase is a variation on passwords that uses a sequence of characters or words instead of a single password. Although they are generally more difficult to break than passwords, they are also inconvenient to enter and share the same problems associated with passwords.

The username and password can be stored in a normal text file. To prevent anyone looking at the text file to see the password, the password is hashed and the hashed value is stored in the text file. When a user logs in, the system will look at the text file and go down the list until it finds a matching name. It then hashes the password that was supplied and compares it to the hashed password stored in the file. Of course, if the username and password match, the user is given access.

Similar to a password is a **personal identification number (PIN),** which is a code made of numbers. PINs are commonly assigned to bank customers for use with automatic cash dispensers, and they are also used, sometimes with a security token, for individual access to computer networks or other secure systems.

Unfortunately, passwords (including passphrase and PINs) are generally insecure for several reasons. They are:

- **Human nature**—In the case of user-generated passwords, users will normally choose passwords that are easily remembered and consequently easily guessed. In addition, users may share them with other users or may write them down, especially if they were generated by the system and not the user.
- **Transmission and storage**—Many applications and protocols, such as FTP and PAP, transmit passwords in clear text, store them in a ordinary text file, or protect them with a weak hashing algorithm, which can be easily broken.
- **Easily broken**—Passwords are susceptible to brute force and dictionary attacks.
- **Inconvenient**—Many users see passwords as inconvenient. Therefore, they try to bypass these controls by selecting easily typed or weak passwords, automate their logons such as when a browser remembers a password for an Internet website, or neglect to lock their workstation or log out when they leave their computer.
- **Refutable**—If a system only uses passwords for authentication, there is no guarantee or absolute proof that it was the user that used the password to log in. In other words, there is no guarantee for nonrepudiation.

Passwords have the following login controls and management features that should be configured in accordance with an organization's security policy and security best practices:

- **Length**—Since a password is, in effect, an encryption key, just as larger encryption keys are better, so, too, are longer passwords. Systems should be configured to require a password of minimum character length.
- **Complexity**—Strong passwords contain a mix of upper- and lowercase letters, numbers, and special characters such as # and $.
- **Aging**—Maximum password aging should be set to require passwords at regular intervals; 30 to 45 days is usually recommended. On the other hand, you should have a minimum of password aging so that users don't keep resetting passwords to circumvent password history controls so that they can reset their password back to their original password. It is recommended to have a minimum of 1 day.
- **History**—Password history allow a system to remember previously used passwords so that users cannot keep reusing the same passwords over and over or alternate between two or three familiar passwords when required to change their passwords.

■ **Limited attempts**—This control limits the number of unsuccessful logon attempts and consists of two components: counter threshold (3 is usually recommended) and counter reset (30 minutes is usually recommended).

■ **Lockout duration**—When the counter threshold has been exceeded, the account is locked out for a preset duration (commonly set to 30 minutes) or is set to forever, which requires an administrator to unlock the account. When a lockout occurs by too many attempts, depending on the system, the system administrator could be automatically notified or the lockout could be written in a log. In both cases, the system administrator can use these notifications or logs to detect possible break-in attempts.

■ **Time and system restrictions**—On some systems, you can restrict the time of day that a user can log in and from which system they can log in to. Of course, today, these features are not as commonly used as they have been in the past because of long or erratic work hours or when a company conducts global business.

In addition, to the previous guidelines, you also have control over system messages including logon banners, last usernames, and last successful logon. A logon banner is the welcome message that is displayed before or after a login. You should disable any welcome message and replace it with a legal warning that requires the user to click OK to acknowledge the message. There have been several court cases against hackers that have been dismissed because after they hacked into a system, the system told them welcome, meaning it was OK to access the system. Many popular operating systems display the username of the last successful logon. While this feature is convenient for users, security is based on knowing both the correct username and password. Lastly, after successfully logging on to the system, some systems can be configured to display a message that tells the user the last time that he or she logged on. If the system shows that the last successful logon is different from when the user actually logged on, the user can assume that his or her account has been compromised, change his or her password immediately and report the incident.

5.4.2   Challenge-Response Authentication

A challenge-response authentication is a protocol that challenges a user or system to verify its identity. Instead of transmitting the password over the Internet, the client sends a logon request from the client to the server. The server sends a challenge (such as a number) back to the client. The challenge is encrypted with a secret key (most likely with the user's password) and then sent back to the server. Since the server knows the password, it performs the same encryption. If the response from the client is the same as the encryption done by the server, the server grants authorization.

5.4.3   Digital Envelopes

A **digital envelope** is a type of security that encrypts the message using symmetric encryption and encrypts the key to decode the message using public-key encryption. This technique overcomes one of the problems of public-key encryption being slower than symmetric encryption because only the key is protected with public-key encryption, providing little overhead.

5.4.4   Digital Signature

Security+ Objective 4.2.2.1—Digital Signatures

Security+ Objective 4.2.4.1—Digital Signatures

A **digital signature** is a digital code that can be attached to an electronically transmitted message that uniquely identifies the sender. Like a written signature, the purpose of a digital signature is to guarantee that the individual sending the message really is who he or she claims to be. In addition, it can be used to verify that the person who supposedly sent the message really did (this is nonrepudiation). This is done by encrypting a hash result using an asymmetric algorithm.

For example, if the sender wants to sends a message to the receiver, and it is important that the message not be altered, the sender uses a public key to create a hash value that is stored in the message digest. The sender sends the message to the receiver. The receiver can use his or her private key and compare the value of the message digest. If the message value that he or she gets from this private key is the same as the message digest sent with the message, he or she will know that the method is authentic.

The digital signature is derived from a hash process known only by the originator. The receiver uses a key provided by the sender or a key that will provide the same result when performed. The receiver compares the signature area referred to as a message digest in the message with the value he or she calculated. If the values match, the message has not been tampered with, and the originator is verified as the person he or she claims to be. The process provides both message integrity and authentication.

5.4.5 Digital Certificates

Security+ Objective 1.2.3—Certificates

Security+ Objective 4.3.1—Certificates—Make a distinction between what certificates are used for what purpose. Basics only.

A **digital certificate** is an attachment to an electronic message used for security purposes such as authentication and to verify that a user sending a message is who he or she claims to be; it also provides the receiver with a means to encode a reply without providing a password to authenticate. It accomplishes this by securely binding a public key to the digital certificate to the entity that holds the corresponding private key. Certificates are generally issued by a Certificate Server. By using key information distributed in certificates, a user can:

- Encrypt a message (privacy)
- Confirm a message was not modified (integrity)
- Confirm the sender's identity (nonrepudiation)

A digital certificate typically includes the following information:

- Owner's name, company or organization, and contact information.
- Owner's public key
- The certificate's activation date
- The certificate's expiration date
- What the certificate is used for
- The name of the trusted party or issuer that issued the certificate
- A unique serial number assigned by the issuer

The issuer of the digital certificate digitally signs the contents of the certificate by using its own private key. The issuer's public key can be used to verify that the certificate is authentic and that its contents have not been altered. The owner's public key is then used to verify the identity of the individual named on the certificate.

X.509 certificates are the most widely used digital certificates. The X.509 describes two levels of authentication: simple authentication based on a password to verify user identity and strong authentication using credentials formed using cryptographic techniques. Of course, strong authentication is recommended to provide secure service. Note: X.509 is actually an ITU recommendation, which means that it hasn't been officially defined or approved.

Another important set of standards are the **Public Key Cryptography Standards (PKCS),** which are not really standards at all but are still widely recognized and used in public key cryptography. The PKCS standards were developed by RSA Data Security, Inc. The PKCS standards are numbered PKCS #1 through PKCS #12. PKCS #7 and PKCS #10 are two of the more commonly known standards. PKCS#7 provides a general syntax for digital signatures, and PKCS #10 provides a standard syntax for certification requests.

A **public key infrastructure (PKI)** enables secure e-commerce through the integration of public key cryptography, digital signatures, and other services necessary to ensure confidentiality, integrity, authentication, nonrepudiation and access control. See section 5.6 for more information about PKIs.

An individual wishing to send an encrypted message applies for a digital certificate from a **Certificate Authority (CA).** The CA issues an encrypted digital certificate containing the applicant's public key and a variety of other identification information. The CA makes its own public key readily available through print publicity or the Internet. The recipient of an encrypted message uses the CA's public key to decode the digital certificate attached to the message, verifies it as issued by the CA, and then obtains the sender's public key and identification information held within the certificate. With this information, the recipient can send an encrypted reply.

5.4.6   Security Tokens

Security+ Objective 1.2.5—Tokens

Authentication can be done with something that you have such as a plastic magnetic-strip card, smart card, or some other type of hardware token. A security token is a physical device that is a portable storage for an authenticator. Tokens support authentication by their physical possession. The traditional token is the metal key that has stood the test of time. The drawback of a metal key is that, if lost, it enables its finder to enter the house. This is why most digital tokens combine another factor (two-factor authenticators): an associated secret PIN to protect a lost or stolen token. Since these devices are designed for security applications, most are resistant to physical and electronic tampering. ATM magnetic stripe cards are at the lower end of security and cryptographically-enabled smart cards are at the high end.

Security tokens can be bankcards or smart cards that contain passwords, or active devices that yield time-changing or challenge-based passwords. While the token can store human-chosen passwords, it has the advantage of storing longer codewords that a human cannot remember. A codeword is similar to a password, except it is machine-generated and machine-stored, so it can be longer, more random, and perhaps changing.

Token devices come in two forms: synchronous and asynchronous. A synchronous token is time-based and generates a value that is used in authentication. The token value is valid for a set period of time before it changes and is based on a secret key held by both the token (usually a sealed device) and the server providing authentication services. An asynchronous token uses a challenge-response mechanism to determine whether the user is valid. After the user enters the identification value, the authentication server sends a challenge value. The user then enters that value into the token device, which then returns a value called a token. The user sends that value back to the server, which validates it to the username.

There are two categories of tokens:

- Passive or Stored Value such as a bank card
- Active, such as a one-time password generator

Passive tokens are simply storage devices that store some type of key. Typically, they will use a magnetic strip, which is read by a card reader, or an optical bar code, which is read by a scanner. The most common passive tokens are plastic cards with magnetic strips embedded in them.

The plastic magnetic strip card is increasingly used for controlling access and verifying the authenticity of the user. Bank credit cards, automatic teller machine cards, and cards for authorizing bank teller transactions are common examples. Plastic cards carry a fixed password or key that is invisible to the user and difficult to duplicate. To read the password or key, you would use a port or reader to convey information to the machine. Plastic cards are very appealing because of their low cost and high-security features. However, cards can be lost, stolen, or duplicated and, therefore, are frequently used in conjunction with passwords or personal identification numbers. More sophisticated techniques include requiring the use of two separate valid cards, or coding the card to allow access only within specific time periods. These techniques, however, reduce the flexibility of the system if immediate access is important. Note: Since the plastic magnetic strip cards do not do any processing, the cards are considered dumb tokens.

The active device usually contains a processor that computes a one-time password, either by time-synchronization or challenge-response. A **one-time password (OTP)** is a password that is used only once for a very limited period of time and then is no longer valid. If someone intercepts the password at any point, the password is useless because it has already expired. One-time passwords are typically counter-based or clock-based tokens.

Security+ Objective 3.2.4.6—Smart Cards

Smart cards resemble a plastic magnetic strip except that they contain a processor and electronic memory. In addition, they may include pictures, biometric data storage, bar codes, a magnetic stripe, and a very small antenna (for wireless communication). One card may allow an individual physical access to a restricted area, logical access to a computer system, and authorized access to specified computer files and programs. Smart cards can be designed to be inserted into a slot and read by a special reader or to be read at a distance, such as when you approach a toll booth or locked door. Cards can be disposable (as at a trade-show) or reloadable (for most applications). The card may be modified to remind the user to perform certain tasks, to allow different levels of access according to the time period, to authenticate messages transferred, and a host of other functions including being used for telephone calling and electronic cash payments. Additionally, the chip, by virtue of being embedded in the card, is tamper-resistant, and each card has its own serial number. Protection is further increased by encrypting the processing done by the microprocessor chip. One of the disadvantages of this device is that it is relatively expensive.

Most smart cards support at least one standard encryption algorithm, since without encryption, anyone who can read the card can retrieve the data from it. Encryption algorithms that may be available on smartcards include DES, 3DES, Diffie-Hellman, MD5, SHA-1 and RSA.

There are many standards for the smart card, including ISO/IEC, FIPS, ANSI, X.509 (certificate), and EMV standards, which define physical, electronic, algorithmic and formatting standards. Important from a security standpoint would be the FIPS-140, Level 3 standards level, a NIST security requirement for cryptographic modules. A de facto standard for programmable cards that is gaining in popularity is that of Java support, with other options being Visual Basic or MULTOS. Of course, when selecting a smart card, you must make sure that the smart card reader and smart card lifecycle management software you choose works with the operating systems and OS versions on which you plan to use them.

Like the magnetic strip card, smart cards are often used as part of an authentication process. Since a smart card can be lost or stolen, it is important that the authentication process depend on something you know, like a PIN, or something you are, like biometric data. To protect the information on the smart card means that the data stored on the card should be encrypted to protect against unauthorized access. Some active tokens can also perform cryptographic calculations to encrypt and decrypt.

5.4.7   Biometrics

Security+ Objective 1.2.8—Biometrics

A **biometric** is a feature measured from the human body that is distinguishing enough to be used for user authentication. Biometrics include fingerprints, eye (iris and retina), face, hand, voice, and signature. A biometric offers something passwords and tokens cannot do, since they can be lent or stolen. When used to verify the person involved in a transaction, this inextricable link can offer nonrepudiation, proof that a transaction did take place involving the authenticated user though that user denies it.

To use biometric authentication requires comparing a registered sample against a new captured biometric sample captured during a logon. The biometric authentication mechanism typically has two modes: enrolling and verifying.

To initially use the biometric system, an administrator must enroll each user to verify that each individual being enrolled is authorized. The enrolling process includes storing the user's biological feature that can be used later to verify the user's identity. This typically requires using a sensor that can record this particular such as a thumbprint scanner, retina scanner, or microphone.

When a person logs on using the biometric information, the user is verifying his or her identity. Therefore, the user has a sensor on his or her computer that can capture the same biometric information that was used for enrollment and then transmit that information to the authenticating server. The server then compares the two sets of information.

When selecting a biometric authentication method, you should consider its performance, difficulty, reliability, acceptance, and cost. For the biometric authentication method to be usable, it must perform quickly and not be difficult to use. It must be reliable because you don't want to falsely accuse anyone of trying to break into a system, misidentify an employee or customer, or deny anyone access who needs to use the system to perform his or her job. The accuracy of a biometric system is normally stated as a percentage, in the following terms:

- **False Reject Rate (FRR) or Type I error**—Authorized users who are incorrectly denied access.
- **False Accept Rate (FAR) or Type II error**—Unauthorized users who are incorrectly granted access.
- **Crossover Error Rate (CER)**—The point at which the FRR equals the FAR. Since you can adjust the system's sensitivity, you indirectly can adjust the FRR and FAR. Therefore, the CER can be the most important measure of biometric system accuracy.

The generally accepted standards for biometric systems are:

- **Accuracy**—The CER should be less 10 percent.
- **Speed**—No more than 5 seconds.
- **Throughput**—6 to 10 per minute.
- **Enrollment time**—Less than 2 minutes.

While it may be more acceptable to use on employees, it may be more intrusive to customers. And last but not least, a biometric system will cost more than using a magnetic strip card or smart card.

5.5   PUBLIC KEY INFRASTRUCTURE

Security+ Objective 4.3—PKI

Security+ Objective 4.3.1.1—Certificate Policies

Security+ Objective 4.3.1.2—Certificate Practice Statements

Security+ Objective 4.3.2—Revocation

Security+ Objective 4.3.3—Trust Models

Security+ Objective 4.5—Key Management/Certificate Lifecycle

Security+ Objective 4.5.1—Centralized vs. Decentralized

Security+ Objective 4.5.2—Storage

Security+ Objective 4.5.2.1—Hardware vs. Software

Security+ Objective 4.5.2.2—Private Key Protection

Security+ Objective 4.5.3—Escrow

Security+ Objective 4.5.4—Expiration

Security+ Objective 4.5.5—Revocation

Security+ Objective 4.5.5.1—Status Checking

Security+ Objective 4.5.6—Suspension

Security+ Objective 4.5.6.1—Status Checking

Security+ Objective 4.5.7—Recovery

Security+ Objective 4.5.7.1—M of N Control

Security+ Objective 4.5.8—Renewal

Security+ Objective 4.5.9—Destruction

Security+ Objective 4.5.10—Key Usage

Security+ Objective 4.5.10.1—Multiple Key Pairs (Single, Dual)

Using asymmetric key pairs (private and public keys) is simple enough to implement in small networks, but it becomes much more difficult in larger networks to distribute public keys and hard to track and manage private keys. When a private key is compromised, it is difficult to locate and remove that key.

The security infrastructure created to solve these problems is known as the public key infrastructure (PKI). PKI uses asymmetric key pairs and combines software encryption technologies and services to provide a means of protecting the security of communications and business transactions. RFC 2459 defines the X.509 PKI, which is the PKI defined for use on the Internet. According to Netscape Communications, PKI protects your information assets in a variety of ways:

- **Authenticate identity**—Individual users, organizations, and their websites use digital certificates, issued as part of your PKI, to validate the identity of the parties to a transaction.
- **Verify integrity**—Ensure that the signed message has not changed since being signed.

- **Ensure privacy**—Ensure that unauthorized individuals cannot make use of confidential data.
- **Authorize access**—Digital certificates can replace user IDs and passwords for login security, reducing IT overhead.
- **Authorize transactions**—The enterprise can control access privileges for specified transactions.
- **Support nonrepudiation**—Protects against forging and users' later challenging transactions.

The Public Key Infrastructure (PKI) provides security for conversations between computers. PKI relies on these components to achieve its purpose:

- **Digital signature (certificate)**—Like a person's cursive signature, this verifies that a message is actually from the stated source. In a networking computer environment, users, computers, routers, and organizations can use digital certificates to certify their identities. Certificates thus provide authentication
- **Encryption**—Like the snapping lid on a bottle of ketchup verifies that the tasty red contents have not been tampered with, encryption verifies that the message has not been corrupted or viewed. Encryption thus provides privacy as well as integrity to the communicating entities

As stated earlier in the chapter, a certificate, also known as a digital certificate or public key certificate, is a digital document that attests to the binding of a public key to an entity. The main purpose of a certificate is to generate confidence that the public key contained in the certificate actually belongs to the entity named in the certificate.

When implementing a PKI scheme, you need to look at whether you require a centralized key management mechanism, in which a central authority manages keys, or whether a decentralized model, in which each individual user manages his/her own key pair, is sufficient.

Improper protection of private keys would prove a major disruption of business and costly in terms of revenue. This does not even begin to address the security aspects between compromising of private keys and the time when the compromise was discovered. It's not uncommon to hear of organizations keeping copies of private keys in vaults, or even off-site, in case needed for disaster recovery.

A software device might be something as simple as a text file maintained by a user, which contains his or her private keys, decrypted as needed to obtain the appropriate private key. Or it might be a key management database specifically intended for the centralized storage and retrieval of keys.

A hardware device for key storage might either:

- Store the key itself (for instance, a smart card which can be read by an appropriate reader when a PIN is provided)
- Not store the key at all (just an algorithm for generating a key based on the input of a user-provided pass phrase or PIN number.

A private key holder is responsible for taking all adequate precautions to secure their primary key and ensure that no one has access to it. This is important because anyone who obtains a user's private key can forge a message and claim it was sent by that user, and can decrypt any sensitive communications encrypted by that user's public key.

Key escrow is the procedure of keeping a copy of a user's private key in a centralized location that is only accessible to security administrators, or of implementing a mechanism whereby the private key can be recovered without having to be physically stored. Escrow allows for the future recovery of the key, should it be lost in a disaster or by its owner, or needed by someone authorized to view the information encrypted by it, such as in certain regulatory environments or situations in which law enforcement is involved.

The certificates are issued by Certificate Authorities (CA), which can be any trusted service or entity willing to verify and validate the identities of those to whom it issues certificates, and their association with specific keys. The **Registration Authority (RA)** is an entity that is designed to verify certificate contents for the CA. When a person requests a certificate, the CA verifies that individual's identity, constructs the certificate, signs it, delivers it to the requester, and maintains the certificate over its lifetime. When another person wants to communicate with this person, the CA will vouch for that person's identity. See figure 5.3.

The following six steps describe the process of requesting and issuing a certificate:

1. **Generating a key pair**—The applicant generates a public and private key pair or is assigned a key pair by some authority in his or her organization.

Figure 5.3   A Certificate Gives Out and Validates Certificates

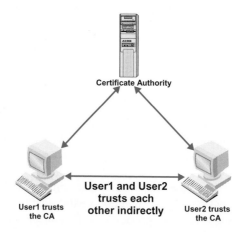

2. **Collecting required information**—The applicant collects whatever information the CA requires to issue the certificate. The information could include the applicant's email address, birth certificate, fingerprints, or notarized documents, wherever the CA needs to be certain that the applicant is who he or she claims to be.

3. **Requesting the certificate**—The applicant sends a certificate request, consisting of his or public key and the additional required information to the CA. The certificate request may be encrypted using the CA's public key. Many requests are made using email, but requests can also be sent by postal or courier service, for example, when the certificate requests itself must be notarized.

4. **Verifying the information**—The CA applies whatever policy rules it requires to verify that the applicant should receive a certificate. As with identification requirements, CA's verification policy and procedures influence the amount of confidence generated by the certificate it issues.

5. **Creating the certificate**—The CA creates and signs a digital document containing the applicant's public key and other appropriate information. The signature of the CA authenticates the binding of the subject's name to the subject's public key. The signed document is the certificate.

6. **Sending or posting the certificate**—The CA sends the certificate to the applicant or posts the certificate in a directory as appropriate.

NOTE: A certificate has a validity period, by default, 2 years. After this period, the certificate expires and the CA must then renew the certificate.

In a brief summary, when a user establishes a public and private key pair for him- or herself, he or she makes a request to the CA. The CA requests certain identification from the user and verifies the information. The CA registers him or her in the database, performs a key pair generation, and creates a certificate with the user's public key and identity information embedded.

When User1 wants to communicate with User2, User1 will requests User2 public key from the CA. The CA sends User2's public key, and User1 uses this to encrypt a session key that will be used to encrypt that he or she wants to send. User1 sends the encrypted session key to User2. User1, then sends his or her certificate, containing his public key, to User2. When User2 receives User1's certificate, his or her application (such as a browser or email application) looks to see if it trusts the CA that digitally signed the certificate. User2's application trusts this CA and User2 makes a request to the CA to see if User1's certificate is still valid. When the certificate has been validated, User2 decrypts the session key with his or her private key. Now the both can communicate using public key cryptography. Of course, most of this happens in the background, so the users don't really see this happen. See figure 5.4.

5.5.1   CA Models

For PKI to work, the capabilities of CAs must be readily available to users. Therefore, there are several models in which CAs can be established. Microsoft Windows uses the hierarchical model. Certificate Services include two policy modules that permit two classes of CAs: enterprise CAs and stand-alone CAs. Within these two classes, there can be two types of CAs: a root CA or a subordinate

Figure 5.4 When a user wants to send a message to another user, he or she will use the certificate authority to get the receiving user's key to encrypt a message and send it to the receiving user.

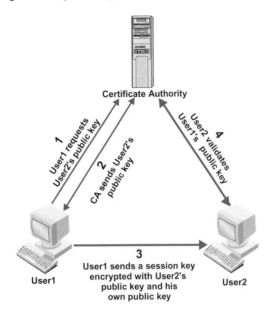

CA. The policy modules define the action that a CA can take when it receives a certificate request, and it can be modified if necessary. CAs are usually organized in a hierarchy in which the most trusted CA is at the top.

In the enterprise, the enterprise root CA is the most trusted CA. There can be more than one enterprise root CA in a Windows domain, but there can be only one enterprise root CA in any given hierarchy. All other CAs in the hierarchy are enterprise subordinate CAs.

An organization should install an enterprise CA if it will be issuing certificates to users or computers within the organization. It is not necessary to install a CA in every domain in the organization. Enterprise CAs have a special policy module that enforces how certificates are processed and issued. The policy information used by these modules is stored in Windows Active Directory. Note: An Active Directory and a DNS server must be running prior to installing an enterprise CA.

An organization that will be issuing certificates to users or computers outside the organization should install a stand-alone CA. There can be many stand-alone CAs, but there can only be one stand-alone CA per hierarchy. All other CAs in a hierarchy are either stand-alone subordinate CAs or enterprise subordinate CAs.

A stand-alone CA has a relatively simple default policy module and does not store any information remotely. Therefore, a stand-alone CA does not need to have Active Directory available.

A Root CA is at the top of a hierarchy of CAs and is self-certified. It should be highly secured and, if possible, taken offline to protect its certificate and keys. This way, if a child CA gets "compromised," the child can be disabled and the overall CA hierarchy is still intact; i.e., the Root CA still contains a clean list of certificates. It communicates with either issuing or intermediate CAs. A Subordinate CA is either an Intermediate or Issuing CA that must communicate with an intermediate or root CA to obtain information about certificates. Moreover a parent CA certifies a subordinate ("child") CA. A Certification Path is the trust chain from the certificate all the way up to the Root CA. Before the Certification Path works, the certificate of the Root CA must be placed in the Trusted Root Certification Authorities store. For security reasons, a Subordinate CA cannot have a certificate expire after a certificate higher up in the hierarchy expires.

When you want Internet users and their browsers to trust executable programs, ActiveX controls, and scripts on your website, you should obtain a Code Signing certificate with which to sign active content. Internet browsers may be configured at security levels that will not allow programs, controls and scripts to be downloaded unless they are signed. Internet users are more likely to trust a Code Signing certificate that was issued from a well-known commercial CA (such as VeriSign) than one that was distributed from your company's own CA. See figure 5.5.

Figure 5.5   When UserA presents a certificate to ServerA, ServerA verify UserA certificate with Subordinate CA3 and ServerA verifies Subordinate CA3 certificate with Root CA.

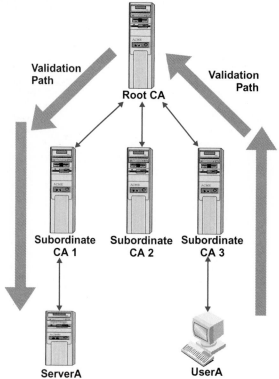

Other models include the bridge trust model, the mesh model, and the hybrid model. The bridge trust model is a peer-to-peer relationship between the root CAs. Each of the root CAs can communicate with each other, allowing cross certification. This allows a certification process to be established between organizations. The mesh model expands the concept of the bridge model by supporting multiple paths with multiple root CAs. Each of the root CAs has the ability to cross certify with the other root CAs in the mesh. A hybrid structure can mixes the capability of the other three.

5.5.2   Trust Lists

A certificate trust list (CTL) is a signed list of root certification authority certificates that an administrator considers reputable for designated purposes, such as client authentication or secure email. You will find embedded root certificates within web browsers. Unfortunately, CTL provides very weak trust compared to other models. For example, it cannot support a specific certificate policy and certification practice statements, and it does not support revocation of a certificate. See figure 5.6.

5.5.3   Managing Certificates

Nonrepudiation means the sender cannot deny the previous actions or message. If, for example, you encrypted the message with a private key, the only way the message can be decrypted properly is with the public key. So while the user would have, in fact, received the message, you still would have no way of verifying that the user is really who that user says he or she is and that the user is a valid user. PKI can solve this problem because it manages the public keys and issues certificates that verify the validity of the sender's message.

The certificate is then valid for use by the requester until its expiration date, at which point the certificate is automatically revoked. Private keys are typically stored in a secure location, possibly including hardware designed expressly for this purpose. If a key is lost, your PKI may allow for its retrieval via a process known as key recovery.

Figure 5.6 Trusted Root Certificates Found on a Browser

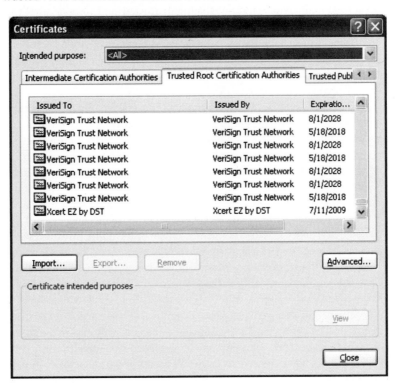

Renewal is the process of revalidating a certificate that has neared or passed its expiration date. There are two variations on certificate renewal, according to VeriSign:

- Use your current public key from your public/private key pair from the existing certificate
- Create and use a new public key that you provide from a newly created public/private key pair. This is essentially a new certificate.

If a certificate is not renewed before its expiration date, then it is considered to be expired and can no longer be relied upon.

You may have to revoke a certificate in situations in which an employee leaves a company, you suspect a private key has been compromised, you accidentally issued a certificate when you did not mean to, or a subscriber has not accepted the certificate within the required acceptance period after it has been issued. Revoked certificates are published in the **certification revocation list (CRL).**

Before trusting a party based on their digital certificate, you should check the status of the certificate to make sure that it is still valid and has not been revoked or expired. Often, if the status is anything other than valid, the status check response will list a reason for the current status, such as "compromise suspected."

Suspension of a certificate places a temporary hold on the validity of a digital certificate without causing irreversible revocation. If it later turns out that the certificate should still be considered valid after all, the suspension can be removed, and the certificate will once again be valid. Suspension can be accomplished by placing a digital certificate into a CRL with a suspended status and a reason code for that suspension. Just as it's generally unwise to trust the data in a revoked certificate, because it may or may not be valid, it's unwise to trust the data in a suspended certificate.

Recovery is the process of reacquiring a private key of your own that has been lost (because of disaster, hardware failure, a personal mistake, etc.), or someone else's private key that you are authorized to possess (perhaps because it is required for a business function or law enforcement investigation).

Another issue around key recovery involves who is authorized to do it. Giving someone key recovery privileges implies that that person is being given the ability to obtain anyone's keys, decrypt any private messages, and perhaps even digitally sign messages with others' identity. Therefore, personnel given this privilege should be highly trusted, and appropriate record-keeping methods should be in effect to help ensure that this privilege is not abused.

Because of the significant exposure presented by a single person having key recovery privileges, organizations have come up with a variety of ways to see that the cooperation of multiple staffers is required to recover a key. This is implemented differently depending on the key escrow system used, but usually involves some degree of "M of N" control

M of N control is a policy of dividing up a task among multiple entities so that no one person acting alone can perform the entire task. As stated above, it is used to help minimize an organization's exposure to the risk of one person misusing a privilege, and performing a sensitive action like key recovery without authorization. One simple approach to M of N control might be to double-encrypt the database of keys, such that two staffers, each assigned one of the keys to the database, are required in order to obtain someone's private key.

M of N control is also provided by some hardware-based key recovery systems, such as the smart-card based KEON KRM (Key Recovery Module) by RSA to control the private key used for key recovery. Each entity is issued some percentage of the entire private key used for recovery, in the form of a token. In order to perform a key recovery, some number of these entities (M) out of the (N) to whom a portion of the recovery key was distributed, must come together and combine their key fragments. This adds additional security to the key recovery process and minimizes opportunities for abuse of Key Recovery Operator privileges.

Destruction refers to the permanent removal of a key or certificate that you no longer need. This is accomplished by destroying the private key and any certificates. In the case of public keys, they tend to be difficult to destroy since they are sometimes passed around indiscriminately. However, if the private key is destroyed, it is not necessary to destroy all copies of the public key, since, because of the way asymmetric cryptography works, no compromise of information will be possible without the other half of the key pair.

Conventional hierarchical PKI uses a single key pair: one public key and one private key. According to VeriSign, "Key Pairs are used for one or more of three basic purposes: encryption, authentication and nonrepudiation." A single key used for multiple purposes violates nonrepudiation. RSA recommends that you assign two key pairs per person, one key pair for signing messages, providing authentication and nonrepudiation, and a second key pair for encryption. This allows someone to recover the encryption key and decrypt documents that were encrypted using it, without their gaining the ability to sign documents with that user's private key as well, which could lead to forgery and violation of nonrepudiation).

With a single key pair, this protection is not available. When a single key pair is used, key recovery gives the individual recovering the key the ability to masquerade as the user whose key was recovered, if desired, in addition to allowing him or her to encrypt/decrypt communications from and to that user.

Since an organization already has to have infrastructure in place to manage a single set of keys, it's generally not that much more difficult, from an administrative point of view, to add a second set of keys for each user (as long as any key management software/hardware used supports this). Because of the low incremental cost and the potential value of implementing a PKI with dual key pairs, it's something to consider.

5.5.4   Certificate Policies

Two important elements associated with a PKI are the Certificate Policy (CP) and the Certification Practice Statement (CPS). The CP and CPS must be formalized within an organization to ensure a level of trust beyond the organization. Although both documents are similar in format, they each have a separate, distinct purpose.

The **Certificate Policy (CP)** is a very broad, high-level security policy that provides the basis for issuing and use of certificates. A CP needs to identify which CAs are acceptable, how certificates are used, and how they are issued. CPs are defined in the X.509 standard as "a named set of rules that indicates the applicability of a certificate to a particular community and/or class of application with common security requirements" and are fully described in RFC 2527. The CP is represented by an Object Identifier (OID) in the X.509 Version 3 digital certificate.

Certification Practice Statements (CPSs) provide the process through which certificates are issued, maintained, and revoked by a Certification Authority. A CPS is generally more detailed than a CP.

You can think of Certificate Policies as analogous to policies and standards and Certification Practice Statements as analogous to procedures. The CPS tells what must be done by the CA, while the CPS tells how it will be done by the CA.

5.6   OPERATING SYSTEM AUTHENTICATION

Today's modern network operating systems use a wide range of authentication systems. Some of these even allow you to select between different authentication systems. UNIX and Linux use the Data Encryption Standard to encrypt passwords and older Windows servers use NTLM. One of the more popular authentication systems is Challenge Handshake Authentication Protocol (CHAP) and Kerberos. Note: CHAP will be discussed in chapter 9.

5.6.1   UNIX and Linux Logins

When you first enter the password in UNIX or Linux, the password is encrypted in a way that it cannot be decrypted. When a person logs in, the password is entered, and it is encrypted in the same way. It is then compared to the stored encrypted password to see if they match. If they match, the user is allowed access to the system. So in reality, the operating system does not really know the password but only the encrypted form of the password.

In UNIX, the password is encrypted by default using the AT&T-developed (and National Security Agency-approved) algorithm called Data Encryption Standard (DES). Unfortunately, until recently, the U.S. government banned export of DES outside of the United States.

FreeBSD had to find a way to both comply with U.S. law and retain compatibility with all the other UNIX variants that still used DES. The solution was to divide up the encryption libraries so that U.S. users could install the DES libraries and use DES, but international users still had an encryption method that could be exported abroad. This is how FreeBSD came to use MD5 as its default encryption method. MD5 is similar to DES and is believed to be a bit more secure, so installing DES is offered primarily for compatibility reasons. While DES passwords are limited to 8 characters, MD5 allows passwords to be as long as 256 characters.

It is pretty easy to identify which encryption method FreeBSD is set up to use. Examining the encrypted passwords in the /etc/passwd file is one way. Passwords encrypted with the MD5 hash are longer than those encrypted with the DES hash and also begin with the characters 1. DES password strings do not have any particular identifying characteristics, but they are shorter than MD5 passwords and are coded in a 64-character alphabet, which does not include the $ character, so a relatively short string which does not begin with a dollar sign is very likely a DES password. When created, user accounts are placed in the file/etc/passwd file. Although administrators often use tools to avoid editing this file directly, it is important to be familiar with the file as part of system maintenance.

The syntax of an entry in the /etc/passwd file is:

```
username:password:UID:GUID:name:home:shellUser
```

If the password entry is an "x," it means that shadow passwords are in use, and that the user's password is stored in /etc/shadow. If the account does not have a password at all, it will be indicated with an asterisk (*). This is typically used for daemons and system programs such as shutdown. If the password is series of characters, then the password is encrypted into /etc/passwd. Note: Do not edit this password manually. Instead, use the passwd command instead.

The name entry is the real name assigned to the user. Since the username is not always intuitive to others, the name entry is used often by programs to display the user's name.

The shell entry is the path to the shell used by default for this account. The default for Linux is /bin/bash unless the administrator uses a custom shell instead of the general user.

Traditionally, Unix and Linux systems have stored passwords and other account information in an encrypted form in a file called /etc/passwd. Various tools need access to this file for non-password information, so it needs to be readable to all users. Shadow passwords take the encrypted password entries that were removed from the password file and placed in a separate file called shadow. This way, the regular password file would continue to be readable by all users on the system, and the actual encrypted password entries would be readable only by the root user (the login prompt is run with root permission). Note: During the installation of Red Hat Linux, shadow password protection for your system is enabled by default, as are MD5 passwords.

Shadow passwords offer a few distinct advantages over the previous standard of storing passwords on UNIX and Linux systems, including:

- Improved system security by moving the encrypted passwords (normally found in `/etc/passwd`) to `/etc/shadow`, which is readable only by root.
- Information concerning password aging (how long it has been since a password was last changed).
- Control over how long a password can remain unchanged before the user is required to change it.
- The ability to use the `/etc/login.defs` file to enforce a security policy, especially concerning password aging.

If you did not enable shadow passwords and your version of Linux supports shadow passwords, you can convert your regular passwords to shadow passwords by using the `pwconv` program. If you have a need to convert the shadow passwords to regular passwords, you would use the `pwunconv` command.

If shadow passwords are enabled on the system, the `/etc/shadow` contains the password information. The syntax for the `/etc/ shadow` file is:

```
username:password:lchange:mchange:change:wchange:disable:expire:
system
```

The lchange is the number of days since January 1, 1970, since the password was last changed. Mchange is the number of days before the password can be changed again. This value is set to zero by default. Change is the number of days until the password must be changed. Wchange is the number of days before the password is set to expire that the system will begin warning the user to change the password.

Once the password reaches the time when it must be changed, the disable value is the count of days before the account is automatically disabled if the password is not changed. Expire is the count of days since January 1, 1970, which equates to the date the account is to expire. System is reserved for the system.

5.6.2   Pluggable Authentication Modules for Linux

Some distributions include newer versions of Red Hat Linux ship with a united authentication scheme called **Pluggable Authentication Modules (PAM)** for Linux. PAM allows you to change your authentication methods and requirements on the fly, and encapsulate all local authentication methods without recompiling any of your programs.

Originally, the PAM configuration file was `/etc/pam.conf` but more recent versions of PAM use a separate file for each PAM-using program, in the directory `/etc/pam.d`. Having separate files for each program prevents misconfigurations in one program from affecting others. In addition, the service name of every PAM-enabled application is the name of its configuration file in the `/etc/pam.d`. Each program that uses PAM defines its own service name.

PAM includes four different types of modules for controlling access to a particular service:

- An auth module provides the actual authentication (perhaps asking for and checking a password) and sets credentials, such as group membership or Kerberos tickets.
- An account module checks to make sure that access is allowed for the user (the account has not expired, the user is allowed to log in at this time of day, and so on).
- A password module is used to set passwords.
- A session module is used after a user has been authenticated. A session module performs additional tasks which are needed to allow access.

These modules may be stacked, or placed upon one another, so that multiple modules are used. The order of a module stack is very important in the authentication process, because it makes it very easy for an administrator to require that several conditions exist before allowing user authentication to occur.

For more information on Configuring PAM, be sure to take a look at the following websites:

PAM website

http://www.kernel.org/pub/linux/libs/pam/index.html

The Linux-PAM System Administrator's Guide

http://www.kernel.org/pub/linux/libs/pam/Linux-PAM-html/pam.html

5.6.3   LAN Manager and NTLM Authentication

To authenticate a user name and password, Windows can use either LAN Manager, NTLM, or Kerberos. Kerberos V5 is the default in a Windows 2000 or Windows Server 2003 environment, while NTLM authentication is used with earlier Windows operating systems such as Windows 9X or Windows NT, Windows 2000 and Windows Server 2003 provide NTLM authentication for backward compatibility.

LAN Manager authentication was developed to connect computers running MS-DOS, IBM OS/2, and UNIX operating systems, and it was the first Windows authentication used only when connecting to shared folders on computers running Microsoft Windows for Workgroups, Windows 95, Windows 98, and Windows Me. The LanMan password representation is extremely weak and can be easily cracked. No matter how complex and obscure your password is, an attacker can crack it in no time because of the incredibly feeble encryption used to formulate the LanMan hash.

To significantly improve your security, your best bet is to eliminate the LanMan hashes altogether.

■ On Windows 2000 and Windows Server 2003, you can accomplish this by creating the registry key:

    `HKEY_LOCAL_MACHINE\System\CurentControlSet\Control\LSA\NoLMHash`.

■ On Windows XP, use regedit to create the registry key:

    `HKEY_LOCAL\_MACHINE\System\CurrentControlSet\Control\Lsa\NoLMHash`
    as a `"REG_DWORD—Number"` and give it the value of 1.

Note that these registry entries only stop the creation of new LanMan hashes when user passwords are changed. Your current LanMan hashes will still hang around until your users select new passwords. Of course, when you disable LanMan hashes, Windows will not operate in Windows 9X. You can install Directory Services client to upgrade Windows 9X authentication to NTLM version 2 and install Service Pack 4 or greater to provide compatibility with Windows NT. You should also install the latest version of Microsoft Internet Explorer to support 128-bit encryption.

In **NTLM authentication,** the client selects a string of bytes, uses the password to perform a one-way encryption of the string, and sends both the original string and the encrypted one to the server. The server receives the original string and uses the password from the account database to perform the same one-way encryption. If the result matches the encrypted string sent by the client, the server concludes that the client knows the username/password pair.

NTLM authentication is more secure than LAN Manager authentication. It uses 14-character passwords and 56-bit encryption to increase the difficulty of acquiring a password in a brute-force attack. However, NTLM authentication is still not secure enough to withstand a concerted decryption attack. NTLM version 2 increases the security of NTLM encryption by using 128-bit encryption, which provides enough security to make brute-force attacks impractical with today's technology. Dictionary attacks can still be successful, so passwords must be strong enough to avoid compromise.

5.6.4   Kerberos Authentication

Security+ Objective 1.2.1—Kerberos

Kerberos, named after the three-headed dog that guards the entrance in Hades in Greek mythology, is an authentication service developed at MIT for the TCP/IP network. Its purpose is to allow users and services to authenticate themselves to each other without allowing other users to capture the network packet on the network and to resend it so that they can be authenticated over an insecure media such as the Internet. Therefore, Kerberos provides strong authentication for client/server applications by using symmetric secret-key cryptography, but it does not send the user's password across the network, in encrypted or unencrypted form. Instead, the key is used to encrypt information exchanged between the client and server. After a client and server have used Kerberos to prove their identities, they can also encrypt all of their communications to assure privacy and data integrity as they go about their business.

When a user signs onto the local operating system, a local agent or process sends an authentication request to the Kerberos server. The server responds by sending the encrypted credentials for the user attempting to sign on the system. The local agent then tries to decrypt the credentials using the user-supplied password. If the correct password has been supplied, the user is validated and given

Figure 5.7   When a user requests a service from a server, the user is authenticated by the KDC.

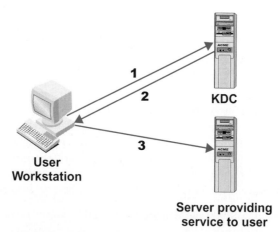

User Workstation

KDC

Server providing service to user

1. User requests access to service running on a different server.
2. KDC authenticates user and sends a ticket to be used between the user and the service on the server.
3. User's workstation sends ticket to service to authenticate and use the requested service.

authentication tickets, which allow the user to access other Kerberos authenticated services. In addition to the tickets, the user is also given a set of cipher keys that can be used to encrypt all data during the sessions so that it doesn't have to reauthenticate each time the user requests access to a new network resource. See figure 5.7. For more detailed explanation of the Kerberos process, see the following material.

The following are some of the definitions used in Kerberos authentication:

- **Realm**—An organizational boundary that is formed to provide authentication boundaries. Each realm has an authentication server (AS) and a ticket-granting server (TGS). Together the AS and TGS form a Key Distribution Center (KDC). All services and users in the realm receive tickets from the TGS and are authenticated with the AS. This provides a single source of authority to register and authenticate with.

- **Key Distribution Center (KDC)**—The authentication server (AS) and ticket-granting server (TGS) that contains the information that allows Kerberos clients to authenticate.

- **Authentication server (AS)**—In a Kerberos realm, the AS is the server that registers all valid users (clients) and services in the realm. The AS provides each client a ticket-granting ticket (TGT) that is used to request a ticket from the TGS.

- **Ticket-granting server (TGS)**—To minimize the workload of the AS in a Kerberos realm, the TGS grants the session tickets used by clients to start a session with a service. The client must use the TGT issued by the AS to request a session ticket from a TGS.

- **Ticket**—A ticket is a block of data that allows users to prove their identity to a service. Each ticket is stored in a ticket cache on the user's local computer and is time stamped, so after a given amount of time (typically 10 hours), the ticket expires and is no longer valid. Limiting the length of time a ticket is valid reduces the chances of a hacker obtaining a ticket and being able to use it for unauthorized access.

- **Ticket-granting ticket (TGT)**—A TGT is a ticket that is granted as part of the Kerberos authenticated process and is stored in the ticket cache. The TGT is used to obtain other tickets that are specific to a service. For example, if a user wanted to gain access to a specific service, his or her TGT would be used in a negotiation process to get the additional ticket. Each service requires its own ticket.

- **Authenticators**—A series of bits, a symbol, or a group of symbols that are inserted into a transmission or message in a predetermined manner and are then used for validation. Authenticators are typically valid for five minutes, and an authenticator can only be used once. This helps prevents someone from intercepting an authenticator and then reusing it.

- **Principal**—A principal is any unique entity to which Kerberos can assign tickets.

To get the initial Kerberos ticket, the user must authenticate him- or herself when logging into the network. Therefore, the user will be prompted for the username and password. The client computer will first send the username to the server. The server checks to see if the user is listed in the security data-base on an authentication server. If the username is valid, a random session key and a ticket consisting of the client's name, the name of the ticket-granting server, the current time, a lifetime of the ticket, the client's IP address, and the random session key is generated. The ticket and random session key en-crypted with the user's password is sent back to the client.

Once the response has been received by the client, the password is converted to a key and is used to decrypt the response from the authentication server. The ticket and the session key are stored for future use, and the user's password and key are erased from memory.

To gain access to the server, the client builds an authenticator for the desired server. The applica-tion builds an authenticator containing the client's name, the IP address, and current time, which is en-crypted with the session key and the ticket for the server and sent to the server. Once the authenticator and ticket have been received by the server, the server decrypts the ticket, uses the session key included in the ticket to decrypt the authenticator, compares the information in the ticket with that in the au-thenticator, the IP address from which the request was received, and the present time. If everything matches, it allows the request to proceed.

If the client specifies that it wants the server to prove its identity, too (mutual authentication), the server adds one of the timestamps the client sent in the authenticator, encrypts the result in the session key, and sends the result back to the client. At the end of the exchange, the server is certain that the client is who it says it is. If mutual authentication occurs, the client is also convinced that the server is au-thentic. Moreover, the client and server share a key, which no one else knows, and they can safely as-sume that a reasonable recent message encrypted in that key originated with the other party.

When a program requires a ticket to access a network service, it sends a request to the ticket-granting server. The request contains the name of the server for which a ticket is requested, along with the ticket-granting ticket and the authenticator. The ticket-granting server then checks the authenticator and ticket-granting ticket. If it is valid, the ticket-granting server generates a new random session key to be used between the client and the new server. It then builds a ticket for the new server containing the client's name, the server name, the current time, the client's IP address, and the new session key it just generated.

The ticket-granting server then sends the ticket, along with the session key and other information, back to the client. This time, however, the reply is encrypted in the session key that was part of the ticket-granting ticket. Of course, this ticket is only good for that service at that server.

During the entire process, the AS creates two session keys. These session keys are temporary in du-ration, lasting only as long as that session lasts. One of the session keys for the user's connection with the ticket-granting service, as well as an expiration date, is included in the ticket. The AS retains the other session key. Distributing the keys in this manner allows both sides of the session to communicate with each other in a secure, encrypted fashion, if desired. In addition, Kerberos is dependent on each system having the correct date and time. Therefore, it is recommended that you use a time server to make sure servers and clients have the correct time.

As you can see, throughout the entire process of getting authentication, the password was never sent on the wire. Therefore, a packet that contains the password cannot be compromised. In addition, many of these tickets and requests are timestamped, to keep track of when the packet was made so that pack-ets are not captured and resent at a later time. The encryption algorithm is different for every client. Lastly, Kerberos assumes the use of a strong password, since it employs conventional encryption mechanisms.

A server decides whether to let a remote access client connect after evaluating the client's creden-tials, accepting a connection only after authenticating and authorizing the client attempt. Authentica-tion is the process of verifying a client's credentials. A client uses an authentication protocol to send either encrypted or unencrypted credentials to the server, depending on the protocol.

Lastly, since Kerberos is scalable enough to operate on the Internet, it can be used as an authentica-tion mechanism on the Internet and other heterogeneous environments. Cross-realm authentication is the capability of users in one realm to be authenticated and access services in another realm. This is accom-plished by the user's realm registering a remote ticket-granting server on the real of the service. Rather than having each realm authenticate with each other, cross-realm authentication can be configured in a hierar-chical fashion. While this eases authentication for the AS and TGS, it might force the client to contact sev-eral remote ticket-granting server to access a service. Note: Kerberos uses TCP port 88 and UDP port 88. When performing authentication across a router boundary, you may need to open those ports on the router.

5.7   IPSEC

Security+ Objective 2.1.7—IPSEC

IP Security, more commonly known as **IPSec,** is a protocol that provides data integrity, authentication and privacy to data being sent from one point to another point. IPSec works at the IP level and works transparently to protect the data from end-to-end. Besides being used to create virtual tunnels over an insecure network such as the Internet, it will be built into IPv6 and it is recommended to be used with wireless technology since the airways transmissions can be easily captured. IPSec is documented in a series of Internet RFCs; the overall IPSec implementation is guided by "Security Architecture for the Internet Protocol," RFC 2401.

IPSec is not a single protocol, but a suite of protocols that can provide either message authentication and/or encryption. IPSec defines a new set of headers to be added to IP datagrams. These new headers are placed after the IP header and before the Layer 4 protocol (typically TCP or UDP). The new protocols/headers that provide information for securing the payload of the IP packet are the authentication header (AH) and the encapsulating security payload (ESP).

While AH and ESP provide the means to protect data from tampering, preventing eavesdropping, and verifying the origin of the data, it is the Internet Key Exchange (IKE), which defines the method for the secure exchange of the initial encryption keys between the two endpoints. IKE allows nodes to agree on authentication methods, encryption methods, the keys to use and the keys' lifespans.

Each pair of hosts communicating with an IPSec session must establish a **security association (SA),** which is negotiated by IKE. The SA is like a contract laying out the rules of the connection for the duration of the SA. An SA is assigned a 32-bit number that, when used in conjunction with the destination IP address and the Security Protocol ID (AH or ESP), uniquely identifies the SA. This number is called the Security Parameters Index or SPI.

Since an SA is a one-way connection between two communicating parties, two SAs are required for each pair of communicating hosts. Additionally, each SA only supports a single protocol (AH or ESP). Thus, if both AH and ESP are used between two communicating hosts, a total of four SAs is required.

Perfect Forward Secrecy (PFS) ensures that no part of a previous encryption key plays a part in generating a new encryption key. This basically means that when a new encryption key is generated, the old key does not play any part in the generation of the new key. Under normal circumstances, for performance reasons, an old key will play a part in generating a new key. When using PFS, this requires a little more overhead, as it requires reauthentication every time a new key is generated.

When the **authentication header (AH)** is added to an IP datagram, the header will ensure the integrity and authenticity of the data, including the fields in the outer IP header. It does not provide confidentiality protection. Thus, while AH provides a method for ensuring the integrity of the packet, it does nothing for keeping its contents secret. In addition, while it provides a mechanism to ensure the integrity of the IP header and the payload of the IP packet that will be transported across an untrusted link, such as the Internet, when used by itself, AH cannot provide a total guarantee of the entire IP header because some of the fields in the IP header are changed by routers as the packet passes through the network. For a truly secure connection, you should use ESP.

AH uses a keyed-hash function rather than digital signatures, because digital signature technology is too slow and would greatly reduce network throughput. If any part of the datagram is changed during transit, this will be detected by the receiver when it performs the same one-way hash function on the datagram and compares the value of the message digest that the sender has supplied. The fact that the one-way hash also involves the use of a secret shared between the two systems means that authenticity can be guaranteed. In addition, AH may also enforce anti-replay protection by requiring that a receiving host set the replay bit in the header to indicate that the packet has been seen. Without it, an attacker may be able to resend the same packet many times.

When added to an IP datagram, the **Encapsulating Security Payload (ESP)** header protects the confidentiality, integrity, and authenticity of the data by performing encryption at the IP packet layer. While the default algorithm for IPSec is 56-bit DES, it does support a variety of symmetric encryption algorithms so that it can provide interoperability among different IPSec products.

ESP operates in two modes:

■ Transport   ■ Tunnel

When used in transport mode, the ESP header is placed between the IP header and the upper-level (transport layer) header, encrypting only the transport layer header and the data portion of the packet. Since the IP header is not encrypted, it shows the actual destination address of the encapsulated datagram, and it can be used with non-IPSec-enabled routers. You would typically use this for encrypting the contents of the IP packet on network connections of limited bandwidth. At the receiving end of the communication path, this clear text header information is saved, the contents of the encrypted packet are decrypted and reassembled with the correct IP header information, and the packet is sent on its way onto the network. It can also be useful for remote users who need to connect to the corporate network via public networks. However, this use is generally not transparent to the client system, because of the need for IPSec to be installed and properly configured on the client. Note: If you want to protect the integrity of the IP header, ESP can be used in conjunction with AH to protect the integrity of the IP header information.

When operating in tunnel mode, ESP is used between two IPSec gateways, such as a set of routers or firewalls. When used in tunnel mode, the ESP header information is inserted directly before the IP or other protocol datagram that is to be protected. Therefore, the entire IP datagram, including the IP header (which has the true source address and destination address) and its payload (usually the upper-level protocol such as TCP or UPD), is encrypted and encapsulated by the ESP protocol. At the destination gateway, this outer wrapper of information is removed, the contents of the packet are decrypted, and the original IP packet is sent out onto the network to which the gateway is attached. This way, the internals of the network are hidden from would-be hackers.

The datagram being protected is encrypted (according to the methods set up by the SA), and additional headers are added in clear text format so that the new IP datagram can be transported to the appropriate gateway. In other words, the original protocol datagram is encrypted, the ESP header is added, and finally, a new IP datagram is created to transport this conglomeration to its destination gateway point. At the receiving gateway, this outer IP header information is stripped off, and according to the parameters defined by the SA, the protected payload of original datagram is decrypted.

ESP uses both a header and a trailer to encapsulate datagrams that it protects. The header consists of an SPI, which is used to identify the security association, and a sequence number to identify the packets, ensure they arrive in the correct order, and to ensure that no duplicate packets are received. The trailer consists of padding from 0 to 255 bytes to make sure that the datagram ends on a 32-bit boundary. This is followed by a field that specifies the length of the padding that was attached so that it can be removed by the receiver. Following this field is a Next Header field, which is used to identify the protocol that is enveloped as the payload.

Additionally, ESP can include an authentication trailer that contains data used to verify the identity of the sender and the integrity of the message. This Integrity Check Value (ICV) is calculated based on the ESP header information, as well as the payload and the ESP trailer. The layout of an ESP datagram is shown in figure 5.8.

AH and ESP can be used independently or together, although for most applications, one of them is sufficient. IPSec also uses other existing encryption standards to make up a protocol suite.

Any routers or switches in the data path between the communicating hosts will simply forward the encrypted and/or authenticated IP packets to their destination. However, if there is a firewall or filtering router, IP forwarding must be enabled for the following IP protocols and UDP port for IPSec to function:

- IPSec uses TCP port 1293 and UDP port 1293.
- **IP Protocol ID of 51**—Both inbound and outbound filters should be set to pass AH traffic.

Figure 5.8   ESP Datagram

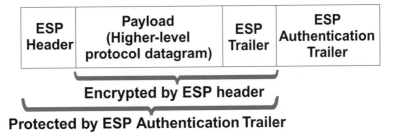

- **IP Protocol ID of 50**—Both inbound and outbound filters should be set to pass ESP traffic.
- **UDP Port 500**—Both inbound and outbound filters should be set to pass ISAKMP traffic. When a NAT is involved, it may use port 4500 instead.

Until recently, IPSec had some issues working with Network Address Translation (NAT). Transport mode IPSec provides end-to-end security between hosts, while tunnel mode protects encapsulated IP packets between security gateways, for example, between two firewalls or between a roaming host and a remote access server. When TCP or UDP are involved, as they are in transport mode ESP, since NAT modifies the TCP/UDP packet, NAT must also recalculate the checksum used to verify integrity. If NAT updates the checksum, ESP authentication will fail. If NAT does not update the checksum, TCP/UDP verification will fail. If the transport endpoint were under your control, you might be able to turn off checksums. To summarize, ESP can pass through NAT in tunnel mode, or in transport mode with checksums disabled or ignored by the receiver.

IPSec and NAT can function together when NAT occurs before the packet is encrypted. This typically works fine in gateway-to-gateway communications, remote access solutions are problematic because IPSec VPN client on a remote laptop computer will encrypt the packet before it travels to the NAT device, subsequently breaking the IPSec VPN connection.

To enable IPSec VPNs to work with NAT devices, some of the leading technology companies created NAT Traversal. The main technology behind this solution is UDP encapsulation, wherein the IPSec packet is wrapped inside a UDP/IP header, allowing NAT devices to change IP or port addresses without modifying the IPSec packet.

For NAT Traversal to work properly, two things must occur. First the communicating VPN devices must support the same method of UDP encapsulation. Second, all NAT devices along the communication path must be identified.

According to the IETF draft standard, IPSec devices will exchange a specific, known value to determine whether or not they both support NAT Traversal. If the two VPN devices agree on NAT Traversal, they next determine whether or not NAT or NAPT occurs anywhere on the communications path between them. NAT devices are determined by sending NAT-D (NAT Discovery) packets. Both endpoints send hashes of the source and destination IP addresses and ports of which they are aware. If these hashes do not match, indicating that the IP address and ports are not the same, then the VPN devices know a NAT device exists somewhere in between.

Usually, NAT assignments last for a short period of time and are then released. For IPSec to work properly, the same NAT assignment needs to remain intact for the duration of the VPN tunnel. NAT Traversal accomplishes this by requiring any endpoint communicating through a NAT device to send a "keepalive" packet, which is a 1-byte UDP packet sent periodically to prevent NAT endpoints from being remapped midsession.

All NAT Traversal communications occur over UDP port 500. This works great because port 500 is already open for IKE (Internet Key Exchange) communications in IPSec VPNs, so new holes do not need to be opened in the corporate firewall. This solution does add a bit of overhead to IPSec communications; namely, 200 bytes are added for the Phase 1 IKE negotiation, and each IPSec packet has about an additional 20 bytes.

5.8   PROTECTING AGAINST PASSWORDS AND ENCRYPTION HACKING

Security+ Objective 1.4—Attacks

Security+ Objective 1.4.11—Password Guessing

Earlier we showed the importance of keeping passwords safe. Most users have more than just one password. As a result, users' memories are taxed, seldom-used systems tend to forget their password, and passwords are forgotten after lengthy vacations, illnesses, or business trips. You would be amazed by how many users use their name, loved-one's names, birthdays, favorite sport team or music band, favorite place or pet's name. In many instances, people also write down their password near their computer.

In addition, many users never change their password. If given enough time, any password can be cracked, either by having someone looking over someone's shoulder, guessing, or by using hacking techniques.

5.8.1   Cracking Passwords

As discussed in this chapter and chapter 4, passwords are generally stored in files or databases ready to be compared with the value entered by a user. To protect the passwords against disclosure by anyone who can obtain a copy of the file or database (such as the passwd or shadow files used in Linux or the SAM database used in Windows), the passwords are generally stored in an encrypted form or by using a mathematical hashing algorithm. If a person can get physical access to the server that holds the password, that person can easily get hold of these passwords. In addition, these files or database can be accessed remotely.

Passwords are also sent over the network, either in clear text such as in telnet or FTP, or in an encrypted form. Both of these passwords can be captured using a protocol analyzer. Brute force is commonly used to "crack" passwords, often for user accounts. It can also be applied to ZIP files and many other types of encrypted data.

Security+ Objective 1.4.11.1—Brute Force

Security+ Objective 1.4.11.2—Dictionary

When a password is not encrypted, you don't have to decrypt the password to determine the password. When the password is encrypted, you will have to decrypt the password. If you have a copy of the file or database or the encrypted password, you can then use one of the following methods to figure out what the password is:

- Dictionary attacks
- Brute force attacks

Both of these attacks are based on trial and error. You try a password. Assuming that you know the password-hashing algorithm such as DES, you perform the password-hashing algorithm on the password and compare it to the encrypted password that you are trying to crack. If two hash values are the same, the password you tried was the correct one. If not, you try another password.

Dictionary attacks are mounted by encrypting a dictionary or words so as to produce all the possible encrypted forms of each word. A simple comparison program then compares the encrypted form of the password file against the encrypted entry from the dictionary. A match indicates the corresponding plaintext of the dictionary entry is the password. Some dictionary lists also use foreign words and propend and append special characters and letters to dictionary words, or even make common numeric or symbol substitutions for letters such as 0 for o and ! for I or L, when trying to determine a password.

While you think that a dictionary attack would be complete, it does not contain every combination of possible characters. **Brute force** attacks attempt to crack the password by trying every possible value. They tend to proceed from A to Z. If the system includes digits and uses both upper- and lowercase combinations, it will also have to include those combinations.

Lastly, the dictionary attack and brute force can also be applied to break the encryption on encrypted files such as encrypted ZIP files. Since they already have a copy of the file, a program will use the dictionary or brute force attack by trying each password until it has decrypted the password.

If an attacker attempts to guess the password for a user account, and is using a password policy that locks account after a set number of failed attempts, the attack can become a DoS attack. If it is a user account, the user is will not be able to log in until the account is unlocked. If it is a service account, such as those that automatically back up servers, the service account cannot perform its job.

Security+ Objective 1.4.10—Birthday

Another type of brute force attack is the **birthday attack,** which is based on statistics. Since there are 365 days per year, it would take 183 people in a single room for a more than 50 percent chance that one of them has the same birthday as you. But it would require only 23 people for there to be a more than even chance that at least two share the same birthday. So you are probably trying to figure out how this relates to decrypting a password or file. A birthday attack is a specific kind of brute force attack that takes advantage of the fact that multiple sets of source data can encrypt to the same hash value. For example, it could be used to find another message that would encrypt to the same MD5 hash value associated with an original message. Theoretically, this would let an attacker change the contents of the message. A birthday attack is an example of attack targeted at the key.

Security+ Objective 1.4.7—Weak Keys

Security+ Objective 1.4.8—Mathematical

So how do you thwart these types of attacks? Of course, if you have control of the encryption algorithm, you want to choose an algorithm that has a long key. While 40-bit and 56-bit keys are considered short keys, 128-bits are considered long keys. In addition, using long passwords and using strong passwords help.

Mathematical attacks are attacks that are based on the fact that a key is generally easier to break the shorter it is, and the less the variety in characters used in the key, than those that somehow "break" an encryption algorithm by finding a way to reverse it without discovering the original key. It has already been stated that a long key is better than a short key because the longer the key, the more possible combinations that you need to try before you find the correct key value using brute force. But with the key length, you also need to look at it mathematically. For example, if a key doesn't use every combination, then when a program is trying brute force, it doesn't have to try as many combinations. Lastly, another factor in the security of a key is the randomness of a key. The security of the key will be useless if a pattern can be figured on what the next key would be.

For example, if you have a 56-bit key and a 128-bit key and someone is trying to figure out the key from a message, the person will have to try more combinations before coming across the correct key that makes the encrypted message meaningful. For example, a 56-bit key could be broken in 1,142 years with today's desktop computer. Of course, if multiple processors and multiple computers work together, the key could be discovered much faster. See table 5.2.

Since it takes time to use a dictionary or brute force attack, if you occasionally change your passwords, you would make the previous captured password invalid. You should also have some form of password policy that will limit the number of login attempts before the account is disabled. You need to physically secure your server that holds the passwords and secure the password files or databases so that

Table 5.2   Average Time Required for Exhaustive Key Search

Key Size	Total Number of Keys Available	Time Required to Break at 1 Encryption per $1\mu s$	Time Required to Break at 10^6 Encryption per $1\mu s$
32-bits	$2^{32} = 4.3 \times 10^9$	35.8 minutes	2.14 milliseconds
56-bits	$2^{56} = 7.2 \times 10^{16}$	1,142 years	10.01 hours
128-bits	$2^{128} = 3.4 \times 10^{38}$	5.4×10^{24} years	5.4×10^{18} years
168-bits	$2^{168} = 3.7 \times 10^{50}$	5.9×10^{36} years	5.9×10^{30} years
6 characters[1]	$36^6 = 2.18 \times 10^9$	36.3 minutes	2.20 milliseconds
8 characters[1]	$36^8 = 2.82 \times 10^{12}$	783.6 hours	2.82 seconds
14 characters[1]	$36^{14} = 6.14 \times 10^{21}$	1.9×10^8 years	190 years
6 characters[2]	$94^6 = 6.90 \times 10^{11}$	191.6 hours	690 milliseconds
8 characters[2]	$94^8 = 6.10 \times 10^{15}$	193.3 years	1.69 hours
14 characters[2]	$94^{14} = 4.21 \times 10^{27}$	1.33×10^{14} years	1.33×10^8 years

[1]Based on 36 different characters [Characters (A–Z) and digits (0–9)]
[2]Based on 94 different characters [uppercase characters (A–Z), lower case characters (a–z), digits (0–9) and symbols ('~!@#$%^&*()_+−={}|[]\:";'<>?,./)]

people cannot copy them. If you have encrypted files, you will need to secure those files so that hackers cannot get hold of them to begin with. Lastly, you need to actively look for signs of people trying to hack a password such as looking for patterns in failed login attempts. Of course, another way to thwart password guessing is not to use passwords. Instead use smart cards with a personal pin number or a biometric identifier.

5.8.2   Key Logging Program

A key logging program is a program that invisibly records every keystroke on a computer, stores the keystrokes in a file, and sends the file to a predefined email address. Therefore, every time that you visit a website and type in a username and password or you access a network resource that requires a password, it will record what you type in.

A key logging program is installed by someone without your knowledge, installed by you in the form of a Trojan virus or as an attachment of an email. To protect your system from a key logging program, use antivirus software that can detect such software. In addition, physically secure your computer so that only authorized personnel can approach your system and install applications. Lastly, document the system's state with applications, such as Tripwire, which can verify if system files have been altered from their original state.

WHAT YOU NEED TO KNOW

Security+ Objective 1.2—Authentication

Security+ Objective 4.2.3—Authentication
1. Authentication is the process by which the system validates the user's logon information.
2. Users must be able to prove their identity to those with whom they communicate and must be able to verify the identity of others.
3. A user who logs on with a valid user ID and password combination is considered an authenticated user.
4. Authentication requires a user to provide some proof or credential that represents proving what you know, showing what you have, demonstrating who you are or identifying where you are before allowing access to your company's resources.

Security+ Objective 1.2.1—Kerberos
1. Kerberos is an authentication service developed at MIT for the TCP/IP network.
2. Its purpose is to allow users and services to authenticate themselves to each other without allowing other users to capture the network packet on the network, and to resend it so that they can be authenticated over an insecure media such as the Internet.
3. Therefore, Kerberos provides strong authentication for client/server applications by using symmetric secret-key cryptography, but it does not send the user's password across the network, in encrypted or unencrypted form. Instead, the key is used to encrypt information exchanged between the client and server.
4. After a client and server have used Kerberos to prove their identity, they can also encrypt all of their communications to assure privacy and data integrity as they go about their business.

Security+ Objective 1.2.5—Tokens
1. A security token is a physical device that is a portable storage for an authenticator.
2. Tokens support authentication by their physical possession.
3. Most digital tokens combine another factor (two-factor authenticators) an associated secret PIN to protect a lost or stolen token.

Security+ Objective 1.2.6—Multifactor
1. When two or more authentication methods are used to authenticate someone, you are implementing a multifactor authentication system.

Security+ Objective 1.2.7—Mutual Authentication
1. The authentication process can be a one-way process, where only the user's credentials are authenticated, or a mutual authentication process, in which both the user and resource authenticate to each other.

Security+ Objective 1.2.8—Biometrics
1. A biometric is a feature measured from the human body that is distinguishing enough to be used for user authentication.
2. Biometrics include fingerprints, eye (iris and retina), face, hand, voice, and signature.

Security+ Objective 1.4—Attacks

Security+ Objective 1.4.10—Birthday

Security+ Objective 1.4.11—Password Guessing

Security+ Objective 1.4.11.1—Brute Force

Security+ Objective 1.4.11.2—Dictionary

Security+ Objective 1.4.7—Weak Keys

Security+ Objective 1.4.8—Mathematical

1. If given enough time, any password can be cracked, either by having someone looking over someone's shoulder, guessing, or by using hacking techniques.
2. Dictionary attacks are mounted by encrypting a dictionary or words so as to produce all the possible encrypted forms of each word. A simple comparison program then compares the encrypted form of the password file against the encrypted entry from the dictionary. A match indicates the corresponding plaintext of the dictionary entry is the password.
3. Brute force attacks attempt to crack the password by trying every possible value.
4. A birthday attack is a specific kind of brute force attack that takes advantage of the fact that multiple sets of source data can encrypt to the same hash value.
5. For example, it could be used to find another message that would encrypt to the same MD5 hash value associated with an original message. Theoretically, this would let an attacker change the contents of the message.
6. Mathematical attacks are attacks that are based on the fact that a key is generally easier to break the shorter it is and the less the variety in characters used in the key, than those that somehow "break" an encryption algorithm by finding a way to reverse it without discovering the original key.
7. A long key is better than a short key because the longer the key, the more possible combinations that you need to try before you find the correct key value using brute force.
8. Since it takes time to use a dictionary or brute force attack, if you occasionally change your passwords, you would make the previous captured password invalid.
9. You should also have some form of password policy that will limit the number of login attempts before the account is disabled.
10. Another way to thwart password guessing is not to use passwords. Instead use smart cards with a personal pin number or a biometric identifier.

Security+ Objective 2.1.7—IPSEC

1. IP Security, more commonly known as IPSec, is a protocol that provides data integrity, authentication and privacy to data being sent from one point to another point.
2. IPSec works at the IP level and works transparently to protect the data from end-to-end.
3. The new protocols/headers that provide information for securing the payload of the IP packet are the authentication header (AH) and the encapsulating security payload (ESP).
4. When the authentication header (AH) is added to an IP datagram, the header will ensures the integrity and authenticity of the data, including the fields in the outer IP header. It does not provide confidentiality protection.

5. When added to an IP datagram, the Encapsulating Security Payload (ESP) header protects the confidentiality, integrity, and authenticity of the data by performing encryption at the IP packet layer.
6. ESP operates in two modes: transport and tunnel.

Security+ Objective 3.2.4.6—Smart Cards

1. Smart cards resemble a plastic magnetic strip except that they contain a processor and electronic memory.
2. Smart cards can be designed to be inserted into a slot and read by a special reader or to be read at a distance, such as when you approach a toll booth or locked door.

Security+ Objective 4.1—Algorithms

Security+ Objective 4.1.1—Hashing

Security+ Objective 4.1.2—Symmetric

Security+ Objective 4.1.3—Asymmetric

1. Symmetric cryptography uses a single key (secret key) for both encryption and decryption
2. Algorithms that use private-key encryption are DES, 3DES, AES, and IDEA/PGP.
3. Asymmetric cryptography uses one key (shared key) for encryption and another key (secret key) for decryption. The two keys are mathematically related.
4. Public encryption is used by Diffie-Hellman, RSA, and ECC.
5. Hash encryption, also called message digests and one-way encryption, uses algorithms that don't really use a key. Instead, it converts data from a variable-length to a fixed-length piece of data called a hash value.
6. Hashing is always a one-way operation.
7. Hash algorithms are typically used to provide a digital fingerprint of a file or message contents, often used to ensure that the file has not been altered by an intruder or virus.
8. Hash algorithms include MD4 and MD5.

Security+ Objective 4.2—Concepts of Using Cryptography

Security+ Objective 4.2.1—Confidentiality

Security+ Objective 4.2.2—Integrity

Security+ Objective 4.2.5—Access Control

1. The initial unencrypted data is referred to as plaintext or clear text.
2. Encryption is the process of disguising a message or data in what appears to be meaningless data (cipher text) to hide and protect the sensitive data from unauthorized access (confidentiality).
3. Decryption is the process of converting data from encrypted format back to its original format.
4. Cryptography is the art of protecting information by transforming it (encrypting it) into cipher text.

5. In data and telecommunications, cryptography is necessary when communicating over any untrusted medium.

6. Cryptography not only protects data from theft or alteration (integrity), but can also be used for user authentication.

7. Modern cryptography uses algorithms to encrypt and decrypt data by using a mathematical function.

8. To encrypt and decrypt a file, you must use a key.

9. A key is a string of bits used to map text into a code and a code back to text.

10. Since private-key encryption uses a private key and you share the secret key with someone else, that person would also be able to encrypt and decrypt messages to and from you.

Security+ Objective 4.2.2.1—Digital Signatures

Security+ Objective 4.2.4—Nonrepudiation

Security+ Objective 4.2.4.1—Digital Signatures

1. A digital signature is a digital code that can be attached to an electronically transmitted message that uniquely identifies the sender.

2. Like a written signature, the purpose of a digital signature is to guarantee that the individual sending the message really is who he or she claims to be.

3. In addition, it can be used to verify that the person who supposedly sent the message really did (this is nonrepudiation). This is done by encrypting a hash result using an asymmetric algorithm.

Security+ Objective 1.2.3—Certificates

Security+ Objective 4.3.1—Certificates—Make a distinction between what certificates are used for what purpose. Basics only.

1. A digital certificate is an attachment to an electronic message used for security purposes such as authentication and to verify that a user sending a message is who he or she claims to be and to provide the receiver with a means to encode a reply without providing a password to authenticate.

2. It accomplishes this by securely binding a public key to the digital certificate to the entity that holds the corresponding private key.

3. Certificates are generally issued by a Certificate Server.

4. A digital certificate typically includes the owner's name, owner's public key, the certificate's activation date, the certificate's expiration date, what the certificate is used for, the name of the trusted party or issuer that issued the certificate, and a unique serial number assigned by the issuer

5. X.509 certificates are the most widely used digital certificates.

Security+ Objective 4.3—PKI

Security+ Objective 4.3.1.1—Certificate Policies

Security+ Objective 4.3.1.2—Certificate Practice Statements

Security+ Objective 4.3.2—Revocation

Security+ Objective 4.3.3—Trust Models

Security+ Objective 4.5—Key Management/ Certificate Lifecycle

Security+ Objective 4.5.1—Centralized vs. Decentralized

Security+ Objective 4.5.10—Key Usage

Security+ Objective 4.5.10.1—Multiple Key Pairs (Single, Dual)

Security+ Objective 4.5.2—Storage

Security+ Objective 4.5.2.1—Hardware vs. Software

Security+ Objective 4.5.2.2—Private Key Protection

Security+ Objective 4.5.3—Escrow

Security+ Objective 4.5.4—Expiration

Security+ Objective 4.5.5—Revocation

Security+ Objective 4.5.5.1—Status Checking

Security+ Objective 4.5.6—Suspension

Security+ Objective 4.5.6.1—Status Checking

Security+ Objective 4.5.7—Recovery

Security+ Objective 4.5.7.1—M of N Control

Security+ Objective 4.5.8—Renewal

Security+ Objective 4.5.9—Destruction

1. A public key infrastructure (PKI) enables secure e-commerce through the integration of public key cryptography, digital signatures, and other services necessary to ensure confidentiality, integrity, authentication, nonrepudiation and access control.

2. An individual wishing to send an encrypted message applies for a digital certificate from a Certificate Authority (CA).

3. Key Escrow is the procedure of keeping a copy of a user's private key in a centralized location that is only accessible to security administrators, or of implementing a mechanism whereby the private key can be recovered without having to be physically stored.

4. The certificates are issued by Certificate Authorities (CA), which can be any trusted service or entity willing to verify and validate the identities of those to whom it issues certificates, and their association with specific keys.

5. The Registration Authority (RA) is an entity that is designed to verify certificate contents for the CA.

6. Revoked certificates are published in the certification revocation list (CRL).

7. M of N control is a policy of dividing up a task among multiple entities so that no one person acting alone can perform the entire task. It is used to help minimize an organization's exposure to the

risk of one person misusing a privilege, and performing a sensitive action like key recovery without authorization.

8. Destruction refers to the permanent removal of a key or certificate that you no longer need.

9. Suspension of a certificate places a temporary hold on the validity of a digital certificate without causing irreversible revocation. If it later turns out that the certificate should still be considered valid after all, the suspension can be removed, and the certificate will once again be valid.

10. Suspension can be accomplished by placing a digital certificate into a CRL with a suspended status and a reason code for that suspension.

11. Recovery is the process of reacquiring a private key of your own that has been lost (due to disaster, hardware failure, a personal mistake, etc.), or someone else's private key that you are authorized to possess (perhaps because it is required for a business function or law enforcement investigation).

12. The Certificate Policy (CP) is a very broad, high-level security policy that provides the basis for trust between organizations.

13. Certification Practice Statements (CPSs) provide the process through which certificates are issued, maintained, and revoked by a Certification Authority.

14. There are several PKI models including the hierarchical model, the bridge trust model, the mesh model and the hybrid model.

Security+ Objective 5.4.1—Username/Password

1. One of the common methods used on networks is to use a username and password.

2. A username is used to identify a user account, so that it can keep track of the user.

3. The password is used to validate the person's identity when that person logs on.

4. Similar to a password is a personal identification number (PIN), which is a code made of numbers.

QUESTIONS

1. Which two of the following are symmetric-key algorithms used for encryption?
   a. Stream-cipher
   b. Block
   c. Public
   d. Secret

2. You have decided to implement biometrics as part of your security system. Before purchasing a locking system that uses biometrics to control access to secure areas, you need to decide what will be used to authenticate users. Which of the following options relies solely on biometric authentication?
   a. Username and password
   b. Fingerprints, retinal scans, PIN numbers, and facial characteristics
   c. Voice patterns, fingerprints, and retinal scans
   d. Strong passwords, PIN numbers, and digital imaging

3. As the security analyst for your company's network, you want to implement AES. What algorithm will it use?
   a. Rijndael
   b. Nagle
   c. Spanning Tree
   d. PKI

4. Advanced Encryption Standard (AES) is an encryption algorithm for securing sensitive but unclassified material by U.S. government agencies. What type of encryption is it from the list below?
   a. WTLS
   b. Symmetric
   c. Multifactor
   d. Asymmetric

5. Which of the following is an example of an asymmetric algorithm?
   a. CAST (Carlisle Adams Stafford Tavares)
   b. RC5 (Rivest Cipher 5)
   c. RSA (Rivest Shamir Adelman)
   d. SHA-1 (Secure Hashing Algorithm 1)

6. What kinds of attacks are hashed password vulnerable to?
   a. Man in the middle
   b. Dictionary or brute force
   c. Reverse engineering
   d. DoS (Denial of Service)

7. In order to establish a secure connection between headquarters and a branch office over a public network, the router at each location should be configured to use IPSec (Internet Protocol Security) in _____ mode.
   a. Secure
   b. Tunnel
   c. Transport
   d. Data link

8. By definition, how many keys are needed to lock and unlock data using symmetric-key encryption?
   a. 3+
   b. 2
   c. 1
   d. 0

9. Users who configure their passwords using simple and meaningful things such as pet names or birthdays are subject to having their account used by an intruder after what type of attack?
   a. Dictionary attack
   b. Brute force attack
   c. Spoofing attack
   d. Random guess attack
   e. Man-in-the-middle attack
   f. Change list attack
   g. Role-based access control attack
   h. Replay attack
   i. Mickey Mouse attack

10. What are two common methods when using a public key infrastructure for maintaining access to servers in a network?
    a. ACL and PGP
    b. PIM and CRL
    c. CRL and OCSP
    d. RSA and MD2

11. What two functions does IPSec perform? (Choose two.)
    a. Provides the Secure Shell (SSH) for data confidentiality

b. Provides the Password Authentication Protocol (PAP) for user authentication

c. Provides the authentication header (AH) for data integrity

d. Provides the Internet Protocol (IP) for data integrity

e. Provides the Nonrepudiation Header (NH) for identity integrity

f. Provides the Encapsulation Security Payload (ESP) for data confidentiality

12. What type of authentication may be needed when a stored key and memorized password are not strong enough and additional layers of security are needed?
    a. Mutual   b. Multifactor
    c. Biometric   d. Certificate

13. If a private key becomes compromised before its certificate's normal expiration, X.509 defines a method requiring each CA (Certificate Authority) to periodically issue a signed data structure called a certificate:
    a. Enrollment list.   b. Expiration list.
    c. Revocation list.   d. Validation list.

14. Many intrusion detection systems look for known patterns or _____ to aid in detecting attacks.
    a. Viruses   b. Signatures
    c. Hackers   d. Malware

15. Asymmetric cryptography ensures that:
    a. Encryption and authentication can take place without sharing private keys.
    b. Encryption of the secret key is performed with the fastest algorithm available.
    c. Encryption occurs only when both parties have been authenticated.
    d. Encryption factoring is limited to the session key.

16. In order for a user to obtain a certificate from a trusted CA (Certificate Authority), the user must present proof of identity and a:
    a. Private key   b. Public key
    c. Password   d. Kerberos key

17. When a user clicks to browse a secure page, the SSL (Secure Sockets Layer) enabled server will first:
    a. Use its digital certificate to establish its identity to the browser.
    b. Validate the user by checking the CRL (Certificate Revocation List).
    c. Request the user to produce the CRL (Certificate Revocation List).
    d. Display the requested page on the browser, then provide its IP (Internet Protocol) address for verification.

18. Data integrity is best achieved using a(n):
    a. Asymmetric cipher.
    b. Digital certificate.
    c. Message digest.
    d. Symmetric cipher.

19. As the security analyst for your company's network, you are concerned about your systems being penetrated via password cracking. Which system of password cracking will always break through and is only limited by time?
    a. Logical bomb
    b. Dictionary
    c. Sentry
    d. Brute force

20. RSA is an encryption and authentication system that uses an algorithm developed in 1977 by Ron Rivest, Adi Shamir, and Leonard Adleman. The RSA algorithm is the most commonly used encryption and authentication algorithm. Where would you most likely find RSA encryption?
    a. When using IPSec on the LAN
    b. When configuring digital signatures on an RA
    c. In web browsers from Microsoft and Netscape
    d. In DES encryption packets

21. In cryptography, what system uses a private key generated randomly is used only once to encrypt a message that is then decrypted by the receiver using a matching one-time pad and key?
    a. RTP   b. OTP
    c. RDP   d. ACL

22. As the security analyst for your company's network, you want to implement a network layer (OSI Model) level of security. What should you select from the list below?
    a. ARP   b. RSA
    c. IPsec   d. AES

23. As the security analyst for your company's network, you want to use a certificate authority and set up security with digital certificates. Some digital certificates conform to a standard. Which standard is it?
    a. X.507   b. Z.509
    c. X.509   d. X.409

24. As the security analyst for your company's network, you want to implement digital certificates. From the list below, which choice allows you to get a digital certificate issued to you?
    a. RE   b. MA
    c. CA   d. TA

25. Data Encryption Standard (DES) is a widely used method of data encryption using a private (secret) key that was judged so difficult to break by the U.S. government that it was restricted for exportation to other countries. Like other private key cryptographic methods, both the sender and the receiver must know and use the same private key. DES applies which of the following?
    a. 56-bit key to each 64-bit block of data
    b. 65-bit key to each 64-bit block of data
    c. 56-bit key to each 46-bit block of data
    d. 65-bit key to each 46-bit block of data

26. As the security analyst for your company's network, you want to implement hashing. Hashing is the transformation of a string of characters into

a usually shorter fixed-length value or key that represents the original string. What is the biggest benefit to hashing?

a. It is a form of PKI.

b. It is the strongest level of encryption you can get.

c. Hashing is the code used to attempt a Smurf attack.

d. Hashing increases Speed.

27. From the list below, what algorithm is used to verify data integrity through the creation of a 128-bit message digest from data input (which may be a message of any length) that is claimed to be as unique to that specific data as a fingerprint is to the specific individual?

a. RSA-1   b. PIM

c. AEST   d. MD5

28. As the security analyst for your company's network, you want to enable users of a basically unsecure public network such as the Internet to securely and privately exchange data and money through the use of a public and a private cryptographic key pair that is obtained and shared through a trusted authority. What can you use?

a. DMZ   b. IDS

c. PKI   d. ACL

29. A method of trying to gain access to a network by trying a specific list of passwords is called a _____ . (Select the correct answer for the blank.)

a. Dictionary attack

b. Mickey Mouse attack

c. Brute force attack

d. Change list attack

e. Role-based access control attack

f. Man-in-the-middle attack

g. Replay attack

h. Spoofing attack

i. Random guess attack

30. As the security analyst for your company's network, you need a level of authentication that supports both authentication of the sender and encryption of data as well. Which one should you select when using IPsec?

a. Encapsulating Security Payload (ESP)

b. Encapsulating System Payload (ESP)

c. Authentication header (AH)

d. Access header (AH)

31. Kerberos uses _____ to control access to resources. (Select the correct answer for the blank.)

a. Tickets   b. Coupons

c. Slips   d. Chits

e. Papers   f. Notes

32. As the Security Analyst for your company's network, you want to implement a form of cryptography that is a public key encryption technique based on elliptic curve theory that can be used to create faster, smaller, and more efficient cryptographic keys. What would you use?

a. ATEC   b. RDP

c. ACC   d. ECC

33. Pat is implementing a multi-factor authentication system for his network. What can this type of solution consist of? (Choose all correct answers.)

a. Something you have, such as a user name

b. Something you know, such as a password

c. Something you are, such as a network administrator

d. Something you have, such as a smart card

e. Something you know, such as the location of the server

f. Something you are, such as a fingerprint

g. Something you have, such as a desktop computer

h. Something you know, such as the topology of the network

i. Something you are, such as an employee

34. Pat is using a special software program to audit passwords in her network. The software is randomly trying all combinations of letters, numbers and characters from 4 to 10 characters in length. What type of attack is this audit similar to?

a. Dictionary attack

b. Mickey Mouse attack

c. Brute force attack

d. Change list attack

e. Role-based access control attack

f. Man-in-the-middle attack

g. Replay attack

h. Spoofing attack

i. Random guess attack

35. _____ is the process of collecting information about network usage and access. (Select the correct answer for the blank.)

a. Monitoring   b. Watching

c. Recording   d. Logging

e. Typing   f. Keylogging

36. ActiveX applets are typically protected and verified by which of the following means?

a. Secure connections

b. Digital certificates

c. Usernames and passwords

d. Firewalls

e. Virus scanners

f. Gateways

g. Routers

37. A user who has access an information system with a valid user ID and password combination is considered a(n):

a. Manager.

b. User.

c. Authenticated user.

d. Security office.

38. How many characters should the minimum length of a password be to deter dictionary password cracks?

a. 6   b. 8

c. 10   d. 12

39. An attack whereby two different messages using the same hash function produce a common message digest is also known as a:
    a. Man-in-the-middle attack.
    b. Ciphertext-only attack.
    c. Birthday attack.
    d. Brute force attack.

40. Digital certificates can contain which of the following items:
    a. The CA's (Certificate Authority) private key.
    b. The certificate holder's private key.
    c. The certificate's revocation information.
    d. The certificate's validity period.

41. Which encryption key is used to verify a digital signature?
    a. The signer's public key
    b. The signer's private key
    c. The recipient's public key
    d. The recipient's private key

42. An organization is implementing Kerberos as its primary authentication protocol. Which of the following must be deployed for Kerberos to function properly?
    a. Dynamic IP routing protocols for routers and servers
    b. Separate network segments for the realms
    c. Token authentication devices
    d. Time synchronization services for clients and servers

43. The Diffie-Hellman algorithm allows:
    a. Access to digital certificate stores from a certificate authority.
    b. A secret key exchange over an insecure medium without any prior secrets.
    c. Authentication without the use of hashing algorithms.
    d. Multiple protocols to be used in key exchange negotiations.

44. A user logs onto a workstation using a smart card containing a private key. The user is verified when the public key is successfully factored with the private keys. What security service is being provided?
    a. Authentication   b. Confidentiality
    c. Integrity   d. Nonrepudiation

45. In cryptographic operations, digital signatures can be used for which of the following systems?
    a. Encryption
    b. Asymmetric key
    c. Symmetric and encryption
    d. Public and decryption

46. Digital signatures can be used for which of the following?
    a. Availability   b. Encryption
    c. Decryption   d. Nonrepudiation

47. Which of the following keys is contained in a digital certificate?
    a. Public key   b. Private key
    c. Hashing key   d. Session key

48. Which of the following describes a challenge-response session?
    a. Workstation or system that generates a random challenge string that the user enters when prompted along with the proper PIN (Personal Identification Number)
    b. Workstation or system that generates a random login ID that the user enters when prompted along with the proper PIN (Personal Identification Number)
    c. Special hardware device that is used to generate random text in a cryptography system
    d. The authentication mechanism in the workstation or system does not determine if the owner should be authenticated

49. Message authentication codes are used to provide which service?
    a. Integrity
    b. Fault recovery
    c. Key recovery
    d. Acknowledgement

50. A VPN (Virtual Private Network) using IPSec in the tunnel mode will provide encryption for the:
    a. One-time pad used in handshaking.
    b. Payload and message header.
    c. Hashing algorithm and all email messages.
    d. Message payload only.

51. When implementing Kerberos authentication, which of the following factors must be accounted for?
    a. Kerberos can be susceptible to man-in-the-middle attacks to gain unauthorized access.
    b. Kerberos tickets can be spoofed using replay attacks to network resources.
    c. Kerberos requires a centrally managed database of all user and resource passwords.
    d. Kerberos uses clear text passwords.

52. A public key _____ is a pervasive system whose services are implemented and delivered using public key technologies that include CAs (Certificate Authority), digital certificates, non-repudiation, and key history management.
    a. Cryptography scheme
    b. Distribution authority
    c. Exchange
    d. Infrastructure

53. The integrity of a cryptographic system is considered compromised if which of the following conditions exist?
    a. A 40-bit algorithm is used for a large transaction.
    b. The public key is disclosed.
    c. The private key is disclosed.
    d. The validity of the data source is compromised.

54. Nonrepudiation is based on what type of key infrastructure?
    a. Symmetric   b. Distributed trust
    c. Asymmetric   d. User-centric

55. Which of the following provides the strongest authentication?
    a. Token
    b. Username and password
    c. Biometrics
    d. One-time password

56. Which are the three main components of a Kerberos server?
    a. Authentication server, security database, and privilege server
    b. SAM (sequential Access Method), security database, and authentication server
    c. Application database, security database, and system manager
    d. Authentication server, security database, and system manager

57. The standard encryption algorithm based on Rijndael is known as:
    a. AES (Advanced Encryption Standard).
    b. 3DES (Triple Data Encryption Standard).
    c. DES (Data Encryption Standard).
    d. Skipjack.

58. A CPS (Certificate Practice Statement) is a legal document that describes a CA's (Certificate Authority):
    a. Class-level issuing process.
    b. Copyright notice.
    c. Procedures.
    d. Asymmetric encryption schema.

59. The primary disadvantage of symmetric cryptography is:
    a. Speed.
    b. Key distribution.
    c. Weak algorithms.
    d. Memory management.

60. What is a good practice in deploying a CA (Certificate Authority)?
    a. Enroll users for policy-based certificates.
    b. Create a CPS (Certificate Practice Statement).
    c. Register the CA (Certificate Authority) with a subordinate CA (Certificate Authority).
    d. Create a mirror CA (Certificate Authority) for fault tolerance.

61. Which of the following is a field of a X.509 v.3 certificate?
    a. Private key
    b. Issuer
    c. Serial number
    d. Subject

62. The greater the keyspace and complexity of a password, the longer a _____ attack may take to crack the password.
    a. Dictionary
    b. Brute force
    c. Inference
    d. Frontal

63. When a cryptographic system's keys are no longer needed, the keys should be:
    a. Destroyed or stored in a secure manner.
    b. Deleted from the system's storage mechanism.
    c. Recycled.
    d. Submitted to a key repository.

64. Which of the following is the best reason for a CA (Certificate Authority) to revoke a certificate?
    a. The user's certificate has been idle for two months.
    b. The user has relocated to another address.
    c. The user's private key has been compromised.
    d. The user' public key has been compromised.

65. Which of the following correctly identifies some of the contents of an end user's X.509 certificate?
    a. User's public key, object identifiers, and the location of the user's electronic identity
    b. User's public key, the CA (Certificate Authority) distinguish name, and the type of symmetric algorithm used for encryption
    c. User's public key the certificate's serial number, and the certificate's validity dates
    d. User's public key, the serial number of the CA (Certificate Authority) certificate, and the CRL (Certificate Revocation List) entry point

66. Which protocol is used to negotiate and provide authenticated keying material for security associations in a protected manner?
    a. ISAKMP (Internet Security Association and Key Management Protocol)
    b. ESP (Encapsulating Security Payload)
    c. SSH (Secure Shell)
    d. SKEME (Secure Key Exchange Mechanism)

67. Regarding security, biometrics are used for:
    a. Accountability.
    b. Certification.
    c. Authorization.
    d. Authentication.

68. Most certificates used for authentication are based on what standard?
    a. ISO19278
    b. X.500
    c. RC 1205
    d. X.509 v3

69. In order for User A to send User B an e-mail message that only User B can read, User A must encrypt the e-mail with which of the following keys?
    a. User B's public key
    b. User B's private key
    c. User A's public key
    d. User A's private key

70. What does the message recipient use with the hash value to verify a digital signature?
    a. Signer's private key
    b. Receiver's private key
    c. Signer's public key
    d. Receiver's public key

71. The public key infrastructure model where certificates are issued and revoked via a CA (certificate Authority) is what type of model?
    a. Managed
    b. Distributed
    c. Centralized
    d. Standard

72. When a user A applies to the CA (Certificate Authority) requesting a certificate to allow the start of communicating with User B, User A must supply the CA (Certificate Authority) with:
    a. User A's public key only.
    b. User B's public key only.

c. User A's and User B's public keys.

d. User A's and User B's public and private keys.

73. One of the primary concerns of a centralized key management system is that:

a. Keys must be stored and distributed securely.

b. Certificates must be made readily available.

c. The key repository must be publicly accessible.

d. The certificate contents must be kept confidential.

74. A network administrator is having difficulty establishing a L2TP (Layer Two Tunneling Protocol) VPN (Virtual Private Network) tunnel with IPSec (Internet Protocol Security) between a remote dial-up client and the firewall, through a perimeter router. The administrator has confirmed that the client's and firewall's IKE (Internet Key Exchange) policy and IPSec (Internet Protocol Security) policy are identical. The appropriate L2TP and IKE transport layer ports have also been allowed on the perimeter router and firewall. What additional step must be performed on the perimeter router and firewall to allow AH (Authentication Header) and ESP (Encapsulation Security Payload) tunnel-encapsulated IPSEC traffic to flow between the client and the firewall?

a. Configure the perimeter router and firewall to allow inbound protocol number 51 for ESP encapsulated IPSec traffic

b. Configure the perimeter router and firewall to allow inbound protocol number 49 for ESP encapsulated IPSec traffic

c. Configure the perimeter router and firewall to allow inbound protocol numbers 50 and 51 for ESP and AH encapsulated traffic

d. Configure the perimeter router and firewall to allow inbound protocol numbers 52 and 53 for AH and ESP encapsulated IPSec traffic

75. The main purpose of digital certificates is to security bind a:

a. Public to the identity of the signer and recipient.

b. Private key to the identify of the signer and recipient.

c. Public key to the entity that holds the corresponding private key.

d. Private key to the entity that holds the corresponding public key.

HANDS-ON EXERCISES

Exercise 1: Cracking Passwords in Windows

1. Make sure that you have a one or more accounts on your computer with the password of password. In addition, have another account with the password of test0 and another account with a strong password. Make sure that you have logged in at least once with these accounts.

2. Download LC (L0phtCrack) program from http://www.atstake.com/research/lc/download.html.

3. Install the LC program that you download on a Windows computer.

4. Press the Ctrl+Alt+Del keys and start the Task Manager.

5. Click on the Performance tab and view your processor performance. Close the Task Manager.

6. Click the Start button, select Programs, select LC (or LC4), and start the LC (or LC4) program.

7. If the Trial version dialog box appears, click on the Trial button. Note: If you have strong passwords and you want to use Brute Force to break it, you will have to register the software.

8. When the wizard appears, click the Next button.

9. Select the Retrieve from the local machine and click on the Next button.

10. Select Strong Password Audit and click on the Next button.

11. Enable the Display encrypted password hashes option.

12. Click the Finish button.

13. While it tries to figure out the passwords, start the Task Manager and view the performance again. Close the Task Manager.

14. Look at the password that it finds and their LM Hash and NTLM Hash.

NOTE: If you have strong passwords and you are using brute force, it may take a while before it figures out the passwords.

Exercise 2: Using Certificate Authority and Certificates in Windows

To Install Certificate Services

1. Click the Start button, select Settings, and select Control Panel.
2. In the Control Panel, double-click the Add/Remove Programs.
3. In the Add/Remove Programs dialog box, click the Add/Remove Windows Components.
4. In the Windows Components wizard, select the check box for Certificate Services. Click the Yes button to acknowledge the warning that the computer cannot be renamed or have its domain affiliation changed.
5. Click on the Next button.
6. When the Certificate Authority Type page appears, select the Enterprise Root CA, select Advanced Options, and click Next.
7. When the Public and Private Key Pair page appears, select Microsoft Enhanced Cryptographic Provider as the CSP and click Next.
8. Type Acme Inc. in the Organization box. Type in your city, state and country/region. Type rootca@acmeXX.com in the E-mail box. Type Acme Root Certifier in the CA description box. Click on the Next button.
9. When asked, insert your Windows Installation CD.
10. Click the Finish button. Close the Add/Remove Programs window and Control Panel.

To Revoke a Certificate

1. Click the Start button, select Programs, select Administrative Tools and choose Certificate Authority.
2. In the Certificate Authority console, expand Certificate Authority, Acme Enterprise Root Certifier and select Issued Certificates.
3. In the right pane of the console, right-click the certificate with the Issued Common Name of Acme Web SSL and S/MIME Extranet Certifier, select all Tasks, and then choose Revoke Certificate.
4. When the Certificate Revocation dialog box appears, select Cease of Operating in the Reason Code box and click the Yes button.
5. Click the Revoked Certificates folder and note that the certificate now appears in this folder.

Managing the CRL

1. Click Start, select Programs, select Administrative Tools, and select Certificate Authority.
2. In the Certificate Authority console, expand the Certification Authority and Acme Enterprise Root Certifier.
3. Right-click the Revoked Certificates and choose Properties. The Revoked Certificates Properties dialog box appears.
4. Click View Current CRL and notice that it is empty.
5. Click OK to close the Certificate Revocation List dialog box.
6. Click OK to close the Revoked Certificates Properties dialog box.
7. Right-click the Revoked Certificates, point to All Tasks, and choose Publish.
8. When a message appears informing you that the current CRL is still valid, click Yes to publish the new CRL.
9. View the revoked certificates again.

Deploying Computer Certificates Manually

1. Click the Start button, and click the Run option.
2. Type mmc and click the OK button.
3. From the Console menu, choose Add/Remove Snap-in. The Add/Remove Snap-in dialog box appears.
4. Click Add. The Add Standalone Snap-in dialog box appears with a list of snap-ins.
5. Double-click certificates. The Certificates Snap-in Wizard appears with a list of the types of certificates that the snap-in can manage.
6. Select Computer Account, and click Next. Select Local Computer and click Finish.
7. Click Close to the close the Add Standalone Snap-in dialog box. The Certificates snap-in is now in the Add/Remove snap-ins list name.
8. Click OK to close the Add/Remove Snap-in dialog box.
9. From the Console menu, choose Save. The Save As dialog box appears.
10. Select the Desktop for the location and type Certificates in the File Name box. Click the Save button.
11. With the Certificates management console still open, right-click the Personal folder, click All Tasks and select Request Net Certificate. The Certificate Request Wizard appears. Click the Next button.
12. When the Certificate Template dialog box appears with Computer is the only option, click the Next.

13. Type Workstation Certificate as the Friendly Name for the certificate. Type IPSec enabling certificate as the description for the certificate.
14. Click Next, and then click Finish. A message box appears indicating that the certificate request was successful.
15. Click OK to acknowledge that the certificate request was successful.
16. Click the Certificates folder under the Personal folder.
17. Double-click the client certificate to view the certificate information.

Exercise 3: Enabling IPSec for Windows

1. From the Start menu, click the Run option and execute the MMC command.
2. On the Console menu, click the Add/Remove Snap-in and click the Add button.
3. In the list of available snap-ins, select IP Security Policy Management, and click on the Add button.
4. Make sure Local Computer option button is selected, and then click the Finish button.
5. In the Adds Standalone Snap-in dialog box, click the Close
6. In the add/Remove Snap-in dialog box, click OK.
7. On the console menu, click the Save As and save it to the desktop with the name of ipsec.msc.
8. In the right pane, right-click the Client (Respond Only) IPSec Policy, and then click Assign. Notice that Yes appears in the Policy Assigned column for the Client (Respond Only) policy.
9. Open Control Panel and double-click the Network and Dial-Up Connections icon. The Network and Dial-Up Connections
10. Right-click Local Area Network, and then click Properties. The Internet Protocol (TCP/IP) dialog box appears.
11. Click the Advanced button.
12. Click the Options tab.
13. In the Optional Settings list, select IP Security, and then click Properties. Notice that the Use This IP Security Policy option button is selected, and the Client (Respond Only) Policy from the drop-down menu is enabled.
14. Select the Do Not Use IPSEC option button, then click OK.
15. Click OK to close the Advanced TCP/IP Settings dialog box.
16. Click OK to close the Internet Protocol (TCP/IP) Properties dialog box.
17. Click OK to close the Local Area Connection Properties dialog box.
18. Close the Networking and Dial-Up Connections dialog box, and then switch to your custom management console. If you close the costume management console, you just need to double-click on the ipsec icon on the desktop. Notice that No appears in the Policy Assigned column for the Client (Respond Only) policy.
19. From the custom console (ipec.msc), in the left pane, right-click the IP Security Policy On Local Machine file. From the shortcut menu, click the Create IP Security Policy.
20. When the IPSec Policy wizard appears, click the Next Button.
21. Type the policy named IPSec Custom1, and then click the Next button. The Requests for Secure Connection Page appears.
22. Verify that the Activate the Default Response Rule check box is selected, and then click the Next button.
23. Accept the default response rule for Kerberos Authentication, and then click the Next button.
24. Leave the Edit properties check box selected, and then click the Finish button. The IPSec Custom1 Properties dialog box appears.
25. At the bottom of the Properties dialog box, clear the Use Add Wizard check box.
26. In the Rules tab of the Properties dialog box, click the Add button.
27. Click the Add button in the IP Filter List tab.
28. In the Name box, name the filter CustomFilter1.
29. Clear the Use Add Wizard check box.
30. In the IP Filter List tab, click the Add button.
31. In the Source Address drop-down list, select A Specific IP Address.
32. Type your IP address.
33. In the Destination Address list, select A Specific IP Address.
34. Type your lab partner's IP address, and then click OK.
35. Click Close.
36. In the IP Filter List tab, select the CustomFilter1 option button.
37. Open the Filter Action tab, clear the Use Add Wizard check box, and then click Add.
38. In the Security Methods tab, click Add.
39. In the New Security Method dialog box, select the Medium (AH) option button, then click OK.
40. In the New Filter Action Properties dialog box.

41. Select the option button next to MediumFilter.
42. Open the Authentication Methods tab.
43. Click the Add button.
44. Select the Use this String to Protect the Key Exchange (Preshared Key) option button.
45. Type password in the text box, and then click OK.
46. Select PreShared Key in the list, and then click the Move Up button.
47. Click Close to return to the Policy Properties dialog box and to complete the creation of the rule.
48. Click Close in the Policy Properties dialog box.
49. To activate your new custom IPSec policy, in the right pane of your custom console, right-click the IPSec Custom1 policy file and then click Assign. The Policy Assigned column value is set to Yes.
50. When your lab partner is ready to enable the policy on his or her computer, open a command prompt and attempt to ping your partner's computer.
51. Have your partner activate his or her policy and try the ping again.
52. Disable your IPSec policy and try the ping again.
53. Have you and your partner disable your IPSec policy on both machines.
54. Close your custom console and click the Yes button when prompted to save changes.

Exercise 4: Using the pwconv and pwunconv Commands in Linux

1. Login as your user1 account.
2. Use the su command to switch to the root user.
3. If you installed Red Hat Linux using the default values for password usage, you should be using shadow passwords. To view the passwd file, change into the /etc directory and use the following command:

```
cat passwd
```

4. Now view the shadow file.
5. To convert from shadow passwords, use the following command:

```
pwunconv
```

6. View the passwd file.
7. Attempt to view the shadow file.
8. Execute the following command to convert to shadow passwords, use the following command:

```
pwconv
```

9. View the passwd and shadow file.

CHAPTER **6**

Network Infrastructure Security

Topics Covered in this Chapter

Introduction

This chapter focuses on how to protect the network as a whole. If someone really wanted to, it does not take much to take a network or at least a part of a network down. If someone walks by a cable and cuts the cable or disconnects the cable, data cannot travel through the cable. You also need to secure the individual devices, physically and remotely. Lastly, any computer or networking equipment that can be physically touched also needs to be protected. Therefore, computers and disks also need to be protected.

Objectives

1. Security+ Objective 3.1.1—Firewalls
2. Security+ Objective 3.1.2—Routers
3. Security+ Objective 3.1.11—Workstations
4. Security+ Objective 3.1.12—Servers
5. Security+ Objective 3.1.13—Mobile Devices
6. Security+ Objective 3.1.3—Switches
7. Security+ Objective 3.2—Media
8. Security+ Objective 3.2.1—Coax
9. Security+ Objective 3.2.2—UTP/STP
10. Security+ Objective 3.2.3—Fiber
11. Security+ Objective 3.2.4—Removable Media
12. Security+ Objective 3.2.4.1—Tape
13. Security+ Objective 3.2.4.2—CDR
14. Security+ Objective 3.2.4.3—Hard drives
15. Security+ Objective 3.2.4.4—Diskettes
16. Security+ Objective 3.2.4.5—Flashcards
17. Security+ Objective 3.2.4.6—Smart Cards
18. Security+ Objective 3.3.1—Security Zones
19. Security+ Objective 3.3.1.1—DMZ
20. Security+ Objective 3.3.1.2—Intranet
21. Security+ Objective 3.3.1.3—Extranet
22. Security+ Objective 3.3.2—VLANs
23. Security+ Objective 3.3.3—NAT
24. Security+ Objective 5.1—Physical Security
25. Security+ Objective—5.1.1 Access Control
26. Security+ Objective—5.1.1.1 Physical Barriers
27. Security+ Objective—5.1.1.2 Biometrics

6.1   PHYSICAL SECURITY

Security+ Objective 5.1—Physical Security

Security+ Objective 5.1.1—Access Control

Security+ Objective 5.1.1.1—Physical Barriers

Security+ Objective 5.1.1.2—Biometrics

To protect your corporate resources, you should consider hiring security guards to help monitor your site or building. In addition, you should also consider using sensors, alarms, and cameras to help monitor everything, and you should use physical access badges and security cards to limit access to your building or site. You need to also provide training and reminders for all employees to report anything suspicious.

Walls are used to create barriers between one area and another. They can separate work areas and provide protected areas for sensitive systems and devices. Unfortunately, many buildings have hung ceilings, meaning the wall may not extend above the ceiling. An intruder can lift a ceiling panel and climb over the partition wall. If you need a room to be secure, you must verify that the walls go beyond the hung ceiling.

6.1.1   Securing Servers

Security+ Objective 3.1.12—Servers

People often forget when planning security to plan for the security of servers and user computers. The reason to secure servers is that they provide network services for multiple users. In addition, they often contain confidential information. Therefore, it is important to protect your servers. Of course, the best location to place a server would be the server room. Of course, to further secure a server, you should consider the following:

- The server should be physically locked when not in use.
- The server should have a BIOS password set so that you must enter the password.
- You should always log out when the server is not being used.
- Use passwords on screensavers. Note: Do not select complex screensavers that will take up a lot of processing away from the network services.
- The server should be locked so that it cannot be opened.
- Your server should include intruder detection sensors that will notify you when the server has been physically opened.

6.1.2   Securing User Computers

Security+ Objective 3.1.11—Workstations

While most user computers don't provide network services, they often contain confidential information, and they may aid in unauthorized user access to the rest of the network. You also don't want someone to steal the computer or any of its components. Therefore, it is just as important to protect the individual computers. Consequently, you should use passwords to boot the computer and you should use a password for the operating system. You should always log out when the computer is not being used, and you should always use passwords on screensavers. Lastly, you should use a lock preventing users from opening the computer.

6.1.3   Security Portable Computers

Security+ Objective 3.1.13—Mobile Devices

In addition to the requirements for the user computers, you should have a couple of additional requirements for portable computers. When you are not in a secure environment, you need to use a locking cable, which you can use to physically secure the notebook so that no one will steal it. In addition, portable computers should have hard drive passwords so that if someone steals the computer, he or she will still not be able to access the hard drive, even when the hard drive is used in another system. You should also consider using file encryption to further protect your system. Lastly, since notebook computers are smaller and easier to steal, you might consider requiring smart cards or biometrics to access the notebook and to log on to the network with the notebook.

6.1.4   Securing Removable Storage Media

Security+ Objective 3.2.4—Removable Media

Security+ Objective 3.2.4.1—Tape

Security+ Objective 3.2.4.2—CDR

Security+ Objective 3.2.4.3—Hard drives

Security+ Objective 3.2.4.4—Diskettes

Security+ Objective 3.2.4.5—Flashcards

Security+ Objective 3.2.4.6—Smart Cards

Removable storage media is any device that stores information and can be easily carried. It includes floppy disks, CDs, hard disks, Zip disks, backup tapes, and flash cards. Unfortunately, while they are useful for transporting programs and data and are used for backup purposes, they can also be a security risk since they can be used to copy confidential information and can be removed from your building or site. The first step in securing these devices would be to include what is allowed and not allowed in your security policies. Second, there are steps that you can do to minimize or reduce the use of these devices.

Depending on your security requirements, you might consider encrypting data on removable media, especially if the removable data is removed from a secure area. Therefore, if it is lost or stolen, unauthorized personnel still cannot read it.

For floppy disks, you can use diskless workstations or you can disable floppy disk drives in the BIOS. Note: Of course, the BIOS needs to be password-protected. To avoid using writable CDs, you should not purchase writable CD drives for every system. If you need to have writable CDs, you need to limit access to the writable CD drives by putting them behind locked doors, using BIOS passwords, and/or by using OS rights and permissions. On some operating systems such as Windows 2000 or Windows XP, you can also limit users from adding additional hardware items to their system. This will prevent them from adding additional devices that could give them the ability to copy confidential information to removable media.

When you are done using a disk and you no longer want to use that disk, you need to properly erase the information off the disk so that it cannot be retrieved. For hard drives, you can use a low-level format program which comes from the hard drive manufacturer. For floppy disks, you can also do an unconditional format. For CDs, it is best to break the disk into several pieces.

A memory card (sometimes called a flash memory card or a storage card) is a small storage medium used to store data such as text, pictures, audio, and video, for use on small, portable, or remote computing devices. Most of the current products use flash memory, although other technologies are being developed. A number of memory cards are on the market, including the SD card (secure digital card), the CF card (CompactFlash card), the SmartMedia card, the Memory Stick, and the MultiMediaCard (MMC). These cards vary in size, and each is available in a range of storage capacities that typically correspond directly to the price. The CompactFlash card is about the size of a matchbook, while the MultiMediaCard and Secure Digital card are each about the size of a postage stamp. Flash memory is also being used in USB devices, which are not bigger than a car or house key, which are used much like a disk would be. You connect it to your USB port, and you can save or retrieve information from it.

Most available cards have constantly powered nonvolatile memory, which means that data are stable on the card, are not threatened by a loss of power source, and do not need to be periodically refreshed. Because memory cards are solid state media, they have no moving parts and, therefore, are unlikely to suffer mechanical difficulties. Earlier removable storage media, such as the PC Card, the smart card, and similar cards used for game systems, can also be considered to be memory cards. However, the newer cards are smaller, require less power, have higher storage capacity, and are portable among a greater number of devices. Because of these features, memory cards are influencing the production of an increasing number of small, lightweight, and low-power devices. Memory cards offer a number of advantages over the hard disk drive: They're much smaller and lighter, extremely portable, completely silent, allow more immediate access, and are less prone to mechanical damage.

Unfortunately, because of their very small size, flashcards are vulnerable to theft. Depending on the type of media, a gigabyte of data or more may be stored on a small device about the size of a large postage stamp or small key chain. Additionally, the USB version of these devices may be attached to any computer's USB port, and provide a way to pull data off that computer and remove the data from the site, even if that PC has been carefully locked down by removing floppy drive and CD-R capability.

Flashcards are most often used in combination with electronic devices, such as digital cameras and MP3 player/recorders, which do not support reading or writing encrypted files. Because of this, you should be aware that data exchanged with these devices via flashcard will be stored unencrypted and are thus available for access by anyone who obtains the card. If you are using a flashcard as storage for a Palm or Pocket PC, numerous programs will encrypt data, so that loss of the device or card does not necessarily mean that the data on it are accessible by unauthorized personnel.

Along the same lines, some people have begun to use flashcards (and their cousins, solid-state USB "storage units") as portable storage media, copying data off one computer and then onto another. If you're copying a file off a Windows 2000 system, and that file is encrypted using Windows 2000's built-in encryption, be aware that when you copy it to the flashcard, whose file system does not support encryption, the portable copy of the file will not be encrypted.

Flashcards tend to allow a more limited number of write/read cycles before failure, than hard disks and RAM. If you plan to use flash memory for frequent data transfer, it's a good idea to estimate the useful life of the media, and make sure that you have spare cards on hand toward the end of its anticipated life so that bad media do not interrupt operations.

6.1.5 Handling Sensitive Information

Sensitive information such as financial records or employee or customer information must be handled according to these guidelines:

- **Marking**—The words that appear on sensitive documents saying that they are sensitive. For example marking could be: Company confidential, handle according to company policy.
- **Handling**—The organization should have established procedures for handling marked documents. These procedures would detail how such documents may be transported, faxed, emailed, or sent over networks.
- **Storage**—Similar to the handling guideline, the organization must have procedures and requirements specifying how marked information must be stored.
- **Destruction**—Sooner or later a document with sensitive information must be destroyed. The organization must have procedures detailing how to destroy sensitive information, whether hard or soft copy.

6.2 THE NETWORK INFRASTRUCTURE

Security+ Objective 3.2—Media

Security+ Objective 3.2.1—Coax

Security+ Objective 3.2.2—UTP/STP

Security+ Objective 3.2.3—Fiber

While wireless networks are growing in popularity, most networks are primarily wired networks. The cabling system used in networks is the veins of the network that connects all of the computers together and allows them to communicate with each other. In addition, network connectivity devices are used to connect the different types of cables and to connect multiple networks together.

6.2.1 Topologies

Topology describes the appearance or layout of the network. Depending on how you look at the network, there is the physical topology and the logical topology. The most common used topologies are the bus topology and the star topology.

A **bus topology** looks like a line, and it is where data is sent along the single cable. The two ends of the cable do not meet and the two ends do not form a ring or loop. See figure 6.1. All nodes (devices connected to the computer including networked computers, routers, and network printers) listen to all of the traffic on the network but only accept the packets that are addressed to them. The single cable is sometimes referred to as a **segment, backbone cable,** or **trunk.** Since all computers use the same backbone cable, the bus topology is very easy to set up and install, and the cabling costs are minimized. Unfortunately, traffic easily builds up on this topology, and it is not a recommended topology for large networks. Examples of a bus topology include Ethernet (10Base2 and 10Base5).

Typically with a bus topology network, the two ends of the cable must be terminated. This is because when signals get to the end of a cable segment, they have a tendency to bounce back and collide with new data packets. If there is a break anywhere or one system does not pass the data along

Figure 6.1   The Bus Topology

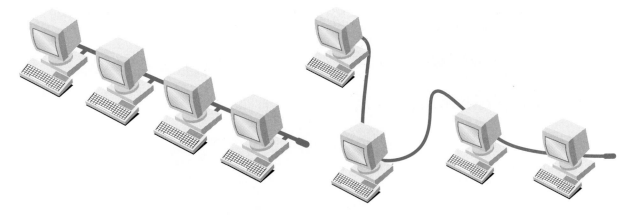

Figure 6.2   The Star Topology

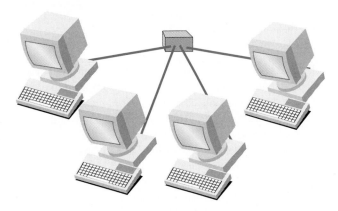

correctly, the entire network will go down. This is because a break divides the trunk into two pieces, each with an end that is not terminated. In addition, these problems are difficult to troubleshoot since a break causes the entire network to go down with no indication of where the break is.

A **star topology** is the most popular topology in use. It has each network device connect to a central point such as a hub or switch, which acts as a multipoint connector. Other names for a hub would be a concentrator, multipoint repeater, or media access unit (MAU). See figure 6.2.

Star networks are relatively easy to install and manage, but may take some time to install, since each computer requires a cable that runs back to the central point. If a link fails (hub port or cable), the remaining workstations are not affected like the bus topology. If the central point fails (hub or switch), the entire network fails.

6.2.2   Types of Cables

A conductor is material in which electrical current can flow easily. Most metals are good conductors, particularly silver and copper. Copper is often used as a conductor within electrical circuits and wires because it is inexpensive. Unshielded twisted pair, shielded twisted pair, and coaxial cable are made of copper wires that carry electrical signals to represent the data.

A **twisted pair** consists of two insulated copper wires twisted around each other. While each pair acts as a single communication link, twisted pairs are usually bundled together into a cable and wrapped in a protective sheath. See figure 6.3. Twisted pairs come in **unshielded twisted pairs (UTP)** and shielded twisted pairs (STP). Of these, unshielded twisted pairs are the same type of cable that is used with telephones and is the most common cable used in networks. See figure 6.4.

Figure 6.3   Twisted Pair Cable

Figure 6.4   UTP Cable

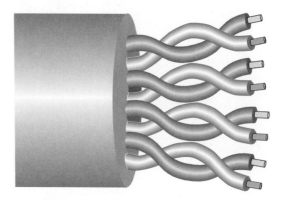

UTP cable consists of four pairs of wires in each cable. Each pair of wires is twisted about each other and used together to make a connection. Compared to other cable types (unshielded twisted pair, shielded twisted pair, coaxial cable, and fiber optics), UTP is inexpensive and is the easiest to install. The biggest disadvantages of UTP are its limited bandwidth of 100 meters and its susceptibility to interference and noise. Traditional, UTP has had a limited network speed, but more recently UTP can be used in networks running between 4 Mbps and 1 Gbps. Some companies, such as Hewlett-Packard, are working on a 10 Gbps network standard. UTP is the most commonly used type in Ethernet.

Early networks that used UTP typically used Category 3, while today's newer high-speed networks typically use Category 5 or Enhanced Category 5 cabling. Category 3 has three to four twists per foot and could operate up to 16 MHz, while Category 5 uses three to four twists per inch, contains Teflon insulation, and can operate at 100 MHz. Enhanced Category 5 is a higher-quality cable designed to reduce crosstalk even further and support applications that require additional bandwidth.

While your telephone uses a cable with 2 pairs (4 wires) and a RJ-11 connector, computer networks use a cable with 4 pairs (8 wires) and a RJ-45 connector. See figure 6.5. In a simple network, one end of the cable attaches to the network card on the computer and the other end attaches to a hub (multi-ported connection) or switch. As more computers and network devices connect to the hub or switch, they form a star topology.

In a larger network, one end of the cable will connect the network card of the computer to a wall jack. The wall jack is connected to the back of a patch panel kept in a server room or wiring closet. A cable then is attached to the patch panel and connected to a hub or switch. The cables that connect to the computer to the wall jack and the cable that connects the patch panel and the hub or switch are called patch cables. See figure 6.6.

Shielded twisted pair (STP) is similar to unshielded twisted pair except that it is usually surrounded by a braided shield that serves to reduce both EMI sensitivity and radio emissions. See figure 6.7. Shielded twisted pair cable was required for all high-performance networks such as IBM Token Ring until a few years ago and is commonly used in IBM Token Ring networks and Apple's LocalTalk network. STP is relatively expensive compared to UTP and is more difficult with which to work.

Coaxial cable, sometimes referred to as Coax, is a cable that has a center wire surrounded by insulation and then a grounded shield of braided wire (mesh shielding). See figure 6.8. The copper core carries the electromagnetic signal, and the braided metal shielding acts as both a shield against noise and a ground for the signal. The shield minimizes electrical and radio frequency interference and provides a connection to ground. Coaxial cable is the primary type of cable used by the cable television industry and is widely used for computer networks.

Figure 6.5   UTP Cable with a RJ-45 Connector and a UTP Cable with a RJ-11 Connector

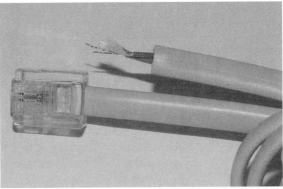

Figure 6.6   Patch Panel Allows for Easy Connection of Computers

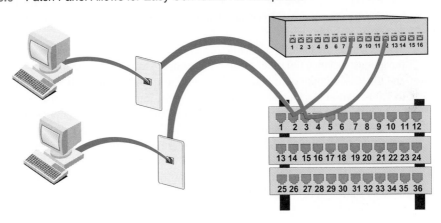

Figure 6.7   Shielded Twisted Pair Cable

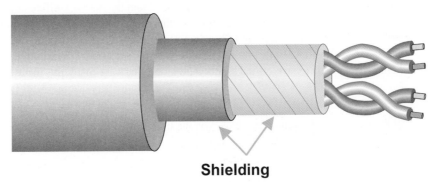

Shielding

Figure 6.8   Coaxial Cable

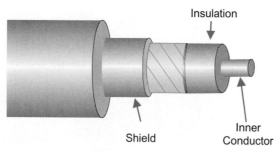
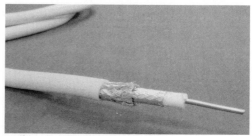

For computer networks, coaxial cables are usually used for the backbone cable for older Ethernet networks. The network devices are attached by cutting the cable and using a T-connector or by applying a vampire tap (a mechanical device that uses conducting teeth to penetrate the insulation and attach directly to the wire conductor). To maintain the correct electrical properties of the wire, you must terminate both ends of the cable, and you must ground one end of the cable. The termination dampens signals that bounce back or reflect at the end of the cable. The ground completes the electrical circuit. Not grounding at all can lead to an undesirable charge in the coax cable, whereas grounding at both ends can lead to a difference in ground potential, causing an undesirable current on the coax cable, especially if they are between two buildings.

A **fiber optic** cable consists of a bundle of glass or plastic threads, each of which is capable of carrying data signals in the forms of modulated pulses of light. While glass can carry the light pulses (several kilometers) even further than plastic, plastic is easier to work with. Since each thread can only carry a signal in one direction, a cable consists of two threads in separate jackets—one to transmit and one to receive. The fiber optic cable uses cladding that surrounds the optical fiber core, which helps reflect light back to the core and to ensure that little of the light signal is lost. Lastly, the cable contains Kevlar strands to provide strength.

Fiber has the largest bandwidth (up to 10 GHz) of any media available. It can transmit signals over the longest distance (20 times farther than copper segments) at the lowest cost, with the fewest repeaters and the least amount of maintenance. In addition, since it has such a large bandwidth, it can support up to 1,000 stations and it can support faster speeds introduced during the next 15 to 20 years.

Fiber optic cables use several connectors, but the two most popular and recognizable connectors are the straight tip (ST) and subscriber (SC) connectors. The ST fiber optic connector, developed by AT&T, is probably the most widely used fiber optic connector. It uses a BNC attachment mechanism similar to the Thinnet connector mechanism.

SC connectors (sometimes known as the square connector) are typically latched connectors. This makes it impossible for the connector to be pulled out without releasing the connector's latch (usually by pressing some kind of button or release).

A new connector called the MT-RJ uses a connector that is similar to a RJ-45 connector. It offers a new small two-fiber connector that is lower in cost and smaller than the duplex SC interface. See figure 6.9.

Fiber optics are extremely difficult to tap, making them very secure and highly reliable. Since fiber does not use electrical signals running on copper wire, interference does not affect fiber traffic, and as a result, the number of retransmissions is reduced and the network efficiency is increased.

The main disadvantage of fiber optics is that the cables are expensive to install and require special skills and equipment to split or splice. In addition, they are more fragile than wire. Fortunately, in recent years, while fiber optics products are being mass-produced more often, the cost gap between the high grades of UTP have closed significantly, and there are many pre-made products available.

6.2.3   Network Connectivity Devices

Now that you understand the cables, you need to look at the common network connectivity devices to which the cables will connect. These include:

- Hubs
- Switches
- Bridges
- Routers

Figure 6.9 Fiber Optics Cable and Common Connectors (ST, SC, and MT-RJ)

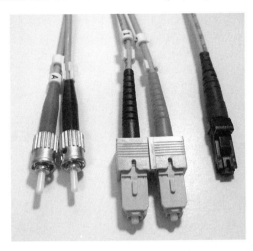

Figure 6.10 A Hub

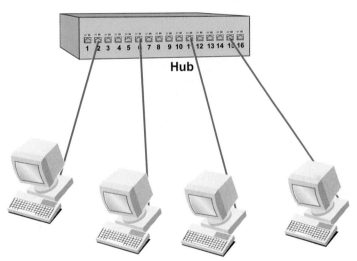

A **hub,** which works at the physical OSI layer, is a multiported connection point used to connect network devices via a cable segment. When a PC needs to communicate with another computer, it sends a data packet to the port, which the device is connected to. When the packet arrives at the port, it is forwarded or copied to the other ports so that all network devices can see the packet. In this way, all of the stations "see" every packet just as they do on a bus network. Of course, a standard hub is not very efficient on networks with heavy traffic since it causes a lot of collisions and retransmitted packets. See figure 6.10.

Hubs can be categorized as passive hubs or active hubs. A passive hub serves as a simple multiple connection point, which does not act as a repeater for the signal. An active hub, which always requires a power source, acts as a multi-ported repeater for the signal. Note: When installing an active hub, if the hub has a fan (which provides cooling), make sure that the fan is operating.

The most advanced hub is called the intelligent hub (also known as a manageable hub). An intelligent hub includes additional features that enable an administrator to monitor the traffic passing through the hub and to configure each port in the hub. For example, you can prevent certain computers from communicating with other computers or you can stop certain types of packets from being forwarded. In addition, you can gather information on a variety of network parameters, such as the numbers of packets that pass through the hub and each of its ports, what types of packets they are, whether the packets contain errors, and how many collisions have occurred.

Figure 6.11   A Bridge

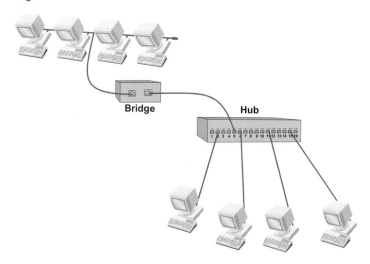

A bridge analyzes the incoming data packet and will forward the packet if its destination is on the other side of the bridge. Many bridges today filter and forward packets with very little delay, making them good for networks with high traffic. See figure 6.11.

There are two kinds of bridges: basic and learning. A basic bridge is used to interconnect LANs using one (or more) of the IEEE 802 standards. Packets received on one port may be retransmitted on another port. Unlike a repeater, a bridge will not start retransmission until it has received the complete packet. As a consequence, stations on both sides of a bridge can transmit simultaneously without causing collisions.

Security+ Objective 3.1.3—Switches

A **switching hub** (sometimes referred to as switch or a layer 2 switch) is a fast multi-ported bridge, which builds a table of the MAC addresses of all the connected stations. It then reads the destination address of each packet and then forwards the packet to the correct port. A major advantage of using a switching hub is that it allows one computer to open a connection to another computer (or LAN segment). While those two computers communicate, other connections between the other computers (or LAN segments) can be opened at the same time. Therefore, several computers can communicate at the same time through the switching hub. As a result, the switches are used to increase performance of a network by segmenting large networks into several smaller, less congested LANs, while providing necessary interconnectivity between them. Switches increase network performance by providing each port with dedicated bandwidth, without requiring users to change any existing equipment, such as NICs, hubs, wiring, or any routers or bridges that are currently in place.

Many switching hubs also support load balancing, so that ports are dynamically reassigned to different LAN segments based on traffic patterns. In addition, some include fault tolerance, which can reroute traffic through other ports when a segment goes down.

Switches can be used to segment a large network into several smaller, less congested segments (breaking up collision domains) while providing necessary interconnectivity between them. Switches increase network performance by providing each port with dedicated bandwidth, without requiring users to change any existing equipment, such as NICs, hubs, wiring, or any routers or bridges that are currently in place.

Switches are more secure than hubs. Since Ethernet works with broadcast technology, switches will reduce the effectiveness of network traffic sniffing because the traffic is not forwarded to all ports, only the destination ports of the packets. Therefore, if someone plugs a protocol analyzer to a port on the switch, they will not see communications between the other ports of the switch.

Security+ Objective 3.1.2—Routers

A router, which works at the network ISO layer, is a device that connects two or more LANs. As multiple LANs are connected together, multiple routes are created to get from one LAN to another.

NOTE: Since a router needs to know which network to route to, each port must have a unique network address. The primary role of a router is to transmit similar types of data packets from one local area network or wide area communications link (such as a T-1 or Fiber links) to another.

A multi-homed computer is a PC with two or more network cards. Each card is configured to a different network or subnet and is configured to act as a router. While a multi-homed computer is not as fast as an actual router, it is relatively inexpensive to implement.

The second role of a router is to select the best path between the source and destination. When you send a packet from one computer to another computer, it first determines if the packet is sent locally to another computer on the same LAN or if the packet is sent to router so that it can be routed to the destination LAN. If the packet is meant to go to a computer on another LAN, it is sent to the router (or gateway). The router will then determine what is the best route to take and forward the packets to that route. The packet will then go to the next router, and the entire process will repeat itself until it gets to the destination LAN. The destination router will then forward the packets to the destination computer.

To determine the best route, the routers use complex routing algorithms, which take into account a variety of factors including the speed of the transmission media, the number of network segments, and the network segment that carries the least amount of traffic. Routers then share status and routing information to other routers so that they can provide better traffic management and bypass slow connections. In addition, routers provide additional functionality, such as the ability to filter messages and forward them to different places based on various criteria. Most routers are multiprotocol routers because they can route data packets using many different protocols.

A metric is a standard of measurement, such as hop count, that is used by routing algorithms to determine the optimal path to a destination. A hop is the trip a data packet takes from one router to another router or a router to another intermediate point to another in the network. On a large network, the number of hops a packet has taken toward its destination is called the hop count. When a computer communicates with another computer, and the computer has to go through 4 routers, it would have a hop count of 4. With no other factors taken in account, a metric of 4 would be assigned. If a router had to choose between a route with 4 metrics and a route with 6 metrics, it would choose the route with 4 metrics over the route with 6 metrics. Of course, if you want the router to choose the route with 6 metrics, you can overwrite the metric for the route with 4 hops in the routing table to a higher value.

Static routing algorithms are hardly algorithms at all, but are table mappings established by the network administrator prior to the beginning of routing. These mappings do not change unless the network administrator alters them. Algorithms that use static routes are simple to design and work well in environments where network traffic is relatively predictable and where network design is relatively simple.

Because static routing systems cannot react to network changes, they generally are considered unsuitable for today's large, changing networks. Most of the dominant routing algorithms are dynamic routing algorithms, which adjust to changing network circumstances by analyzing incoming routing update messages. If the message indicates that a network change has occurred, the routing software recalculates routes and sends out new routing update messages. These messages flow through the network, stimulating routers to rerun their algorithms and change their routing tables accordingly.

Dynamic routing algorithms can be supplemented with static routes where appropriate. A router of last resort (a router to which all unroutable packets are sent), for example, can be designated to act as a repository for all unroutable packets, ensuring that all messages are at least handled in some way. Examples of dynamic routers include RIP, OSPF, and NLSP.

Dynamic router algorithms are often divided into two categories: distance vector-based routing protocols and link-state routing protocols. Routers that use distance vector-based routing protocols periodically advertise or broadcast the routes in their routing tables, but they only send it to their neighboring routers. Routing information exchanged between typical distance vector-based routers is unsynchronized and unacknowledged. Distance vector-based routing protocols are simple, easy to understand, and easy to configure. The disadvantage is that multiple routes to a given network can reflect multiple entries in the routing table, which leads to a large routing table. In addition, if you have a large routing table, network traffic increases as it periodically advertises the routing table to the other routers, even after the network has converged. Lastly, with distance vector protocols, convergence of large internetworks can take several minutes. RIP for TCP/IP and RIP for IPX are examples of distance vector routing protocols.

Link-state algorithms are also known as shortest path first algorithms. Instead of using broadcast, link-state routers send updates directly (or by using multicast traffic) to all routers within the network. Each router, however, sends only the portion of the routing table that describes the state of its own links. In essence, link-state algorithms send small updates everywhere. Because they converge more quickly, link-state algorithms are somewhat less prone to routing loops than distance-vector algorithms. In addition, link-state algorithms do not exchange any routing information when the internetwork has converged. They have small routing tables since they store a single optimal route for each network ID. On the other hand, link-state algorithms require more CPU power and memory than distance-vector algorithms. Link-state algorithms, therefore, can be more expensive to implement and support and are considered harder to understand. OSPF for TCP/IP and NLSP for IPX are examples of link-state routing protocols.

To keep track of the various routes in a network, the routers will create and maintain routing tables based on both network and node addresses (Layer 3—Network Layer of the OSI model). The routers communicate with one another to maintain their routing tables through a routing update message. The routing update message can consist of all or portion of a routing table. By analyzing routing updates from all other routers, a router can build a detailed picture of network topology.

In addition to performing these basic functions, routers may perform any of the following options:

- Filter out broadcast transmissions to alleviate network congestion.
- Prevent certain types of traffic from getting to a network or from leaving a network, enabling customized segregation and security.
- Monitor network traffic and report statistics to a Management Information Base (MIB).
- Diagnose internal or other connectivity problems and trigger alarms.

Another routing hybrid, a **layer 3 switch** or routing switch combines a router and a switch. It has been optimized for high-performance LAN support and is not meant to service wide area connections (although it could easily satisfy the requirements for high-performance MAN connectivity, such as SONET). Because it is designed to handle high-performance LAN traffic, a layer 3 switch can be placed anywhere within a network core or backbone, easily and cost-effectively replacing the traditional collapsed backbone router. The layer 3 switch communicates with the WAN router using industry-standard routing protocols like RIP and OSPF. Therefore, if you need a router to segment your network, you can use a layer 3 switch, in which it could use its high performance. If you need to connect through a WAN connection, you would use a router. Of course, for your campus or large building, you can use the level 3 switches to connect your segments and then link the level 3 switches to the router to connect to the WAN.

6.2.4   VLANS

Security+ Objective 3.3.2—VLANs

As networks have grown in size and complexity, many companies have turned to virtual local area networks (VLANs) to provide some way for structuring this growth logically. Basically, a VLAN is a collection of nodes that are grouped together in a single broadcast domain that is based on something other than physical location. A VLAN is a switched network that is logically segmented on an organizational basis, by functions, project teams, or applications, rather than on a physical or geographical basis. In a VLAN, member hosts can communicate as if they were attached to the same wire, when in fact they can be located on any number of physical LANs. Because VLANs form broadcast domains, members enjoy the connectivity, shared services, and security associated with physical LANs. Reconfiguration of the network can be done through software rather than by physically unplugging and moving devices or wires. In addition, you can use VLAN technology to break a single physical subnet into multiple logical subnets, reducing collisions and broadcast overhead.

In a traditional network with a hub connected to a router, you might often have your network divided by function. For example, let's say that the second floor of your building contains all of the salespeople and their computers, and the third floor contains all of the marketing people and their computers. The computers on the second floor are connected to a hub or hubs, which is connected to a router, the computers on the third floor are connected to different hubs, which are also connected to the router. You run out of space on the second floor, and you need to add another salesperson. Unfortunately, if you connect the new salesperson into the hubs used by the third floor, the person has to go through a slower router to get to the resources that have been assigned to the second floor and the system will see all of the broadcasts meant for the marketing people. Therefore, as you can see, this can be a security issue and a performance issue.

Some older applications have been rewritten to reduce their bandwidth needs. But today, a new generation of multimedia applications consume more bandwidth than every before, consuming all they can find. These applications use broadcast and multicasts extensively. In addition, faulty equipment, inadequate segmentation and poorly designed firewalls only serve to compound the problem that these broadcast-intensive applications create. All of this has added a new dimension to network design. Making sure the network is properly segmented in order to isolate one segment's problems and keep those problems from propagating throughout the internetwork is imperative. The most effective way of doing this is through strategic switching and routing.

A broadcast domain is a set of NICs for which a broadcast frame sent by one NIC will be received by all other NICs in the broadcast domain. While a bridge and switch isolate collision domains on the same subnet, a VLAN (defined using a switch) will isolate broadcast domains.

NOTE: Since routers typically do not allow broadcasts, they also define broadcast domains. See figure 6.12 and 6.13.

Just as switches isolate collision domains for attached hosts and only forward appropriate traffic out a particular port, VLANs provide complete isolation between VLANs. A VLAN is a bridging domain, and all broadcast and multicast traffic is contained within it. Therefore, a VLAN can be thought of as a broadcast domain that exists within a defined set of switches. Since switches have become more cost-effective lately, many companies are replacing their flat hub networks with a pure switched network and VLANs environment. See figure 6.14.

VLANs also improve security by isolating groups. High-security users can be grouped into a VLAN, possible on the same physical segment, and no users outside that VLAN can communicate with them. Administrators can now have control over each port and whatever resources that port could access. This prevents a user from plugging their workstation into any switch port and gaining access to network resources. To make it more flexible, servers can be members of multiple VLANs so that the users can get access to the resources that they need.

6.3   SECURING THE NETWORK INFRASTRUCTURE

Now that this chapter reviewed the basic components of the network infrastructure, this section will look at the security risks associated with the network infrastructure and how you can protect your network infrastructure.

Figure 6.12   A Broadcast Domain

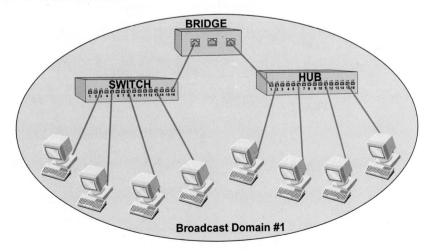

Figure 6.13 A Broadcast Domain is Defined by Routers

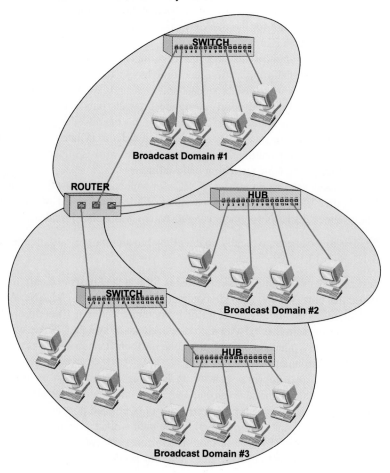

Figure 6.14 A Sample Network Using VLAN

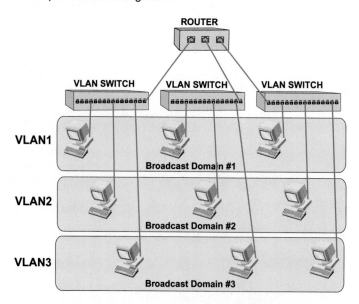

6.3.1   Protecting the Cables and Network Connectivity Devices

One of the easiest ways to disable a network is to disconnect or unplug a cable connector. Some managed hub, switches, and routers can alert you when a cable is unplugged.

Another easy way is to cut one of the cables with wire cutters or even a pair of scissors. Copper cables can be disabled by excessively bending the cable, and fiber optic cables can be disabled by crushing, bending, or snapping them. If someone unplugs or cuts an unshielded twisted pair cable, you disable that computer or network device that is using that cable. If that cable is connected to a workstation, it only affects that single person who uses the workstation. If the cable is connected to a server, it affects the people who use the network resources on the server. If you cut a coaxial cable or remove one of the terminator resistors used in a bus topology, the entire network will fail and users will not be able to connect.

One way to disable multiple hosts is to disable the hub or switches that the PCs connect to. If someone shuts off the hub or switch, unplugs the power cable for the hub or switch, or even steals the hub or switch, everyone who is trying to connect to the hub or switch will not be able to access the network.

If you want to disable an entire LAN, you can disconnect or cut a cable that leads to a router or WAN link, shut down the router, disconnect the power cable of a router, or steal the router. While people should still be able to connect to network resources that are located on the local network, those users on the local network will not be able to connect to other networks including the Internet.

To prevent an attack on your cabling system or network connectivity devices is to prevent attackers from ever gaining access to your network infrastructure. Unfortunately, this can be extremely difficult. But some of the ways may include the following:

- Hire security guards.
- Install sensors, alarms, closed-circuit TV cameras and monitoring equipment.
- Use a man-trap to enter a building or a security area.
- Use physical access badges and security cards to enter a building.
- Bury or enclose network cables.
- Lock wiring closets and server rooms.

A man-trap is a security measure in which a narrow passageway permits visual, electronic, and biometric identification of personnel before entering the co-location space. The doors at either end are never open at the same time. By using a man-trap, this protects against physical piggybacking, in which one or more people sneak in with another person.

Most of your network connectivity devices and major cable links should be located in a server room or wiring closet. It is therefore very important that these rooms are locked and possibly have sensors, alarms, cameras, or some other forms of monitoring equipment. Of course, you would restrict access to these rooms to a limited number of people. The other cables can be protected by either burying or enclosing the network cable. Lastly, you should consider hiring security guards, using physical access badges and security cards to enter the building, physically inspecting your cable infrastructure on a routine basis, and training everyone to report anything suspicious. In addition, when a network goes down and you diagnose a cable or network connectivity device as the problem, you should look for signs of tampering.

Networks can also be hampered or disabled by heat, radio frequency interference, or electromagnetic interference. Too much heat has always been bad for computer and networking equipment. Therefore, you should always make sure that cables, computers, and network devices are away from any heat sources. In addition, since computers and network devices have fans to help cool the system, you should make sure that computers and network devices have enough air ventilation and that the fans are operating properly. You should also consider a maintenance program to clean out dust and dirt from these systems, which would cause heat to build up.

Interference occurs when undesirable electromagnetic waves affect the desired signal. Interference can be caused by **electromagnetic interference (EMI),** caused by large electromagnets used in industrial machinery, motors, fluorescent lighting and power lines, and **radio frequency interference (RFI),** which is caused by transmission sources such as a radio station. Therefore, when inspecting your network infrastructure, you should make sure that computers, network devices, and cables are not near any of these devices that can generate EMI or RFI. In addition, you may need to put servers and other sensitive equipment on their own power circuit to limit the AC line noise.

6.3.2   Securing Hubs, Switches, and Routers Operations

Security+ Objective 3.1.3—Switches

Intelligent devices, including intelligent hubs, intelligent switches, and all routers, need to be configured to operate properly. These are configured by connecting a PC through a console port, or by connecting remotely through the network. Therefore, it is imperative that you limit access to these devices.

It has already been discussed that these types of devices should be physically secured in a server room or wiring closet. Then you should disable any methods of connecting to the device that are not being used. And, most importantly, you need to enable and configure passwords for these devices. If the devices have a choice of the type of passwords, you should always choose an encrypted password, such as the secret passwords available with Cisco devices. In addition, you should always use strong passwords. You should also make sure not to use the default passwords that come with these devices. It should be mentioned once more that if a person can physically access a hub, switch, or router, they can disable or bypass any security configured within the device such as passwords. You should also have documented the configuration of each of your network devices, and you should routinely check to see if they have been reconfigured.

Like a network operating system, these intelligent hubs, switches, or routers run an operating system. Occasionally, these devices might have software configuration problems or security vulnerabilities. So like a network operating system, you need to keep checking for vendor patches and install them when available. If possible, you should test the patches before rolling them out to production systems.

While routers add networks to their routing table that they are directly connected to, routers learn of other networks through router packets from other routers. Attackers easily perform RIP spoofing by utilizing routing protocols such as Router Information Protocol (RIP) to update routing tables with invalid information. To protect yourself against RIP spoofing, RIP version 2 (RIPv2) specifies which routers it will receive router updates from, and it will allow passwords to validate those messages. Note: While simple password authentication was originally defined, newer authentication mechanism such as Message Digest 5 (MD5) are available.

Lastly, you can use access list entries to prevent inappropriate connections and routing of traffic. For example, packets with the IP address of your internal network should not be coming from the outside through the external interface on the router. If this happens, it usually indicates that someone is trying to perform IP address spoofing.

For example, you can configure each RIP router with a list of routers (by IP address) which RIP announcements are accepted from. By configuring a list of RIP peers, RIP announcements from unauthorized RIP routers are discarded. In addition, to prevent RIP traffic from being received by any node except neighboring RIP routers, you can set up some routers to use unicast RIP announcements to neighboring RIP routers.

In addition, you can configure route filters on each RIP interface so that the only routes considered for addition to the routing table are those that reflect reachable network IDs within the internetwork. For example, if an organization is using subnets of the private network ID 10.0.0.0, route filtering can be used so that the RIP routers discard all routes except those within the 10.0.0.0 network ID.

6.3.3   Unauthorized Access and Eavesdropping

Security+ Objective 3.1.3—Switches

Security+ Objective 3.2—Media

Ethernet was originally designed as a technology that broadcast all packets on a bus. For a bus topology network using a coaxial cable, when one PC needs to communicate with another PC, the packet is sent along the bus. All PCs can see the packet on the bus, but only the PC that it was destined for processes the packet. Ethernet that uses unshielded twisted pair cable connected to a hub works in a similar way. While the network may use a star topology, the logical path of the signal is actually a bus. When one PC communicates with another PC, again, all of the PCs can see the packets, but only the one that it is destined for will process the packet. In both of these cases, you can see all of the data packets that go on the network by using a protocol analyzer. In addition, with twisted pair cabling, you could splice into the twisted-pair cable or use special devices that can read escaping electromagnetic signals that pass through the wire.

Any connection along the coaxial segment or the hub is susceptible to eavesdropping. If someone decides to connect to a coaxial cable, the network must be temporarily disconnected to insert the new node. To help prevent eavesdropping, protect your network cable as much as possible by burying it underground, placing it inside walls or protecting it within tamper-proof containers. You should also document your cable infrastructure and inspect your cable infrastructure on a routine basis. Of course, you should investigate any outages on your coaxial cable, and you should investigate all undocumented hosts and connections.

To protect a twisted-pair network connected together with a hub, you need to physically secure your network connectivity devices. In addition, since switches only forward packets to their destination port, you could use switches instead of hubs.

Promiscuous mode is a condition in which a network adapter can be placed to gather all passing information. Normally, network adapters do not gather information that is not specifically destined for the adapter or broadcast to all adapters. But certain programs including protocol analyzers can put the adapter into promiscuous mode. While network card manufacturers and operating system have instructions on how to disable promiscuous mode, it can usually be easily reenabled by someone with a little knowledge. However, some network card manufacturers offer network cars on which promiscuous mode can be permanently disabled.

Switches often have a function called port mirroring or port spanning, which allows the administrator to map the input and output from one or more ports on the switch to a single port. This is meant to be used to troubleshoot problems on the network when the administrator wants to view every packet being sent. However, if an attacker is configuring port mirroring, he or she could watch all network traffic that passes through the switch. To protect against this, you need to secure your switch physically and with passwords.

As discussed earlier, bridges and switches segment the network and forward packets from one port to another port based on MAC addresses. The MAC addresses that it collects are stored in an ARP cache. It might be possible for an attacker to use **Address Resolution Protocol (ARP) cache poisoning,** which allows a user to put false addresses in the cache, which then causes the packets to be forwarded to the wrong destination.

For an attacker to conduct ARP cache poisoning, he or she must typically gain physical connectivity to the local segment. The attacker must then access and compromise the ARP cache of the hosts on that segment. ARP cache poisoning involves overwriting entries in the ARP cache to cause a computer to send all network traffic directly to the attacker's computer. If an attacker is able to do this to all the computers on the segment, he or she could effectively listen to (and forward) data packets without the network users realizing it. The attacker would then be able to listen to the network traffic sent on the network, most likely to steal sensitive information or obtain passwords.

To prevent someone from connecting unauthorized PCs (either by connecting their own personal PC or by connecting a hub to their network jack in their office or cubicle and connecting several PCs), you could use port security found in many of the high-level switches. With these switches, you can specify the number of devices that can connect through each switch port, and you can specify the MAC address of the network devices that you want to connect to the network so that other network devices will be denied accessed. It will also prevent the switch or bridge from learning new addresses.

On some managed hubs, switches and routers can alert you when a cable is connected. You can also monitor your network with management tools (such as ARPWATCH, which can alert you of changes to the ARP mappings) that alert you to unauthorized connections.

You can use VLANs, configured on switches, to improve security by isolating groups. You could control each port or the device that connects to the switch and specify which network resources that port can access. This prevents users plugging their workstations into a switch port and gaining access to network resources. To make it more flexible, servers can be members of multiple VLANs so that the users can get access to the resources that they need.

Electronic eavesdropping on fiber optic cables is almost impossible because they uses light pulses instead of electrical signals. To eavesdrop on a fiber network, you must cut the cable, polish the ends and attach the two ends to a network interface.

6.3.4   Protecting Documentation

As mentioned in chapter 2, to help you troubleshoot your network and for new IT people to learn about your network, you should have network infrastructure documented, including how the network is cabled and how each network connection is addressed. However, you must also take care in protecting this documentation so that it cannot be used to hack into your network.

6.4   FIREWALLS AND PROXY SERVERS

Security+ Objective 3.1.1—Firewalls

Firewalls, which are often routers, serve as a primary defense against external threats to an organization's computer network system. The firewall is usually a combination of hardware and software used to implement an organization's security policy governing network traffic. This network traffic is between two or more networks, one of which is under the organization's control. Two objectives common to all firewall systems is to allow the flow of network traffic that has been determined to be consistent with the organization's security policy and to minimize the amount and usefulness of information about the organization's computer network system that is disclosed to those outside the firewall. A firewall is a barrier to keep destructive forces away from an organization's computer system. The organization's computer system could be directly accessible to anyone on the Internet if a firewall is not in place.

Without a firewall, an organization will not be able to prevent many forms of undesirable access to their computer systems and information assets. The undesirable access could lead to loss of confidential business information; loss of availability of mission critical services; exposure of system infrastructure to those who might attack the system, and vandalism of public information services, such as the organization's website. Firewall technology provides the organization with one of the most effective tools available to manage network risk by providing access control mechanisms that can implement complex security policies.

Firewalls are customizable so that filters can be added or removed based on several conditions. The firewall administrator can control how an organization's employees connect to Internet sites and whether files are allowed to leave the organization via the Internet. A firewall can give the organization tremendous control over how employees use the Internet. For example, a security rule could be implemented to allow only one computer within the organization to be able to receive public FTP traffic. A firewall can also do the following:

- Access control based on time of day or an authenticated user ID, allowing access to a service only during certain times of the day or by certain user ID's, and disallowing it at other times or for other users
- Session logging, useful for tracking connection utilization.
- Intrusion detection and notification (and optionally, network reconfiguration in response to an intrusion).

A firewall can be as simple as a router that filters packets or as complex as a multicomputer, multirouter solution that combines packet filtering and application-level proxy services. An organization's network security policy must contain procedures to safeguard the network and its contents against damage or loss. A network security policy identifies network resources and threats, defines network use and responsibilities, and details action plans to follow when policy is violated. The network security policy needs to be strategically enforced at defensible boundaries within the organization's network. These strategic boundaries are called perimeter networks.

To establish an organization's perimeter networks, the system administrator must designate the computers that are to be protected and define the network security mechanisms that protect them. To establish a successful network security perimeter, the firewall sever must be the gateway for all communications between trusted networks within the organization's control and untrusted external networks such as the Internet. The firewall server defines the point of focus or choke point through which all communications between the internal and external networks pass.

To help monitor the network traffic, two main approaches have proven extremely valuable:

- Packet filters—You can examine traffic at the network layer, looking at the source and destination addresses. The filter can disallow traffic to or from specific addresses or address ranges and can disallow traffic with suspect address patterns.
- Firewalls—You can also examine traffic as high as the application layer, checking ports in message addresses or even checking the internal content of specific application messages. Traffic that fails any of those tests can be rejected.

There are two approaches to designing a set of rules. The best protection will result from rules that specify what traffic is allowed to be passed through a router: All other traffic should be rejected, hence the common name for this strategy—"default-deny." The alternative "default-permit" strategy can effectively block particular, known, attacks but it is unlikely to provide protection against new attacks. It should not, therefore, be regarded as a long-term solution. However, even blocking a few well-chosen services is better than nothing.

6.4.1   Packet Filters

As you recall, TCP/IP addresses are composed of both a machine address and, within the machine, a port number identifying the program to handle the message. The combined address/port information is available in every TCP/IP message, with the exception of broadcasts and some messages exchanged while a TCP/IP address is being assigned via the DHCP protocol, and is available for both the sender and the receiver of the message.

Packet filters are based on protecting the network by using an **access control list (ACL).** This list resides on your router and determines which machine (IP address) can use the router, what traffic can pass, and in what direction. For example, if you want to allow selected users to surf the Web, but not allow access to the Internet by others, you could set up the firewall to allow only port 80 and 443 connections from those users' workstations outbound to the Internet. Note: The security method of routers that use ACL's to disable ports is Mandatory Access Control (MAC).

Typically, the router will permit all outgoing traffic, but it will deny any new incoming connections. If a machine has established a connection with a machine on the outside, it will accept those packets. Therefore, it will reject unsolicited connection attempts from the Internet to your computer.

If your packet filter software is sophisticated enough to examine the subnet of the source address based on which the physical port delivers the message to the router, you can set up rules to avoid spoofed TCP/IP addresses. The idea behind spoofing is for messages from the Internet to appear to have originated from your LAN; the spoofing filter prevents this by rejecting messages coming on a port with impossible source addresses.

The anti-spoofing filter is an important part of protecting machines on your network on which you've installed filters to limit particular services to machines on your subnet. For instance, suppose that you've installed software on a Linux machine to act as a Windows network file server. You can configure Linux to reject all network traffic originating outside your subnet, preventing computers on the Internet from seeing the file server. If an attacker could pretend to be on your LAN, that safeguard would be bypassed. To defeat that attack, you would have to use anti-spoofing filter.

The anti-spoofing filter, also known as Egress and Ingress filtering, will only route outgoing packets if they have a valid internal IP address. By rule, your routers should disregard and drop any outgoing packets that have not originated from a valid internal IP address. When you perform this setting change, you will effectively prevent your network from becoming a participant in any spoofing attack. These address filters are:

    Historical Low End Broadcast: 0.0.0.0/8
        Limited Broadcast: 255.255.255.255/32
        RFC 1918 Private Networks: 10.0.0.0/8
        RFC 1918 Private Networks: 172.16.0.0/12
        RFC 1918 Private Networks: 192.168.0.0/16
        The Loop Back Address: 127.0.0.0/8
        Link Local Networks: 169.254.0.0/16

Class D Addresses: 224.0.0.0/4
Class E Reserved Address: 240.0.0.0/5
Unallocated Address: 248.0.0.0/5

There may be other addresses that need to be blocked by your router. However, the addresses listed above should help provide protection against DoS and/or spoofing attacks.

The U.S. National Security Agency (NSA) has published the *Router Security Configuration Guide*, which provides technical guidance intended to help network administrators and security officers improve the security of their networks. It contains principles and guidance for secure configuration of IP routers, with detailed instructions for Cisco Systems routers. The information presented can be used to control access, resist attacks, shield other network components, and protect the integrity and confidentiality of network traffic.

Help Defeat Denial of Service Attacks: Step-by-Step

http://www.sans.org/dosstep/index.htm

Router Security Configuration Guide

http://nsa2.www.conxion.com/cisco/download.htm

One disadvantage of a packet filter is that they generally don't protect against attacks using the UDP protocol. This is because there is no formal connection opened with UDP as there is with TCP and therefore, the filter cannot reject the opening message.

Besides analyzing the source and destination TCP/IP address, it can also examine the source and destination port numbers and the content of the packet data. This gives it far more power such as it can allow or disallow specific application services such as FTP or web pages, and it can allow or disallow access to services based on the content of the information being transferred. You can even combine these functions such as allowing incoming FTP access from the Internet, but only to a specific, designated server.

When you decide which port numbers to block, you need to choose with care. If you decide to block a specific port, any service or application that uses a specific port will not function through the firewall. For example, if you block port 80, you will not be able to contact http web servers that are using the default port 80.

6.4.2   Dynamic Packet Filters

Some firewalls are considered static packet filters, while others are considered dynamic packet filters. The static packet filter, the packet filtering mechanism, allows you to set rules based on protocol and port number to control inbound and outbound access on the external interface.

The dynamic packet filter is an extension of packet filtering and is often referred to as **stateful inspection.** It is a firewall facility that can monitor the state of active connections and use this information to determine which network packets to allow through the firewall. By recording session information such as IP addresses and port numbers into a dynamic state list (also known as a state table), a dynamic packet filter can implement a much tighter security posture than a static packet filter.

For example, assume that you wish to configure your firewall so that all users in your company are allowed out to the Internet, but only replies to users' data requests are let back in. With a static packet filter, you would need to permanently allow in replies from all external addresses, assuming that users were free to visit any site on the Internet. This kind of filter would allow an attacker to sneak information past the filter by making the packet look like a reply (which can be done by indicating "reply" in the packet header). By tracking and matching requests and replies, a dynamic packet filter can screen for replies that don't match a request. When a request is recorded, the dynamic packet filter opens up a small inbound hole so only the expected data reply is let back through. Once the reply is received, the hole is closed. This dramatically increases the security capabilities of the firewall such as preventing someone from replaying a packet to get access because it is not part of an active connection.

6.4.3   Circuit-level Gateway

While the application gateway operates on the OSI model's application layer, the circuit-level gateway operates on the transport level of the OSI model. As a second-generation firewall, **circuit-level gateways** validate TCP and UDP sessions before opening a connection. Since it operates at the transport layer, this means a circuit-level firewall actually establishes a virtual circuit between the client and the host on a session-by-session basis. Once a handshake has taken place, it passes everything through until the session is ended.

A circuit-level gateway translates IP addresses between the Internet and your internal systems. The gateway receives outbound packets and transfers them from the internal network to the external network. Inbound traffic is transferred from the outside network to the internal network. Circuit-level gateways provide a complete break between your internal network and the Internet. Unlike a packet filter, which simply analyzes and routes traffic, a circuit-level gateway translates packets and transfers them between network interfaces. This helps shield your network from external traffic since the packets appear to have originated from the circuit-level gateway's Internet IP address.

To validate and create a session, the circuit-level firewall examines each connection setup to ensure it follows a legitimate handshake for the transport layer being used, typically TCP. No data packets are forwarded to until the handshake is complete. The firewall maintains a table of valid connections, which includes session state and sequencing information, and let network packets containing data pass through when the network packet information matches an entry in the virtual circuit table. When a connection is terminated, its table entry is removed and that virtual circuit between the two peers is closed.

Circuit-level firewalls permit access through the firewall with a minimum amount of scrutiny by building a limited form of connection state, i.e., handshake, established, or closing. Only those packets that are associated with an established connection are allowed through the firewall. When a connection establishment request is received, the circuit-level firewall checks its rule base to determine whether or not the connection should be allowed. If it is allowed, all network packets associated with that connection are routed through the firewall with no further security checks. This method provides very fast service and a minimal amount of state checking.

Security+ Objective 3.3.3—NAT

Circuit-level application gateways often provide **network address translation (NAT),** in which a network host alters the packets of internal network hosts so they can be sent out across the Internet. NAT allows an Intranet to use addresses that are different from what the Internet sees. NAT allows insiders to get out without allowing outsiders to get in. NAT rewrites the IP headers of internal packets going out making it appear as if the packets originated from firewall. Reply packets coming back are translated and forwarded to the appropriate internal machine. With NAT, inside machines are allowed to connect to the outside world but outside machines cannot. In fact, outside machines cannot find the internal machines because they are aware of only one IP address—the firewall. The ability to attack internal machines is greatly reduced by employing NAT.

NAT can be static or dynamic. In static NAT, there is one-to-one mapping between each private address and a public address. The NAT process consists of modifying the source IP address on outgoing packets to the public address, and modifying the destination IP address on incoming packets to the private address. In this situation, an organization is required to have as many public network addresses as private network addresses, which sometimes isn't possible (for technical or political reasons).

In dynamic NAT (also known as hide NAT), NAT hides a number of network objects, or your entire network behind a single externally visible IP address. To use dynamic NAT, you only need to use a single IP address connected to the Internet (although you can have more). IP Masquerading is when you hide your network behind the external IP address of your firewall.

A variation of the dynamic NAT is when you have a pool of public addresses, and internal hosts needing Internet connectivity will be mapped to the next available public address on an as-needed basis. When the connection is terminated, the public address is returned to the pool, to be used again. Because of this reuse, it is possible to have a smaller number of public addresses than you have machines with private addresses, as long as all of the internal machines aren't using the Internet simultaneously.

Another variation on dynamic NAT is Port Address Translation (PAT). PAT, sometimes known as "single address NAT," is a specific case of NAT in which there is one external address, and multiple internal computers connecting to Internet hosts through it. In this case, not only does the IP address in the packet change but so does the TCP/IP port number. This is required because multiple internal connections are sharing the same public IP address simultaneously, and a connection using the same port number on the public address cannot be guaranteed, since someone else may already have it. An alternate explanation of PAT is that it is used to redirect requests for access to a specific port number on the external address, to a specific internal machine, based on a table of address/port redirections set up by the administrator. For example, if you have one external address, you might redirect port 80 packets to a web server in your network, port 25 packets to a mail server, etc. In this case, the port number of the packet doesn't change, but the address does.

Additionally, NAT eases administration by insulating an organization from external IP address changes. Without NAT, if an organization switches providers and is assigned a new Class C address, the organization would have to change every hard-coded address used in their organization (including configuration information like DHCP servers, DNS servers, etc.).

6.4.4   Application Gateway

Application-level gateways take requests for Internet services and forward them to the actual services. Application-level gateways sit between a user on the internal network and a service on the Internet. Instead of talking to each other directly, each system talks to the gateway. Your internal network never directly connects to the Internet.

Application-level gateways help improve security by examining all application layers, and they bring context information into the decision process. However, they do this by breaking the client/server model into two connections: one from the client to the firewall and one from the firewall to the server. Unfortunately, since each application gateway requires a different application process, or daemon, you will need to add a different application processor or daemon to support new applications.

A proxy server is a server that sits between a client application, such as a web browser, and a real server. It intercepts all requests to the real server to see if it can fulfill the requests itself. If not, it forwards the request to the real server. If it can fulfill the request itself, the user gets increased performance. In addition, it provides a means for sharing a single Internet connection among a number of workstations. While this has practical limits in performance, it can still be a very effective and inexpensive way to provide Internet services, such as email, throughout an office.

NOTE: Proxy servers typically refer to application gateways, but a circuit-level gateway is also a form of proxy server.

Besides increasing performance, a proxy server sits between a client program (typically a web browser) and some external server (typically another server on the Web), which acts as an application-level firewall. It acts as a type of firewall that manages packet sequence and origin to reduce the chance of hackers hijacking communication sessions.

NOTE: Proxy servers are often used with firewalls and sometimes are the same machine or device as a firewall.

The proxy server can monitor and intercept any and all requests being sent to the external server or that comes in from the Internet connection. Therefore, besides the proxy server improving performance and sharing connections, it can also filter requests.

Filtering requests is the security function and the original reason for having a proxy server. Proxy servers can inspect all traffic (in and out) over an Internet connection and determine if there is anything that should be denied transmission, reception, or access. Since this filtering cuts both ways, a proxy server can be used to keep users out of particular websites (by monitoring for specific URLs) or restrict unauthorized access to the internal network (by authenticating users). Before a connection is made, the server can ask the user to log in. To a web user, this makes every site look like it requires a login. Because proxy servers are handling all communications, they can log everything the user does. For HTTP (web) proxies this includes logging every URL. For FTP proxies this includes every downloaded file. A proxy can also examine the content of transmissions for "inappropriate" words or scan for viruses, although this may impose serious overhead on performance.

To the user, the proxy server is almost totally invisible. All Internet requests and returned responses appear to be directly with the addressed Internet server. The reason it is not totally invisible is that the IP address of the proxy server has to be specified as a configuration option to the browser or other protocol program.

For the browser to go through a proxy server, the browser must be configured. These configuration settings include automatic configuration, configuring through scripts or by manually specifying the settings. The automatic configuration and configuring through scripts enable you to change settings after you deploy Internet Explorer. By providing a pointer to configuration files on a server, you can change

Figure 6.15   Configuring the Proxy Selection and Proxy Bypass Settings In Internet Explorer

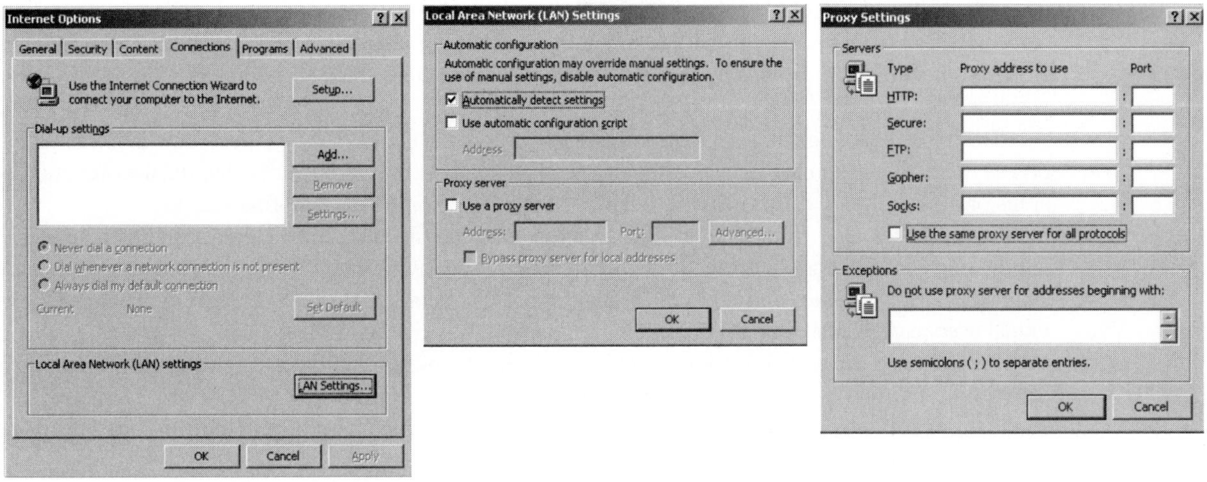

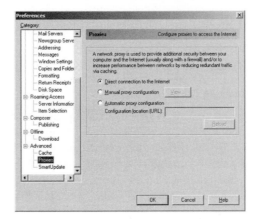

Figure 6.16   Configuring the Proxy Settings for Netscape Navigator

the settings globally without having to change each user's computer. This can help reduce administrative overhead and potentially reduce help desk calls about browser settings.

To configure the proxy selection and proxy bypass settings in Internet Explorer:

1. Open the Tools menu, and then click Internet Options.
2. Click the Connections tab, and then click LAN Settings.
3. In the Proxy Server area, select the Use a proxy server check box.
4. Click Advanced, and then fill in the proxy location and port number for each Internet protocol that is supported. See figure 6.15.

    NOTE: In most cases, only a single proxy server is used for all protocols. In those cases, enter the proxy location and port number for the HTTP setting, and then select the "Use the same proxy server for all protocols" check box. If you want to manual set the addresses, then enable the "Use a proxy server" and specify the address and port number of the proxy server. If you need to specify different addresses and/or port numbers for the various Internet services, click on the Advanced button.

For Netscape, the same basic options are available if you:

1. Open the Edit menu and select the Preferences option.
2. Find and open the Advanced option
3. Click on the Proxy option. See figure 6.16.

6.4.5   Advanced Firewall Features

Most firewalls today are a hybrid of stateful inspection, circuit-level gateways, and application-level gateways. Only packets dealing with acceptable activities are allowed in and out of your internal network. Some firewalls provide advanced firewalls features that make them more effective in your perimeter.

The firewall is a logical place to install authentication mechanisms to help overcome the limitations of TCP/IP. You can also use a reverse lookup on an IP address to try and verify that the user is actually at his or her reported location. This activity helps identify and prevent spoofing attacks.

Firewalls can also provide user authentication. Some application-level gateways contain an internal user account database or integrate with UNIX and Windows domain accounts. These accounts can be used to limit activities and services by user or provide detailed logs of user activity. Because individual users can be easily identified, more granular rule sets can be implemented.

You can also use authentication for remote access. Allowing employees to connect to the internal network from home or while traveling increases productivity, but how can you ensure that the person making the request is who he or she is supposed to be? Most firewalls support third-party authentication methods to provide strong authentication.

Lastly, almost every firewall performs some type of logging. Most packet filters do not enable logging by default because it degrades performance of traffic analysis. So if you want logging, make sure it is enabled and active. Extensive logging can help you track and potentially capture a hacker. Since your firewall is the single point of entry to your network, an attacker will have to pass through it. Your log files should provide information to show you what the hacker was up to on your systems.

6.4.6   Demilitarized Zone (DMZ)

Security+ **Objective 3.3.1**—Security Zones

Security+ **Objective 3.3.1.1**—DMZ

Security+ **Objective 3.3.1.2**—Intranet

Security zones are areas of your network with specific security-related attributes and requirements. They are typically broken into intranets, internets, extranets, and DMZ.

If you set a firewall between the Internet and your private network (intranet), it provides no good place to locate publicly accessible servers. If you place the servers out on the Internet in front of the firewall, they will be unprotected. If you have them behind the firewall, you have to create holes in the firewall protection to permit access to the servers. It is those holes that can be exploited on the rest of the network.

To get around this problem, you create a **demilitarized zone (DMZ).** Instead of having two ports, the public network on one port of the firewall and the private network on another port, you have three ports. The third port is the DMZ, which is a less secure area than the private network. The DMZ will include the Web and FTP servers and the rest of your computers will be in the private network. See figure 6.17.

Each segment—the public, the private, and the DMZ—that are connected to the firewall have a different set of security rules. The private and the public is no different from what we discussed before. On the DMZ LAN, you still want to use antispoofing filters, limit the allowable ports to those used by the servers on the LAN, and disallow access from known attacking sites. Note: Remember that firewalls themselves aren't a guarantee of security. You will have to get in the habit of examining firewall logs for suspicious events, and you have to be vigilant about discovering and applying software security patches.

6.4.7   TCP Wrappers

Linux computers (and some other network devices) use TCP Wrappers. For Linux, any network services managed by xinetd can use TCP wrappers to manage access to the Linux computer by using the `/etc/hosts.allow` and `/etc/hosts.deny files.`

The first of these (`/etc/hosts.allow`) specifies computers that are allowed access to the system in a particular way, the implication being that systems not listed are not allowed access. The `hosts.deny` file, by contrast, lists computers that are not allowed access; all others are given permission to use the system. If a system is listed in both files, hosts.allow takes precedence. By default, Linux allows connections from everywhere by default.

Figure 6.17   A DMZ

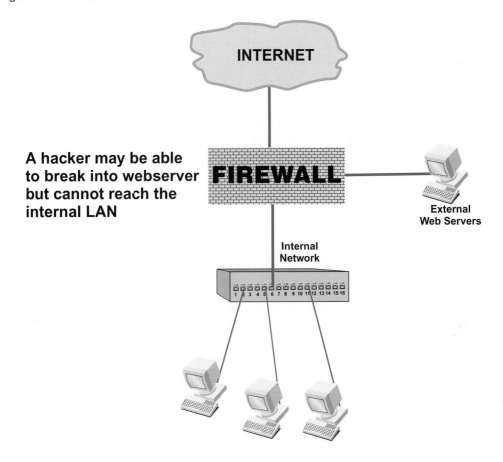

Both files use the same basic format. The files consist of the following lines:

```
daemon-list : client-list
```

The *daemon-list* is a list of services, using the names for the services that appear in /etc/services. There are also wildcards available, such as ALL to represent all services.

The client-list is a list of computers to be granted or denied access to the specified daemons. You can specify computers by name or by IP addresses, and you can specify a network by using (respectively) a leading or trailing dot (.). For instance, .acme.com blocks all computers in the acme.com domain, and 192.168.7. blocks all computers in the 192.168.7.0/24 network. You can also use wildcards in the client-list, such as ALL (all computers). EXCEPT causes an exception. For instance, when placed in `hosts.deny, 192.168.7. EXCEPT 192.168.7.105` blocks all computers in the 192.168.7.0/24 network except for 192.168.7.105.

Not all servers are protected by TCP Wrappers. Normally, only those servers that inetd runs via tcpd are so protected. Such servers typically include, but are not limited to, Telnet, FTP, TFTP, rlogin, finger, linuxconf, POP, and IMAP servers. In Linux distributions that have switched from inetd to xinetd, TCP Wrappers isn't normally used in conjunction with xinetd. Instead, they include its own access control features. For example, Samba provides hosts allow and hosts deny options that work much like TCP Wrappers file entries.

6.4.8   Ipchains and Iptables

The Linux kernel has support for packet filtering and masquerading. This support is provided by the package called IP chains. Installing and configuring IP chains is highly recommended when security is a must. There is always the danger of some unscrupulous individual breaking into your computer from the Internet or even from within your corporate network. If you take the time to install and configure IP chains properly, you can minimize the danger of this happening.

An IP chain is a set of related TCP/IP packet handling rules. The ipchains package always has at least three chains: input, forward, and output. All rules can be placed under one of these three chains, or new chains can be created if that is what the administrator prefers.

When establishing the chains, you should keep related rules together so they can be checked against one another. In addition, chain order is important. When a packet enters a chain, it is tested to determine if it matches each of the rules on the chain. If it does, it is passed to the target of that rule. If it reaches the end of the chain, it is passed to the chain's default target. A target specifies what to do with a packet that matches a particular rule or, in the case of the default targets, that reaches the end of a chain. There are six system targets as shown in table 6.3. Table 6.1 and table 6.2 show the ipchains commands and most common ipchains options.

Table 6.1   Ipchains Commands

Command	Action
-A chain	Adds rule to *chain*.
-D chain [rulenum]	Deletes rule number *rulenum* from *chain*. If *rulenum* is omitted, the default is the first rule (number 1).
-I chain [rulenum]	Inserts rule into *chain* before rule number *rulenum*.
-R chain [rulenum]	Replaces rule number *rulenum* in *chain*.
-F chain	Flushes *chain*. Equivalent to using -D on all rules one by one.
-L chain	Lists the rules in *chain*.
-N chain	Creates new user-defined chain.
-X chain	Deletes user-defined chain.
-P chain target	Sets default target for *chain* to *target*.

Table 6.2   Most Common Ipchains Options

Option	Specifies
-s [!] *address*[/*mask*] [!] [*port*[:*port*]]	Source address and port of the packet.
-d [!] *address*[/*mask*] [!] [*port*[:*port*]]	Destination address and port of the packet.
-i [!] *interface*	Interface the packet is arriving on (in the input chain) or leaving on (in the *output* and *forward* chains).
-p [!] *protocol*	Packet protocol. It may be any protocol specified in the /etc/protocols file.
-j *target* [port]	Target to send the packet to.
[!] -y	Packet is a SYN packet; only for rules that specify -p tcp.
—icmp-type *type*	ICMP type is type; only for rules that specify -p icmp.
-l	Log the packet to syslog.–n or–numeric. Used with the -L option. Displays numeric host and port addresses instead or names.

For incoming data, the first chain applied is the input chain. The forwarding chain examines it and passes it on to the appropriate local machine. This is typically used when the host is being used as a firewall or router. On the other hand, for outgoing data the first applied is the forwarding chain, and then the output chain.

There are two broad ways of thinking about firewall policies, mostly open and mostly closed. In a mostly-open firewall, your system lets everything through except the packets you specify. A mostly-closed firewall does the reverse, denying or rejecting everything except that which you specifically allow. This second kind of firewall is usually regarded as more secure, because you know exactly what is going through and won't be subject to future attacks based on unused protocols.

Consider a network that has an internal network using private addresses which is connected to the public Internet. You want all hosts in the internal network to access the Internet, while providing protection from external hackers. No one needs to access the internal hosts from the outside (thus, this kind of firewall is known as a one-way firewall). Figure 6.18 shows a script that will setup a one-way firewall. As you can see in this listing, you first set the default target of all chains to deny or reject and then add rules to accept those packets that you want to let through.

Table 6.3   The System Targets used in IP Chains

Name	Function
ACCEPT	Lets the packet through.
DENY	Drops the package silently.
REJECT	Drops the package, notifying the sender.
MASQ	Valid only if the forward chain or chains called from it. Masquerades the package.
REDIRECT	Valid only in the input chain or chains called from it. Sends the package to a port on the firewall host itself, regardless of its real destination. May be followed by a port specification to redirect the package to a different port regardless of its destination port.
RETURN	Transfers immediately to the end of the current chain; the package will be handled according to the chain's default target.

Figure 6.18   A Script to Set up a Basic Firewall Using Ipchains

```
#!/bin/sh -x
#To enable logging if necessary
#LOG=-1

#Constants
ANYWHERE=0.0.0.0/0
EXT_IF=eth0
INT_IF=eth1

#Networks
INTERNAL_NET=10.0.1.0/24
EXTERNAL_ADDR=205.142.24.1/32

#Disable packet forwarding while we set up the firewall
echo 0 > /proc/sys/net/ipv4/ip_forward

#Flush all rules
/sbin/ipchains -F input
/sbin/ipchains -F output
/sbin/ipchains -F forward
```

Figure 6.18   Continued

```
#Deny all packets by default - this is a mostly-closed firewall
/sbin/ipchains -P input DENY
/sbin/ipchains -P output DENY
/sbin/ipchains -P forward DENY

#Accept anything to/from localhost
/sbin/ipchains -A input -j ACCEPT -p all -s localhost -d localhost -I lo $LOG
/sbin/ipchains -A output -j ACCEPT -p all -s localhost -d localhost -I lo $LOG

#Spoofing protection - deny anything coming from an outside with #an internal address
/sbin/ipchains -A input -j RETURN -p all -s $INTERNAL_NET -d $ANYWHERE -I @EXT_IF $LOG

#Accept TCP packets belonging to already-established connections
/sbin/ipchains -A input -j ACCEPT -p tcp -s $ANYWHERE -d $ME -I $EXT_IF \! -y $LOG

#Accept and masquerade all packets from the inside going #anywhere
/sbin/ipchains -A input -j ACCEPT -p all -s $INTERNAL_NET -d $ANYWHERE -I $INT_IF $LOG
/sbin/ipchains -A forward -j MASQ -p all -s $INTERNAL_NET -d $ANYWHERE -I $INT_IF $LOG

#Accept all TCP packets going to the outside net
/sbin/ipchains -A output -j ACCEPT -p all -s $ME -d $ANYWHERE -I $EXT_IF $LOG

#Accept type 3 ICMP queries (Destination Unreachable)
/sbin/ipchains -A input -j ACCEPT -p icmp -s $ANYWHERE -d $ME -I $EXT_IF \
--icmp-type destination-unreachable $LOG
/sbin/ipchains -A output -j ACCEPT -p icmp -s $ME -d $ANYWHERE -I $EXT_IF \
--icmp-type destination-unreachable $LOG

#Catch-all rules to provide logging
/sbin/ipchains -A input -j DENY -l
/sbin/ipchains -A output -j DENY -l
/sbin/ipchains -A forward -j DENY -l

#Enable packet forwarding
echo 1 > /proc/sys/net/ipv4/ip_forward
```

When you make changes to the ipchain rules, keep in mind that the rules are not saved. Therefore, when you shut down or reboot the computer, these rules are lost and have to be rebuilt the next time the machine comes up. To work around this, two scripts have been created. The ipchains-save script will save the rules. For example, if you execute the following command:

```
ipchains-save > /root/ipchains-rules
```

it will save the rules to the ipchains-rules file.

The ipchains-restore script reads the rules saved from the last shutdown and reimplements them so they are put back in place. Rather than running this script by hand, you should add the following command to the init files such as rc.local:

```
/sbin/ipbinchains-restore < /root/ipchains-rules
```

Iptables used to filter packets are very similar to ipchains. Note: The chain names INPUT, OUTPUT, and FORWARD are all uppercase letters. It still uses lists of packet filtering rules (chains) and the common command-line arguments are identical.

Different from ipchains, the iptables uses a simpler model. The INPUT chain applies only to packets that are destined for the local machine itself. The OUTPUT chain applies to locally generated packets only. The FORWARD chain only sees packets that are just passing through. Therefore, in this architecture, there is only one place (or one chain) to do the packet filtering for any given packet. Not only does this reduce confusion, it also simplifies the filtering rules. See figure 6.19.

Figure 6.19   Sample Packet Filter

```
# Let everything out.
iptables -A FORWARD -o ppp+ -j ACCEPT

# Only let replies in.
iptables -A FORWARD -i ppp+ -m state --state ESTABLISHED,RELATED -j ACCEPT
```

Figure 6.20   Internet Connection Firewall (personal firewall) Used In Windows XP

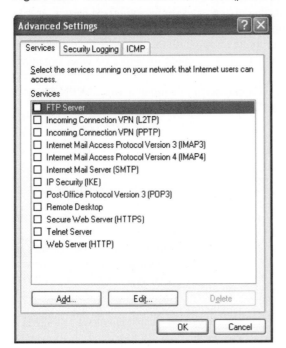

For more information on iptables, see the following website:

Netfilter/Iptables Home Page

http://www.iptables.org/

6.4.9   Personal Firewalls

Today, many operating systems offer personal firewalls to protect an individual computer when connecting to the Internet. For example, Windows XP has the Internet Connection Firewall (ICF) (see figure 6.20) and Linux has GNOME Lokkit. Much like a full-blown firewall, a personal firewall restricts what information is communicated from your home or small office network to and from the Internet to your computer.

Most of the personal firewalls are considered "stateful" firewalls. A stateful firewall is one that monitors all aspects of the communications that cross its path and inspects the source and destination address of each message that it handles. To prevent unsolicited traffic from the public side of the connection from entering the private side, the private firewall keeps a table of all communications that have originated from the computer. Some of these firewalls can be used in conjunction with Internet sharing, which, in turn, will keep track of all traffic originated from the computers sharing the Internet link. All inbound traffic from the Internet is compared against the entries in the table. Inbound Internet traffic is only allowed to reach the computers in your network when there is a matching entry in the table that shows that the communication exchange began from within your computer or private network. Communications that originate from a source on the Internet are dropped by the firewall unless an entry using the configuration options of the personal firewall is made to allow passage.

With these personal firewalls, the firewall can be configured to allow unsolicited traffic from the Internet to be forwarded by the computer to the private network. For example, if you are hosting an HTTP web server service, and have enabled the HTTP service on your ICF computer, unsolicited HTTP traffic will be forwarded by the computer with the personal firewall to the HTTP web server.

6.4.10   Extranets

Security+ Objective 3.3.1.3—Extranet

An extranet is another type of logical network, which allows a business to connect with suppliers, vendors, customers, stockholders or others related to its business. An extranet is usually run over the Internet, often using a VPN for security. Alternatively, some companies limit their extranet functionality to data exchange via SSL-protected web pages that can only be accessed by authorized parties, and do not implement a VPN. The extranet's primary components are normally situated within the company's internal network, allowing limited access to some corporate resources to those outside the organization on a need-to-know basis, and allowing corporate staff to access limited resources on other organizations' networks as needed.

If you are employing a VPN for your intranet, you may wish to employ a second VPN for your extranet, to best separate this "restricted public access" traffic from your completely internal traffic.

WHAT YOU NEED TO KNOW

Security+ Objective 3.1.1—Firewalls

1. Firewalls, which are often routers, serve as a primary defense against external threats to an organization's computer network system.
2. The firewall is usually a combination of hardware and software used to implement an organization's security policy governing network traffic.
3. To establish an organization's perimeter networks, the system administrator must designate the computers that are to be protected and define the network security mechanisms that protect them.
4. To establish a successful network security perimeter, the firewall sever must be the gateway for all communications between trusted networks within the organization's control and untrusted external networks such as the Internet.
5. Packet filters are based on protecting the network by using an access control list (ACL). This list resides on your router and determines which machine (IP address) can use the router, what traffic can pass and in what direction.
6. The anti-spoofing filter is an important part of protecting machines on your network on which you've installed filters to limit particular services to machines on your subnet.
7. The anti-spoofing filter, also known as Egress and Ingress filtering, will only route outgoing packets if they have a valid internal IP address.
8. By rule, your routers should disregard and drop any outgoing packets that have not originated from a valid internal IP address.
9. The dynamic packet filter is an extension of packet filtering and is often referred to as stateful inspection. It is a firewall facility that can monitor the state of active connections and use this information to determine which network packets to allow through the firewall.
10. Circuit-level gateways validate TCP and UDP sessions before opening a connection.
11. Application-level gateways sit between a user on the internal network and a service on the Internet. Instead of talking to each other directly, each system talks to the gateway. Your internal network never directly connects to the Internet.
12. An example of a application-level gateway is a proxy server.
13. A proxy server is a server that sits between a client application, such as a Web browser, and a real server.
14. Most firewalls today are a hybrid of stateful inspection, circuit-level gateways, and application-level gateways.

Security+ Objective 3.1.2—Routers

Security+ Objective 3.1.3—Switches

1. A router, which works at the network ISO layer, is a device that connects two or more LANs.
2. Switches are more secure than hubs.
3. Since Ethernet works with broadcast technology, switches will reduce the effectiveness of network traffic sniffing because the traffic is not forwarded to all ports, only the destination ports of the packets.
4. Intelligent devices including intelligent hubs, intelligent switches, and all routers need to be configured to operate properly.
5. These are configured by connecting a PC through a console port, or by connecting remotely through the network. Therefore, it is imperative that you limit who can access these devices.

6. You can use access list entries to prevent inappropriate connections and routing of traffic.

7. On some managed hubs, switches and routers can alert you when a cable is connected.

8. You can also monitor your network with management tools (such as ARPWATCH, which can alert you of changes to the ARP mappings) that alert you to unauthorized connections.

Security+ Objective 3.1.11—Workstations

Security+ Objective 3.1.12—Servers

Security+ Objective 3.1.13—Mobile Devices

1. People often forget when planning security to plan for the security of servers and user computers.

2. The reason to secure servers is that they provide network services for multiple users. In addition, they often contain confidential information.

3. While most user computers don't provide network services, they often contain confidential information, and they may aid in an unauthorized user access to the rest of the network.

4. You should use passwords to boot the computer, and you should use a password for the operating system.

5. You should always log out when the computer is not being used, and you should always use passwords on screensavers.

6. You should use a lock preventing users from opening the computer.

7. When you are not in a secure environment, you need to use a locking cable, which you can use to physically secure the notebook so that no one will steal it.

8. Portable computers should have hard drive passwords so that if someone steals the computer, they will still not be able to access the hard drive, even when the hard drive is used in another system.

9. For portable computers, you should also consider using file encryption to further protect your system.

10. Since notebook computers are smaller and easier to steal, you might consider requiring smart cards or biometrics to access the notebook and to logon to the network with the notebook.

Security+ Objective 3.2—Media

Security+ Objective 3.2.1—Coax

Security+ Objective 3.2.2—UTP/STP

Security+ Objective 3.2.3—Fiber

1. A twisted pair consists of two insulated copper wires twisted around each other. While each pair acts as a single communication link, twisted pairs are usually bundled together into a cable and wrapped in a protective sheath.

2. Twisted pairs come in unshielded twisted pairs (UTP) and shielded twisted pairs (STP).

3. In a larger network, one end of the cable will connect the network card of the computer to a wall jack. The wall jack is connected to the back of a patch panel kept in a server room or wiring closet. A cable then is attached to the patch panel and connected to a hub or switch. The cables that connect to the computer to the wall jack and the cable that connects the patch panel and the hub or switch are called patch cables.

4. The biggest disadvantages of UTP are its limited bandwidth of 100 meters, and it is quite susceptible to interference and noise.

5. Shielded twisted pairs are similar to unshielded twisted pairs except that they are usually surrounded by a braided shield that serves to reduce both EMI sensitivity and radio emissions.

6. Coaxial cable, sometimes referred to as coax, is a cable that has a center wire surrounded by insulation and then a grounded shield of braided wire (mesh shielding).

7. A fiber optic cable consists of a bundle of glass or plastic threads, each which is capable of carrying data signals in the forms of modulated pulses of light.

8. Fiber optics are extremely difficult to tap, making them very secure and highly reliable.

9. To help prevent eavesdropping, protect your network cable as much as possible by burying it underground, placing it inside walls, or protecting it within tamper-proof containers.

Security+ Objective 3.2.4—Removable Media

Security+ Objective 3.2.4.1—Tape

Security+ Objective 3.2.4.2—CDR

Security+ Objective 3.2.4.3—Hard Drives

Security+ Objective 3.2.4.4—Diskettes

Security+ Objective 3.2.4.5—Flashcards

Security+ Objective 3.2.4.6—Smart Cards

1. While removable storage media are useful for transporting programs and data and are used for backup purposes, they can also be a security risk since they can used to copy confidential information and removed from your building or site.

2. You should have a security policy that specifies what can be and what cannot be copied and/or removed from your building or site.

3. You might consider encrypting data on removable media, especially if the removable data is removed from a secure area.

4. To prevent someone from copying files to a floppy disk, you can use diskless workstations or you can disable floppy disk drives in the BIOS.

5. To avoid using writable CDs, you should not purchase writable CD drives for every system. If you have a need to have writable CDs, you need to limit access to the writable CD drives by putting them behind locked doors, using BIOS passwords, and/or by using OS rights and permissions.

6. On some operating systems such as Windows 2000 or Windows XP, you can also limit users from adding additional hardware items to their system. This will prevent them from adding additional devices that could give them the ability to copy confidential information to removable media.

7. When you are done using a disk and you no longer want to use that disk, you need to properly erase the information off the disk so that it cannot be retrieved.

8. A memory card (sometimes called a flash memory card or a storage card) is a small storage medium used to store data such as text, pictures, audio, and video, for use on small, portable, or remote computing devices.

9. Unfortunately, because of their very small size, flashcards are vulnerable to theft.

10. If you are using a flashcard as storage for a Palm or Pocket PC, there are numerous programs that will encrypt data, so that loss of the device or card does not necessarily mean that the data on it is accessible by unauthorized personnel.

Security+ Objective 3.3.1—Security Zones

Security+ Objective 3.3.1.1—DMZ

Security+ Objective 3.3.1.2—Intranet

Security+ Objective 3.3.1.3—Extranet

1. Security zones are areas of your network with specific security-related attributes and requirements. They are typically broken into intranets, internets, extranets, and DMZ.

2. A demilitarized zone (DMZ) has three ports. Two ports are the public network on one port of the firewall and the private network on another port. The third port is the DMZ, which is a less secure area than the private network. The DMZ will include the web and FTP servers and the rest of your computers will be in the private network.

3. An extranet is another type of logical network, which allows a business to connect with suppliers, vendors, customers, stockholders, or others related to its business.

4. An extranet is usually run over the Internet, often using a VPN for security.

Security+ Objective 3.3.2—VLANs

1. Basically, a VLAN is a collection of nodes that are grouped together in a single broadcast domain that is based on something other than physical location.

2. A VLAN is a switched network that is logically segmented on an organizational basis, by functions, project teams, or applications rather than on a physical or geographical basis.

3. Because VLANs form broadcast domains, members enjoy the connectivity, shared services, and security associated with physical LANs.

4. High-security users can be grouped into a VLAN, possible on the same physical segment, and no users outside that VLAN can communicate with them. Administrators can now have control over each port and whatever resources that port could access.

5. This prevents a user from plugging their workstation into any switch port and gaining access to network resources.

Security+ Objective 3.3.3—NAT

1. Circuit-level application gateways often provide network address translation (NAT), in which a network host alters the packets of internal network hosts so they can be sent out across the Internet.

2. NAT allows an Intranet to use addresses that are different from what the Internet sees.

3. NAT allows insiders to get out without allowing outsiders to get in.

Security+ Objective 5.1—Physical Security

Security+ Objective 5.1.1—Access Control

Security+ Objective 5.1.1.1—Physical Barriers

Security+ Objective 5.1.1.2—Biometrics

1. To protect your corporate resources, you should consider hiring security guards to help monitor your site or building.

2. In addition, you should also consider using sensors, alarms, and cameras to help monitor everything, and you should use physical access badges and security cards to limit access to your building or site.

3. You need to also provide training and remind all employees to report anything suspicious.

QUESTIONS

1. The primary purpose of NAT (network address translation) is to:
   a. Translate IP (Internet Protocol) addresses into user-friendly names.
   b. Hide internal hosts from the public network.
   c. Use a public IP (Internet Protocol) address on the internal network as a name server.
   d. Hide the public network from internal hosts.

2. Which of the following media types is most immune to RF (Radio Frequency) eavesdropping?
   a. Coaxial cable
   b. Fiber optic cable
   c. Twisted-pair wire
   d. Unbounded

3. A company consists of a main building with two smaller branch offices at opposite ends of the city. The main building and branch offices are connected with fast links so that all employees have good connectivity to the network. Each of the buildings has security measures that require

visitors to sign in, and all employees are required to wear identification badges at all times. You want to protect servers and other vital equipment so that the company has the best level of security at the lowest possible cost. Which of the following will you do to achieve this objective?

a. Centralize servers and other vital components in a single room of the main building, and add security measures to this room so that they are well protected.

b. Centralize most servers and other vital components in a single room of the main building, and place servers at each of the branch offices. Add security measures to areas where the servers and other components are located.

c. Decentralize servers and other vital components, and add security measures to areas where the servers and other components are located.

d. Centralize servers and other vital components in a single room in the main building. Because the building prevents unauthorized access to visitors and other persons, there is no need to implement physical security in the server room.

4. One way to limit hostile sniffing on a LAN (local area network) is by installing:

a. An Ethernet switch.

b. An Ethernet hub.

c. A CSU/DSU (Channel Service Unit/Data Service Unit).

d. A firewall.

5. What technology was originally designed to decrease broadcast traffic but is also beneficial in reducing the likelihood of having information compromised by sniffers?

a. VPN (Virtual Private Network)

b. DMZ (Demilitarized Zone)

c. VLAN (Virtual Local Area Network)

d. RADIUS (Remote Authentication Dial-in User Service)

6. You are running cabling for a network through a boiler room where the furnace and some other heavy machinery reside. You are concerned about interference from these sources. Which of the following types of cabling provides the best protection from interference in this area?

a. STP   b. UTP

c. Coaxial   d. Fiber-optic

7. A DMZ (demilitarized zone) typically contains:

a. A customer account database

b. Staff workstations

c. An FTP (File Transfer Protocol) server

d. An SQL (Structured Query Language)–based database server

8. What is a computer host or small network inserted as a "neutral zone" between a company's private network and the outside public network. It prevents outside users from getting direct access to a server that has company data?

a. DMZ   b. ACL
c. ART   d. CERT

9. As the security analyst for your company's network, you need to configure Internet access so that your clients are hidden behind a single IP address. From the list below, what is your best choice?

a. ACL List   b. IDS
c. Switch   d. Proxy Server

10. What type of server sits between an internal client and the Internet to help protect the internal client and also cache web pages?

a. Port scanner   b. Firewall
c. Proxy server   d. Packet server
e. Packet inspector   f. Web server
g. Firewall

11. A device that is placed between the internal network and the Internet to protect internal assets is a _____ . (Select the correct answer for the blank.)

a. Proxy server   b. RADIUS server
c. Firewall   d. FTP server
e. Web server   f. File server

12. A _____ is a network device that is designed to prevent unauthorized or unwanted network traffic from entering the private internal network from the Internet. (Select the correct answer for the blank)

a. Web server

b. File server

c. RADIUS server

d. RRAS server

e. Firewall

f. Quarantine server

13. A _____ is a network device that connects two or more networks to each other. (Select the correct answer for the blank)

a. Firewall   b. Proxy server
c. Router   d. Web server
e. File server

14. Thinnet has which of the following characteristics? (Choose all that apply.)

a. 100 MB/Sec

b. 1000 MB/Sec

c. 10 MB/Sec

d. Up to 200 feet in length

e. Up to 185 meters in length

f. Up to 2 kilometers in length

g. Up to 185 meters in length

h. Uses coaxial cabling

i. Uses twisted pair cabling

15. What makes fiber optic networks superior to those running on standard copper wire? (Choose all that apply.)

a. Increased security

b. Easier to install

c. Faster data throughput

d. Cheaper to install

e. No interference

f. Fiber optic has no advantages

16. What advantage does a VLAN offer?
    a. The benefits of a subnet can be realized, while the actual hosts are distant from each other.
    b. It is cheaper to configure than a regular subnet.
    c. It is easier to configure than a regular subnet.
    d. It takes no special hardware.
    e. It requires no special protocols.

17. _____ uses light impulses transmitted across thin glass wires to transmit data.
    a. Coaxial   b. Fiber optic
    c. UTP   d. STP
    e. CAT 3   f. RJ 45

18. Most commonly, a _____ operates at the Data Link layer and forwards packets to computers based on the MAC address of the destination computer. (Select the correct answer for the blank.)
    a. Router   b. Firewall
    c. Proxy   d. Switch
    e. Hub   f. Repeater

19. If you only have one public IP address from your ISP, but you have three servers you want to make accessible to the Internet, what technology can you use?
    a. DHCP   b. RRAS
    c. NAT   d. TCP/IP
    e. DNS   f. RADIUS

20. NAT is typically performed by _____ and _____ . (Choose the two correct answers.)
    a. FTP servers   b. Firewalls
    c. Web servers   d. Proxy servers
    e. SMTP servers   f. NNTP servers
    g. RADIUS servers   h. RIS servers
    i. RRAS servers

21. What makes removable media an inherently insecure product?
    a. It is easily destroyed.
    b. It can be easily stolen or transferred to an unauthorized location.
    c. It is relatively inexpensive.
    d. It does not last long when used often.

22. The first step in effectively implementing a firewall is:
    a. Blocking unwanted incoming traffic.
    b. Blocking unwanted outgoing traffic.
    c. Developing a firewall policy.
    d. Protecting against DDoS attacks.

23. What physical access control most adequately protect against physical piggybacking?
    a. Man-trap
    b. Security guard
    c. Closed-circuit television
    d. Biometrics

24. What is the advantage of a multi-homed firewall?
    a. It is relative inexpensive to implement.
    b. The firewall rules are easier to manage.

    c. If the firewall is compromised, only the systems in the DMZ (Demilitarized Zone) are exposed.
    d. An attacker must circumvent two firewalls.

25. What should a firewall employ to ensure that each packet is part of an established TCP session?
    a. Packet filter
    b. Stateless inspection
    c. Stateful like inspection
    d. Circuit level gateway

26. The basic strategy that should be used when configuring the rules for a secure firewall is:
    a. Permit all.
    b. Deny all.
    c. Default permit.
    d. Default deny.

27. An employer gives an employee a laptop computer to use remotely. The user installs personal applications on the laptop and overwrites some system files. How might this have been prevented with minimal impact on corporate productivity?
    a. Users should not be given laptop computers in order to prevent this type of occurrence.
    b. The user should have received instructions as to what is allowed to be installed.
    c. The hard disk should have been made read only.
    d. Biometrics should have been used to authenticate users before allowing software installation.

28. A fundamental risk management assumption is, computers can *never* be completely:
    a. Secure until all vendor patches are installed.
    b. Secure unless they have a variable password.
    c. Secure.
    d. Secure unless they have only one user.

29. Which of the following will let a security administrator allow only HTTP (Hypertext Transfer Protocol) traffic for outbound Internet connections and set permissions to allow only certain users to browse the Web?
    a. Packet filtering firewall
    b. Protocol analyzer
    c. Proxy server
    d. Stateful firewall

30. The system administrator concerned about security has designated a special area in which to place the web server away from other servers on the network. This area is commonly known as the:
    a. Honey pot   b. Hybrid subnet
    c. DMZ   d. VLAN

31. Which of the following IP address schemes will require NAT to connect to the Internet?
    a. 204.180.0.0/24   b. 172.16.0.0/24
    c. 192.172.0.0/24   d. 172.48.0.0/24

32. A network administrator wants to restrict internal access to other parts of the network. The network restrictions must be implemented with the least

amount of administrative overhead and must be hardware based. What is the best solution?

  a. Implement firewalls between subnets to restrict access.

  b. Implement a VLAN to restrict network access.

  c. Implement a proxy server to restrict access.

  d. Implement a VPN.

33. What are TCP wrappers used for?

  a. Preventing IP spoofing

  b. Controlling access to selected services

  c. Encrypting TCP traffic

  d. Sniffing TCP traffic to troubleshoot

34. Which is of greatest importance when considering physical security?

  a. Reduce overall opportunity for an intrusion to occur

  b. Make alarm identification easy for security professionals

  c. Barricade all entry points against unauthorized entry

  d. Access the impact of crime zoning and environmental considerations in the overall design

35. The flow of packets traveling through routers can be controlled by implementing what type of security mechanism?

  a. ACLs

  b. Fault tolerance tables

  c. OSPF

  d. Packet locks

HANDS-ON EXERCISES

Exercise 1: Using IP Filtering in Windows 2000

1. By default, the telnet service is disabled. To enable it, click the Start button, select Programs, select Administrative Tools and select Services. In the left pane, right-click telnet and select Start.
2. Close the Services console.
3. Have your partner telnet into your computer.
4. Click the Start button, select Settings, select Network and Dial-up Connections.
5. Right-click Local Area Connection and then select Properties.
6. Select Internet Protocols (TCP/IP), then click Properties.
7. Click Advanced.
8. On the Options tab, select TCP/IP Filtering, and click Properties.
9. On the TCP/IP Filtering dialog box, click Enable TCP/IP Filtering (All Adapters). Then select Permit Only on the TCP Ports. Click the Add button and type 80. This will allow access to a web server. Click on the OK button.
10. Click OK two more times. Close the Local Area Connection dialog box.
11. Have your partner try to telnet into your computer.
12. Disable your TCP/IP Filtering.

Exercise 2: Using Firewalls

1. To test your Internet security, go to the Gibson Research Corporation website located at http://grc.com/default.htm and click on the ShieldsUp! link.
2. On the Shields Up page, click the Test My Shields! button.
3. After your system is tested, print the results of the test noting any system vulnerabilities.
4. Toward the bottom of the window, load the free IP Agent executable file to your computer.
5. When the IP Agent dialog box appears, click on the Test My Shields button.
6. Click the Test My Shields button again.
7. Compare this test report with the previous test report.
8. Print out the test report.
9. Click the Probe My Ports option and view its results.
10. Go to the Zone Alarm Web site at http://www.zonealarm.com.
11. Find, download, and install the free trial version of Zone Alarm Pro.
12. On the Zone Alarm Pro Welcome screen, click on the Next button.
13. If you want to enable private control or cache cleaner, do so. Click on the Next button.
14. Select the Alert me when blocked traffic is probably hacker activity and click on the Next button.
15. Do not choose a password and click the Finish option.

16. When it asks if you want preconfigure access permissions, select the Yes option and click the Finish option.
17. To view the ZoneAlarm Pro tutorial click the Next option. Go through the tutorial.
18. After viewing the tutorial, ZoneAlarm Pro should find the new network. Click the OK button.
19. Run the ShieldsUp test again and compare it with your other results.

Exercise 3: Installing and Configuring a Proxy Server (ISA Server Enterprise Edition)

1. Insert the Microsoft Internet Security and Acceleration Server Enterprise Edition CD-ROM into your CD-ROM drive. If the ISA Server Setup screen does not open automatically, double-click the ISA Server icon in My Computer to open it manually.
2. Select Run ISA Server Enterprise Initialization from the Microsoft ISA Server Setup screen. Click Yes to continue.
3. In the ISA Initialization dialog box, select the Use Array Policy Only radio button.
4. Select the Allow Publishing Rules check box. Clear the Force Packet Filtering On the Array check box. Click the OK button.
5. Click the OK button again.
6. Back on the ISA Server Setup screen, select Install ISA Server.
7. In the Microsoft ISA Server (Enterprise Edition) Setup message box, click Continue.
8. Enter the ISA Server CD key. Click the OK button.
9. Read the license agreement and click I agree.
10. On the Microsoft ISA Server (Enterprise Edition) Setup dialog box, click Full Installation.
11. Click Yes to install the server as an array member.
12. In the text box of the New Array dialog box, highlight your server and type ArrayXX. Click the OK button.
13. Click the Use Custom Enterprise Policy Settings radio button.
14. Click the use Array Policy Only radio button.
15. Click the Continue button. Click the Continue button again.
16. Click the OK button.
17. When the cache settings dialog box appears, use the Set button and Cache Size text box to specify a single cache location on the C: drive of 105 MB. Click the OK button.
18. Click the Construct Table button.
19. When the Local Address Table dialog box appears, clear the Add the Following Private Ranges check box.
20. Verity that the Add Address Ranges Based On the Windows 2000 Routing Table check box is selected.
21. Select the 192.168.0.1 check box appearing in the bottom pane. If any other check boxes appear in the bottom pane, make sure they are not checked. Click OK.
22. Click OK to close the message box, and click OK again to continue.
23. Click OK two more times.
24. Click the Start button, select Programs, select Microsoft ISA Server, and select ISA Management.
25. Click the View menu, and verity the Taskpad is selected.
26. In the console tree, expand the Servers and Arrays node, and then expand the ArrayXX node.
27. Expand the Access Policy node, and select the Protocol Rules folder.
28. In the details pane, click the Create A Protocol Rule icon.
29. In the Rule Action screen, verify that the Allow radio button is selected. Click on the Next button.
30. On the Protocols screen, verify that All IP Traffic appears in the Apply This Rule To dropdown list box, and then click Next.
31. On the Schedule screen, verify that Always appears in the Use This Schedule drop-down list box, and then click the Next button.
32. On the Client Type screen, verify that the Any Request radio button is selected, and then click the Next button.
33. On the Completing the New Protocol Rule Wizard screen, click Finish.

Exercise 4: Configuring the Browser for a Proxy Server

This exercise is based on completing exercise 3.
1. Open Internet Explorer.
2. If the Internet Connection Wizard appears, advance through the wizard by configuring a manual (LAN) connection.
3. On the Tools menu, click Internet Options.

4. On the Connections tab, click LAN Settings.
5. Select the Use A Proxy Server check box.
6. In the Address text box, type 192.168.0.1 and in the Port text box, type 8080.
7. Click OK to close the Local Area Network (LAN) Settings dialog box.
8. Click OK to close the Internet Options dialog box.

Exercise 5: Using a Personal Firewall in Linux

1. To start GNOME Lokkit, type the following command at the command prompt:

```
gnome-lokkit
```

2. Set the personal firewall to high security and on the Next button. Finish the wizard.
3. Try to use the telnet command again.

## CHAPTER 7

Remote Access Security

Topics Covered in this Chapter

Introduction

In the last chapter, you learned how to physically secure your network and how to setup security zones. In this chapter, you learn how to secure your network being accessed through remote access. This includes dial-up connection and virtual tunnels. Lastly, this book will briefly discuss issues dealing with your PBX.

Objectives

1. Security+ Objective 1.2.2—CHAP
2. Security+ Objective 2.1—Remote Access
3. Security+ Objective 2.1.2—VPN
4. Security+ Objective 2.1.3—RADIUS
5. Security+ Objective 2.1.4—TACACS/+
6. Security+ Objective 2.1.5—L2TP/PPTP
7. Security+ Objective 2.1.7—IPSEC
8. Security+ Objective 2.1.8— Vulnerabilities
9. Security+ Objective 3.1.5—Modems
10. Security+ Objective 3.1.6—RAS
11. Security+ Objective 3.1.7—Telecom/PBX
12. Security+ Objective 3.1.8—VPN
13. Security+ Objective 3.3.4—Tunneling

7.1 PUBLIC SWITCHED TELEPHONE NETWORK (PSTN)

Security+ Objective 2.1—Remote Access

Public Switched Telephone Network (PSTN) is the international telephone system based on copper wires (UTP cabling) carrying analog voice data. The PSTN, also known as the plain old telephone service (POTS), is the standard telephone service that most homes use. The PSTN is a huge network with multiple paths that link source and destination devices. PSTN uses circuit switching when you make a call. Therefore, the data is switched to a dedicated path throughout the conversation.

The original concept of the Bell system was a series of PSTN trunks connecting the major U.S. cities. The PSTN network originally began with human operators sitting at a switchboard manually routing calls. Today, the PSTN systems still use analog signals from the end node (phone) to the first switch. The switch then converts the analog signal to a digital signal and routes the call on to its destination. Since the digital signal travels on fiber optic cabling, the signals are switched at high speeds. Once the call is received on the other end, the last switch in the loop converts the signal back to analog, and the call is initiated. The connection will stay active until the call is terminated (user hangs up). The active circuit enables you to hear the other person almost instantaneously.

The **subscriber loop** or **local loop** is the telephone line that runs from your home or office to the telephone company's central office (CO) or neighborhood switching station (often a small building with no windows). While its cable length can be as long as 20 miles, it is referred to as the **last mile**, not because of its length, but because it is the slow link in the telecommunications infrastructure as it carries analog signals on a twisted-pair cable. The point where the local loop ends at the customer's premises is called the **demarcation point (demarc)**. Note: unless you have an agreement with the phone company, the phone company is only responsible from the central office to the demarc. See figure 7.1.

The standard home phone communicates over the local loop using analog signals. Therefore, when a PC needs to communicate over the local loop, it must use an analog modem to convert the PC's digital data to analog signals. Unfortunately, the analog lines can only reach a maximum speed of 53 Kbps because of FCC regulations that restrict the power output. Unfortunately, the speed is not guaranteed and is often not reached.

Integrated Services Digital Network (ISDN) is the planned replacement for POTS so that it can provide voice and data communications worldwide using circuit switching while using the same wiring that is currently being used in homes and businesses. Because ISDN is a digital signal from end to end, it is faster and much more dependable with no line noise. ISDN has the ability to deliver multiple simultaneous connections, in any combination of data, voice, video, or fax, over a single line and allows for multiple devices to be attached to the line.

Figure 7.1   Public Switched Telephone Network

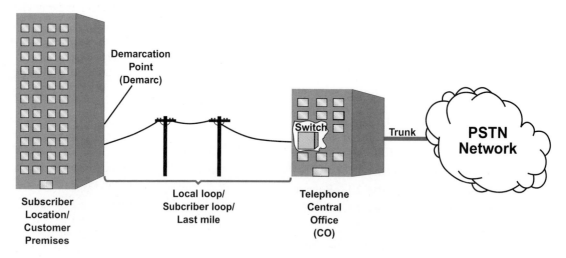

The ISDN network uses two types of channels: a B channel and a D channel. The **bearer channels (B channels)** transfer data at a bandwidth of 64 Kbps (kilobits per second) for each channel. The **data channels (D channels)** uses a communications language called DSS1 for administrative signaling, such as to instruct the carrier to setup or terminate a B-channel call, to ensure that a B-channel is available to receive a call, or to provide signaling information for such features as caller identification. Since the D channel is always connected to the ISDN network, the call setup time is greatly reduced to 1 to 2 seconds (versus 10 to 40 using an analog modem) as it establishes a circuit. Note: the bandwidth listed here are the uncompressed speed of the ISDN connections. The compressed bandwidth has a current maximum transmission speed of four times the uncompressed speed. Of course, you will probably see a much lower speed, as much of the data flowing across the network already compressed.

Today, two well-defined standards are used, including the **Basic Rate Interface (BRI)** and **Primary Rate Interface (PRI).** The Basic Rate Interface defines digital communication lines consisting of three independent channels, two Bearer (or B) channels, each carrying 64 Kilobytes per second and one Data (or D) channel at 16 Kilobits per second. For this reason, the ISDN Basic Rate Interface is often referred to as 2B+D. BRIs were designed to enable customers to use their existing wiring in the home or business. This provided a low-cost solution for customers and is why it is the most basic type of service today intended for small business or home use.

To use BRI services, you must subscribe to ISDN services through a local telephone company or provider. By default, you must be within 18,000 feet (about 3.4 miles) of the telephone company central office. Repeater devices are available for ISDN service to extend this distance, but these devices can be very expensive.

7.2   DSL AND CABLE TELEVISION

Digital subscriber line (DSL) is a special communication line that uses sophisticated modulation technology to maximize the amount of data that can be sent over plain twisted-pair copper wiring, which is already carrying phone service to subscribers' homes. It was originally aimed to transmit video signals to compete against the cable companies, but it soon found use as a high-speed data connection with the explosion of the Internet. DSL is sometimes expressed as xDSL, because there are various kinds of digital subscriber line technologies including ADSL, R-DSL, HDSL, SDSL, and VDSL.

The best thing about DSL technologies is their ability to transport large amounts of information across existing copper telephone lines. This is possible because DSL modems leverage signal-processing techniques that insert and extract more digital data onto analog lines. The key is modulation, a process in which one signal modifies the property of another.

In the case of digital subscriber lines, the modulating message signal from a sending modem alters the high-frequency carrier signal so that a composite wave, called a modulated wave, is formed. Because this high-frequency carrier signal can be modified, a large digital data payload can be carried in the modulated wave over greater distances than on ordinary copper pairs. When the transmission reaches its destination, the modulating message signal is recovered, or demodulated, by the receiving modem.

To create upstream and downstream channels, ADSL modems divide the phone line's available bandwidth using one of two methods: frequency-division multiplexing (FDM) or echo cancellation. FDM assigns one band or frequency for upstream data and another band or frequency for downstream data. The downstream path is further divided by time-division multiplexing (TDM) into one or more high-speed channels for data and one or more low-speed channels, one of which is for voice. The upstream path is multiplexed into several low-speed channels.

Currently, existing POTS data is transmitted over a frequency spectrum that ranges from 0 to 4 kHz. Copper phone lines can actually support frequency ranges much greater than those, and ADSL takes advantage of these ranges by transmitting data in the ranges between 4 kHz and 2.2 MHz. Therefore, ADSL relies on advanced digital signal processing (DSP) and complex algorithms to compress all the information into the phone line. In addition, ADSL modems correct errors caused by line conditions and attenuation. With this technology, any computer or network can easily become connected to the Internet at speeds comparable to T1 access for a fraction of the cost and it can serve as a suitable medium for video streaming and conferencing.

As its name implies, **asymmetrical DSL (ADSL)** transmits an asymmetric data stream, with much more going downstream to the subscriber and much less coming back. The reason for this has less to do with transmission technology than with the cable plant itself. Twisted-pair telephone wires are bundled together in large cables. Fifty pair to a cable is a typical configuration towards the subscriber, but cables coming out of a central office may have hundreds or even thousands of pairs bundled together. An individual line from a CO to a subscriber is spliced together from many cable sections as they fan out from the central office (Bellcore claims that the average U.S. subscriber line has 22 splices). Alexander Bell invented twisted-pair wiring to minimize crosstalk. Since a small amount of crosstalk does occur, the amount of crosstalk increases as the frequencies and the length of line increases. Therefore, if you have symmetric signals in many pairs within the same cable, the crosstalk significantly limits the data rate and the length of the line.

Since most people are downloading information as they view web pages and download files, the amount of information downloaded is far greater than the amount of information that a user uploads or transfers to the other computers. This asymmetry, combined with "always on" access (which eliminates call setup), makes ADSL ideal for Internet/intranet surfing, video-on-demand, and remote LAN access.

ADSL modems usually include a POTS splitter, which enables simultaneous access to voice telephony and high-speed data access. Some vendors provide active POTS splitters, which enable simultaneous telephone and data access. However, if the power fails or the modem fails with an active POTS splitter, then the telephone fails. A passive POTS splitter, on the other hand, maintains lifeline telephone access even if the modem fails (because of a power outage, for example), since the telephone is not powered by external electricity. Telephone access in the case of a passive POTS splitter is a regular analog voice channel, the same as customers currently receive to their homes.

Downstream, ADSL supports speeds between 1.5 and 8 Mbps, while upstream, the rate is between 640 Kbps and 1.544 Mbps. ADSL can provide 1.544 Mbps transmission rates at distances of up to 18,000 feet over one wire pair. Optimal speeds of 6 to 8 Mbps can be achieved at distances of 10,000 to 12,000 feet using standard 24-gauge wire.

If you order DSL for your home, it is most likely ADSL Lite. ADSL Lite specification, also known as g.lite, is a low-cost, easy-to-install version of ADSL specifically designed for the consumer marketplace. ADSL Lite is a lower-speed version of ADSL (up to 1.544 Mbps downstream, up to 512 Kbps upstream) that will eliminate the need for the telephone company to install and maintain a premises-based POTS splitter. ADSL Lite is also supposed to work over longer distances than full-rate ADSL, making it more widely available to mass market consumers. It will support both data and voice and provide an evolution path to full-rate ADSL.

To connect to an ADSL line, you install an ADSL modem via an expansion card, a USB port, or external standalone device connected to a network card. If you are using the expansion card or USB device, you would assign and configure the TCP/IP protocol. If you are using the external standalone device, you assign and configure the TCP/IP protocol for the network card.

At home and in small offices, it is very common for the office to connect their network to the Internet by ordering a DSL line and using a DSL router or using some other form to have several computers share the DSL line. The DSL router will allow multiple computers to connect to the router, and the router will act as a DHCP server for the clients connected to it.

Cable systems were originally designed to deliver broadcast television signals efficiently to subscribers' homes. To ensure that consumers could obtain cable service with the same TV sets they use to receive over-the-air broadcast TV signals, cable operators recreate a portion of the over-the-air radio frequency (RF) spectrum within a sealed coaxial cable line.

Traditional coaxial cable systems typically operate with 330 MHz or 450 MHz of capacity, whereas modern hybrid fiber/coax (HFC) systems are expanded to 750 MHz or more. Logically, downstream video programming signals begin around 50 MHz, the equivalent of channel 2 for over-the-air television signals. Each standard television channel occupies 6 MHz of the RF spectrum. Thus a traditional cable system with 400 MHz of downstream bandwidth can carry the equivalent of 60 analog TV channels, and a modern HFC system with 700 MHz of downstream bandwidth has the capacity for about 110 channels.

A **hybrid fiber coaxial (HFC) network** is a telecommunication technology in which optical fiber cable and coaxial cable are used in different portions of a network to carry broadband content (such as video, data, and voice). Using HFC, a local CATV company installs fiber optic cable from the cable head-end (distribution center) to serving nodes located close to business and residential users and from these nodes uses coaxial cable to individual businesses and homes. An advantage of HFC is that some of the characteristics of fiber optic cable (high bandwidth and low noise and interference susceptibility) can be brought close to the user without having to replace the existing coaxial cable that is installed all the way to the home and business. Both cable TV and telephone companies are using HFC in new and upgraded networks and, in some cases, sharing the same infrastructure to carry both video and voice conversations in the same system.

While regular cable is analog, digital cable uses digital signals. The digital signals can be compressed much more than analog signals. Digital cable can give you 200 to 300 channels of the same bandwidth as analog cable.

To deliver data services over a cable network, one television channel in the 50 to 750 MHz range is typically allocated for downstream traffic to homes and another channel in the 5 to 42 MHz band is used to carry upstream signals. A cable modem termination system (CMTS) communicates through these channels with **cable modems** located in subscriber homes to create a virtual local area network (LAN) connection. Most cable modems are external devices that connect to a personal computer (PC) through a standard 10Base-T Ethernet card and twisted-pair wiring, though external Universal Serial Bus (USB) modems and internal PCI modem cards.

A single downstream 6 MHz television channel may support up to 27 Mbps of downstream data throughput from the cable using 64 QAM (quadrature amplitude modulation) transmission technology. Speeds can be boosted to 36 Mbps using 256 QAM. Upstream channels may deliver 500 Kbps to 10 Mbps from homes using 16 QAM or QPSK (quadrature phase shift key) modulation techniques, depending on the amount of spectrum allocated for service. This upstream and downstream bandwidth is shared by the active data subscribers connected to a given cable network segment, typically 500 to 2,000 homes on a modern HFC network.

An individual cable modem subscriber may experience access speeds from 500 Kbps to 1.5 Mbps or more, depending on the network architecture and traffic load, blazing performance compared to dial-up alternatives. However, when surfing the Web, performance can be affected by Internet backbone congestion. In addition to speed, cable modems offer another key benefit: constant connectivity. Because cable modems use connectionless technology, much like in an office LAN, a subscriber's PC is always online with the network. That means there's no need to dial-in to begin a session, so users do not have to worry about receiving busy signals. Additionally, going online does not tie up their telephone line.

Similar to DSL routers, cable modems can be replaced with the cable routers. The cable router will allow multiple computers to connect to the router and the router will act as a DHCP server for the clients connected to it.

7.3   DIAL-UP TECHNOLOGY

Dial-up networking is when a remote access client makes a nonpermanent, dial-up connection to a physical port on a remote access server by using the service of a telecommunications provider such as analog phone or ISDN. The best example of dial-up networking is that of a dial-up networking client who dials the phone number of one of the ports/modem of a remote access server.

Today, modern networks offer **remote access service (RAS),** which allows users to connect remotely using various protocols and connection types. A **remote access server,** sometimes called a **communication server** or **network access server (NAS),** is the computer and associated software that is set up to handle users seeking access to network remotely. A remote access server usually includes or is associated with a firewall server to ensure security and a router that can forward the remote access request to another part of the corporate network.

A **modem (modulator-demodulator)** is a device that enables a computer to transmit data over telephone lines. Since the computer information is stored and processed digitally, and the telephone lines transmit data using analog waves, the modem converts digital signals to analog signals (modulates) and analog signals to digital signals (demodulates).

7.3.1   Traditional Remote Access

The typical dial-in session is actually composed of six distinct steps or stages, each of which must be completed successfully before the user gains access to centralized resources. Each step is subject to its own unique set of problems or failures that individually could jeopardize the entire connection. These steps include:

1. Modem connection
2. Dial-out
3. Handshake
4. Authentication
5. IP address negotiation
6. Access to resources

During the modem connection, the modem checks the phone line for a dial tone. If the modem fails, or if the modem cannot detect a dial tone, the connection process fails immediately. A "no dial tone" error can be caused by problems with the phone cable, the phone jack, the modem, the dialer, or any combination of conditions related to these items or devices.

If a dial tone is detected, the remote PC proceeds with the connection process by dialing the remote access number. Any number of events, such as no answer, a busy signal, no carrier, etc., could cause the connection process to fail.

If the call gets through, the remote (dialing) modem will begin negotiating a common data rate and other transmission parameters with the answering modem. This is referred to as the **handshaking** stage because both modems must agree on the same parameters before continuing. Technology advancements have produced a variety of ways to encode, compress, modulate, and transfer bits over the phone line, adding complexity—and processing time—to the process. These factors make it critical for IT managers to monitor and measure both the final outcome of the negotiation process and the length of time it takes for the negotiation to complete. Connection failures and delays are typically the result of the local and remote modems disagreeing on one or more transmission parameters.

Once authentication is complete, the remote PC is assigned a dynamic IP address for identification purposes. The remote PC must agree to use the specified IP address or the local system will refuse to establish the link. The remote PC is also assigned a DNS server at this time; if the assignment isn't recorded or is unsuccessful for some reason, attempts to connect will appear as application problems.

Once the previous five stages of the remote connection process have successfully been completed, the dial-in client PC is finally granted access to the corporate network. At this stage, the user can then check e-mail, send messages, copy or transfer files, run application programs, etc. But the connection is still not entirely safe; connectivity problems can occur if the call is abnormally terminated, if the modem speed is too slow or if the dial-up network has an excessive amount of line noise.

7.3.2   SLIP and PPP Protocols

The first protocol used to connect to an IP network using dial-up lines was **Serial Line Interface Protocol (SLIP)**. SLIP is a simple protocol, in which you send packets down a serial link delimited with special END characters. SLIP doesn't do a number of desirable things that data-link protocols can do. First, it only works with TCP/IP. Therefore, it cannot be used with other protocols such as IPX. It doesn't perform error checking at the OSI data layer, and it doesn't authenticate users who are dialing into an access router. Next, with SLIP, you have to know the IP address assigned to you by your service provider. You also need to know the IP address of the remote system into which you will be dialing. If IP addresses are dynamically assigned (depends on your service provider), your SLIP software needs to be able to pick up the IP assignments automatically or you will have to set them up manually. You will have to configure certain parameters of the device such as maximum transmission unit (MTU) and maximum receive unit (MRU) and the use of compression. Lastly, SLIP does not support encrypted passwords and therefore transmits passwords in clear text, which is not secure at all. You would typically use SLIP when you are dialing into an older server that does not use PPP connections.

Point-to-Point Protocol (PPP) has become the predominant protocol for modem-based access to the Internet that provides full-duplex, bidirectional operations between hosts and can encapsulate multiple network-layer LAN protocols to connect to private networks. PPP is a full-duplex protocol that can be used on various physical media, including twisted pair or fiber optic lines or satellite transmission. PPP supports asynchronous serial communication, synchronous serial communication, and ISDN. Furthermore, a multilink version of PPP is also used to access ISDN lines, inverse multiplexing analog phone lines and high-speed optical lines. PPP is one of the many variants of an early, internationally standardized data-link protocol known as the High-level Data Link Protocol (HDLC).

There are four distinct phases of negotiation of a PPP connection. Each of these four phases must be completed successfully before the PPP connection is ready to transfer user data. The four phases of a PPP connection are:

1. PPP configuration
2. Authentication
3. Callback (optional)
4. Protocol configuration

PPP configures PPP protocol parameters using the LCP (Link Control Protocol). During the initial LCP phase, each device on both ends of a connection negotiates communication options that are used to send data and include:

- PPP parameters (address and control)
- Compression
- Protocol ID compression
- Which authentication protocols are used to authenticate the remote access client
- Multilink options

NOTE: An authentication protocol is selected but not implemented until the authentication phase.

After LCP is complete, the authentication protocol agreed upon by the remote access server and the remote access client is implemented. The nature of this traffic is specific to the PPP authentication protocol.

7.3.3   Authentication Protocols

Security+ Objective 3.1.6—RAS

When a client dials in to a RAS server, the server will have to verify the client's credentials for authentication by using the client's user account properties and remote access policies to authorize the connection. If authentication and authorization succeed, the server allows a connection.

There are a number of PPP authentication protocols, and each protocol has advantages and disadvantages in terms of security, usability, and breadth of support. See table 7.1.

Table 7.1   Various Security Protocols

Protocols	Security	Description	Use When
Password Authentication Protocol (PAP)	Low	Passwords are sent across the link as unencrypted plaintext. Not a secure authentication method.	The client and server cannot negotiate by using a more secure form of validation.
Shiva Password Authentication Protocol (SPAP)	Medium	Sends password across link in reversibly encrypted form. Not recommended in situations where security is an issue.	Connecting to a Shiva LanRover, or when a Shiva client connects to a Windows–based remote access server.
Challenge Handshake Authentication Protocol (CHAP)	High	Uses MD5 hashing scheme. Client computer sends a hash of the password to the RAS, which checks the client hash against a hash it generates with the password stored on the RAS server. CHAP does provide protection against server impersonation.	You have clients that are not running Microsoft operating systems.
Microsoft Challenge Handshake Authentication Protocol (MS-CHAP) v1	High	Similar to CHAP. Provides nonreversible, encrypted password authentication. Does not require the password on the server to be in plaintext or reversibly encrypted form. It only supports one-way authentication. Therefore, MS-CHAP v1 does not provide protection against remote server impersonation, which means that a client can't determine the authenticity of a RAS server it connects to. It is more secure than CHAP.	You have clients running Windows.
Microsoft Challenge Handshake Authentication Protocol (MS-CHAP) v2	High (Most Secure)	An improved version of MS-CHAP v1. It provides stronger security for remote access connections and allows for mutual authentication where the client also authenticates the server.	You have clients running Windows.

Password Authentication Protocol (PAP) is the least secure authentication protocol because it uses **clear text** (plain text) passwords. The steps when using PAP are:

1. The remote access client sends a PAP Authenticate-Request message to the remote access server containing the remote access client's user name and clear text password. Clear text, also referred to as plain text, is textual data in ASCII format.
2. The remote access server checks the user name and password and sends back either a PAP Authenticate-Acknowledgment message when the user's credentials are correct, or a PAP Authenticate-No acknowledgement message when the user's credentials are not correct.

Therefore, the password can easily be read with a protocol analyzer. In addition, PAP offers no protection against replay attacks, remote client impersonation, or remote server impersonation. Therefore, to make your remote access server more secure, ensure that PAP is disabled. Another disadvantage of using PAP is that if your password expires, PAP doesn't have the ability to change your password during authentication.

Shiva Password Authentication Protocol (SPAP), Shiva's proprietary version of PAP, offers a bit more security than PAP's plain-text password with its reversible encryption mechanism. SPAP is more secure than PAP but less secure than CHAP or MS-CHAP. Someone capturing authentication packets won't be able to read the SPAP password, but this authentication protocol is susceptible to playback attacks (i.e., an intruder records the packets and resends them to gain fraudulent access). Playback attacks are possible because SPAP always uses the same reversible encryption method to send the passwords over the wire. Like PAP, SPAP doesn't have the ability to change your password during the authentication process.

Security+ Objective 1.2.2—CHAP

Historically, **Challenge Handshake Authentication Protocol (CHAP)** is the most common dial-up authentication protocol used, which uses an industry Message Digest 5 (MD5) hashing scheme to encrypt authentication. A **hashing scheme** scrambles information in such a way that it's unique and can't be reversed back to the original format.

CHAP doesn't send the actual password over the wire; instead, it uses a three-way challenge-response mechanism (or handshake) with one-way MD5 hashing to provide encrypted authentication without sending the password over the link.

1. The remote access server sends a CHAP Challenge message containing a session ID and an arbitrary challenge string.
2. The remote access client returns a CHAP Response message containing the user name in clear text and a hash of the challenge string, session ID, and the client's password using the MD5 one-way hashing algorithm.
3. The remote access server duplicates the hash and compares it to the hash in the CHAP Response. If the hashes are the same, the remote access server sends back a CHAP Success message. If the hashes are different, a CHAP Failure message is sent.

Because standard CHAP clients use the plain text version of the password to create the CHAP challenge response, passwords must be stored on the server to calculate an equivalent response.

CHAP performs the handshake process when establishing a connection and at any time the connection is established. Since CHAP uses an arbitrary challenge string per authentication attempt, it protects against replay attacks. In addition, CHAP protects against session hijacking by performing this handshake multiple again at random times during a session. However, CHAP does not protect against remote server impersonation. In addition, because the algorithm for calculating CHAP responses is well-known, it is very important that passwords be carefully chosen and sufficiently long. CHAP passwords that are common words or names are vulnerable to dictionary attacks if they can be discovered by comparing responses to the CHAP challenge with every entry in a dictionary. Passwords that are not sufficiently long can be discovered by brute force by comparing the CHAP response to sequential trials until a match to the user's response is found.

Microsoft Challenge Handshake Authentication Protocol (MS-CHAP) is Microsoft's proprietary version of CHAP. Unlike PAP and SPAP, it lets you encrypt data that is sent using the Point-to-Point Protocol (PPP) or PPTP connections using Microsoft Point-to-Point Encryption (MPPE). The challenge response is calculated with an MD4 hashed version of the password and the NAS challenge. Note: The two flavors of MS-CHAP (versions 1 and 2) allow for error codes, including a "password expired" code and password changes.

1. The remote access server sends an MS-CHAP challenge message containing a session ID and an arbitrary challenge string.
2. The remote client must return the user name and an MD4 hash of the challenge string, the session ID, and the MD4-hashed password.
3. The remote access server duplicates the hash and compares it to the hash in the MS-CHAP response. If the hashes are the same, the remote access server sends back a CHAP Success message. If the hashes are different, a CHAP Failure message is sent.

MS-CHAP v1 is that it supports only one-way authentication. Therefore, MS-CHAP v1 does not provide protection against remote server impersonation, which means that a client can't determine the authenticity of a RAS server it connects to.

MS-CHAP v2 provides stronger security for remote access connections and allows for mutual authentication where the client authenticates the server.

1. The remote access server sends an MS-CHAP v2 Challenge message to the remote access client that consists of a session identifier and an arbitrary challenge string.
2. The remote access client sends an MS-CHAP v2 Response that contains the user name, an arbitrary peer challenge string, an MD4 hash of the received challenge string, the peer challenge string, the session identify, and the MD4 hashed versions of the user's password.

3. The remote access server checks the MS-CHAP v2 Response message from the client and sends back an MS-CHAP v2 Response message containing an indication of the success or failure of the connection attempt. An authentication response is based on the sent challenge string, the peer challenge string, the client's encrypted response and the user's password.
4. The remote access client verifies the authentication response and, if it is correct, uses the connection. If the authentication response is not correct, the remote access client terminates the connection.
5. If a user authenticates by using MS-CHAP v2 and attempts to use an expired password, MS-CHAP prompts the user to change the password while connecting to the server. Other authentication protocols do not support this feature effectively locking out the user who used the expired password.

If you configure your connection to use only MS-CHAP 2 and the server you're dialing in to does not support MS-CHAP 2, the connection will fail. This behavior is different from Windows NT where the RAS servers negotiate a lower-level authentication if possible. In addition, MS-CHAP passwords are stored more securely at the server but have the same vulnerabilities to dictionary and brute force attacks as CHAP. When using MS-CHAP, it is important to ensure that passwords are well-chosen and long enough that they cannot be calculated readily. Many large customers require passwords to be at least six characters long with upper- and lowercase characters and at least one digit.

Another form of authentication is EAP. Since security and authentication is a constantly changing field, embedded authentication schemes into an operating system is impractical at times. To solve this problem, Microsoft has included support for **Extensible Authentication Protocol (EAP),** which allows new authentication schemes to be plugged in as needed. Therefore, EAP allows third-party vendors to develop custom authentication schemes, such as retina scans, voice recognition, fingerprint identification, smart card, Kerberos, and digital certificates. In addition, EAP offers mutual authentication. Note: Mutual authentication is where both computers authenticate each other so that the client also knows that the server is who it says it is.

Extensible Authentication Protocol Message Digest 5 Challenge Handshake Authentication Protocol (EAP-MD5 CHAP) is an EAP type that uses the same challenge-handshake protocol as PPP-based CHAP, but the challenges and responses are sent as EAP messages. A typical use for EAP-MD5 CHAP is to authenticate the credentials of remote access clients by using username and password security systems.

EAP-Transport Level Security (EAP-TLS) is an EAP type that is used in certificate-based security environments. If you are using smart cards for remote access authentication, you must use the EAP-TLS authentication method. The EAP-TLS exchange of messages provides mutual authentication, negotiation of the encryption method, and secured private key exchange between the remote access client and the authenticating server. EAP-TLS provides the strongest authentication and key exchange method.

EAP-RADIUS is not an EAP type, but the passing of EAP messages of any EAP type by a remote access server to a RADIUS server for authentication. The EAP messages sent between the remote access client and remote access server are encapsulated and formatted as RADIUS messages between the remote access server and the RADIUS server.

EAP-RADIUS is used in environments where RADIUS is used as the authentication provider. An advantage of using EAP-RADIUS is that EAP types do not need to be installed at each remote access server, only at the RADIUS server. In a typical use of EAP-RADIUS, a remote access server is configured to use EAP and to use RADIUS as its authentication provider. When a connection is made, the remote access client negotiates the use of EAP with the remote access server. When the client sends an EAP message to the remote access server, the remote access server encapsulates the EAP message as a RADIUS message and sends it to its configured RADIUS server. The RADIUS server processes the EAP message and sends a RADIUS-encapsulated EAP message back to the remote access server. The remote access server then forwards the EAP message to the remote access client. In this configuration, the remote access server is only a pass-through device. All processing of EAP messages occurs at the remote access client and the RADIUS server.

The unauthenticated access method allows remote access users to log on without checking their credentials. It does not verify the user's name and password. The only user validation performed in the unauthenticated access method is authorization. Enabling unauthenticated access presents security risks that must be carefully considered when deciding whether to enable this authentication method.

7.3.4   PPPoE

With the arrival of low-cost broadband technologies in general and DSL (digital subscriber line) in particular, the number of computer hosts that are permanently connected to the Internet has greatly increased. Computers connected to the Internet via DSL do so through an Ethernet link has no additional protocols including protocols for security. Modem dial-up connections, on the other hand, use PPP (Point-to-Point Protocol) which provides secure login and traffic metering, among other advanced features. **PPPoE (PPP over Ethernet)** was designed to bring the security and metering benefits of PPP to Ethernet connections such as those used in DSL. DSL is discussed in the next section.

7.3.5   Remote Authentication Dial-In User Service

Security+ Objective 2.1.3—RADIUS

Adding a remote access point to the centralized corporate network increases the chance of a break in. Therefore, a secure authentication scheme is required to provide security and protect against remote client impersonation. During the authentication stage, the remote access server collects authentication data from the dial-in client and checks it against its own user database or against a central authentication database server, such as RADIUS or TACACS+.

RADIUS, short for **Remote Authentication Dial-In User Service,** is the industry standard client/server protocol and software that enables remote access servers to communicate with a central server to authenticate dial-in users and authorize their access to the requested system or service for authenticating remote users. See figure 7.2. RADIUS allows a company to maintain user profiles in a central database that all remote servers can share. It provides better security, allowing a company to set up a policy that can be applied at a single administered network point. Lastly, since RADIUS has a central server, it also means that it is easier to perform accounting of network usage for billing and for keeping network statistics.

RADIUS supports a variety of authentication protocols, such as clear text, CHAP, or MS-CHAP. When a user dials in to a remote access device or server, the remote server communicates with the central RADIUS server to determine if the user is authorized to connect to the LAN. When an authentication request is received, the authentication server validates the request and then decrypts the data packet to access the username and password information and accesses a centralized database such as UNIX/Linux password file, Kerberos, Microsoft's Active Directory, or its own database. If the username and password are correct, the server sends an authentication acknowledgement that includes information on the user's network system and service requirements (protocol used such as TCP/IP or IPX/SPX) or encryption such as Microsoft Point-to-Point Encryption (MPPE) or DES. The acknowledgement can also filter information to limit a user's access to specific resources on the network. Note: Besides being deployed in remote access servers, it can also be deployed on routers and firewalls.

Figure 7.2   RADIUS Servers Authenticate Remote Users

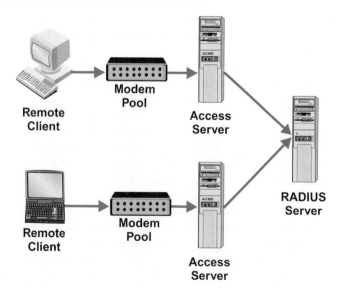

7.3.6   TACACS and TACACS+

Security+ Objective 2.1.4—TACACS/+

TACACS (Terminal Access Controller Access Control System) is an older authentication protocol common to UNIX networks that allows a remote access server to forward a user's logon password to an authentication server to determine whether access can be allowed to a given system. TACACS is an encryption protocol and therefore less secure than the later TACACS+ and Remote Authentication Dial-In User Service protocols. A later version of TACACS is XTACACS (Extended TACACS). Both are described in RFC 1492.

In spite of its name, TACACS+ is an entirely new protocol made to replace TACACS, developed by Cisco systems to address the need for a scalable solution that RADIUS did not provide. TACACS+ uses the Transmission Control Protocol (TCP), and RADIUS uses the User Datagram Protocol (UDP). Some administrators recommend using TACACS+ because TCP is seen as a more reliable protocol. Whereas RADIUS combines authentication and authorization in a user profile, TACACS+ separates the two operations.

When a user attempts to remotely access a central LAN, the user sends an authorization request to the TACACS+ server. The server then sends a reply asking for the username. The user inputs a username, and this is sent to the TACACS+ server, which then requests a password. The user inputs a password, which is verified against a database the TACACS+ server. Note: The username and password information is encrypted with MD5. If successful, the authorization portion of the logon process is complete. At this point, the user's computer negotiates with the TACACS+ server what the authorization settings are. While this happens, the TACACS+ server records the activities being performed by the remote user into a database for future security audits.

While RADIUS only encrypts the password in the packet that is passed from client to server, TACACS+ encrypts the entire body of the packet including username, authorized services, and other information.

Different from RADIUS which combines the authentication and authorization packets, TACACS+ separates authentication, authorization, and accounting, which allows for separate authentication solutions such as Kerberos. Once the authentication takes place, the remote server contacts the TACACS+ server for authorization without having to reauthenticate. The TACACS+ then handles all authorization and accounting functions on the network.

7.3.7   Securing Remote Access

Security+ Objective 2.1.8—Vulnerabilities

Security+ Objective 3.1.5—Modems

Security+ Objective 3.1.6—RAS

War dialing is the act of using a modem to dial every telephone number in a local area to find out where computers are available, then attacking them, trying to gain access by guessing passwords. A war dialer is a computer program used to identify the phone numbers that can successfully make a connection with a computer modem. The program automatically dials a defined range of phone numbers and logs and enters in a database those numbers that successfully connect to the modem. Some programs can also identify the particular operating system running in the computer and may also conduct automated penetration testing. In such cases, the war dialer runs through a predetermined list of common usernames and passwords in an attempt to gain access to the system.

A war dialer, usually obtained as freeware, is typically used by a hacker to identify potential targets. If the program does not provide automated penetration testing, the intruder attempts to hack a modem with unprotected log-ins or easily cracked passwords. Commercial war dialers, also known as modem scanners, are also used by system administrators, to identify unauthorized modems on an enterprise network. Such modems can provide easy access to a company's intranet.

Like someone trying to hack into a network, someone will also try to dial into a RAS server and guess the password. Like networks, the best protection for this is to use password policies to limit the number of times users can guess their password before their account is locked. In addition, it is recommended that users use strong passwords. To protect against war dialing, as well as unauthorized users, you can configure remote access policies to verify the caller, either by caller-ID, calling back the user, or calling back a preset phone number. Lastly, you can also smart cards or some form of biometrics.

Attackers might attempt to eavesdrop on the dial-up circuit of the user. This is difficult to do because the hacker must connect to the physical telephone line that is used to make the connection, which requires a highly skilled attacker. But if this is a risk that you want to protect against, just be sure to use strong authentication and encryption. You can also be vulnerable to man-in-the-middle attacks and spoof-user identifies. To avoid these types of attacks, you should use more advanced authentication such as certificates or challenge-response technology and strong encryption.

Lastly, like any operating system or program, there may be security holes within the software which an attacker might try to exploit. Like any operating system or program, you should check for services packs, software patches, or security fixes.

7.4   VIRTUAL PRIVATE NETWORKING

Security+ Objective 2.1.2—VPN

Security+ Objective 2.1.5—L2TP/PPTP

Security+ Objective 3.1.8—VPN

Security+ Objective 3.3.4—Tunneling

Virtual private networking (VPN) is the creation of secured, point-to-point connections across a private network or a public network such as the Internet. In other words, a VPN connects the components of one network using another network. A VPN can support:

- Traditional, host-based remote access (dial-in from a PC)
- LAN-to-LAN access (wide area networking)
- An extra level of communications security within an intranet (encrypting sensitive traffic so that it cannot be "sniffed" by personnel using your internal network)

The basic technology that defines a VPN is tunneling. **Tunneling** is the method for transferring data packets over the Internet or other public network, providing the security and features formerly available only on private networks. A tunneling protocol encapsulates the data packet in a header that provides routing information to enable the encapsulated payload to securely traverse the network. The entire process of encapsulation and transmission of packets is called tunneling, and the logical connection through which the packets travel is known as a tunnel.

You can compare tunneling similar to sending internal mail from one building to another building that belongs to the corporation but are located in two different cities. You take your letter and send it through the corporation mail services. When the letter gets to the mail root, it will then be sent using the US mail. The US mail then delivers it to the second building. The letter is then sent through the corporate mail to the correct office.

The main two types of tunneling protocols are:

- Point-to-Point Tunneling Protocol (PPTP)
- Layer 2 Tunneling Protocol (L2TP)

7.4.1   Point-to-Point Tunneling Protocol

Remote users who can gain access to their networks via the Internet are probably using **Point-to-Point Tunneling Protocol (PPTP).** PPTP, developed by Microsoft and Ascend Communications, uses the Internet as the connection between remote users and a local network, as well as between local networks. It is easy to see that the PPTP is the most popular implementation of the virtual private network (VPN) and is an inexpensive way to create wide area networks (WAN) with PSTN, ISDN, and X.25 connections. PPTP wraps various protocols inside an IP datagram, an IPX datagram, or a NetBEUI frame. This lets the protocols travel through an IP network tunnel, without user intervention. In addition, PPTP saves companies the need to build proprietary and dedicated network connections for their remote users and instead lets them use the Internet as the conduit.

PPTP is based on the Point-to-Point Protocol. The difference between PPP and PPTP is that PPTP allows access using the Internet as the connection medium, rather than requiring a direct connection between the user and the network. In other words, instead of having to dial up the corporate network directly, a remote user could log in to a local Internet service provider, and PPTP will make the connection from that provider to the corporate network's Internet connection. From there, it continues into the corporate network the same as if the user dialed in directly.

1. The remote client makes a point-to-point connection to the front-end processor via a modem.
2. The front-end processor connects to the remote access server, establishing a secure "tunnel" connection over the Internet. This connection then functions as the network backbone.
3. The remote access server handles the account management and supports data encryption through IP, IPX, or NetBEUI protocols.

Microsoft Point-to-Point Encryption (MPPE) is a data encryption method that is used to encrypt data on PPTP connections. MPPE uses the RSA RC4 stream cipher to encrypt data, and MPPE can use a 40-bit, 56-bit, or 128-bit encryption key. Windows NT 4.0 only supports 40-bit MPPE encryption, so Windows 2000 and Windows Server 2003 MPPE provide 40-bit encryption for backward compatibility with down-level clients. The level of MPPE encryption that will be used on a virtual private network (VPN) connection is negotiated as the link is being established.

PPTP has drawbacks. PPTP is not the strongest encryption technology and authentication feature available. Therefore, for highly secure transmission over the Internet, most corporations tend to prefer L2TP with IPSec.

7.4.2   L2TP with IPSec

Security+ Objective 2.1.7—IPSEC

The more secure alternative to PPTP is **L2TP (Layer 2 Tunneling Protocol).** L2TP is another Microsoft development merging elements of PPTP with Layer 2 Forwarding, a Cisco Systems Inc. packet encapsulation scheme. L2TP alone is not secure, so it is almost invariably paired with IPSec **(IP security),** which supports end-to-end encryption between clients and servers.

L2TP encapsulates PPP frames to be sent over IP, X.25, Frame Relay, or ATM networks. These encapsulated PPP frames can be encrypted or compressed. L2TP uses UDP port 1701 and includes a series of L2TP control messages for tunnel maintenance. When L2TP tunnels appear as IP packets, they take advantage of standard IPSec security using IPSec transport mode for strong integrity, replay, authenticity, and privacy protection. While MPPE only supports link encryption, IPSec supports end-to-end encryption between clients and servers. If implemented properly, IPSec is virtually impenetrable because IPSec employs triple Data Encryption Standard (3DES) based on ANSI X.509 security certificates. Electronic certificates, issued internally or by a public authority such as Verisign Inc., irrefutably identify the client and server. 3DES encryption (ANSI X9.52) stiffens standard 56-bit encryption keys, which can be broken only with considerable effort, by applying the encryption algorithm three times.

7.4.3   High-level Tunneling

Higher-level tunneling, when you wish to tunnel traffic related to some applications, but not all traffic on the network, is most often accomplished via Secure Shell (SSH), or Secure Sockets Layer (SSL). SSH seems to be the protocol of choice when tunneling login connections (providing a more secure remote connection than telnet and related commands). And SSL is, of course, the protocol used to implement a secure version of HTTP communication used between web browsers and servers. In addition, SSL has evolved into the IETF-standard Transport Layer Security (TLS), which uses digital certificates for authentication and confidentiality.

7.5   PBX

Security+ Objective 3.1.7—Telecom/PBX

In many businesses, the phones are digital phones. Therefore, the voice is digitized immediately by the phone. The signal then travels to a PBX. A **PBX (private branch exchange)** is a telephone system within an enterprise that switches calls between enterprise users on local lines while allowing all users to share a certain number of external phone lines. The main purpose of a PBX is to save the cost of requiring a line for each user to the telephone company's central office. The PBX is owned and operated by the company, supplier, or service provider rather than the telephone company. The PBX is the closest thing that the PBX has to an Internet access router.

A PBX includes:

- Telephone trunk (multiple phone) lines that terminate at the PBX.
- A computer with memory that manages the switching of the calls within the PBX and in and out of it.
- The network of lines within the PBX.
- Usually a console or switchboard for a human operator.
- In some situations, alternatives to a PBX include centrex service (in which a pool of lines are rented at the phone company's central office), key telephone systems, and, for very small enterprises, primary-rate Integrated Services Digital Network.

Today, almost all PBXs are now computers, which handle digitized voice usually at the standard 64 Kbps. Because of the processing power of the computer driving these modern PBXs, most products have an array of features that many users do not even know about. Some companies actually hire consultants to come in and tell the users about the features available on the PBX and how to access them. For instance, many PBXs have a make-busy feature that allows users to set their office telephone to give a busy signal to all callers, even if the telephone is not in use. This is good for getting some privacy to work undisturbed. While enhanced features are common on the business PBX, they are not as common, or as extensive, on residential systems.

Telephones connected to the PBX have a unique extension number enabling intra-switch phone calls, bypassing the need for an external telephone line. Incoming calls may be sent to an onsite operator or automatically routed using dialed number information provided by the CO switch. PBXs may also be connected to other PBXs over dedicated trunk lines.

PBXs often offer voice mail which is kept secure by giving individual voice-mail boxes and passwords to each user. Each person's voice mail should be kept confidential and may contain company secrets, which should not be revealed to other people.

Attackers who gain unauthorized access to the PBX system could potentially use it to do the following:

- Make free long-distance calls by changing billing records.
- Compromise or shut down the phone system or voice-mail system.
- Reroute incoming, transferred, or outgoing calls.
- If the PBX system is part of your network infrastructure, compromise the rest of your organization's network.
- Access confidential voice mail.

While many organizations put a lot of time and effort into securing their network, many organizations don't really put much time and effort into securing their phone system. The first thing you should do is establish passwords for voice mail, have users change their passwords from time to time, and educate your users on the voice-mail security. In addition, you should establish a password change and audit policy much like you do with the password policies for networks.

To protect your PBX, you should restrict access to the room where the PBX and switching equipment is controlled. Like your network infrastructure, you should have your telecommunications infrastructure documented and routinely checked for unauthorized connections. Log maintenance, software updates, remote management, and all other system access.

Like a file server, the PBX also has a maintenance password, which allows someone to reconfigure the PBX. First, you should always change the password from its default password. In addition, you should insist on strong authentication. In addition, if possible, establish a system that tracks system access, checks for fraud, and performs audits.

Since PBXs are expensive machines and often difficult to upgrade, many companies still have older PBXs. Those PBXs may not have features that would help you secure them. In addition, some of the older PBXs may have unencrypted databases. Therefore, you should consider upgrading these older PBXs.

Lastly, many employees don't think twice about using a company telephone system for extended personal use, including long distance calls. Even company-supplied mobile phones and pagers are also easily abused. The simplest and most effective countermeasure against internal abuses is to publish and enforce a corporate telephone use policy. Of course, you should also regularly audit telephone records to deter and detect telephone abuse.

7.6   FACSIMILE SECURITY

Facsimile (fax) machines are used extensively for transmitting and receiving text and graphics over public telephone circuits. However, while fax transmissions are often taken for granted, they can be a major security issue. A fax transmission, which transmits and receives data in plain text, can be easily intercepted or recreated. However, software and hardware products are available for encrypting fax data. When communicating sensitive data with a facsimile machine, implement the following guidelines to reduce the likelihood of disclosure.

Guidelines:

- Place any facsimile machine in a secured area to eliminate or at least minimize access by users not having a "need-to-know" for very sensitive data.
- Coordinate the use of data encryption equipment or dedicated communications lines with IT.
- Make sure that you have staff present in areas at all times that contain facsimile machines when the room is open.
- Verify the telephone number of the facsimile machine receiving the information before transmitting sensitive data.
- Notify the recipient of the time when sensitive information will be transmitted and agree to have that authorized person present at the destination machine when the material is sent.
- Never send sensitive information to an unattended facsimile machine.
- Use cover pages with appropriate routing and classification markings
- Distribute facsimile phone numbers only to personnel and authorized vendors so that it will help eliminate unsolicited documents that can tie up the machine.

WHAT YOU SHOULD KNOW

Security+ Objective 1.2.2—CHAP

1. Password Authentication Protocol (PAP) is the least secure authentication protocol because it uses clear text (plain-text) passwords.
2. Historically, Challenge Handshake Authentication Protocol (CHAP) is the most common dial-up authentication protocol used, which uses an industry Message Digest 5 (MD5) hashing scheme to encrypt authentication.
3. CHAP doesn't send the actual password over the wire; instead, it uses a three-way challenge-response mechanism (or handshake) with one-way MD5 hashing to provide encrypted authentication without sending the password over the link.
4. Microsoft Challenge Handshake Authentication Protocol (MS-CHAP) is Microsoft's proprietary version of CHAP.
5. MS-CHAP v2 provides stronger security for remote access connections and allows for mutual authentication where the client authenticates the server.

6. Extensible Authentication Protocol (EAP) allows new authentication schemes to be plugged in as needed, which allows third-party vendors to develop custom authentication schemes such as retina scans, voice recognition, finger print identification, smart card, Kerberos, and digital certificates.

Security+ Objective 2.1—Remote Access

Security+ Objective 3.1.5—Modems

Security+ Objective 3.1.6—RAS

1. Dial-up networking is when a remote access client makes a nonpermanent, dial-up connection to a physical port on a remote access server by using the service of a telecommunications provider such as analog phone or ISDN.
2. Today, modern networks offer remote access service (RAS), which allows users to connect remotely using various protocols and connection types.

3. A remote access server, sometimes called a communication server or network access server (NAS), is the computer and associated software that is set up to handle users seeking access to a network remotely.

4. A remote access server usually includes or is associated with a firewall server to ensure security and a router that can forward the remote access request to another part of the corporate network.

5. The first protocol used to connect to an IP network using dial-up lines was Serial Line Interface Protocol (SLIP).

6. Point-to-Point Protocol (PPP) has become the predominant protocol for modem-based access to the Internet that provides full-duplex, bi-directional operations between hosts and can encapsulate multiple network layer LAN protocols to connect to private networks.

7. When a client dials in to a RAS server, the server will have to verify the client's credentials for authentication by using the client's user account properties and remote access policies to authorize the connection.

8. PPPoE (PPP over Ethernet) was designed to bring the security and metering benefits of PPP to Ethernet connections such as those used in DSL.

Security+ Objective 2.1.3—RADIUS

1. Adding a remote access point to the centralized corporate network increases the chance of a break in.

2. Therefore, a secure authentication scheme is required to provide security and protect against remote client impersonation.

3. During the authentication stage, the remote access server collects authentication data from the dial-in client and checks it against its own user database or against a central authentication database server, such as RADIUS or TACACS+.

4. RADIUS, short for Remote Authentication Dial-In User Service, is the industry standard client/server protocol and software that enables remote access servers to communicate with a central server to authenticate dial-in users and authorize their access to the requested system or service for authenticating remote users.

5. RADIUS allows a company to maintain user profiles in a central database that all remote servers can share. It provides better security, allowing a company to set up a policy that can be applied at a single administered network point.

Security+ Objective 2.1.4—TACACS/+

1. TACACS (Terminal Access Controller Access Control System) is an older authentication protocol common to UNIX networks that allows a remote access server to forward a user's logon password to an authentication server to determine whether access can be allowed to a given system.

2. In spite of its name, TACACS+ is an entirely new protocol made to replace TACACS, developed by Cisco systems to address the need for a scalable solution that RADIUS did not provide.

3. Whereas RADIUS combines authentication and authorization in a user profile, TACACS+ separates the two operations.

4. Different from RADIUS which combines the authentication and authorization packets, TACACS+ separates authentication, authorization, and accounting, which allows for separate authentication solutions such as Kerberos.

Security+ Objective 2.1.8—Vulnerabilities

1. War dialing was the act of using a modem to dial every telephone number in a local area to find out where computers are available, then attacking them, trying to gain access by guessing passwords.

2. A war dialer is a computer program used to identify the phone numbers that can successfully make a connection with a computer modem. The program automatically dials a defined range of phone numbers and logs and enters in a database those numbers that successfully connect to the modem.

3. Some programs can also identify the particular operating system running in the computer and may also conduct automated penetration testing.

4. In such cases, the war dialer runs through a predetermined list of common usernames and passwords in an attempt to gain access to the system.

5. Like people trying to hack into a network, people will also try to dial into a RAS server and guess the password. Like networks, the best protection for this is to use password policies to limit the number of times they can guess the password before their account is locked.

Security+ Objective 3.1.7—Telecom/PBX

1. A PBX (private branch exchange) is a telephone system within an enterprise that switches calls between enterprise users on local lines while allowing all users to share a certain number of external phone lines.

2. The PBX is the closest thing that the PBX has to an Internet access router.

3. Attackers who gain unauthorized access to the PBX system could potentially use it to make free long-distance calls by changing billing records; compromising or shutting down the phone system or voice-mail system; rerouting incoming, transferred, or outgoing calls, or accessing confidential voice mail.

4. While many organizations put a lot of time and effort in securing their network, many organizations don't really put much time and effort into securing their phone system.

5. If you have a PBX, you should establish a password change and audit policy much like you do with the password policies for networks.

6. To protect your PBX, you should restrict access to the room where the PBX and switching equipment is controlled.

7. The simplest and most effective countermeasure against internal abuses of an internal phone system is to publish and enforce a corporate telephone use policy.

Security+ Objective 2.1.2—VPN

Security+ Objective 3.1.8—VPN

Security+ Objective 3.3.4—Tunneling

Security+ Objective 2.1.5—L2TP/PPTP

Security+ Objective 2.1.7—IPSEC

1. Virtual private networking (VPN) is the creation of secured, point-to-point connections across a private network or a public network such as the Internet.
2. Tunneling is the method for transferring data packets over the Internet or other public network, providing the security and features formerly available only on private networks.

3. The main two types of tunneling protocols are Point-to-Point Tunneling Protocol (PPTP) and Layer 2 Tunneling Protocol (L2TP).
4. PPTP is based on the Point-to-Point Protocol. The difference between PPP and PPTP is that PPTP allows access using the Internet as the connection medium, rather than requiring a direct connection between the user and the network.
5. Microsoft Point-to-Point Encryption (MPPE) is a data encryption method that is used to encrypt data on Point-to-Point Tunneling Protocol (PPTP) connections.
6. PPTP does not have the strongest encryption technology and authentication features available. Therefore, for highly secure transmission over the Internet, most corporations tend to prefer L2TP with IPSec.
7. L2TP alone is not secure, so it is almost invariably paired IPSec (Internet Protocol security), which supports end-to-end encryption between clients and servers.

QUESTIONS

1. The best protection against the abuse of remote maintenance of PBX (Private Branch Exchange) system is to:
   a. Keep maintenance features turned off until needed.
   b. Insists on strong authentication before allowing remote maintenance.
   c. Keep PBX (Private Branch Exchange) in locked enclosure and restrict access to only a few people.
   d. Check to see if the maintenance caller is on the list of approved maintenance personnel.
2. As the security analyst for your company's network, you need to implement a client/server protocol and software that enables remote access servers to communicate with a central server to authenticate dial-in users and authorize their access to the requested system or service. From the list below, what should you use?
   a. RADIUS   b. ICMP
   c. IPSEC   d. DVMRP
3. A device that is used to allow access to the Internet from the private network without exposing the internal clients to the Internet directory is known as a _____ . (Select the correct answer for the blank.)
   a. Port scanner   b. Firewall
   c. Proxy server   d. Packet server
   e. Packet inspector f. Web server
   g. Firewall
4. _____ and _____ are the two protocols supported in Windows 2000 for establishing secure VPN tunnels. (Choose two correct answers.)
   a. SMB   b. CDP
   c. RDP   d. PPTP

   e. L2TP with IPSec f. TCP/IP
   g. LEAP   h. BGP
   i. IMAP4
5. The _____ serves as a central point for the authentication and authorization of all remote access clients attempting to gain access to your network. (Select the correct answer for the blank.)
   a. Firewall   b. RADIUS server
   c. Proxy server   d. Web server
   e. File server   f. Print server
   g. DHCP server
6. _____ is typically used to allow users to connect to your internal network even if they are not located in the same physical location as the network. (Select the correct answer for the blank.)
   a. Routing   b. Fire walling
   c. Filtering   d. Remote Access
   e. Media Access   f. RF hopping
7. A _____ is built on top of an existing network connection between two computers to add security and encryption. This type of connection is often times performed over insecure public networks, such as the Internet. (Select the correct answer for the blank.)
   a. PPP connection
   b. AppleTalk connection
   c. RIP update
   d. Virtual private network
   e. Encapsulated tunnel connection
8. _____ performs a similar function to a RADIUS server, but is most commonly seen in UNIX networks. (Select the correct answer for the blank.)
   a. TACACS/+   b. Bluesocket

c. LEAP   d. RDP
e. CDP   f. NetBEUI
g. Daemon

9. IPSec is used with what protocol to create secure, encrypted VPN tunnels?
   a. RADIUS   b. PPTP
   c. MPPE   d. SMB
   e. S-HTTP   f. L2TP
   g. NNTP

10. A _____ is a secure tunneled connection between two computers over an insecure medium such as the Internet. (Select the correct answer for the blank.)
    a. AH   b. VPN
    c. PPP   d. MD5
    e. RADIUS   f. RRAS
    g. FTP

11. PAP transmits your username and password in _____ . (Select the correct answer for the blank.)
    a. An MD5 encrypted packet
    b. Clear text
    c. PAP encryption
    d. An HTML encoded packet

12. The best protection against the abuse of remote maintenance of a PBX (Private Branch Exchange) system is to:
    a. Keep maintenance features turned off until needed.
    b. Insist on strong authentication before allowing remote maintenance.
    c. Keep PBX in locked enclosure and restrict access to only a few people.
    d. Check to see if the maintenance caller is on the list of approved maintenance personnel.

13. A perimeter router is configured with a restrictive ACL (Access Control List). Which Transport Layer Protocol and ports must be allowed in order to support L2TP and PPTP connections, respectively, through the perimeter?
    a. TCP port 635 and UDP port 654
    b. TCP port 749 and UDP port 781
    c. UDP port 1701 and TCP port 1723
    d. TCP port 1812 and UDP port 1813

14. The process to which remote users can make a secure connection to internal resources after establishing an Internet connection could correctly be referred to as:
    a. Channeling.   b. Tunneling.
    c. Throughput.   d. Forwarding.

15. When does CHAP (Challenge Handshake Authentication Protocol) perform the handshake process?
    a. When establishing a connection and at anytime after the connection is established
    b. Only when establishing a connection and disconnecting
    c. Only when establishing a connection
    d. Only when disconnecting

16. What is the greatest advantage to using RADIUS for multiside VPN supporting a large population of remote users?
    a. RADIUS provides for a centralized database.
    b. RADIUS provides for a decentralized user database.
    c. No user database is required with RADIUS.
    d. User database is replicated and stored locally on all remote systems.

17. What type of security mechanism can be applied to modems to better authenticate remote users?
    a. Firewalls   b. Encryption
    c. SSH   d. Callback

18. Tunneling is best described as the act of encapsulating:
    a. Encrypted/secure IP packets inside of ordinary/non-secure IP packets.
    b. Ordinary/non-secure IP packets inside of encrypted/secure IP packets.
    c. Encrypted/secure IP packets inside of encrypted/non-secure IP packets.
    d. Ordinary/secure IP packets inside of ordinary/non-secure IP packets.

19. An attacker attempting to penetrate a company's network through its remote access system would most likely gain access through what method?
    a. War dialer   b. Trojan horse
    c. DoS   d. Worm

20. In the context of the Internet, what is tunneling? Tunneling is:
    a. Using the Internet as part of a private secure network.
    b. The ability to burrow through three levels of firewalls.
    c. The ability to pass information over the Internet within the shortest amount of time.
    d. Creating a tunnel which can capture data.

21. Which authentication protocol could be employed to encrypt passwords?
    a. PPTP   b. SMTP
    c. Kerberos   d. CHAP

HANDS-ON EXERCISES

Exercise 1: Remote Access Server

Configure the Remote Access Server

Perform the following on your Windows Computer
  1. Log on as the Administrator for your domain.
  2. In the Administrative Tools, start Open Routing and Remote Access console.
  3. In the left pane, right-click the your server and select the Configure and Enable Routing and Remote Access option. Click on the Next button.
  4. On the Common Configurations page, select the Remote access server option and select the Next button.
  5. On the Remote Client Protocols page, TCP/IP is listed. Keep the default option of Yes, all of the required protocols are on this list option and click the Next page.
  6. On the Network Selection page, select your network connection and click on the Next button.
  7. On the IP Address Assignment page, select the From a specified range of addresses option and click on the Next button.
  8. On the Address Range Assignment page, click the New button.
  9. In the Start IP address box, type 10.x.
  10. Use 140.100.100.XX for the Start address and 140.100.100.XX+1 for the End address, whereas XX is your computer number. Click on the OK button. Click on the Next button.
  11. On the Managing Multiple Remote Access Servers page, keep the default setting of "No, I don't want to set up this server to use RADIUS now" is selected and click the Next button. Click on the Finish button. Click OK to close the Routing and Remote Access message box.
  12. Close the Routing and Remote Access console.

Granting Dial-in Permissions

Perform the following on your computer
  1. In the Administrative Tools, open Active Directory Users and Computers console from the Administrative Tools menu.
  2. In the console tree in the left pane, expand your domain.
  3. Click on Users in the left pane and double-click Administrator in the right pane.
  4. On the Dial-in tab, select the Allow access option and click the OK button.
  5. Close the Active Directory Users and Computers console.

Configure a VPN Connection

Perform the following on your partner's computer
  1. Right-click My Network Places and then click Properties.
  2. In the Network and Dial-up Connections, double-click the Make New Connection icon. Click on the Next button.
  3. On the Network Connection Type page, select the Connect to a private network through the Internet option and click the Next button.
  4. On the Destination Address page, type in the address of your partner's computer and click the Next button.
  5. On the Connection Availability page, click the Only for myself option. Click the Next button followed by the Finish button.
  6. Click on the Cancel button.

Making a VPN Connection

Perform the following on your partner's computer
  1. Right-click My Network Places and select the Properties button.
  2. Double-click the Virtual Private Connections icon.
  3. Connect as the Administrator with the Connect Virtual Private Connection dialog box.
  4. After a message appears indicating that you are connected, you will see an icon in the system tray. Click OK button.
  5. Close Network and Dial-up Connections.
  6. At the command prompt, execute IPCONFIG to verify the IP address for the connection.
  7. Double-click the Connection icon in the system tray.
  8. Click the Disconnect button.

CHAPTER 8

Wireless Security

Topics Covered in this Chapter

Introduction

As networks advanced and have gotten faster, so has the wireless technology. Today, wireless technology can be used for a wide variety of applications including data networks, cell phones, and GPS systems. In addition, wireless technology is useful when certain factors do not allow you to use a wired network.

Objectives

1. Security+ Objective 2.1.1—802.1x
2. Security+ Objective 2.6.1—WTLS
3. Security+ Objective 2.6.2—802.1x
4. Security+ Objective 2.6.3—WEP/WAP
5. Security+ Objective 2.6.4—Vulnerabilities
6. Security+ Objective 2.6.4.1—Site Surveys
7. Security+ Objective 3.1.4—Wireless
8. Security+ Objective 5.1.3.1—Wireless Cells
9. Security+ Objective 5.1.3.2—Location
10. Security+ Objective 5.1.3.3—Shielding

8.1   THE WIRELESS SPECTRUM

For decades, radio and television stations have used the atmosphere to transport information via analog signals. The atmosphere is also capable of carrying digital signals. Networks that transmit signals through the atmosphere are known as wireless networks.

All wireless signals are carried through the air along electromagnetic waves. Electromagnetic waves are waves of energy composed of both electric and magnetic components. Sound and light are both examples of electromagnetic waves. The waves that belong to the wireless spectrum (waves used for broadcasting, cellular phones, and satellite transmission) are not visible or audible, except by the receiver.

When radio waves are described as the technology used to broadcast radio and TV programs, some people assume radio waves are a little like sound waves. Thus the term "airwaves." A sound is made when something causes the air to vibrate. This vibration is transferred to our eardrums when the sound wave arrives. The vibration is then translated into a signal transmitted to our brains, where we perceive the sound.

In reality, radio waves are really not at all like sound waves. They do not create vibrations in our ears. They do not rely on vibrations in the air; in fact, they do not need air for transmission. Instead of being a vibration, they are a form of energy. They are part of what is called the electromagnetic spectrum. This energy spectrum includes the full range of radiation created by the interaction of electrons and magnetic fields. These types of radiation include radio waves, microwaves, infrared light, visible light, ultraviolet light, and x-rays.

All are forms of radiation, created by the properties of electromagnetic fields. For example, radio waves are created when electrons are passed through a conductor, like an electrical wire. The current creates a magnetic field. Fluctuations in the current produce changes in the magnetic field, creating waves of electromagnetic energy or radiation. Other forms of electromagnetic radiation are produced through other atomic processes.

These changes in the magnetic field are called waves because the energy oscillates—rises in intensity to a peak, fades to a minimum, and then rises to its peak level again. The distance between two successive peaks or troughs is called the energy's wavelength.

All of these forms of energy travel at the same speed, the speed of light. The only difference between them is their wavelengths. Radio waves are the longest. Gamma rays are the shortest. Because gamma rays are shorter, and they travel the same speed as radio waves, more of them can pass a specified point in a single second. The number of waves passing a point in one second is called the energy's frequency. Gamma rays have much, much higher frequencies than radio waves.

Like data transfer rates, frequencies can be very large, so the standard large units are used to note them: kilo (K), mega (M), and giga (G). Radio waves have frequencies from about 150 KHz (kilohertz)

Table 8.1 Electromagnetic Spectrum

Band Name	Range	Applications
VLF (Very Low Frequency)	3–30 kHz	Used mainly in submarine communications.
LF (Low Frequency)	30–300 kHz	Used mainly in low-capacity radio communications.
MF (Medium Frequency)	0.3–3 MHz	Used mainly in low-capacity radio communications.
HF (High Frequency)	3–30 MHz	High-capacity long-distance communication. However: Interference and fading.
VHF (Very High Frequency)	30–300 MHz	Lower VHF frequencies: High-capacity long-distance communication up to 100 km is possible. Higher VHF frequencies: High-capacity line-of-sight communication (up to 40–50 km).
UHF (Ultra High Frequency)	0.3–3 GHz	High-capacity line-of-sight communication (up to 40–50 km).
SHF (Super High Frequency)	3–30 GHz	Communication up to 10 km. Over longer distances than 10km: Too much interference from rain and obstacles.
EHF (Extremely High Frequency)	30–300 GHz	High-capacity communication over short distances.
Infrared	300–1,000 GHz	Wireless local area networks. Infrared is not capable of penetrating walls or rain.

through 300 GHz (gigahertz). In contrast, light waves are much shorter and have much higher frequencies. Light wave frequencies are in the area of about 100 trillion hertz, or 100 THz (terahertz).

It is possible to encode a few bits per hertz at low frequencies with current technology. However, more bits can be encoded at high frequencies. Therefore the high frequencies are in general much more popular. However, it stops at the high end because high frequencies are not able to cover great distances.

The **wireless spectrum** is a continuum of electromagnetic waves, with varying frequencies and wavelengths that are used for telecommunications. See table 8.1. The wireless spectrum as defined by the FCC spans frequencies between 9 KHz and 300,000 GHz. Each type of wireless service is associated with one area of the wireless spectrum. AM broadcasting, for example, involves the low-frequency end of the wireless communication spectrum, using frequencies between 535 and 1605 KHz. Its wavelengths are between 560 meters and 190 meters long. Infrared waves make use of a wide band of frequencies at the high-frequency end of the spectrum, between 300 GHz and 300,000 GHz. Infrared wavelengths can be between 1 millimeter and 1 micrometer long.

The wireless spectrum is a subset of the spectrum of all electromagnetic waves. Electromagnetic waves with higher or lower frequencies exist in nature but are not used for telecommunications. Frequencies lower than 9 KHz are used for specialized applications, such as wildlife tracking collars and garage door openers.

Frequencies higher than 300,000 GHz are visible to humans and, for that reason, cannot be used for communications through the air. For example, the color red is 428,570 GHz. At the very highest end of the electromagnetic spectrum are X-rays and gamma rays.

Wireless networks typically use infrared or radio frequency signaling. See table 8.2. By using a wireless network, these networks are suited to very specialized network environments that require mobility, long distances or isolated locations. Note: Radio and infrared are considered unbound media because they are not carried or bound with a physical cable.

When two senders use the same frequency for transmitting their information chaos will be the result. To prevent this chaos, there are national and international agreements about who can use which frequencies. Worldwide, an agency of the ITU (WARC) is supervising these agreements. In the United States, the FCC allocates spectrum. Unfortunately the FCC is not bound by WARC's recommendations, so some chaos does exist.

Table 8.2 Wireless Technology

Media	Frequency Range	Cost	Ease of Installation	Capacity Range	Attenuation	Immunity for Interference and Signal Capture
Low-power single frequency	Entire RF, high GHz is most common	Moderate (depends on equipment)	Simple	<1 to 10 Mbps	High	Extremely low
High-power single frequency	Entire RF, high GHz is most common	Moderately expensive	Difficult	<1 to 10 Mbps	Low	Extremely low
Spread spectrum radio	Entire RF, 902 to 928 MHz in US, 2.4 GHz band is most common	Moderate (depends on equipment)	Simple to Moderate	2 to 6 Mbps	High	Moderate
Terrestrial microwave	Low GHz, 4 to 6 or 21 to 23 is most common	Moderate to high (depends on equipment)	Difficult	<1 to 10 Mbps	Variable	Low
Satellite microwave	Low GHz, 11 to 14 GHz most common	High	Extremely difficult	<1 to 10 Mbps	Variable	Low
Point-to-Point infrared	100 GHz to 1,000 THz	Low to moderate	Moderate to difficult	<1 to 16 Mbps	Variable	Moderate
Broadcast infrared	100 GHz to 1,000 THz	Low	Simple	≤1 Mbps	High	Low

Figure 8.1 Cellular Topology

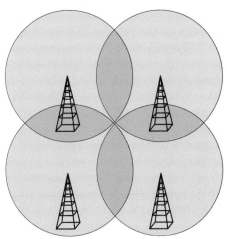

Security+ Objective 5.1.3.1—Wireless Cells

When discussing wireless technology, many technologies that are wireless use a **cellular topology,** in which an area is divided into cells. A broadcast device is located at the center and is broadcasting in all directions to form an invisible circle (cell). All network devices located within the cell communicate with the network through the central station or hub, which are interconnected with rest of the network infrastructure. If the cells are overlapped, devices may roam from cell to cell while maintaining connection to the network as the devices. See figure 8.1. The best-known example of cellular topology is cellular phones.

8.1.1   Radio Systems

Radio frequency (RF) resides between 10 KHz to 1 GHz of the electromagnetic spectrum. It includes shortwave radio, very-high frequency (VHF) and ultra-high frequency (UHF). Radio frequencies have been divided between regulated and unregulated bandwidths. Users of the regulated frequencies must get a license from the regulatory bodies that have jurisdiction over the desired operating area (the FCC in the United States and CDC in Canada). While the licensing process can be difficult, licensed frequencies typically guarantee clear transmission within a specific area.

The properties of radio waves are strongly dependent on the frequency used:

- **Low frequencies**—Radio waves pass through obstacles easily, but the power declines sharply with the distance from the transmitter. The main problem with using these low frequencies for data communication is the relatively small bandwidth they offer.
- **High frequencies**—Radio waves tend to travel in straight lines and bounce off obstacles like buildings. Transmitter and receiver need a direct line of sight connection. However, the waves that reach the ionosphere, a layer of charged particles circling the earth at a height of about 300 km, are refracted by it and sent back to earth. Amateur radio operators (hams) use these bands to talk long distance.

At all frequencies, radio waves are subject to interference from other electrical equipment.

In radio network transmissions, a signal is transmitted in one or multiple directions, depending on the type of antenna that is used. The wave is very short in length with a low transmission strength (unless the transmission operator has a special license for a high-wattage transmission), which means it is best suited to short-range line-of-sight transmissions. A line-of-sight transmission is one in which the signal goes from point to point, rather than bouncing off the atmosphere over great distances. Of course, a limitation of line-of-sight transmissions is that they are interrupted by land masses such as mountains. Because of its ability to travel long distances, interference between users is a problem. Therefore, all governments tightly license the user of radio transmitters.

In unregulated bands, you must operate at regulated power levels (under 1 watt in the United States) to minimize interference with other signals. Of course, if a device broadcast uses less power, the effective area will be smaller. The Federal Communications Commission (FCC) allocated the following bands for unregulated broadcast: 902–928 MHz, 2,400–2,483.5 MHz and 5,752.5–5,850 MHz. Note: These are called the ISM bands, short for Industrial, Scientific, and Medical bands. See table 8.3. While you don't require a license from the FCC to use these frequencies, you must meet FCC regulations, which include power limits and minimizing interference (antenna gain of 6 dB and 1 watt of radiated power).

Since the bandwidth available increases in the higher-frequency ranges, these higher-frequencies will support higher data transfer rates. Therefore, many wireless bridge products being sold today operate in the 2.4 GHz and 5.7 GHz frequencies. As throughput increases, computer networking becomes more of a real possibility. And with more companies producing RF wireless networking products, prices are continuing to fall, making wireless networking a viable alternative to land-based lines in many local areas.

A **band** is a contiguous group of frequencies, which are used for a single purpose. Commercial radio stations often refer to the band of frequencies they are using as a single frequency. However, typical radio transmissions actually cover a range of frequencies and wavelengths. Because most tuning equipment is designed to address the entire bandwidth at the kilohertz or megahertz level, the distinction between one frequency and a band is often overlooked.

A **narrowband radio system** transmits and receives user information on a specific radio frequency. Narrowband radio keeps the radio signal frequency as narrow as possible just to pass the information. Undesirable crosstalk between communications channels is avoided by carefully

Table 8.3   ISM Bands

Frequency	Range Band Description	Bandwidth Available
902–928 MHz	Industrial Band	26.0 MHz
2.40–2.4835 GHz	Scientific Band	83.5 MHz
5.725–5.850 GHz	Medical Band	125.0 MHz

coordinating different users on different channel frequencies. In a radio system, privacy and noninterference are accomplished by the use of separate radio frequencies. The radio receiver filters out all radio signals except the ones on its designated frequency. Depending on the power and frequency of the radio signal, the range could be a room, an entire building or long distances. A low power (1–10 watts) single-frequency signal has a data capacity in the range of 1–10 Mbps.

Spread-spectrum signals are distributed over a wide range of frequencies and then collected onto their original frequency at the receiver. Different from narrowband signals, spread-spectrum signals use wider bands, which transmit at a much lower spectral power density (measured in watts per Hertz). Unless the receiver is not tuned to the right frequency or frequencies, a spread-spectrum signal resembles noise, making the signals harder to detect and harder to jam. As an additional bonus, spread-spectrum and narrow-band signals can occupy the same band, with little or no interference. There are two types of spread spectrum: direct sequence and frequency hopping. Spread-spectrum frequency ranges are very high, in the 902–928 MHz range and higher, and typically send data at a rate of 2–6 Mbps.

Direct-sequence spread-spectrum (DSSS) generates a redundant bit pattern for each bit to be transmitted. This bit pattern is called a chip (or chipping code). The intended receiver knows which specific frequencies are valid and deciphers the signal by collecting valid signals and ignoring the spurious signals. The valid signals are then used to reassemble the data. Because multiple subsets can be used within any frequency range, direct-sequence signals can coexist with other signals. Although direct-sequence signals can be intercepted almost as easily as other RF signals, eavesdropping is ineffective because it is quite difficult to determine which specific frequencies to make up the bit pattern, retrieve the bit pattern, and interpret the signal. Because of modern error detection and correction methods, the longer the chip, the greater the probability that the original data can be recovered even if one or more bits in the chip are damaged during transmission.

Frequency hopping quickly switches between predetermined frequencies, many times each second. Both the transmitter and receiver must follow the same pattern and maintain complex timing intervals to be able to receive and interpret the data being sent. Similar to direct-sequence spread-spectrum, intercepting the data being sent is extremely difficult unless the person aiming to intercept knows the signals to monitor and timing pattern. In addition, dummy signals can be added to increase security and confuse eavesdroppers. The length of time that the transmitter remains on a given frequency is known as the dwell time.

8.1.2   Microwave Signals

Before fiber optics came upon the scene, for decades microwaves formed the heart of the long-distance telephone transmission system. Microwave communications is a form of electromagnetic energy that operates at a higher frequency (low GHz frequency range) than radio wave communications. These days, microwaves are widely used for long-distance telephone communication, cellular telephones, television distribution, and many other areas. Since microwaves provide higher bandwidths than those available using radio waves and they can carry more bits on each wave, they are currently one of the most popular long-distance transmission technologies.

Above 10^8 Hz (or 100 MHz), waves travel in straight lines. Therefore, the signals can be narrowly focused into a small beam using a parabolic antenna (like the familiar satellite TV dish). The transmitting and receiving antennas must be accurately aligned with each other. Since the microwaves travel in a straight line, repeaters placed in a tower are needed periodically. The higher the towers are, the further apart they can be. Using 100-m high towers, 80 km can be covered.

Microwave signals propagate in straight lines and are affected very little by the lower atmosphere. In addition, they are not refracted or reflected by ionized regions in the upper atmosphere. The attenuation of microwave systems highly depends on atmospheric conditions; for example, both rain and fog can reduce the maximum distance possible. Higher-frequency systems are usually affected most by such conditions. In addition, microwaves do not pass through buildings. The systems are not particularly resistant to EMI and protection for eavesdropping can only be achieved by encryption techniques.

Terrestrial systems are often used where cabling is difficult or the cost is prohibitively expensive. Relay towers are used to provide an unobstructed path over an extended distance. These line-of-sight systems use unidirectional parabolic dishes that must be aligned carefully.

The cost of these systems is relatively high, and technical expertise is required to install them, as accurate alignment is required. But putting up two towers with antennas is, in many cases, cheaper than getting 100 km of copper cable or fiber into the ground. Often, this service is leased from a service provider, which reduces installation costs and provides the required expertise.

8.1.3   Satellite Signals

Satellite transmission is much like line-of-sight microwave transmission in which one of the stations is a satellite orbiting the earth. This requires that the sending and receiving antennas be locked onto each other's location at all times. The satellite must move at the same speed as the earth so that it seems to remain fixed above a certain spot. These satellites must be in **geosynchronous (GEO) orbits** and are in positioned 22,300 miles (35,800 km) above the earth's equator. Satellite systems provide far bigger areas of coverage than can be achieved using other technologies because they can either relay signals between sites directly or via another satellite. The huge distances covered by the signal result in propagation delays of up to 5 seconds. The costs of launching and maintaining a satellite are enormous, and consequently customers usually lease the services from a provider.

For satellite transmission, information sent to earth from a satellite first has to be transmitted to the satellite in an uplink. An uplink is a broadcast from an earth-based transmitter to an orbiting satellite. Often the uplink information is scrambled before transmission to prevent unauthorized interception. At the satellite, a transponder receives the uplink, then transmits the signals to another earth-based location in a downlink. A typical satellite contains 24 to 32 transponders. Each satellite uses unique frequencies for its downlink. Back on earth, the downlink is picked up by a dish-shaped antenna. The disk shape concentrates the signal, which has been weakened by traveling over 22,300 miles so that it can be interpreted by a receiver.

To prevent total chaos in the sky, there have been international agreements about who may use which frequencies. The main frequency bands are shown in table 8.4.

An alternative to GEO satellites are low earth-orbiting (LEO) satellites. LEO satellites orbit the earth with an altitude roughly between 700 and 1,400 km. But different from GEO satellites, LEO satellites are not placed above the equator. While their altitude is lower, they can only cover a smaller geographical range than GEO satellites. But less power is required to issue signals between earth and an LEO satellite than a GEO satellite. While LEO satellites can be used for data communications, they are very popular with mobile telephone service.

The medium earth-orbiting (MEO) satellites orbit the earth between 10,350 and 10,390 km above its surface. Similar to LEO satellites, they are not placed above the equator. MEOs are used to carry voice and data signals.

8.1.4   Infrared Systems (IR)

Another form of wireless technology is **infrared (IR) systems,** which are based on infrared light (light that is just below the visible light in the electromagnetic spectrum). Similar to your TV or VCR remote controls, infrared links use light-emitting diodes (LEDs) or injection laser diodes (ILDs) to transmit signals and photodiodes to receive signals. It transmits in light frequency ranges of 100 GHz to 1,000 THz.

Table 8.4   Satellite Frequency Bands

Band	Freq. Range [GHz]	Applications
C	4–8	The most heavily used piece of the satellite spectrum. The large size of the antennae of the earth station is a drawback.
X	8–12.5	Military usage
Ku	12.5–17.7	Digital Direct To Home (DTH) services
K	17.7–26.5	VSAT
Ka	26.5–40	VSAT

Unfortunately, IR only transmits up to 1 Mbps for omnidirectional communications and 16 Mbps for directional communications.

Since IR is essentially light, it cannot penetrate opaque objects. Infrared devices work using either directed or diffused technology. **Directed IR** uses line-of-sight or point-to-point technology. **Diffused** (also known as **reflective** or **indirect**) IR technology spreads the light over an area to create a cell, limited to individual rooms. Since infrared light can bounce off walls, ceilings, and any other objects in the path, the indirect infrared is not confined to a specific pathway. Unfortunately, since it is not confined to a specific pathway, this means that the transmission of data is not very secure. Lastly, since infrared signals are not capable of penetrating walls or other opaque objects and are diluted by strong light sources, infrared is most useful in small or open indoor environments.

8.2   COMPONENTS OF A WIRELESS NETWORK

To see how electrical signals get changed into radio signals, let's look at the two radio components of a wireless data connection: the radio transceiver and the antenna. To create a computer network connection over radio waves, you will first need a network device such as a bridge or a router. The network bridge/router handles the data traffic. It routes the appropriate data signals bound from the computer network in one building to the network at the other end of the radio connection. Second, a radio transmitter and receiver, commonly called a transceiver, is required. The radio transceiver handles the radio signal communications between locations.

The interesting part of this marriage of technologies is that radios have always dealt with electrical signals. The radio transmitter modulates, or changes, an electrical signal so that its frequency is raised to one appropriate to radio communications. Then the signal is passed on to a radio antenna.

At the other end of the transmission, the receiving portion of the radio transceiver takes the radio signal and demodulates it back to its normal frequency. Then the resulting electrical signal is passed to the bridge/router side for processing by the network. While the actual process of modulation/demodulation is technical, the concept of radio transmission is very simple.

Likewise, when a response is sent back to the originating site, the radio transceiver "flips" from reception mode to transmission mode. The radio transceivers at each end have this characteristic: transmit-receive, transmit-receive. They change modes as many as thousands of times per second. This characteristic leads to a delay in communications called latency. It is idiosyncratic to radio communications and negatively affects data throughput.

In the middle of the radio transmission/reception process sit two antennas, one at the building from which the signal is transmitted and one at the building receiving the signal. Of course, it is possible to have one central location and several remote locations connected to the network. For discussion's sake, though, let's think of the communication process as a straight line, from one antenna to the other. In order to transmit the modulated radio signal, an electrical current passes through the antenna, inducing a magnetic field, which oscillates at the given frequency. The variations in the current create slight variations in the radio frequency. These radio waves radiate outward from the antenna in a "beam" according to the antenna's design.

On the other end, when the radio is in receive mode, the antenna is passive. The electromagnetic radiation from the originating antenna passes across the receiving antenna. This creates a magnetic field, which, in turn, induces an electrical current through the antenna. The current passes through the radio receiver and is demodulated back into an electrical signal with the same form as the original electrical signal from the first network bridge/router. This electrical signal passes to the bridge/router portion of the receiving unit as a normal data signal.

As a result, the data signal is transferred from one network bridge/router to another without the necessity or expense of an interconnecting wire. Because the radio equipment used in wireless networking must by law be very low-powered to minimize interference with other devices, the antennas required are much more focused than those used in radio or television applications. The amount of focus they use in transmitting a signal, and their corresponding ability to "pick out" specific radio signals, is called gain. The gain is measured in decibels, abbreviated dB.

There are two major categories of antennas: directional and omni-directional. Directional antennas focus their energy in tight, narrow beams. When receiving signals, directional antennas do not "see" any signals coming from outside the "beam" on which they are focused. This eliminates a great deal of potential interference from other radio sources and contributes to the ability of multiple wireless communications systems to coexist with a minimum of interference.

Omni-directional antennas transmit their energy in a full circle. Spreading the radio signal over such a large area reduces the energy in the signal. This severely restricts the distance the signal can be transmitted and received effectively. Therefore, transmissions via an omni-directional antenna do not travel as far before being degraded as do those from directional antennas. However, amplifiers are available for both types of antennas to lengthen the transmit distance.

These characteristics make each type of antenna optimal in different situations. For those networks involving more than two buildings, called multi-point connections, an omni-directional antenna at the central site will be most cost-effective.

A directional antenna is installed at each remote site, aimed back at the central site omni-directional antenna. Since the omni-directional antenna transmits in all directions, every remote antenna can pick up its signal and transmit back to it.

On the other hand, some network connections involve only two distinct buildings. These are called point-to-point connections. In these situations, a directional antenna is used at each site, each aimed at the other. Both types of antennas are available with various levels of gain.

In addition to the wireless bridge and antenna a few more items are required to make a functional wireless network connection. They are:

- **Feature sets**—Some manufacturers sell their wireless bridges in separate units. In such instances, the physical radio/bridge unit has a base cost. Software features, such as individual protocol routing and encryption, are sold as a separate unit. However, these may be required in your implementation. Be sure to define your needs completely to the reseller/integrator/installer who installs your wireless connection.
- **External cables**—For all wireless installations there must be a cable which connects the antenna to the radio in the wireless bridge. Because it runs to the outside of the building, this is called an external cable. When purchasing all the components as part of a kit, an external cable is included. Depending on where the wireless bridge is located inside your building, and where the antenna is mounted, an additional length of cable may be required. In order to keep the wireless system within specifications, it is important to minimize the length of the cable. If necessary, it is possible to locate the wireless bridge at one location in your building and run a network cable from it to your network connection at an alternate location in the building. Be sure to physically secure the bridge if it is located in a public area.
- **Lightning arrestor**—Since external antennas are involved, the threat of a lightning strike can be very real. Make sure that proper measures are implemented to minimize the risk of lightning strikes. Most manufacturers of wireless bridges sell an optional device called a lightning arrestor. It is normally installed between the antenna and the bridge. Also make sure the antenna is properly grounded.
- **Emissions filter**—Some manufacturers provide another optional component known generally as an emissions filter. It reduces the level of extraneous noise that might interfere with the electrical signal on its way from the antenna to the wireless bridge. It also is installed inline between the antenna and bridge.
- **Mast or tower**—When it is not possible to obtain a clear line of sight between the two antennas involved in a wireless connection, a mast or radio tower may provide additional height for the antenna, clearing obstacles such as trees or buildings that lie in the path of the radio signal. Masts are generally mounted on the roof and may be 10 to 50 feet in height. If a mast is used in your implementation, be sure it is tied down properly to minimize the risk of wind damage. Radio towers are generally independent structures erected to raise antennas when extended distances are desired. They may also be required when tall buildings (higher than three stories) or topographical features lie directly in the path of the radio signal between two antennas. Towers can be erected at heights of 50 feet and higher. Obviously, depending on the application, the cost of erecting tall towers can be prohibitive.
- **Data cable**—A network data cable is required to connect the wireless bridge to your internal network (to a hub, switch, or repeater). This cable is generally the responsibility of the individual entity. If the wireless bridge is a significant distance from the network equipment, installation of this cable may require a cable installer. In this case, be sure to discuss the cable run with your wireless installer when the system is being specified.

8.3   WIRELESS LAN (WLAN)

A wireless LAN (WLAN) is a local area network without wires. WLANs have been around for more than a decade but are just beginning to gain momentum because of falling costs and improved standards. WLANs transfer data through the air using radio frequencies instead of cables. They can reach a radius of 500 feet indoors and 1,000 feet outdoors, but antennas, transmitters, and other access devices can be used to widen that area. WLANs require a wired access point that plugs all the wireless devices into the wired network.

Wireless LAN system can provide LAN users with access to real-time information anywhere in their organization. Installing a wireless LAN system can be fast and easy and can eliminate the need to pull cable through walls and ceilings. In addition, wireless technology allows the network to go where wire cannot go. Thus, WLANs combined data connectivity with user mobility, and through simplified configuration, enable movable LANs.

WLAN configurations vary from simple, independent, peer-to-peer connections between a set of PCs, to more complex, intrabuilding infrastructure networks. There are also point-to-point and point-to-multipoint wireless solutions. A point-to-point solution is used to bridge between two local area networks, and to provide an alternative to cable between two geographically distant locations (up to 30 miles). Point-to-multipoint solutions connect several, separate locations to one single location or building. Both point-to-point and point-to-multipoint can be based on the 802.11b standard or on more costly infrared-based solutions that can provide throughput rates up to 622 Mbps (OC-12 speed).

8.4   802.11 WIRELESS STANDARD

The 802.11 standards can be compared to the IEEE 802.3 standard for Ethernet for wired LANs. A new standard put out by the Institute of Electrical and Electronics Engineers (IEEE) called 802.11b or **Wi-Fi** is making WLAN use faster and easier, and the market is growing quickly. The number of IEEE 802.11b users grew from almost zero in early 2001 to more than 15 million at the end of the 2002. That still isn't much compared to cell phones and wired Ethernet, but the growth will likely continue.

8.4.1   802.1X

Security+ Objective 2.1.1—802.1x

Security+ Objective 2.6.2—802.1x

The IEEE 802.1X standard is a relatively recent protocol enhancement that creates a standard for how authentication is performed over an 802 standards-based network. The 802.1X standard is designed to enhance the security of wireless local area networks (WLANs) that follow the IEEE 802.11 standard. 802.1X provides an authentication framework for wireless LANs, allowing a user to be authenticated by a central authority. The actual algorithm that is used to determine whether a user is authentic is left open and multiple algorithms are possible. 802.1X uses an existing protocol, the Extensible Authentication Protocol (EAP), specified in RFC 2284, that works on Ethernet, Token Ring, or wireless LANs, for message exchange during the authentication process.

In a wireless LAN with 802.1X, a user (known as the supplicant) requests access to an access point (known as the authenticator). The access point forces the user (actually, the user's client software) into an unauthorized state that allows the client to send only an EAP start message. The access point returns an EAP message requesting the user's identity. The client returns the identity, which is then forwarded by the access point to the authentication server, which uses an algorithm to authenticate the user and then returns an accept or reject message back to the access point. Assuming an accept was received, the access point changes the client's state to authorized and normal traffic can now take place. The authentication server may use the Remote Authentication Dial-In User Service (RADIUS), although 802.1X does not specify it.

EAP provides an extensible authentication mechanism for use over PPP, allowing new authentication mechanisms (biometrics, smart cards, etc.) to be "plugged in" without the PPP protocol needing to understand them. EAP on LAN (EAPOL) is an adaptation of EAP. It allows authentication information to be passed in network frames, rather than requiring that it be embedded in a higher-level protocol such as PPP. This reduces network overhead for authentication and removes the necessity for the network to be running a particular protocol suite such as TCP/IP.

The potential network client passes authentication information through a wireless access point to a centralized authentication server, who validates the logon and permits certain network activities based on the identity of the client. For instance, the authentication server may install a certain set of firewall security rules or a specific VPN configuration for that client's address, based on user identity. Until a user is authenticated, the wireless network will only forward 802.1X traffic for that connection. Nothing else, such as attempts to browse the Web, send email, or obtain a local IP address via DHCP, will be permitted.

Optionally, it can be used to improve the privacy of wireless LAN communication by dynamically varying the keys used to encrypt the wireless traffic. It does this by returning encryption keys to users, allowing the network to dynamically vary the encryption used by each connection, rather than requiring that all stations be pre-configured with a fixed key (currently a time-consuming activity).

802.1X is only the framework allowing EAP transactions to be passed on the media. It is not EAP itself. To get authentication functionality, you must choose a particular flavor of EAP and install it on your authentication server. Here's a listing of the choices:

- Transport Layer Security (EAP-TLS)
- EAP Tunneled Transport Layer Security (EAP-TTLS)
- RADIUS
- LEAP

You can change the flavor of EAP that you use at any time, without needing to replace 802.1X-compliant access points, because the exact mechanics of EAP are transparent to the access points.

8.4.2   802.11 Physical Layer and Architecture

The 802.11 standard defines three physical layers for WLANs, two radio frequency specifications (RF—direct sequence and frequency-hopping spread spectrum) and one infrared (IR). Most WLANs operate in the 2.4 GHz license-free frequency radio band and have throughput rates up to 2 Mbps.

NOTE: The 2.4 GHz band is particularly attractive because it enjoys worldwide allocations for unlicensed operations. The most popular 802.11 types are:

- **802.11a**—Operate in the 5 GHz license-free frequency band and is expected to provide throughput rates up to 54 Mbps in normal mode or 75 Mbps in turbo mode, but most commonly, communications take place at 6 Mbps, 12 Mbps, or 24 Mbps. It uses a modulation scheme known as orthogonal frequency-division multiplexing (OFDM)
- **802.11b (Wi-Fi)**—standard is direct sequence only, and initially provided throughput rates up to 11 Mbps with the potential of three simultaneous channels, but has been recently increased to 22 Mbps. The modulation method selected for 802.11b is known as complementary code keying (CCK), which allows higher data speeds and is less susceptible to multipath-propagation interference. 802.11b is the clear leader in business and institutional wireless networking and is gaining share for home applications as well.

- **802.11g**—Has a nominal maximum throughput of 54 Mbps. But because it is using the 2.4 GHz frequency band, its products should be compatibility with 802.11b products.

For other 802.11 types, see table 8.5.

There are two operation modes defined in IEEE 802.11:

- Infrastructure mode
- Ad-hoc mode

The ad-hoc network, also referred to as the Independent Basic Service Set (IBSS), stands alone and is not connected to a base. The wireless stations communicate directly with each other without using an access point or any connection to a wired network. This basic topology is useful in order to quickly and easily set up a wireless network anywhere a wireless infrastructure does not exist such as a hotel room, a convention center, or an airport.

Table 8.5 802.11 Standards

IEEE Working Group	Primary Task	Status of Work
802.11a	Worked to establish specification for wireless data transmission in the 5 GHz band.	Approved 1999
802.11b	Worked to establish specifications for wireless data transmission in the 2.4 GHz band.	Approved 1999
802.11c	Worked to establish wireless MAC bridging functionality.	Folded into 802.1d
802.11d	Working to determine requirements that will allow 802.11 to operate outside the United States.	The work of this group is ongoing.
802.11e	Working to add multimedia and quality of service (QoS) capability to wireless MAC layer	Proposal in draft form
802.11.f	Working to allow for better roaming between multivendor access points and distribution systems.	The work of this group is ongoing.
802.11g	Working to provide raw data throughput over wireless networks at a rate of up to 54 Mbps.	Draft created in January 2002 and final approval expected soon.
802.11h	Worked to allow for European implementation requests regarding the 5 GHz band.	The work of this group is ongoing.
802.11i	Working to fix security flaws in WLANs by developing new security standards	The work of this group is ongoing.
802.11j	Worked to create a global standard in the 5 GHz band by making high-performance LAN (HiperLAN) and 802.11 interoperable	Disbanded

Figure 8.2 Wireless End Station and Wireless Access Point

In infrastructure mode, also known as Extended Service Set (ESS), the wireless network consists of at least one access point (AP) connected to the wired network infrastructure and a set of wireless end stations. See figure 8.2. An access point controls encryption on the network and may bridge or route the wireless traffic to a wired Ethernet network (or the Internet). Access points that act as routers can also assign an IP address to your PC's using DHCP services. APs can be compared with a base station used in cellular networks.

An Extended Service Set (ESS) consists of two or more BSSs forming a single subnetwork. Traffic is forwarded from one BSS to another to facilitate movement of wireless stations between BSSs using cellular topology. Almost always the distribution system which connects this networks is an Ethernet LAN. Since most corporate WLANs require access to the wired LAN for services (file servers, printers, Internet links) they will operate in infrastructure mode.

One of the requirements of IEEE 802.11 is that it can be used with existing wired networks. 802.11 solved this challenge with the use of a portal. A **portal** is the logical integration between wired LANs and 802.11. It also can serve as the access point to the DS. All data going to an 802.11 LAN from an 802.X LAN must pass through a portal. It thus functions as a bridge between wired and wireless.

Today, 802.11a still has some issues to work out, particularly in the area of compatibility. Currently, products aren't backward compatible with 802.11b products, which clearly dominate the market. And although all 802.11a products use the same chip set, their implementation by each manufacturer differs enough to make them incompatible. Until an interoperability standard is established, 802.11a products from one company may not communicate with those of another.

The Wireless Ethernet Compatibility Alliance (WECA) is an industry consortium that tests for interoperability. Those 802.11b products tests that pass WECA's tests are given the wireless fidelity (Wi-Fi) seal of approval. WECA is working on an 802.11a certification called WiFi5.

8.4.3   Framing

Frame formats are specified for wireless LAN systems by 802.11. Each frame consists of a MAC header, a frame body and a frame check sequence (FCS). The MAC header consists of seven fields and is 30 bytes long. The fields are frame control, duration, address 1, address 2, address 3, sequence control, and address 4. The frame control field is 2 bytes long and is comprised of 11 subfields.

The duration/ID field is 2 bytes long. It contains the data on the duration value for each field and for control frames it carries the associated identity of the transmitting station. The address fields identify the basic service set, the destination address, the source address, and the receiver and transmitter addresses. Each address field is 6 bytes long. The sequence control field is 2 bytes and is split into 2 subfields, fragment number and sequence number. Fragment number is 4 bits and tells how many fragments the MSDU is broken into. The sequence number field is 12 bits, which indicates the sequence number of the MSDU. The frame body is a variable length field from 0 to 2312. This is the payload. The frame check sequence is a 32-bit cyclic redundancy check, which ensures there are no errors in the frame.

8.4.4   Medium Access Control Protocol

Most wired LANs products use Carrier Sense Multiple Access with Collision Detection (CSMA/CD) as the MAC protocol. Carrier Sense means that the station will listen before it transmits. If there is already someone transmitting, then the station waits and tries again later. If no one is transmitting, then the station goes ahead and sends what it has. When two stations send at the same time, the transmissions will collide and the information will be lost. This is where Collision Detection comes into play. The station will listen to ensure that its transmission made it to the destination without collisions. If a collision occurs then the stations wait and try again later. The time the station waits is determined by a different random amount of time. This technique works great for wired LANs but wireless topologies can create a problem for CSMA/CD. The problem is the hidden node problem.

The Hidden Node problem is shown in figure 8.3. Node C cannot hear node A. So if node A is transmitting, node C will not know and may transmit as well. This will result in collisions. The solution to this problem is Carrier Sense Multiple Access with Collision Avoidance or CSMA/CA. In CSMA/CA, the station listens before it sends. If someone is already transmitting, it will wait for a random period and try again. If no one is transmitting, then it sends a short message called the Ready To Send message (RTS). This message contains the destination address and the duration of the transmission. Other stations now know that they must wait that long before they can transmit. The destination then sends a short message, which is the Clear To Send message (CTS). This message tells the source that it can send without fear of collisions. Each packet is acknowledged. If an acknowledgement is not received, the MAC layer retransmits the data. This entire sequence is called the 4-way handshake as shown by figure 8.4 on the following page. This is the protocol that 802.11 chose for the standard.

Figure 8.3   The Hidden Node Problem

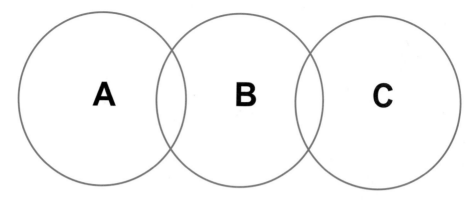

Figure 8.4   The 4-way Handshake

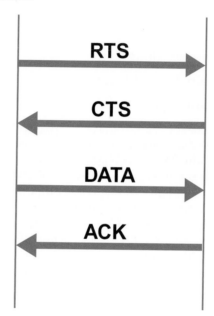

8.4.5   Wireless Application Protocol

Security+ Objective 2.6.3—WEP/WAP

WAP (Wireless Application Protocol) is a specification for a set of communication protocols to standardize the way that wireless devices with limited capability, such as cellular telephones and radio transceivers, can be used for Internet access, including e-mail, the World Wide Web, newsgroups, and Internet Relay Chat (IRC). While Internet access has been possible in the past, different manufacturers have used different technologies. In the future, devices and service systems that use WAP will be able to interoperate.

Wireless Application Protocol (WAP) is a universal open standard developed by the WAP forum and governs wireless communication. The programming used for WAP is based on the WWW programming model. The model has three components: the client, the gateway, and the original server. HTTP is used between the gateway and the original server to transfer the content of the message, and the gateway acts as a proxy server for the wireless domain.

Another component of the WAP is the wireless markup language (WML). WML documents are subdivided into small well-defined units of user interaction known as cards. The users navigate by moving from card to card. The communications protocol stack of WAP has six layers—application, session, transaction, security, transport, and network—which can adapt to the standard web protocols.

The WAP layers are:

- **Wireless Application Environment (WAE)**—Defines the user interface on the phone.
- **Wireless Session Layer (WSL)**—The WAP equivalent of HTTP. This layer links the WAE to two session services: a connection-oriented one operating over the WTP, and a connectionless service operating above the WDP.
- **Wireless Transport Layer Security (WTLS)**—Incorporates security features that are based on TLS.
- **Wireless Transport Layer (WTP)**—The WAP equivalent of TCP or UDP, that provides reliable or unreliable communications. WTP supports Protocol Data Unit concatenation and delayed acknowledgment to help reduce the number of messages sent.
- **Wireless Datagram Protocol (WDP)**—Allows WAP to be bearer independent by adapting the transport layer of the underlying bearer. WDP presents a consistent data format to the higher layers of the WAP protocol stack.
- **Network Carrier Method**—Type of wireless signal.

The WAP was conceived by four companies: Ericsson, Motorola, Nokia, and Unwired Planet (now Phone.com). The Wireless Markup Language (WML) is used to create pages that can be delivered using WAP.

8.4.6   Accessing the Wireless LAN

Security+ Objective 2.6.4—Vulnerabilities

Security+ Objective 3.1.4—Wireless

The way 802.11b works is that if you possess a couple of pieces of information, which are shared among network users, you can access the network. There is generally no individual authentication when gaining access to the network. The two pieces of information required to communicate over an 802.11b LAN are the SSID and, if encryption is enabled, the WEP key.

The Service Set Identifier (SSID) is a 32-character identifier that is attached to each packet, identifying the wireless LAN to which the traffic belongs, so that multiple wireless LANs can exist in the same physical area. Much like multiple Windows, workgroups can exist on a single physical LAN, and an individual can select the workgroup to join by setting its name in their system configuration. A user can select the 802.11b LAN to participate in by setting the proper SSID. All users who desire to communicate with each other typically set their SSID to the same value. Since the SSID can be "sniffed" from the network via programs that monitor wireless LAN activity, and once known, anyone can set their wireless network adapter's SSID to the desired value, the SSID really is only a LAN selection feature for user convenience, not an access control feature designed to add security.

To protect an 802.11b network from unauthorized, use and "snooping," you can enable packet encryption via WEP. Different cards have different levels of support for WEP. WEP works by using a RC4 encryption scheme, (refer to encryption for details on RC4) with a key that can be 40, 64, 128, or 256 bits in length. The design in 802.11 for RC4 uses a shared key. The access point sends a random number at the registration request. The receiving node assigns the key with a secret key that was pre-shared. The access point checks the results and allows the node to sign on.

Data between the devices is encrypted by one of the values listed. The method described is known as one-way authentication. Stated another way, the access point knows it is from some group of computers that has the pre-shared key and cannot identify a specific computer. Given this, it is possible for a rogue computer to pretend it is an access point. When enabling WEP (Wired Equivalent Privacy) on a network, the encryption key must be the same among all the devices, including the wireless base station providing network connectivity.

Another difficulty with WEP is that it is possible to "break" this WEP encryption and gain access to the network. Another issue with WEP is RC4 being used in wireless. RC4 was designed for a synchronous stream. The nature of wireless communications is such that the signal can be dropped very easily. The designers address this challenge by changing the key for every packet. This uses up unique keys very rapidly, which forces key reuse, which hurts security. In addition, RC4 has as part of the logic a number known as an initialization vector that is not encrypted. Because of this, anyone can capture a bunch of packets and figure out the WEP pattern.

8.4.7   Security

Security+ Objective 2.6.3—WEP/WAP

Security+ Objective 2.6.4—Vulnerabilities

Security+ Objective 3.1.4—Wireless

War driving is the act of locating and possibly exploiting connections to wireless local area networks while driving around a city or elsewhere. To do war driving, you need a vehicle, a computer (which can be a laptop), a wireless Ethernet card set to work in promiscuous mode, and some kind of an antenna which can be mounted on top of or positioned inside the car. Because a wireless LAN may have a range that extends beyond an office building, an outside user may be able to intrude into the network, obtain a free Internet connection, and possibly gain access to company records and other resources.

Some people have made a sport out of war driving, in part to demonstrate the ease with which wireless LANs can be compromised. With an omnidirectional antenna and a geophysical positioning system (GPS), the war driver can systematically map the locations of 802.11b wireless access points. Companies that have a wireless LAN are urged to add security safeguards that will ensure only intended users have access.

New wireless LAN hacking tools are introduced every week and are widely available on the Internet for anyone to download. The table 8.6 lists some of these hacking tools.

Security+ Objective 2.6.1—WTLS

Wireless Transport Layer Security (WTLS) is the security level for Wireless Application Protocol (WAP) applications. Based on Transport Layer Security (TLS) v1.0 (a security layer used in the Internet, equivalent to Secure Socket Layer 3.1), WTLS was developed to address the problematic issues surrounding mobile network devices—such as limited processing power and memory capacity, and low bandwidth—and to provide adequate authentication, data integrity, and privacy protection mechanisms.

Wireless transactions, such as those between a user and the user's bank, require stringent authentication and encryption to ensure security to protect the communication from attack during data transmission. Because mobile networks do not provide end-to-end security, TLS had to be modified to address the special needs of wireless users. Designed to support datagrams in a high-latency, low-bandwidth environment, WTLS provides an optimized handshake through dynamic key refreshing, which allows encryption keys to be regularly updated during a secure session.

Table 8.6   Software Used To Crack Wireless Networks

Netstumbler http://www.netstumbler.com/	Freeware wireless access point identifier—listens for SSIDs and sends beacons as probes searching for access points
Kismet http://www.kismetwireless.net/	Freeware wireless sniffer and monitor—passively monitors wireless traffic and sorts data to identify SSIDs, MAC addresses, channels, and connection speeds
WEPCrack http://wepcrack.sourceforge.net/	Freeware encryption breaker—cracks 802.11 WEP encryption keys using the latest discovered weakness of RC4 key scheduling
AirSnort http://airsnort.shmoo.com/	Freeware encryption breaker—passively monitoring transmissions, computing the encryption key when enough packets have been gathered
Airopeek http://www.wildpackets.com	A comprehensive commercial packet analyzer for IEEE 802.11 wireless LANs, is designed to identify and solve wireless network anomalies. It quickly isolates security problems, fully decodes all 802.11 WLAN protocols, and analyzes wireless network performance with accurate identification of signal strength, channel, and data rates.

Wired Equivalent Privacy (WEP) is a security protocol, specified in the IEEE Wireless Fidelity (Wi-Fi) standard, 802.11b, that is designed to provide a wireless local area network (WLAN) with a level of security and privacy comparable to what is usually expected of a wired LAN. A wired local area network (LAN) is generally protected by physical security mechanisms (controlled access to a building, for example) that are effective for a controlled physical environment, but may be ineffective for WLANs because radio waves are not necessarily bound by the walls containing the network. WEP seeks to establish similar protection to that offered by the wired network's physical security measures by encrypting data transmitted over the WLAN. Data encryption protects the vulnerable wireless link between clients and access points; once this measure has been taken, other typical LAN security mechanisms such as password protection, end-to-end encryption, virtual private networks (VPNs), and authentication can be put in place to ensure privacy.

A research group from the University of California at Berkeley recently published a report citing "major security flaws" in WEP that left WLANs using the protocol vulnerable to attacks (called wireless equivalent privacy attacks). In the course of the group's examination of the technology, they were able to intercept and modify transmissions and gain access to restricted networks. The Wireless Ethernet Compatibility Alliance (WECA) claims that WEP—which is included in many networking products—was never intended to be the sole security mechanism for a WLAN, and that, in conjunction with traditional security practices, it is very effective.

Minimum steps that should be taken to protect your network should include:

- Change the default network name, ESSID, and the default password, which is needed to sign on to a WLAN on your access points. Each manufacturer's defaults settings are commonly known by hackers.
- Disable the ESSID broadcast in the Access Point Beacon. By default, access points periodically transmit their ESSID values. Wireless utilities included with Windows XP and as freeware programs can capture these values to present a list of available networks to the user. Disabling this broadcast makes it more difficult for intruders to recognize your network.
- Enable Wired Equivalent Privacy (WEP). Without encryption, your data is transmitted in readable form. Anyone within radio range using a wireless protocol analyzer or a promiscuous-mode network adapter may capture the data without joining the network. REP employs RC4 encryption, the same algorithm used for secure online shopping. WEP encryption can generally be found in 64-bit or 128-bit flavors. Of course, use the 128-bit variety if available.
- Change your encryption keys periodically. While the WEP is reasonably strong, the algorithm can be broken in time. The relationship between breaking the algorithm is directly related to the length of time that a key is in use. So WEP allows changing of the key to prevent brute force attach of the algorithm. Note: WEP can be implemented in hardware or in software. One reason that WEP is optional is because encryption may not be exported from the United States. This allows 802.11 to be a standard outside the United States albeit without the encryption.
- Enable Media Access Control (MAC) filtering on your access point (AP). Each wireless PC card has a unique identifier known as the MAC address. Many access points let you build a list of MAC addresses that are allowed on the network. Those not listed are denied.

While WEP is probably adequate for most home use, depending on the confidentiality of the data, corporate administrators should add strong encryption to the WLAN. Virtual private networks (VPNs) can be used so that you can also use IPSec or PPTP encryption over the wireless segment.

802.11i is a developing IEEE standard for security in a wireless local area network (WLAN). A subset of the 802.11i is Wi-Fi Protected Access (WPA), which solves the problem by abandoning WEP in favor of 802.11i's vastly improved Temporal Key Integrity Protocol (TKIP). WPA ensures that TKIP keys vary for each packet through key mixing. WPA also increases part of the keyspace and adds encrypted packet integrity to reject inserted packets. Current Wi-Fi puts weak integrity outside the encrypted payload. WPA includes full support for server-based authentication using the 802.1x protocol and EAP (Extensible Authentication Protocol).

WPA requires the user to provide a master key, but this does not become a static encryption key. Instead, the master key is simply a password used as a starting point through which WPA derives the key it will use to encrypt network traffic. Moreover, the key is regularly and automatically changed (and never reused), reducing the likelihood that it will be compromised. The master key also serves as a password by which users can be authenticated and granted network access.

Temporal Key Integrity Protocol (TKIP, pronounced tee-kip) fixes the key reuse problem of WEP, that is, periodically using the same key to encrypt data. The TKIP process begins with a 128-bit "temporal key" shared among clients and access points. TKIP combines the temporal key with the client's MAC address and then adds a relatively large 16-octet initialization vector to produce the key that will encrypt the data. This procedure ensures that each station uses different key streams to encrypt the data. TKIP uses RC4 to perform the encryption, which is the same as WEP. A major difference from WEP, however, is that TKIP changes temporal keys every 10,000 packets. This provides a dynamic distribution method that significantly enhances the security of the network. TKIP also includes a message integrity check.

An advantage of using TKIP is that companies having existing WEP-based access points and radio NICs can upgrade to TKIP through relatively simple firmware patches. In addition, WEP-only equipment will still interoperate with TKIP-enabled devices using WEP. TKIP is a temporary solution, and most experts believe that stronger encryption is still needed.

In addition to the TKIP solution, the 802.11i standard will likely include the Advanced Encryption Standard (AES) protocol. An issue, however, is that AES requires a coprocessor (additional hardware) to operate. This means that companies need to replace existing access points and client NICs to implement AES. Based on marketing reports, the installed base today is relatively small compared to what future deployments will bring. As a result, there will be a very large percentage of new wireless LAN implementations that will readily take advantage of AES when it becomes part of 802.11. Companies that have installed wireless LANs, on the other hand, will need to determine whether it's worth the costs of upgrade for better security.

A number of third-party manufacturers have stepped into the breach to offer a new class of hardware-based VPN products designed specifically for wireless networks. In addition, IEEE formed a task group, TGi, specifically to tighten up WLAN security in a nonproprietary systematic format.

TGi proposed a stopgap measure called the Temporary Key Integrity Protocol (TKIP) which is intended to work with existing and legacy hardware. Your WLAN provider may add this feature through a firmware revision. TKIP uses a mechanism called fast-packet rekeying, which changes the encryption keys frequently.

In addition, TGi also ratified the use of 802.1X, that requires a WLAN client to initiate an authorization request to the access point, which authenticates the client with an Extensible Authentication Protocol (EAP)-compliant RADIUS server. This RADIUS server may authenticate either the user (via passwords) or the machine (by MAC address). In theory, the wireless client is not allowed to join the network until the transaction is complete.

One form of EAP that was created by Cisco and is not supported my Microsoft is PEAP. PEAP, short for Protected Extensible Authentication Protocol, is a form of EAP that is combined with Transport Layer Security (TLS) to create a TSL-encrypted channel between client and server. To provide mutual authentication, PEAP uses Microsoft Challenge Authentication Protocol (MS-CHAP) Version 2. Because the challenge/response packets are sent over a TLS-encrypted channel, the password and the key are not exposed to offline dictionary attacks.

Security+ Objective 2.6.4.1—Site Surveys

Security+ Objective 5.1.3.2—Location

Security+ Objective 5.1.3.3—Shielding

Security+ Objective 5.1.3.1—Wireless Cells

The first step in a successful wireless installation is to conduct a site survey. It's virtually impossible to identify the ideal wireless solution and location of wireless access points without first conducting a site survey. Wireless site surveys analyze the conditions required to provide an optimal radio link, including:

- The users, applications, and equipment on the LANs that need to be internetworked.
- The wireless system best suited for the application (e.g, the level of security, speed and distance required).

- The line-of-sight requirements between antennas (using calculations for antenna size and cable length).
- The specific places where each component should be located (e.g., keeping access points as close to clients as possible).
- Whether to use a point-to-point or multipoint configuration. Typically, point-to-point configuration is used when two buildings need to communicate to one another, while multipoint is ideal when two or more buildings need to communicate in a "triangle" configuration.
- Potential sources of interference in alternative RF bands (e.g, cordless phones, microwaves, natural interference, or other access points using the same channel).
- Any federal, state, and local regulations (e.g, FCC regulations and right-of-way mandates).

When considering location issues, a prime area of concern is wireless networking, because too little attention paid to wireless network positioning can increase the likelihood that your network is available to unauthorized individuals. When considering wireless network components, minimizing transmission power reduces the changes your data will leak out of the intended area. Careful antenna placement will also have an effect. Attempt to place antennas as far from exterior walls as possible. Consider the RF pattern options with different types of antennas.

Typically the interface between the wired network and the transceiver is placed in a corner in an effort to hide the electronics. If that corner is along the outside of your building, that places the network signal outside and easy to intercept. In effect, you have put an Ethernet jack for your network in the parking lot.

Wireless networks can also be interrupted by EMI or RFI and the only real countermeasure to that is a strong signal. This is done by either purchasing an amplifier or new APs that offer a stronger signal. Of course, when installing your wireless network, you should ensure that you don't place workstations or APs near any obvious sources of EMI and RFI. Lastly, if another business or person uses wireless networking near your wireless network, you may need to use a different channel from their network. Of course, you should not use the default channel that is set on your wireless equipment.

Shielding (paint with metal and Mylar window covering can attenuate the RF signals) reduces the distance that radio and other electronic waves can travel, decreasing the chance someone can get to your network. In addition, shielding reduces the risk of a wireless denial of service attack (such as using a heavy duty antenna or even using a consumer microwave and disabling the safety interlock). The downside could be a negative impact on pagers and cellular phones.

More sensitive environments may wish to either hire someone to perform a Technical Surveillance Counter Measures (TSCM) sweep on a periodic basis. Extremely sensitive sites would be wise to consider installing in-place monitoring in addition to periodic searches for unauthorized infrared (IR) or cellular phone-based equipment.

8.5   BLUETOOTH

BlueTooth refers to a short-range radio technology aimed at simplifying communications among Net devices and between devices and the Internet. It also aims to simplify data synchronization between Net devices and other computers. An advantage of BlueTooth is its similarity to many other specifications already deployed and its borrowing of many features from these specifications. The BlueTooth standard is becoming more and more of a short time network between devices for a small amount of information.

BlueTooth has a present nominal link range of 10 cm to 10 m, which can be extended to 100 m, with increased transmitting power. BlueTooth operates in the 2.4-GHz Industrial-Scientific-Medical (ISM) Band and uses a frequency-hop spread-spectrum technology in which packets are transmitted in defined time slots on defined frequencies. A full duplex information interchange rate of up to 1 Mbps may be achieved in which a Time-Division Duplex (TDD) scheme is used. The second generation of BlueTooth supports up to 2 Mbps.

Work on the BlueTooth specification is progressing and is primarily the responsibility of the Blue-Tooth Special Group (SIG).This is an industry group consisting of leaders in telecommunications and computing industries. The promoter group within the SIG currently consists of 3Com, Ericsson, IBM, Intel, Lucent Technologies, Microsoft, Motorola, Nokia, and Toshiba.

A BlueTooth system comprises of the following four major components:

- **Radio unit**—Consisting of a radio transceiver, which provides the radio link between the Blue-Tooth devices.
- **Baseband unit**—A hardware consisting of flash memory and a CPU. This interfaces with the radio unit and the host device electronics.
- **Link management software**—A driver software or firmware which enables the application software to interface with the baseband unit and radio unit.
- **Application software**—This implements the user interface and is the application that can run on wireless. For example, this could be chat software that allows two laptop users in a conference hall to talk to each other using wireless technology.

Each device has a unique 48-bit address from the IEEE 802 standard. In addition, a frequency hop scheme allows devices to communicate even in areas with a great deal of electromagnetic interference and it includes built-in encryption and verification.

One BlueTooth standard is **HomeRF SWAP** (SWAP is short for Shared Wireless Access Protocol). It is designed specifically for wireless networks in homes, which in contrast to 802.11 was created for use in businesses. HomeRF networks are designed to be more affordable to home users than other wireless technologies. It is based on frequency hopping and using radio frequency waves for the transmission of voice and data with a range of up to 150 ft.

The Shared Wireless Access Protocol works together with the PSTN network and the Internet through existing cordless telephone and wireless LAN technologies to enable voice activated home electronic systems, accessing the Internet from anywhere in the home and forward fax, voice and email messages. SWAP uses Time Division Multiple Access for interactive data transfer and CSMA/CA for high-speed packet transfer. SWAP operates in the 2,400 MHz band at 50 hops per second to provide a data rate between 1 Mbps and 2 Mbps.

WHAT YOU NEED TO KNOW

Security+ Objective 2.1.1—802.1X

Security+ Objective 2.6.2—802.1X

1. 802.1X provides an authentication framework for wireless LANs, allowing a user to be authenticated by a central authority.
2. 802.1X uses an existing protocol, the Extensible Authentication Protocol (EAP) that works on Ethernet, Token Ring, or wireless LANs, for message exchange during the authentication process.

Security+ Objective 2.6.1—WTLS

1. Wireless Transport Layer Security (WTLS) is the security level for Wireless Application Protocol (WAP) applications.
2. Based on Transport Layer Security (TLS) v1.0 (a security layer used in the Internet, equivalent to Secure Socket Layer 3.1), WTLS was developed to address the problematic issues surrounding mobile network devices—such as limited processing power and memory capacity, and low bandwidth—and to provide adequate authentication, data integrity, and privacy protection mechanisms.

Security+ Objective 2.6.3—WEP/WAP

1. While WEP is probably adequate for most home use, depending on the confidentiality of the data, corporate administrators should add strong encryption to the WLAN.

2. WAP (Wireless Application Protocol) is a specification for a set of communication protocols to standardize the way that wireless devices with limited capability, such as cellular telephones and radio transceivers, can be used for Internet access, including e-mail, the World Wide Web, newsgroups, and Internet Relay Chat (IRC).
3. The two pieces of information required to communicate over an 802.11b LAN are the SSID and, if encryption is enabled, the WEP key.
4. The Service Set Identifier (SSID) is a 32-character identifier that is attached to each packet, identifying the wireless LAN to which the traffic belongs, so that multiple wireless LANs can exist in the same physical area.
5. To protect an 802.11b network from unauthorized, use and "snooping," you can enable packet encryption via WEP.
6. Wired Equivalent Privacy (WEP) is a security protocol, specified in the IEEE Wireless Fidelity (Wi-Fi) standard, 802.11b, that is designed to provide a wireless local area network (WLAN) with a level of security and privacy comparable to what is usually expected of a wired LAN.
7. Virtual private networks (VPNs) can be used so that you can also use IPSec or PPTP encryption over the wireless segment.
8. A subset of the 802.11i is Wi-Fi Protected Access (WPA), which solves the problem by abandoning

WEP in favor of 802.11i's vastly improved Temporal Key Integrity Protocol (TKIP).

9. WPA ensures that TKIP keys vary for each packet through key mixing.

Security+ Objective 2.6.4—Vulnerabilities

1. War driving is the act of locating and possibly exploiting connections to wireless local area networks while driving around a city or elsewhere.
2. To do war driving, you need a vehicle, a computer (which can be a laptop), a wireless Ethernet card set to work in promiscuous mode, and some kind of an antenna that can be mounted on top of or positioned inside the car.
3. Because a wireless LAN may have a range that extends beyond an office building, an outside user may be able to intrude into the network, obtain a free Internet connection, and possibly gain access to company records and other resources.
4. Wireless networks can also be interrupted by EMI or RFI, and the only real countermeasure to that is a strong signal. This is done by either purchasing an amplifier or new APs that offer a stronger signal.

Security+ Objective 2.6.4.1—Site Surveys

1. The first step in a successful wireless installation is to conduct a site survey.
2. Wireless site surveys analyze the conditions required to provide an optimal radio link.
3. When considering wireless network components, minimizing transmission power reduces the changes your data will leak out of the intended area.

Security+ Objective 3.1.4—Wireless

1. For decades, radio and television stations have used the atmosphere to transport information via analog signals. The atmosphere is also capable of carrying digital signals.
2. Networks that transmit signals through the atmosphere are known as wireless networks.
3. All wireless signals are carried through the air along electromagnetic waves.
4. The wireless spectrum is a continuum of electromagnetic waves, with varying frequencies and wavelengths that are used for telecommunications.
5. Radio frequency (RF) resides between 10 KHz to 1 GHz of the electromagnetic spectrum. It includes shortwave radio, very high frequency (VHF) and Ultra-high frequency (UHF).
6. In unregulated bands, you must operate at regulated power levels (under one watt in the U.S.) to minimize interference with other signals.
7. A band is a contiguous group of frequencies, which are used for a single purpose. Commercial radio stations often refer to the band of frequencies they are using as a single frequency.

8. A narrowband radio system transmits and receives user information on a specific radio frequency.
9. Spread-spectrum signals are distributed over a wide range of frequencies and then collected onto their original frequency at the receiver. Unless the receiver is not tuned to the right frequency or frequencies, a spread spectrum signal resembles noise, making the signals harder to detect and harder to jam.
10. Direct-sequence spread-spectrum (DSSS) generates a redundant bit pattern for each bit to be transmitted. The intended receiver knows which specific frequencies are valid and deciphers the signal by collecting valid signals and ignoring the spurious signals. The valid signals are then used to reassemble the data.
11. Frequency hopping quickly switches between predetermined frequencies, many times each second. Both the transmitter and receiver must follow the same pattern and maintain complex timing intervals to be able to receive and interpret the data being sent.
12. Before fiber optics came along, for decades microwaves formed the heart of the long-distance telephone transmission system. Microwave communications is a form of electromagnetic energy that operates at a higher frequency (low GHz frequency range) than radio wave communications.
13. Satellite transmission is much like line-of-sight microwave transmission in which one of the stations is a satellite orbiting the earth. This requires that the sending and receiving antennas be locked onto each other's location at all times.
14. Another form of wireless technology is Infrared (IR) systems, which are based on infrared light (light that is just below the visible light in the electromagnetic spectrum).
15. Infrared devices work by using either directed or diffused technology.
16. A wireless LAN (WLAN) is a local area network without wires.
17. A new standard established by the Institute of Electrical and Electronics Engineers (IEEE) called 802.11b or Wi-Fi is making WLAN use faster and easier, and the market is growing quickly.
18. The ad-hoc network, also referred to as the Independent Basic Service Set (IBSS), stands alone and is not connected to a base. The wireless stations communicate directly with each other without using an access point or any connection to a wired network.
19. In infrastructure mode, also known as Extended Service Set (ESS), the wireless network consists of at least one access point (AP) connected to the wired network infrastructure and a set of wireless end stations.

20. BlueTooth refers to a short-range radio technology aimed at simplifying communications among Net devices and between devices and the Internet. It also aims to simplify data synchronization between Net devices and other computers.

21. One BlueTooth standard is HomeRF SWAP (SWAP is short for Shared Wireless Access Protocol). It is designed specifically for wireless networks in homes, which in contrast to 802.11 was created for use in businesses.

22. The new 802.11b standard is direct sequence only, and initially provided throughputs rates up to 11 Mbps, but has been recently increased to 22 Mbps.

23. The new standard, 802.11a, will operate in the 5 GHz license-free frequency band and is expected to provide throughput rates up to 54 Mbps in normal mode or 75 Mbps in turbo mode.

24. The newest standard is the 802.11g standard, which has a nominal maximum throughput of 54 Mbps.

Security+ Objective 5.1.3.1—Wireless Cells

1. When discussing wireless technology, many technologies that are wireless use a cellular topology, whereas an area is divided into cells.

2. A broadcast device is located at the center and broadcasting in all directions to form an invisible circle (cell).

3. All network devices located within the cell communicate with the network through the central station or hub, which are interconnected with rest of the network infrastructure.

4. If the cells are overlapped, devices may roam from cell to cell while maintaining connection to the network as the devices.

Security+ Objective 5.1.3.2—Location

1. Careful antenna placement will also have an effect. Attempt to place antennas as far from exterior walls as possible. Consider the RF pattern options with different types of antennas.

2. Of course, when installing your wireless network, you should ensure that you don't place workstation or APs near any obvious sources of EMI and RFI.

Security+ Objective 5.1.3.3—Shielding

1. Shielding (paint with metal and Mylar window covering can attenuate the RF signals) reduces the distance that radio and other electronic waves can travel, decreasing the chance someone can get to your network.

QUESTIONS

1. A company uses WEP (Wired Equivalent Privacy) for wireless security. Who may authenticate to the company's access point?
   a. Only the administrator
   b. Anyone can authenticate
   c. Only users within the company
   d. Only users with the correct WEP (Wired Equivalent Privacy) key

2. In the context of wireless networks, WEP (Wired Equivalent Privacy) was designed to:
   a. Provide the same level of security as a wired LAN (local area network).
   b. Provide a collision preventive method of media access.
   c. Provide a wider access area that that of wired LANs (local area network).
   d. Allow radio frequencies to penetrate walls.

3. As the security analyst for your company's network, you have been hacked via your wireless system all week during the evening. The term used for attacking a wireless system from afar is called:
   a. War driving   b. ICMP exploiting
   c. ARP spoofing   d. War dialing

4. Which protocol is specified in the IEEE Wireless Fidelity (Wi-Fi) standard, 802.11b, that is designed to provide a wireless local area network (WLAN) with a level of security and privacy comparable to what is usually expected of a wired LAN?
   a. WEP   b. PIM
   c. IPSEC   d. 802.11SD

5. As the security analyst for your company's network, you want to enable WLAN technologies. You need to ensure that you will have proper bandwidth. From the following list, what is the proper range and bandwidth for 802.11b?
   a. 802.11b (Wi-Fi) operates in the 2.4 GHz range offering data speeds up to 2 Mbps
   b. 802.11b (Wi-Fi) operates in the 3.4 GHz range offering data speeds up to 11 Mbps
   c. 802.11b (Wi-Fi) operates in the 2.4 GHz range offering data speeds up to 11 Mbps
   d. 802.11b (Wi-Fi) operates in the 1.4 GHz range offering data speeds up to 15 Mbps

6. WAP stands for _____ ? (Select the correct answer for the blank.)
   a. Wireless Acceptable Privacy
   b. Wired Account Protection
   c. Wireless Application Protocol
   d. Wired Application Protocol
   e. Wireless Account Privacy

7. Wireless Ethernet (802.11) uses _____ in an effort to prevent packet collisions. (Select the correct answer for the blank.)
   a. Collision sensing
   b. Collision avoidance
   c. Collision preemptive tasking
   d. Collision detection
   e. Collision prevention
   f. Collision retransmission

8. In a 128-bit WEP key, how long is the actual secret key?
   a. 24 bits
   b. 40 bits
   c. 64 bits
   d. 104 bits
   e. 128 bits
   f. 256 bits

9. Hidden node occurs in a wireless network when:
   a. The administrator cannot physically locate a wireless client.
   b. A wireless client cannot see the network due to interferences.
   c. A wireless client has been removed from the cell diameter of the nearest access point.
   d. A wireless access point has been powered off.

10. WEP stands for _____? (Select the correct answer for the blank.)
    a. Wireless Enterprise Privacy
    b. Wired Enterprise Protection
    c. Wired Equivalent Protection
    d. Wired Equivalent Privacy
    e. Wireless Everywhere Privacy

11. Network transmission of data via radio, laser, infrared, or microwave is said to be sent on what?
    a. Switching media
    b. Bound media
    c. Pulse media
    d. Unbounded media

12. Which of the following types of antennas issues signals with equal strength and clarity in all directions?
    a. Directional
    b. Bidirectional
    c. Tri-directional
    d. Omni-directional

13. Which of the following wireless services uses the lowest range of frequencies?
    a. AM radio
    b. FM radio
    c. Cellular telephone service
    d. Wireless LANs

14. Which of the following is an advantage of using spread-spectrum signaling over narrowband signaling?
    a. Spread spectrum is easier to install.
    b. Spread spectrum is more secure.
    c. Spread spectrum is less expensive to deploy.
    d. Spread spectrum can achieve higher throughput.

15. The 802.11g WLAN standard is compatible with what other WLAN standard?
    a. BlueTooth
    b. 802.11a
    c. 802.11b
    d. HomeRF

16. What frequency band do 802.11b, 80211g, Blue-Tooth, and HomeRF WLANs share?
    a. 1.25 GHz
    b. 2.4 GHz
    c. 5 GHz
    d. 12.5 GHz

17. At what altitude does a geosynchronous satellite orbit the earth?
    a. 700 km
    b. 1400 km
    c. 10,400 km
    d. 34,800 km

18. The _____ encryption algorithm is used in WEP. (Select the correct answer for the blank.)
    a. RC4
    b. MD4
    c. Rijndael
    d. RC5
    e. Blowfish
    f. PAP
    g. L2TP

19. The WAP (Wireless Application Protocol) programming model is based on the following three elements:
    a. Client, original server, WEP.
    b. Code design, code review, documentation.
    c. Client, original review, wireless interface card.
    d. Client, gateway, original server.

20. Which of the following provides privacy, data integrity, and authentication for handheld devices in a wireless network?
    a. WEP (Wired Equivalent Privacy)
    b. WAP (Wireless Application Protocol)
    c. WSET (Wireless Secure Electronic Transaction)
    d. WTLS (Wireless Transport Layer Security)

21. A wireless network with three access points, two of which are used as repeaters, exists at a company. What step should be taken to secure the wireless network?
    a. Ensure that employees use complex passwords.
    b. Ensure that employees are only using issued wireless cards in their systems.
    c. Ensure that WEP (Wired Equivalent Privacy) is being used.
    d. Ensure that everyone is using adhoc mode.

22. WTLS (Wireless Transport Layer Security) provides security services between a mobile device and a:
    a. WAP (Wireless Application Protocol) gateway.
    b. Web server.
    c. Wireless client.
    d. Wireless network interface card.

23. What is the first step before a wireless solution is implemented?
    a. Ensure ad-hoc mode is enabled on the access points.
    b. Ensure that all users have strong passwords.
    c. Purchase only Wi-Fi (Wireless Fidelity) equipment.
    d. Perform a thorough site survey.

24. IEEE 802.11b is capable of providing data rates of up to:
    a. 10 Mbps.   b. 10.5 Mbps.
    c. 11 Mbps.   d. 12 Mbps.

25. A protocol specified in IEEE 802.11b intended to provide a WLAN with the level of security associated with a LAN is:
    a. WEP.   b. ISSE.
    c. ISDN.   d. VPN.

HANDS-ON EXERCISES

Exercise 1: Researching the Internet for Wireless LANs

1. Use your browser and open the following URL: http://support.intel.com/support/network/wireless/pro5000/onlineuserguide/admin/contents.htm
2. Click on the Researching the Site and the Site Survey links and read their content.
3. Answer the following questions:

   Is simple drywall almost transparent or mostly opaque to microwaves?
   If the range is shorter, what can be said about the speed of the data?
   What is the loss through a typical office window?
   What is the loss through a typical brick wall?
   What is the loss through a typical office wall?
   What is the loss through a typical metal door in an office wall?

4. If you are interested, view the content of Using the Site Survey Tool.
5. Download and read the Administrator's and Site Survey Guide located at the following website: http://support.intel.com/support/network/wireless/pro2011b/accesspoint/ssurvey.htm
6. Read the following webpage: http://support.intel.com/support/network/wireless/pro5000/onlineuserguide/admin/trouble.htm
7. Using the above URLs and guides, perform a site survey for a wireless network.

Exercise 2: Installing and Configuring a WLAN

Install and Configure Your Access Point

1. Locate and read the installation manual for your wireless access point and wireless network adapters.
2. Take the wireless access point and connect the power cable. After the access point is powered, look to see if the access point has any LEDs. By using the manuals, determine what the LED's mean.
3. Attach to the access point using a null serial cable from a computer to the access point 9-pin serial connector.
4. Refer to the access point manual to gather the correct COM port settings. Then use HyperTerminal or some other serial communications program to access the access point.
5. Using the access point configuration menu or commands, establish an IP address on your network for the access point. You should also set the subnet mask and default gateway.
6. Using the access point manual, determine what the default SSID.
7. Using the configuration mode or configuration commands, change the SSID to WLAN.
8. Using the configuration mode or configuration commands, change the admin system password to password.
9. Using the configuration mode or configuration commands, enable WEP and select the highest possible encryption that is allowed by the access point and your wireless adapters.
10. By looking at the manual, determine how to restrict access by MAC address to the access point.

Install and Configure Your Wireless Adapter

1. Install the adapter and install any drivers and configuration software that comes with the adapter.
2. Using the configuration software, set your card to the same SSID, encryption mode, and encryption key as the access point.

3. Try to ping the access point.
4. Try to telnet into the access point.
5. Try to ping your neighbor

Exercise 3: War Driving with Network Stumbler

1. Find and Download Network Stumbler.
2. Load Network Stumbler on your system with a wireless adapter that has not been configured for your wireless LAN.
3. Run the Network Stumbler program and see what information can be retrieved.

## CHAPTER 9

Directory and File Security

Topics Covered in this Chapter

Introduction

If you have more than one person use a computer (locally or remotely), it is important to be able secure the system and data files on that computer. Directory and file security allows you to specify who can access those files and how the files can be accessed.

Objectives

1. **Security+ Objective 2.5.3**—File sharing
2. **Security+ Objective 2.5.4**—Vulnerabilities
3. **Security+ Objective 2.5.4.1**—Packet Sniffing
4. **Security+ Objective 3.5.3.7**—File/Print Servers

9.1   DATA ACCESS CONTROL

Data access controls protect systems and information by restricting access to system files and user data based on object (user) identity. Data access controls also provide authorization and accountability, relying on system access controls to provide identification and authentication.

Data access control techniques are generally categorized as either discretionary or mandatory. As you recall from chapter 2, the discretionary access control (DAC) is an access policy determined by the owner of a file (or other resource). The owner decides who is allowed access to the file and what privileges they have.

In terms of file and data ownership, because the access policy is determined by the owner of the resource (including files, directories, data, system resources, and devices), every object in a system must have an owner. Theoretically, an object without an owner is left unprotected. Normally, the owner of a resource is the person who created the resource (such as a file or directory), but in certain cases, the owner may need to be explicitly identified as an administrative function.

In the area of access rights and permissions, these are the controls that an owner can assign to individual users or groups for specific resources. Various systems (Windows, UNIX/Linux, and Novell) define different sets of permissions that are essentially variations or extensions of three basic types of access:

- **Read (R)**—The subject can read contents of a file or list contents of a directory.
- **Write (W)**—The subject can change the contents of a file or directory (including add, rename, create, and delete).
- **Execute (X)**—If the file is a program, the subject can run the program.

Access control lists (ACLs) provide a flexible method for applying discretionary access controls. An ACL lists the specific rights and permissions that are assigned to a subject for a given object.

9.2   WINDOWS FILE AND DISK SYSTEMS

Throughout the life of the PC, a few different file systems have been used. Today, the most common include FAT, FAT32, and NTFS. See table 9.1.

9.2.1   FAT

The **File Allocation Table (FAT)** is a simple and reliable file system, which uses minimal memory. It supports file names of 11 characters, which include the 8 characters for the file name and 3 characters for the file extension.

Table 9.1   Common Microsoft File Systems

	FAT	FAT32	NTFS
Operating Systems	Used by DOS and all Microsoft Windows versions	Used by Windows versions since 95B/OSR2	Used by the Windows NT Family
Volume Size	Floppy disk to 4 GB	512 MB to 32 GB	10 MB to 2 TB
Maximum File Size	2 GB	4 GB	Limited by size of volume
Limit on entries in root directory	Yes	No	No
File and Directory Security	No	No	Yes
Directory and File Compression	No	No	Yes
Cluster Remapping	No	No	Yes

Table 9.2   DOS File Attributes

Attributes	Abbreviations	Description
Read-Only	R or RO	When a file is marked as read-only, it can not be deleted or modified. Note: the opposite of read-only is read-write.
Hidden	H	When a file is marked as hidden, it can not be seen during normal directory listings.
System	S or Sy	When a file is marked as system, it should not be moved. In addition, it usually can't be seen during normal directory listings.
Volume Label		The name of the volume.
Subdirectory		A table that contains information about files and subdirectories.
Archive	A	When a file is marked as archive, the file has not been backed up. Anytime a file is new or has been changed, the archive attribute comes on automatically. When the archive attribute is off, the file has been backed up.

VFAT is an enhanced version of the FAT structure, which allows Windows to support long file names (LFN) up to 255 characters. If someone refers to FAT, they probably mean VFAT. Since it is built on ordinary FAT, each file has to have an 8 character name and 3 character extension to be backward compatible for DOS and Windows 3.XX applications. Therefore, programs running in DOS and Windows 3.XX will not see the longer file names. When running a WIN32 program (programs made for Windows 9X and the Windows NT Family), they can see and make use of the longer names.

After the filename and file extension, 1 byte is used for attributes. The **file attribute** field stores a number of characteristics about each file. Attributes can be either on or off. The most common attributes include Read-only, Hidden, System, and Archive. Note: One of these attributes indicates if the file is a real file or a directory. Since DOS reserves 1 byte for attributes, it can keep track up to 8 attributes. Remember, 1 byte equals 8 bits (on/off switch). To change the attributes, you would use the ATTRIB command or Explorer (right-clicking the file and select the Properties option) or Explorer. See table 9.2.

9.2.2   FAT32

FAT32, which uses 32-bit FAT entries, was introduced in the second major release of Windows 95 (OSR2/Windows 95B) and is an enhancement of the FAT/VFAT file system. It supports hard drives up to 2 terabytes. It uses space more efficiently, such as 4-KB clusters for drives up to 8 GB, which resulted in 15% more efficient use of disk space relative to large FAT drives.

The root directory is an ordinary cluster chain. Therefore, it can be located anywhere in the drive. In addition, it allows dynamic resizing of FAT32 partitions (without loosing data) and allows the FAT mirroring to be disabled, which allows a copy of the FAT other than the first to be active. Consequently, FAT32 drives are less prone to failure of critical data areas such as the FAT.

9.2.3   NTFS

NTFS is a file system for the Windows NT Family OSs designed for both the server and workstation. It provides a combination of performance, reliability, security and compatibility. It supports long file names, yet maintains an 8.3 name for DOS and Windows 3.XX programs. Since the NTFS is a 64-bit architecture, NTFS is designed to support up to 2^{64} bytes = 18,446,744,073,709,551,616 bytes = 16 exabytes.

Since Windows NT Family OSs include enhanced security, it supports a variety of multiuser security models and allows computers running other operating systems to save files to the NTFS volume on a server. This includes DOS, Microsoft Windows, UNIX, Linux, and even Macintosh computers. It does not allow DOS to access an NTFS volume directly, only through the network (assuming you have the proper permissions or rights to access the volume).

To make a NTFS volume more resistant to failure, NTFS write updates to a log area (making NTFS a journaled filesystem) and supports remapped clusters. If a system crash occurs, the log area can be used to quickly clean up problems. If a cluster is found to be bad, it can move the data to another cluster and mark the cluster as bad so that the operating system doesn't use it.

FAT is simpler and smaller than NTFS and uses an unsorted directory structure. NTFS is generally faster because NTFS uses a B-tree directory structure, which minimizes the number of disk accesses required to find a file, making access to the file faster, especially if it is a larger folder.

NTFS supports volume set and directory/file compression. A volume set combines several hard drives (or parts of hard drives) to be combined into a single volume. If the volume needs to be expanded again, you just add another hard drive and expand the volume. NTFS allows an individual file or directory to be compressed without compressing the entire drive.

To convert FAT or FAT32 to NTFS, you would use the following command at the command prompt.

```
convert x: /fs:ntfs
```

whereas *x*: is the drive that you are trying to convert. Note: you cannot convert NTFS volume to FAT or FAT32 using Microsoft utilities.

9.2.4   CDFS

The **CDFS (CD-ROM File System)** is the read-only file system used to access resources on a CD-ROM disk. Windows supports CDFS so as to allow CD-ROM file sharing. Because a CD-ROM is read-only, you cannot assign specific permissions to files through CDFS.

9.3   NTFS PERMISSIONS

A primary advantage of NTFS over FAT and FAT32 is that NTFS volumes have the ability to apply NTFS permissions to secure folders and files. By setting the permissions, you specify the level of access for groups and users for accessing files or directories. For example, to one user or group of users, you can specify that they can only read the file; another user or group of users can read and write to the file while others have no access. No matter if you are logged on locally at the computer or accessing a computer through the network, NTFS permissions always apply.

Table 9.3 Standard NTFS Folder Permissions

NTFS Folder Permissions	Description
Read	The Read permission allows the user to display the file's data, attributes, owner, and permissions.
Write	The Write permission allows a user to create new files and subfolders within the folder, write to the file, append to the file, read and change folder attributes, and view ownership.
List Folder Contents	The List Folder Contents permission allows the user to see the names of folders and subfolders in the folder.
Read & Execute	The Read & Execute permission allows the user to display the folder's contents and display the data, attributes, owner, and permissions for files within the folder, and execute files within the folder. In addition, it allows the user to navigate a folder to reach other files and folders, even if the user does not have permissions for these folders.
Modify	The Modify permission allows the user to read the files, execute files, write and modify files, create folders and subfolders, delete subfolders and files, and change attributes of subfolders and files.
Full Control	The Full Control permission allows the user to read the files, execute files, write and modify files, create folders and subfolders, delete subfolders and files, and change attributes of subfolders and files, change permissions, and take ownership of the file.

NOTE: Groups or users granted Full Control for a folder can delete files and subfolders within that folder regardless of the permissions protecting the files and subfolders.

Table 9.4 NTFS Folder Permissions

Special Permissions	Full Control	Modify	Read & Execute	List Folder Contents	Read	Write
Traverse Folder/Execute File	X	X	X	X		
List Folder/Read Data	X	X	X	X	X	
Read Attributes	X	X	X	X	X	
Read Extended Attributes	X	X	X	X	X	
Create Files/Write Data	X	X				X
Create Folders/Append Data	X	X				X
Write Attributes	X	X				X
Write Extended Attributes	X	X				X
Delete Subfolders and Files	X					
Delete	X	X				
Read Permissions	X	X	X	X	X	X
Change Permissions	X					
Take Ownership	X					
Synchronize	X	X	X	X	X	X

NOTE: Although List Folder Contents and Read & Execute appear to have the same permissions, these permissions are inherited differently. List Folder Contents is inherited by folders but not files, and it should only appear when you view folder permissions. Read & Execute is inherited by both files and folders and is always present when you view file or folder permissions.

All of the folder and file NTFS permissions (also known as special permissions) are listed in tables 9.4 and 9.6. To simplify the task of administration, the permissions have been logically grouped into the standard folder and file NTFS permissions as shown in tables 9.3 and 9.5. The standard folder permissions include Full Control, Modify, Read & Execute, List Folder Contents, Read and Write and the standard file permissions include Full Control, Modify, Read & Execute, Read, and Write.

Table 9.5 Standard NTFS File Permissions

NTFS File Permissions	Description
Read	The Read permission allows the user to display the file's data, attributes, owner, and permissions.
Write	The Write permission allows the user to write to the file, append to the file, overwrite the file, change file attributes, and view file ownership and permissions.
Read & Execute	The Read & Execute permission allows the user to display the data, attributes, owner, and permissions for file and execute the file.
Modify	The Modify permission allows user to read the file, execute the file, write, modify, and delete the files, and change attributes of file.
Full Control	The Full Control permission allows the user to read the file, execute the file, write, modify, and delete the files, and change attributes of the file, change permissions, and take ownership of the file.

NOTE: Groups or users granted Full Control for a folder can delete files and subfolders within that folder regardless of the permissions protecting the files and subfolders.

Table 9.6 NTFS File Permissions

Special Permissions	Full Control	Modify	Read & Execute	Read	Write
Traverse Folder/Execute File	x	x	x		
List Folder/Read Data	x	x	x	x	
Read Attributes	x	x	x	x	
Read Extended Attributes	x	x	x	x	
Create Files/Write Data	x	x			x
Create Folders/Append Data	x	x			x
Write Attributes	x	x			x
Write Extended Attributes	x	x			x
Delete Subfolders and Files	x				
Delete	x	x			
Read Permissions	x	x	x	x	x
Change Permissions	x				
Take Ownership	x				
Synchronize	x	x	x	x	x

The NTFS permissions that are granted are stored in an **access control list (ACL)** with every file and folder on an NTFS volume. The ACL contains an **access control entry (ACE)** for each user account and group that has been granted access for the file or folder as well as the permissions granted to each user and group.

To assign NTFS permissions you would right-click a drive, folder, and file (using My Computer or Windows Explorer), select the properties option, and click on the Security tab. To assign the special permissions, click on the Advanced button within the security tab and click on the View Edit/button. See figure 9.1.

Permissions are given to a folder or file as explicit permission and inherited permissions. Explicit permissions are those that are granted directly to the folder or file. Some of these permissions are granted automatically, such as when a file or folder is created, while others have to be assigned manually.

To explicitly grant a permission to a folder or file, you would select the permission by putting a check in the respective checkbox. To remove an explicit permission, deselect the permission to remove the check in the respective checkbox. To remove a user or group from being assigned explicit permissions, click to highlight the user, and click on the Remove button.

Since a user can be a member of several groups, it is possible for the user to have several sets of explicit permissions to a folder or file. When this happens, the permissions are added together to form the effective permissions. The effective permissions are the actual permissions when logging in and accessing a file or folder. They consist of explicit permissions plus any inherited permissions. Inherited permissions will be discussed a little bit later.

NTFS file permissions override folder permissions. Therefore, if a user has access to a file, the user will still be able to gain access to a file even if he or she does not have access to the folder containing the file. Of course, since the user doesn't have access to the folder, the user cannot navigate or browse through the folder to get to the file. Therefore, a user would have to use the universal naming convention (UNC) or local path to open the file.

When you set permissions to a folder (explicit permissions), the files and subfolders created in the folder inherit these permissions (inherited permissions). In other words, the permissions flow down from the folder into the subfolders and files, indirectly giving permissions to a user or group. Inherited permissions ease the task of managing permissions and ensure consistency of permissions among the subfolders and files within the folder.

Figure 9.1   NTFS Permissions

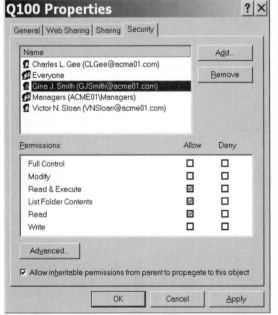
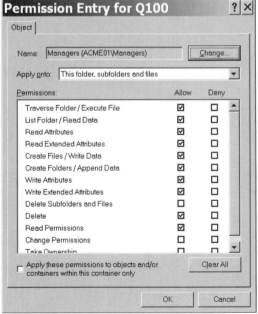

When viewing the permissions, the permissions will be checked, cleared (unchecked), or shaded. If the permission is checked, the permission was explicitly assigned to the folder or file. If the permission is clear, the user or group does not have that permission explicitly granted to the folder or file. Note: A user may still obtain permission through a group permission or a group may still obtain permission through another group. If the checkbox is shaded, the permission was granted through inheritance from a parent folder.

When you copy and move files and folders from one location to another, you need to understand how the NTFS folder and file permissions are affected. If you copy a file or folder, the new folder and file will automatically acquire the permissions of the drive or folder that the folder and file is being copied to.

If the folder or file is moved within the same volume, the folder or file will retain the same permissions that were already assigned. When the folder or file is moved from one volume to another volume, the folder or file will automatically acquire the permissions of the drive or folder and file is being copied to. An easy way to remember the difference is, when you move a folder or file from within the same volume, the folder and file is not physically moved but the Master File Table is adjusted to indicate a different folder. When you move a folder or file from one volume to another, it copies the folder or file to the new location and then deletes the old location. Therefore, the moved folder and files are new to the volume and acquire the new permissions.

9.4 SHARING DRIVES AND DIRECTORIES

Security+ Objective 2.5.3—File sharing

Security+ Objective 3.5.3.7—File/Print Servers

As mentioned earlier in this chapter, File and Print Sharing for Microsoft networks gives you the ability to share your files or printers with Windows computers using the SMB/CIFS protocol. Note: Just because you enable file and print sharing for an individual computer, you must still share a drive, directory, or printer before it can be accessed through the network.

9.4.1 Enabling Drives and Directories Sharing

If you enabled file sharing, you can share any drive or directory by right-clicking the drive or directory and selecting the Sharing option from the File menu or by selecting the Sharing option from the short-cut menu of the drive or directory. You would then provide a Share Name, the name seen by other clients and type of access that users can have. A shared drive and directory will be indicated with a hand under the drive or directory. See figure 9.2. Note: If you are using Windows XP, you need to open a folder, select the Tools menu, and select the Folder Options option. Then click the View tab and deselect the simple file sharing. This will allow you to access the same file sharing and NTFS permissions interface as available in the other Windows version.

The shared drive or directory can then be accessed in one of three ways:

1. Using Network Neighborhood and accessing the resources under the server. See figure 9.3.
2. Specifying the Universal Naming Convention (UNC) using the Run . . . option under the Start button. The UNC format is specified as \\computername\sharename.
3. By selecting the Map Drive button on the toolbar of Network Neighborhood or Microsoft Explorer on machines using the Active Desktop.

9.4.2 Share Rights

To control how users gain access to a shared folder, you assign shared folder permissions. Note: These permissions are not needed or used if the user is accessing the directory locally (logged on to the computer that has the shared drive or directory). The Shared Folder/Drive permissions are shown in table 9.7.

To grant or change shared permissions to a shared folder, you would right-click the shared folder or drive, select the Sharing option and click on the Permissions button. To add a user or group, click on

Figure 9.2 Sharing Drive/Directory

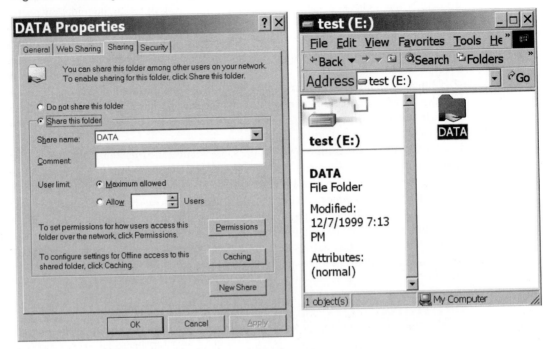

Figure 9.3 Access a Shared Folder Using Windows Explorer

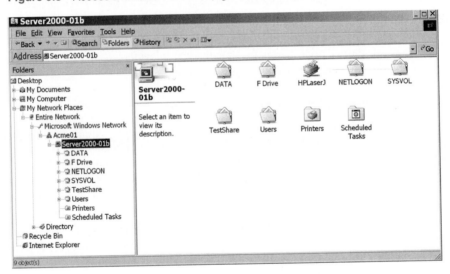

Table 9.7 Share Permissions

Share Permissions	Description
Read	The Read permission allows the user to view folder names and file names, open and view subfolders files and their attributes, and to navigate the tree structures.
Change	Allows all permissions granted by the Read permission, and it also allows the user to create folders, add files to folders, change data in files, append data to files, change file attributes, and delete folders and files.
Full Control	The Full Control Permissions allows all permissions granted by the Change permission, and it also allows the user to change file permissions and take ownership of files.

the Add button. To remove a user or group, click to highlight the user or group and click on the Remove button. To specify which permissions to grant, click to highlight the user or group and select or deselect the Allow and Deny options.

Different from NTFS permissions, there is only one level of permissions assigned to a shared folder. For example, on the SERVER1 server, you share a folder called FOLDER1 and assign the Full Control permission. In the FOLDER1 folder, you share a folder called FOLDER2 and assign the Modify permission. Therefore, if you access the \\SERVER1\FOLDER1 folder, you are using the Full Control share permission, even when accessing the \\SERVER1\FOLDER1\FOLDER2 folder. If you access the \\SERVER folder, you are using the Change share permission. The permissions assigned to FOLDER1 are not an issue.

Since a user can be a member of several groups, it is possible for the user to have several sets of explicit permissions to a shared drive or folder. The effective permissions are the combination of all of the user and group permissions. For example, if the user has a Write permission to the user and the Read permission to the group that a user is a member of, the effective permission would be the Write permission. Note: Like NTFS permissions, Deny permissions override the granted permission.

When accessing a shared folder on an NTFS volume, the effective permissions that a person can do in the share folder are calculated by combining the shared folder permissions and the NTFS permissions. When combining the two, you first determine the cumulative NTFS permissions and the cumulative shared permissions and apply the more restrictive permission or the permissions that give the person the lesser permissions.

In Windows 2000 and Windows Server 2003, several special shared folders are automatically created by Windows for administrative and system use. See table 9.8. Different from regular shares, these shares do not show when a user browses the computer resources using Network Neighborhood, My Network Place or similar software. In most cases, special shared folders should not be deleted or modified. For Windows 2000 Professional and Windows XP Professional computers, only members of the Administrators or Backup Operators group can connect to these shares. For Windows 2000 and Windows Server 2003 Servers, members of Administrators, Backup Operators and Server Operators group are the only members that can connect to these shares.

Table 9.8 Special Shares

Special Share	Description
Drive letter $	A shared folder that allows administrative personnel to connect to the root directory of a drive, also known as an administrative share. It is shown as A$, B$, C$, D$, and so on. For example, C$ is a shared folder name by which drive C might be accessed by an administrator over the network.
ADMIN$	A resource used by the system during remote administration of a computer. The path of this resource is always the path to the Windows 2000 system root (the directory in which Windows 2000 is installed by default is C:\Winnt and Windows Server 2003 by default is C:\WINDOWS.
IPC$	A resource sharing the named pipes that are essential for communication between programs. It is used during remote administration of a computer and when viewing a computer's shared resources.
PRINT$	A resource used during remote administration of printers.
NETLOGON	A resource used by the Net Logon service of a Windows 2000 Server computer while processing domain logon requests. This resource is provided only for Windows 2000 Server computers. It is not provided for Windows 2000 Professional or Windows XP computers.
FAX$	A shared folder on a server used by fax clients in the process of sending a fax. The shared folder is used to temporarily cache files and access cover pages stored on the server.

An **administrative share** is a shared folder typically used for administrative purposes. To make a shared folder or drive into an administrative share, the share name must have a $ at the end of it. Since the share folder or drive cannot be seen during browsing, you would have to use a UNC name, which include the share name (including the $). Instead, it would have to be accessed using the Start button, selecting the Run option and typing the UNC name and clicking the OK button. By default, all volumes with drive letters automatically have administrative shares (C$, D$, E$, and so on). Other administrative shares can be created as needed for individual folders.

9.4.3   Home Directories Permissions

To create a home folder on a network file server, you should first create and share a folder such as home or users in which to store all home folders on a network server. The home folder for each user will reside below the shared folder. Then remove the default permission the default Full Control from the Everyone group and assign Full Control to the Users group. This ensures that only users with domain user accounts can gain access to the shared folder.

To provide the home folder path, you open the properties of the user in input the path in the Home folder section. Since the home folder is on a network server, click Connect and specify a drive letter to use to connect. As a result, when the user logs on to the network, the drive letter you assign will appear in the My Computer. In the text box, a UNC name appears in the form of `servername\sharename\ userlogonname`. If you use the %username% variable as the user's logon name, it will automatically name and create the user's home folder as the same name as the user's logon name. In addition, the user and the built-in Administrator group are assigned the NTFS Full Control permission. All other permissions are removed for the folder, including those for the Everyone group. This way, it is secure for the individual users. Lastly, you can further enhance the home folder feature by redirecting the user's My Documents pointer to the location of his or her home directory.

9.4.4   Combining Shared Folder Permissions and NTFS Permissions

As a review, NTFS permissions apply if you logged on locally or if you connect to the computer using a network connection. Share permissions are the only protection for FAT and FAT32 drives. Unfortunately, share permissions only protect the network resource when you connect to the computer using a network connection. If you logon locally to the computer, share permissions do not matter. Remember that you help protect the local files by only allowing a small group of people to logon on locally.

When accessing a shared folder on an NTFS volume, the effective permissions that a person can do in the share folder is calculated by combining the shared folder permissions and the NTFS permissions. When combining the two, you first determine the cumulative NTFS permissions and the cumulative shared permissions and apply the more restrictive permission or the permissions that gives the person the lesser permissions.

Example 9.1:

On the E drive (NTFS partition), you have a DATA folder and under the DATA folder you have a FINANCE folder. In the FINANCE folder, you have the DOC1.TXT file. The DATA folder is shared.

For USER1, you assign the Read (R) NTFS permission to the DATA folder and Full Control (FC) Share permission to the DATA folder. What are is the effective rights to the DOC1.TXT file for USER1?

To determine the effective rights when accessing the server remotely, take the more restrictive permission or the permissions that are more limiting. Since the Read permission is the more limiting than the FC permission, the effective rights when USER1 is accessing the DATA folder over the network is those permissions granted by the Read permission. As the rights flow down to the FINANCE folder, again, the R is more limiting then the FC. Therefore, the effective rights when USER1 is accessing the DATA folder over the network is those permission granted by the Read permission. Lastly, the rights flow into the DOC1.TXT file and again the effective permissions is Read.

Remote Access Effective Permissions

		NTFS	Shared	Combined
DATA	Explicit	R	FC	
	Effective	R	FC	
FINANCE	Inherited	R	FC	
	Explicit	–	–	
	Effective	R	FC	R
DOC1.TXT	Inherited	R	FC	
	Explicit	–	–	
	Effective	R	FC	R

If USER1 logs on locally on the server, the share permissions do not matter and the only permissions to look at is the Read permission.

Remote Access Effective Permissions

		NTFS	Shared	Combined
DATA	Explicit	R	FC	
	Effective	R	NA	
FINANCE	Inherited	R	NA	
	Explicit	–	–	
	Effective	R	NA	R
DOC1.TXT	Inherited	R	NA	
	Effective	–	–	
	Explicit	R	NA	R

Example 9.2:

On the E drive (NTFS partition), you have a DATA folder and under the DATA folder you have a FINANCE folder. In the FINANCE folder, you have the DOC1.TXT file. The DATA folder is shared. USER1 is a member of the local group called MANAGERS.

For USER1, you assign the Modify (M) NTFS permission to the DATA folder and Read and Execute (R&E) permission to the FINANCE folder. For the Managers group, you assign the Write permission to the FINANCE folder. In addition, for the Managers group, you assign Full Control (FC) Share permission to the DATA folder. What are the effective permissions to the DOC1.TXT file for USER1 when USER1 logs on remotely?

To determine the effective rights when accessing the server remotely, take the more restrictive permission or the permissions that are more limiting. For the USER1 NTFS permission, the R&E permission will stop the FINANCE folder from inheriting the Modify permission from the DATA folder. The DOC1.TXT file will inherit the R&E permission. For Managers, DOC1.TXT file will inherit the Write permission from the FINANCE folder. When you combine all of the NTFS permissions for the DOC1.TXT file, USER1 will have Read and Execute and Write permissions.

For the shared permissions, the Managers were assigned Full Control to the shared Data folder. Therefore the effective shared permission is the Full Control permission.

When you combine the two at the DOC1.TXT level, you must take the permissions that are the most restrictive. Since the Read and Execute and Write permissions are more restrictive then Full Control, USER1 will have Read and Execute and Write permission when accessing the DOC1.TXT file.

		USER1 NTFS	MANAGERS NTFS	Combined NTFS	USER1 Shared	MANAGERS Shared	Combined Shared	Combined Overall
DATA	Explicit	M	–		–	FC		
	Effective	M	–	M	–	FC	FC	M
FINANCE	Inherited	R&E	–		–	FC		
	Explicit	–	W		–	–		
	Effective	R&E	W	R&E & W	–	FC	FC	R&E & W
DOC1.TXT	Inherited	R&E	W		–	FC		
	Explicit	–	–		–	–		
	Effective	R&E	W	R&E & W	–	FC	FC	R&E & W

9.4.5   Distributed File System

The **distributed file system (Dfs)** groups and organizes shared folders that reside on the same or different computers into a single hierarchical tree structure. By using Dfs, a user can easily gain access to network resources without knowing the actual location of the underlying resources. To create a Dfs share, you must first create a Dfs root followed by creating child nodes that represent the shared folders, which can be physically located on different servers. See figure 9.4. Note: Any Windows 2000 server or Windows Server 2003 can host one Dfs root located in a FAT or NTFS volume. Of course, NTFS would be a better choice because of its extra security features.

There are two types of Dfs. They are:

Dfs Type	Description
Stand-alone Dfs	A stand-alone Dfs stores the Dfs topology on a single computer. It does not provide any fault tolerance if the computer that stores the Dfs topology or any of the shared folders fail.
Domain Dfs (Fault Tolerance)	Domain Dfs provides fault tolerance by having the child nodes point to multiple identical shared folders. Different from the stand-alone Dfs, the domain Dfs stores its topology in the Active Directory. By using Active Directory, it supports DNS. Each child node can have up to 32 replicas.

Figure 9.4 Distributed File System

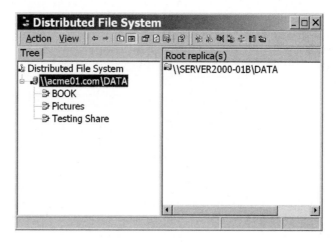

To create the stand-alone Dfs root:

1. On the Action menu, click the New Dfs Root, and click on the Next button.
2. Select Create a stand-alone Dfs root, and click on the Next button.
3. Type in the name of the host server for the DNS Root and click on the Next button.
4. Select an existing share, or select the Create a new share and specify the path to share and the share name; click on the Next button.
5. Specify a unique Dfs Share name, and click on the Next button.
6. Click on the Finish button.

To create the domain (fault-tolerant) Dfs root:

1. On the Action menu, click the New Dfs Root, and click on the Next button.
2. Select Create a domain Dfs root, and click on the Next button.
3. Type in the name of the host domain for the Dfs root, and click on the Next button.
4. Type in the name of the host server for the DNS Root, and click on the Next button.
5. Select an existing share or select the Create a new share and specify the path to share and the share name; click on the Next button.
6. Specify a unique Dfs Share name, and click on the Next button.
7. Click on the Finish button.

Replicating the Dfs root to another server in the domain ensures that if the host server becomes unavailable for any reason, the distributed file system associated with that Dfs root is still available to domain users. To set up a replication of the root, right-click the root, select the New Root Replica and use the wizard.

By replicating a Dfs shared folder, Dfs stores a duplicate copy of the contents of the original shared folder into another shared folder. To replicate a Dfs shared folder, right-click the Dfs link and select the New Replica option. Then specify an alternate shared folder that will act as a replication partner to the original shared folder, select the type of replication policy and click on the OK button. If Automatic replication is selected, it automatically will replicate the files from the one share to the other. Note: Automatic replication can only be used for files stored on NTFS volumes on Windows servers. If manual replication is selected, you must manually copy the files. Note: when using Stand-Alone Dfs, you can only select manual replication. See figure 9.5.

To remove a link, right-click the link and select the Remove Dfs Link option and click on the Yes button. To delete a Dfs root share, right-click the Dfs root share, select the Delete Dfs Root option and click on the Yes button.

To access Dfs resources, the operating system must include Dfs client software. Dfs client software is included in Windows 98, Windows Millennium, Windows NT 4.0, Windows 2000, Windows XP, and Windows Server 2003. If you have a Windows 95 computer, you must download and install a Dfs client. If your system has the Dfs client, you then access the Dfs just like a shared folder or directory.

Figure 9.5   Setting Up Replicas in Dfs

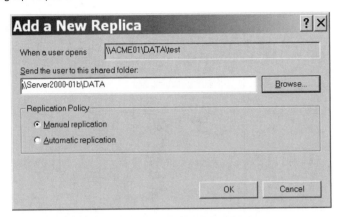

Figure 9.6   Network Neighborhood Showing a Computer with Network Services

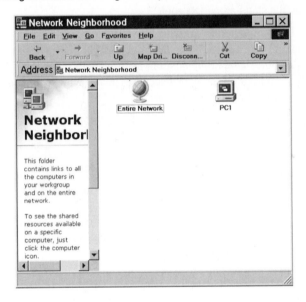

9.4.6   Browsing the Network

Windows uses a Computer Browser service to easily find network computers and their services. An example of using the Computer Browser service is when you use Network Neighborhood, My Network Places, the NET VIEW command and Windows Explorer to show the available network resources such as shared drives, directories and printers in a graphical environment and allows easy access to these resources. See figure 9.6.

After installing the appropriate network software (client software, network card driver, and protocol), the Network Neighborhood is automatically placed on the desktop. When you double-click on the icon, it will open a window that displays computers that have network resources available. By double-clicking on one of the computers listed in the network neighborhood, a new window will open and display the network resources (mostly shared drives, directories, and printers) provided by that computer. See figure 9.7.

Windows uses a browser service to discover all shared devices on the network and compile a database of those resources. A browser is a network computer that tracks the location, availability, and identity of shared devices. Several kinds of browsers exist including a domain master browser, master browser and backup browser. A domain master browser tracks resources for a group of domains. A master browser maintains a database (called a browse list) of shared resources for its domain. Every time a

Figure 9.7 Network Resources Shown in Network Neighborhood

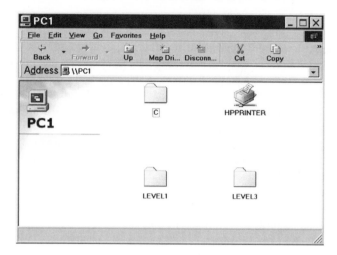

computer on the network starts, it registers itself with the master browser. In an environment containing two or more domains, each master browser will pass along its browse list to the domain master browser. A backup browser keeps a copy of the master browser browse list in case the master browser goes down. Although every server on a Windows NT network has the potential to act as a browser, by default the PDC is the master browser for its domain. In Windows 2000 and Windows Server 2003 networks, Active Directory can provide Computer Browser service by using global catalogs.

When Windows clients need to perform NetBIOS name resolution, the client will first look in its local cache to see if it knows its IP address by talking to it recently. If not, it will then check the lmhosts file. If the entry is not in the file, it will by default, do a broadcast looking for that computer (if the client is a B node) or by checking with a WINS server (if the client is a P or H node).

B node broadcast don't go through routers. So typically NT4 domains with B nodes that don't have any WINS servers to access will have a truncated browse list featuring only those workstations on the same side of the router as they were located. Additionally, master browser election wars would frequently occur when more than one domain was on the same subnet causing more confusion. So with Windows NT4, the Network Neighborhood list was created via a highly unreliable network of master browsers on each subnet.

Windows 2000 or Windows Server 2003 domain master browser (the DC with the PDC emulator role) actively queries its configured WINS server for a list of all registered domains. It uses this list to contact the other domain master browsers to coordinate browser lists with. This means that the browse list presented to the workstation should be more complete than before. All workstations should be represented, assuming that the domain master browser of every domain (or workgroup) is configured to use a central WINS server, and at least one workstation from every domain (or workgroup) on each router segment is able to contact its domain master browser.

9.4.7 Securing Microsoft Shares

Any time you share drives or directories, the shared drives and directories become targets of an attacker. Therefore, they will attempt to make unauthorized connections to shared resources on the network, access shared drives and directories that do not have the permissions configured incorrectly and by packet sniffing. To help secure these shares, you can first block access to the shares at the firewall so that no one can access them from outside of your network. You should therefore block TCP/UDP ports 137, 138, and 139. You should use the highest security and authentication available and you need to verify share permissions. Remember to use the rule of least privilege to secure your shares. Therefore, you would typically remove the everyone from the shared permissions and assign the appropriate user and group names with only the necessary permissions. You can also use IPSec or VPNs to encrypt communications between clients and servers.

9.5   WINDOWS FILE ENCRYPTION

Encryption is the process of converting data into a format that cannot be read by another user. Once a user has encrypted a file, the file automatically remains encrypted whenever the file is stored on disk. Decryption is the process of converting data from encrypted format back to its original format. Once a user has decrypted a file, the file remains decrypted whenever the file is stored on disk.

Windows 2000, Windows Server 2003, and Windows XP include the **Encrypting File System (EFS),** which allows a user to encrypt and decrypt files that are stored on a NTFS volume. By using EFS, folders and files are still kept secure against those intruders who might gain unauthorized physical access to the drive such as stealing a notebook computer or a removable drive. EFS is not intended to support accessing an encrypted file by multiple users and EFS does not decrypt or encrypt files that are transmitted over the network. Instead, another protocol would have to be used to secure the data sent over the network.

When EFS is enabled, the encrypting and decrypting of a file is transparent to the user. As a file is encrypted, each file has a unique file encryption key, which is later used to decrypt the file's data. The file encryption key is also encrypted by the user's public key. When a decryption of files, the file encryption key must first be decrypted. The file encryption is decrypted when the user has a private key that matches the public key. If a user that doesn't have the right private key tries to open, copy, move, or rename an encrypted file, the user will get an access denied message.

You should follow certain guidelines when using EFS:

- You cannot encrypt files or folders that are compressed.
- Encrypted files can become decrypted if you copy or move the file to a volume that is not an NTFS volume.
- Use cutting and pasting to move files into an encrypted folder. If you use a drag-and-drop operation to move the files, they will not automatically be encrypted in the new folder.
- System files cannot be encrypted.
- Encrypting a folder or file does not protect against deletion. Anyone with delete permission can delete encrypted folders or files.
- Temporary files, which are created by some programs when documents are edited, are also encrypted as long as all the files are on an NTFS volume and in an encrypted folder. It is recommended that you encrypt the Temp folder on your hard disk for this reason.
- Encrypt the My Documents folder if this is the place where you save most of your documents. This ensures that your personal documents are encrypted by default.

9.5.1   Encrypt Attribute

To encrypt a folder or file:

1. Right-click the folder or file and select the Properties option.
2. Click on the Advanced button. See figure 9.8.
3. Select the Encrypt contents to secure data option.

NOTE: When a folder is encrypted, the folder itself is not encrypted, but all of the files in the folder are encrypted.

To decrypt the folder or file, unselect the Encrypt contents to secure data option.

You can also encrypt or decrypt a file or folder by using the CIPHER command. For more information on the CIPHER command, type CIPHER /? at the command prompt. See figure 9.9.

9.5.2   Recovering Encrypted Files

If a person leaves the company and his or her data is encrypted, the data will have to be decrypted before someone else can use it. A recovery agent is an administrator authorized to decrypt data that was encrypted by another user. Before you can add a recovery agent for a domain, you must ensure that each recovery agent has been issued an X.509 Version 3 certificate.

The recovery agent has a special certificate and associated private key that allow data recovery for the scope of influence of the recovery policy. If you are the recovery agent, you should be sure to use

Figure 9.8 Encryption and Compression Attributes

Figure 9.9 Cipher /? Command

```
C:\>cipher /?
Displays or alters the encryption of directories [files] on NTFS partitions.

  CIPHER [/E | /D] [/S:dir] [/A] [/I] [/F] [/Q] [/H] [/K] [pathname [...]]

   /E        Encrypts the specified directories. Directories will be marked so
             that files added afterward will be encrypted.

   /D        Decrypts the specified directories. Directories will be marked so
             that files added afterward will not be encrypted.

   /S        Performs the specified operation on directories in the given
             directory and all subdirectories.

   /A        Operation for files as well as directories. The encrypted file
             could become decrypted when it is modified if the parent directory
             is not encrypted. It is recommended that you encrypt the file and
             the parent directory.

   /I        Continues performing the specified operation even after errors have
             occurred. By default, CIPHER stops when an error is encountered.

   /F        Forces the encryption operation on all specified objects, even
             those which are already encrypted. Already-encrypted objects are
             skipped by default.

   /Q        Reports only the most essential information.

   /H        Displays files with the hidden or system attributes. These files
             are omitted by default.

   /K        Create new file encryption key for the user running CIPHER. If this
             option is chosen, all the other options will be ignored.

   pathname specifies a pattern, file, or directory.

   Used without parameters, CIPHER displays the encryption state of the current
   directory and any files it contains. You may use multiple directory names
   and wildcards. You must put spaces between multiple parameters.
```

Figure 9.10 File Recovery Certificate

the Export command from Certificates in Microsoft Management Console (MMC) to back up the recovery certificate and associated private key to a secure location. After backing them up, you should use Certificates in MMC to delete the recovery certificate. Then, when you need to perform a recovery operation for a user, you should first restore the recovery certificate and associated private key using the Import command from Certificates in MMC. After recovering the data, you should again delete the recovery certificate. You do not have to repeat the export process. See figure 9.10.

9.6   NETWARE DISK STRUCTURE

NetWare offers its own high-performance file system that supports DOS, Macintosh, UNIX, OS/2 and Windows long filenames. While NetWare supports DOS filenames by default, you have to load the proper NLM to support other filenames including the long file names.

The NetWare file system is organized much like the DOS file system. In NetWare, volumes are the major division of NetWare file system. A **volume** is physical amount of storage on a hard disk or other storage device, such as CD ROM. A volume may be fully contained on a single hard drive or may be spread across multiple hard drives.

The physical storage space that makes up a volume is allocated and named during the installation of the NetWare operating system on the server. These are some of the rules for naming a volume:

- The name must be 2 to 15 characters long.
- The physical volume name must be followed by a colon (:).
- Spaces, commas, back slashes, and periods are not permitted within the volume name.
- Use only the letters A–Z, the numbers zero through nine, and the following symbols: (~), (!), (#), ($), (%), (^), (&), (()), (-), (_) and ({ }).
- Two physical volumes on the same NetWare server cannot have the same name.
- The back slash (\) or the forward slash (/) must be used to separate the NetWare server name from the physical volume name.

The main volume for NetWare is the **SYS volume.** During installation, it is automatically created and several directories are placed in them:

- **Login**—Contains the programs necessary for logging in to the network.
- **Public**—Holds the NetWare commands and utilities available to network users.
- **System**—Stores files used by the NetWare server operating system or by the SUPERVISOR. The SYSTEM directory holds NLMs and files specific to the NetWare server.
- **Mail**—Used by the NetWare operating system. It contains subdirectories for each user. They are named after the user's hexadecimal ID number and contain the user's login script.
- **Etc**—Contains sample files to help configure the server for TCP/IP protocols.
- **Deleted.Sav**—Contains deleted files from directories that have been removed.

In addition, you need to add additional volumes to hold the directories and files for your users. Novell breaks down these directories into the following:

- **Home Directories**—Users should have a "home" directory in which to store individual user-created files. Usually, individual users are given full access to their own directories so that they can manage (create, delete, modify, move, copy, and so on) their own files.
- **Application directories**—These contain application files and establish security over the application files. A user must be given access to an application directory in order to use the application. User-created data files generated using the applications are usually not kept here.
- **Configuration File Directories**—Many applications use configuration files to allow a user to set up or customize how an application functions for him or her without affecting how the application functions for the other users. Configuration files allow users to make changes to an application without affecting the application for other users.
- **Shared Data Directories**—Shared data directories facilitate the distribution of information needed by groups of users. These directories are also used to ensure data security.

To access the NetWare file system starts with accessing the volume containing the needed directories and files. Applications that use NetWare volume-naming procedures can access file systems through the server\volume or volume object name. For example, NetWare utilities can access the NetWare file system in this manner. Many legacy applications cannot access NetWare volumes by their volume names. These applications require the use of a drive mapping.

Newer Windows-based programs do not require drive mappings. Instead, they locate workstation and network resources by object name as displayed in My Computer or Network Neighborhood.

The full path to a directory can be used when identifying a directory. The path consists of the names of the levels in the file system structure, beginning with the server name followed by the volume name or the name of the volume object in the NDS tree followed by the names of all directories leading to the specific directory or file. The directory name with a full path would look like this:

```
SERVER\VOLUME:DIRECTORY\SUBDIRECTORY
```

or

```
VOLUME_OBJECT:DIRECTORY\SUBDIRECTORY
```

To mount a CD on a Novell Server, you need to load the cdrom.nlm. This would be done by executing the following command at the server console:

```
load cdrom
```

Rights determine the type of access a user has to network directories and files. A user cannot do anything to a directory or a file without the assignment of rights. See table 9.9. If rights are granted to a directory for a trustee, the rights will flow down to, or are inherited by, all files and directories within and below the directory. Because directory and file rights are the same, all rights to a directory can be inherited by the files in the directory.

There are two ways to block the inheritance of rights. The first way is to make a trustee assignment lower in the directory structure. The rights inherited by an object are overwritten when the same object is given a trustee assignment lower in the directory structure, unless the assignment above the new assignment is the Supervisor right.

Table 9.9 NetWare Directory/File Rights

Right	Abbreviation	Description
Supervisor	S	Grants users all rights to the directory and its files and subdirectories and their files. Users grant any right to other users. This right cannot be blocked by an Inherited Rights Filter (IRF).
Read	R	Grants users the right to open files in the directory and read their contents or run the programs.
Write	W	Grants users the right to open and change the contents of files.
Create	C	Grants users the right to create new files and subdirectories.
Erase	E	Grants users the right to delete the directory and its files and subdirectories.
Modify	M	Grants users the right to change the attributes or name of a file or directory.
File Scan	F	Grants users the right to see files and directories.
Access Control	A	Grants users the right to change trustee assignments and the IRF so that all rights, except the Supervisor right, are given.

The second way to block the inheritance of rights is to setup Inheritance Rights Filters (IRFs). An IRF controls the rights that a trustee can inherit from parent directories. The IRF of a directory or file does not block rights that are granted to a trustee of the same directory or file. Only those rights inherited from trustee assignments made higher in the file structure are affected. Note: In file system security, the Supervisor right cannot be blocked by an IRF.

9.7 STORING FILES IN LINUX

Linux supports various file systems for storing data including ext2 file system (developed specifically for Linux), journaled file systems including ext3 and reiserfs, Microsoft's VFAT file systems (used in Windows 95/98) and ISO 9660 CD-ROM file system. In addition, it is the Linux computer, acting as a server, allows various computer systems to store files on the server include DOS, Windows, Apple Macintosh, UNIX, and Linux.

9.7.1 Disk Names in Linux

Linux treats all devices as files and has actual files that represent each device. In Linux, these device files are located in the /dev directory. Linux filenames are similar to MS-DOS filenames, except that they do not use drive letters such as A and C and they substitute the slash (/) for the MS-DOS backslash as the separator between directory names.

Because Linux treats a device as a file in the /dev directory, the hard disk names start with /dev. Table 9.10 lists the hard disk and floppy drive names that you may have to use. Of course, when you use the Red Hat Disk Druid or Linux fdisk program to prepare the Linux partitions, you have to identify the disk drive by its name such as /dev/hda.

When Disk Druid or fdisk displays the list of partitions, the partition names are of the form /dev/hda1, /dev/hda2, etc. Linux constructs each partition name by appending the partition number (1 through 4 for the four primary partitions on a hard disk) to the disk name. Therefore, if your PC's single IDE hard drive has two partitions, the installation program uses /dev/hda1 and /dev/hda2 as the names of these partitions.

Table 9.10 Hard Disk and Floppy Drive Names

Device Type	Name	Description
IDE Hard Drives	/dev/hda	First IDE hard drive (typically the C drive)
	/dev/hdb	Second IDE hard drive
SCSI Hard Drives	/dev/sda	First SCSI hard drive
	/dev/sdb	Second SCSI hard drive
Floppy Disk	/dev/fd0	First floppy drive (A drive)
	/dev/fd1	Second floppy drive (B drive)

9.7.2   Linux File System

Under most operating systems (including Linux), there is the concept of a file, which is just a bundle of information given a filename. Examples of files might be your paper or report, an email message, or an actual program that can be executed. Essentially, anything saved on disk is saved as an individual file.

Files are identified by their file names. These names usually identify the file and its contents in some form that is meaningful to you. There is no standard format for file names as there is under MS-DOS and some other operating systems; in general, a file name can contain any character (except the / character) and is limited to 256 characters in length.

With the concept of files comes the concept of directories. A directory is a collection of files. It can be thought of as a folder that contains many different files. Directories are given names, with which you can identify them. Furthermore, directories are maintained in a tree-like structure, in which directories may contain other directories.

Most Linux systems use a standard layout for files so that system resources and programs can be easily located. This layout forms a directory tree, which starts at the root directory (designated as the / directory). Note: This is different from DOS and the command prompt under Windows, which use the backslash (\) as the root directory and as a separator for directories. Directly underneath / are important subdirectories: /bin, /etc, /dev, and /usr among others. See figure 9.11.

Figure 9.11   Sample File System

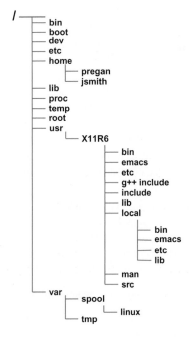

Red Hat and other Linux distributors are committed to the Filesystem Hierarchy Standard (FHS), a collaborative document that defines the names and locations of many files and directories. The current FHS document is the authoritative reference to any FHS compliant filesystem. The complete standard can be viewed at http://www.pathname.com/fhs/. Unfortunately, the standard leaves many areas undefined or extensible. See table 9.11 for a list of well-known directories used in Linux.

Table 9.11   Key Directories Used in Red Hat Linux File System Hierarchy

Directory Name	Description
root (/)	In this setup, all files (except those stored in /boot) reside on the root partition. For Red Hat Linux, a 900-MB root partition will permit the equivalent of a workstation-class installation with very little free space, whereas a 1.7-GB root partition will let you install every package in Red Hat Linux.
/bin	Contains the executable programs that are part of the Linux operating system that are available to all users. Many commands, such as cat, cp, ls, more, and tar, are located in /bin.
/boot	The /boot directory contains the operating system kernel (which allows your system to boot Linux), along with files used during the bootstrap process. Due to the limitations of older PC BIOSes, creating a small partition to hold these files is a good idea. This partition should be no larger than 16 MB.
/dev	Contains all device files. The /dev directory contains files divided into subdirectories that contain files for a specific device. These directories are named based on type of device files they contain. Some examples of these hda1 for the first IDE hard drive, fd0 for the floppy disk and cdrom, which is the symbolic link created to the CD-ROM device that Linux was installed from.
/etc	The location for configuration files and for the system boot scripts. These boot scripts are located under the /etc/rc.d/ directory. The services that run at boot up are located under /etc/rc.d/init.d/.
/home	The /home directory is where users store their own files. When planning out the size of the /home partition, you must consider how many users you have and how much space you want to allocate for each user.
/lib	Contains library files for C and other programming languages
/lost+found	The system's directory for placing lost files that are found or created by disk errors or improper system shutdowns. At boot, programs such as fsck find the inodes, which have no directory entries, and reattach them as files in this directory. Directory for lost files. Every disk partition has a lost+found directory
/mnt	An empty directory, typically used to mount devices temporarily such as floppy disks and disk partitions. Also contains the /mnt/floppy directory for mounting floppy disks, and the /mnt/cdrom directory for mounting the CD-ROM drive. *NOTE:* You also can mount the CD-ROM drive on another directory.
/opt	The location for optional packages.
/proc	A special directory that contains information about various aspects of the Linux system configuration information (interrupt usage, I/O port use, and CPU type) and the running processes (programs).
/root	The home directory for the root user.
/sbin	The location of some system configuration and system administrator executable files. Most of your general administration commands such as lilo, fdisk, fsck, and route are located here are typically available only to root.
/swap	The /swap directory is where the swap files (virtual memory). If you have more swap space, it will allow more programs to run simultaneously or larger programs to run with more data. If you have 16 MB or less, you must have a swap partition. Even if you have more memory, a swap partition is still recommended. The minimum size of your swap partition should be equal to the amount of RAM in your system or 16 MB, whichever is larger. Linux allows each up to 16 swap partitions.
/tmp	The /tmp directory used to hold temporary files, typically needed in larger multi-user systems and network file servers.

Continued

Table 9.11   Continued

Directory Name	Description
/usr	The /usr directory is where most of the software on the Linux system resides. It should be about 150 MB to 600 MB, depending on which packages are installed.
	/usr/bin—Contains executable files for many Linux commands including utility programs commonly available in Linux, but not part of the core Linux operating system
	/usr/doc—Contains the documentation files for the Linux operating system, as well as many utility programs such as the Bash shell, mtools, the xfm File Manager, xv image viewer.
	/usr/games—Contains some old Linux games such as fortune, banner, and trojka
	/usr/include—Contains the header files (files with names ending in .h) for the C and C++ programming languages.
	/usr/lib—Contains the libraries for C and C++ programming languages
	/usr/local—The /usr/local is used for storing programs that you want to separate from the rest of the Red Hat Linux software.
	/usr/man—Contains the online manual, which can can be read by using the man command
	/usr/sbin—Contains many administrative commands, such as commands for electronic mail and networking
	/usr/share—Contains shared data such as default configuration files and images for many applications.
	/usr/src—The /usr/src contains much of the Linux source code.
	/usr/X11R6—Contains the Xfree86 (X Window System) software
/var	Short for various. It is used to store files that change often such as for spooling, logging, and other data.

9.7.3   Mount Points

DOS and Windows use drive letters to identify logical drives or partitions that may be one the one hard drive or several hard drives. Each drive has a root directory and its hierarchical file system.

In Linux, all of the drives and their partitions make up a single directory file system. If you have more than one physical disk partition, it is associated with a specific part of the file system. All you have to do is decide which part of the Linux directory tree should be located on each partition. This process is known in Linux as mounting a file system on a device (the disk partition). The term mount point refers to the directory you associate with a disk partition or any other device. In other words, each mount point is a disk partition, and that disk partition is mounted on the directory of the limb above it.

Although you can get by with a single large partition for the entire Linux file system and another for the swap space, you can better manage the disk space if you create separate partitions for the key parts of the Linux file system. This is probably more important if Linux is running as a server where you need to do a better job in managing disk space. See figure 9.12. Some of the recommended partitions are:

- /bin
- /home
- /root
- /var
- /boot
- /lib
- /tmp

At the very minimum, you will need two partitions for your system: root (/) and swap. For performance reasons, Linux likes to have swap on its own partition. For most other installations, I would recommend three partitions: swap, root, and home. If you require complicated system requirements and decide to use multiple partitions, you should refer to table 9.12.

The size of the swap partition usually varies between the amount of physical memory (RAM) and twice the amount of physical memory. There are situations, such as certain databases, where an increased swap partition is desired. But if the swap file is too big, you will most likely see a degradation in performance since disk is much slower than RAM.

Figure 9.12   Sample Linux File System Using Mounted Points

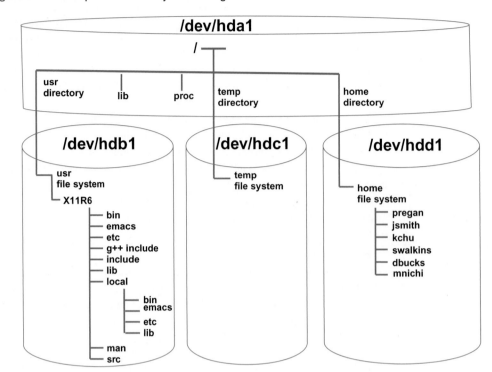

Table 9.12   Directory Guidelines for a Complicated Disk Structure for Linux

Name	Min Size	Usage
Swap	128 MB	Virtual Memory, which is used to store inactive memory to disk until it is later used.
/	250 MB	Root file system including basic libraries, programs and configuration
/var	250 MB	For files that change frequently including logs, spool files, lock files
/usr	500 MB	Used by most applications
/boot	16 MB	Used to store the kernel
/home	500 MB	Home directory of users including user specific configuration and data

Partitions like /usr and /home tend to fill up quickly, so if you have extra space, it should be put there. Depending on the function of the computer, extra space could go to other partitions. For example, if you are using it as a mail server, you would have little need for the /home partition, but you would want lots of space in /var to store all the mail. If you have a file server, you would not have many binary files in /bin, but its /home will most likely need to be quite large.

9.7.4   Second Extended File System (EXT2)

The second extended file system, referred to as EXT2, is considered the native Linux filesystem. It is very similar to other modern Unix filesystems but most closely resembles the Berkeley Fast Filesystem used by BSD systems. The maximum size of an EXT2 filesystem is 4 TB, while the maximum file size is currently limited to 2 GB by the Linux kernel.

The EXT2 file system, like a lot of the file systems, is built on the premise that the data held in files is kept in data blocks. You can think of data blocks as being similar to clusters or allocation units. These data blocks are all the same length, and although that length can vary between different EXT2 file systems, the block size of a particular EXT2 file system is set when it is created (during formatting with the mke2fs program).

As far as each file system is concerned, block devices are just a series of blocks which can be read and written. A file system does not need to concern itself with where on the physical media a block should be put, that is the job of the device driver. Whenever a file system needs to read information or data from the block device containing it, it requests that its supporting device driver reads an integral number of blocks.

EXT2 defines the file system topology by describing each file in the system with an inode data structure. An inode describes which blocks of data belong to which files, the access rights of the file, the file's modification times, and the type of the file.

9.7.5   Journaling Filesystems

EXT2 is not perfect. EXT2 is a static filesystem, which does not guarantee that all updates to your hard drive are performed safely. If the computer is shut down improperly, for example because of a power outage or a system crash, it can take several minutes for Linux to verify the integrity of the partition when the computer reboots. In addition, to make things worse, EXT2 is not fault tolerant. To overcome such situations, journaling filesytems were created, which becomes more important with mission critical servers and maintaining large datasets.

Journaling filesystems are superior to static filesystems when it comes to guaranteeing data integrity and increasing overall filesystem performance. Journaling and logging filesystems can either keep track of the changes to a file's "metadata" (information such as ownership, creation dates, and so on), or to the data blocks associated with a file, or to both, rather than maintaining a single static snapshot of the state of a file.

When modifying the blocks in the middle of a file and then adding new blocks to the end, a journaling filesystem would first store the pending changes (modified and new blocks) in a special section of the disk known as the "log." The filesystem would then update the actual file and directory inodes using the data from the log, and would then mark that log operation as having been completed ("committed," in logging terms).

Whenever a file is accessed, the last snapshot of the file is retrieved from the disk, and the log is consulted to see if any uncommitted changes have been made to the file since the snapshot was taken. Every so often, the filesystem will update file snapshots and record the changes in the log, thereby "trimming" the log and reducing access time. Committing operations from the log and synchronizing the log and its associated filesystem is called a checkpoint.

Journaling and logging filesystems get around the problem of inconsistencies introduced during a system crash by using the log. Before any on-disk structures are changed, an "intent-to-commit" record is written to the log. The directory structure is then updated and the log entry is marked as committed. Since every change to the filesystem structure is recorded in the log, filesystem consistency can be checked by looking in the log without the need for verifying the entire filesystem. When disks are mounted, if an intent-to-commit entry is found but not marked as committed, then the file structure for that block is checked and fixed if necessary.

After a crash, filesystems can come online almost immediately because only the log entries after the last checkpoint need to be examined. Any changes in the log can be quickly "replayed," and the corrupted part of the disk will always correspond to the last change added to the log. The log can then be truncated since it will be invalid, and no data is lost except for any changes that were being logged when the system went down. Mounting a heavily populated directory that requires subsequent validation for database partitions might take 10 to 20 minutes to fsck with a standard static filesystem. A journaled filesystem can reduce that time to a few seconds.

The disadvantage of logging is it generally requires more disk writes because you have to first append log records to the log, then replay them against the filesystem. However, in practice, the system can operate more efficiently by using its "free time" to commit entries from the log and checkpoint the file system records. Also, because logs are stored separately on the disk from filesystem data and are only appended to, logging changes happen much faster than actually making those changes.

There are multiple offerings from commercial software vendors who have released journaled filesystems for Linux, and there are a few contenders from the open source community. The most popular two are EXT3 and Reiserfs.

EXT3 is designed to make the migration from static ext2fs filesystems to ext3fs as easy as possible. The initial proposal of EXT3 had simply adding logging capabilities to ext2fs through a log file in that filesystem. Although it is slow, it is extremely reliable.

Reiserfs is a new, general-purpose filesystem for Linux that is designed for flexibility and efficiency. In some cases it still extracts a slight performance penalty in the interests of increased reliability and faster restart times. Reiserfs is more space efficient than most files as it can pack many small files into a single block. In addition, Reiserfs supports filesystem plug-ins that make it easy to create your own types of directories and files. This guarantees Reiserfs a place in the Linux filesystems of the future by making it easy to extend reiserfs to support the requirements for protocols that are still being finalized, such as streaming audio and video. For example, a system administrator can create a special filesystem object for streaming audio or video files, and then create his/her own special item and search handlers for the new object types. The content of such files can already be stored in TCP/IP packet format, reducing processing latency during subsequent transmission of the actual file.

9.7.6   Virtual File System (VFS)

The virtual file system (VFS) is a kernel software layer that handles all system calls related to the Linux file system. It must manage all of the different file systems that are mounted at any given time. It provides a common interface to several kinds of file systems including disk-based file systems, network-based file systems, and special file systems, including the /proc file system and /dev file systems. To do this, it maintains data structures that describe the whole (virtual) file system and the real mounted file systems. Similar to the EXT2 file system, VFS describes the system's files in terms of superblocks and inodes, in much the same way that the EXT2 file system uses superblocks and inodes.

As each file system is initialized, it registers itself with the VFS. This happens as the operating system initializes itself at system boot time. The file systems drivers are either built into the kernel itself or are built as loadable modules. File System modules are loaded as the system needs them, so, for example, if the VFAT file system is implemented as a kernel module then it is only loaded when a VFAT file system is mounted. When a block device based file system is mounted, and this includes the root file system, the VFS must read its superblock. Each file system type's superblock read routine must work out the file system's topology and map that information onto a VFS superblock data structure. The VFS keeps a list of the mounted file systems in the system together with their VFS superblocks. Each VFS superblock contains information and pointers to routines that perform particular functions.

For example, the superblock representing a mounted EXT2 file system contains a pointer to the EXT2 specific inode reading routine. This EXT2 inode read routine, like all of the file system specific inode read routines, fills out the fields in a VFS inode. Each VFS superblock contains a pointer to the first VFS inode on the file system. For the root file system, this is the inode that represents the "/" directory. This mapping of information is very efficient for the EXT2 file system but moderately less so for other file systems.

9.7.7   The /proc and /dev File System

The flexibility of the virtual file system is shown in the /proc and /dev file systems. The file systems and their files and directories do not actually exist, yet they act like real file systems for quick and easy access.

The /proc file system, like a real file system, registers itself with the virtual file system. The /proc file system does not store data, rather, its contents are computed on demand according to user file I/O requests. When the VFS makes calls to it requesting inodes as its files and directories are opened, the /proc file system collects the appropriate information, formats it into text form and places it into the requesting process's read buffer. Note: If you need to analyze your system and its performance, much of the information can be found in the /proc file system.

Linux represents its hardware devices as special files. A device file does not use any data space in the file system, it is only an access point to the device driver. The EXT2 file system and the Linux VFS both implement device files as special types of inode. There are two types of device file; character and block special files. Within the kernel itself, the device drivers implement file semantics: you can open them, close them and so on. Character devices allow I/O operations in character mode and block devices require that all I/O is via the buffer cache. When an I/O request is made to a device file, it is forwarded to the appropriate device driver within the system. Often this is not a real device driver but a psuedo-device driver for some subsystem such as the SCSI device driver layer. Device files are referenced by a major number which identifies the device type, and a minor type, which identifies the unit, or instance of that major type. For example, the IDE disks on the first IDE controller in the system have a major number of 3 and the first partition of an IDE disk would have a minor number of 1.

9.8   LINUX FILE SECURITY

Besides login security, when you think of security, you think of file security whereby you determine who can access what directories and files and how they can access those directories and files. Therefore, it is obvious that if you are going to be setting up a network server or if you want to secure a Linux workstation, you will need to understand file security and how to configure file security.

There are three components to Linux's file permission handling:

- **Username (or UID)**—A username (or UID) is associated with each file on the computer. This is frequently referred to as the file owner.
- **Group (or GID)**—Every file is associated with a particular GID, which links the file to a group. This is something referred to as the group owner. Normally, the group of a file is one of the groups to which the file's owner belongs, but root may change the file's group to one unassociated with the file's owner.
- **File access permissions**—The file access permission is a code that represents who may access the file, relative to the file's owner, the file's group, and all others.

You can see all three elements by using the ls –l command on a file. See figure 9.13.

- **Permission string**—The output of this command has several different components, each with a specific meaning. The first component (for example, `-rwxr-xr-x`), is the permission string. Along with the user and group names, it's what determines who may access a file. As displayed by ls –l, the permission string is a series of codes. Sometimes the first character of this is string is omitted, particularly when discussing ordinary files, but it's always present in an ls –l listing.
- **Number of hard links**—Linux supports hard links in its filesystems. A hard link allows one file to be referred to by two or more different file names. Internally, Linux uses a data structure known as an inode to keep track of the file, and multiple filenames point to the same inode. The number 1 in the preceding example output means that just one filename points to this file; it has no hard links. Larger numbers indicate that hard links exist. For instance, 3 means that the file may be referred to by three different filenames.
- **Owner**—The next field, root is this example of the owner of the file. in the case of long usernames, the username may be truncated.
- **Group**—The manager is the group to which the example file belongs. Many system files belong to the root owner and root group.
- **File size**—The next field, 33,026 in this example, is the size of the file in bytes.
- **Creation time**—The next field contains the file creation time and date. If the file is older than a year, you'll see the year rather than the creation time, although the time is still stored with the file.
- **Filename**—The final field is the name of the file. When using the ls command, if the complete path to the file is used, the complete path appears in the output.

Figure 9.13   Using the ls –l Command to View the File Permissions

```
[root@host1-1 data]# ls -l
total 148
drwxr-xr-x    2 root     root         4096 Apr 15 17:38 archive
-rwxr-xr-x    1 user1    manager     33026 Apr 15 17:36 file1.txt
-rwxrwxrwx    1 user1    manager     35812 Apr 15 17:36 file2.txt
-rwxr-----    1 user1    user1       48738 Apr 15 17:36 file3.txt
-rwxrwx---    1 root     root        23196 Apr 15 17:36 file4.txt
```

9.8.1   File Access Codes

The file access control string is 10 characters in length. The first character is the file type code, which determines how Linux will interpret the file such as ordinary data, a directory or a special file type (see table 9.13).

The remaining 9 characters represent the permissions (for example, rwxr-xr-x), which are broken into three groups of three characters. The first group controls the file owner's access to the file, the second controls the group's access to the file, and the third controls all other users' access to the file. This is often referred to as world permissions.

In each of the three groupings, the permission string determines the presence or absence of each of three types of access: read, write, and execute. The absence of the permission is denoted by a hyphen (-) in the permission string. The presence of the permission is indicated by a letter (r for read, w for write, and x for execute).

- **Read permission (r)**—For a file, the read permission enables you to read the file. For a directory, read permission allows the ls command to list the names of the files in the directory. You must also have execute permission for the directory name to use the –l option of the ls command or to change to that directory. It has a value of 4.
- **Write permission (w)**—For a file, the write permission means you can modify the file. For a directory, you can create or delete files inside that directory. It has a value of 2.
- **Execute permission (x)**—For a file, the execute file means that you can type the name of the file and execute it. For a directory, execute permission means that you can change to that directory (with the cd command). It has a value of 1.

You cannot view or copy the file unless you also have read permission. This means that files containing executable Linux commands, called shell scripts must be both executable and readable by the person executing them. Programs written in a compiled language such as C, however, can have only executable permissions, to protect them from being copied where they shouldn't be copied.

If you have the execute command and you do not have the read permission for the directory, you can change into the directory but ls –l will not work. You can list directories and files in that directory, but you cannot see additional information about the file or directory by just doing a ls –l command. This is a highly desirable characteristic for directories, so you'll almost never find a directory on which the execute bit is not set in conjunction with the read bit.

Directories can be confusing with respect to write permission. Recall that directories are files that are interpreted in a special way. As such, if a user can write to a directory, that user can create, delete, or rename files in the directory, even if the user isn't the owner of those files and does not have permission to write to those files.

Table 9.13   File Type Codes

Code	Meaning
-	Normal data file—It may be text, an executable program, graphics, compressed data, or just about any other type of data.
d	Directory—Disk directories are files just like any other, but they are marked as a directory and they contain filenames and pointers to disk inodes.
l	Symbolic link—The file contains the name of another file or directory. When Linux accesses the symbolic link, it tries to read the linked-to-file.
p	Named pipe—A pipe allows two running Linux programs to communicate with each other. One opens the pipe for reading, and the other opens it for writing, allowing data to be transferred between the programs.
s	Socket—A socket is similar to a named pipe, but it permits network and bidirectional links.
b	Block device—A hardware device to and from which data is transferred in blocks of more than 1 byte. Disk devices (hard disks, floppies, CD-ROMs, and so on) are common block devices.
c	Character device—a hardware device to and from which data is transferred in units of one byte. Examples include parallel and serial port devices.

Thus, the example of a permission string of rwxr-xr-x means that the file's owner, the file's group, and all other users can read and execute the file. Only the file's owner has write permission to the file. You can easily exclude those who don't belong to the file's group, or even all but the file's owner, by changing the permission string.

Individual permissions, such as execute access for the file's owner are often referred to as permission bits. This is because Linux encodes this information in binary form. Because it is binary, the permission information can be expressed as a single 9-bit number. This number is usually expressed in octal (base-8 form because a base-8 number is 3 bits in length, which means that the base-8 representation of a permission string is 3 digits long, 1 digit for each of the owner, group, and world permissions. The read, write, and execute permissions each correspond to one of these bits. The result is that you can determine owner, group, and world permissions by adding base-8 numbers, 1 for execute permission, 2 for write permission, and 4 for read permission. See table 9.14 for more examples.

Permissions								
Owner			**Group**			**World**		
r	w	x	r	w	x	r	w	x
4	2	1	4	2	1	4	2	1

Example 9.3:

If you give the owner of the file all rights (read, write, and execute, you give the group read and execute and you give everyone else no rights, the base-8 rights would be expressed as 750.

Permissions								
Owner			**Group**			**World**		
r	w	x	r	–	x	r	–	–
4	2	1	4	–	1	–	–	–
7			5			0		

Table 9.14   Example Permissions and Their Likely Uses

Permission String	Octal Code	Meaning
rwxrwxrwx	777	Read, write, and execute permissions for all users.
rwxr-xr-x	755	Read and execute permission for all users. The file's owner also has write permission.
rwxr-x---	750	Read and execute permission for the owner and group. The file's owner also has write permission. Nongroup members have no access to the file.
rwx------	700	Read, write, and execute for the file's owner only; all others have no access to the file.
rw-rw-rw-	666	Read and write permissions for all users. No execute permissions to anybody.
rw-rw-r--	664	Read and write permissions for all users. No execute permissions to anybody.
rw-rw----	660	Read and write permissions to the owner and group. No world permissions.
rw-r--r--	644	Read and write permissions to the owner. Read-only permission to all others.
rw-r----	640	Read and write permissions to the owner, and read-only permission to the group. No permission to others.
rw-------	600	Read and write permissions to the owner. No permission to anybody else.
r--------	400	Read permissions to the owner. No permission to anybody else.

Many of the permission rules do not apply to root. The superuser can read or write any file on the computer, even files that grant access to nobody (that is, those that have 000 permissions). The superuser still needs the execute bit to be set to run a program file, but the superuser has the power to change the permissions on any file, so this limitation isn't very substantial.

There are a few special permissions options that are also supported, and they may be indicated by changes to the permission string:

- **Set user ID (SUID)**—The set user ID (SUID) option is used in conjunction with executable files, and it tells Linux to run the program with the permissions who runs the program. For instance, if a file is owned by root and has its SUID bit set, the program runs with root privileges and can therefore read any file on the computer. Some servers and other system programs run in this way, which is often called SUID root.

  IMPORTANT NOTE: The SUID represent a security risk if they are not carefully controlled. SUID programs are indicated by an s in the owner's execute bit position of the permission string, as in `rwsr-xr-x`.

- **Set group ID (SGID)**—The set group ID (SGID) option is similar to the SUID option, but it sets the group of the running program to the group of the file. It's indicated by an s in the group execute bit position of the permission string, as in `rwxr-sr-x`.

  IMPORTANT NOTE: The SUID represent a security risk if they are not carefully controlled.

- **Sticky bit**—In modern Linux implementations, it is used to protect files from being deleted by those who don't own the files. When this bit is present on a directory, the directory's files can only be deleted by their owners, the directory's owner or root. The sticky bit is indicated by a t in the world execute bit position, as in `rwxr-xr-t`.

A file's owner and root are the only users who may adjust a file's permissions. Even if other users have write access to a directory in which a file resides and write access to the file itself, they may not change the file's permission (but they may modify or even delete the file). To understand why this is so, you need to know that the file permissions are stored as part of the file's inode, which isn't part of the directory entry. Read/write access to the directory entry, or even the file itself, doesn't give a user the right to change the inode structures (except indirectly—for instance, if a write changes the file's size or a file directory eliminates the need for the inode).

9.8.2   Setting Default Permissions

When a user creates a file, that file has default ownership and permissions. The default owner is, understandably, the user who creates the file. The default group is the primary group of the user that created the file. The default permissions, however, are configurable. These are defined by the usermask (umask), which is an octal file creation mask. The umask contains the bits that are off by default when a new file is created. This umask takes an input an octal value that represents the bits to be removed from 777 permissions for directories, or from 666 permissions for files. Note: you can not set the execute bit of a file with a usermask. The usermask is set by the umask command.

Example 9.4:

If you have an umask of 022 and you create a new file, the 022 will be subtracted from 666.

- Owner Permissions:
  - If you look at the first 6 of the 666 represents 42-, which represents RW permissions.
  - If you look at the 0 of the 022, you notice that 0 represents ---, which represents no permissions.
  - If you subtract the bit by bit, you get 4 - 0 = 4, 2 - 0 = 2 and 0 - 0 = 0 gives you a 6 for the resultant group permission.
- Group Permissions:
  - If you look at the second 6 of the 666 represents 42-, which represents RW permissions.
  - If you look at the first 2 of the 022, you notice that 2 represents -2-, which represents the write permissions.

- If you subtract the bit by bit, you get 4 - 0 = 4, 2 - 2 = 0 and 0 - 0 = 0 gives you a 4 for the resultant owner permission.
- World Permissions:
  - If you look at the last 6 of the 666 represents 42-, which represents RW permissions.
  - If you look at the second 2 of the 022, you notice that 2 represents -2-, which represents the write permissions.
  - If you subtract the bit by bit, you get 4 - 0 = 4, 2 - 2 = 0 and 0 - 0 = 0 gives you a 4 for the resultant owner permission.

All Permissions								
Owner			Group			World		
r	w	x	r	w	x	r	w	x
4	2	–	4	2	–	4	2	–
	6			6			6	

Unmask								
Owner			Group			World		
r	w	x	r	w	x	r	w	x
–	–	–	–	2	–	–	2	–
	0			2			2	

Resulting Permissions								
Owner			Group			World		
r	w	x	r	w	x	r	w	x
4	2	–	4	–	–	4	–	–
	6			4			4	

Therefore, with an umask of 022, any file created, the owner of the file will automatically have read and write permissions. The group that the file is assigned to will have the read permission and everyone else will have the read permission.

If you had an umask of 002, the owner and the group will have read and write permission, and everyone else will only have read permission.

Example 9.5:

Let's say that you want the owner to have the read and write permission, the group only to have read permission, and everyone else to have no permission, you would do the following:

- The read and write permission means that you don't want to shut off any of the permissions for the owner. Therefore, it will be represented by ---=0.
- The read permission for the file means that you want to shut off the write permission for the group. Therefore, –W–, represented by –2–=2.
- The no permissions for the file means that you want to shut off the read and write permission 42–=6.

Therefore, the umask should be 026. It would be set with the following command:

```
umask 026
```

To find what the current umask is, type umask alone, without any parameters. Typing umask -S produces the umask expressed symbolically, rather than in octal form. You may also specify an umask in this way when you want to change it, but in this case, you specify the bits that you do want set. For instance umask u=rwx, g=rx, o=rx is equivalent to umask 022.

Ordinary users can enter the umask command to change the permissions on new files they create. The superuser can also modify the default setting for all users by modifying a system configuration file. Typically, /etc/profile contains one or more umask commands. Setting the umask in /etc/profile might or might not actually have an effect, because it can be overridden at other points, such as user's own configuration files. Nonetheless, setting the umask in /etc/profile or other system files can be useful procedure if you want to change the default system policy. Most Linux distributions use a default umask of 002 or 022.

9.9   GROUP STRATEGIES

The traditional way of creating user accounts is that you create one or more groups in /etc/group and then assign one of these groups to be the primary group for each new user account that is added. For example, you may create one group for the accounting department, and a group for the information systems department in your organization. When you create accounts for new hires in the accounting department, each user account receives a unique user account, but the same group as the other accountants. Note that user accounts can belong to more than one group; the primary group for an account is simply the default group for that account.

The purpose of having groups is to allow users who are members of a particular group to share files. Typically, this is done by creating a directory and changing the group ownership of the directory to the group that is going to share files in the directory. For example, suppose you have a group set up for the users in the accounting department called accgrp, and you would like to create a shared called accshared under /home, you would do the following:

```
mkdir /home/accshared
chown nobody.accgrp /home/accshared
chmod 775 /home/accshared
```

Any user who is a member of the accgrp group can now create files in the /home/accshared directory.

9.9.1   User Private Group

Several problems can arise when sharing files. For example, suppose that a user, who happens to be a member of accgrp but whose primary group is something other than accgrp, creates a file in the /home/accshared directory. The user who created the file will be the owner of the file, and the group ownership of the file will be the user's primary group. Unless the user who created the file remembers to use the chgrp command on the file to set the ownership of the file to the accgrp group, other users in that group may not have the necessary permissions to access the file.

To solve this problem, Red Hat uses the user private group (UPG) scheme as the default behavior for creating accounts under Red Hat Linux. Every user has a primary group; the user is the only member of that group. The solution to this particular problem is to use something called the set group id bit or setgid bit. The setgid bit is applied to a directory with the chmod command. When the setgid bit is set for a directory, any files that are created in that directory automatically have their group ownership set to be that of the group owner for the directory. The command to set the setgid bit for the /home/accshared directory is:

```
chmod g+s /home/accshared
```

or, alternately

```
chmod 2775 /home/accshared
```

Setting the setgid bit solves the problem of making sure all files that are created in a shared directory belong to the correct group. The other problem that can arise has to do with permission settings. Typically, most users run with an umask setting of 022, which specifies that any files that they create are not modifiable by any account that is a member of the user's group or by anyone else on the system. If the user is creating a file in a shared directory and he or she wishes to allow others update access to the file, he or she will have to remember to issue a chmod command to make the file group writable. The way around this problem is to set the default umask (usually in /etc/profile) to be 002. With this umask, any files that are created will be modifiable by the user and any member of the group assigned the file.

At this point, you might think that with a umask of 002, anyone who is a member of that user's primary group will automatically have write access to any file that user creates in his or her home directory. But you must remember that the advantage behind the user private group scheme is since every user account is the only member in his or her private group, having the umask set to 002 has no effect on file security.

9.9.2   Project Groups

One approach to group configuration is to create separate groups for specific purposes or projects. As most companies have multiple projects, most employees work on just one product, and for security reasons, you don't want users working on one product to have access to information relating to the other two products. In such an environment, a Linux system may be well served by having three main user groups, one for each product. Most users will be members of precisely one group. If you configure the system with a umask that denies world access, those who don't belong to a specific product's group won't be able to read files realating to that product. You can set read or read/write group permission to allow group members to easily exchange files. Of course, individual users may use chmod to customize permissions on particular files and directories. If a user needs access to files associated with multiple products, you can assign that user to as many groups as are needed to accommodate the need. For instance, a supervisor might have access to all three groups.

9.9.3   Multiple Group Membership

On today's networks, you will find that many people will be members of multiple groups. This means that users will be able to do the following things:

- Read files belonging to any of the user's groups, provided that the file has group read permission.
- Write files belonging to any of the user's groups, provided that the file has group write permission.
- Run programs belonging to any of the user's group, provided that the file has group execute permission.
- Change the group ownership of any of the user's own files to any of the groups to which the user belongs.
- Use newgrp to make any of the groups to which the user belongs the user's primary group. Files created thereafter will have the selected group as the group owner.

Since you can only be logged in under one group at a time, when the user create files for another project that is not their primary group, he or she will become the owner of the file and his or her primary group will become the group owner of the file. Unless you can teach all of your users to use the newgrp command to temporarily change their primary group before creating such files or to use the chgrp command to change group ownership of a group (both of these tasks will be difficult for novice users), you are going to have problems.

Therefore, when having users assigned to several group members, it is extremely important to use user private groups. By using the UPG scheme, groups are automatically assigned to files created within that directory, which makes managing group projects that share a common directory very simple.

For example, let's say you have a big project called devel, with many people editing the devel files in the devel directory. Make a group called devel, chgrp the devel directory to devel group and add all of the devel users to the devel group. If you then set the setgid bit for the devel directory, all devel users will be able to edit the devel files and create new files in the devel directory. The files they create will always retain their devel group status, so other devel users will always be able to edit them.

If you have multiple projects like *devel* and users who are working on multiple projects, these users will never have to change their umask or group when they move from project to project. If set correctly, the setgid bit on each project's main directory "selects" the proper group for all files created in that directory.

9.10   NETWORK FILE SYSTEM

Security+ Objective 2.5.3—File sharing

Security+ Objective 3.5.3.7—File/Print Servers

Network File System (NFS) was developed by Sun Microsystems in the 1980s as a way for UNIX to share files and applications across the network. It allows you to attach a remote drive or directory to a virtual file system and work with it as if it were a local drive. NFS is available in UNIX, Linux, and through add-ons for Microsoft operating systems and Novell NetWare.

NFS is a stateless protocol, which means that each request made between the client and server is complete and does not require knowledge of prior transactions. This allows servers to go down and come back up without having to reboot the clients.

When a user accesses a NFS directory on another computer, the NFS access is handled by remote procedure calls (RPCs). RPCs are responsible for handling the requests between the client and server. Whenever a service wants to make itself available on a server, it needs to register itself with the RPC service manager, portmapper. Portmapper takes care of telling the client where the actual service is located on the server.

9.10.1   Configuring an NFS Server

The key configuration file for NFS on a NFS server is the /etc/exports file. The exports file specifies which directories are to be shared with which clients (hosts) and each client's access rights. Note: If you do not plan out your export rules well, the NFS can be a massive security hole. The /etc/exports file have the following format:

```
/directory_to_export  host1(permissions) host2(permissions)
host3(permissions)
# Comments
/another_directory_to_export  host1(permissions) host2(permissions)
```

The *directory_to_export* and *another_directory_to_export* are directories that you want to make available to other machines on your network. In these examples, you must supply the absolute pathname for this entry. On the same line, you then list which computers can access the specified directory. You can specify the the names of hosts in four ways:

- Their direct hostname.
- Using @*group*, where *group* is the specific netgroup. Wildcard hosts in the group are ignored.
- Wildcards in the hostname. The asterisk (*) can match an entire network. For example, *.animals. acme.com matches all hosts that end in animals.acme.com.
- IP subnets can be matched with address/netmask combinations. For example, to match everything in the 192.168.42.0 network where the netmask is 255.255.255.0, you use 192.168.42.0/24.

After the computers, you can specify the permissions. See table 9.15. If the list is longer than the line size permits, you can use the standard backslash (\) continuation character to continue on the next line. Some examples would be:

```
/export/data     daffy(rw,root_squash) bugs(rw,root_squash)
/export/reports  *.acme.com(rw,all_squash)
```

The first line creates an NFS statement that allows users from the machine daffy and bugs to mount the /export/data with read and write capability. But by using the root_squash option, root is automatically mapped to be an anonymous user called nobody, which effectively "squashes" the power of the remote root user to the lowest local user, preventing remote root users from acting as though they were the root user on the local system. The second line creates an NFS statement that allows anyone from the acme domain to NFS mount the /export/reports directory with read-write access. However, everyone who mounts this item is forced into anonymous user permissions.

Table 9.15   Access Options Commonly Used While Setting NFS Exports

Option	Purpose
all_squash	All visitors are set to be anonymous users.
insecure	No limits on which port NFS mounts can originate from.
noaccess	The visitor is not allowed to descend into subdirectories.
ro	The visitor is given read-only access.
root_squash	Accessing the mount as the user root is forcibly mapped to the user nobody for security reasons (default).
rw	The visitor is given full read-write access (default).
no_root_Squash	Acknowledge and trust the client's root account.
Secure	Requires all NFS mounts to originate from a port below 1024 (default)

It is considered a good convention to place all the directories you want to export in the /export directory. This makes the intent clear and self-documenting. If you need the directory to also exist elsewhere in the directory tree, use symbolic links. For examples, if your server is exporting its /usr/local directory, you should place the directory in /export, thereby creating /export/usr/local. Because the server will need access to the /export/usr/local directory, you should create a symbolic link from /usr/local that points to the real location, /export/usr/local.

Unfortunately, NFS is not a very secure method for sharing disks. Although taking some steps to protect yourself from hackers pretending to be common users provides a moderate level of security, there is not much more you can do. Any time you share a disk with another machine via NFS, you need to give the users of that machine (especially the root user) a certain amount of trust. If you believe that the person you are sharing the disk with is untrustworthy, you need to explore alternatives to NFS for sharing data and disk space. As always, stay up-to-date on the latest security bulletins coming from the Computer Emergency Response Team (www.cert.org) and keep up with all the patches from your distribution vendor.

After you set up your /etc/exports file, run the exportsfs command with the –r option:

```
exportsfs -r
```

This sends the appropriate signals to the rpc.nfsd and rpc.mountd daemons to reread the /etc/exports file and update their internal tables.

9.10.2   Mounting an NFS Drive or Directory

To mount an NFS drive or directory to your file system, you would use the mount command:

```
mount servername:/exported_dir /dir_to_mount
```

Servername is the name of the server from which you want to mount a filesystem. The *exported_dir* is the directory listed in its /etc/exports file on the specified server (*servername*) and /*dir_to_mount* is the location on your local machine where you want to mount the filesystem. For example, to mount the /export/home directory located on the server1 computer and you want to mount it as the /home directory, you would type in the following command:

```
mount server1:/export/home /home
```

Of course, the directory must exist in your local filesystem before anything can be mounted there.

You can pass options to the mount command. The most important characteristics are specified in the –o option. These options are listed in table 9.16. An example of these parameters in use would be:

```
mount -o rw,bg,intr, soft,retrans=6 server1:/export/home /home
```

Table 9.16   The –o Option Used with the Mount Command

Characteristics	Decription
rw	Read/write.
ro	Read-only.
bg	Background mount. Should the mount initially fail, such as when the server is down or the network connection is having problems, the mount place will place itself in the background and continue trying until it is successful. This is useful for filesystems mounted at boot time because it keeps the system from hanging at the mount if the server is down.
intr	Interruptible mount. If a process is pending I/O on a mounted partition, it will allow the process to be interrupted and the I/O call to be dropped.
soft	By default, NFS operations are hard, meaning that they require the server to acknowledge completion before returning to the calling process. The soft option allows the NFS client to return a failure to the calling process after retrans number of retries.
retrans	Specifies the maximum number of retried transmissions to a soft-mounted filesystem.
wsize	Specifies the number of bytes to be written across the network at once. The default is 8,192 (for example, wsize = 2,048). You shouldn't change this value unless you are sure of what you are doing. Setting this value too low or too high can have a negative impact on your system's performance.
rsize	Specifies the number of bytes to be read across the network at once. Like wsize, the default is 8,192 bytes. Setting this value too low or too high can have a negative impact on your system's performance.

To unmount the nfs mount, use the umount command:

```
umount /home
```

To mount each directory automatically during bootup, you can use add entries to the /etc/fstab file. These entries in the /etc/fstab file use the following format:

```
/dev/device /directory_to_mount  ftype parameters fs_freq fs_passno
```

The */dev/device* is the device to be mounted. The */directory_to_mount* is the location at which the filesystem should be mounted on your directory tree. The *ftype* represents the filesystem type. In these cases, the filesystem type should be nfs. The *parameters* are the same parameters that you passed to mount using the –o option. The *fs_freq* is used by dump to determine whether a filesystem needs to be dumped. The *fs_passno* is used by the fsck program to determine the order to check disks at boot time. The root filesystem should be set to 1 and other filesystems should have a 2. Filesystems on the same drive will be checked sequentially, but filesystems on different drives will be checked at the same time. An example would look like this:

```
server1:/usr/local/pub  /pub  nfs resize=8192,wsize=8192,timeo=
14,intr
```

If you need to mount a new filesystem while the machine is live, you must perform the mount by using the mount command at the command prompt. If you want to mount this automatically the next time the system is rebooted, you would add it to the fstab file.

9.10.3 Securing NFS

Security+ Objective 2.5.4—Vulnerabilities

Security+ Objective 2.5.4.1—Packet Sniffing

It has already been mentioned that NFS is not a very secure solution for sharing files and if you had a choice between NFS or using NetBIOS shares via Samba, you should use NetBIOS shares so that your directories and files will be more secure. Samba is explained in the next section. Yet, if you have to use NFS, like NetBIOS shares, you can block TCP/UDP port 2049 so that no one from outside your network can access the NFS shares. In addition, it is recommended to use strong authentication and encryption using IPSec or a VPN.

9.11 SAMBA

Security+ Objective 2.5.3—File sharing

Security+ Objective 3.5.3.7—File/Print Servers

Samba used in Linux uses the Common Internet File System (CIFS), which is basically an updated SMB protocol to provide file sharing and print sharing among Linux and Microsoft computers. Samba needs two daemons to operate. The smbd daemon provides the file and print services to SMB clients by using port 139 and the nmbd daemon provides NetBIOS nameserving and browsing support by using port 137. You can also run nmbd interactively to query other name service daemons. Smbd and nmbd are located in the /usr/sbin directory.

Before you start configuring Samba, you should make sure that the smb is automatically loaded during boot. Again, use the Linuxconf, ntsysv or similar utility to activate the smb daemon for Runlevel 3 and 5.

Samba uses the following programs:

- The SMB client program (smbclient) implements a simple FTP-like client on a Linux computer.
- The SMB mounting program (smbmount) enables mounting of server directories on a Linux machine.
- The testparm utility allows you to test your smb.conf configuration file for proper syntax.
- The smbstatus utility tells you who is currently using the smbd server.

All of these are located in the /usr/bin directory.

Samba Web Page

http://www.samba.org/
http://us1.samba.org/samba/samba.html

Samba Documentation

http://us1.samba.org/samba/docs/

Samba HOWTO Documentation

http://us1.samba.org/samba/docs/Samba-HOWTO-Collection.html
http://us1.samba.org/samba/docs/Samba-HOWTO-Collection.pdf

9.11.1 SWAT

The easiest way to configure Samba is to use the Samba Web Administration Tool (SWAT), which uses a browser interface. What makes SWAT a little different from other browser-based administration tools is that SWAT does not rely on a Web server like Apache.

If you have Red Hat 7.0 or higher, SWAT is disabled by default. To enable it you need to do the following:

1. Verify the /etc/services contains the following line:

   ```
   swat        901/tcp
   ```

2. Comment out the following line in the /etc/xinetd.d/swat file by adding a pound sign (#) before it:

   ```
   disable = yes
   ```

3. You can then restart samba by typing in the following command

   ```
   /etc/rc.d/init.d/smb restart
   ```

For Red Hat Linux 7.0 or higher, you can start Samba in one of two ways:

1. If you are using the GNOME desktop, you can open the main menu, select Programs, select System and select Samba Configuration.
2. Open an Internet browser such as Netscape Navigator and type in the

   ```
   http://127.0.0.1:901 URL.
   ```

A dialog box will appear asking for a user ID and password. You have to be root in order to configure Samba, so enter root as the user ID and the password for root.

When the main SWAT screen appears, you will first configure the [globals] section by clicking on the Global icon button at the top of the screen. The values shown are being read from the smb.conf file (the SWAT configuration file) that already exists on the system. After you have entered the appropriate values for your system, click the Commit Changes button to save them to the file.

Next, you will create shares by clicking on the Shares icon. This will open the Share Parameters page as shown in figure 9.14. To create a new share, fill in a name for the share and click the Create Share button. An expanded Share Parameters page will appear. You then enter the appropriate information and click Commit Changes to save them to the smb.conf file.

The Status page can be used to verify if smbd and nmbd daemons are running. You can then start, stop, or restart these daemons by clicking on the start/stop, buttons or the restart button. See figure 9.15.

Figure 9.14   Configuring a Share Using Samba html Page

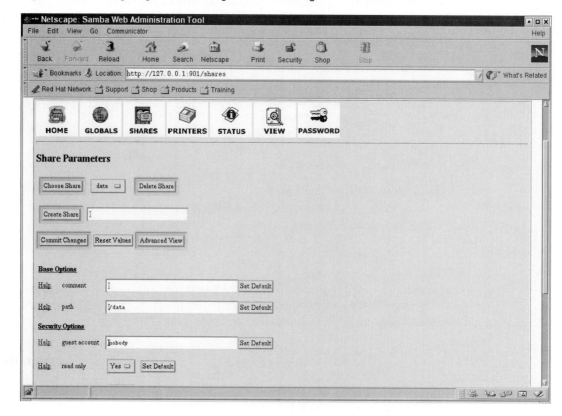

Figure 9.15   The Samba html Pages Can Also Show the Status of Samba

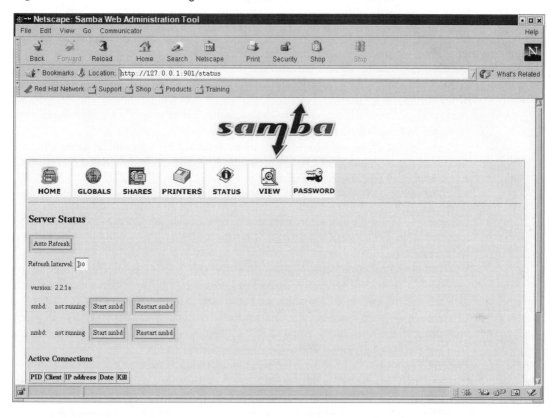

9.11.2   Accessing a Samba Share

Samba shares can be accessed by SMB clients on Windows and Linux platforms. Linux access is via the smbmount command. The smbmount command allows you to mount a smb share. Smbclient provides command-line options to query a server for the shared directories available or to exchange files. To list all of the available shares on the machine with an IP address of 192.168.100.1:

```
smbclient -NL 192.168.100.1
```

Any name resolving to the IP address can be substituted for the IP address. The -N parameter tells smbclent not to query for a password if one isn't needed, and the -L parameter requests the list.

Most of the time, you will most likely use the smbmount command which enables you to mount a Samba share to a local directory. To create a /mnt/test directory on your local workstation, you would run the following command:

```
mount -t smbfs //192.168.100.1/homes /mnt/test -o username=
pregan,dmask=777,fmask=777
```

This command is a smbmount command, even though it looks like an ordinary mount command. The -t smbfs tells the mount command to call smbmount to do the work. The preceding command grants all rights to anyone, via the directory mask (dmask) and the file mask (fmask) arguments.

Another way to do the same command is:

```
smbmount //192.168.100.1/homes /mnt/test -o username=pregan,
dmask=777,fmask=777
```

To unmount it, simply run the following command as user root:

```
umount /mnt/test
```

You can also use smbmount to mount shared Windows resources on a Linux computer. The following mounts Windows share called sharedirectory to the Linux directory /mnt/test directory:

```
mount -t smbfs //computername/sharedirectory /mnt/test
```

This must be done as root. You will be asked for a password. If Windows is in share mode, you would input the password of the share. If you mounting a user share, use the -U option followed by a valid username on the Windows computer. Of course, the user must have rights to the share and the /mnt/test directory must exist.

9.11.3   Using Smpasswd

If the security is set to user, it enforces security by user and password. The Smbpasswd is the Samba encrypted password file that contains the username, Linux user ID, the SMB hashed passwords of the user, account flag information and the time the password was last changed.

The format of the smbpasswd file used by Samba 2.2 is very similar to the Unix passwd file. It is an ASCII file containing one line for each user. Each field within each line is separated from the next by a colon. Any entry beginning with the pound symbol (#) is ignored.

The smbpasswd file contains the following information for each user:

- **name**—This is the user name. It must be a name that already exists in the standard UNIX passwd file.
- **uid**—This is the UNIX uid. It must match the uid field for the same user entry in the standard UNIX passwd file.
- **Lanman Password Hash**—This is the LANMAN hash of the user's password, encoded as 32 hex digits. The LANMAN hash is created by DES encrypting a well known string with the user's password as the DES key. This is the same password used by Windows 95/98 machines. If the user has a null password this field will contain the characters "NO PASSWORD" as the start of the hex string. If the hex string is equal to 32 'X' characters then the user's account is marked as disabled and the user will not be able to log onto the Samba server.
- **NT Password Hash**—This is the Windows NT hash of the user's password, encoded as 32 hex digits. The Windows NT hash is created by taking the user's password as represented in 16-bit, little-endian UNICODE and then applying the MD4 (internet rfc1321) hashing algorithm to it. This password hash is considered more secure than the LANMAN Password Hash as it preserves the case of the password and uses a much higher quality hashing algorithm.
- **Account Flags**—This section contains flags that describe the attributes of the users account. In the Samba 2.2 release this field is bracketed by '[' and ']' characters and is always 13 characters in length (including the '[' and ']' characters). The contents of this field may be any of the characters.
  - **U**—This means this is a "User" account, i.e., an ordinary user. Only User and Workstation Trust accounts are currently supported in the smbpasswd file.
  - **N**—This means the account has no password (the passwords in the fields LANMAN Password Hash and NT Password Hash are ignored). Note that this will only allow users to log on with no password if the null passwords parameter is set in the smb.conf config file.
  - **D**—This means the account is disabled and no SMB/CIFS logins will be allowed for this user.
  - **W**—This means this account is a "Workstation Trust" account. This kind of account is used in the Samba PDC code stream to allow Windows NT Workstations and Servers to join a Domain hosted by a Samba PDC.
  - Other flags may be added as the code is extended in future. The rest of this field space is filled in with spaces.
- **Last Change Time**—This field consists of the time the account was last modified. It consists of the characters 'LCT-' (standing for "Last Change Time") followed by a numeric encoding of the UNIX time in seconds since the epoch (1970) that the last change was made.

When you make changes to the smbpasswd file, you will typically use the smbpasswd command.

```
smbpasswd [options] [username] [password]
```

See table 9.17.

To add users, you would, type the following:

```
smbpasswd -a username
```

You will then be asked to specify the password for the new user.

Table 9.17   Smbpasswd Options

Options	Description
-a	add user
-x	delete user
-d	disable user
-e	enable user
-n	set no password
-r *remote_machine_name*	Allows a user to specify what machine they wish to change their password on. Without this parameter smbpasswd defaults to the local host. The `remote_machine_name` is the NetBIOS name of the SMB/CIFS server to contact to attempt the password change.
-U username	This option may only be used in conjunction with the `-r` option. When changing a password on a remote machine it allows the user to specify the user name on that machine whose password will be changed. It is present to allow users who have different user names on different systems to change these passwords.
-R *name_resolve_order*	This option allows the user of smbpasswd to determine what name resolution services to use when looking up the NetBIOS name of the host being connected to. • lmhosts—Lookup an IP address in the Samba lmhosts file. • host—Do a standard host name to IP address resolution, using the system /etc/hosts, NIS, or DNS lookups. • wins—Query a name with the IP address listed in the wins server parameter. If no WINS server has been specified this method will be ignored. • bcast—Do a broadcast on each of the known local interfaces listed in the interfaces parameter. This is the least reliable of the name resolution methods as it depends on the target host being on a locally connected subnet. The default order is lmhosts, host, wins, bcast and without this parameter or any entry in the smb.conf file the name resolution methods will be attempted in this order.

Smbpasswd also allows a user to change their encrypted smb password. Ordinary users can only run the command with no options. It will prompt them for their old smb password and then ask them for their new password twice, to ensure that the new password was typed correctly. No passwords will be echoed on the screen while being typed. If you are the root, you can change other people's password by typing:

```
smbpasswd username
```

WHAT YOU NEED TO KNOW

Security+ **Objective 2.5.3**—File sharing

Security+ **Objective 3.5.3.7**—File/Print Servers

1. File and Print Sharing for Microsoft networks gives you the ability to share your files or printers with Windows computers using the SMB/CIFS protocol.

2. Samba allows UNIX and Linux computers to access and provide Microsoft's shares based on the SMB/CIFS protocol.

3. If you enabled file sharing, you can share any drive or directory by right-clicking the drive or directory and selecting the Sharing option from the File menu or by selecting the Sharing option from the

shortcut menu of the drive or directory. You would then provide a Share Name, the name seen by other clients and type of access that users can have.

4. A shared drive and directory will be indicated with a hand under the drive or directory.

5. To control how users gain access to a shared folder, you assign shared folder permissions.

6. To grant or change share permissions to a shared folder, you would right-click the shared folder or drive, select the Sharing option and click on the Permissions button.

7. When accessing a shared folder on an NTFS volume, the effective permissions that a person can do in the share folder is calculated by combining the shared folder permissions and the NTFS permissions.

8. When combining the two, you first determine the cumulative NTFS permissions and the cumulative shared permissions and apply the more restrictive permission or the permissions that gives the person the lesser permissions.

9. An administrative share is a shared folder typically used for administrative purposes.

10. To make a shared folder or drive into an administrative share, the share name must have a $ at the end of it.

11. Since the administrative share folder or drive cannot be seen during browsing, you would have to use a UNC name, which include the share name (including the $). Instead, it would have to be accessed using the Start button, selecting the Run option and typing the UNC name and clicking the OK button.

12. By default, all volumes with drive letters automatically have administrative shares (C$, D$, E$, and so on).

13. Share permissions are the only protection for FAT and FAT32 drives.

14. Unfortunately, share permissions only protect the network resource when you connect to the computer using a network connection.

15. Network File System (NFS) was developed by Sun Microsystems in the 1980s as a way for UNIX to share files and applications across the network.

16. NFS allows you to attach a remote drive or directory to a virtual file system and work with it as if it were a local drive.

17. NFS is available in UNIX, Linux and through add-ons for Microsoft operating systems and Novell NetWare.

Security+ Objective 2.5.4—Vulnerabilities

Security+ Objective 2.5.4.1—Packet Sniffing

1. Any time you share drives or directories, the shared drives and directories become targets of an attacker.

2. Therefore, they will attempt to make unauthorized connections to shared resources on the network, access shared drives and directories that do not have the permissions configured incorrectly and by packet sniffing.

3. To help secure these shares, you can first block access to the shares at the firewall so that no can access them from the outside of your network. You should therefore block TCP/UDP ports 137, 138, and 139.

4. You should use the highest security and authentication available and you need to verify share permissions.

5. Remember to use the rule of least privilege to secure your shares. Therefore, you would typically remove the everyone from the shared permissions and assign the appropriate user and group names with only the necessary permissions.

6. You can also use IPSec or VPNs to encrypt communications between clients and servers.

7. NFS is not a very secure solution for sharing files and if you had a choice between NFS or using NetBIOS shares via Samba, you should use NetBIOS shares so that your directories and files will be more secure.

8. If you have to use NFS, like NetBIOS shares, you can block TCP/UDP port 2049 so that no one from outside your network can access the NFS shares. In addition, it is recommended to use strong authentication and encryption using IPSec or a VPN.

QUESTIONS

1. What is one advantage if the NTFS file system over the FAT16 and FAT32 file systems?
   a. Integral support for streaming audio files
   b. Integral support for UNIX compatibility
   c. Integral support for dual-booting with Red Hat Linux
   d. Integral support for file and folder level permissions

2. Which of the following Microsoft files systems supports file level security?
   a. FAT32   b. NTFS
   c. FAT12   d. FAT16

3. Which of the following are features of the NTFS file system on Windows 2000?
   a. Support for on-disk compression
   b. Support for file and folder-level security
   c. Support for disk quotas
   d. Support for on-disk file encryption

4. You have just modified the permissions on an NTFS folder. By default, which permissions will be changed?
   a. The permissions on the folder and files in the folder, but not subfolders
   b. The permissions on the folder only

c. The permissions on the folder, files, and subfolders

d. The permissions on the folder and subfolders but not on any files

5. Pat is about to access a Word document from a shared folder in another domain that belongs to the same forest. The folder's share name is FI-NANCE. The Domain Accountants group of the trusted domain has Change permission to the folder and its Word document files. The folder is stored on an NTFS partition. Pat's user account only has Read permission for the FINANCE share, and the Accountants group has Full Control permission for the FINANCE share. Assuming Pat is not logging on locally to the server containing the Word document files, what will be his level of access?

   a. No Access   b. Read

   c. Change   d. Full Control

6. A Windows 2000 Server contains a shared folder on an NTFS partition. Which of the following statements concerning access to the folder is correct?

   a. A user accessing the folder remotely has the same or more restrictive access permissions than if he or she accesses the folder locally.

   b. A user accessing the folder remotely has less restrictive access permissions than if he or she accesses the folder locally.

   c. A user accessing the folder remotely has the same access permissions as when accessing the folder locally.

   d. A user accessing the folder remotely has more restrictive access permissions than if he or she accesses the folder locally.

7. Pat is a member of the Manager group. There is a shared folder called DATA on an NTFS partition on a remote server. Pat is given the write NTFS permission, the Manager group is given the Read and Execute NTFS permissions and the Everyone has the Read NTFS permission to the DATA folder. In addition, Pat, Manager and Everyone are assigned the shared Change permission to the DATA folder. When Pat logs on his client computer and access the DATA folder, what would Pat's permissions be? (Choose all that apply)

   a. Read the files in the folder

   b. Write to the files in the folder

   c. Execute the files in the folder

   d. Delete the files in the folder

   e. Have no access to the files in the folder

8. Pat is a member of the Manager group. There is a shared folder called DATA on an NTFS partition on a remote server. Pat is given the write NTFS permission, the Manager group is given the Deny all NTFS permissions and the Everyone group has the Read NTFS permission to the DATA folder. In addition, Pat and Everyone is assigned

the shared Change permission to the DATA folder and the Manager group is assigned the Full Control shared permission. When Pat logs on his client computer and accesses the DATA folder, what would Pat's permissions be? (Choose all that apply)

   a. Read the files in the folder

   b. Write to the files in the folder

   c. Execute the files in the folder

   d. Delete the files in the folder

   e. Have no access to the files in the folder

9. Your company, the Acme Corporation, has a human resources (HR) manager named Pat. He keeps the confidential HR files in a shared folder. To increase the security of the HR files, Pat set the folder to encrypt the files. Pat leaves the company without resetting the permissions and encryption settings for the HR files. The files must be made accessible to the new HR manager. Which two actions should you take to allow this access? (Choose two)

   a. Select the file permissions on the HR files to allow access to the new manager.

   b. Back up the shared folder to tape and restore the files to a different folder.

   c. Log on as an administrator and remove the encryption attribute from the HR files.

   d. Log on the new manager, connect to the shared folder, and run the cipher/e/s*.* command.

   e. Configure the new manager's account to be an Encrypted Date Recovery Agent for Pat's account.

10. You are the administrator of your company's network. Your network has 200 Windows 2000 Professional computers and 15 Windows 2000 Server computers. Users on the network save their work files in home folders on a network server. The NTFS partition that contains the home folders has Encrypting File System (EFS) enabled. A user named Pat leaves the company. You move all of the files from Pat's home folder to his manager's folder. When the manager attempts to open any of the files, she receives the following error message; "Access denied." You want the manager to be able to access the files. What should you do?

   a. Grant the manager NTFS Full control permission to the files.

   b. Grant the manager NTFS Take Ownership permission to the files.

   c. Log on to the network as a Recovery Agent. Decrypt the files for the manager.

   d. Log on to the network as a member of the Backup Operators Group. Decrypt the files for the manager.

11. In Linux, which command is used to add the read permission to the file yourfile.txt?

   a. chmod   b. chgrp

   c. chown   d. chedit

12. In Linux, which of the following umask values will result in files with rw-r----- permissions?
    - a. 640
    - b. 210
    - c. 022
    - d. 027

13. In Linux, which file permission allows only the user and members of the user's group to change or erase a file, while allowing everyone to read it?
    - a. -rw--r-rw-
    - b. -r-xr-xr--
    - c. -rw-rw-r--
    - d. -r--rw-rw-

14. In Linux, what permission is needed to delete a file?
    - a. The w permission for the file
    - b. The x permission for the file
    - c. The w permission for the directory that the file is in
    - d. The x permission for the directory that the file is in.

15. In Linux, what permission is needed to view a directory listing?
    - a. The r permission on the files in the directory
    - b. The x permission on the files in the directory
    - c. The r permission on the directory
    - d. The x permission on the directory

16. In Linux, what is the octal representation of the permission rw-r--r--?
    - a. 322
    - b. 422
    - c. 741
    - d. 644

17. What must a Linux computer run in order to access network resources in a Windows networking environment that uses WINS?
    - a. NFS
    - b. NIS
    - c. Samba
    - d. Apache

18. Which file sharing protocol also handles print sharing?
    - a. SMB/CIFS
    - b. NFS
    - c. FTP
    - d. HTTP

19. Which of the following file systems are supported by Windows 2000? (Choose three)
    - a. NFS
    - b. FSN
    - c. NTFS
    - d. HPFS
    - e. CDFS
    - f. FAT32

20. Which file system supports encryption on Windows 2000?
    - a. NTFS
    - b. CDFS
    - c. FAT16
    - d. FAT32

HANDS-ON EXERCISES

Exercise 1: Understanding NTFS Rights in Windows

1. Delete the M drive and create a new FAT32 volume. Assign the M drive.
2. On your C drive (which should be NTFS volume) create a folder called DIRN1.
3. In the DIRN1 folder, create a DIR2 folder.
4. In the DIRN2 folder, create a DIR3 folder.
5. In the DIRN3 folder, create a text file called FILE1.TXT. To create a text file, open the DIRN3 folder and right-click the empty space and select New Text file. In the FILE1.TXT file, put in your first name.
6. Right-click the DIRN1 folder and select the Properties option. Click on the Security tab.
7. Click on the Add button. Pick Charlie Brown and click on the Add button. Click on the OK button.
8. Logout as Administrator and login as Charlie Brown.
9. Try to open the FILE1.TXT file.
10. Try to add your last name to the FILE1.TXT file, save the changes and exit the program.
11. Try to delete the FILE1.TXT file and try to delete the DIRN2 folder.
12. Try to create a new text file called FILE2.TXT in the DIR1 folder.
13. Logout as Charlie Brown and login as the Administrator.
14. Right-click the DIRN1 folder and click the Properties options.
15. From the Security tab, click to highlight Charlie Brown. Give Charlie Brown the Write right.
16. Try to open the FILE1.TXT file.
17. Try to add your last name to the FILE1.TXT file, save the changes and exit the program.
18. Try to delete the FILE1.TXT file and try to delete the DIRN2 folder.
19. Try to create a new text file called FILE2.TXT in the DIR1 folder.
20. Log out as Charlie Brown and login as Administrator
21. For the DIRN1 folder, assign the Modify right also to Charlie Brown.
22. Try to open the FILE1.TXT file.

23. Try to add your last name to the FILE1.TXT file, save the changes and exit the program.
24. Try to delete the FILE1.TXT file and try to delete the DIRN2 folder.
25. Try to create a new text file called FILE2.TXT in the DIR1 folder.
26. Log out as Charlie Brown and login as Administrator
27. In the DIRN1 folder, recreate the DIRN2 folder. In the DIRN2 folder, recreate the DIRN3 folder. In the DIRN3 folder, recreate the FILE1.TXT file.
28. Right-click the DIRN2 and select the Properties option. From the Security tab, specify Charlie Brown to have the Read permission.
29. Log out as the Administrator and login as Charlie Brown.
30. Open the FILE1.TXT file and try to add your last name to it. Again try to save it.

Exercise 2: Share Rights in Windows

1. Log in as Administrator.
2. In the M drive, create a folder called DIRS1.
3. In the DIRS1 folder, create a folder called DIRS2 folder.
4. In the DIRS2 folder, create a text file called FILE1.TXT, with your first name listed in the file.
5. Right-click the DIRS1 folder, and select the Sharing option.
6. Click the Share this folder option. Keep the default share name, click on the Permissions button to set the Share rights.
7. With the Everyone account highlighted, click on the Remove button.
8. Click on the Add button and add Charlie Brown.
9. For Charlie Brown share rights, assign only the Read permission. Click on the OK button.
10. From your partners computer, log in as Charlie Brown, and access the DIRS1 share through the My Network Places.
11. Close the DIRS1.
12. Click on the Start button, select the Run option, and execute \\SERVER2000-XXx\DIRS1.
13. Try to open the FILE1.TXT file.
14. Try to add your last name to the FILE1.TXT file, save the changes, and exit the program.
15. Try to delete the FILE1.TXT file.
16. Try to create a new text file called FILE2.TXT in the DIR1 folder.
17. As the Administrator back at your own computer, change the share rights to include Read and Change permissions for Charlie Brown.
18. From your partners computer, try to open the FILE1.TXT file.
19. Try to add your last name to the FILE1.TXT file, save the changes, and exit the program.
20. Try to delete the FILE1.TXT file.
21. Try to create a new text file called FILE2.TXT in the DIR1 folder.
22. As the Administrator back at your own computer, change the rights to Deny all rights for Charlie Brown.
23. From your partners computer, try to access the shared folder.
24. Back at your own computer, log out as the administrator, and log in as Charlie Brown.
25. Try to delete the FILE2.TXT file. Try to figure out why Charlie Brown was able to delete the folder.

Exercise 3: File Encryption

1. Log in as Charlie Brown.
2. In the C: drive, create a folder called Encrypted.
3. In the Encrypted folder, create a text file with your first and last name in the file.
4. Right-click the Encrypted folder in the C: drive and select the Properties option.
5. Click on the Advanced button. Select the Encrypt contents to secure data option and click on the OK button.
6. Click on the OK button to close the Uncompressed properties dialog box. Select the Apply Changes to this folder, subfolders, and files. Click on the OK button.
7. Log out as Charlie Brown and login as the Administrator.
8. Try to access the text file in the Encrypted folder.

Exercise 4: Groups and Permissions

1. Log in as the Administrator. Make sure that Charlie Brown is a member of the Sales group.
2. In the C: drive, create a folder called GROUP1.
3. In the GROUP1 folder, create a GROUP2 folder.

4. In the GROUP2 folder, create a new text file with your name in it.
5. Assign the NTFS Read and Execute and List Folder Contents to the Sales group for the GROUP1 folder.
6. Assign the NTFS Modify to Charlie Brown for the GROUP1 folder.
7. Assign the NTFS List Folder Contents to Everyone for the GROUP1 folder.
8. Right-click the text file and select the Properties option. Click on the Permissions tab. Notice the rights assigned to Charlie Brown. Of those rights, you should notice which ones are grayed out.
9. Assign Full Control to Charlie Brown for the GROUP1 folder.
10. Assign Full Control to Sales for the GROUP1 folder.
11. Deny all rights to Everyone for the GROUP1 folder.
12. Share the GROUP1 folder, and assign full control share permissions to Charlie Brown, Sales group, and Everyone.
13. From your partner's computer, log in as Charlie Brown and try to access the text file.
14. Back on your own computer, log out as administrator and log in as Charlie Brown. See if you can access the text file in the GROUP2 folder.
15. Log out as Charlie Brown and login as the administrator.
16. Remove Everyone from the NTFS permissions for the GROUP1 folder.
17. Log out as the administrator and log in as Charlie brown. Try to access the text file.
18. Back on your partner's computer, logged in as Charlie Brown, try to access the text file.

Exercise 5:Working with File Permissions

1. Create a user2 account.
2. Create a group2 group.
3. Assign user2 to group2.
4. If you don't already have one, create a /data directory.
5. Change into the /data directory.
6. Create three text files called file10.txt, file20.txt and file30.txt with your name in them.
7. Use the `ls -l` command and record the permissions.
8. Change to the 2nd virtual console.
9. Log in as user2.
10. Change into the data directory.
11. View the contents of the file10.txt by using the cat command.
12. Try to add your age to the file10.txt file.
13. Try to delete the file10.txt file using the rm command.
14. Change back to the 1st virtual console.
15. Assuming that you are still in the /data directory, to change owner of the files to user2 and group2, type the following command:

    ```
    chown user2.group2 *
    ```

16. Change to the 2nd virtual console.
17. View the contents of the file10.txt by using the cat command.
18. Try to delete the file.
19. Change back to the 1st virtual console.
20. Change the permissions by typing the following command:

    ```
    chmod 660 file20.txt
    ```

21. Use the `ls -l` command to view the permissions.
22. Change back to the 2nd virtual console.
23. Open the file20.txt file and add your age to the file. Save the file.
24. Try to delete the file. Remember that to delete a file, you must have the write permission for the directory that the file is in.
25. Change back to the 1st virtual console.
26. Change to the root directory. Execute the following command to directory permissions:

    ```
    chmod 660 data
    ```

27. Change back to the 2nd virtual console.
28. Try to perform a listing of the data directory. Remember, that for you to see a directory listing, you must have the execute permission for the directory.
29. Change back to the 1st virtual console.
30. Change the permissions for the data directory.

    ```
    chmod 770 data
    ```

31. Perform a directory listing for the /data directory.
32. Delete the file10.txt.

33. Change back to the 1st virtual console.
34. At the command prompt, type in the following command to view the current umask:

    umask

35. To change the umask, type the following command:

    umask 007

36. To create an empty text file called file40.txt, type the following command.

    touch file40.txt

37. Use the ls –l command to view the permissions.

Exercise 6: Setting up a Samba Share

On Your Computer

1. If you don't already have a /data directory, create it.
2. Create a text file called name.txt in the /data directory with your name in the file and "samba share - /data directory."
3. Make sure that the data directory has the read, write and execute permissions by using the following command:

    chmod 777 /data

4. Make sure that the files in the directory have the read, write and execute permissions by using the following command:

    chmod 777 /data/*

5. Use Linuxconf or ntsysv or similar utility to activate the smb daemon for Runlevel 3 and 5.
6. Open the /etc/xinetd.d/swat file and comment out the following line:

    disable = yes

    Save the changes.

7. To restart the xinetd.d so that the changes can be read for the swat file, run the following command:

    service xinetd restart

8. To start Samba, type in the following command:

    /etc/rc.d/init.d/smb start

9. Start X Window. Open an Internet browser such as Netscape Navigator and enter the following URL:

    http://127.0.0.1:901

    Login as root.

10. Click on the Status option at the top of the web page. Notice if the smbd and nmbd daemons are running. If they are not, start them.
11. Click on the View option to view your smb.conf file.
12. Click on the Globals option.
13. Make sure that your workgroup is GROUPXXX.
14. For your Netbios name, be sure it is host*XXX-YY* where as *XXX* is your room number and *YY* is your computer number. If you are not in a class room, use host1-1 and your partner/2nd computer should be host1-2.
15. Currently, the security is set to user. Click on the Security help hyperlink. If you want to mainly setup shares without passwords, what options would you select? _____
16. Close the help window. For the security option, change it to share.
17. Click on the update encrypted help hyperlink. For the best security, should this be set to yes or no? _____
18. Close the help window.
19. Set the encrypt password to yes.
20. Click on the Commit changes button.
21. Click on the shares option at the top of the screen.
22. In the create share text box, type data and click on the create share button.
23. In the path text box, specify the /data directory.
24. Make sure that the Read-only option is set to yes and that the guest OK option is set to yes.
25. At the top of the screen, click on the Commit Changes button.
26. Open a terminal window and execute the following command:

    smbclient -NL your_IP_Address

On Your Partner's Computer

27. Create a /mnt/sambaremote directory.

28. Execute the following command:

    ```
    chmod 775 /mnt/sambaremote
    ```

29. Execute the following command for your computer:

    ```
    smbclient -NL your_IP_Address
    ```

30. Execute the following command:

    ```
    smbclient //your_IP_address/data
    ```

    When it is asked for a password, just press enter.
31. At the smb prompt, execute the ls command.
32. At the smb prompt, execute the following command:

    ```
    get name.txt
    ```

33. At the smb prompt, execute the `exit` command.
34. At the command prompt, execute the following command:

    ```
    mount -t smbfs //your_IP_address/data /mnt/sambaremote
    ```

    When it is asked, just press enter.
35. Change to the /mnt/sambaremote directory.
36. Perform the ls command.
37. Try to delete the file.
38. Unmount the /mnt/sambaremote directory.

On Your Computer

39. Open the data share using SWAT.
40. Change the guest OK option to No.
41. Commit the changes.
42. At the command prompt, execute the following command:

    ```
    smbpasswd -a user1
    ```

    Enter `password` for the password.

On Your Partner's Computer

43. Perform the following command:

    ```
    smbmount //your_IP_address/data /mnt/sambaremote -o U=user1
    ```

    Provide the appropriate password
44. Open the name.txt file in the share, add your age to the file and try to save the changes.
45. Try to delete the file.

On Your Computer

46. Open the data share using SWAT.
47. Change the Read-Only option to no.
48. Commit the changes.

On Your Partner's Computer

49. Perform the following command:

    ```
    smbmount //your_IP_address/data /mnt/sambaremote -o username=user1,
    dmask=777,fmask=777
    ```

50. Open the name.txt file in the share, add your age to the file and save the changes.
51. Delete the file.
52. Open the /etc/fstab file and add the following line:

    ```
    //Your_IP_Address/data /mnt/sambaremote smb  username=user1,password=
    password  1 2
    ```

## CHAPTER 10

Application Security

Topics Covered in this Chapter

Introduction

The primary purpose of a server is to provide services. Typically, these services are provided through applications. For example, when you access a web server, an application or program running on the server provides the web pages. To keep your server running and to keep the content of the server safe, you must secure these applications.

Objectives

10.1 INTRODUCTION TO DOMAIN NAMING SYSTEM (DNS) NAME RESOLUTION

Security+ Objective 3.5.3.5—DNS Servers

There are two services that can be used to find and provide IP addresses. If a computer knows the destination's NetBIOS name, it can send the NetBIOS name to the WINS service and the WINS service will send back the corresponding IP address of the destination. If a computer knows the fully qualified domain names (FQDN), it can send that to a DNS service and the DNS service will return the corresponding IP address. Most modern OS's and programs can use FQDNs.

Domain Name System (DNS) is a hierarchical client/server-based distributed database management system that translates Internet domain names such as MICROSOFT.COM to an IP address. As mentioned in previous chapters, it is used because domain names are easier to remember than IP addresses. The DNS clients are called **resolvers** and the DNS servers are called **name servers.**

The DNS system can be thought of as its own little network. If one DNS server doesn't know how to translate a particular domain name, it will ask another DNS server. DNS is most commonly associated with the Internet, but private networks can also use DNS to resolve computer names and to locate computers within their local networks without being connected to the Internet.

The most popular implementation of the DNS protocol is the Berkeley Internet Name Domain (BIND), which was developed for the UC Berkeley's BSD UNIX operating system. The primary specifications for DNS are defined in Requests for Comments (RFC) 1034 and 1035. DNS uses either UDP port 53 or TCP port 53 as the underlying protocol. Windows NT Family Servers, Linux, and Novell NetWare include all the necessary software to operate as a DNS server.

10.1.1   Domain Name Space

The **DNS name space** describes the hierarchical structure of the DNS database as an inverted logical tree structure. Each node on the tree is a partition of the name space called a domain. Domains can be further partitioned at node points within the domain into subdomains. The names of the domain and subdomains can be up to 63 characters long. See figure 10.1.

The top of the tree is known as the **root domain.** It is sometimes shown as a period (.) or as empty quotation marks (""), indicating a null value. Immediately below the root domain, you will find the **top-level domains.** The top-level domains indicate a country, region, or type of organization. Three-letter codes indicate the type of organization. For example, COM indicates commercial (business) and EDU stands for educational institution. They are listed in table 10.1.

Two-letter codes indicate countries, which follow the International Standard 3166. For example, CA stands for Canada, AU for Australia, FR for France, and UK for United Kingdom. For a list of two letter codes, go to:

http://www.din.de/gremien/nas/nabd/iso3166ma/codlstp1/index.html

Figure 10.1   DNS Namespace

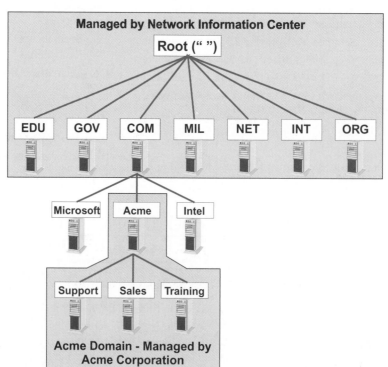

Table 10.1   Top-level Domain Codes Indicating the Type of Organization

Traditional Top-level Domains		New Top-level Domains	
Code	Meaning	Code	Meaning
com	Commercial	**aero**	airline-related services
edu	Educational	**biz**	businesses
gov	Government	**coop**	cooperatives
int	International Organization	**info**	web sites providing information
mil	Military	**museum**	museums
net	Network related	**name**	personal web sites and email addresses
org	Miscellaneous Organization	**pro**	professionals such as doctors and lawyers

The **second-level domain names** are variable-length names registered to an individual or organization for use on the Internet. These names are almost always based on the appropriate top-level domain, depending on the type of organization or geographic location where a name is used.

Example 10.1:

Domain Name	Second-Level Domain Name
MICROSOFT.COM	Microsoft Corporation
CISCO.COM	Cisco Corporation
MTI.EDU	MTI University
ED.GOV	United States Department of Education
ARMY.MIL	United States Army
W3.ORG	World Wide Web Consortium
NATO.INT	North Atlantic Treaty Organization
PM.GOV.AU	Prime Minister of Australia

The second-level domain names must be registered by the authorized party. For example, for years, Network Solutions Inc. ran a government-sanctioned monopoly on registrations for .COM, .NET, and .ORG domain names. But as the U.S. government handed the control of the Internet to an international body, several companies now handle the registration of these three-letter codes. Note: Since most of the common top-level domain names are already taken, some countries such as Tonga (TO) and Tuvalu (TV) are selling their domain name. Therefore, some commercial and user sites may be using one of these two-letter codes. This is especially true with the TV domain name since it is easily linked to television.

Subdomain names are additional names that an organization can create that are derived from the registered second-level domain name. The subdomain allows an organization to divide a domain into a department or geographical location, allowing the partitions of the domain name space to be more manageable. A subdomain must have a contiguous domain name space. This means that the domain name of a zone (child domain) is the name of that zone added to the name of the domain or parent domain.

A **host name** is a name assigned to a specific computer within a domain or subdomain by an administrator to identify the TCP/IP host. Multiple host names can be associated with the same IP address, although only one host name can be assigned to a computer. If the DNS is seen as a tree, it represents the leaf or object of the tree. Much like a subdomain, it is the leftmost label of the DNS domain name. The host name can then be used in place of an IP address such as the PING or other TCP/IP utilities. Total length of an FQDN cannot exceed 255 characters. Note: The host name does not have to be the same as the NetBIOS (computer) name.

A **fully qualified domain name (FQDN)** describes the exact position of a host (computer) within the domain hierarchy, and it is considered to be complete. When used in a DNS domain name, it is stated by a trailing period (.) to designate the name of the host is located off the root or highest level of the domain hierarchy.

Example 10.2:

SERVER1.SALES.ACME.COM

COM indicates a commercial business.
ACME is the name of the domain name.
SALES is the name of the subdomain.
SERVER1 is the name of the server located within the SALES subdomain.

When you create a domain name space, consider the following domain guidelines and standard naming conventions:

- To minimize the level of administrative tasks, limit the number of domain levels.
- If possible, each subdomain should have a unique name throughout the entire domain to ensure the subdomain name is unique.
- Use simple, yet meaningful names so that domain names are easy to remember and navigate.
- Use standard DNS characters including A–Z, a–z, 0–9, and hyphen and Unicode characters, which include the additional characters needed for foreign languages such as French, German, and Spanish.
- The names of the domain and subdomains can be up to 63 characters long.
- Total length of an FQDN cannot exceed 255 characters.

10.1.2   DNS Zones

A **DNS zone** is a portion of the DNS namespace whose database records exist and are managed in a particular DNS database file. See figure 10.2 and table 10.2. Each zone is based on a specific domain node, which is also referred to as the zone's root domain. It is the authority source for that node. Zone files do not necessarily contain the complete DNS branch since subdomains may be its own zone. Note: If subdomains are added below the domain, the subdomains can be part of the same zone or belong to another zone.

The computer that maintains the master list for a zone is the primary name server for that zone, which is considered the authority for that zone. A DNS server might be configured to manage one or more zones.

Most BIND implementations have two types of zones that you can configure: a standard primary and a standard secondary zone. Windows 2000 and Windows Server 2003 servers also use a third type called the Active Directory Integrated zone. See table 10.3.

The **primary name server** is a name server that stores and maintains the zone file locally. Changes to a zone, such as adding domains or hosts, are done by changing files at the primary name server. A **secondary name server** gets the data from its zone from another name server, either a primary name server or another secondary name server. The process of obtaining this zone information across the network is referred to as a zone transfer. Zone transfers occur over TCP port 53. The **Active Directory integrated zone** has the zone defined using the Active Directory, not the zone files.

The source of the zone information for a secondary name server is referred to as a master name server. A master name server can be either a primary or secondary name server for the requested zone.

Figure 10.2 Sample Zone Database Files

```
;

;   Database file acme.com.dns for acme.com zone.

;     Zone version:     6

;

@                          IN     SOA server1.acme.com.

administrator.acme.com.(

                           6                      ; serial number

                           900                    ; refresh

                           600                    ; retry

                           86400                  ; expire

                           3600            ) ; minimum TTL

;

;   Zone NS records

;

@                          NS server1.acme.com.

;

;   Zone records

;

server2000-01a    A    132.132.60.45

server1           A    132.132.20.1

testserver        A    132.132.20.20
```

Question:

Why do you want to have a secondary name server?

Answer:

There are three reasons. The first reason is for fault tolerance. You should have at least two DNS name servers serving each zone. In each client's configuration, both name servers would be listed. If the first server listed cannot be contacted, the client will than contact the second name server. The second reason would be to divide the load between different name servers so that the performance for name resolution will be increased. Lastly, the DNS servers could be used to service computers that are located in remote locations so that they would not have to use a slow WAN link.

Table 10.2   Common Resource Record Types Used in DNS Database Files

Resource Record	Purpose
SOA (Start of Authority)	Identifies the name server that is the authoritative source of information for data within a domain. An SOA record is created automatically when you create a new zone. A primary server for a given zone lists itself in SOA record to show that it's the source for this zone. The first record in the zone database file must be the SOA Record.
NS (Name Server)	Provides a list of name servers that are assigned to a domain.
A (Host Address)	Provides a host name to an Internet Protocol (IP) version 4 32-bit address. For more information, see RFC 1035.
PTR (Pointer)	Resolves an IP address to a host name (reverse mappings). For more information, see RFC 1035.
CNAME (Canonical Name) - Alias	Creates an alias or alternate DNS domain name for a specified host name. The most common or popular use of an alias is to provide a permanent DNS aliased domain name for generic name resolution of a server-based name such as www.acme.com and ftp.acme.com to more than one computer or IP address used in a web server. This way, you can assign acme.com to one server, www.acme.com to second server and ftp.acme.com to a third server. If you do not use the same server for all three entries and you decide to split the service to separate servers, you just have to change the CNAME resource record to point to the new server.
SRV (Service)	Locates servers that are hosting a particular service. Note: SRV records are new in Windows 2000 DNS Server Services. This record enables you to maintain a list of servers for a well-known server port and transport protocol type ordered by preference for a DNS domain name. For more information, see the Internet draft "A DNS RR for specifying the location of services (DNS SRV)."
MX (Mail Exchanger)	Identifies which mail exchanger to contact for a specified domain and in what order to use each mail host.

Table 10.3   Zone Types

Zone Type	Description
Standard Primary	The master copy of a new zone.
Standard Secondary	A replica of an existing zone. Standard secondary zones are read-only.
Active Directory Integrated	A zone that is stored in Active Directory (Windows 2000/Windows Server 2003 only). Updates of the zone are performed during Active Directory replication.

10.1.3   Dynamic DNS

Since DNS has become the primary naming resolution tool, every computer that will hold a network service such as file or print sharing would have to be registered. A large network that has a lot of computers that use DHCP to obtain a new IP address needs to dynamically register and update the DNS servers resource records. Windows 2000, Windows Server 2003, newer versions of Linux, and Novell NetWare 5.1 and higher provide client and server support for the use of dynamic updates, as described in RFC 2136.

10.1.4 Securing DNS

One of the uses of DNS servers for attackers is to use them to help map out your network. Since anyone can query the DNS servers, you should limit the information that is there. In addition, you need to secure the zone transfers so that they cannot steal them to gather the same information. Therefore, you need to configure your DNS servers to only allow zone transfers to specific secondary servers. In addition, you can secure the zone transfers by allowing zone transfers so that secondary servers can verify the credentials of the primary server or by using Active Directory zones. Since many companies have a need to have servers available to the public and servers available for the internal network, you should divide your network into two zones, one for your internal network and one for the public network. Of course, you should not put any information in your public DNS server that you don't want the public to see. Next, you should limit the amount of additional information you provide in DNS.

There are two types of attacks aimed at hampering or disabling your DNS server. In either of these two cases, users will not be able to access the web using FQDN names. They are:

■ DNS spoofing—When someone establishes a bogus DNS server to answer client requests for name resolution and the server responds with invalid information.
■ DNS cache poisoning—Since DNS servers maintain caches of IP name resolutions, it allows a DNS server to quickly answer a DNS name query that it has previously answered. Flaws have been found in some DNS servers that allow attackers to insert bogus information into a DNS cache.

To prevent these types of attacks, use secure dynamic updates (Windows 2000 and Windows Server 2003) or signed DNS updates (BIND version 9 or higher) where allows a cross-check of client computer credentials before an update takes place. To prevent cache poisoning, you need to use an updated version of the DNS server or install a security patch that does not allow the DNS cache to be poisoned.

10.2 INTRODUCTION TO WINDOWS INTERNET NAME SERVICE (WINS)

If you try to access a computer using its NetBIOS (computer) name, such as using a UNC name to specify a network resource, the computer needs to determine what the IP address is. Initially, it would broadcast onto the network asking for the IP address of the computer. Unfortunately, the broadcast usually doesn't go across routers, which means that computers on other subnets don't get resolved. In addition, if you have a lot of computers doing these types of broadcast, the broadcasts will slow the performance of the network.

Other methods to resolve NetBIOS names would be to use either LMHOSTS files or to access a WINS server. Like HOSTS files, using LMHOSTS files, it would be extremely difficult to maintain and distribute the LMHOSTS files to all of the computers in a large network, especially since addresses may change frequently under a network using DHCP servers.

10.2.1 Using a WINS Server

A **WINS server** contains a database of IP addresses and NetBIOS (computer names) that update dynamically. For clients to access the WINS server, the clients must know the address of the WINS server. Therefore, the WINS server needs to have a static address that does not change. When the client accesses the WINS server, the client doesn't do a broadcast, the client sends a message directly to the WINS server. When the WINS server gets the requests, it knows which computer sent the request and can reply directly to the originating IP address. The WINS database stores the information and makes it available to the other WINS clients. Note: The WINS database is located at *systemroot*\System32\ WINS\Wins.mdb. The WINS registration generates little excessive network traffic because it doesn't use broadcast. Note: The WINS protocol is based on and is compatible with the protocols defined for NetBIOS Name Server (NBNS) in RFCs 1001/1002.

When a WINS client starts up, it registers its name, IP address, and type of services within the WINS server's database. The type of service is designated by a hexadecimal value, which is placed at the end of the name. For example, when starting a Windows 2000 computer called Server2, it will register 3 mappings, including Server2[00h] (workstation), Server2[03h] (messenger) and Server2[20h]

Table 10.4   NetBIOS Network Services

NetBIOS Name Suffix	Network Service/Resource Identifier
\\computer_name[00h]	Workstation service
\\computer_name[03h]	Messenger service
\\computer_name[06h]	RAS
\\computer_name[20h]	Server service
\\computer_name[21h]	RAS client service (on a RAS client)
\\computer_name[BEh]	Network monitoring agent service
\\domain_name[1Bh]	The PDC in its role as the domain master browser
\\domain_name[1Dh]	The master browser for each subnet
\\domain_name[1Ch]	The domain controllers (up to 25 IP addresses) within the domain

(File server). Note: The NetBIOS can only be up to 15 characters not counting the hexadecimal value, which represents the service. See table 10.4 for the list of NetBIOS network services.

Since WINS was only made for Windows operating systems, other network devices and services (such as a network printer and UNIX machines) cannot register with a WINS service. Therefore, these addresses would have to added manually.

Names that are held in the WINS database are given a Time to Live (TTL) or Renewal interval during name registration. A name must be refreshed before this interval ends or the name will be released from the database. Names are refreshed by sending a Name Refresh Request to the WINS server by the WINS client. Windows clients will attempt a refresh at half of the Renewal interval and will keep trying until it contacts the WINS server or the time has expired. NetBIOS names are explicitly released when the client performs a proper shutdown or silent when the name is not refreshed within the Renewal interval.

When a client node registers a name that already exists in the WINS database that has a different IP address, the WINS server must determine if the name with the old IP address still exists. Therefore, the WINS server will send a Name Query Request to the old IP address. If the old address responds with a Positive Name Query Response, the WINS server will reject the new registration with a Negative Name Registration Response. If the old address does not respond to the Name Query, the new registration is accepted.

10.2.2   WINS Clients

A WINS client can be configured to use one of four NetBIOS name resolution methods. They include B (broadcast) node, P (point-to-point) node, M (mixed) node, and H (hybrid) node. See table 10.5. In either case, when trying to resolve a computer name, it will always check its own local NetBIOS name cache. Just like the DNS name cache, it remembers names and addresses of computers which it recently communicated with. By default, when a system is configured to use WINS for its name resolution, it adheres to h-node for name registration. By using DHCP servers or by using the registry, you can force the client into one of these modes.

Example 10.3:

If you are using H (hybrid)-node, it will first check to see if the name is the local machine name. It will then check the NetBIOS cache area for remote names. Resolved Names will remain in the cache area for 10 minutes. If the name hasn't been resolved yet, it will try the WINS server followed by a broadcast. Lastly, it looks in the LMHOSTS file if the system has one followed by using the HOSTS file and DNS server if it was configured.

Table 10.5   NetBIOS Resolution Modes

Node Types	Windows Registry Value	Description
B (broadcast) node	1	A computer doing B-node name resolution relies on broadcasts to convert names into IP addresses. B-node name resolution is not the best option on larger networks because the broadcast will load the network and will usually not go through routers. Note: Microsoft uses B-node, which will check the LMHOSTS file after during a broadcast.
P (point-to-point) node	2	A computer doing P-node name resolution uses a NetBIOS Name Server (NBNS)/WINS server to look up NetBIOS names to get IP addresses. All systems must know the IP address of the NBNS. The main drawback of p-node name resolution is that if the NBNS cannot be accessed, there will be no way to resolve names and thus no way to access other systems on the network by using NetBIOS names.
M (mixed) node	3	An M-node computer first tries a broadcast to resolve a name. If that attempt fails, the computer looks up the name in a NetBIOS name server. In other words, an M-node computer first acts as a B-node, and if that fails, tries to act as a P-node. M-node has the advantage over p-node in that if the NBNS is unavailable, systems on the local subnet can still be accessed through b-node resolution. M-node is typically not the best choice for larger networks because it uses b-node and thus results in broadcasts. However, when you have a large network that consists of smaller subnetworks connected via slow wide area network (WAN) links, M-node is a preferred method since it will reduce the amount of communication across the slow links.
H (hybrid) node (Default)	8	Finally, an H-node computer first does a P-node lookup, if that fails, the computer does a broadcast. In either case, the NetBIOS name resolution will try the LMHOSTS file after trying a broadcast and/or WINS server.

10.2.3   WINS Server Replication

To provide fault tolerance, it is recommended to have more than one WINS server with the same WINS database. By having more than one WINS server, a WINS client can go to the second WINS server when the first one is unavailable. To make sure that the WINS server has the same information, you must replicate the information from one WINS server to the other WINS server. These servers are known as replication partners.

A **WINS replication partner** can be added and configured as either a pull partner, a push partner, or a push/pull partner. The push/pull partner type is the default configuration and is the type recommended for use in most cases. A **pull partner** is a WINS server that requests new database entries from its partner. The pull occurs at configured time intervals or in response to an update notification from a push partner. A **push partner** is a WINS server that sends update notification messages. The update notification occurs after a configurable number of changes to the WINS database.

Since pull partners configure at certain time intervals, you should use a pull partner across slow links. For example, you could have it replicate every 24 hours beginning at 12:00 at night. Therefore, the replication will occur when traffic is at a minimum. A push parent should be used with servers connected across fast links because push replication occurs when a particular number of updated WINS entries are reached. Note: If you need certain changes to replicate immediately, you can force the WINS servers to replicate using WINS console.

You can configure a WINS server to automatically configure other WINS server computers as its replication partners using periodic multicasts to announce their presence. These announcements are sent as IGMP messages for the multicast group address of 224.0.1.24 (the well-known multicast IP address reserved for WINS server use). With this automatic partner configuration, other WINS servers are discovered when they join the network and are added as replication partners.

10.2.4   WINS Proxy Agent

A **WINS proxy agent** is a WINS-enabled computer configured to act on behalf of other host computers that cannot directly use WINS. WINS proxies help resolve NetBIOS name queries for computers located on a subnet where there is not a WINS server by hearing broadcasts on the subnet of the proxy agent and forwarding those responses directly to a WINS server. This keeps the broadcast local, yet gets responses from a WINS server without using the P-node. Since most WINS proxies are only useful or necessary on networks that include NetBIOS broadcast-only (B-node) clients. Therefore, for most networks, WINS proxies are typically not needed.

10.2.5   Securing WINS

Since WINS is an aging service, you may consider using DNS or a directory service for users to locate their network resources. But if you choose to use WINS and if you have WINS traffic crossing the Internet, remember that the data is in cleartext. Therefore, if you need WINS information to be replicated between sites, you should use IPSec or VPNs. To allow WINS traffic to go through a firewall, you will need to open UDP/TCP port 137, UDP port 138, and TCP port 139. If you don't need to have WINS information between sites and you want to protect your internal site from public browsing, block these ports at the firewall.

10.3   INTRODUCTION TO DHCP SERVICES

Security+ Objective 3.5.3.8—DHCP Servers

A DHCP server maintains a list of IP addresses called a pool. When a user needs an IP address, the server removes the address from the pool and issues it to the user for a limited amount of time. Issuing an address is called leasing. Using a DHCP server to issue an address is more reliable and requires less labor than setting every computer manually, and you can get by with fewer IP addresses because computers not on the network are not using IP addresses.

Created for diskless workstations, the **Bootstrap protocol (BOOTP)** enabled a booting host to configure itself dynamically. See table 10.6. **DHCP,** which stands for **Dynamic Host Configuration Protocol,** is an extension of BOOTP. It is used to automatically configure a host during boot up on a

Table 10.6   Common RFC for DHCP

RFC Number	Description
RFC 2131	Dynamic Host Configuration Protocol
RFC 2132	DHCP Options and BOOTP Vendor Extensions
RFC 951	The Bootstrap Protocol (BOOTP)
RFC 1534	Interoperation Between DHCP and BOOTP
RFC 1542	Clarifications and Extensions for the Bootstrap Protocol
RFC 2136	Dynamic Updates in the Domain Name System (DNS UPDATE)
RFC 2241	DHCP Options for Novell Directory Services
RFC 2242	Netware/IP Domain Name and Information

TCP/IP network and to change settings while the host is attached. There are many parameters that you can automatically set with the DHCP server. Some of the more common parameters include:

- IP address
- Subnet mask
- Gateway (router) address
- Address of DNS Servers
- Address of WINS Servers
- WINS client mode

10.3.1   The DHCP Requests

A host computer that is configured to get a DHCP address sends a DHCPDISCOVER message on the local IP subnet to find the DHCP server or servers. The client doesn't know the address or addresses of the DHCP server, so it uses an IP broadcast address for the DHCPDISCOVER message. All available DHCP servers respond with a DHCPOFFER message. If more than one server is available, the client usually selects the first server to respond, but no rule specifies which server the client has to use. Regardless of how many servers respond, the client broadcasts a DHCPREQUEST message that identifies which server the client will use and implicitly informs all other servers that the client won't use them. The selected server responds to the client with a DHCPPACK message that contains the assigned IP address, any other network parameter assignments, and the lease or amount of time for which the DHCP server assigns the client the IP address. The client sends messages to UDP port 67 on the DHCP server and the server sends messages to UDP port 68 on the DHCP client.

To provide fault tolerance, you can assign two or more DHCP servers for every subnet. With two DHCP servers, if one server is unavailable, the other server can take its place and continue to lease new addresses or renew existing clients. When setting up the two DHCP servers, the scopes of the two servers should include scopes with different addresses to avoid both servers handed out the same address to two different computers. Before installing a DHCP server, you must make sure that the TCP/IP protocol is installed and a static IP address is assigned to the DHCP server.

If you have a client that must always use the same address, you can reserve an address by using client reservation. The DHCP server will then assign the reserved address to the computer with the specified MAC address. If multiple DHCP servers are configured with a scope that covers the range of the reserved IP address, the client reservation must be made and duplicated at each of these DHCP servers. Otherwise, the reserved client computer can receive a different IP address, depending on which DHCP responds.

10.3.2   DHCP Relay Agent

A **DHCP relay agent** is a computer that relays DHCP and BOOTP messages between clients and servers on different subnets. This way, you can have a single DHCP server handle several subnets without the DHCP server being connected directly to those subnets. You should enable the DHCP Relay Agent on those router interfaces that are attached to subnets that contain network client computers and do not contain a DHCP server. When you want to use DHCP to configure TCP/IP information on computers that reside on remote subnets from the DHCP server, you must ensure either that the routers can function as BOOTP/DHCP relay agents or that a server on each remote subnet has a BOOTP/DHCP relay agent installed. A router that has a BOOTP relay agent installed is RFC-1542 compliant.

10.3.3   Securing DHCP

Attackers can interrupt the handing out of addresses by using a rogue DHCP server. A rogue DHCP server can hands out bogus information such as an incorrect gateway or DNS address. This will cause the client to be unable to use resources on other networks, access network resources by FQDN or misdirect the clients to resources controlled by the attacker.

In addition, an attacker can get a foothold on your network by obtaining a legitimate IP address and related information. This allows them to learn part of your internal addressing scheme. By using an internal address, an attack could then attack other systems on your network.

To protect your network, you should scan for rogue DHCP servers by using protocol analyzers or by using an intrusion-detection system to discover DHCP Offer packets from unauthorized DHCP servers. Since manual settings are not overwritten by DHCP settings, if you configure the DNS settings on each client machine, they cannot get an invalid DNS server. You can also restrict which computers the DHCP server will respond to by using address reservation of MAC addresses. Lastly, to prevent DHCP servers from getting queries answered outside your network, you should block TCP/UDP ports 67 and 68 on your firewall.

10.4   SIMPLE NETWORK MANAGEMENT PROTOCOL (SNMP)

The **Simple Network Management Protocol (SNMP)** has become the de facto standard for internetwork management. It allows configuring of remote devices, monitors network performance, detects network faults, detects inappropriate access, and audits network usage. Remote devices include hubs, bridges, routers, and servers. Note: SNMP uses UDP.

SNMP contains two primary elements: a manager and agents. The **SNMP manager** is the console through which the network administrator performs network management functions. The SNMP works by sending messages called protocol data units (PDUs), to different parts of a network. Agents store data about themselves in **Management Information Bases (MIB).** The manager, which is the console through which the network administrator performs network management functions, will request the information from the MIB. The **SNMP agent** returns the appropriate information to the manager.

A **trap** is an unsolicited message sent by an SNMP agent to a SNMP management system when the agent detects that a certain type of event has occurred locally on the managed host. The SNMP management console receives a trap message, which is known as a trap destination. For example, a trap message might be sent when a system restarts or when a router link goes down.

Each SNMP management host and agent belongs to an SNMP community. An **SNMP community** is a collection of hosts grouped together for administrative purposes. Deciding which computers should belong to the same community is generally, but not always, determined by the physical proximity of the computers. Communities are identified by the names you assign to them.

While most networks use a username and a password for authentication, SNMP messages are only authenticated by the community name. Although a host can belong to several communities at the same time, an SNMP agent does not accept requests from a management system in a community that is not on its list of acceptable community names. If the community name is incorrect, the agents send an "authentication failure" trap to its trap destination. Therefore, it is the responsibility of the administrator to set hard-to-guess community names.

After the SNMP authenticates a message, the request is evaluated against the agent's list of access permissions for that community. The types of permissions that can be granted to a community are shown in table 10.7.

Table 10.7   Community Permissions

Permission	Description
None	The SNMP agent does not process the request. When the agent receives an SNMP message from a management system in this community, it discards the request and generates an authentication trap.
Notify	This is currently identical to the permission of None.
Read-Only	The agent does not process SET requests from this community. It processes only GET, GET-NEXT, and GET-BULK requests. The agent discards SET requests from manager systems in this community and generates an authentication trap.
Read Create	The SNMP agent processes or creates all requests from this community. It processes SET, GET, GET-NEXT, and GET-BULK requests, including SET requests that require the addition of a new object to a MIB table.
Read Write	Currently identical to Read Create.

Community names are transmitted as clear text, that is, without encryption. Because unencrypted transmissions are vulnerable to attacks by hackers with network analysis software, the use of SNMP community names represents a potential security risk. However, Windows 2000 and Windows Server 2003 IP Security can be configured to help protect SNMP messages from these attacks. In addition, you can use IPSec or VPNs to encrypt SNMP messages.

The SNMP service requires configuring at least one default community name. The name Public is generally used as the community name because it is the common name that is universally accepted in all SNMP implementations. Since these default names are well-known to attackers, you should delete or change the default community name or add multiple community names. If no community names are defined, the SNMP agent will deny all incoming SNMP requests.

When an SNMP agent receives a message, the community name contained in the packet is verified against the agent's list of acceptable community names. After the name is determined to be acceptable, the request is evaluated against the agent's list of access permissions for that community. The types of permissions that can be granted to a community are detailed below.

There are two versions of SNMP. SNMPv1 reports only whether a device is functioning properly. The industry has attempted to define a new set of protocols called SNMPv2 that would provide additional information, but the standardization efforts have not been successful. Instead, network managers have turned to a related technology called RMON that provides more detailed information about network usage.

In 1998, the IETF SNMPv3 working group produced a set of Proposed Internet Standards, current RFCs 2570 through 2576. This document set defines a framework for incorporating security features into an overall capability that includes with SNMPv1 or SNMPv2 functionality. In addition, the documents define a specific set of capabilities for network security and access control. SNMPv3 provides secure access to devices by a combination of authenticating and encrypting packets over the network. The security features provided in SNMPv3 are:

- **Message Integrity**—Ensuring that a packet has not been tampered with in-transit.
- **Authentication**—Determining the message is from a valid source.
- **Encryption**—Scrambling the contents of a packet prevent it from being seen by an unauthorized source.

SNMPv3 provides for both security models and security levels. A security model is an authentication strategy that is set up for a user and the group in which the user resides. A security level is the permitted level of security within a security model. A combination of a security model and a security level will determine which security mechanism is employed when handling an SNMP packet. Three security models are available: SNMPv1, SNMPv2c, and SNMPv3. See table 10.8.

For SNMPv3, each user belongs to a group and a group defines the access policy for a set of users. An access policy is what SNMP objects can be accessed for reading, writing, and creating. A group

Table 10.8   SNMP Security Models and Levels

Model	Level	Authentication	Encryption	Description
v1	noAuthNoPriv	Community String	No	Uses a community string match for authentication.
v2c	noAuthNoPriv	Community String	No	Uses a community string match for authentication.
v3	noAuthNoPriv	Username	No	Uses a username match for authentication.
v3	authNoPriv	MD5 or SHA	No	Provides authentication based on the HMAC-MD5 or HMAC-SHA algorithms.
v3	authPriv	MD5 or SHA	DES	Provides authentication based on the HMAC-MD5 or HMAC-SHA algorithms. Provides DES 56-bit encryption in addition to authentication based on the CBC-DES (DES-56) standard.

determines the list of notifications its users can receive, and it also defines the security model and security level for its users.

To help protect users from threats outside your network, you need to block UDP ports 161 and 162 on your firewall or gateway. SNMP utilizes port 161 to issue and respond to SNMP queries and commands. Port 162 is used to send trap messages. Port 161 should be set to block both inbound and outbound, thereby preventing someone from sending or receiving information on these ports. Port 162 should block outbound traffic. Other ports that you may consider blocking would be TCP/UDP port 199, TCP/UDP 391, TCP port 705, and UDP port 1993.

10.5   TERMINAL EMULATION

Telecommunication Network (Telnet) is a virtual terminal protocol (**terminal emulation**) allowing a user to log on to another TCP/IP host to access network resources. Such a computer is frequently called a host computer while the client is called a dumb terminal. With Telnet, you log on as a regular user with whatever privileges, you may have been granted to the specific applications and data on that computer. You can then enter commands through the Telnet program and they will be executed as if you were entering them directly on the server console. This enables you to control the server and communicate with other servers on the network. Telnet is a common way to remotely control Web servers. The default port for telnet is TCP port 23.

A popular terminal program/brand of terminal from DEC was Visual Terminal 100 (vt100). It was extremely popular with the companies and universities that ran Berkeley UNIX on their VAXes (also from DEC). Most communication packets support vt100.

DOS, Windows, and Linux computers can start a telnet session by executing the telnet command at the command prompt, which can be used with or without a computer name. If no computer name is used, telnet provides command mode and provides a prompt to the user. After a connection is established, Telnet enters input mode.

The telnet command can be used to test TCP connections. You can telnet to any TCP port to see if it is responding, which is especially useful when checking SMTP and HTTP ports. The syntax for the telnet command is:

> telnet hostname port

whereas the hostname could be the hostname or the IP address. If you do not specify the port number, it will default to port 23. For example, to verify HTTP is working on a computer, you can type in the following command:

> telnet acme.com 80

If you connect to a SMTP server (port 25), you can further test your email server by actually sending an email message from the telnet session.

Telnet, in other related commands (rlogin and rsh), have one major problem. They send the username and password in cleartext for any one to see. This is the reason that these utilities and services are typically disabled by default.

Security+ Objective 2.1.6—SSH

To overcome this security weakness of these utilities, a more secure protocol had to be developed. **Secure Shell (SSH)** is a program to log into another computer over a network, to execute commands in a remote machine, and to move files from one machine to another. It provides strong authentication (RSA public key cryptography) and secure communications over insecure channels (encryption algorithms include Blowfish, DES, and IDEA, with IDEA being the default). When using ssh's slogin, the entire login session, including transmission of password, is encrypted; therefore, it is almost impossible for an outsider to collect passwords. See figure 10.3.

SSH protects a network from attacks such as IP spoofing, IP source routing, and DNS spoofing. An attacker who has managed to take over a network can only force ssh to disconnect. He or she cannot play back the traffic or hijack the connection when encryption is enabled. SSH comes with Linux and is available for Windows, UNIX, Macintosh, and OS/2, and it also works with RSA authentication. The most popular SSH packages can be found from OpenSSH (http://www.openssh.com).

Figure 10.3   SSH Login Session

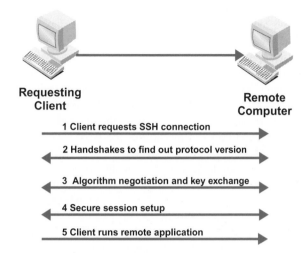

```
                    Requesting                              Remote
                      Client                               Computer

              1 Client requests SSH connection
              ────────────────────────────────────────►

              2 Handshakes to find out protocol version
              ◄────────────────────────────────────────

              3  Algorithm negotiation and key exchange
              ◄────────────────────────────────────────

              4 Secure session setup
              ◄────────────────────────────────────────

              5 Client runs remote application
              ────────────────────────────────────────►
```

10.6   WEB SERVICES SECURITY

Security+ **Objective 2.3**—Web

Security+ **Objective 2.3.4**—Vulnerabilities

Security+ **Objective 3.5.3.2**—Web Servers

The terms the Internet and the World Wide Web are often used interchangeably, but they have different meanings. As was pointed out before, the **Internet** refers to the huge global WAN. Until the early 1990s for one to be able to use the computer to communicate with another computer via the Internet required a good deal of knowledge and the ability to understand and use some fairly unfriendly commands. The **World Wide Web (WWW)** was created in 1992, and refers to the means of organizing, presenting, and accessing information over the Internet.

To access the web, a user would be using the following technologies:

1. HTML
2. Web Server
3. Web Browser
4. http and ftp

10.6.1   Introduction to Web Servers

Web pages are written using the **HyperText Markup Language (HTML).** This language is pretty simple and is implemented as special ASCII tags or codes that you embed within your document to give the browser a general idea of how the information should be displayed. The browsers understand the standard HTML tags, although they may display the same document a little differently. If you want your documents to be accessible by people using different browsers, you should stick with the standard tags. The HTML standard is still actively evolving, so new tags are constantly becoming available to support new browser features. Note: A plain HTML web page is a static document that doesn't change.

A **Web server** is a computer equipped with the server software that uses Internet protocols such as Hypertext Transfer Protocol (HTTP) and File Transfer Protocol (FTP) to respond to Web client requests on a TCP/IP network via web browsers. One server can service a large number of clients. There are several free server programs available on the Internet. Most web browsers are built to process two basic types of requests: file server and database server. New features are always being added to provide additional support for new technology. A web server acting as a file server simply accepts a request for a document, validates the request, and sends the requested files back to the browser. In addition, the browser can act as a front-end tool or interface to collect data and feed it in a database or script. The database can be located either on the same server as the web server or on a different server. When the database responds with the results, it will then send the results back to the browser.

The **web browser** is the client program/software that you run on your local machine to gain access to a web server. It receives the HTML commands, interprets the HTML and displays the results. It is strictly a user-interface/document presentation tool. It knows nothing about the application it is attached to and only knows how to take the information from the server and present it to the user. It is also able to capture data entry made into a Form and get the information back to the server for processing. The most common browsers are Microsoft Internet Explorer and Netscape Communicator. Both of these tools are available for little or no charge on the Internet.

The application protocol that makes the web work is **Hypertext Transfer Protocol** or **HTTP.** While the HTML is the language used to write web pages, HTTP is the protocol that web browsers and web servers use to communicate with each other over the Internet. It is an application-level protocol because it sits on top of the TCP layer in the protocol stack and is used by specific applications to talk to one another. In this case, the applications are web browsers and web servers.

HTTP is a text-based protocol. Clients (web browsers) send requests to web servers for web elements such as web pages and images. Most protocols are connection-oriented, two computers communicating with each other keep the connection open over the Internet. Although HTTP uses the connection-oriented service of TCP (a connection-oriented data transmission service guarantees that packets will arrive at their destination in the order that they were sent and that they will arrive error-free), HTTP does not keep a connection open. Before an HTTP request can be made by a client, a new connection must be made to the server. After the request is serviced by a server, the connection between client and server across the Internet is disconnected. A new connection must be made for each request.

Currently, most web browsers and servers support HTTP 1.1. One of the main features of HTTP 1.1 is that it supports persistent connections. This means that once a browser connects to a web server, it can receive multiple files through the same connection. This should improve performance by as much as 20%.

HTTP is called a stateless protocol because each command is executed independently, without any knowledge of the commands that came before it. This is the main reason that it is difficult to implement websites that react intelligently to user input. This shortcoming of HTTP is being addressed in a number of new technologies, including ActiveX, Java, JavaScript, and cookies.

10.6.2 Scripting Languages

Security+ Objective 2.3.4.1—Java Script

Security+ Objective 2.3.4.2—ActiveX

Security+ Objective 2.3.4.5—Signed Applets

In an effort to make browsing more functional, web developers created and enabled active content. Active content is done by using small executables or script code that is executed and shown within the client's web browser. Unfortunately, like a Trojan horse virus, this enhancement adds an added security risk where some scripts could be used to perform harmful actions on a client machine. Some of the most popular types of active content are, VBScript, JavaScript, and ActiveX components.

VBScript, Short for Visual Basic Scripting Edition, is a scripting language developed by Microsoft and supported by Microsoft's Internet Explorer Web browser. VBScript is based on the Visual Basic programming language, but it is much simpler. It enables web authors to include interactive controls, such as buttons and scrollbars, on their web pages.

An **applet** is a component in a distributed environment that is downloaded and executed by a web browser. Web browsers, which are designed to display text and graphics and also accept data input on forms, aren't very good at processing information locally on the client system, so applets were invented to solve this problem. Applets are also known as mobile code because they are downloaded from a server and run on a client.

Java is a programmable language developed by Sun Microsystems that has a number of features that make it well suited for use on the Web. **Java applets** are self-contained Internet applications that are written in Java. Initially, Java applets are stored on a web server. When you first access a web page that contains HTML code to access the Java applet, the Java applet is downloaded onto the client computer. When the client subsequently accesses the server, the applet is already cache on the client's computer and is accessed with a download delay. The Java source code is run through a client-side engine or Java Virtual machine (VM).

By default, and for security reasons, Java applets are contained within a **sandbox.** This means that the applets cannot do anything which might be construed as threatening to the user's machine (e.g., reading, writing, or deleting local files; putting up arbitrary message windows; communicating with arbitrary other machines; or querying various system parameters). Any attempt to access a resource outside of the sandbox will result in a security violation and the program will terminate. Early browsers had no provisions for Java applets to reach outside of the sandbox. Recent browsers, however, have provisions to give "trusted" applets the ability to work outside the sandbox. For this power to be granted to one of your applets, the applet's code must be digitally signed with your unforgeable digital ID, and then the user must state that he trusts applets signed with your ID.

The Java sandbox relies on a three-tiered defense. If any one of these three elements fails, the security model is completely compromised and vulnerable to attack:

- **Byte code verifier**—This is one way that Java automatically checks untrusted outside code before it is allowed to run. When a Java source program is compiled, it compiles down to platform-independent Java byte code, which is verified before it can run. This helps to establish a base set of security guarantees.
- **Applet class loader**—All Java objects belong to classes, and the applet class loader determines when and how an applet can add classes to a running Java environment. The applet class loader ensures that important elements of the Java run-time environment are not replaced by code that an applet tries to install.
- **Security manager**—The security manager is consulted by code in the Java library whenever a dangerous operation is about to be carried out. The security manager has the option to veto the operation by generating a security exception.

Netscape Corporation created **JavaScript,** which is not Java nor is it a lightweight version of Java, although it does share many of the structure and features of Java. It is a scripting language that was originally called LiveScript. Most web browsers support JavaScript, which is typically embedded inside a HTML page and read by the client browser. A SCRIPT tag inside the HTML code is used to denote the JavaScript. JavaScript is commonly used to communicate with other components or to accept user input. JavaScript can be used to open Java applets.

Since JavaScript is a simple scripting language, it has no built-in means of accessing resources on the client machine and it doesn't have the means to subvert the security of a machine. As long as the web page containing dynamic HTML written in JavaScript runs in a sandbox within the web browser, the dynamic HTML will be contained within the web page in much the same way as Java applets. It, therefore, does not have access to the resources of the host machine. Like Java applets, it can have more access to the system if it is digitally signed. An Active Server Page (ASP) containing JavaScript or a Windows Scripting Host (WSH) script containing JavaScript is potentially hazardous since these environments allow scripts unrestricted access to machine resources (file system, registry, etc.) and application objects (via COM).

In both cases of Java applets and JavaScripts, from time to time, there are vulnerabilities that are found. Therefore, you must keep checking for service packs, patches, and security fixes for your browsers. Another option to stop Java applets and JavaScripts from compromising your client system is to disable Java in the web browser.

An ActiveX control is similar to a Java applet. **ActiveX** is not a programming language, but rather a set of rules for how applications should share information. Programmers can develop ActiveX controls and plug-ins in a variety of languages, including C, C++, Visual Basic, and Java. Unlike Java applets, however, ActiveX controls are downloaded and executed by a web browser (Internet Explorer) and have full access to the Windows operating system. For example, ActiveX technology allows users to view Word and Excel documents directly from a browser interface. In addition, Microsoft Office applications (Microsoft Word, Excel, Access, and PowerPoint) are examples of built-in ActiveX components. This gives them much more power than Java applets, but with this power comes a certain risk that the applet may damage software or data on your machine.

ActiveX uses code signing, specifically the Microsoft Authenticode technology. Authenticode allows you to verify the origin of a control and thus assess its reliability and safety. If a control destroys your system, at least you'll know whom to blame. Independent certificate authorities (CAs) like VeriSign issue the digital signatures to mark the code. Developers have to pay for the certificates, and in order to be considered for a certificate you must pass through a screening process. The digital signature is 1,024 bits and thus essentially impossible to reverse engineer.

Authenticode is based on Microsoft's code-signing proposal now being evaluated by the World Wide Web Consortium. Authenticode uses X.509 v3 cryptography certificates, as well as the PKCS #7 and #10 signature standards. The digital signature uses both a public key and a private key, known as a key pair. Only the private key owner knows the private key, while the public key is available to the world. The private key is used to generate the signature, and the public key is used to validate it.

10.6.3 CGI Programs

Security+ Objective 2.3.4.6—CGI

The **Common Gateway Interface (CGI)** is a standard for interfacing external applications with web servers. For example, you can transfer information between an application and a web server. A CGI program, on the other hand, is executed in real-time, so that it can output dynamic information. For example, let's say that you wanted to "hook up" your server database to the World Wide Web, to allow people from all over the world to query it. Basically, you need to create a CGI program that the PC with the web page will execute to transmit information to the database engine, receive the results back and display them to the client.

When a web server executes a CGI program, it typically begins by displaying an HTML form on the screen. The form provides space for specific data items in the form of text boxes, pull-down boxes, check boxes, radio buttons, and so on. The form typically has a submit button that a user can click on to submit the entry and some will have a clear button to put the data values back to their default values. The FORM tag in the HTML web page specifies a form to fill out. More than one fill-out form can be in a single document, but forms cannot be nested (one inside of another).

The security risk with CGI is that you are allowing anyone on the Internet to execute a program on your web server. Just like any other program, a CGI program might contain security holes that allow an attacker to access your network or its systems. In addition, CGI programs are typically a target for attackers because they are frequently used on public web servers. Some of the examples might include having a CGI program run over and over again from multiple web browsers, which will use up system resources and slow or halt the machine. They can also be used to send bogus data to CGI programs in an attempt to compromise the application or exploiting hidden fields within your CGI programs and modify the information as it is returned to the server. Lastly, if server-side includes (SSIs) are enabled, it allow one document to be inserted into another, which can compromise your scripts.

CGI programs are executed when the web server receives a URL that contains the CGI program name and any parameters required by the program. If your CGI program is compiled into an executable file (.exe), you must give the directory that contains the program Execute permission so that users can run the program. If your CGI program is written as a script, for example a Perl script, then you can give the directory either Execute permission or Script permission. To use Script permission, the script interpreter must be marked as a script engine. If you give read permission, then someone can read and download the script or executable program to their computer. If you enable the write permission, an attacker could load a malicious CGI program to that directory and run it to compromise your web server.

You should limit CGI programs to run as the least privileged user possible and remove all default and sample programs from your web server. Check all CGI applications for security holes, have the CGI application check for properly formatted data that is being submitted and reject the data if it is invalid, too long or improperly formatted. Lastly, disable SSI. If your web server must support SSI, turn them off on your script directories.

10.6.4 Cookies

Security+ Objective 2.3.4.4—Cookies

A cookie is a small amount of data (a text file) that a web server stores about a user on the user's own computer. The message is then sent back to the server each time the browser requests a page from the server. A command line in the HTML of a document tells the browser to set a cookie of a certain name or value. An example of using a cookie would be:

Set-Cookie: NAME=VALUE; expires=DATE; path=PATH; domain=DOMAIN_NAME;

The main purpose of cookies is to identify users and possibly prepare customized web pages for them. When you enter a website using cookies, you may be asked to fill out a form providing such information as your name and interests. This information is packaged into a cookie and sent to your web browser, which stores it for later use. The next time you go to the same website, your browser will send the cookie to the web server. The server can use this information to present you with custom web pages. So, for example, instead of seeing just a generic welcome page you might see a welcome page with your name on it. Some uses of cookies including keeping track of what a person buys using online ordering systems, personalizing a website, storing a person's profile, storing user ID's, and providing support to older web browsers that do not support host header names. Some servers also use cookies for client authentication purposes.

A cookie cannot be used to get data from your hard drive, get your email address, or steal sensitive information about your person. Early implementations of Java and JavaScript could allow people to do this, but for the most part these security leaks have been plugged. While cookies typically make things easier for the user, these tasks can be easily done without using cookies.

By now, you should realize that cookies are considered a security risk because they contain your personal information. If someone gets hold of your cookies, that person can use them to gain illegal access to your user accounts on the Internet, and they can be sold to advertisement companies that target the user with unwanted ads.

So how do you protect yourself? First, a good portion of the security should come from the website owners to design security measures that handle cookies. This should be in their interest because it is protecting their user base and the sensitive data stored on their servers. The other option would be to disable cookies with the browser.

10.6.5   SSL, TLS, and HTTPS

Security+ Objective 2.3.1—SSL/TLS

Security+ Objective 2.3.2—HTTP/S

Most companies with connections to the Internet have implemented firewall solutions to protect the corporate network from unauthorized users coming in—and unauthorized Internet sessions going out via the Internet. But, while firewalls guard against intrusion or unauthorized use, they cannot guarantee the security of the link between a workstation and server on opposite sides of a firewall or the security of the actual message being conveyed.

To create this level of security, two related Internet protocols, Secure Sockets Layer (SSL) and Secure Hypertext Transfer Protocol (S-HTTP), ensure that sensitive information passing through an Internet link is safe from prying eyes. Whereas SSL is designed to establish a secure connection between two computers, S-HTTP is designed to send individual messages securely. Since SSL and S-HTTP have very different designs and goals, it is possible to use the two protocols together. S-HTTP is not available on all browsers.

Secure Sockets Layer (SSL) operates between the application and transport and layer and operates with application layer services such as at the HTTP, FTP, NNTP, and SMTP. When both a client (usually in the form of a web browser) and a server support SSL, any data transmitted between two becomes encrypted. It supports both server and client authentication and is designed to negotiate encryption keys, as well as to authenticate the server before any data is exchanged. SSL is based on PKI encryption methods developed by RSA Corporation to provide encryption and authentication to maintain the integrity of the transmission channel. Note: In order for an SSL connection to be established between a web client and server automatically, the web client and server should have a certificate signed by a trusted root CA.

When an SSL client wants to communicate with an SSL-compliant server, an SSL handshake will occur, which starts when the client initiates a request to the server. The server then sends a X.509 standard certificate back to the client. The certificate includes the server's public key and server's preferred cryptographic algorithms, or ciphers.

The client then creates a key to be used for that session, encrypts the key with the public key sent by the server, and sends the newly created session key to the server. After it receives this key, the server authenticates itself by sending a message encrypted with the key back to the client, proving that the message is coming from the proper server. After this handshake process, which results in the client and server agreeing on the security level, all data transfer between that client and that server for a particular session is encrypted using the session key. When a secure link has been created, the first part of the URL will change from http:// to https://. SSL supports several cryptographic algorithms to handle the authentication and encryption routines. Although SSL is optimized for use with HTTP, it can also be used with FTP or other relevant protocols. Note: While HTTP uses TCP port 80, HTTPS uses port 443.

The **Transport Layer Security (TLS)** protocol is based on and similar to SSL version 3 and is a draft standard of the IETF. TLS is essentially the latest version of SSL, but it is not as widely available in browsers. Its primary goal is to provide privacy and data integrity between two communicating applications. While TLS protocol is based on Netscape's SSL 3.0 protocol, TLS and SSL are not interoperable. The TLS protocol does contain a mechanism that allows TLS implementation to back down to SSL 3.0. The most recent browser versions support TLS.

TLS consists of two layers. The lower level is termed the TLS Record protocol and is layered on top of some reliable transport protocol, such as TCP. The TLS Record protocol provides connection security with some encryption method such as the Data Encryption Standard so that it can keep the connection private and reliable. It is used for encapsulation of various higher-level protocols but can also be used without encryption. Where encryption is used, as would be normal, the secret keys for this are generated uniquely for each connection and are based on a secret key negotiated by another protocol, such as the higher-level TLS Handshake protocol. The TLS Handshake Protocol allows the server and client to authenticate each other using asymmetric cryptography and to negotiate an encryption algorithm and cryptographic keys before data is exchanged.

As with SSL, TLS is application-protocol independent and uses a similar range of ciphers. The TLS standard, however, leaves the decisions on how to initiate TLS handshaking and how to interpret the authentication certificates to the judgment of the designers and implementers of the protocols that run on top.

Common 40- or 56-bit web browsers are considered to have weak encryption because their keys can be cracked in a short time. The stronger browsers will use 128-bit ciphers, which would require more time and commitment of resources to break. Most SSL/TLS-enabled web servers allow the customization of types of encryption and what key sizes can and cannot be used while a connection is made.

Secure Hypertext Transfer Protocol (S-HTTP), also referred to as **HTTP/S,** is simply an extension of HTTP. S-HTTP is created by SSL running under HTTP. Note: Don't confuse S-HTTP with HTTPS (HTTP over SSL). Each S-HTTP file is encrypted, contains a digital certificate or both. The protocol was developed as implementation of the RSA encryption standard. While SSL operates at the Transport layer, S-HTTP supports secure end-to-end transactions by adding cryptography to messages at the application layer. Of course, while SSL is application independent, S-HTTP is tied to the HTTP protocol.

An S-HTTP message consists of three parts:

- The HTTP message
- Sender's cryptographic preferences
- Receiver's preferences

The sender integrates both preferences, which results in a list of cryptographic enhancements to be applied to the message.

S-HTTP, like SSL, can be used to provide electronic commerce without customers worrying about who might intercept their credit card number or other personal information. To decrypt an S-HTTP message, the recipient must look at the message headers, which designate which cryptographic methods were used to encrypt the message. Then, to decrypt the message, the recipient uses a combination of his or her previously stated and current cryptographic preferences and the sender's previously stated cryptographic preferences. S-HTTP doesn't require that the client possess a public key certificate, which means secure transactions can take place at any time without individuals needing to provide a key (as in session encryption with SSL).

10.6.6   Browser Options

As mentioned before, software publisher certificates are used to validate software code. If a user accesses a website that is trying to download a Java or ActiveX control or a plug-in, depending on your browser settings, a security warning may appear giving you the option to download the program. In Internet Explorer, you open the Tools menu and select Internet Options. Then on the Security tab, you select Customer Level and click on the Custom Level button. From there, you can enable, disable, or prompt to download ActiveX controls (signed and unsigned) and scripting of Java applets. See figure 10.4. For Netscape Navigator, you would open the Edit menu and select Preferences. Under the Advanced option, you can select Scripts & Plugins to enable Javascript.

For Internet Explorer, you would select the Privacy tab and use the slider to adjust your cookie settings or click on the Advanced button to override automatic settings. See figure 10.5. In Netscape Navigator, you can select Cookies under the Privacy & Security section. From there, you can enable or disable cookies or enable cookies based on security settings.

To view the certificates for Internet Explorer, click on the Content button and click on the Certificates button. To see a list of certificates, click on the appropriate certificates. From here, you can also import and export individual certificates. See figure 10.6. For Netscape, you would select Certificates under Privacy & Settings.

10.6.7   Secure Electronic Transaction

Secure Electronic Transaction (SET) is an open encryption and security specification designed to protect credit card transactions on the Internet. It was supported initially by Mastercard, Visa, Microsoft, Netscape, and others. With SET, a user is given an electronic wallet (digital certificate) and a transaction is conducted and verified using a combination of digital certificates and digital signatures among the purchaser, a merchant, and the purchaser's bank in a way that ensures privacy and confidentiality. SET makes use of Netscape's Secure Sockets Layer (SSL), Microsoft's Secure Transaction Technology (STT), and Terisa System's Secure Hypertext Transfer Protocol (S-HTTP). SET uses some but not all aspects of a public key infrastructure (PKI).

SET incorporates important features needed for secure credit card transactions over the Internet:

■ **Confidentiality of information**—Cardholder account and payment information is secured as it travels across the network. An interesting and important feature of SET is that it prevents the merchant from learning the cardholder's credit card number; this is provided only to the issuing bank. Conventional encryption by DES is used to provide confidentiality.

Figure 10.4   Security Settings within Internet Explorer

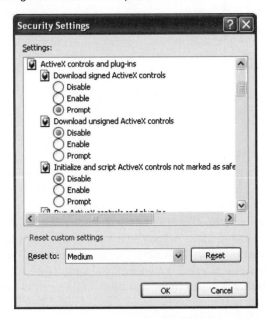

Figure 10.5   Privacy Settings within Internet Explorer

Figure 10.6   Certificates Shown in Internet Explorer

■ **Integrity of data**—Payment information sent from cardholders to merchants includes order information, personal data, and payment instructions. SET guarantees that these messages' contents are not altered in transit. RSA digital signatures, using SHA-1 hash codes, provide message integrity. Certain messages are also protected by the message authentication code HMAC, using SHA-1.

■ **Cardholder account authentication**—SET enables merchants to verify that a cardholder is a legitimate user of a valid card account number. SET uses X.509v3 digital certificates with RSA signatures for this purpose.

▪ **Merchant authentication**—SET enables cardholders to verify that a merchant has a relationship with a financial institution allowing it to accept payment cards. SET uses X.509v3 digital certificates with RSA signatures for this purpose.

SET is not itself a payment system. Rather, it's a set of security protocols and formats enabling users to employ the existing credit card payment infrastructure on an open network, such as the Internet, in a secure fashion. In essence, SET consists of three services:

▪ Providing a secure communications channel among all parties involved in a transaction.
▪ Providing trust by the use of X.509v3 digital certificates.
▪ Ensuring privacy because the information is only available to parties in a transaction when and where necessary.

Assume that a customer has a SET-enabled browser such as Microsoft's Internet Explorer or Netscape Navigator and that the transaction provider (bank, store, etc.) has a SET-enabled server, SET follows the following steps:

1. The customer opens a Mastercard or Visa bank account. Any issuer of a credit card is some kind of bank.
2. The customer receives a digital certificate. This electronic file functions as a credit card for online purchases or other transactions. It includes a public key with an expiration date. It has been through a digital switch to the bank to ensure its validity.
3. Third-party merchants also receive certificates from the bank. These certificates include the merchant's public key and the bank's public key.
4. The customer places an order over a web page, by phone, or some other means.
5. The customer's browser receives and confirms from the merchant's certificate that the merchant is valid.
6. The browser sends the order information. This message is encrypted with the merchant's public key, the payment information, which is encrypted with the bank's public key (which can't be read by the merchant), and information that ensures the payment can only be used with this particular order.
7. The merchant verifies the customer by checking the digital signature on the customer's certificate. This may be done by referring the certificate to the bank or to a third-party verifier.
8. The merchant sends the order message along to the bank. This includes the bank's public key, the customer's payment information (which the merchant can't decode), and the merchant's certificate.
9. The bank verifies the merchant and the message. The bank uses the digital signature on the certificate with the message and verifies the payment part of the message.
10. The bank digitally signs and sends authorization to the merchant, who can then fill the order.

10.6.8   Introduction to FTP Services

Security+ Objective 2.5—File Transfer

Security+ Objective 2.5.1—S-FTP

Security+ Objective 2.5.2—Blind FTP/Anonymous

Security+ Objective 2.5.3—File sharing

Security+ Objective 3.5.3.4—FTP Servers

Two other common protocols are the **File Transfer Protocol (FTP)** and the **Trivial File Transfer Protocol (TFTP)**, which are used on the Internet to send files. FTP, the more popular of the two, use TCP, the connection-oriented service of the TCP/IP protocol suite. A connection-oriented data transmission service guarantees that packets will arrive at their destination in the order that they were sent and that they will arrive error-free. TFTP uses UDP to send and receive data packets. UDP is the connectionless service provided by the TCP/IP protocol suite. A connectionless service sends data packets but does not guarantee that those packets will arrive in the order that they were sent or that they will arrive error-free. You would typically use TFTP is when you need to send small files over a reliable link. Cisco routers use TFTP to backup and update their configuration files.

When setting up your FTP server, you need to know which directories in which the files are available through the FTP server and you have to configure the permissions. Often, some people specify the wrong directories. For example, they may include their operating system files or private data. Some organizations allow users write permissions, while others do it my mistake. If you don't want the changes to your files, you should disable the write permission.

When transferring files with FTP, the data including the user name and password are sent in clear text. Therefore, anyone can capture this information with a protocol analyzer modified using a man in the middle attack. To overcome these problems, you need to encrypt the data using an IPSec, a tunnel or by using secure FTP. **Secure FTP (S-FTP)** is a program that uses SSH to transfer files or you need to transfer them over an encrypted pathway. Unlike standard FTP, it encrypts both commands and data, preventing passwords and sensitive information from being transmitted in the clear over the network. It is functionally similar to FTP, but because it uses a different protocol, you cannot use a standard FTP client to talk to an S-FTP server, nor can you connect to an FTP server with a client that supports only S-FTP.

If S-FTP is not a viable option, you do have some other options. First, if the files that you need shared are not considered confidential, such as a form that you are providing, you do not want your users to log in and have their username and password sent in clear text. In this case, you can set up an **anonymous FTP,** where anyone can download files without providing a user name or password.

Blind FTP means that the user cannot see the names of any files in the directory. They can only retrieve a file if they know its full name. If the directory is configured to allow uploads, the user can upload a file to the site, but they and other users cannot see it in the FTP site's directory once it has been uploaded.

FTP uses TCP ports 20 and 21 for data and control while TFP uses UDP ports 20 and 21. While it is recommended to put public FTP servers on an DMZ, if you have internal FTP servers (private network), you should block ports 20 and 21 (both TCP and UDP) from coming in.

Like any network application, there may be software bugs or vulnerabilities which may be used to exploit your FTP server. You should then check for service packs, patches, and security fixes for your web server on a regular basis. One such exploit is the FTP bounce, which allows attackers to run scans against other computers though your FTP server. This makes it look like your FTP server is scanning client computers. While this attack is related to the proper functioning of FTP, many vendors have found solutions for preventing it in the form of security updates or configuration changes.

10.6.9   8.3 Naming Convention Vulnerability

Security+ Objective 2.3.3.2—8.3 Naming Conventions

When DOS was introduced with the IBM PC, DOS identified each file with a filename and its extension. When displaying the filename and the extension, it would be divided by a period(.):

```
filename.ext
```

The filename could be from 1 to 8 characters and the extension could be from 0 to 3 characters. In DOS, and latter Windows programs, the extension would identify the type of file it was. This became known as the 8.3-compliant filename.

When Windows 95 was introduced, Windows used long file names, the same type of long file names that is used today with Microsoft Windows. However, to be backward compatible with DOS and Windows 3.X programs, it would store the file under two filenames, the 8.3 filename (the short filename) and the long filename. For example, when you look at the name of a folder called "Program Files," it is also has a filename of "PROGRA~1."

Some Win32-based web servers have not compensated for the two filename versions when restricting access to files that have long names. The web servers attempt to restrict access by building an internal list of restricted filenames. However, for files with long names, only the long, and not the short, file name is added to this internal list. This leaves the file unprotected by the web server because the file is still accessible via the short file name. To overcome this vulnerability, first look for a software patch or security fix. If none are available, then you will have to restrict both the long and short filenames. For Windows environments, you can also use NTFS-based ACLs (directory or file level access control lists) to augment or replace web server–based security.

10.6.10   Other Web Vulnerabilities

The first step in securing a web or FTP server is to check for any vulnerabilities and to apply any service packs, patches, and security fixes to the operating system and to the web and FTP server software. In addition, any services not needed on the server and any ports not be used should be blocked.

In addition to the vulnerabilities mentioned earlier, there are various other types of other security issues with the Web. Some people may try security through obscurity where they have a document on a web server but the document is not listed in any links. The only way to get to it is to know the exact URL. Unfortunately, while this is secure for a while, eventually, one person will give the URL to someone who is not authorized to access the document.

Other people may go to a document and try to learn more about the website by altering the valid URL in certain ways to access other pages, pages that may be advertise or not advertised. One example would be that you are accessing a checklist located at http://www.acme.com/security/checklist.html, so you try to type in http://www.acme.com/security to see what comes up. The way to avoid this type of problem is by not allowing browsing on the directory structure and being sure to secure each document.

While companies have internal web servers and external web servers, external web servers should be placed on a DMZ so that you can establish different access to the public than the rest of your internal site. In addition, like any network application, there may be software bugs or vulnerabilities which may be used to exploit your web server. You should then check for service packs, patches, and security fixes for your web server on a regular basis.

10.7   EMAIL OVERVIEW

Security+ Objective 2.2—Email

Security+ Objective 3.5—Email Servers

Electronic mail (email) is the transmission of messages over communications networks. The messages can be notes entered from the keyboard or electronic files stored on disk. Most mainframes, minicomputers, and computer networks have an email system. Some electronic-mail systems are confined to a single computer system or network, but others have gateways to other computer systems, enabling users to send electronic mail anywhere in the world. Companies that are fully computerized make extensive use of email because it is fast, flexible, and reliable. In recent years, the use of email has exploded.

Most email systems include a rudimentary text editor for composing messages, but many allow you to edit your messages using any editor you want. You then send the message to the recipient by specifying the recipient's address. You can also send the same message to several users at once.

10.7.1   Email and the Internet

No matter which email package that you use or which service you use to host the email, your email travels the same road that all Internet-based information such as web page downloads. That is, your email traverses the Internet backbone. The sender creates an email message on an application. The client system is known as a user agent, or UA. When the user sends the message, it is transmitted to the user's Internet mail server.

Once the message reaches the Internet mail server, it enters the Internet's message transfer system, or MTS. The MTS relies on other Internet mail servers to act as **message transfer agents (MTAs),** which relay the message toward the receiving UA. Once an MTA passes the message to the recipient's Internet mail server, the receiving UA can access the message.

RFC 822 defines the standard format for email messages, treating an email message as having two parts: an envelope and its contents. The envelope contains information needed to transmit and deliver an email message to its destination. The contents are the message that the sender wants delivered to the recipient.

The envelope contains the email address of the sender, the email address of the receiver, and a delivery mode, which in our case states that the message is to be sent to a recipient's mailbox. We can divide the contents of the message into two parts, a header and a body. The header is a required part of the message format, and the sending UA automatically includes it at the top of the message; the user does not input this information. The receiving UA may reformat the header information or delete it entirely to make the message easier for the recipient to read.

The header contains detailed information about who sent the message, who received the message, and how the message got from the sending point to the receiving point. In addition, the header displays the date of the message, the times at which the different MTAs received the message, and the unique ID of the message.

The body of the message contains the actual text the sender typed and is separated from the header by a "null" line. RFC 822 doesn't define the message body, as it can be anything the user enters, as long as it is ASCII text.

A standard email address usually follows the following form:

```
<mailbox ID>@<domain name>
```

The mailbox ID is the name of an individual mailbox on a local machine. The domain name is the name of a valid domain registered in the domain name service (DNS). The DNS servers are key to Internet email because they allow MTAs to find the machine specified in the recipient's email address.

10.7.2   Simple Mail Transfer Protocol (SMTP)

The transmission of an email message through the Internet relies on the **Simple Mail Transfer Protocol,** which is defined in RFC 821. SMTP specifies the way a UA establishes a connection with an MTA and the way it transmits its email message. MTAs also use SMTP to relay the email from MTA to MTA, until it reaches the appropriate MTA for delivery to the receiving UA.

The interactions that happen between two machines, whether a UA to an MTA or an MTA to another MTA, have similar processes and follow a basic call-and-response procedure. The main difference between a UA-to-MTA transaction and an MTA-to-MTA transaction is that with the latter, the sending MTA must locate a receiving MTA.

To do this, the sending MTA contacts the DNS to look up the domain name specified in the recipient email address. The DNS may return the IP address of the domain name—in which case the sending MTA tries to establish a mail connection to the host at that domain—or the DNS may return a set of mail relaying records that contain the domain names of intermediate MTAs that can act as relays to the recipient. In this case, the sending MTA tries to establish a mail connection to the first host listed in the mail relaying record.

When an MTA is sending to an MTA, the sending MTA chooses a receiving MTA, which may be the final destination of the message or an intermediate MTA that will relay the message to another MTA. Next, the sending MTA requests a TCP connection to the receiving MTA. The receiving MTA responds with a server ID and a status report, which indicates whether or not it is available for the mail transaction. If it isn't, the transaction is over; the sending MTA can try again later or attempt another route. If the receiving MTA is free to handle a session, it will accept the TCP connection.

The sending MTA then sends a Hello command followed by its domain name information to the receiving MTA, which responds with a greeting. Next, the sending MTA sends a Mail From command that identifies the email address from which the message originated, as well as a list of the MTAs that the message has passed through. This information is also known as a return path. If the receiving MTA can accept mail from that address, it responds with an OK reply.

The sending MTA then sends a Rcpt To command, which identifies the email address of the recipient. If the receiving MTA can accept mail for that recipient (it may perform a DNS lookup to verify this, particular using the Mail Exchange (MX) records) it responds with an OK reply. If not, it rejects that recipient. (An email message may be addressed to more than one recipient, in which case this process is repeated for each recipient address.)

Once the receiving MTA identifies the recipient's address, the sending MTA sends the Data command. The receiving MTA accepts command by responding with OK. It then considers all succeeding lines of data to be the message text. Once the sending MTA gets an OK reply, it starts sending the message. The sending MTA signals the end of the message by transmitting a line that contains only a period (.).

When the receiving MTA receives the signal for the end of the message, it replies with an OK to signal its acceptance of the message. If for some reason, the receiving MTA can't process the message, it will signal the sending MTA with a failure code. After the message has been sent to the receiving MTA and the sending MTA gets an OK reply, the sending MTA can either start another message transfer or use the Quit command to end the session.

Once the receiving MTA accepts the message, it reverses its role and becomes a sending MTA, contacting the MTA next in line for the relay of the message. The process stops once the message reaches the Internet mail server that services the recipient specified in the Rcpt To email address.

If at any point along the way an MTA can't deliver the email, it generates an error report, also known as an undeliverable mail notification. The MTA uses MTAs identified in the return path to relay the error report back to the original sender.

10.7.3   MIME

Initially, the Internet email system was limited to simple text messages because SMTP, the protocol used to transport mail across the Internet, could carry only 7-bit ASCII text. In the United States, the main ASCII standard used for email is US-ASCII. This version of ASCII offers only a basic set of characters—128 characters in all, each represented as a 7-bit binary number. This ASCII set was designed to cover the English alphabet, including both uppercase and lowercase letters, and the numbers 0 through 9, as well as some other characters.

If you have used email today, you know that email is not just simple text anymore. You can use rich text with italics, boldface, bullets, and other types of enriched formatting. You can even embed graphics in documents. But because SMTP was developed to handle only basic text messages in a 7-bit format—as laid out by RFC 822, which defines the standard for Internet text messaging—these more sophisticated data formats can't be sent via email. The problem with the 128-character set is that it cannot accommodate rich text. In addition, you cannot use foreign language characters that aren't represented in US-ASCII. Therefore, the 7-bit format required by SMPT prevents users from sending other types of data via email, for example, the 8-bit binary data found in many executable files and in files created by applications such as Microsoft Word. For email to handle diverse data such as text, word processing documents and images users could share all sorts of data without having to ship disks or make any actual real-time network connections to copy or download files.

To work around the limitation of SMPT's 7-bit ASCII format, today's email uses **Multipurpose Internet Mail Extensions (MIME).** MIME makes the data appear as standard email messages to the Internet's SMTP servers regardless of the data it contains although the SMTP didn't have to change the way it handles such data. In other words, the solution didn't require that all Internet mail servers be upgraded to a new version of SMTP. In effect, the transport system remained untouched.

As defined in RFC 2045, MIME provides three main enhancements to standard email. First, with MIME, email can contain text that goes beyond basic US-ASCII, including various keystrokes such as different line and page breaks, foreign language characters, and enriched text. Second, users can attach different types of data to their email, including such files as executables, spreadsheets, audio, and images. And third, users can create a single email message that contains multiple parts, and each part can be in a different data format. For example, you could compose a single email message that consists of a plain text message, an image file, and a binary-based document, such as a Word file.

The application type supports two types of data, data that's meant to be processed by an application, and data that do not fall into any of the other categories. For now, it supports the octet-stream subtype, which means the message can carry arbitrary binary data. Also, it supports the postscript subtype, meaning the message can be sent to print as a PostScript file. Note: If a mail agent receives a message whose content subtype it doesn't recognize, by default it will attempt to pass the message on as an application type message with a subtype of octet-stream (or, application/octet-stream).

The remaining two content types allow for special handling of an email message. For instance, the message type allows an email to contain an encapsulated message. The external-body subtype allows an email to indicate an external location where the intended body of the message resides. That way, the user can choose whether or not to retrieve the message body. The message type also allows MIME to send a large email message as several small ones (the subtype for this is partial). The receiving MIME-enabled mail agent can then open the smaller email messages and reassemble them into the original long version.

Finally, the multipart type allows an email message to contain more than one body of data. The mixed subtype allows users to mix different data formats into one email message. The alternative subtype allows a message to contain different versions of the same data, each version in a different format. MIME mail agents can then select the version that works best with the local computing environment. The digest subtype allows users to send a collection of messages in one email, such as the kind used with Internet mailing lists sent in digest form. Finally, the parallel subtype allows mixed body parts, but the ordering of the body parts is not important.

To package the different data formats into the 7-bit ASCII format, MIME uses five different encoding schemes: 7-bit, 8-bit, binary, quoted-printable, and base64. But, as you'll soon see, only the quoted-printable and base64 schemes actually encode data. The 7-bit, 8-bit, binary quoted-printable, and base-64. But, as you'll soon see, only the quoted-printable and base64 schemes actually encode data.

Using MIME is simple. If your mail system supports MIME, it automatically chooses the data type and encoding scheme. It then adds MIME headers to the body of the message. These headers tell receiving mail agents that they've received a MIME message and indicate how the mail agents should handle the message.

The main headers are MIME-Version, Content-Type, and Content-Transfer-Encoding. The last two headers refer to the data type found in the message and the scheme used to encode the data, respectively. Some other headers are Content-Description, which lets you type in a description of the message (much like SMTP's Subject header), and Content-ID, which is similar to SMTP's Message-ID.

10.7.4   Retrieving Email

When the email arrives at the recipient's Internet mail server, the user agent can employ different methods to access, or retrieve, its email from the MTA. For instance, the majority of companies rely on proprietary email packages, such as Microsoft Exchange or cc:Mail, to handle email operations on the local network. There are a few different models for this operation and a few different protocols that can handle the task, including proprietary protocols found in commercial email packages and two Internet standards-based protocols, Post Office Protocol-3 (POP-3) and the Internet Message Access Protocol 4 (IMAP-4).

When an email reaches the designated recipient's mail server, the message is placed in a message store, which is also called a post office. In its most basic form, the message store, located on a server, is usually some type of file system that holds delivered mail for access by users. You can think of the message store as one large directory with subdirectories dedicated to each user. These subdirectories are also known as mailboxes. A more advanced form of message store would allow users to create personal folders to store read and unread messages, and it would allow users to create archives for groups of messages. Other advanced features include the ability to perform keyword searches and to create a hierarchy of folders.

The message store component of an email system is usually located on a different machine than the message transport component, which handles the delivery of incoming messages and the transmission of outgoing ones. The reason for their separation is that the transport component usually handles a high volume of operations. So, if both systems were on the same machine, the traffic of inbound and outbound mail would experience slower performance, as would users when they try to retrieve and manipulate mail in their mailboxes. Once an email message is delivered to the message store, it's ready for retrieval by the recipient.

One of the first email access protocols developed was the **Post Office Protocol,** the latest version of which is POP-3. In essence, **POP-3** follows the offline model of message access, and it revolves around send-and-receive types of operation. However, there have been recent attempts to remodel POP-3 so that it has some online capabilities, such as saved-message folders and status flags that display message states. But using POP-3 in online mode usually requires the additional presence of some type of remote file system protocol.

IMAP-4 is the more advanced of the standards-based message access protocols. It follows the online model of message access, although it does support offline and disconnected modes. IMAP-4 offers an array of up-to-date features, including support for the creation and management of remote folders and folder hierarchies, message status flags, new mail notification, retrieval of individual MIME body parts, and server-based searches to minimize the amount of data that must be transferred over the connection.

10.7.5   PGP and S/MIME

Security+ Objective 2.2.2—PGP-like technologies

Unfortunately, anyone can collect and read messages (including username and passwords) by using a protocol analyzer. In addition, email messages can be easily forged by modifying the sender field of an email message so that it can appear to come from anyone. Therefore, you need to encrypt these messages so that only the intended recipient can decrypt them and you need a way to digitally sign messages so that your message recipients can be sure that the message is really from you. Two common solutions to these problems is PGP and S/MIME.

Pretty Good Privacy (PGP) is a popular program used to encrypt and decrypt email over the Internet. It can also be used to send an encrypted digital signature that lets the receiver verify the sender's identity and know that the message was not changed en route. Available both as freeware and in a low-cost commercial version, PGP is the most widely used privacy-ensuring program by individuals and is also used by many corporations. Developed by Philip R. Zimmermann in 1991, PGP has become a de facto standard for email security. PGP can also be used to encrypt files being stored so that they are unreadable by other users or intruders.

PGP uses a variation of the public key system. In this system, each user has a publicly known encryption key and a private key known only to that user. You encrypt a message you send to someone else using their public key. When they receive it, they decrypt it using their private key. Since encrypting an entire message can be time-consuming, PGP uses a faster encryption algorithm to encrypt the message and then uses the public key to encrypt the shorter key that was used to encrypt the entire message. Both the encrypted message and the short key are sent to the receiver who first uses the receiver's private key to decrypt the short key and then uses that key to decrypt the message.

PGP comes in two public key versions—Rivest-Shamir-Adleman (RSA) and Diffie-Hellman. The RSA version, for which PGP must pay a license fee to RSA, uses the IDEA algorithm to generate a short key for the entire message and RSA to encrypt the short key. The Diffie-Hellman version uses the CAST algorithm for the short key to encrypt the message and the Diffie-Hellman algorithm to encrypt the short key.

For sending digital signatures, PGP uses an efficient algorithm that generates a hash (or mathematical summary) from the user's name and other signature information. This hash code is then encrypted with the sender's private key. The receiver uses the sender's public key to decrypt the hash code. If it matches the hash code sent as the digital signature for the message, then the receiver is sure that the message has arrived securely from the stated sender. PGP's RSA version uses the MD5 algorithm to generate the hash code. PGP's Diffie-Hellman version uses the SHA-1 algorithm to generate the hash code.

To use PGP, you download or purchase it and install it on your computer system. Typically, it contains a user interface that works with your customary email program. You also need to register the public key that your PGP program gives you with a PGP public-key server so that people you exchange messages with will be able to find your public key. PGP is available at:

- **PGP Freeware version**—http://web.mit.edu/network/pgp.html
- **Commercial versions of PGP to be purchased and freeware versions of PGP from the PGP Corporation**—http://www.pgp.com.

Originally, the U.S. government restricted the exportation of PGP technology. Today, however, PGP-encrypted email can be exchanged with users outside the United States if you have the correct versions of PGP at both ends. Unlike most other encryption products, the international version is just as secure as the domestic version.

The freely available PGP cannot legally be used for commercial purposes—for that, one must obtain the commercial version from Network Associates (formerly PGP, Inc.). There are several versions of PGP in use. Add-ons can be purchased that allow backwards compatibility for newer RSA versions with older versions. However, the Diffie-Hellman and RSA versions of PGP do not work with each other since they use different algorithms.

Security+ Objective 2.2.1—S/MIME

S/MIME (Secure Multi-Purpose Internet Mail Extensions) is a secure method of sending email that uses the Rivest-Shamir-Adleman encryption system. S/MIME is included in the latest versions of the Web browsers from Microsoft and Netscape and has also been endorsed by other vendors that make messaging products. S/MIME describes how encryption information and a digital certificate can be included as part of the message body. S/MIME follows the syntax provided in the Public-Key Cryptography Standard format #7. Of course, to utilize S/MIME, you must have access to a PKI certificate. This certificate can come from an internal PKI provided by your organization or an external infrastructure such as Verisign.

Client email settings for digital signatures and encryption are often independently configurable. For example, Microsoft's Outlook email client allows you to digitally sign all or select messages and separately digitally encrypt all or selected messages.

10.7.6   Email Spam, Hoaxes, and Scams

Security+ Objective 2.2.3—Vulnerabilities

Security+ Objective 2.2.3.1—Spam

Security+ Objective 2.2.3.2—Hoaxes

Security+ Objective 2.3.4.7—SMTP Relay

While email has become one of the most popular forms of communications, it has also been a target of email scams, hoaxes, spam, and viruses. **Spam** is unsolicited email on the Internet. From the sender's point-of-view, it's a form of bulk mail, often to a list obtained by companies that specialize in creating email distribution lists. To the receiver, it usually seems like junk email. Some apparently unsolicited email is, in fact, email people agreed to receive when they registered with a site and checked a box agreeing to receive postings about particular products or interests. This is known as both opt-in email and permission-based email.

Email spoofing is the forgery of an email header so that the message appears to have originated from someone or somewhere other than the actual source. Spam distributors often use spoofing in an attempt to get recipients to open, and possibly even respond to, their solicitations. Spoofing can be used legitimately. Classic examples of senders who might prefer to disguise the source of the email include a sender reporting mistreatment by a spouse to a welfare agency or a "whistleblower" who fears retaliation. However, spoofing anyone other than yourself is illegal in some jurisdictions.

Although most spoofed email falls into the "nuisance" category and requires little action other than deletion, the more malicious varieties can cause serious problems and security risks. For example, spoofed email may purport to be from someone in a position of authority, asking for sensitive data, such as passwords, credit card numbers, or other personal information—any of which can be used for a variety of criminal purposes. One type of email spoofing, self-sending spam, involves messages that appear to be both to and from the recipient.

Email spoofing is possible because Simple Mail Transfer Protocol (SMTP), the main protocol used in sending email, does not include an authentication mechanism. Although an SMTP service extension allows an SMTP client to negotiate a security level with a mail server, this precaution is not often taken. If the precaution is not taken, anyone with the requisite knowledge can connect to the server and use it to send messages. To send spoofed email, senders insert commands in headers that will alter message information. It is possible to send a message that appears to be from anyone, anywhere, saying whatever the sender wants it to say. Thus, someone could send spoofed email that appears to be from you with a message that you didn't write.

Some spammers attempt to funnel their junk mail through other email servers that permit SMTP relay. If spammers can forward mail from a server not linked to spam, they can get more spam to more people. When someone else's email server is used for spam without permission, the spamming becomes an attack as their email service is bogged down. In addition, some ISPs may block mail from your email server because the email appears to come from it.

To protect your organization's server from becoming a spammer mail relay station, you must restrict access to SMTP relay. In addition, SMTP relay should be disabled on any device that the organization does not intend to use for mail transfer. In addition, to prevent malicious users from sending emails from non-existing domains, you need to enable DNS reverse lookup on the email server so that it can verify the domains.

Email hoaxes continue to be problems for network users. An email hoax is often spread like a chain letter or rumor. Hoaxes contain false information that is believable. Since email messages ask you to forward the message to colleagues, making it possible for a single email to spread exponentially. As a result, the emails can use valuable network resources. Other hoaxes have been warnings to check for a virus that they might have received off the Internet or through their email. Instructions in the email tell people to search their computers for files that are said to be viruses, when the files are actually part of popular operating systems. The hoaxes tell users to delete these files and forward this information to everyone in their address book.

For a list of the more common Internet hoaxes, visit the Hoax Busters website (http://www.hoaxbusters.org/). Hoax Busters also give the five telltale signs of a hoax:

- Urgent, Warning, Important, Virus, often with a lot of exclamation points (!).
- Tell your friends
- This isn't a hoax
- Dire consequences
- The email contains a history of many people in which the email has been sent to and forwarded from.

To protect your organization from hoaxes, you should create a written policy that prohibits the forwarding of known hoaxes. The policy should also be posted to help users identify potential hoaxes. Be sure to educate your network users on the existence of these hoaxes and the damage and loss of productivity they can cause. In addition, be sure to communicate that users should not delete any files that an email instructs them to delete. Instead, they should forward such messages to your support team for an official response and action plan. Lastly, an up-to-date virus scanner can be used to check for actual viruses.

In addition to spam and hoaxes, we have email scams. Scams do not offer legitimate products or services. Instead, they want to steal money, products, or services. Usually, they ask the intended victim to transfer money or provide bank account or credit card information. Some emails will forge the source of the email to make the email look legitimate and sometimes point to a fake website that looks like a legitimate website. You could then be asked to type in credit card information or username and passwords. They will then use that information to access your personal information or make transactions under your name.

An old scam that started in the 1980s with fax machines is now being used in emails. The Nigerian money laundering scam induces the recipient into believing they are going to get something for nothing. Usually the letters claim there are extensive funds available for immediate transfer into the recipient's bank account(s). Emphasizing the fact that all that is required of the recipient is to provide the details of their personal or company bank accounts. Should they reply to the invitation there then follows a series of further communications usually by fax but email is now being used. Further instructions are passed to the potential victim explaining the finer points of the scheme and the fact that they will be required to provide some form of advanced payment. The explanation for this is that the negotiations for this deal are highly secretive and money is required to bribe officials in Nigeria to arrange customs clearance or exchange control procedures. After sometimes investing hundreds, if not thousands of dollars, they receive nothing. The Better Business Bureau reported that Americans loss $100 million per year. Note: This scam does not have to come from Nigeria, and there may be many deviations of this scam.

So how do you protect your company from such scams? First, you need to create a policy prohibiting the release of sensitive information through the inappropriate channels. In addition, educating your users to the existence and prevalence of email scams is essential. The FTC has compiled a list of common email scams which can be found at the following website:

http://www.ftc.gov/bcp/conline/pubs/alerts/doznalrt.htm

10.7.7   Other Security Concerns

Any network service may have vulnerabilities that may be exploited. Therefore, you need to check for service packs, patches, and security fixes on a regular basis from the email server vendor. In addition, if you are concerned about viruses being sent through email attachments, you should filter executable files from your email messages

10.8   NNTP

Security+ Objective 3.5.3.6—NNTP Servers

NNTP servers handle the distribution of Usenet News. The NNTP (or Net News Transfer Protocol) uses port 119, so if you need to provide NNTP access to clients outside your network, make sure you allow incoming connections to port 119 on your NNTP server. Through an NNTP server, users can read and post news "articles" which are then made available to other sites participating in Usenet through bulk transfers of batches of articles among cooperating sites.

NNTP software tends to be fairly complex, and security holes are discovered in various implementations from time to time, with results including an attacker obtaining system administrator access to the news server, creating a denial of service situation, reconfiguration of the news server, etc., so do keep up with patches.

NNTP originally controlled access based on the host from which users connected (or they allowed everyone, anywhere, access). When most users read news from multi-user UNIX machines, this model worked well enough, but with the advent of single-user workstations and dynamically assigned IP addresses, became difficult to manage. Add the problem of users making inappropriate posts, and even "forging" news articles (making it look like someone else posted an article they created), and news server suppliers began to place more emphasis on authenticating those who connect to them.

Some require users to authenticate themselves before access is provided, and some don't. If possible, run a news server that requires authentication and takes steps to ensure that articles are not submitted with forged identity information. Based on the provided authentication information, users can be authorized to read news, post or bulk transfer news (which allows the user to upload/download entire sets of multiple articles, a capability which is usually only needed for servers). Most commonly, you would only allow the first two privileges, unless a peer server with whom you exchange news used the user ID in question.

As with email messages headers, NNTP article headers listing the poster's identity and other information can be forged. Additionally, NNTP client connections can consume a lot of bandwidth. Therefore, it is best if you can run a news server that requires authentication and takes steps to ensure that forged articles are not accepted.

10.9   USING INSTANT MESSENGERS AND PEER-TO-PEER APPLICATIONS

Security+ Objective 2.3.3—Instant Messaging

Security+ Objective 2.3.3.1—Vulnerabilities

Security+ Objective 2.3.3.3—Packet Sniffing

Security+ Objective 2.3.3.4—Privacy

While Instant Messaging (IM) and Peer-to-Peer (P2P) applications are now being deployed in enterprises as productivity-enhancing communications tools, the vast majority of IM and P2P applications in the enterprise today are installed and used without the enterprises' oversight, exposing data and networks to theft and damage. IM allows users to chat, videoconference, share applications, transfer files, and even remotely access their PC. IM is now included with the most Windows XP and America Online.

P2P applications such as Kazaa, Morpheus, or Gnutella enable people around the world to share music, video, and software applications, often exposing data on their computer to thousands of people on the Internet. These applications are not designed for use in enterprise networks, and, as a result, introduce serious security vulnerabilities to enterprise networks if installed on networked PCs. Since P2P allows a user to download files, these files may contain viruses or may be Trojan horses. Lastly, your business or corporation may be liable for software or media piracy.

IM and P2P applications effectively circumvent most enterprise security architectures in the same way that a Trojan horse does. The IM or P2P application is installed on a trusted device that is allowed to communicate through the enterprise firewall with an outside IM server, or other P2P users. Once there is a connection made from a "trusted device" to the public Internet, malicious users can gain remote access to that trusted device for the purpose of stealing enterprise data, launching a Denial of Service attack (such as buffer overflow), gaining control of network resources or running malicious programs. In addition, people often send confidential or private information using IM, such as usernames, passwords, or trade secrets. However many popular IM applications transfer information unencrypted. In addition, when transferring files using message, the files bypass the network virus scanners.

One alternative to Internet messenger software is to use Microsoft NetMeeting, which offers a secure connection option, which encrypts all traffic between clients. NetMeeting is software that enables groups to teleconference using the Internet or corporate networks as the transmission medium. Net-Meeting supports Voice on the Net, chat sessions, a whiteboard, and application sharing. NetMeeting is included in newer versions of Windows. Microsoft NetMeeting uses port 389, 522, 1503, 1720, and 1731.

Existing security infrastructures lack the ability to effectively control IM and P2P application communication at the host level. Network-based solutions to the IM and P2P problem such as perimeter firewalls, routers, and network-IDS cannot accurately detect, control, and enforce security policy related to the usage of IM and P2P. For example, you could attempt to block perimeter firewall ports used by some of the more popular IM and P2P applications, but some operate on port 80 or can be configured to change the port automatically.

IM applications used registered ports are follows:

- MSN messenger uses TCP port 1863 to connect to the messenger servers and to carry text messages, UDP port 6501 for voice communications and TCP ports 6891–6900 for file transfers.
- AOL Instant Messenger uses TCP port 5190 for file transfers and file sharing, but transportation not IM images take place on TCP port 4443.
- Yahoo's Messenger typically uses TCP port 5050 for server communication and TCP port 80 for direct file transfers.
- ICQ messages are sent via TCP port 3570, and voice and video transfer utilizes UDP port 6701.

You could implement Network IDS to detect known attacks that exploit IM and P2P applications, but most of the exploits are part of the normal operation of the product (file sharing, remote access) and cannot be identified accurately, or are not recognized as illegitimate communication by any signature libraries. IDS cannot detect new vulnerabilities until a signature is created and distributed.

Another problem with IM is that there is a lack of logging or audit trail. While on some IM users can log IM conversations on there personal computer. Unfortunately, most if not all of these are of short duration and are not kept in a central location. Some organizations would like a centralized audit trail that lets them know which users within the organization are communicating via IM, and when they're doing it.

Some organizations protect themselves from potential IM applications exploits by prohibiting the use of IM and P2P applications. Other organizations allow the use of IM, but define an IM application that they can support and secure. If removing IM completely from your organization's network is not an option, consider the following:

Restrict the types of IM that are authorized so that you don't have to figure out the security risk of each of the different types of messengers. If the data transmitted between IM clients should be private, obtain an IM application that encrypts communications. Some IM products allow you to implement PKI encryption, audit usage, and configure security settings centrally. Since messages have become more popular, some companies even offer corporate versions (such as Microsoft Exchange server can be configured as an IM server) of their messenger service that can be used within your corporation. Note: Top Secret Messenger and Message Inspector are two products that address IM security issues.

Create a written policy regarding the acceptable use of IM applications. You should probably prohibit the downloading of files over IM and P2P to protect your network users from potentially unsafe content. Of course, with that, you will need to educate your users about the risks of IM and P2P. Each machine that has IM should have updated virus scanners to help protect against viruses. If you have to use messengers between sites and the packets are not encrypted, use IPSec or some type of virtual tunnel.

10.10   DATABASES

Security+ Objective 3.5.3.9—Data Repositories

Security+ Objective 3.5.3.9.2—Databases

A **database** is a collection of information organized in such a way that a computer program can quickly select desired pieces of data. You can think of a database as an electronic filing system.

Traditional databases are organized by fields, records, and files. A field is a single piece of information; a record is one complete set of fields; and a file is a collection of records. For example, a telephone book is analogous to a file. It contains a list of records, each of which consists of three fields:

name, address, and telephone number. Each person with his or her address and phone number would be one record. Another example of a database is a collection of information about a company's products, its customers, its financial records and so on.

In a flat-based database you will find a table, which refers to data arranged in rows and columns. A spreadsheet, for example, is a table. In relational database management systems, all information is stored in the form of tables and the tables are linked together. When you access a record, you may be accessing information from the various tables.

To access information from a database, you need a **database management system (DBMS),** which is a collection of programs that enables you to enter, organize, and select data in a database. There are many different types of DBMSs, ranging from small systems that run on personal computers to huge systems that run on mainframes. Some examples include computerized library systems, automated teller machines, flight reservation systems and computerized parts inventory systems.

For database security, the granularity of access control is a description of how finely you can control who can see which tables, rows, and fields. An example of low granularity is read or read/write access to all rows and fields in a table. High granularity restricts access to certain fields and even certain rows.

A view is a particular way of looking at a database. A single database can support numerous different views. Typically, a view arranges the records in some order and makes only certain fields visible. It does not affect the physical organization of the database.

Aggregation is the process of combining low-sensitivity data items to produce a high-sensitivity data item. For example, dates of birth or a home address don't mean a lot, but when they are aggregated with a name, they become a high-sensitivity data item. If someone is able to get enough information such as a social security number or a driver's license number, then the person that the information represents is vulnerable to identity theft. On the other hand, inference is the ability to deduce or infer sensitive information that is beyond normal reach because of its sensitivity level.

Structured query language, more commonly referred to as **SQL** (pronounced either see-kwell or as separate letters) is a standardized query language for requesting information from a database. SQL was first introduced as a commercial database system in 1979 by Oracle Corporation. Historically, SQL has been the favorite query language for database management systems running on minicomputers and mainframes. Increasingly, however, SQL is being supported by PC database systems because it supports distributed databases (databases that are spread out over several computer systems). This enables several users on a local area network to access the same database simultaneously.

Although there are different dialects of SQL, it is nevertheless the closest thing to a standard query language that currently exists. In 1986, ANSI approved a rudimentary version of SQL as the official standard, but most versions of SQL since then have included many extensions to the ANSI standard. In 1991, ANSI updated the standard. The new standard is known as SAG SQL.

For SQL servers, the three entities of the SQL security model are:

- users (authentication using a logon process at the OS or database level)
- actions (commands like SELECT, DELETE, etc.)
- objects (tables, views, etc.)

In SQL servers, permissions can be assigned to allow users to execute certain statements and to access certain database objects. Statement permissions restrict who can execute statements such as CREATE DATABASE, CREATE TABLE, or CREATE VIEW. Object permissions restrict access to objects such as tables, views, or stored procedures. Object permissions are dependent on the object being referenced. For example, object permissions for tables include the SELECT, INSERT, UPDATE, DELETE, and REFERENCES permissions, while the object permissions on a stored procedure include EXECUTE permissions. Permissions can be granted to roles and users.

Unfortunately, a database server, such as a SQL server, is a good target for any hacker. Like hardening a web server, hardening a database server tends to be a multi-step process, in which you harden the database server software itself, and then any custom applications/databases your organization's staff has set up. Don't overlook the step of checking for security updates for your database server software.

The most straightforward issue with databases is simply configuration of the database for appropriate levels of data privacy and integrity. Your database administrator should be responsible for maintaining the necessary security on the sets of data stored in the database. Each data table can often be assigned its own permissions, which may, for example, allow web users to just read, or just add to a table. If you need to apply different rules to different users, many databases can be configured to accept individual user logins as well as general connections without authentication, and then match the user login with access rules for the data in the database, to determine what kind of access (delete records, add new records, change records, read-only) the user has to each type of data in the database.

Because of programming errors or oversights or because applications are written by others and attached to the database, some databases/DBMSs offer access to the command line prompt to the operating system, sometimes with system administrator privileges. In addition, some databases/DBMSs have small programs or macros stored in the database server to do a series of tasks or commands when they are invoked by database users. Since these small programs and macros sometimes take user inputs, they can be used to cause a buffer overflow or cause the server to crash if the user inputs something that the server did not expect. In both of these situations, you will need to check for these possible vulnerabilities and see if you can configure the database or DBMS or apply patches to close these vulnerabilities.

In addition to considering the server itself, you should also consider how the database communicates over the network. Some database systems, like SQL server, communicate on a well-known port. If you have an internal database server that is accessed by your employees, you can external block traffic from the Internet that uses that port. In fact, ideally, you can put rules (by using ACLs) into place on your network that allow your web server and a couple of internal workstations to connect to the database server port and disallow access to it by everyone else. For example, if SQL server is your database, only allow inbound access to the database server machine TCP ports 1433 and 1434 from your web server and a minimal number of trusted internal hosts.

Lastly, some databases have default passwords. Therefore, be sure to change the password of any account installed with your database installation (or use a method of authentication that verifies identity other than by password).

WHAT YOU NEED TO KNOW

Security+ Objective 2.1.6—SSH

1. Telecommuncation Network (Telnet) is a virtual terminal protocol (terminal emulation) allowing a user to log on to another TCP/IP host to access network resources.
2. The telnet command can be used to test TCP connections. You can telnet to any TCP port to see if it is responding, which is especially useful when checking SMTP and HTTP ports.
3. Telnet, and other related commands (rlogin and rsh), have one major problem. They send the username and password in cleartext for any one to see.
4. To overcome this security weakness of telnet and related utilities, Secure Shell (SSH) had to be developed by proividing strong authentication (RSA public key cryptography) and secure communications over insecure channels (encryption algorithms include Blowfish, DES, and IDEA, with IDEA being the default).
5. When using ssh's slogin, the entire login session, including transmission of password, is encrypted; therefore it is almost impossible for an outsider to collect passwords.

Security+ Objective 2.2—Email

Security+ Objective 2.2.1—S/MIME

Security+ Objective 2.2.2—PGP-like Technologies

Security+ Objective 2.2.3—Vulnerabilities

Security+ Objective 2.2.3.1—Spam

Security+ Objective 2.2.3.2—Hoaxes

Security+ Objective 2.3.4.7—SMTP Relay

Security+ Objective 3.5—Email Servers

1. Electronic mail (email) is the transmission of messages over communications networks.
2. Unfortunately, anyone can collect and read messages (including username and passwords) by using a protocol analyzer.
3. In addition, email messages can be easily forged by modifying the sender field of an email message so that it can appear to come from anyone.
4. Therefore, you need to encrypt these messages so that only the intended recipient can decrypt them, and you need a way to digitally sign messages so that your message recipients can be sure that the message is really from you. Two common solutions to these problems is PGP and S/MIME.
5. Pretty Good Privacy (PGP) is a popular program used to encrypt and decrypt email over the Internet. It can also be used to send an encrypted digital signature that lets the receiver verify the sender's identity and know that the message was not changed en route.
6. PGP has become a de facto standard for email security.

7. PGP can also be used to encrypt files being stored so that they are unreadable by other users or intruders.

8. S/MIME (Secure Multi-Purpose Internet Mail Extensions) is a secure method of sending email that uses the Rivest-Shamir-Adleman encryption system.

9. S/MIME is included in the latest versions of the web browsers from Microsoft and Netscape and has also been endorsed by other vendors that make messaging products.

10. Client email settings for digital signatures and encryption are often independently configurable. For example, Microsoft's Outlook email client allows you to digitally sign all or select messages and separately digitally encrypt all or selected messages.

11. While email has become one of the most popular forms of communications, it has also been a target of email scams, hoaxes, spam, and viruses.

12. Spam is unsolicited email on the Internet.

13. Email spoofing is the forgery of an email header so that the message appears to have originated from someone or somewhere other than the actual source.

14. Although most spoofed email falls into the "nuisance" category and requires little action other than deletion, the more malicious varieties can cause serious problems and security risks.

15. Email spoofing is possible because Simple Mail Transfer Protocol (SMTP), the main protocol used in sending email, does not include an authentication mechanism.

16. Although an SMTP service extension allows an SMTP client to negotiate a security level with a mail server, this precaution is not often taken.

17. Some spammers attempt to funnel their junk mail through other email servers that permit SMTP relay. If spammers can forward mail from a server not linked to spam, they can get more spam to more people.

18. When someone else's email server is used for spam without permission, the spamming becomes an attack as their email service is bogged down. In addition, some ISP may block mail from your email server because the email appears to come from it.

19. To protect your organization's server from becoming a spammer mail relay station, you must restrict access to SMTP relay.

20. SMTP relay should be disabled on any device that the organization does not intend to use for mail transfer.

21. To prevent malicious users from sending emails from nonexisting domains, you need to enable DNS reverse lookup on the email server so that it can verify the domains.

22. Email hoaxes continue to be problems for network users. An email hoax is often spread like a chain letter or rumor. Hoaxes contain false information that is believable.

23. Other hoaxes have been warnings to check for a virus that they might have received off the Internet or through their email. Instructions in the email tell people to search their computers for files that are said to be viruses, when the files are actually part of popular operating systems. The hoaxes tell users to delete these files and forward this information to everyone in their address book.

24. To protect your organization from hoaxes, you should create a written policy that prohibits the forwarding of known hoaxes. The policy should also be posted to help users identify potential hoaxes. Be sure to educate your network users on the existence of these hoaxes and the damage and loss of productivity they can cause. In addition, be sure to communicate that users should not delete any files that an email instructs them to delete. Instead, they should forward such messages to your support team for an official response and action plan. Lastly, an up-to-date virus scanner can be used to check for actually viruses.

25. Scams do not offer legitimate products or services. Instead, they want to steal money, products, or services. Usually, they ask the intended victim to transfer money or provide bank account or credit card information.

26. To protect against scams, you need to create a policy prohibiting the release of sensitive information through the inappropriate channels. In addition, educating your users to the existence and prevalence of email scams is essential.

Security+ Objective 2.3—Web

Security+ Objective 3.5.3.2—Web Servers

1. The World Wide Web (WWW) was created in 1992, and refers to the means of organizing, presenting, and accessing information over the Internet.

2. A web server is a computer equipped with the server software that uses Internet protocols such as Hypertext Transfer Protocol (HTTP) and File Transfer Protocol (FTP) to respond to web client requests on a TCP/IP network via web browsers.

3. A web server acting as a file server simply accepts a request for a document, validates the request, and sends the requested files back to the browser.

4. Other people may go to a document and they try to learn more about the website by altering the valid URL in certain ways to access other pages, pages that may be advertised or not advertised. To avoid this type of problem is don't allow browsing on the directory structure and be sure to secure each document.

5. While companies have internal web servers and external web servers, external web servers should be placed on a DMZ so that you can establish different access to the public than the rest of your internal site.

6. In addition, like any network application, there may be software bugs or vulnerabilities which may be used to exploit your web server. You should then check for service packs, patches, and security fixes for your web server on a regular basis.

Security+ Objective 2.3.1—SSL/TLS

1. Secure Sockets Layer (SSL) ensure that sensitive information from passing through an Internet link is safe from prying eyes by establishing a secure connection between two computers,

2. SSL is based on PKI encryption methods developed by RSA Corporation to provide encryption and authentication to maintain the integrity of the transmission channel.

3. When an SSL client wants to communicate with an SSL-compliant server, an SSL handshake will occur, which starts when the client initiates a request to the server. The server then sends a X.509 standard certificate back to the client. The certificate includes the server's public key and server's preferred cryptographic algorithms, or ciphers.

4. When a secure link has been created, the first part of the URL will change from http:// to https://. Although SSL is optimized for use with HTTP, it can also be used with FTP or other relevant protocols.

5. While HTTP uses TCP port 80, HTTPS uses port 443.

6. The Transport Layer Security (TLS) protocol is based on and similar to SSL version 3.

7. TLS is essentially the latest version of SSL, but it is not as widely available in browsers.

8. Its primary goal is to provide privacy and data integrity between two communicating applications.

9. While TLS protocol is based on Netscape's SSL 3.0 protocol, TLS and SSL are not interoperable.

10. Common 40- or 56-bit web browsers are considered to have weak encryption because their keys can be cracked in a short time. The stronger browsers will use 128-bit ciphers, which would require more time and commitment of resources to break.

11. Most SSL/TLS-enabled web servers allow the customization of types of encryption and what key sizes can and cannot be used while a connection is made.

Security+ Objective 2.3.2—HTTP/S

1. Secure Hypertext Transfer Protocol (S-HTTP), also referred to as HTTP/S, is simply an extension of HTTP.

2. S-HTTP is created by SSL running under HTTP.

3. Don't confuse S-HTTP with HTTPS (HTTP over SSL).

4. While SSL operates at the Transport layer, S-HTTP supports secure end-to-end transactions by adding cryptography to messages at the application layer.

5. While SSL is application independent, S-HTTP is tied to the HTTP protocol.

6. S-HTTP doesn't require that the client possess a public key certificate, which means secure transactions can take place at any time without individuals needed to provide a key (as in session encryption with SSL).

Security+ Objective 2.3.3—Instant Messaging

Security+ Objective 2.3.3.1—Vulnerabilities

Security+ Objective 2.3.3.3—Packet Sniffing

Security+ Objective 2.3.3.4—Privacy

1. While Instant Messaging (IM) applications are now being deployed in enterprises as productivity-enhancing communications tools, the vast majority of IM and P2P applications in the enterprise today are installed and used without the enterprises' oversight, exposing data and networks to theft and damage.

2. IM allows users to chat, videoconference, share applications, transfer files, and even remotely access their PC.

3. IM and P2P applications effectively circumvent most enterprise security architectures in the same way that a Trojan horse does. The IM or P2P application is installed on a trusted device that is allowed to communicate through the enterprise firewall with an outside IM server, or other P2P users.

4. Once there is a connection made from a "trusted device" to the public Internet, malicious users can gain remote access to that trusted device for the purpose of stealing enterprise data, launching a Denial of Service attack (such as buffer overflow), gaining control of network resources or running a malicious programs.

5. In addition, people often send confidential or private information using IM, such as user names, passwords, or trade secrets. However many popular IM applications transfer information unencrypted. In addition, when transferring files using message, the files bypass the network virus scanners.

6. Another problem with IM is that there is a lack of logging or audit trail.

7. Some organizations protect themselves from potential IM applications exploits by prohibiting the use of IM and P2P applications. Other organizations allow the use of IM, but define an IM application that they can support and secure.

8. Create a written policy regarding the acceptable use of IM applications. You should probably prohibit the downloading of files over IM to protect your network users from potentially unsafe content.

9. Of course, with that, you will need to educate your users about the risks of IM.

10. Each machine that has IM should have updated virus scanners to help protect against viruses.

11. If you have to use messengers between sites and the packets are not encrypted, use IPSec or some type of virtual tunnel.

Security+ Objective 2.3.3.2—8.3 Naming Conventions

1. When DOS was introduced with the IBM PC, DOS identified each file with a filename and its extension (8.3 naming convention).

2. When Windows 95 was introduced, Windows used long filenames, the same type of long filenames that is used today with Microsoft Windows.

3. To be backward compatible with DOS and Windows 3.X programs, it would store the file under two filenames, the 8.3 filename (the short filename) filename and the long filename.

4. Some Win32-based web servers have not compensated for the two filename versions when restricting access to files that have long names.

5. To overcome this vulnerability, first look for a software patch or security fix.

6. If none are available, then you will have to restrict both the long and short filenames.

7. For Windows environments, you can also use NTFS-based ACLs (directory or file level access control lists) to augment or replace web server–based security.

Security+ Objective 2.3.4—Vulnerabilities

Security+ Objective 2.3.4.1—Java Script

Security+ Objective 2.3.4.2—ActiveX

Security+ Objective 2.3.4.4—Cookies

Security+ Objective 2.3.4.5—Signed Applets

Security+ Objective 2.3.4.6—CGI

1. JavaScript is a scripting language that was originally called LiveScript. Most web browsers support JavaScript, which is typically embedded inside a HTML page and read by the client browser.

2. Since JavaScript is a simple scripting language, it has no built-in means of accessing resources on the client machine and it doesn't have the means to subvert the security of a machine.

3. As long as the web page containing dynamic HTML written in JavaScript runs in a sandbox within the web browser in much the same way as Java applets within a web page, it does not have access to the resources of the host machine.

4. Like Java applets, java scripts can have more access to the system if it is digitally signed.

5. An Active Server Page (ASP) containing JavaScript or a Windows Scripting Host (WSH) script containing JavaScript is potentially hazardous since these environments allow scripts unrestricted access to machine resources (file system, registry, etc.) and application objects (via COM).

6. Java is a programmable language developed by Sun Microsystems that has a number of features that make it well suited for use on the web.

7. Java applets are self-contained Internet applications that are written in Java. Initially, Java applets are stored on a web server.

8. When you first access a web page that contains HTML code to access the Java applet, the Java applet is downloaded onto the client computer. When the client subsequently accesses the server, the applet is already cache on the client's computer and is accessed with a download delay.

9. The Java source code is run through a client-side engine or Java Virtual machine (VM).

10. By default, and for security reasons, Java applets are contained within a sandbox. This means that the applets cannot do anything which might be construed as threatening to the user's machine.

11. Any attempt to access a resource outside of the sandbox will result with a security violation and the program will terminate.

12. An ActiveX control is similar to a Java applet. ActiveX is not a programming language, but rather a set of rules for how applications should share information.

13. Unlike Java applets, however, ActiveX controls are downloaded and executed by a web browser (Internet Explorer) and have full access to the Windows operating system.

14. ActiveX uses code signing, specifically the Microsoft Authenticode technology.

15. Authenticode allows you to verify the origin of a control and thus assess its reliability and safety.

16. Independent certificate authorities (CAs) like VeriSign issue the digital signatures to mark the code.

17. Authenticode uses X.509 v3 cryptography certificates as well as the PKCS #7 and #10 signature standards.

18. A cookie is a small amount of data (a text file) that a web server stores about a user on the user's own computer.

19. The main purpose of cookies is to identify users and possibly prepare customized web pages for them.

20. A cookie cannot be used to get data from your hard drive, get your email address, or steal sensitive information about your person.

21. You should realize that cookies are considered a security risk because they contain your personal information.

22. If someone gets hold of your cookies, they can use it to gain illegal access to your user accounts on the Internet and they can be sold to advertisement company that targets the user with unwanted ads.

23. Website owners have to design security measures to handle web-based cookies in order to protect their user base and the sensitive data stored on their servers. To protect your system, you can disable cookies with the browser.

24. An applet is a component in a distributed environment that is downloaded and executed by a web browser.

25. Like Java applets, Java scripts can have more access to the system if it is digitally signed.

26. The Common Gateway Interface (CGI) is a standard for interfacing external applications with web servers.

27. Basically, you need to create a CGI program that the PC with the web page will execute to transmit information to the database engine, receive the results back and display them to the client.

28. The security risk with CGI is that you are allowing anyone on the Internet to execute a program on your web server.

29. Just like any other program, a CGI program might contain security holes that allow an attacker to access your network or its systems.

30. CGI programs are typically a target for attackers because they are frequently used on public web servers.

31. Lastly, if server-side includes (SSIs) are enabled, it allows one document to be inserted into another, which can compromise your scripts.

32. If you enable the write permission when using CGI programs, an attacker could load a malicious CGI program to that directory and run it to compromise your web server.

33. You should limit CGI programs to run as the least privileged user possible and remove all default and sample programs from your web server.

34. Check all CGI applications for security holes, have the CGI application check for properly formatted data that is being submitted and reject the data if it is invalid, too long, or improperly formatted.

35. Lastly, disable SSI. If your web server must support SSI, turn them off on your script directories.

Security+ Objective 2.5—File Transfer

Security+ Objective 2.5.1—S-FTP

Security+ Objective 2.5.2—Blind FTP/Anonymous

Security+ Objective 2.5.3—File sharing

Security+ Objective 3.5.3.4—FTP Servers

1. Two other common protocols are the File Transfer Protocol (FTP) and the Trivial File Transfer Protocol (TFTP), which are used on the Internet to send files.

2. FTP, the more popular of the two, File Transfer Protocol (FTP) use TCP, the connection-oriented service of the TCP/IP protocol suite.

3. When setting up your FTP server, you need to which directories in which the files are available through the FTP server and you have to configure the permissions.

4. If you don't want the changes to your files, you should disable the write permission.

5. When transfer files with FTP, the data including the user name and password are sent in clear text.

6. Secure FTP (S-FTP) is a program that uses SSH to transfer files or you need to transfer them over an encrypted pathway. Unlike standard FTP, it encrypts both commands and data, preventing passwords and sensitive information from being transmitted in the clear over the network.

7. You can set up an anonymous FTP, where anyone can download files without providing a username or password.

8. Blind FTP means that the user cannot see the names of any files in the directory. They can only retrieve a file if they know its full name.

9. FTP uses TCP ports 20 and 21 for data and control while TFP uses UDP ports 20 and 21.

10. While it is recommended to put public FTP servers on an DMZ, if you have internal FTP servers (private network), you should block ports 20 and 21 (both TCP and UDP) from coming in.

11. Like any network application, there may be software bugs or vulnerabilities which may be used to exploit your FTP server. You should then check for service packs, patches, and security fixes for your web server on a regular basis.

12. The FTP bounce allows attackers to run scans against other computers though your FTP server. This makes it look like your FTP server is scanning client computers.

13. While the FTP bounce is related to the proper functioning of FTP, many vendors have found solutions for preventing it in the form of security updates or configuration changes.

Security+ Objective 3.5.3—Application Hardening

Security+ Objective 3.5.3.1—Updates (Hotfixes, Service Packs, Patches)

1. For all network applications, you need to take steps to secure each application.

2. To overcome many security problems for all operating systems, network operating systems, and applications, you need to check for hotfixes, service packs, and patches.

Security+ Objective 3.5.3.5—DNS Servers

1. One of the uses of DNS servers for attackers is to use them to help map out your network.

2. Since anyone can query the DNS servers, you should limit the information that is there.

3. In addition, you need to secure the zone transfers so that they cannot steal them to gather the same information. Therefore, you need to configure your DNS servers to only allow zone transfers to specific secondary servers.

4. You can secure the zone transfers by allowing zone transfers so that secondary servers can verify the credentials of the primary server or by using Active Directory zones.

5. Since many companies have a need to have servers available to the public and servers available for the internal network, you should divide your network into two zones, one for your internal network and one for the public network. Of course, you should not put any information in your public DNS server that you don't want the public to see.

6. There are two types of attacks aimed at hampering or disabling your DNS server that users will not be able to access the web using FQDN names. They are DNS spoofing and DNS cache poisoning.

7. DNS spoofing is when someone establishes a bogus DNS server to answer client requests for name resolution and the server responds with invalid information.

8. DNS cache poisoning is based on flaws, which have been found in some DNS servers that allow attackers to insert bogus information into a DNS cache.

9. To prevent these types of attacks, use secure dynamic updates (Windows 2000 and Windows Server 2003) or signed DNS updates (BIND version 9 or higher) where allows a cross-check of client computer credentials before an update take place.

10. To prevent cache poisoning, you need to use an updated version of the DNS server or install a security patch that does not allow the DNS cache to be poisoned.

Security+ Objective 3.5.3.6—NNTP Servers

1. The NNTP (or Net News Transfer Protocol) uses port 119, so if you need to provide NNTP access to clients outside your network, make sure you allow incoming connections to port 119 on your NNTP server.

2. As with email message headers, NNTP article headers listing the poster's identity and other information can be forged.

3. Additionally, NNTP client connections can consume a lot of bandwidth.

4. It is best if you can run a news server that requires authentication and takes steps to ensure that forged articles are not accepted.

Security+ Objective 3.5.3.8—DHCP Servers

1. Attackers can interrupt the handing out of addresses by using a rogue DHCP server.

2. A rogue DHCP server can hand out bogus information such as an incorrect gateway or DNS address. This will cause the client unable to use resources on other networks, access network resources by FQDN, or misdirect the clients to resources controlled by the attacker.

3. An attacker can get a foothold on your network by obtaining a legitimate IP address and related information. This allows them to learn part of your internal addressing scheme and it could allow the attacker to use the address to attack other systems on your network.

4. To protect your network, you should scan for rogue DHCP servers by using protocol analyzers or by using an intrusion-detection system to discover DHCP Offer packets from unauthorized DHCP servers.

5. Since manual settings are not overwritten by DHCP settings, if you configure the DNS settings

on each client machine, they cannot get an invalid DNS server.

6. You can also restrict which computers the DHCP server will respond to by using address reservation of MAC addresses.

7. Lastly, to prevent DHCP servers from getting queries answered outside your network, you should block TCP/UDP ports 67 and 68 on your firewall.

Security+ Objective 3.5.3.9—Data Repositories

Security+ Objective 3.5.3.9.2—Databases

1. A database is a collection of information organized in such a way that a computer program can quickly select desired pieces of data.

2. To access information from a database, you need a database management system (DBMS), which is a collection of programs that enables you to enter, organize, and select data in a database.

3. For database security, the granularity of access control is a description of how finely you can control who can see which tables, rows, and fields.

4. A view is a particular way of looking at a database. A single database can support numerous different views. Typically, a view arranges the records in some order and makes only certain fields visible.

5. A view does not affect the physical organization of the database.

6. Aggregation is the process of combining low-sensitivity data items to produce a high-sensitivity data item.

7. Structured query language, more commonly referred to as SQL (pronounced either see-kwell or as separate letters) is a standardized query language for requesting information from a database. Database server, such as a SQL server, is a good target for any hacker.

8. Like hardening a web server, a hardening a database server tends to be a multi-step process, in which you harden the database server software itself, and then any custom applications/databases your organization's staff has set up.

9. Don't overlook the step of checking for security updates for your database server software.

10. The most straightforward issue with databases is simply configuration of the database for appropriate levels of data privacy and integrity.

11. Because of programming errors or oversights, or because applications are written by others and attached to the database, some databases/DBMSs offer access to the command line prompt to the operating system, sometimes with system administrator privileges.

12. Some databases/DBMSs have small programs or macros stored in the database server to do a series of tasks or commands when they are invoked by database users.

13. Since these small programs and macros sometimes take user inputs, they can be used to cause a buffer overflow or cause the server to crash if the user inputs something that the server did not expect.

14. You will need to check for these possible vulnerabilities and see if you can configure the database or DBMS or apply patches to close these vulnerabilities.

15. In addition to considering the server itself, you should also consider how the database communicates over the network.

16. Lastly, some databases have default passwords. Therefore, be sure to change the password of any account installed with your database installation (or use a method of authentication that verifies identity other than by password).

QUESTIONS

1. Pat is increasing the security of his web site by adding SSL (Secure Sockets Layer). Which type of encryption does SSL use?
   a. Asymmetric
   b. Symmetric
   c. Public Key
   d. Secret

2. Users of instant messaging clients are especially prone to what?
   a. Theft of root user credentials.
   b. Disconnection from the file server.
   c. Hostile code delivered by file transfer.
   d. Slow Internet connections.
   e. Loss of email privileges.
   f. Blue Screen of Death errors.

3. While connected from home to an ISP (Internet Service Provider), a network administrator performs a port scan against a corporate server and encounters four open TCP (Transmission Control Protocol) ports: 25, 110, 143, and 389. Corporate users in the organization must be able to connect from home, send and receive messages on the Internet, read email by beams of the IMAPv.4 (Internet Message Access Protocol version 4) protocol, and search into a directory services database for user email addresses, and digital certificates. All the email relates services, as well as the directory server, run on the scanned server. Which of the above ports can be filtered out to decrease unnecessary exposure without affecting functionality?
   a. 25
   b. 110
   c. 143
   d. 389

4. IMAP4 requires port _____ to be open.
   a. 80
   b. 3,869
   c. 22
   d. 21
   e. 23
   f. 25
   g. 110
   h. 143
   i. 443

5. Packet sniffing can be used to obtain username and password information in clear text from which one of the following?
   a. SSH (Secure Shell)
   b. SSL (Secure Sockets Layer)
   c. FTP (File Transfer Protocol)
   d. HTTPS (Hypertext Transfer Protocol over Secure Sockets Layer)

6. You are explaining SSL to a junior administrator and come up to the topic of handshaking. How many steps are employed between the client and server in the SSL handshake process?
   a. Five
   b. Six
   c. Seven
   d. Eight

7. What is the greatest benefit to be gained through the use of S/MINE /Secure Multipurpose Internet Mail Extension) The ability to:
   a. Encrypt and digitally sign email messages.
   b. Send anonymous emails.
   c. Send emails with a return receipt.
   d. Expedite the delivery of email.

8. John wants to encrypt a sensitive message before sending it to one of his managers. Which type of encryption is often used for email?
   a. S/MIME
   b. BIND
   c. DES
   d. SSL

9. What transport protocol and port number does SSH (Secure Shell) use?
   a. TCP (Transmission Control Protocol) port 22
   b. UDP (User Datagram Protocol) port 69
   c. TCP (Transmission Control Protocol) port 179
   d. UDP (User Datagram Protocol) port 17

10. What design feature of instant messaging makes it extremely insecure compared to other messaging systems?
    a. It is a peer-to-peer network that offers most organizations virtually no control over it.
    b. Most IM clients are actually Trojan Horses.
    c. It is a centrally managed system that can be closely monitored.
    d. It uses the insecure Internet as a transmission medium.

11. An application that appears to perform a useful function but instead contains some sort of malicious code is called a _____ .
    a. Worm
    b. SYN flood
    c. Virus
    d. Trojan horse
    e. Logic Bomb

12. When securing a FTP (File Transfer Protocol) server, what can be done to ensure that only authorized users can access the server?
    a. Allow blind authentication.
    b. Disable anonymous authentication.
    c. Redirect FTP (File Transfer Protocol) to another port.
    d. Only give the address to users that need access.

13. Users of instant messaging clients are especially prone to what?
    a. Hostile code delivered by file transfer.
    b. Theft of root user credentials.
    c. Slow Internet connections.
    d. Loss of email privileges.
    e. Disconnection from the file server.
    f. Blue Screen of Death errors.

14. You want to implement security on your web site. To do this, you want to use a protocol that will allow secure transmissions over the Internet. When you view the browser URL, it start with: https://. What protocol are you going to use?
    a. SSH
    b. SSL
    c. ARP
    d. PGP

15. As the security analyst for your company's network, you want to impliment a secure protocol for web transmissions as an alternative to SSL. From the list below, what should you use?
    a. TLA
    b. IPSEC
    c. TLS
    d. PIM

16. Pat is responsible for a group of remote access servers in his network. Which, if any, of the services listed should he consider disabling on these servers? (Choose all correct answers.)
    a. Routing and Remote Access
    b. POP3
    c. Kerberos
    d. SMTP
    e. IMAP4
    f. Print Services for Macintosh
    g. None of these services should be disabled on a Remote Access Server
    h. All of these services should be disabled on a Remote Access Server

17. As the security analyst for your company's network, you want to implement personal email security. From the list below, what would you suggest that your users use?
    a. MD8
    b. PIM
    c. PGP
    d. AST

18. As the security analyst for your company's network, you need to find an alternative to using Telnet as an in band connection tool. Since Telnet sends data in cleartext, what can you use as an alternative?
    a. SSH
    b. SSL
    c. IPSEC
    d. PGP

19. In relation to email, MIME stands for _____ . (Select the correct answer for the blank.)
    a. Mail Industrial Multipurpose Environment
    b. Multipurpose Internet Mail Extensions
    c. Multipurpose Internet Mail Environment
    d. Mail Internet Multiple Environments

20. _____ are small executable programs that are downloaded to you computer and then executed to enhance experience on the Web. (Select the correct answer for the blank.)
    a. Macros
    b. ActiveX applets

    c. Viruses
    d. Service Packs
    e. Hot Fixes

21. ICQ and AIM are examples of what type of messaging application?
    a. Email client
    b. Email server
    c. Instant Messaging
    d. Web browser
    e. Filter server
    f. File server
    g. Firewall

22. _____ is/are written in plain-text and be easily modified or copied for use.
    a. ActiveX applets
    b. Java applets
    c. Macros
    d. Javascript
    e. Trojans
    f. Backdoors

23. MIME uses _____ in an email message to specify what type of content has been attached.
    a. Footnotes
    b. References
    c. Tags
    d. Static placeholders
    e. Footers
    f. Headers
    g. Captions

24. You have made a connection to a website for the purpose of buying a new coat for your dog. You notice that the URL starts with http://. You are concerned about your privacy and don't want your credit card information to be jeopardized. Is there a problem?
    a. No problem here, http:// is the normal protocol for web pages.
    b. Yes, there is a problem, your URL should start with ftp:// which denotes secure connections.
    c. Yes, there is a problem, your URL should start with shttp:// which denotes secure http connections.
    d. Yes, there is a problem, your URL should start with https:// which denotes secure http connections.

25. Because most Instant Messaging systems do not support strong authentication or encryption routines, _____ is a strong concern when using these services.
    a. Protection
    b. Privacy
    c. Popularity
    d. Proper usage
    e. Service quality
    f. Connection speed

26. POP3 requires port _____ to be open. (Select the correct answer for the blank.)
    a. 21
    b. 22
    c. 23
    d. 25
    e. 80
    f. 110
    g. 143
    h. 443

27. What protocol was developed by Netscape to make sending confidential information over the Internet protected?
   - a. HTTP
   - b. S/MIME
   - c. CHAP
   - d. IPSec
   - e. SSL
   - f. FTP

28. Yesterday you were able to connect to your financial institution and view your account information. Today you cannot. What is the most reason for this?
   - a. The Internet is down.
   - b. The server at your financial institution has been hacked.
   - c. Port 443 on your company's firewall has been closed.
   - d. You need to clear your browser cache.

29. What is designed to be a secure replacement for telnet?
   - a. IPSec
   - b. MPPE
   - c. SSH
   - d. RADIUS
   - e. S-HTTP
   - f. Authentication
   - g. Authorization

30. One of the major security problems with instant messaging is what?
   - a. Instant Messaging provides strong encryption for all communications.
   - b. Instant Messaging almost always provides no encryption for communications.
   - c. Instant Messaging is an extremely resource intensive application.
   - d. Instant Messaging can quickly flood a firewall and cause it to lock up.
   - e. Instant Messaging often causes Blue Screen of Death errors.
   - f. Instant Messaging often requires you to enter your Windows username and password to login.

31. Closing port 25 on a firewall will impact users internal to the network in what way?
   - a. POP3 traffic will be blocked.
   - b. HTTP traffic will be blocked.
   - c. FTP traffic will be blocked.
   - d. IMAP4 traffic will be blocked.
   - e. SMTP traffic will be blocked.
   - f. GOPHER traffic will be blocked.
   - g. NNTP traffic will be blocked.
   - h. SNMP traffic will be blocked.

32. What are the methods available to secure email messages? (Choose all that apply.)
   - a. IMAPv4
   - b. PGP
   - c. S/MIME
   - d. S-HTTP
   - e. HTTPS
   - f. LDAP
   - g. MIME

33. In which email security solution does a sender use a recipients public key to encrypt a message so that only the legitimate recipient can decrypt it using his or her private key.
   - a. Kerberos
   - b. S/MIME
   - c. IPSec
   - d. PGP

   - e. MPPE
   - f. PPTP
   - g. L2TP
   - h. SSH2

34. Spam, as it refers to the Information Technology community, is also known as _____ .
   - a. A luncheon meat
   - b. Junk email messages
   - c. Websites that use pop-up and pop-under advertising
   - d. Stock trading websites
   - e. Web sites that propagate urban legends

35. An SMTP server that does not preclude access to users outside of its domain is known as a what?
   - a. Easy mark
   - b. Closed relay
   - c. Relay point
   - d. Open relay
   - e. SMTP trapdoor
   - f. Loose server

36. Should proper attention not be given to securing an SMTP server, what can reasonably be expected to happen?
   - a. Nothing, SMTP servers are inherently secure by design.
   - b. If you are running a UNIX SMTP server, then you have nothing to worry about.
   - c. It is possible for unauthorized individuals to use your SMTP server to send spam, making it appear to have come from your server.
   - d. The SMTP will certainly crash as it must be watched carefully 24/7.

37. _____ are usually plain text files placed on the local computer by web servers that can often times contain confidential information. (Select the correct answer for the blank.)
   - a. Resumes
   - b. Cookies
   - c. Crumbs
   - d. Cache
   - e. History
   - f. Trace files

38. What problem exists with using FTP?
   - a. It is not as fast as using HTTP.
   - b. User names and passwords are sent in clear text.
   - c. FTP requires a preconfigured user account on the FTP server.
   - d. It can only be used by Windows users.

39. When security a FTP (File Transfer Protocol) server, what can be done to ensure that only authorized users can access the server?
   - a. Allow blind authentication
   - b. Disable anonymous authentication
   - c. Redirect FTP to another port
   - d. Only give the address to users that need access

40. When a user clicks to browse a secure page, the SSL (Secure Sockets Layer) enabled server will first:
   - a. Use its digital certificate to establish its identity to the browser.
   - b. Validate the user by checking the CRL (Certificate Revocation List).
   - c. Request the user to produce the CRL.
   - d. Display the requested page on the browser, then provide its IP (Internet Protocol) address for verification.

41. User A needs to send a private email to User B. User A does not want anyone to have the ability to read the email except for User B, thus retaining privacy. Which tenet of information security is User A concerned about?
    a. Authentication
    b. Integrity
    c. Confidentiality
    d. Nonrepudiation

42. When securing a DNS server, and shutting down all unnecessary ports, which port should NOT be shut down?
    a. 21   b. 23
    c. 53   d. 55

43. What is the main advantage SSL has over HTTPS?
    a. SSL offers full application security for HTTP while HTTPS does not.
    b. SSL supports additional application layer protocols such as FTP and NNTP while HTTPS does not.
    c. SSL and HTTPS are transparent to the application.
    d. SSL support user authentication and HTTPS does not.

44. What functionality should be disallowed between a DNS server and untrusted node?
    a. Names resolution
    b. Reverse ARP requests
    c. System name resolutions
    d. Zone transfers

45. How must a firewall be configured to only allow employees within the company to download files from a FTP server?
    a. Open port 119 to all inbound connections
    b. Open port 119 to all outbound connections
    c. Open port 20/21 to all inbound connections
    d. Open port 20/21 to all outbound connections

46. Administrators currently use telnet to remotely manage several servers. Security policy dictates that passwords and administrative activities must not be communicated in clear text. Which of the following is the best alternative to using telnet?
    a. DES (Data Encryption Standard)
    b. S-Telnet
    c. SSH (Secure Shell)
    d. PKI (Public Key Infrastructure)

47. The best way to harden an application that is developed in house is to:
    a. Use an industry-recommended hardening tool.
    b. Ensure that security is given due considerations throughout the entire development process.
    c. Try attacking the application to detect vulnerabilities, then develop patches to fix any vulnerabilities found.
    d. Ensure that the auditing system is comprehensive enough and to detect and log any possible intrusion, identifying existing vulnerabilities.

48. Which of the following is required to use S/MIME?
    a. Digital certificate
    b. Server side certificate
    c. SSL certificate
    d. Public certificate

49. Which of the following is likely to be found after enabling anonymous FTP read/write access?
    a. An upload and download directory for each user
    b. Detailed logging information for each user
    c. Storage and distribution of unlicensed software
    d. Fewer server connections and less network bandwidth utilization

50. Which of the following is the greatest problem associated with instant messaging?
    a. Widely deployed and difficult to control
    b. Created without security in mind
    c. Easily spoofed
    d. Created with file sharing enabled.

51. An email relay server is mainly used to:
    a. Block all spam, which allows the email system to function more efficiently without the additional load of spam.
    b. Prevent viruses from entering the network.
    c. Defend the primary email server and limit the effects of any attack.
    d. Eliminate email vulnerabilities since all email is passed through the relay first.

52. Which of the following is an HTTP extension or mechanism used to retain connection data, user information, history of sites visited, and can be used by attackers for spoofing an on-line identity?
    a. HTTPS
    b. cookies
    c. HTTP/1.0 Caching
    d. vCard v3.0

53. ActiveX controls _____ to prove where they originated.
    a. Are encrypted
    b. Are stored on the web server
    c. Use SSL
    d. Are digitally signed

54. What should be done to secure a DHCP service?
    a. Block ports 67 and 68 at the firewall
    b. Block port 53 at the firewall
    c. Block ports 25 and 26 at the firewall
    d. Block port 110 at the firewall

55. Which one of the following would most likely lead to a CGI security problem?
    a. HTTP protocol
    b. Compiler or interpreter that runs the CGI script
    c. The web browser
    d. External data supplied by the user

56. Which of the following protocols is most similar to SSLv3.
    a. TLS   b. MPLS
    c. SASL   d. MLS

57. How should a primary DNS server be configured to provide the best security against DoS and hackers?
    a. Disable DNS cache function
    b. Disable application service other than DNS
    c. Disable the DNS reverse lookup function
    d. Allow only encrypted zone transfer to a secondary DNS server

58. Which of the following protocols is used by web servers to encrypt data?
    a. TCP/IP   b. ActiveX
    c. IPSec   d. SSL

59. SSL is used for secure communications with:
    a. File and print servers
    b. Radius servers
    c. AAA servers
    d. Web servers

60. What is the best method to secure a web browser?
    a. Do not upgrade, as new versions tend to have more security flaws
    b. Disable any unused features of the web browser.
    c. Connect to the Internet using only a VPN connection
    d. Implement a filtering policy for illegal, unknown, and undesirable sites

61. Which of the following methods may be use to exploit the clear text nature of an instant messaging session?
    a. Packet sniffing
    b. Port scanning
    c. Cryptanlysis
    d. Reverse engineering

62. When an ActiveX control is executed, it executes with the privileges of the:
    a. Current user account
    b. Administrator account
    c. Guest account
    d. System account

63. Which of the following would best protect the confidentiality and integrity of an email message?
    a. SHA-1   b. IPSec
    c. Digital signature   d. S/MIME

64. What determines if a user is presented with a dialog box prior to downloading an ActiveX component?
    a. The user's browser setting
    b. The <script> meta tag
    c. The condition of the sandbox
    d. The negotiation between the client and the server

65. To reduce vulnerabilities on a web server, an administrator should adopt which preventative measure?

    a. Use packet sniffing software on all inbound communications
    b. Apply the most recent manufacturer updates and patches to the server
    c. Enable auditing on the web server and periodically review the audit logs
    d. Block all DNS requests coming into the server

66. Which of the following statements most clearly outlines a major security vulnerability associated with instant messaging?
    a. Instant messaging does not support any form of encryption.
    b. Instant messaging negatively impacts user production
    c. Instant messaging uses TPC port for 25 for message exchange.
    d. Instant messaging allows file attachments which could potentially contain viruses

67. A company's web server is configured for the following services: HTTP, SSL, FTP, and SMTP. The web server is placed into a DMZ. What are the standard ports on the firewall that must be opened to allow traffic to and from the server?
    a. 119, 23, 21, and 80
    b. 443, 119, 21, and 1250
    c. 80, 443, 21, and 25
    d. 80, 443, 110, and 21

68. What is the primary disadvantage of a third-party relay?
    a. Spammers can utilize the relay
    b. The relay limits access to specific users
    c. The relay restricts the types of email that may be sent
    d. The relay restricts spammers from gaining access

69. With regards to the use of instant messaging, which of the following type of attack strategies is effectively combated with user awareness training?
    a. Social engineering
    b. Stealth
    c. Ambush
    d. Multipronged

70. An administrator is concerned with viruses in email attachments being distributed and inadvertently installed on users workstations. If the administrator sets up an attachment filter, what types of attachments should be filtered from emails to minimize the danger of viruses?
    a. Text files   b. Image files
    c. Sound files   d. Executable files

71. In order for an SSL connection to be established between a web client and server automatically, the web client and server should have a(n):
    a. Shared password.
    b. Certificate signed by a trusted root CA.
    c. Address on the same subnet.
    d. Common operating system.

72. When hosting a web server with CGI (Common Gateway Interface) scripts, the directories for public view should have:
    a. Execute permissions.
    b. Read and write permissions.
    c. Read, write, and execute permissions.
    d. Full control permissions.

73. What are the three entities of the SQL (Structured Query Language) security model?
    a. Actions, objects, and tables
    b. Actions, objects, and users
    c. Tables, objects, and users
    d. Users, actions, and tables

74. How can an email administrator prevent malicious users from sending emails form non-existing domains?
    a. Enable DNS reverse lookup on the email server
    b. Enable DNS forward lookup on the email server
    c. Enable DNS recursive queries on the DNS server

d. Enable DNS reoccurring queries on the DNS server

75. SSL session keys are available in what two lengths?
    a. 40-bit and 64-bit
    b. 40-bit and 128-bit
    c. 64-bit and 128-bit
    d. 128-bit and 1024-bit

76. A FTP bounce attack is generally used to:
    a. Exploit a buffer overflow vulnerability on the FTP server
    b. Reboot the FTP server
    c. Store and distribute malicious code
    d. Establish a connection between the FTP server and another computer

77. S/MIME is used to:
    a. Encrypt user names and profiles to ensure privacy.
    b. Encrypt messages and files.
    c. Encrypt network sessions acting as a VPN client.
    d. Automatically encrypt all outbound messages.

HANDS-ON EXERCISES

Exercise 1: Installing and Using PGP in Windows

Installing PGP

1. Go the http://web.mit.edu/network/pgp.html and download PGP v6.5.8 for Windows.
2. Open the downloaded zip file and execute the setup.exe file.
3. Click the Next button on the Welcome screen.
4. Click Yes on the Software License Agreement.
5. Click Next on the Importance Product Information screen.
6. Enter your name and company on the User Information screen
7. Accept the default installation path by clicking Next or select your own path by selecting Browse.
8. On the Select Components screen, make sure you have the Outlook Express Plugin checked and click Next.
9. Click Next to start copying files.
10. When prompted, select the network adapter you want protected by PGPnet (a lock will appear in the box). This allows you to communicate securely using IPSec.
11. When asked if you have any existing keyrings you would like to use, select No.
12. When you see the Setup Complete screen, make sure the "Yes, I want to restart my computer" box is checked and click Finish.

Generating a Key Pair in PGP on Windows

1. From the Start menu, select Programs, select PGP, select PGPkeys.
2. The Key Generation Wizard will start. Click Next on the Welcome screen.
3. Enter the Full Name and Email Address that will be associated with this key. Click Next when finished.
4. On the next screen, select Diffie-Hellman/DSS as your Key Pair Type. Click Next.
5. The Key Pair Size establishes encryption strength. The higher the key size, the stronger the encryption. The default 2048 bits is sufficient for our use. Make sure it is selected and click Next.
6. Choose the default selection: Key pair never expires. Click Next.
7. Select passphrase. This phrase is what is used to protect your private key. Only you should know your passphrase. Enter your passphrase in the Passphrase box.

8. Enter the passphrase again in the Confirmation box. Click Next.
9. PGP will now generate your key pair. When you see the word Complete, the process is finished. Click Next to continue.
10. Leave the "Send my key to the root server now" box unchecked and click Next.
11. Click Finish to end the Key Generation Wizard.
12. Your PGPkeys window will open. PGP comes with many keys pre-installed. Find the key you just created. Right-click and select Key Properties. Notice that your key is fully trusted.
13. Click the Subkeys tab. Your subkey is used for encryption and can be revoked at any time if you think it has been compromised.

Exporting PGPKeys

1. Launch PGP keys if it is not already open.
2. Find your public key and right-click. Select Export.
3. The Export key to File box opens. Keep the default settings and save the file.
4. A file with the name associated with the key and an .asc extension should appear in the saving location.
5. Launch Microsoft Outlook Express. Make sure it is configured to send and receive email.
6. Send a message to your partner and attach your key file to the message as an attachment. Have your partner do the same, sending you his or her key life.
7. When you receive your partner's message with his key attached, save the attachment to your system.
8. Now add your partner's key to your key ring. In PGPkeys, select Keys, then Import.
9. When the dialog box opens, highlight your partner's key and select Import.
10. You now have your partner's key in your keyring. But his or her key is not signed, so it is not trusted. Change this by right-clicking your partner's key and selecting during the installation process to protect your private key.
11. When a green icon appears next to your partner's key, it is not signed.
12. Right-click your partner's key and select Key Properties.
13. At the bottom, slide the bar from Untrusted to Trusted.

Exchanging Encrypted Message Using PGP on Windows

1. Open Outlook Express and type a message to your partner.
2. Before sending the message, select the PGP Encrypt and PGP Sign icons.
3. Enter your passphrase for your private key when prompted.
4. Have your partner do the same to send you a message.
5. When you receive the encrypted message your partner sent you, double-click it open it in its own window.
6. Click the Decrypt PGP Message icon.
7. When prompted for the passphrase for your private key, enter it. This will decrypt the message that your partner's encrypted with your public key.
8. You can now read the message, as well as see who signed it.

Exercise 2: Utilizing Telnet to Generate a Spoofed Email Message

1. Using Telnet, connect to an SMTP server on port 25.
2. Enter the following text:

Hello.↵
mail from: **spoof.sender@spoof.com.**↵
rcpt to: **gullible.recipient@company.com.**↵
data:↵
This is a spoofed message.↵
.↵
quit.↵

3. Send the message to an account you can access. Check your mail for the message you just sent and make sure you check the From field.

Exercise 3: Using the SSH Command on a Linux Machine

1. At the command prompt, login to your partner's machine with the ssh command by typing the following command:

```
ssh partner's_ipaddress
```

2. When it ask you if you want to continue connecting, type in yes.

3. Login with the user1 account.
4. Exit the telnet session by typing exit at the prompt.

Exercise 4: Securing DHCP

Installing and Configuring DHCP on a Windows Server

On a computer on your network running Windows Server

1. Open the Add/Remove Programs applet in the Control Panel.
2. Click on the Add/Remove Windows Components.
3. Click on the Next button.
4. Click to highlight the Networking Services option.
5. Click on the Details button.
6. In the subcomponents of Networking Services, make sure that there is a check mark in the check box next to the DHCP.
7. Click on the OK button.
8. Click on the Next button.
9. In the Insert Disk dialog box appears, insert the Windows installation CD-ROM, ensure that the path to the source files is correct, and click on the OK button.
10. Click on the Finish button.
11. Open the DHCP console from the Administrative Tools.
12. Right-click the server and click the New scope option. Click on the Next button.
13. On the Scope Name page, type the name of your server in the Name text box and click on the Next button.
14. Use 192.168.1.150 for the Start address and 192.168.1.190 for the End address. Change the subnet mask to 255.255.255.0. Click on the Next button.
15. On the Lease Duration, click the Next button to keep the default of 8 days.
16. On the Configure DHCP Options page, select the Yes, I want to configure these options now and click the Next button.
17. On the Router (Default Gateway) page, type in the address of your gateway or local router. If you don't have one, for now, type in 192.168.1.254. Click on the Add button and then click the Next button.
18. On the Domain Name and DNS Servers page, type in ACME.COM for the parent domain and type in the address of your DNS server. Click the Add button and then the Next button.
19. Select the Yes, I want to activate this scope now and click the Next button. Click the Finish button. Click on the Scope option and look at the various options that were configured with the wizard.

Testing the DHCP Server

Other Windows computers in the room

1. At the command prompt, execute the IPCONFIG /ALL command.
2. Right-click My Network Places and select the Properties option.
3. Right-click Local Area Connection and select the Properties.
4. Click the Internet Protocol (TCP/IP) dialog box, click the Obtain an IP address automatically option.
5. Click the Obtain DNS server address automatically option.
6. Click on the Advanced button.
7. In the WINS tab, click the WINS address and click the Remove button.
8. Click the OK button to close the Advanced TCP/IP Settings, click OK to close the Internet Protocol (TCP/IP) Properties dialog box, and click OK to close the Local Area Connection Properties dialog box. Remember, any settings set manually will override settings given by a DHCP server.
9. At the command prompt, execute the IPCONFIG/ALL command and study the current setting. Notice the address of the DHCP server that configured the TCP/IP parameters.

Using Protocol Analyzer

On the Windows Server not running DHCP

1. Click the Start button, select Settings, select Control Panel, and then select Add/Remove Programs.
2. In Add/Remove Programs, click Add/Remove Windows Components.
3. In the Windows Component Wizard, highlight Management and Monitoring Tools and then click the Details button.
4. In the Management and Monitoring Tools window, select the Network Monitor Tools check box and then click OK.

5. Click the Next button in the Windows Components Wizard to continue. If you are prompted for additional files, insert your Windows Server disk or type a push to the location of the files on the network.

6. Click Finish to complete the installation.

7. Click the Start button, select Programs, select Administrative Tools, and choose Network Monitor. If you are prompted for a default network on which to capture frames, select the local network from which you want to capture data by default.

8. On the Capture menu, click Start.

9. Open a DOS window and execute the two commands:
   ipconfig /release
   ipconfig /renew

10. Change back to Network Monitor and click on the Stop button (fourth from the right on the tool bar).

11. Double-click a packet and analyze its parts. Look for DHCPOFFER messages and the addresses that they come from.

12. Close Network Monitor

Exercise 5: Securing Browsers

To be performed on Windows Server computer.

1. Start Internet Explorer.
2. Open the Tools menu and select Internet Options
3. On the General tab, click the Delete Cookies button, to delete the saved cookies.
4. Select the Security tab.
5. With Internet selected, click the Custom Level button.
6. Make sure that the downloading of unsigned ActiveX controls is disabled.
7. At the bottom of the list, determine which type of user authentication login is selected.
8. Click on the ? button and click on the Anonymous logon option. Read the help box.
9. Click on the Cancel button.
10. Select the Privacy tab.
11. Record the current Privacy Setting.
12. Move the slider to each setting and read the description of each setting.
13. Click on the Content tab.
14. Click the Certificates button. View any certificates that are there and when they expire.
15. Select the Advanced tab.
16. Scroll down to the bottom of the list to the Security section.
17. View the options that are available. If you do not know what one is, use help to see what they are.
18. Click on the OK button to close Internet Options.
19. Close Internet Explorer.
20. Open the C:\Documents and Settings folder.
21. Open the folder of the account that you are currently logged in as.
22. Open the Cookies folder and notice if any cookies are in there.
23. Start Internet Explorer and open the http://www.msn.com page.
24. If you have a passport account, log in with that account. If you don't have a passport account, click on the login button, click the register button and create a passport account. Then login as that account.
25. Close Internet Explorer.
26. Go back to the Cookies folder and look at the new cookies that have been created.
27. Open the passport and msn cookies by double-clicking on them and view their content.
28. Close the notepad files.
29. Change the date of the computer to 2060.
30. Open the http://www.msn.com page and log in. View the security alert that appears.
31. Click on the OK button and notice that you are still not logged in.
32. Change the date back to the correct date.

Exercise 6: Looking at MSN Messenger

1. Start MSN messenger. Login with your MSN passport account.
2. Open the Tools menu and select Add Contact.
3. Add your partner's passport email address.
4. Start Network Monitor and start capturing packets.
5. In MSN messenger, start a conversation with your partner. Be sure to say hello and anything else that comes to mind.
6. Use Network Monitor to view the packets. Look for your conservation with your partner.

## CHAPTER 11

Windows Group Policies and Security Templates

Topics Covered in this Chapter

Introduction

While the information in this chapter is not tested in the Security+ exam, if you are using a Windows network, you should be familiar with Windows group policies and security templates. By using group policies and security templates, you can easily establish password policies, account lockout policies, and user rights throughout the entire domain. In addition, you can secure the registry so that it cannot be changed, causing security and reliability problems.

Objectives

1. Describe the purpose of group policy and security templates and how they can secure a Windows system.

2. Given a situation, secure the registry.

11.1   POLICIES

A **policy** is a tool used by administrators to define and control how programs, network resources, and the operating system behave for users and computers in the Active Directory structure. These settings include:

System settings—Application settings, desktop appearance, and behavior of system services
Security settings—local computer, domain, and network security settings
Software Installation settings—management of software installation, updates, and removal
Scripts settings—Scripts for when a computer starts and shuts down and when a user logs on and off
Folder Redirection settings—Stores users' folders on the network

Using Group Policies, administrators can create, manage, and deploy many different computer configurations to create a consistent work environment for various classes of workers across any number of client computers in an organization. They can also be used to manage administrative and security settings for groups of users and computers based on their memberships in domains, sites, or organizational units.

Since the Active Directory is a structured hierarchy, there are different levels of policies so that you can have a customized configuration. The different levels of policies are applied in this order:

1. Windows NT 4.0-style policies
2. Unique local Group Policy object
3. Site Group Policy objects, in administratively specified order
4. Domain Group Policy objects, in administratively specified order
5. Organizational unit Group Policy objects, from the highest to lowest organizational unit, and in administratively specified order

Local GPOs are stored directly on client computers rather than downloaded from a domain controller. Because they are stored locally, they are always available even when the computer has no connection to the network or is not a member of a domain.

Non-local Group Policies (site, domain, and organization group policies) settings are stored in Group Policy Objects (GPOs). A GPO is a directory containing all files that are required to enact a Group Policy. Every GPO has two components:

- A Computer Configuration portion that is applied before anyone logs on.
- A User Configuration portion that is applied based on the identity of the logged-on user.

After Windows applies local Group Policy to computers in a domain when they start, it downloads the Computer Configuration portion of any GPOs from Active Directory that apply to them. It then applies the Computer Configuration portion of all GPOs before displaying the logon prompt. When users log on, the process is repeated for the User Configuration portion of the same set of GPOs.

Computer Configuration and User Configuration policies each have three major divisions:

- The Software Settings portion of a configuration contains settings extensions provided by independent software vendors for software installation.
- The Windows Settings portion of a configuration settings that apply to Windows, as well as startup/shutdown scripts (Computer Configuration) or logon/logoff scripts (User Configuration). The Windows Settings portion of a configuration contains most of the settings that are security specific.
- The Administrative Templates portion of a configuration can be extended by administrators using .adm files, and it contains settings that modify the behavior of Internet Explorer, Windows Explorer, and other programs.

Unless a GPO is specifically set not to allow overrides, Group Policy settings are inherited, cumulative, and affect all computers and user accounts in the Active Directory container with which the Group Policy is associated. If you have settings that are in conflict with each other, the later policies will overwrite the previous policies. Therefore, settings in the Organizational unit group policy will overwrite any settings in the other policies.

For example, if you have the site group policy, 2 domain group policy, 1 parent organization unit group policy, and 3 child organizational unit group policies, the site group policy will be executed first. Next, the first listed domain group policy will be executed. If any settings from the first domain group policy are in conflict with the default domain controller group policy, it will overwrite those setting. Then the second listed domain group policy will be executed, again overwriting any settings that conflict. It then executes the parent organizational unit group policy followed by the child organizational unit group policy in the order that they are listed. Again, as they are executed, they will overwrite any settings that are in conflict.

In the Domain GPO, Account Policies (Password Policies, Account Lockout, and Kerberos Policies) are defined on a domain basis only. This is a very important consideration since GPO's for account settings defined for lower level OU's will not work for domain users. Settings at lower level OU's will take effect if users logon locally (i.e., using a local account) to a computer, but will not when logging on to the domain. In addition, because domain controllers do not have local accounts like servers and workstations do, account policies that are defined in the Default Domain Controllers organizational unit have no effect. If you need to have different Account Policies for different computers, you will have to break your network into two or more domains, each domain with its own account policy.

Domain controllers pull some security settings only from the domain container. Because domain controllers share the same account database for the domain, certain security settings must be set uniformly on all domain controllers even if the domain controller is in the domain controller organizational unit or not. This ensures that the members of the domain have a consistent experience regardless of which domain controller they use to log on.

11.1.1   Windows NT 4.0–Style Policies and Windows 9X System Policies

Windows NT 4.0–style policies consist of a set of system registry settings that you create and place on workstations as they logon to the network. These registry entries affect machine and user-specific settings on the workstation. The Windows NT 4.0–style policies control what resources are available to users, including what applications appear on the desktop, which applications appear on the Start menu, what access is available to basic system areas including the control panel and what access is available to the command prompt.

Windows 95 and Windows 98 systems policies are contained in the file CONFIG.POL, while Windows NT system policies are contained in the NTCONFIG.POL file. These files are created with the appropriate System Policy Editor, such as POLEDIT.EXE, and stored in the server's NETLOGON shared folder (\SYSTEM32\REPL\IMPORT\SCRIPTS). The system policies can be defined on a user. Note: Although System Policy Editor (Poledit.exe) has been largely replaced by Group Policy, it is still useful under some special circumstances.

11.1.2   Group Policies

Each computer running Windows 2000, Windows Server 2003, or Windows XP has one local group policy object, which can be stored on individual computers whether or not they are part of an Active Directory environment or a networked environment. Of course, these settings can be overwritten by any of the nonlocal group policies (sites, domains, and organizational units). The local group policy can be added as a snap-in to the MMC console or can be executed as a program in the Administrative Tools. The local Group Policy object resides in SystemRoot\System32\GroupPolicy. Note: Computers running Windows NT 4.0 or earlier do not have a local Group Policy object.

The non-local group policies are stored on the domain controller as Group Policy Templates in the SYSVOL volume and are only available in an Active Directory environment. The SYSVOL share is automatically replicated among domain controllers. Different from the local group policies, the non-local group policies are stored in Group Policy Objects (GPO). As objects, the GPOs can be assigned to multiple sites, domains or organizational units and sites, domains and organizational units can have multiple Group Policy Objects.

There are five major categories that group policies can be configured for:

- **Folder redirection**—Store users' folders (My Documents, Start Menu, Application Data, My Pictures, Desktop, and My Pictures) on the network.
- **Security**—Similar to account policies under user manager in NT4—includes settings for the local computer, the domain, and network security.
- **Administrative Templates**—NT4 administrators will recognize this section as system policies—in a much more convenient and flexible configuration. Included are desktop, application, and system settings.
- **Software Installation**—Completely new—enables an administrator to have software installed automatically at the client machine—or removed automatically.
- **Scripts**—similar to logon scripts in NT4, but we can now specify a startup and a shutdown script for the computer as well as a logon and a logoff script for the user.

Group Policy objects other than the local Group Policy object consist of two parts, stored separately: the Group Policy container (GPC) and the Group Policy template (GPT). An administrator can create several Group Policy Objects (GPO) in a given Group Policy Container (GPC) and assign the appropriate GPO to the computers or users that need the settings contained in that GPO. Information that is small and infrequently changed resides in the Group Policy template, while information that is large or frequently changed is kept in the Group Policy container. The Group Policy user interface does not expose them separately.

If you want to exclude certain users or computers from processing the GPO assigned to the Site/Domain/OU that they belong to, you can simply remove the users' or groups' "apply group policy" permissions. This effectively creates a filter. You can also delegate control over GPOs so that a manager can change what a GPO does for his or her department but can't create any new GPOs or change the scope of a GPO.

It is also possible to disable group policy objects without deleting them. If you do this (from Group Policy—Options) it will only disable it for that container and any subcontainers that inherit the settings. If another administrator "linked" to that GPO from another container, then the GPO is still active in that container.

To create a nonlocal group policy:

1. Open the Active Directory Sites and Services console or the MMC console with the Active Directory Sites and Services snap-in.
2. Right-click the site (Domain Controllers folder), the domain or the organizational unit and select the Properties option.
3. Click on the Group Policy tab.
4. Click on the new button and name the profile.

If you have multiple group policies assigned to a site, domain or organizational unit, you can specify the order by clicking on the GPO and using the Up and Down buttons. See figure 11.1.

As mentioned earlier, when a GPO is created and associated with an Active Directory container, the settings from the parent container flow down into the child containers. In other words, the child container inherits those settings from above. Of course, it was also mentioned that those settings could be overwritten by group policies executed later.

The inheritance or flow down of rights can be stopped or blocked by using the Block Policy Inheritance checkbox located with the properties of the container. This means that when the box is checked, the container does not inherit any policy settings from the parent-level group policies.

Figure 11.1   Properties of a Container Showing Group Policies

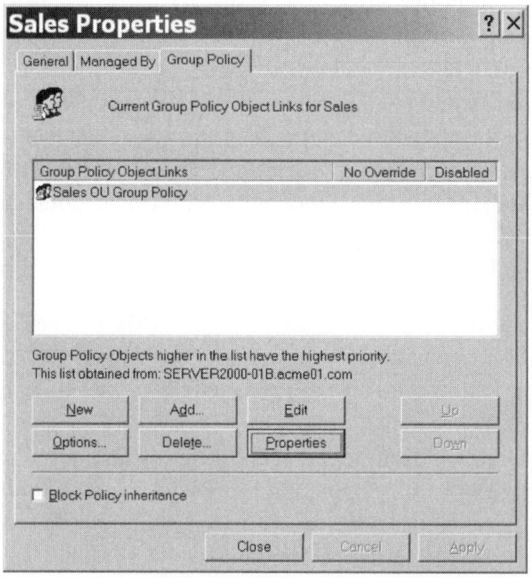

Figure 11.2   The No Override and Disable Options for Group Policies

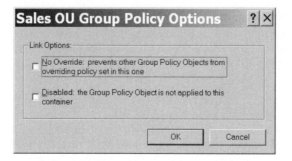

Of course, sometimes, you may not want some of the earlier policies overwritten by the later exe-cuted policies or by blocking the policy inheritance. To maintain these settings, you would open the properties of the GPO and select No Override. You would typically use this in one of the higher levels such as the site or domain GPO to make sure that the administrators of the OUs don't overwrite those settings that you want to assign to everyone. See figure 11.2.

The "*Disabled: the Group Policy Object* is not applied to this container" option is a troubleshoot-ing tool to help isolate which container a setting is coming from. For example, if you have a setting that is not the setting that you want, you may want to see where the setting originated. Since there can be many GPOs, the disable feature allows you to temporarily disable the GPO without removing its link to the container or by deleting the GPO. If the settings that you have a problem with go away when you disable it, you know that the setting is involved in the GPO that you disabled.

If you choose to delete a Group Policy object, you will be given two options. You can either remove the association with the GPO to the container or you can remove the link and delete the GPO. Of course, if other containers were using the GPO, those containers would also lose these settings. See figure 11.3.

11.1.3   Group Policy Permissions

The permissions of a Group Policy can be done using the standard Access Control List (ACL) editor. To use the ACL editor, click a Group Policy object's property sheet and then click the Security tab. The ACL editor can be used by administrators to delegate who can modify the Group Policy object and who is affected by the group policy.

By default, only members of Domain Administrators, Enterprise Administrators, and Group Pol-icy Creator Owners groups can create new Group Policy objects. If the Domain Administrator wants a

Figure 11.3 When you delete Group Policies, you get the Remove the link from List or Remove the Link and delete the GPO.

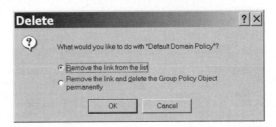

nonadministrator or group to be able to create Group Policy objects, that user or group can be added to the Group Policy Creator Owners security group. When a nonadministrator who is a member of the Group Policy Creator Owners group creates a Group Policy object, that user becomes the creator and owner of the Group Policy object and can edit the object.

For a group policy to apply to a person, the person must have Apply Group Policy and Read Permission for the group policy. By default, Authenticated Users have read access to the Group Policy object with the Apply Group Policy attribute set.

To edit a Group Policy object, the user must have both read and write access to the Group Policy object. The Domain Administrators, Enterprise Administrators, and Group Policy Creator Owners groups have full control without the Apply Group Policy attribute set. This means that they can edit the Group Policy object, but the policies contained in that Group Policy object do not apply to them. Note: Domain Administrators and Enterprise Administrators are also members of Authenticated Users; therefore, members of those groups are, by default, affected by Group Policy objects unless you explicitly exclude them.

11.1.4 Modifying Policy Settings

You can manage Group Policy by navigating through Active Directory using the Active Directory Users and Computer management console or the Active Directory Sites and Services management console. Once you have navigated to the specific Active Directory object to which a Group Policy will apply, you can open the object's Properties dialog box and manage the GPOs that are linked to that object.

You can create GPOs on the Group Policy tab of an Active Directory object's Properties dialog box. Click the New button to create a new GPO in the domain controller's SYSVOL, assign it a GUID, and populate it with default administrative templates. You can then click Edit to modify the default Group Policy for the purpose you intend.

Each GPO is automatically linked to the Active Directory object from which you created it. If you want to link the same GPO to a different Active Directory object, manually create a link by clicking the Add button on the Group Policy tab in the Properties dialog box for the target Active Directory object, and then, in the Add A Group Policy Object Link dialog box, selecting the appropriate GPO from the list. You can link a single GPO to any number of Active Directory objects. Note: You can also create an MMC console with the appropriate snap-ins showing the various Group Profile objects such as that shown in figure 11.4.

Windows 2000 and Windows Server 2003 periodically refreshes group policies throughout the network. By default, the client computers are updated every ninety minutes with an offset of plus or minus 30 minutes. The domain controllers are updated every 5 minutes. The settings that belong to the Computer Configuration are applied when the computer boots. The settings that belong to the User are applied during login.

To refresh the Group Policy immediately, you can do the following:

Windows 2000

1. Click on the Start button and select the Run option.
2. To refresh the User Configuration settings, in the Run dialog box, input `SECEDIT /REFRESHPOLICY USER_POLICY`. To refresh the Computer User Configuration settings, in the Run dialog box, input `SECEDIT /REFRESHPOLICY MACHINE_POLICY`

Figure 11.4   The MMC Console Customized to Show Multiple Group Policies

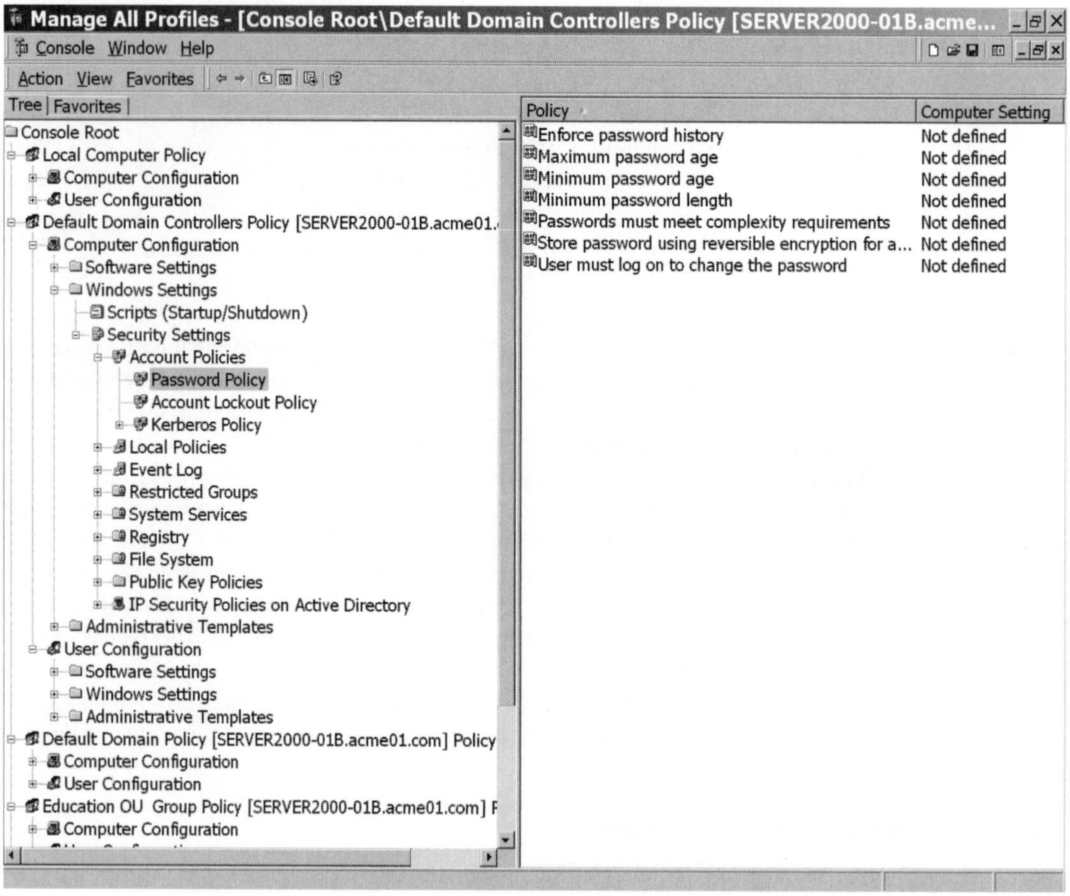

Windows Server 2003

1. Click on the Start button and select the Run option.
2. To refresh the User Configuration settings, in the Run dialog box, input GPUPDATE/TARGET: USER /FORCE. To refresh the Computer Configuration settings, in the Run dialog box, input GPUPDATE /TARGET:COMPUTER /FORCE. To refresh the User and Computer Configuration settings, in the Run dialog box, input GPUPDATE /FORCE.

11.1.5   Computer Security Settings

The Computer Security Settings are used to combat unauthorized access to resources, viruses, theft of data, or disruption of workflow. The Computer Security Settings are broken down to the following categories:

Account Policies—Use account policies to configure password policies, account lockout policies, and Kerberos protocol policies for the domain.

Local Policies—Local policies include auditing policies, the assignment of user rights and privileges, and various security options. Note: Auditing is discussed in chapter 12.

Event Log—Use Event Log to configure the size, access, and retention parameters for the application logs, the system logs, and security logs.

System Services—Use System Services to configure security and startup settings for service running on a computer.

Registry—Use to configure security on registry key.

File System—Use to configure security on specific file paths.

Public Key Policies—Use to configure encrypted data recovery agents, domain roots, trusted certificate authorities, and so forth. Note: you can also configure public key policies in user Configuration.

IP Security Policies on Active Directory—Use to configure network Internet Protocol (IPI) security.

As you open a profile and open the various levels of a profile, you will see that the profile stores hundreds of settings. The following section will discuss some of the more important ones. Note: Since the GPO only modifies user settings and no computer settings are altered, you can reduce the time it takes for a client to process the GPO if you disable the computer configuration settings for the GPO.

11.1.6 Password Policy

Account policies should not be configured for organizational units that do not contain any computers, since organizational units that contain only users will always receive account policy from the domain.

When setting account policies in Active Directory, keep in mind that Windows only allows one domain account policy: the account policy applied to the root domain of the domain tree. The domain account policy will become the default account policy of any Windows 2000 workstation or server that is a member of the domain. The only exception to this rule is when another account policy is defined for an organizational unit. The account policy settings for the organizational unit will affect the local policy on any computers contained in the organizational unit.

When setting account policies in Active Directory, keep in mind that Windows only allows one domain account policy: the account policy applied at the root domain of a domain tree.

The password policy determines the password settings for domain and local user accounts. It can be found by opening the Computer Configuration, opening the Windows Settings, Opening Account Policies, and clicking on Password Policies. The popular password policy settings are:

- **Enforce password history**—The Enforce password history will remember a specified number of passwords. Therefore, when a user changes a password, you cannot use the same password. For example, if the Enforce password history is set to 3, the user would have to change the password 3 times before he or she can use the same password again.
- **Maximum password age**—The maximum password age specifies how often the password must be changed.
- **Minimum password age**—The minimum password age would specify how long a user would have to wait before changing a password.
- **Minimum password length**—The minimum password length specifies the minimum number of characters that a password must be.
- **Passwords must meet complexity requirements**—When enabled, the password must be at least six characters long and must contain characters from at least three of the four classes listed below.
  English uppercase letters (A, B, C, . . . Z)
  English lowercase letters (a, b, c, . . . z)
  Westernized Arabic numerals (0, 1, 2, . . . 9)
  Non-alphanumeric ("special characters") such as punctuation symbols

For a secure network, set the Enforce password history to 5 or more, set the maximum password age to between 30 and 45 days, the minimum password length to 8 characters, and enable passwords must meet complexity requirements.

11.1.7 Account Lockout Policy

The account lockout policy determines when and for whom an account will be locked out of the system. It can be found by opening the Computer Configuration, opening the Windows Settings, Opening Account Policies clicking on Account Lockout Policies. The account lockout policy has the following settings:

- **Account lockout duration**—When an account is locked out, the account lockout duration will specify how long the account will be locked out. If you want the account to be unlocked/reset by an administrator, set the value to 99999.

▓ **Account lockout threshold**—The number of invalid logins within the time specified in the Reset account lockout counter before the account is locked. By using this, this will eliminate someone from hacking their way in by trying passwords until one works.

▓ **Reset account lockout counter after**—The time that the number of invalid logins are counted before the invalid login counter is reset.

For a secure network, set the Account lockout Duration to either 60 minutes or 99999 depending on the situation, set the account lockout threshold to 3 and reset the account lockout counter after to 30 minutes.

11.1.8   Restricted Groups Policies

Restricted groups policies are used to manage and enforce the membership of built-in or user-defined groups that have special rights and permissions. Restricted Groups policies contain a list of members of specific groups whose membership are defined centrally as part of the security policy. Enforcement of Restricted Groups automatically sets any computer local group membership to match the membership list settings defined in the policy. Changes to group membership by the local computer administrator are overwritten by the Restricted Groups policy defined in Active Directory.

Restricted Groups can be used to manage membership in the built-in groups. Built-in groups include local groups such as Administrators, Power Users, Print Operators, and Server Operators, as well as global groups such as Domain Administrators. You can add groups that you consider sensitive or privileged to the Restricted Groups list, along with their membership information. This allows you to enforce the membership of these groups by policy and not allow local variations on each computer.

11.1.9   User Rights Policy

A **right** authorizes a user to perform certain actions on a computer, such as logging on to a system interactively or backing up files and directories. Administrators can assign specific rights to individual user accounts or group accounts. Rights are managed with the User Rights policy. Some of the popular user rights are shown in table 11.1. User rights can be found by opening the group policy, opening Computer Configuration, opening Windows Settings, opening Security Settings, opening Local Policies, and opening User Rights Assignment.

To simplify the administration of rights, user rights are best administered by using groups. If a user is a member of multiple groups, the user's rights are cumulative, which means that the user has more than one set of rights. The only time that rights assigned to one group might conflict with those assigned to another is in the case of certain logon rights. In general, however, user rights assigned to one group do not conflict with the rights assigned to another group. To remove rights from a user, the administrator simply removes the user from the group. In this case, the user no longer has the rights assigned to that group.

While rights can be assigned in any group policy (site or domain controller, domain and organizational unit), the default rights are assigned at the default domain controller group policy. The other group policies, domain and organizational unit, have no rights assigned by default. For example, the domain controller group policy has the Allow Log on Locally right, which is used to logon interactively or directly on the computer assigned to account operators, backup operators, print operators, server operators, and administrators. Therefore, by default, while anyone can logon to a workstation with the proper username and password, only the account operators, backup operators, print operators, server operators, and administrators can log on directly to a domain controller. Yet, the Take Ownership of a File or Other Object right is only assigned to the administrators. Of course, you can assign users or groups to the user rights in the default domain controller group policy or any other nonlocal group policy. Note: Windows Server 2003 has a Domain Controller Security Policy console available in administrative tools.

NOTE: To make the changes effective immediately, you must run one of the following commands:

Windows 2000: `secedit /refreshpolicy machine_policy`

Windows Server 2003: `gpupdate /force`

Table 11.1   Windows 2000 and Windows Server 2003 Rights

Rights	Description	Groups Assigned This Right by Default
Access this computer from a network	Allows you to connect to the computer over the network.	Administrators, Everyone and Power Users
Add workstations to domain	Allows the user to add a computer to a specific domain . The user specifies the domain through an administrative user interface on the computer being added, creating an object in the Computer container of Active Directory. The behavior of this privilege is duplicated in Windows 2000 by another access control mechanism (permissions attached to the Computer container or organizational unit).	Authenticated Users
Back up files and directories	Allows the user to circumvent file and directory permissions to back up the system. Specifically, the privilege is similar to granting the following permissions on all files and folders on the local computer: Traverse Folder/Execute File, List Folder/Read Data, Read Attributes, Read Extended Attributes, and Read Permissions. See also Restore files and directories.	Administrators, Backup Operators
Change the system time	Allows the user to set the time for the internal clock of the computer.	Administrators, Power Users
Create a pagefile	Allows the user to create and change the size of a pagefile. This is done by specifying a paging file size for a given drive in the System Properties Performance Options.	Administrators
Debug programs	Allows the user to attach a debugger to any process. This privilege provides powerful access to sensitive and critical system operating components.	Administrators
Enable Trusted for Delegation on user and computer accounts	Allows the user to set the Trusted for Delegation setting on a user or computer object. The user or object that is granted this privilege must have write access to the account control flags on the user or computer object. A server process either running on a computer that is trusted for delegation or run by a user that is trusted for delegation can access resources on another computer. This uses a client's delegated credentials, as long as the client account does not have the Account Cannot Be Delegated account control flag set. Misuse of this privilege or of the Trusted for Delegation settings could make the network vulnerable to sophisticated attacks using Trojan horse programs that impersonate incoming clients and use their credentials to gain access to network resources.	Administrators
Force shutdown from a remote system	Allows a user to shut down a computer from a remote location on the network. See also the Shut Down the System privilege.	Administrators
Increase quotas	Allows a process with write property access to another process to increase the processor quota assigned to that other process. This privilege is useful for system tuning, but can be abused, as in a denial-of-service attack.	Administrators
Load and unload device drivers	Allows a user to install and uninstall Plug and Play device drivers. Device drivers that are not Plug and Play are not affected by this privilege and can only be installed by administrators. Since device drivers run as trusted (highly-privileged) programs, this privilege could be misused to install hostile programs and give these programs destructive access to resources.	Administrators
Logon locally	Allows a user to log on at the computer's keyboard. Since most protection can be bypassed by being able to log on directly to a machine without going though the network, this right should only be given to a few people.	Administrators, Account Operators, Backup Operators, Print Operators and Server Operators.

Continued

Table 11.1 Windows 2000 and Windows Server 2003 Rights

Rights	Description	Groups Assigned This Right by Default
Manage auditing and security log	Allows a user to specify object access auditing options for individual resources such as files, Active Directory objects, and registry keys. Object access auditing is not actually performed unless you have enabled it in the computerwide audit policy settings under Group Policy or under Group Policy defined in Active Directory; This privilege does not grant access to the computer-wide audit policy.	Administrators
	A user with this privilege can also view and clear the security log from the Event Viewer.	Administrators
Modify firmware environment values	Allows modification of the system environment variables, either by a user through the System Properties or by a process.	Administrators, Power Users
Profile a single process	Allows a user to use Windows NT and Windows 2000 performance-monitoring tools to monitor the performance of non-system processes.	Administrators
Profile system performance	Allows a user to use Windows NT and Windows 2000 performance-monitoring tools to monitor the performance of system processes.	Administrators, Backup Operators
Restore files and directories	Allows a user to circumvent file and directory permissions when restoring backed up files and directories, and to set any valid security principal as the owner of an object. See also the *Backup files and directories* privilege.	Administrators, Backup Operators, Everyone, Power Users, and Users
Shut down the system	Allows a user to shut down the local computer.	Administrators
Take ownership of files or other objects	Allows a user to take ownership of any securable object in the system, including Active Directory objects, files and folders, printers, registry keys, processes, and threads.	

11.1.10 Resolving Group Policies

When using group policies, if someone is getting an extra permission that you did not expect or someone is getting denied something that you did not expect, you can use the resultant set of Policy (RSoP) to help troubleshoot the problem. The RSoP is a query engine that polls existing policies and planned policies and then reports the results of all of the policies. When policies are applied on multiple levels (site, domain, domain controller, and organizational unit), the RSoP can help you resolve the conflict by showing the resultant policy and where the policies are set.

RSoP consists of two modes: planning mode and logging mode. With planning mode, you can simulate the effect of policy settings that you want to apply to a computer and user. Logging mode reports the existing policy settings for a computer and user that is currently logged on. The Resultant Set of Policy Wizard helps you create an RSoP query.

In Windows Server 2003, the Wizard can be started from Microsoft Management Console (MMC), Active Directory Users and Computers, or Active Directory Sites and Services. You must run the Wizard at least once to create an RSoP query. When complete, the query results are displayed in the RSoP snap-in in MMC. From here, you can save, change, and refresh your queries. You can create many RSoP queries by adding multiple Resultant Set of Policy snap-ins to MMC, one RSoP snap-in per query. See figure 11.5.

Another program that you can use to view the RSoP logging mode is the command-line tool called gpresult. gpresult is available in the Windows Tools from the Windows 2000 Server Resource Kit CD and is available with the Windows .net Server 2003. With gpresult, you can get similar detailed information provided by RSoP logging mode.

Figure 11.5   RSoP Console Showing the User Rights Assignments

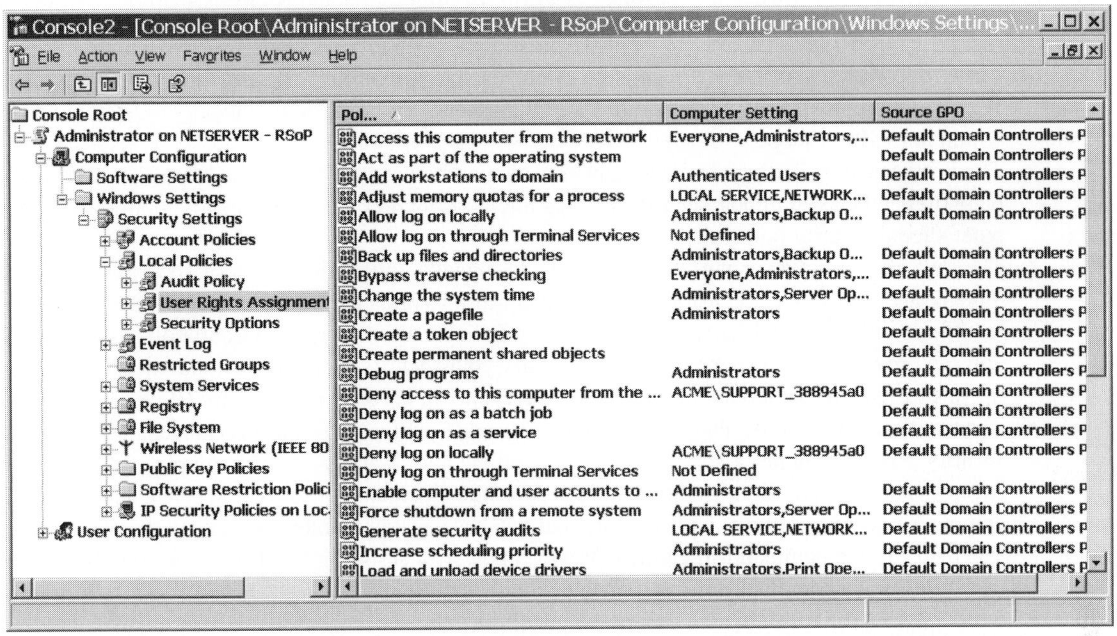

The syntax for the gpresult command is:

```
gpresult [/s computer [/u domain\user /p password]]
[/user TargetUserName] [/scope {user|computer}] [/v] [/z]
```

Parameters:

- **/s computer**—Specifies the name or IP address of a remote computer. The default is the local computer.
- **/u domain\user**—Runs the command with the account permissions of the user that is specified by user or domain\user. The default is the permissions of the current logged-on user on the computer that issues the command.
- **/p password**—Specifies the password of the user account that is specified in the /u parameter.
- **/user TargetUserName**—Specifies the user name of the user whose RSOP data is to be displayed.
- **/scope {user|computer}**—Displays either user or computer results. Valid values for the /scope parameter are user or computer. If you omit the /scope parameter, gpresult displays both user and computer settings.
- **/v**—Specifies that the output display verbose policy information.
- **/z**—Specifies that the output display all available information about Group Policy. Because this parameter produces more information than the /v parameter, redirect output to a text file when you use this parameter (for example, gpresult /z >policy.txt).

11.2   SECURITY TEMPLATES

In Windows 2000 and Windows Server 2003, User Rights assignment has been integrated with Group Policy. While it is possible to change security settings for a local machine in a Group Policy Object, a better approach is to use a security template. A security template provides a single place where all system security can be viewed, analyzed, changed, and applied to a single machine or to a Group Policy Object.

A security template is simply the settings contained in the Computer/Security Settings portion of a GPO that have been exported to a text file so that they can be imported into other GPOs. Security templates do not introduce new security parameters, they simply organize all existing attributes (account policies, local policies, restricted group, registry settings, file system settings, and system services) into one place to ease security administration. Security templates can also be used as a base configuration for security analysis, when used with the Security Configuration and Analysis snap-in.

To manage security templates, you can use one of the following tools:

- The Group Policies management console can be used to import and export security template files. When you import security settings into a GPO, those settings apply automatically to all computers within that GPO's scope.
- The local Security Settings management console can be used to import and export security template files. When you import security settings into a local GPO, you permanently modify the computer's local security policy.
- The Security Templates snap-in can be used to manage entire directories of security templates quickly and easily. The Security Templates snap-in interprets the contents of a security template text file in the same familiar way that the Group Policy Editor interprets Group Policy settings, so you can browse the settings hierarchy and modify your security templates without the risk of making errors and without having to understand the syntax of security template file.
- The Configuration and Analysis snap-in can be used to analyze how closely a machine's effective security posture matches a specific security template and to apply security template settings to a specific machine. The Configuration and Analysis management console can create a database of a computer's security settings and compare that database against numerous security templates.
- The SecEdit.Exe command-line utility provides powerful scripting functions to accomplish tasks that cannot be accomplished using management console snap-ins.

Windows 2000 and Windows Server 2003 come with a number of pre-configured security templates for common machine configurations, like workstations, secure servers, and domain controllers. See table 11.2. The security templates simplify security administration and help to eliminate gaps in security. For servers deployed on the Internet, rather than laboriously going through a checklist to make sure the server is secure, it is now only necessary to apply a security template. This results in a substantial savings of administrator's time.

Table 11.2 Windows Predefined Security Template

Security Template	Description
Basic (basic*.inf)	The basic configurations apply the Windows 2000 and Windows Server 2003 default security settings to all security areas except those pertaining to user rights.
Compatibility (compat*.inf)	The default Windows 2000 or Windows Server 2003 security configuration gives members of the local Users group strict security settings, while members of the local Power Users group have security settings that are compatible with Windows NT 4.0 user assignments so that local users group can use legacy programs. It is not considered a secure environment.
Secure (secure*.inf)	The secure templates implement recommended security settings for all security areas except files, folders, and registry keys. Besides increasing security settings for account policy and auditing, it also removes all members from power users group. These are not modified because file system and registry permissions are configured securely by default.
Highly Secure (hisec*.inf)	The highly secure templates define security settings for Windows 2000 or Windows Server 2003 network communications. The security areas are set to require maximum protection for network traffic and protocols used between computers running Windows 2000 or Windows Server 2003. As a result, such computers configured with a highly secure template can only communicate with other Windows 2000 or Windows Server 2003 computers. They will not be able to communicate with computers running Windows 9X or Windows NT.

To import a security template to a Group Policy object, in a console from which you manage Group Policy settings, click Group Policy object. It can be found by opening the Policy Object Name, Computer Configuration, Windows Settings, Import Policy and selecting the security template that you want to import. The security settings are applied when the computer starts or as the Group Policy settings dictate.

To customize a predefined security template:

1. In the Security Template snap-in, double-click Security Templates.
2. Double-click the default path folder (*Systemroot*\Security\Templates) and right-click the predefined template you want to modify.
3. Click Save As and specify a file name for the security template.
4. Double-click the new security template to display the security policy (such as Account Policies), and double-click the security policy you want to modify.
5. Click the security area you want to customize (such as Password Policy), then double-click the security attribute to modify (such as Minimum Password Length).
6. Check the Define this policy setting in the template check box in order to allow editing.

11.3   REGISTRY SECURITY

The **registry** is a central, secure database in which Windows stores all hardware configuration information, software configuration information and system security policy. Components that use the registry include the Windows NT kernel, Device drivers, setup programs, NTDETECT.COM, hardware profiles, and user profiles.

The data kept in the registry is added and modified by a variety of system modules that start during bootup and modified by various configuration tools such as the Control Panel, Windows Setup program, User Manager, adding or removing a hardware device, adding or removing a printer, and other administrative utilities.

In addition, data is added and modified when installing software that uses a single Application Programming Interface (API). You can think of API as a set of standard commands that can be used by any software package to access the Registry. For example, a software package can find out what type of hardware (including type of processor, resolution and number of colors of the video system and the IRQ and DMA settings for a device), and the version of drivers and other software modules.

If the need arises to view or change the Registry, you can use the **Registry Editor (REGEDIT.EXE)** utilities. REGEDIT.EXE is automatically installed in the WINNT or WINDOWS folder. REGEDIT.EXE is easier to use because of its Explorer-style interface. See figure 11.6.

Once in a while, you may have the need to view or edit the Registry to add or change a value that cannot be changed in the Control Panel or other utility or to add, view, and change hardware settings that cannot be done with the device manager. You should only make changes when following directions in a magazine article, a book or manual or from a support person. If you make the wrong changes, Windows may not run properly or may not boot at all.

The Registry is organized in a hierarchical structure. The Registry is first divided into five **subtrees.** See table 11.3. Subtrees have names that begin with the string HKEY, which stands for "**Handle to a Key.**" A subtree is similar to a root directory of a disk.

Of the different subtrees, the two main subtrees are the HKEY_LOCAL_MACHINE and the HKEY_USERS. The HKEY_LOCAL_MACHINE contains information about the type of hardware installed, drivers, and other system settings. The HKEY_USERS contains information about all users who logon to the computer including the DEFAULT generic user settings. The DEFAULT user is used as a template for any new users.

The root keys are then divided into **subkeys,** which may contain other subkeys. You can think of the subkeys as folders within the subtree.

Within the subkey, you will find a value entry, which consists of three parts: the name of the value, the data type of the value, and the value itself. Data types describe the format of the data. The data types of the values are shown in table 11.4.

Figure 11.6 REGEDIT.EXE

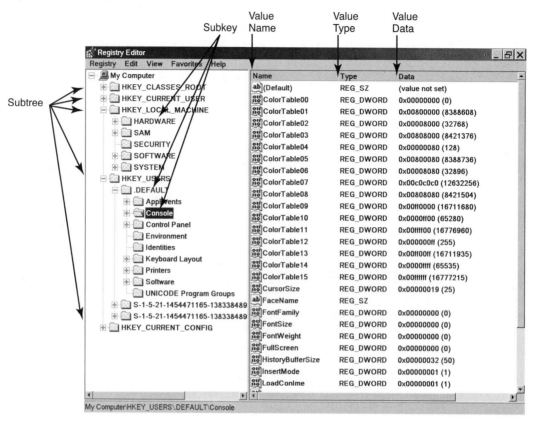

Table 11.3 Windows 2000 and Windows Server 2003 Registry Subtrees

Subtrees	Description
HKEY_CLASSES_ROOT	Contains file associations and OLE information.
HKEY_CURRENT_USER	Contains settings for applications, desktop configurations, and user preferences for the user currently logged on. The information is a copy and is retrieved from the NTUSER.DAT file and stores it in the *systemroot* PROFILES\username key when a user logs on to the computer. This subkey points to the same data contained in HKEY_USERS\SID_ currently_logged_on_user. Note: This subtree takes precedence over HKEY_LOCAL_MACHINE for duplicated values.
HKEY_LOCAL_MACHINE	Contains information about the type of hardware installed, drivers, and other system settings. Information includes the bus type, system memory, device drivers, and startup control data. The data in this subtree remains constant regardless of the user.
HKEY_USERS	Contains information about all users who logon to the computer including the DEFAULT generic user settings. The DEFAULT user is used as a template for any new users.
HKEY_CURRENT_CONFIG	Contains information about the current running hardware configuration. This information is used to configure settings such as the device drivers to load and the display resolution to use. This subtree is part of the HKEY_LOCAL_MACHINE subtree and maps to HKEY_LOCAL_MACHINE\SYSTEM\ CurrentControlSet\Hardware Profiles\Current

Table 11.4   Windows Registry Data Types

Data Type	Description
REG_DWORD	Data represented by a number that is 4 bytes (double word) long. Many parameters for device drivers and services are this type and are displayed in Registry Editor in binary, hexadecimal, or decimal format.
REG_SZ	A fixed-length text string.
REG_EXPAND_SZ	A variable-length data string. This data type includes variables that are resolved when a program or service uses the data.
REG_BINARY	Raw binary data represented as a string of hexadecimal digits. Windows 2000 interprets every two hexadecimal digits as a byte value.
REG_MULTI_SZ	A multiple string. Values that contain lists or multiple values in a form that people can read are usually this type. Entries are separated by spaces, commas, or other marks.
REG_FUL_RESOURCE_DESCRIPTOR	Stores a resource list for hardware components or drivers. You cannot add or modify entries with this data type.

Because the information stored in the registry controls the configuration of the operating system, changes to it can dramatically affect the security of the system as a whole. For examples, hackers could insert keys that would cause kernel-level drivers to be loaded, which would have open access to the system inside the kernel's security boundary. Therefore, controlling access to the registry is critical to keeping a computer secure.

The Registry is protected with an Access Control List (ACL), which allows selected users to modify the contents of the Registry and grant to others read-only access to that data. The permissions include Full Control, Read, and Special Permissions.

WHAT YOU NEED TO KNOW

1. A policy is a tool used by administrators to define and control how programs, network resources and the operating system behave for users and computers in the Active Directory structure.
2. Using Group Policies, administrators can create, manage, and deploy many different computer configurations to create a consistent work environment for various classes of workers across any number of client computers in an organization.
3. Since the Active Directory is a structured hierarchy, there are different levels of policies so that you can have a customized configuration.
4. In the Domain GPO, Account Policies (Password Policies, Account Lockout, and Kerberos Policies) are defined on a domain basis only.
5. As mentioned earlier, when a GPO is created and associated with an Active Directory container, the settings from the parent container flow down into the child containers.
6. The inheritance or flow-down of rights can be stopped or blocked by using the Block Policy In-

heritance checkbox located with the properties of the container.
7. Of course, sometimes, you may not want some of the earlier policies overwritten by the later executed policies or by blocking the policy inheritance. To maintain these settings, you would open the properties of the GPO and select No Override.
8. The "disabled: the Group Policy Object is not applied to this container" option is a troubleshooting tool to help isolate which container a setting is coming from.
9. The permissions of a Group Policy can be done using the standard Access Control List (ACL) editor.
10. By default, only members of Domain Administrators, Enterprise Administrators, and Group Policy Creator Owners groups can create new Group Policy objects.
11. For a group policy to apply to a person, the person must have Apply Group Policy and Read Permission for the group policy.

12. You can manage Group Policy by navigating through Active Directory using the Active Directory Users and Computer management console or the Active Directory Sites and Services management console.

13. Windows 2000 and Windows Server 2003 periodically refresh group policies throughout the network. By default, the client computers are updated every 90 minutes with an offset of plus or minus 30 minutes.

14. To refresh the Group Policy immediately, you would use the SECEDIT command for Windows 2000 computers and GPUPDATE for Windows Server 2003 computers.

15. In Windows 2000 and Windows Server 2003, User Rights assignment has been integrated with Group Policy.

16. Windows 2000 and Windows Server 2003 come with a number of preconfigured security templates for common machine configurations, like workstations, secure servers, and domain controllers.

17. The registry is a central, secure database in which Windows 2000 stores all hardware configuration information, software configuration information, and system security policy.

18. The data kept in the registry is added and modified by a variety of system modules that start during bootup and are modified by various configuration tools such as the Control Panel, Windows Setup program, User Manager, adding or removing a hardware device, adding or removing a printer, and other administrative utilities.

19. If the need arises to view or change the Registry, you can use the Registry Editor (REGEDIT.EXE) utilities.

20. The Registry is protected with an Access Control List (ACL), which allows selected users to modify the contents of the Registry and grant to others read-only access to that data. The permissions include Full Control, Read, and Special Permissions.

QUESTIONS

1. You have just created a GPO for an OU in your enterprise. The GPO only modifies user settings; no computer settings are altered. How can you reduce the time it takes for a client to process this GPO do determine what settings need be applied?
   a. Disable the user configuration settings for the GPO.
   b. Copy the GPO to every local computer.
   c. Split the settings into several GPOs and apply them all.
   d. Disable the computer configuration settings for the GPO.

2. Where in the Group Policy settings would you configure user logon and logoff scripts?
   a. Client configuration
   b. Computer configuration
   c. User configuration
   d. Startup configuration

3. You have associated GPOs with your site, domain, and OUs. In which order are GPOs processed?
   a. Site, Domain, OU
   b. Domain, OU, Site
   c. Domain, Site, OU
   d. OU, Site, Domain

4. You have created a GPO and allocated it to a particular OU in the Active Directory. You do not want this GPO to be applied to all user objects in this OU. How can you apply the OU GPO settings to only some of the user objects in the OU? (Choose all that apply.)
   a. Create a security group containing only the users that will use the GPO settings. Give

only this security group both READ and APPLY GROUP POLICY permissions on the GPO.
   b. This cannot be done. All GPO settings for an OU will apply to all objects in the OU.
   c. Move the user objects that do not require the GPO settings to a sub OU within the parent OU. Use the "block inheritance" setting on the child OU to stop the parent GPO settings being applied.
   d. Create a security group which contains all the users that will not use the GPO settings. DENY this security group APPLY GROUP POLICY permission on the GPO.

5. By default, how often will a client computer refresh its group policy settings?
   a. At user logon only
   b. At computer restart only
   c. Every 90 minutes
   d. Never

6. Most of the Windows 2000 configuration information is kept in _____ .
   a. Initialization files (*.INI)
   b. System files (*.SYS)
   c. The Windows Registry
   d. Configuration files (*.CFG)
   e. Dynamic Link Files (*.DLL)

7. Which utility would you use to search for a particular value in the registry?
   a. Regedit.Exe   b. Regedt32.Exe
   c. Rdisk.Exe   d. Poledit.Exe

HANDS-ON EXERCISES

Exercise 1: User Rights

1. Log out as the Administrator.
2. Try to log in as Charlie Brown. It shouldn't work because Charlie Brown has not been given the right to logon locally to a domain controller.
3. Log in as the Administrator.
4. In the Administrative Tools, open the Domain Controller Security Policy console.
5. If you open Security Settings, Local Policies, User Rights Assignment, you will find Logon Locally. Double-click Logon Locally.
6. Click the Add button, click on the Browse button, select the Charlie Brown account, click on the Add button, and click on the OK button twice.
7. Log out as the Administrator and login as Charlie Brown. When you log in, change the password to PW.
8. As Charlie Brown, try to disable Frank Biggs' account.
9. Log out as Charlie Brown and log in as Administrator.
10. Right-click the Sales Organizational Unit and select the Delegate Control option. Click the Next button.
11. Click the Add button, select Charlie Brown, and click on the Add button. Click the OK button. Click on the Next button.
12. Select the Create, Delete, and Manage User Accounts, and Modify the membership of a group options. Click on the Next button. Click the Finish button.
13. Log out as the Administrator and log in as Charlie Brown.
14. Disable Frank Biggs' account.
15. Log out as Charlie Brown

Exercise 2: Group Policies

1. Log in as Administrator.
2. Using the Run option, start an MMC console.
3. In the MMC console, open the Console menu and select the Add/Remove Snap-in option.
4. In the Add/Remove Snap-in dialog box, click on the Add button.
5. Click-on the Group policy snap-in, click on the Add button. In the Select Group Policy Object dialog box, click on the Browse button.
6. In the Browse for a Group Policy Object dialog box, click the Domain Controllers.AcmeXX.com. Click the OK button.
7. Click the Default Domain Controllers Policy and click the OK button. Click the Finish button.
8. Click on the Group policy snap-in again and click on the Add button. In the Select Group Policy Object dialog box, click on the Browse button.
9. In the Browse for a Group Policy Object dialog box, click the Sales.AcmeXX.com. Click the OK button.
10. Click the New Group Policy Object button (next to the up folder button). Since the New Group Object is highlighted, rename it to the Sales Group Policy and click the OK button. Click the Finish button.
11. Click on the Group policy snap-in; click on the Add button. With the Local Computer selected for the Group Policy Object, click on the Finish button.
12. Click on the Close button. Click on the OK button.
13. Under the Default Domain Controllers Policy, open Computer Configuration, Windows Settings, Security Policy, Account Policies, click on Password Policy.
14. In the detail pane, double-click the Minimum password length option.
15. In the Template Security Policy Setting dialog box, enable Define this policy setting in the template. Specify at least 8 characters. Click the OK button.
16. Under Password Policy, click on Account Policy option.
17. In the Detail pane, double-click the Account Lockout Duration.
18. Enable Define this policy Setting in the template. Keep the default of 30 minutes and click on the OK button. Click on the OK button.
19. Log out as the Administrator.
20. Log in as Charlie Brown.
21. Log in 6 times with the password of test. This should lockout the account.
22. Log in as the Administrator.

23. Using the Active Directory Users and Computers console, right-click Charlie Brown's user account and select the Properties option.
24. In the Account tab, remove the X in the Accounts locked out box.
25. Try to change Charlie Brown's password to LETMEIN. Then change the password to PASSWORD.
26. In the Active Directory Uses and Computers console, right-click the Sales department and select the Properties option.
27. In the Group Policy tab, click the Add button. Click the Up folder button and double-click the Domain Controllers.amcexx.com folder. Select the Default Domain Controllers Policy. Click the OK button.
28. Click the Default Domain Controllers Policy and click on the Up button to make the Default Domain Controller Policy have a higher priority than the Sales Policy. Although we are not going to use the option, notice the Block Policy Inheritance. Click the OK button.

Exercise 3: Comparing Security Templates

1. Click the Start button and select the Run option.
2. In the Run dialog box, type mmc in the Open box and press the Enter key.
3. When the Microsoft Management Console appears, open the Console menu and click the Add/Remove Snap-in dialog box.
4. In the list, double-click both Security Configuration and Analysis and Security Templates.
5. Click Close to close the Add Standalone snap-in dialog box.
6. Click OK to close the Add/Remove span-ins dialog box.
7. Maximize the Console Root window within the console window and then maximize the Console window.
8. Open the Console menu, choose Save As, and type in Security Templates. You should now have a security templates management tool located in the Administrative Tools folder of the Start menu.
9. In the Security Templates management console, right-click Security Configuration and Analysis and click Open Database.
10. In the Open Database dialog box, type in your server name/domain controller as the name of the database and click Open.
11. When the Import template dialog box appears containing a list of security templates from which to choose, select the Hisecdc.inf security template as the template to compare the database to and Click Open.
12. Read the instructions for analyzing security that will appear in the management console.
13. Right-click Security Configuration and Analysis and click Analysis Computer Now.
14. When the Perform Analysis dialog box appears asking for a file name and path for the error log, click OK to accept the error log path.
15. Expand Security Configuration and Analysis, Account Policies, and then select Password Policy. The red X icons indicate a difference between the computer's configuration and the security template while the green check mark icons indicate that the computer settings are the same as the security policy.
16. Double-click Enforce Password History. Notice the number of retained passwords for the computer and the template.
17. Click the OK button.
18. Browse through the remainder of the settings that are marked with red icons.

Exercise 4: Creating and Modifying Security Templates

1. Create a User Defined Templates folder in the `C:\systemroot\Security\Templates`.
2. Open the Security Template management console that you created in exercise 3.
3. Right-click Security Templates in the console tree and click New Template Search Path.
4. Browse to the User Defined Templates and click the OK button.
5. In the console tree, right-click the new User Defined Templates folder and click New Template.
6. Type Passpol as the Template Name.
7. In the Description box, type Company password policy. Click the OK button.
8. Expand the new Passpol security template, expand the Account Policies folder and then click Password Policy.
9. Double-click Enforce Password History.
10. In the Template Security Policy Setting dialog box, select Define This Policy Setting.
11. Type 24 in the Passwords Remembered box and click OK to close the dialog box.
12. Double-click Maximum Password Age. Select Define this policy. Type 120 into the Days box. Click OK.
13. Set the Minimum Password Age to 7 days.

14. Set the Minimum Password Length policy to 8 characters.
15. Enable the Passwords Must Meet Complexity Requirements settings.
16. Close the management console and save the security template file.
17. Using Windows Explorer, browse to C:\systemroot\Security\Templates\User Defined Templates.
18. Right-click Passpol.inf and choose Properties. Notice its size.
19. Close the Properties dialog box.
20. Double-click the Passpol.inf file and view the contents of the file.
21. Close notepad.
22. Click the Start button, select Programs, select Administrative Tools, and select Active Directory Users and Computers.
23. Right-click your domain and select Properties. Click the Group Policy tab. Double-click Domain Security Policy.
24. Expand Domain Security Policy, Computer Configuration, Windows Settings, and then Security Settings.
25. Right-click Security Settings and select Import Policy.
26. Browse to the User Defined Templates folder and double-click Passpol.
27. Expand Security Settings, Account Policies, and then select Password Policy. You should notice that the Enforce Password History is now the same as your settings. The password policy now applies to all computers within your domain.
28. Close the Group Policies management console.
29. Close the Active Directory Users and Computers dialog box.

CHAPTER **12**

Attacks and Intrusion Detections

Topics Covered in this Chapter

Introduction

To better protect your network and the network servers and services, you need to understand what attacks your network is vulnerable and how you can protect your network against such attack. In addition, this chapter discusses how to detect intruders so that you can put a stop to them and protect your network in the future.

Objectives:

1. **Security+ Objective 1.3**—Nonessential Services and Protocols—Disabling unnecessary systems/process/programs
2. **Security+ Objective 1.4**—Attacks
3. **Security+ Objective 1.4.1**—DoS/DDoS
4. **Security+ Objective 1.4.12**—Software Exploitation
5. **Security+ Objective 1.4.2**—Back Door
6. **Security+ Objective 1.4.3**—Spoofing
7. **Security+ Objective 1.4.4**—Man-in-the Middle
8. **Security+ Objective 1.4.5**—Replay
9. **Security+ Objective 1.4.6**—TCP/IP Hijacking
10. **Security+ Objective 1.5**—Malicious Code
11. **Security+ Objective 1.5.1**—Viruses
12. **Security+ Objective 1.5.2**—Trojan Horses
13. **Security+ Objective 1.5.3**—Logic Bombs
14. **Security+ Objective 1.5.4**—Worms
15. **Security+ Objective 1.7**—Auditing—Logging, system scanning
16. **Security+ Objective 2.3.4.3**—Buffer Overflows
17. **Security+ Objective 3.1.1**—Firewalls
18. **Security+ Objective 3.1.2**—Routers
19. **Security+ Objective 3.1.3**—Switches
20. **Security+ Objective 3.1.9**—IDS
21. **Security+ Objective 3.4**—Intrusion Detection
22. **Security+ Objective 3.4.1**—Network-Based
23. **Security+ Objective 3**—Detection
24. **Security+ Objective 3.4.1.2**—Passive Detection
25. **Security+ Objective 3.4.2**—Host-Based
26. **Security+ Objective 3.4.2.1**—Active Detection
27. **Security+ Objective 3.4.2.2**—Passive Detection
28. **Security+ Objective 3.4.3**—Honey Pots
29. **Security+ Objective 3.4.4**—Incident Response
30. **Security+ Objective 3.5**—Security Baselines
31. **Security+ Objective 3.5.1**—OS/NOS Hardening (Concepts and Processes)
32. **Security+ Objective 3.5.1.1**—File System
33. **Security+ Objective 3.5.1.2**—Updates (Hotfixes, Service Packs, Patches)
34. **Security+ Objective 3.5.2**—Network Hardening
35. **Security+ Objective 3.5.2.1**—Updates (Firmware)
36. **Security+ Objective 3.5.2.2**—Configuration
37. **Security+ Objective 3.5.2.2.1**—Enabling and Disabling Services and Protocols
38. **Security+ Objective 3.5.2.2.2**—Access Control Lists
39. **Security+ Objective 3.5.3**—Application Hardening
40. **Security+ Objective 5.4.2**—Incident Response Policy
41. **Security+ Objective 5.5.4**—Auditing (Privilege, Usage, Escalation)
42. **Security+ Objective 5.6**—Forensics (Awareness, Conceptual Knowledge and Understanding—know what your role is)
43. **Security+ Objective 5.6.1**—Chain of Custody
44. **Security+ Objective 5.6.2**—Preservation of Evidence
45. **Security+ Objective 5.6.3**—Collection of Evidence

12.1   DENIAL OF SERVICES

Security+ Objective 1.4—Attacks

Security+ Objective 1.4.1—DoS/DDoS

An attacker does not necessarily have to gain access to a system in order to cause significant problems. **Denial of Service (DoS)** is a type of attack on a network that is designed to bring the network to its knees either by disabling or crippling a server or by flooding it with useless traffic. Many DoS attacks, such as the Ping of Death and Teardrop attacks, exploit limitations in the TCP/IP protocols. In the worst cases, for example, a website accessed by millions of people can occasionally be forced to temporarily cease operation. Other attacks are application specific, which strike at specific flaws within the program.

A Denial of Service attack can also destroy programming and files in a computer system. Although usually intentional and malicious, a Denial of Service attack can sometimes happen accidentally. For all known DoS attacks, there are software fixes that system administrators can install to limit the damage caused by the attacks. But, like viruses, new DoS attacks are constantly being dreamed up by hackers.

Distributed Denial of Service (DDoS) attacks involve installing programs known as zombies on various computers in advance of the attack. A command is issued to these zombies, which launch the attack on behalf of the attacker, thus hiding their tracks. The zombies themselves are often installed using worms. The real danger from a DDoS attack is that the attacker uses many victim computers as host computers to control other zombies that initiate the attack. When the system that is overwhelmed tries to trace back the attack, it receives a set of spoofed addresses generated by a series of zombies.

SANS, short for SysAdmin, Audit, Network, Security Institute is a trusted leader in information security research, certification and education. According to the SANS Institute (http://www.sans.org), the majority of the successful attacks on operating systems come from only a few software vulnerabilities. This can be attributed to the fact that attackers are opportunistic, take the easiest and most convenient route, and exploit the best-known flaws with the most effective and widely available attack tools. They count on organizations not fixing the problems, and they often attack indiscriminately, scanning the Internet for any vulnerable systems. System compromises in the Solar Sunrise Pentagon hacking incident, for example, and the easy and rapid spread of the Code Red and NIMDA worms can be traced to exploitation of unpatched vulnerabilities.

The following defensive steps will help you prevent these types of attacks:

- Keep systems updated with the latest security patches.
- Block large ping packets at the router and firewall, stopping them from reaching the perimeter network.
- Apply antispoof filters on the router; that is, block any incoming packet that has a source address equal to an address on the internal network.
- Filter the ICMP messages on the firewall and router (although this could affect some management tools).
- Develop a defense plan with your Internet service provider (ISP) that enables a rapid response to an attack that targets the bandwidth between your ISP and your perimeter network.
- Disable the response to directed broadcasts.
- Apply proper router and firewall filtering.
- Use an intruder detection system to check for unusual traffic and generate an alert if it detects any. Configure the system to generate an alert if it detects ICMP_ECHOREPLY without associated ICMP_ECHO packets.
- Each week, more DoS attacks are documented and added to bug tracking databases. You should ensure that you always remain current on these attacks and how you can guard against them. To find the most commonly exploited vulnerable services in Windows and Unix, visit the SANS/FBI Top Twenty list located at http://www.sans.org/top20/.

12.1.1   TCP/IP Attacks

Security+ Objective 2.3.4.3—Buffer Overflows

A **buffer** is a data area that is shared by either hardware devices or program processes. Buffer overflows occur when a program tries to store more data in the buffer than it was designed for. The data that do not fit into the designated buffer can overflow into an adjacent buffer. The overflowed data can overwrite and corrupt valid data of another program.

   Buffer overflow attacks, the most common kind of DoS attack, is simply to send more traffic to a network address than the programmers who planned its data buffers anticipated someone might send. The attacker may be aware that the target system has a weakness that can be exploited or the attacker may simply try the attack in case it might work. A few of the better-known attacks based on the buffer characteristics of a program or system include:

- Sending email messages that have attachments with 256-character file names to Netscape and Microsoft mail programs
- Sending oversized Internet Control Message Protocol (ICMP) packets (this is also known as the ping of death)
- Sending to a user of the Pine email program a message with a "From" address larger than 256 characters

In addition, if the application under attack has administrative privileges, it is possible for the attacker to take control of the entire system through the controlled application.

   The best defense against buffer overflow is having software developers follow secure coding practices. This would include safe compiles that help minimize the impact of buffer overflows and design the program to check all user input for validity, so that the wrong data would cause the overflow. Of course, when you don't have direct control over the software, you can minimize their effect by running programs as the least privileged account possible (not as administrator). Of course, this is one of the reasons that for operating systems and network applications, you must constantly check for service packs, patches and security fixes so that it can fix these types of problems.

   SYN Attacks are when a session is initiated between the Transport Control Program (TCP) client and server in a network, a very small buffer space exists to handle the usually rapid "handshaking" exchange of messages that sets up the session. The session-establishing packets include a SYN field that identifies the sequence in the message exchange. An attacker can send a number of connection requests very rapidly and then fail to respond to the reply. This leaves the first packet in the buffer so that other, legitimate connection requests can't be accommodated. Although the packet in the buffer is dropped after a certain period of time without a reply, the effect of many of these bogus connection requests is to make it difficult for legitimate requests for a session to get established. In general, this problem depends on the operating system providing correct settings or allowing the network administrator to tune the size of the buffer and the timeout period. See figure 12.1.

Figure 12.1   The SYN Flood

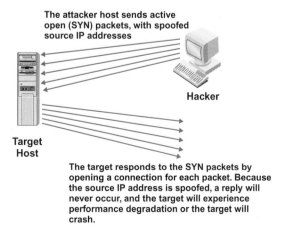

The attacker host sends active open (SYN) packets, with spoofed source IP addresses

Hacker

Target Host

The target responds to the SYN packets by opening a connection for each packet. Because the source IP address is spoofed, a reply will never occur, and the target will experience performance degradation or the target will crash.

Teardrop Attack, a type of Denial of Service attack, exploits the way that the Internet Protocol (IP) requires a packet that is too large for the next router to handle be divided into fragments. The fragment packet identifies an offset to the beginning of the first packet that enables the entire packet to be reassembled by the receiving system. In the teardrop attack, the attacker's IP puts a confusing offset value in the second or later fragment. If the receiving operating system does not have a plan for this situation, it can cause the system to crash.

WinNuke is a Windows program that sends special TCP/IP packets with an invalid TCP header. Windows will crash when it receives one of the packets because of the way Windows TCP/IP stack handles bad data in the TCP header. Instead of returning an error code or rejecting the bad data, it sends the computer to the "**blue screen of death**."

The ICMP protocol is another useful protocol that is used in DOS attacks. The **ping of death (POD)** mentioned above sends an ICMP echo request that is larger than 65,536 bytes to a target. All that the attacker needed to use in the attack was the victim's IP address. Most manufacturers have now provided patches that make their systems invulnerable to the ping of death and other types of IP fragmentation attacks, and Microsoft has removed the ability to generate ICMP packets of invalid sizes.

Another attack that uses the ICMP protocol is the Smurf attack. In a **Smurf attack,** the perpetrator sends an IP ping (or "echo my message back to me") request to a receiving site. The ping packet specifies that it be broadcast to a number of hosts within the receiving site's local network. The packet also indicates that the request is from another site, the target site that is to receive the denial of service. (Sending a packet with someone else's return address in it is called spoofing the return address.) The result will be lots of ping replies flooding back to the innocent, spoofed host. If the flood is great enough, the spoofed host will no longer be able to receive or distinguish real traffic. To prevent Smurf attacks, routers should be configured to drop such packets and not respond to these requests. See figure 12.2.

The UDP flood is very much like an ICMP flood, except the protocol attacked is UDP. The attacker sends a large number of UDP packets to random ports on the target. The target responds with RST packets or ACK packets, depending on whether a service is configured for a particular port. If an attacker is able to send enough of these packets, the target system could become multiple zombie hosts or by spoofing the source address of the UDP service request packet.

A fraggle is a variation of the Smurf attack that uses UDP service request packets instead of ICMP packets. The default method of the attack is identical except that the UDP protocol and UDP echo packets are used.

Note: The following registry key settings can be implemented on Windows 2000 and Windows Server 2003 to enable protection against DoS attacks:

Figure 12.2   The Smurf Attacks

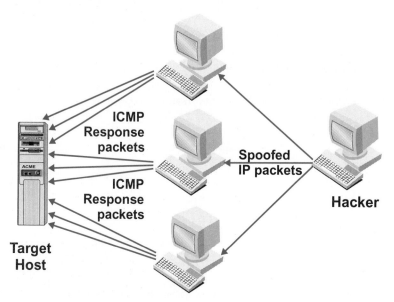

- hkey_local_machine\system\currentcontrolset\services\tcpip\parameters\synattackprotect=1 REG_DWORD
- hkey_local_machine\system\currentcontrolset\services\tcpip\parameters\tcpmaxconnectrespon-seretransmissions=2 REG_DWORD
- hkey_local_machine\system\currentcontrolset\services\tcpip\parameters\tcpmaxdataretransmissi-ons=3 REG_DWORD
- hkey_local_machine\system\currentcontrolset\services\tcpip\parameters\enablepmtudiscovery=0 REG_DWORD

12.1.2 Man-in-the-Middle and Replay Attacks

Security+ Objective 1.4.6—TCP/IP Hijacking

Hijacking is a type of network security attack in which the attacker takes control of a communication, just as an airplane hijacker takes control of a flight, between two entities and masquerades as one of them. One type of hijacking attack is the man-in-the middle attack.

Security+ Objective 1.4.4—Man-in-the Middle

A **man-in-the-middle** attack is one in which the attacker intercepts messages in a public key exchange and then retransmits them, substituting the attacker's own public key for the requested one, so that the two original parties still appear to be communicating with each other directly. The attacker uses a program that appears to be the server to the client and appears to be the client to the server. The attack may be used simply to gain access to the messages, or enable the attacker to modify them before retransmitting them.

The most common example of hijacking is web session hijacking, where an attacker takes control of a user's browser session. Since most web servers use cookies to authenticate and track users, when a user connects to a website and authenticates, an attacker may be able to hijack their session by loading a hacked cookie or by inputting a specific URL on a poorly configured web server into their browser. The legitimate user will most likely be kicked out, or at least be shown an error page indicating their login has failed.

Another opportunity for session hijacking is provided by poorly configured server time-outs. If a web developer makes the session time-out (length of time of no activity before the web server disconnects the user) too long, it provides a larger window of opportunity for an attacker to hijack the session.

Hijacking is also used to make it appear that one or more websites have been taken over. There are two different types of domain name system (DNS) hijacking. In one, the attacker gains access to DNS records on a server and modifies them so that requests for the genuine Web page will be redirected else-where—usually to a fake page that the attacker has created. This gives the impression to the viewer that the website has been compromised, when in fact, only a server has been.

In February 2000, an attacker hijacked RSA Security's website by gaining access to a DNS server that was not controlled by RSA. By modifying DNS records, the attacker diverted requests to a spoof website. It appeared to users that an attacker had gained access to the actual RSA website data and changed it—a serious problem for a security enterprise. This type of hijacking is difficult to prevent, because administrators control only their own DNS records, and have no control over upstream DNS servers.

In the second type of DNS hijack, the attacker spoofs valid email accounts and floods the inboxes of the technical and administrative contacts. This type of attack can be prevented by using authentication for InterNIC records.

In another type of website hijack, the perpetrator simply registers a domain name similar enough to a legitimate one that users are likely to type it, either by mistaking the actual name or through a typo. This type of hijack is currently being employed to send many unwary citizens to porn sites when they were attempting to visit popular commercial or government sites.

Hijacking is not limited to web-based sessions only. Hijacking is especially suited to telnet type plaintext connections, in which an attacker can watch a TCP session being initiated and data being passed between client and server. If the attacker sees something interesting they can break into the conversation and take control of the user's session for their own purposes.

To prevent hijacking attacks, the simplest thing to do is reauthenticate the user before performing important actions. For web servers, creating unique session cookies also reduces the risk. The more unique the cookie, the harder it is to break and hijack. Finally, if possible, use secure protocols, use the latest and most secure encryption techniques for all connections that involve authentication and ensure that the latest security updates are applied to your existing software.

Security+ Objective 1.4.5—Replay

Replay attacks involve listening to and repeating data passed on the network. An attacker tries to capture packets containing passwords or digital signatures as they pass between two hosts on the network using a protocol analyzer. The attacker then filters the data and extracts the portion of the packet that contains the password, encryption key, or digital signature. Later, the attacker resends or replays that information in an attempt to gain access to a secured resource.

An actual replay attack is more difficult than just capturing and repeating information. The attacker must accurately predict or guess TCP sequence numbers to make this work. However, it is possible for an attacker to guess correctly to use a script or utility that automatically makes guesses until the correct sequence is determined.

To protect yourself and your organization's network from replay attacks, ensure that the latest security updates are applied to your existing software. Use the latest and most secure encryption techniques for all connections that involve authentication. For example, IPSEC can provide antireplay services.

12.1.3   Spoofing

Security+ Objective 1.4.3—Spoofing

Some Spoofing attacks were already discussed in chapter 10. As you know spoofing is pretending to be someone else by impersonating, masquerading, or mimicking that person. Some examples of spoofing include:

- IP addressing spoofing is forging the IP source address in one or more IP packets to show that the packet came from a source other than the true source of the packet.
- ARP ache poisoning or spoofing is a method for replacing incorrect information in computers' ARP caches to misroute packets.
- RIP spoofing uses the Routing Information Protocol (RIP) to update routing tables with bogus information.
- Web spoofing occurs when an attacker sets up a web page or website that looks like a legitimate website. The attacker then attempts to redirect other systems to this location in the attempt to steal passwords, credit cards, or other potentially valuable information.
- Email spoofing is the forgery of an email header so that the message appears to have originated from someone or somewhere other than the actual source. Spam distributors often use spoofing in an attempt to get recipients to open, and possibly even respond to, their solicitations.

IP spoofing occurs when a hacker gives his host the same IP address as an existing host on a network. The simplest form of this attack is used to bypass router packet filters designed to limit access to a destination host based on the IP address of the source machine. These filters can be used where the target machine is on one segment and the source host on another. The problem for the hacker is that the router on the permitted segment has a list of IP addresses which are permitted to contact the target. If a host does not appear in that list, his or her packets are discarded by the router.

To prevent address spoofing, you can use a router which will allow you to filter incoming packets on an interface by comparing the source Ethernet address to the permanent ARP entries (or have a table of permitted hosts based on Ethernet and IP address). You should also use an Egress and Ingress Filter. The Egress part of the filter will route outgoing packets if they have a valid internal address, which will disregard and drop any outgoing packets that have not originated from a valid internal IP address. This will prevent your network from becoming a participant in any spoofing attack. The Ingress part of the filter will filter any packets from the outside that originate with an internal address. Internal addresses that are used on other computers that are not part of the internal network indicate that someone is spoofing an internal address on an external computer. See chapter 6 for more information about Egress and Ingress Filters. Lastly, be sure that you have all security updates to the servers, firewalls and routers and be sure to remove all unnecessary network services.

12.2   MALICIOUS SOFTWARE

Security+ Objective 1.5—Malicious Code

Malicious code is software or firmware that is intentionally placed in a system for an unauthorized purpose. These include:

- Viruses
- Worms
- Trojan Horse Program

12.2.1   Viruses

Security+ Objective 1.5.1—Viruses

A **virus** is a program designed to replicate and spread, generally without the knowledge or permission of the user. The characteristics of a virus are a replication mechanism, activation mechanism, and objective. Computer viruses spread by attaching themselves to other programs or to the boot sector of a disk. When an infected file is executed or accessed or the computer is started with an infected disk, the virus spreads into the computer. Some viruses are cute, some are annoying, and others are disastrous. Some of the disastrous symptoms of a virus include the following:

- Computer fails to boot.
- Disks have been formatted.
- The partitions are deleted or the partition table is corrupt.
- Cannot read a disk.
- Data or entire files are corrupt or are disappearing.
- Programs don't run anymore.
- Files become larger.
- System is slower than normal.
- System has less available memory than it should.
- Information being sent to and from a device is intercepted.

Question:

How does a virus spread?

Answer:

Since viruses are small programs that are made to replicate themselves, viruses spread very easily. For example, you are handed an infected disk or you download a file from the Internet or a bulletin board. When the disk or file is accessed, the virus replicates itself to RAM. When you access any files on your hard drive, the virus again replicates itself to your hard drive. If you shut off your computer, the virus in the RAM will disappear. Unfortunately, since your hard drive is infected, the RAM becomes infected every time you boot from the hard drive. When you insert and access another disk, the disk also becomes infected. You then hand the disk or send an infected file to someone else and the cycle repeats itself.

Symantec, developer of Norton Antivirus, says that most current infections are caused by viruses that are at least three years old. Stiller Research, developer of Integrity Master, states that viruses are widespread but only a relatively small number (about 100) account for 90% of all infections. Table 12.1 lists a number of facts about viruses.

Computer viruses can be categorized into four types:

1. Boot sector
2. File
3. Multipartitie
4. Macro

Every logical drive (hard drive partition and floppy disk) has a boot sector with both bootable and nonbootable components. The boot sector contains specific information relating to the formatting of the

Table 12.1   Virus Facts

Viruses can't infect a write-protected disk.	Viruses can infect read-only, hidden, and system files.
Viruses don't typically infect a document (except macro viruses).	Viruses typically infect boot sectors and executable files.
They do not infect compressed files.	A file within a compressed file could have been infected before being compressed.
Viruses don't infect computer hardware such as monitors or chips.	Viruses can change your CMOS values causing your computer not to boot.
You cannot get a virus just by being on the Internet or a bulletin board.	You can download an infected file.

Table 12.2   General Information about Viruses

Virus Information Library	http://vil.mcafee.com/default.asp
Virus Encyclopedia	http://www.symantec.com/avcenter/vinfodb.html
Virus Hoaxes	http://vil.mcafee.com/hoax.asp http://www.symantec.com/avcenter/hoax.html
Virus Reference Area	http://www.symantec.com/avcenter/refa.html

disk and a small program called the boot program, which loads the operating system files. On hard drives, the first physical sector (side 0, track 0, sector 1) contains the master boot record (MBR) and partition table. The master boot program uses the partition table to find the starting location of the bootable partition (active partition). It then tells the computer to go to the boot sector of the partition and load the boot program. A boot sector virus is transmitted by rebooting the machine from an infected diskette. When the boot sector program on the diskette is read and executed, the virus goes into memory and infects the hard drive, specifically the boot sector or the master boot program.

File infector viruses attach themselves to or replace executable files (usually files with the COM or EXE filename extension), but they can also infect SYS, DRV, BIN, OVL, and OVY files. Uninfected programs become infected when they are opened, including from the DOS DIR command. Or the virus simply infects all of the files in the directory from which it was run.

A multipartite virus has the characteristics of both boot sector viruses and file viruses. It may start as a boot sector virus and spread to executable files, or start from an infected file and spread to the boot sector.

A macro, or formula language, used in word processing, spreadsheets, and other application programs, is a set of instructions that a program executes on command. Macros group several keystrokes into one command or perform complex menu selections. They therefore simplify redundant or complex tasks. The macro viruses are the newest strain and are currently the most common type of virus. Unlike previous viruses, macro viruses are stored in a data document and spread when the infected documents are accessed or transferred. Currently, the most vulnerable applications are Microsoft Word and Microsoft Excel. Some macro viruses modify the contents of the document and can even cause documents to be sent out via email.

Some viruses can be characterized as polymorphic viruses or stealth viruses. A polymorphic virus mutates, or changes its code, so that it cannot be as easily detected. Stealth viruses try to hide themselves by monitoring and intercepting a system's call. For example, when the system seeks to open an infected file, the stealth virus uninfects the file and allows the operating system to open it. When the operating system closes the file, the virus reinfects the file.

For more information on viruses, how they work, how they affect your computer and for descriptions of particular viruses, check out table 12.2.

12.2.2   Trojan Horses

Security+ Objectives 1.5.2—Trojan Horses

A Trojan horse is a program that appears to be legitimate software, such as a game or useful utility. Unfortunately, when you run the Trojan horse and the trigger event occurs, the program will do its damage, such as formatting your hard drive. In addition, Trojan horses may have keyboard loggers, backdoor or remote control programs, or other software that may bypass normal security. Trojan horses can be easily given to a user through email, P2P applications, and instant messengers.

On your network, you should use virus protection software. Of course, for this to be effective, you will need to keep the software up-to-date. In addition, it would be advantageous to have solid knowledge of what Trojans are in circulation, what ports they are using, how they operate and what their general purpose in life is. A nice list of Trojans and their associated ports can be found at http://www.simovits.com/nyheter9902.html.

12.2.3   Worms

Security+ Objectives 1.5.4—Worms

A worm is a self-replicating virus that does not alter files but resides in active memory and duplicates itself. Worms use parts of an operating system that are automatic and usually invisible to the user. It is common for worms to be noticed only when their uncontrolled replication consumes system resources, slowing or halting other tasks. Typically, a worm enters the computer because of vulnerabilities available in the computer's operating system. The more known worms include Code Red and Nimda.

Some worms can be detected and removed by using virus checking software. However, since worms function by using operating system, programs, or protocol vulnerabilities, it is important to have the newest service packs, patches, and security fixes installed for your operating system/network operating systems and network applications.

12.2.4   Virus Hoaxes

A virus hoax is a letter or email message warning you about a virus that does not exist. For example, the letter or warning may tell you that certain email messages may harm your computer if you open them. In addition, the letter or message usually tells you to forward the letter or email message to your friends, which creates more network traffic. Some hoaxes will tell you to search for and delete certain files in which it says is a virus. But the file ends up being an important operating system or application file that is needed for the computer to function properly.

12.2.5   Antivirus Software

Security+ Objective 1.5.1—Viruses

Antivirus software will detect and remove viruses and help protect the computer against viruses. Whichever software package is chosen, it should include a scanner-disinfector and an interceptor-resident monitor. The scanner-disinfector software will look for known virus patterns in the RAM, the boot sector, and the disk files. If a virus is detected, the software will typically attempt to remove the virus. The interceptor-resident monitor is a piece of software that is loaded and remains in the RAM. Every time a disk is accessed or file is read, the interceptor-resident monitor software will check the disk or file for the same virus patterns that the scanner-disinfector software does. In addition, some interceptor-resident monitor software will detect viruses within the files as you download them from the Internet or bulletin board.

Unfortunately, scanner-disinfector software has three disadvantages. First, it can detect only viruses that it knows about. Therefore, the antivirus software package must be continually updated. The easiest way to do this is through the Internet. Second, it cannot always remove the virus. Therefore, the file may need to be deleted or a low-level format may need to be performed on the hard drive. Lastly, if it succeeds in removing the virus, the file or boot sector may still have been damaged. Therefore, the infected file still needs to be deleted or replaced, the boot sector may need to be recreated, partitions may need to be recreated or low-level format needs to be performed on the disk.

If you think a virus is present even though the interceptor software is installed, boot from a clean write-protected disk. This will ensure that the RAM does not contain a virus. Without changing to or accessing the hard drive, run an updated virus scanner-disinfector from the floppy disk. If a virus is detected and removed, it is then best to reboot the computer when the scanner-disinfector has finished checking the hard drive. (Note: Also boot from a bootable floppy and check the hard drive before installing any antivirus software.)

12.2.6   Protecting Against Viruses

Security+ Objective 1.5.1—Viruses

To avoid viruses, you should do the following:

1. You should not use pirated software, since there is a greater chance it will have a virus.
2. You should treat files downloaded from the Internet and bulletin boards with suspicion.
3. You should not boot from or access a floppy disk of unknown origin.
4. You should educate your fellow users.
5. You should use an updated anti-virus software package that constantly detects viruses.
6. You should backup your files on a regular basis.
7. You should not use the Administrative accounts for general use.
8. You should not give more rights than what is needed.
9. Keep your operating system up-to-date with patches.

12.2.7   Removing a Virus

Security+ Objective 1.5.1—Viruses

If you suspect that you have a virus, you need to immediately check your hard drive and disk with a current anti-virus software package. If you think that your hard drive is infected, you need to have a non-infected, write-protected, bootable floppy disks that contains the anti-virus software. You need to boot the computer with the noninfected disk without accessing the hard drive. Next, run the software to check the hard drive. If you think that you have a virus on the floppy disk, boot your computer using the hard drive. If you have been using the possible infected disk on your computer, you need to first check the hard drive for viruses. Lastly, execute the anti-virus program to check the floppy drive.

12.2.8   Back Doors, Software Exploits, and Logic Bombs

Security+ Objective 1.4.2—Back Door

A **back door** is the name of an illicit server given a secret access route into the system. Such routes are usually undocumented and almost certainly were not originally specified. In fact, usually only the original developer would be aware of the back door(s) to their system. Some back doors (such as NetBus, Loki, Masters Paradise, NetCat, and Back Orifice) are created because the programmer expects the end-users to mess up the system, that normal ID and password routines would not allow access. However, the existence of a back door allows unauthorized persons to penetrate the system with malicious intent. It is reasonable to assume that a programmer with sufficient skill to build the system in the first place will also have the skills necessary to penetrate the system and withdraw again without leaving any evidence of the incursion. Note: Back door is also the name of several viruses and Trojan horses that attempt to give malicious users access to the computer.

Security+ Objective 1.4.12—Software Exploitation

One of the rules for computers is "that the computer does only what it is told to do." You have to remember that software is written by humans, and humans are far from perfect. Often to make deadlines, sometimes unreasonable deadlines, software goes into production while the product has bugs or flaws. While these bugs are unintentional, nonetheless, these bugs can be exploited to gain access to a system or to disable or cripple a system, usually by unusual conditions that it cannot handle well. For example, sending an excessively large of amount of data to the program, sending the data in a different format, or running out of disk space on the system disk, all of which may cause a blue screen of death in Windows or cause the kernel to crash in Linux are examples of using software exploits. While the user does not have direct control over these types of exploits, you must check for service packs, patches, and security fixes, and apply them when they become available. Note: Don't forget to test these service packs, patches, and security fixes before loading them on production systems. Of course, when you find a problem, you can report this problem back to the vendor or developer of the software so that they can fix the problem and hopefully implement better quality control, checks, and testing to avoid this from happening in the future.

Security+ Objective 1.5.3—Logic Bombs

In a computer program, a **logic bomb,** also known as slag code, is programming code, inserted surreptitiously or intentionally, that is designed to execute (or explode) under circumstances such as the lapse of a certain amount of time or the failure of a program user to respond to a program command. It is in effect a delayed-action computer virus or Trojan horse. A logic bomb, when exploded, may be designed to display or print a spurious message, delete or corrupt data, or have other undesirable effects.

Often logic bombs are created by disgruntled employees, who typically are part of a technical staff with the appropriate access rights and permissions to a company's resources and the programming skill to create a logic bomb. Logic bombs may operate in one of two ways:

- **Triggered Event**—For example, the program will review the payroll records each day to ensure that the programmer responsible is still employed. If the programmer's name is suddenly removed (by virtue of having been fired) the logic bomb will activate another piece of code to slag or destroy vital files on the organization's system. Smarter programmers will build in a suitable delay between these two events (say a couple of months) so that investigators do not immediately recognize cause and effect.
- **Still Here**—In this case, the programmer buries coding similar to the Triggered Event type but in this instance the program will run unless it is deactivated by the programmer (effectively telling the program—"I am still here—do not run") at regular intervals, typically once each quarter. If the programmer's employment is terminated unexpectedly, the program will not be deactivated and will attack the system at the next due date. This type of logic bomb is much more dangerous, since it will run even if the programmer is only temporarily absent, for example through sickness, injury, or other unforeseen circumstances. The fact that it wasn't meant to happen, is of little comfort to an organization with a slagged system.

Logic bombs demonstrate clearly the critical need for audit trails of activity on the system as well as strict segregation of duties and access rights between those staff who create systems—analysts, developers, programmers—and the operations staff who actually run the system on a day-to-day basis.

Some logic bombs can be detected and eliminated before they execute through a periodic scan of all computer files, including compressed files, with an up-to-date anti-virus program. For best results, the auto-protect and email screening functions of the anti-virus program should be activated by the computer user whenever the machine is online. In a network, each computer should be individually protected, in addition to whatever protection is provided by the network administrator. Unfortunately, even this precaution does not guarantee 100% system immunity, especially if it is a disgruntled employee with technical knowledge. In these cases, you would need a thorough scanning of all systems that the employee had access to.

12.3 SECURITY BASELINES

Security+ Objective 3.5—Security Baselines

Security baselines are standards that specify a minimum (that is, "baseline") set of security controls that are suitable for most organizations under normal circumstances. They typically address both technical issues (such as software configuration) and operational issues (such as keeping applications up-to-date with vendor patches). The idea of security baselines is that for any particular platform (hardware, OS, network, application), there is a minimum set of security recommendations which, if followed, will significantly decrease its vulnerability to security threats, and that it shouldn't take an expensive consultant doing an extensive risk analysis of your environment to determine a reasonable set of security controls for you to implement.

When establishing security baselines, you may consider:

- Any existing security baseline documents for the hardware and software you use.
- Any "best practices" guides that exist for hardening the hardware/software you use, which may exceed the recommendations in any proposed baselines for that hardware/software.
- Specific issues you may have experienced in the past which deserve extra attention (suppose your web server has historically been a favorite target of hackers).
- What are other administrators saying and doing?
- Unique characteristics of your environment (in terms of security risks faced, how much collaboration takes place, management's views on the security requirements vs. ease of use tradeoff, etc.)

12.4   AUDITING AND INTRUDER DETECTION

Security + Objective 1.7—Auditing—Logging, system scanning

Security+ Objective 3.4—Intrusion Detection

Security+ Objective 5.5.4—Auditing (Privilege, Usage, Escalation)

Auditing (accounting) is the last item in the AAA of security. It is the process of monitoring a system or network, looking for potential security exposures or incidents, and verifying proper operation and configuration. The "system" that you are auditing may be a network, a computer, or your computing environment as a whole (including disaster recovery, physical security, processes, etc.). The two most common approaches to system and network audit today include configuration analysis/log analysis and vulnerability scanning.

Audit trails are the auxiliary records that are created that record transactions and other auditable events. Of the many reasons for having audit trails, some include:

- Enforcement of accountability
- Investigation
- Reconstruction
- Problem identification

The basic component of an audit record should include the date and time of the event, who performed the event, where the event was performed (for example from which computer or terminal) and details about the event. Of course, audit logs must be protected against sabotage and other attacks that would prevent the audit logs from properly recording events.

Trying to detect intruders can be a very daunting task, and it often requires a lot of hard work and a thorough working knowledge of the network operating system and the network as a whole. You should always see what logs (especially the security logs such as those found in Event Viewer) are available with your network operating system (and firewalls/proxy servers too). For example, you can check the log that lists all of the failed login attempts. If you see that for several days at late hours, the same account has attempted to login but has failed, it could be someone is trying to figure out the password. Sometimes, security logging is enabled by default, other times, it has to be enabled.

For more information on intrusion detection:

http://www.net-security.org/articles_out_cat.php?cat=17

12.4.1   Intrusion Detection Systems

Security+ Objective 3.1.9—IDS

Security+ Objective 3.4.1—Network-Based

Security+ Objective 3.4.1.1—Active Detection

Security+ Objective 3.4.1.2—Passive Detection

Security+ Objective 3.4.2—Host-Based

Security+ **Objective 3.4.2.1**—Active Detection

Security+ **Objective 3.4.2.2**—Passive Detection

Intrusion detection systems (IDS) are monitoring devices on the network that help security administrators to identify attacks in progress, stop them, and to conduct an analysis after the attack is over. Intrusion detection provides monitoring of network resources to detect intrusion and attacks that were not stopped by preventative techniques. Intrusion detection systems gather their information much like a protocol analyzer, collecting and reading each packet. Then like virus scanners, intrusion detection systems compare to files of signatures that indicate specific known types of attacks. These files are usually provided by the hardware or software vendor and are updated on a subscription basis. Intrusion detection systems can also detect anomalies. Any pattern of traffic that deviates from the expected sequence of packets during a session may be suspect and cause a network administrator to be notified. This way, the administrator can look at the traffic pattern and take steps to stop the attack.

One of the most important characteristics about IDS is that they must correctly identify intrusions and attacks. False positives and false negatives refer to situations in which the intrusion detection systems do not correctly categorize network activity. The following are the four possibilities to describe the correctness of IDS determinations:

- **True positive**—Occurs when the IDS correctly identifies undesirable traffic.
- **True negative**—Occurs when the IDS correctly identifies normal traffic.
- **False positive**—Occurs when the IDS incorrectly identifies normal traffic as an attack.
- **False negative**—Occurs when the IDS incorrectly identifies an attack as normal traffic.

Hopefully, when you have false positives or false negatives, the IDS that you are using can be tuned to better identify traffic patterns and minimize the false positives and false negatives. The tuning process allows the administrator to instruct sensors not to alarm, based on parameters such as signature type, and source or destination IP address.

Intrusion detection systems can be categorized based on their ability to take action when they detect suspicious activity. Passive systems do not take any action to stop or prevent the activity, which could potentially be an attack. They usually perform logging, alert administrators and record the offending traffic for analysis. Active systems have all the features of a passive IDS, but they also have the additional ability to take action against the offending traffic. Unfortunately, although active systems seem far superior because of their ability to block undesirable traffic, active IDS need to be well-tuned so that they don't give too many false positives.

The two major types of intrusion detection systems are network-based IDS and host-based IDS. Network-based IDS is by far the most commonly employed form of intrusion detection systems. Since today's networks are typically switched networks, many with multiple subnets, you need to determine where to deploy IDS. It is not cost-effective or manageable to deploy sensors on all network segments. Instead, you need to look at what you consider is the most valuable asset that you are trying to defend. Typical locations for IDS sensors include just inside the firewall, on the DMZ, on the segment where most of your servers are and on network segments connecting mainframe or midrange hosts.

Depending on the type of attack that may be occurring, the network IDS can either perform a TCP reset, or log the attacks and block the attack. The TCP resets operate by sending a TCP reset packet which terminates TCP sessions to the victim host. Of course, you should note that although TCP resets can terminate an attack in progress, they cannot stop the initial packet from reaching the victim. Therefore, TCP resets will not help attacks that only require a single packet to crash or compromise the victim's host. IP session logging records traffic passing between the attacker and victim. This could and should be used for analyzing the attack and preventing the attack in the future. Lastly, most IDS have the ability to block or filter the packets from the attacker. This typically requires a hookup and proper authentication to your firewall or router.

Host-based IDS monitors activity on a host machine. It would typically be used to protect a critical server containing sensitive information since host-based IDS software only protects the hosts on which they are installed. Some host-based IDS will scan file systems and create hashes of critical system files so that it can check if any of these files have changed. Others will audit logs. The more advanced hostbased IDS will offer active monitoring features that can stop attacks before they can access resources on the victim host and cause damage. Some will even intercept requests to the operating system for system resources before they are processed.

12.4.2   Honey Pots

Security+ Objective 3.4.3—Honey Pots

A **honey pot** is a computer set up as a sacrificial lamb on the network. The system is not locked down and has open ports and services enabled. This is to entice a would-be attacker to this computer instead of attacking authentic computers on the network. The honey pot contains no real company information, and thus will not be at risk if and when it is attacked. The administrator can monitor the honey pot so they can see how an attack is occurring without putting your other systems in harm's way and it may give the administrator an opportunity to track down the attacker. The longer the hacker stays at the honey pot, the more will be disclosed about his or her techniques, methodology, and tools. It may also give early warning that a malicious person has access to the network.

12.4.3   Firewalls and Routers

Security+ Objective 3.1.1—Firewalls

Security+ Objective 3.1.2—Routers

To see what kind of attacks are going through your firewalls and routers, you need to look at the firewall and router logs. A typical firewall and router will generate large amounts of log information. The firewall logs can tell you port scans and unauthorized connection attempts, identify activity from compromised systems and much more. Of course, the real trick in using the logs is knowing what to look for.

Traffic moving through a firewall is part of a connection. A connection has two basic components; a pair of IP addresses and a pair of port numbers. The IP addresses identify each computer involved in the communication. The port numbers identify what services or applications are being utilized. More specifically, it is typically the destination port number that will indicate what applications/services are being used. Of course, knowing what port numbers are associated with what services helps identify malicious activity occurring on the firewall.

- **IP addresses that are rejected**—Although a site will be probed from many places and many times, knowing that a probe is occurring and what is being probed for proves useful information when trying to secure a network.
- **Unsuccessful logins**—Knowing when someone is trying to gain access to critical systems proves useful to help secure a network.
- **Outbound activity from internal servers**—If there is traffic originating from an internal server, having a good understanding of the normal activity on that server will help an administrator determine if the server has been compromised.
- **Source routed packets**—Source routed packets may indicate that someone is trying to gain access to the internal network. Since many networks have an address range that is unreachable from the internet (such as 10.x.x.x), source routed packets can be used to gain access to a machine with a private address since there is usually a machine exposed to the Internet that has access to the private address range.

In addition to the security information documented above, you can get a lot out of the firewall logs if you have looked at your logs before so that you can be familiar with normal everyday activities. This way, if you know what is normal, it will be easier to identify malicious activity when they occur.

12.4.4   Auditing Windows Systems

Trying to detect intruders can be a very daunting task, and it often requires a lot of hard work and a thorough working knowledge of the network operating system and the network as a whole. You should always see what logs (especially the security logs such as those found in Event Viewer) are available with your network operating system (and firewalls/proxy servers too). For example, you can check the log that lists all of the failed login attempts. If you see that for several days at late hours, the same account has attempted to log in but has failed, it could be someone is trying to figure out the password. Sometimes, security logging is enabled by default, other times, it has to be enabled. Windows 2000 and Windows Server 2003 have an auditing service by using group policies that allows you to audit a large

Table 12.3 Audit Best Practices

Potential Threat	Audit Event
To watch for users trying random passwords to bypass security.	Failure audit for logon/logoff
To watch for stolen password usage.	Success audit for logon/logoff
To watch for misuse of privileges including those of administrators.	Success audit for user rights, user and group management, security change policies, restart, shutdown, and system events
To watch the use of sensitive files.	Success and failure audit for file-access and object-access events. File Manager success and failure audit of Read/ Write access by suspect users or groups for the sensitive files.
To watch for the improper use of printers.	Success and failure audit for file-access printers and object-access events. Print Manager success and failure audit of print access by suspect users or groups for the printers.
To watch for a virus outbreak.	Success and failure write access auditing for program files (.EXE and .DLL extensions). Success and failure auditing for process tracking. Run suspect programs; examine security log for unexpected attempts to modify program files or create unexpected processes. You should do this when you actively monitor the system log.

array of items including who accesses which files. These auditing features can also be arranged to check everyone including the administrators in an attempt to keep the administrators honest as well.

Auditing is a feature of Windows 2000 and Windows Server 2003 that monitors various security-related events so that you can detect intruders and attempts to compromise data on the system. Some of the events that you can monitor is access to objects such as a folder or file, management of user and group accounts and logging on and off on a system. The security events are then viewed in the Event Viewer. Therefore, the auditing is one way to find security holes in your network and to ensure accountable for people's actions including the administrator's. See table 12.3 to see some recommendations on what to audit.

Events are not audited by default. If you have Administrator permissions, you can specify what types of system events to audit using group policies (Computer Configuration\Windows Settings\Security Settings\Local Policies\Audit Policy). See figure 12.3.

For files and folders, you can only audit files and folders that are volumes formatted with NTFS. To set, view or change auditing a file or folder:

1. Open Windows Explorer and locate the file or folder that you want to audit.
2. Right-click the file or folder and select the Properties option.
3. Click the Security tab, click on the Advanced button and click on the Auditing tab.
    - To setup auditing for a new group or user, click Add, specify the name of the user you want and click the OK button to open the Auditing Entry dialog box.
    - To view or change auditing for an existing group or user, click the name and click the View/Edit button.
    - To remove auditing for an existing group or user, click the name and click the Remove button.

See figure 12.4. Note: To perform auditing, you must be logged on as a member of the Administrator group or have been granted the Manage auditing and security log right in Group Policy.

Lastly, because the security log is limited in size, you should select only those objects that you need to audit and you need to consider the amount of disk space that the security log will need. The maximum size of the security log is defined in Event Viewer by right clicking Security log and selecting the Properties option. See figures 12.5 and 12.6

Figure 12.3 Setting up an Audit Policy in Windows 2000 and Windows Server 2003

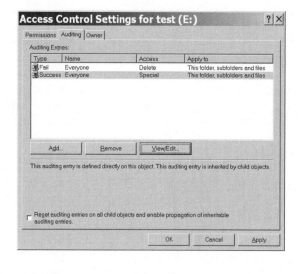

Figure 12.4 Choosing What to Audit in a Windows Audit Policy

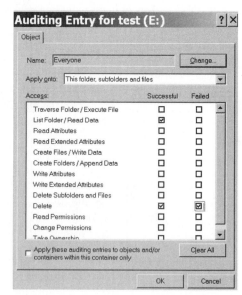

To minimize the risk of security threats, there are a number of auditing steps you can take. Table 12.3 lists various events that you should audit, as well as the specific security threat that the audit event monitors.

12.4.5 Auditing Linux Systems

Trying to detect intruders can be a very daunting task, and it often requires a lot of hard work and a thorough working knowledge of the Linux system. You can start with the log files that are in the /var/log directory. Be sure to include

```
/var/log/boot.log, /var/log/messages and /var/log/secure.
```

Figure 12.5 Configuring the Maximum Log Size for Windows

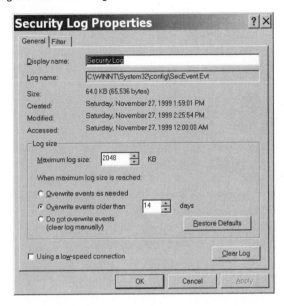

Figure 12.6 Looking at the Security Logs in Windows

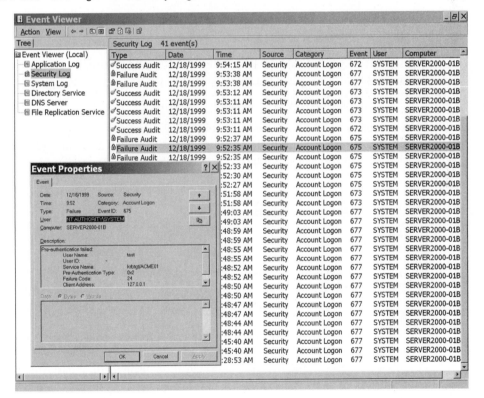

Three files that can become useful in analyzing user login information are the /var/log/wtmp, /var/log/btmp, and /var/log/lastlog files. These files are different from the other log files because they are accounting files and not text files. To access the wtmp file, you would use the `last` command to read the contents which shows who, when and where each person logged from. To access the btmp file, you would use the `lastb` command to see a list of only failed logins. Note: If you do not have a btmp, you just have to use the `touch /var/log/btmp` command to create it and to start its login of failed logins. The `lastlog` command examines the lastlog file, which lists the last time everyone logged in. If a person has never logged in, it will display "Never logged in".

Things to look for in the log files and by using the last command would include:

- Logins by root and attempts to use su to acquire root privileges, both successful and failed attempts. You should also look at where these occurred at and at what time. For example, if you typically work an 8:00 to 5:00 job and you see some logins occurred in the middle of the night, someone is probably trying to break into your system.
- Information logged by firewalls, which may include attempts to access closed ports. Although such accesses may be honest mistakes, they may also indicate malicious activity.
- Failed access attempts logged by TCP Wrappers, xinetd, or individual servers. As with firewalls, these may indicate either honest mistakes or malicious activity.
- System shutdowns and startups. With Linux, these should be rare enough that any shutdown you did not supervise is suspicious.
- Unscheduled server restarts, which may also indicate a successful intrusion.
- Bizarre server error messages, sometimes attempts to break into a system using bugs in particular servers turn up as strange error messages, which may include strings of garbage. Most often, if you see such an error, the attempt was not successful; but it's still good to know the attempt was made. Other errors indicate server misconfiguration.

Before you check individual log files, look for some general clues that someone may have tampered with the log files. Intruders may try to cover their tracks by editing their entries out of your log files or deleting a log file completely. Therefore, check log files for:

- File size (short or incomplete logs)
- Missing logs
- Unusual timestamps
- Incorrect file permissions and/or ownership

You should also regularly check the SETUID and SETGID permissions on files. There should be no setuid and/or setgid that you don't know about. To find these files, you can type in the following command:

```
find / -perm +4000 -print
```

Most user programs don't log their activities. Shells, however, often keep simple records of their last commands. For example, the bash shell uses the .bash_history file in the user's home directory. If you suspect a user of wrongdoing, you can check this file for evidence.

12.5   PENETRATION TESTING

Security + Objective 1.7—Auditing—Logging, system scanning

Penetration testing is the process of probing and identifying security vulnerabilities in a network and the extent to which they might be exploited by outside parties. It is a necessary tool for determining the current security posture of your network. Such a test should determine both the existence and extent of any risk.

The normal pattern for a malicious user to gain information on a target host or network starts with basic reconnaissance. This could be as simple as visiting an organization's website or sites or using public tools to learn more information about the target's domain registrations. After the attacker has gained information to his or her satisfaction, the next logical step is to scan for open ports and services on the target host(s) or network. The scanning process may yield very important information such as ports open through the router and firewall, available services and applications on hosts or network appliances, and possibly the version of the operation system or application. After an attacker has mapped out available hosts, ports, applications, and services, the next step is to test for vulnerabilities that may exist on the target host or network.

When a vulnerability is found and the hacker has gained access to a host, he or she will attempt to keep access and cover their tracks. Covering of tracks almost always involves the tampering of logs or logging servers. The defense in-depth strategy is a layered approach and assumes the perimeter network can be compromised. With this in mind, it is critical to protect logs and logging servers. In the case of an actual intrusion, many times all an organization is left with is their logs. Protect them accordingly because this may be your only evidence of the incident.

12.5.1   Reconnaissance

The reconnaissance phase can be done many different ways depending on the goal of the attacker. Some of the common available tools are:

- **Nslookup**—Available on Unix and Windows Platforms
- **Whois**—Available via any Internet browser client
- **ARIN**—Available via any Internet browser client
- **Dig**—Available on most Unix platforms and some websites via a form
- **Web-based tools**—Hundreds if not thousands of sites offer various recon tools
- **Target website**—The client's web site often reveals too much information
- **Social engineering**—People are an organization's greatest asset, as well as its greatest risk

12.5.2   Scanning

After the penetration engineer or attacker gathers the preliminary information via the reconnaissance phase, he or she will try and identify systems that are alive. The live systems will be probed for available services. The process of scanning can involve many tools and varying techniques depending on what the goal of the attacker is and the configuration of the target host or network. Remember, each port has an associated service that may be exploitable or contain vulnerabilities.

The fundamental goal of scanning is to identify potential targets for security holes and vulnerabilities of the target host or network. Nmap is probably the best known and most flexible scanning tool available today. It is one of the most advanced port scanners available. Nmap provides options for fragmentation, spoofing, use of decoy IP addresses, stealth scans, and many other features. Nmap could be downloaded from the http://www.insecure.org/nmap/ website. Another good software package is GFI LANguard Network Security Scanner (evaluation software available from the http://www. gfisoftware.com/ website).

Below is a list of some common tools to perform scanning:

- **Nmap**—Powerful tool available for UNIX that finds ports and services
- **GFI LANguard Network Security Scanner**—Powerful tool available for Windows that finds ports and services
- **Telnet**—Can report information about an application or service; i.e., version, platform
- **Ping**—Available on most every platform and operating system to test for IP connectivity
- **Traceroute**—Maps out the hops of the network to the target device or system
- **Hping2**—Powerful Unix based tool used to gain important information about a network
- **Netcat**—Some have quoted this application as the "Swiss Army knife" of network utilities
- **Queso**—Can be used for operating system fingerprinting

12.5.3   Vulnerability Testing

Vulnerability testing is the act of determining which security holes and vulnerabilities may be applicable to the target network or host. The penetration tester or attacker will attempt to identify machines within the target network of all open ports, the operating systems, its patch level, service packs applied, and applications running.

The vulnerability testing phase is started after some interesting hosts are identified via the nmap scans or another scanning tool and is preceded by the reconnaissance phase. Nmap will identify if a host is alive or not and what ports and services are available even if ICMP is completely disabled on the target network to a high degree of accuracy.

One of the best vulnerability scanners available today just happens to be free. Nessus is available at the following URL: http://www.nessus.org. The Nessus tool is well supported by the security community and is comparable to commercial products such as ISS Internet Security Scanner and Cyber-Cop by CA.

Other free vulnerability scanners include; SARA available at http://www-arc.com/sara/ and SAINT. A special version of SARA is available to specifically test for the SANS/FBI Top 20 most critical Internet security vulnerabilities located at http://www.sans.org/top20.htm. SARA and SAINT are both prede-cessors of SATAN, an early security administrator's tool for analyzing networks.

Once an attacker has gained a list of potential vulnerabilities for specific hosts on the target net-work they will take this list of vulnerabilities and search for specific exploit to utilize on their victim. Several vulnerability databases are available to anyone on the Internet.

Vulnerability Databases

ISS X-Force—http://www.iss.net/security_center/
Security Focus Database—http://online.securityfocus.com/archive/1
InfoSysSec Database—http://www.infosyssec.com/
Exploit World—http://www.insecure.com/sploits.html

For newer Microsoft operating systems, Microsoft now offers the Microsoft Baseline Security Analyzer (MBSA). It provides a streamlined method of identifying common security misconfigurations. MBSA includes a graphical and command line interface that can perform local or remote scans of Windows systems. MBSA will scan for missing hotfixes and vulnerabilities in the following products: Windows NT 4.0, Windows 2000, Windows Server 2003, Windows XP, Internet Information Server (IIS) 4.0 and 5.0, SQL Server 7.0 and 2000, Internet Explorer (IE) 5.01 and later, and Office 2000 and 2002. MBSA creates and stores individual XML security reports for each computer scanned and will display the re-ports in the graphical user interface in HTML.

Baseline Security Analyzer Home Page and Download Instructions

http://www.microsoft.com/technet/security/tools/Tools/mbsahome.asp

Baseline Security Analyzer White Paper

http://www.microsoft.com/technet/security/tools/tools/mbsawp.asp

12.6   NETWORK DEVICE AND OPERATING SYSTEM HARDENING

Security+ Objective 3.5.1—OS/NOS Hardening (Concepts and Processes)

Hardening is the process of identifying and closing vulnerabilities. To make your network more secure, you need to harden your network as a whole, by hardening your network devices, and you need to harden each system or operating system. When doing all of this, you need to document system and de-vices so that you can repeat the configuration in the future and so you know what has been done already when checking to see if you address certain vulnerabilities and if you installed all of the proper service packs, patches and security fixes.

Security+ Objective 1.3—Nonessential Services and Protocols—Disabling unnecessary systems/ process/programs.

The more services and protocols a host has running, the more targets or potential vulnerabilities an attacker can use. Similarly, unnecessary, but open ports on boundary firewalls are inviting targets for attackers to probe. You can often reduce your network's vulnerability to both random and specifically targeted attacks simply by disabling nonessential components and protocols. In other words, disable or filter out access to all services and protocols except those that are absolutely necessary.

When determining which services to run, and which to disable, there are two possible approaches you can take.

- The first approach involves leaving everything exactly as it is, and only removing services and clos-ing access points (such as firewall ports), as they become an issue.
- The second approach takes the view that nothing on your network is required, and advise closing every port, service, and share before issues arise. This involves changing settings on servers (dis-abling unused services, removing shares) and on the routers and firewalls (setting up "rules" that restrict connections to and from ports on your organization's machines, allowing only those types of connections which are specifically needed). You then open only the ports that are specifically re-quired and justifiable, while keeping firewall rules extremely tight.

The first approach is a little dangerous because a lot of damage can be done while you are learning which services and access points you want to close, especially if you were not in the office at the time of the attack. The second approach may stop some services from operating, and it may cause some frustration for the users until you learn what to enable or open. Of course, if you take the second approach, you should do some testing so that you can see the effect of what you plan to do. You can also use protocol analyzers to look at the traffic to see what is being used before making any decisions.

"Defense in depth" is an important concept that states that you should not rely on a single barrier to protect your sensitive data and system operations. Instead, erect multiple zones of security around your resources, to help ensure that they cannot be compromised if a single security mechanism fails due to a software bug, operator error, etc. Since many data compromises come from within, you should apply the same level of security to your internal systems as you would to your external systems.

12.6.1   Network Hardening

Security+ Objective 3.1.1—Firewalls

Security+ Objective 3.1.2—Routers

Security+ Objective 3.1.3—Switches

Security+ Objective 3.5.2—Network Hardening

Security+ Objective 3.5.2.1—Updates (Firmware)

Security+ Objective 3.5.2.2—Configuration

Security+ Objective 3.5.2.2.1—Enabling and Disabling Services and Protocols

Security+ Objective 3.5.2.2.2—Access control lists

Network hardening involves the steps taken to secure a network and the devices on it. It includes both securing devices which have options set "out of the box" which are generally regarded as insecure, as well as customizing the configuration of the devices to meet the specific security requirements of the organization.

OS/NOS products, being software-based with their code stored on server hard disks, are typically updated via software updates on CD or downloaded from the web. Installing an OS update is much like installing any other program or OS component. The install program copies the code into the proper locations on disk, perhaps makes some configuration changes, and the updated server is ready for use.

With network devices, the program code and data controlling the device is often stored in a form called "firmware." Like OS updates, network device updates are often distributed over the web. However, rather than being stored on a hard disk, code for network devices is usually written into ROM (read only memory) chips with a special firmware update program. Firmware is a combination of hardware and software, in which network device program code and data is stored. As always, stay on top of the latest versions of firmware available for your networking products. These often address security-related vulnerabilities. To locate updates for your network devices, check the vendors' websites.

Configuration deals with setting options on the devices. One key issue to address would be device passwords used to access administrative features of switches, routers, etc. Devices typically ship with a default password used for initial device configuration. Please make sure you change it ASAP. As mentioned earlier in this book, entire web pages are dedicated to lists of default passwords for common network devices, so that intruders can walk right in your front door after turning the key.

When configuring networking equipment, follow along with the standards already set for your network if possible. For example, if your organization has standardized on a particular vendor and model of network switch, the configuration process for one is likely to be very similar to the configuration process for the next. In these situations, it's best not to reinvent the wheel. Create a written document outlining the steps to take when configuring a device of that type, and then follow it each time a similar device needs to be installed. If the device allows you to print out its configuration information, do this, and file it in a safe place (even consider storing a copy offsite). It will be useful to have a record of configuration information should the device fail and need to be replaced in the future.

This can take the form of turning off services at the server, or establishing filtering rules (on your routers or the servers themselves) to completely allow or disallow inbound or outbound connections to certain ports. If you have a multiprotocol router and you have a network that only uses TCP/IP, you can disable IPX and AppleTalk packets through a router. Other items to remember when configuring a new piece of networking equipment include:

1. If you don't specifically need SNMP access to the device, disable it.
2. If you do need SNMP access to the device, use SNMPv3. If this is not an option, change the community name.
3. If installing a router, make sure that you have set it up to not allow inbound packets whose source address is on an internal network, or outbound packets whose source address is *not* on an internal network (these packets are at best, badly damaged, and at worst, forged).
4. Check the manufacturer's site to see if they have specific security related recommendations for their devices. For instance, Cisco provides some hints at http://www.cisco.com/univercd/cc/td/doc/cisintwk/ics/cs003.htm.
5. Does the device offer a handy-dandy web-browser based configuration interface, as many today do? If so, consider implementing a firewall rule to disallow connections to that device on port 80 (or 443) from all but trusted sources.

The next step in hardening a network device is to exert a finer-grained degree of control over what traffic you allow through the router. Instead of just allowing or disallowing based on type of network-layer protocol or service, you can examine a packet's specific origins.

Access Control Lists (ACLs), sometimes called filters, are used to determine which traffic is permitted to pass through a network interface, in which direction, between which addresses. Routers typically manage access control via a text file of access control rules; operating systems and home networking devices including this functionality generally wrap access control lists in a GUI for ease of use. The network device examines the information in each packet, comparing it to the ACLs, and either lets the packet through or stops it depending on the ACL instructions.

Typical attributes that may be examined by rules in ACLs include a packet's:

- Source IP address
- Destination IP address
- Source port number
- Destination port number
- IP protocol number (this is not the same thing as the application port number)
- Direction of travel (incoming to or outgoing from the interface)

Typically an overall default policy is set on each device, specifying whether inbound traffic will be permitted by default, or denied by default. A similar default policy is set for outbound traffic. Often it is appropriate to "deny all" inbound traffic by default and "permit all" outbound traffic by default, but that depends on your organization.

An ACL is a set of rules that specify which traffic will be permitted to pass through the network device, and which will be stopped. Common packet attributes evaluated by access control lists include source and destination IP addresses and port numbers, IP protocol number, and direction of the packet's travel.

A device may permit all outbound traffic (from your network to the Internet) by default, and contain access lists specifying when to deny it, or deny all outbound traffic by default, and contain access lists specifying when to allow it. Similar rules can be configured for inbound traffic (from the Internet to your network).

It is common to deny all inbound traffic, and permit all outbound traffic. You should set up ACLs to enforce your security policies, such as those which specify which Internet services are, and are not, made available from your network to the Internet. ACL rules to implement are:

- Do not allow into your network, any traffic from the outside whose Source IP address is set to an address inside your network (it's a red flag that the incoming traffic was spoofed—to keep the attacker out, don't let the traffic in);
- Do not allow out of your network, any traffic from the inside whose Source IP address is set to an address outside your network (another red flag that the traffic is spoofed—although this time, you've got more problems, because the spoofer is somewhere on your network, at least you're not aiding and abetting him in attacking someone on another network).

12.6.2   Operating System Hardening

Security+ Objective 3.5.1—OS/NOS Hardening (Concepts and Processes)

Security+ Objective 3.5.1.1—File System

Security+ Objective 3.5.1.2—Updates (Hotfixes, Service Packs, Patches)

When you need to harden your network operating systems, you need to first do some planning before you install the systems. First, you need to understand the functions of the system so that you can determine what software will be needed to prove those systems. You need to also plan the disk partition and file system layout with security in mind and plan the system, user account and group structure. Be sure to use a journaling file system such as NTFS, Ext3 or Reiserfs. Before you install, you should gather all required software including operating system installation disks, any service packs, patches and security fixes that are available and any additional software and their service packs, patches and security fixes. Note: You want to verify and test all service packs, patches, and security fixes before you use them on production systems.

Before you actually install the system, you also need to plan the physical system security. You need to select a location which minimizes risk from accidental damage such as no overhead sprinklers. If appropriate, secure the physical system location with locks and other security devices. Secure the cabling to network and other devices. Install an uninterruptible power supply (UPS) on key servers. Assign a BIOS password to prevent unauthorized users from modifying setup settings or perform unauthorized boots. Attach any equipment identification tags or stickers to the computer and its components that are used by your organization.

When you install the operating system, you must set up the disk partitions or volumes, taking into account any security considerations. Then install the operating system and apply all service packs, patches, and security fixes. Next, enable the high-security and trusted operating system options. For Windows, you can enable or disable components that you didn't during installation or using the Add/Remove programs in the Control Panel. For Linux, you may need to build a custom kernel, which supports only the features that you need and remove support for the ones that you don't need. For example, for systems which are not operating as routers, you should remove the IP forwarding capabilities. Intruders cannot exploit features that aren't there. For Linux, secure the boot loader program (lilo or grub) with a password and enable the single user mode password if necessary.

The next step would be to secure the local file systems. Look at the default permissions and correct any security problems. Remember, that when you create a shared directory in Windows, everyone has full control. For Linux, check Group and/or world writable for system executables and directories and group and/or writable for user home directories. You can also use the SetUID and SetGID commands. Lastly, encrypt an sensitive data present on the system.

Security+ Objective 1.3—Nonessential Services and Protocols—Disabling unnecessary systems/process/programs.

The next step would be to remove or disable all unneeded services. For Windows, you would use the MMC to disable services. In Linux, you might want to look in the /etc/inittab, system boot scripts and the inetd file. Of course, when possible, use secure versions of programs or daemons such as using SSH instead of telnet. If at all possible, run service programs and processes as a special user created for that purpose and not as the administrator or root. After you have removed or disabled all unneeded services, you need to specify any auditing or logging of services and any other network resources. Also secure any services such as file sharing, printing or anything else. You should also use penetration testing including vulnerability scanners to identify potential security weaknesses.

Be sure that you select a secure administrator or root password and plan a schedule for changing it regularly. For Windows, you should also limit who can logon directly on the systems and for Linux, you need to prevent direct root logins except on the system console.

To secure your user accounts, you need to choose your user authentication and user account attributes. For Windows, you need to set up the appropriate group policies including password policies and security policies. For Linux, you need to set up shadow passwords, configure PAM as appropriate for the relevant commands, define user account password select and aging settings. You should also remove any unneeded default accounts such as guest. To secure remote authentication, you should make sure that no insecure remote access services are activates including telnet, rlogoin, rsh, ftp, and so on.

The last few things that you need to do include:

- To make sure that you prepare for attacks and disasters, perform two full-system backups and verify the backup media. You will also plan and implement a system backup schedule.
- You will need to add the new host to the security configuration on other systems, in router ACLs and so on as appropriate for your site.
- Sign up for security mailing lists if you have not already done so.
- Get in the habit of checking vendor security web pages on a regular basis.

As you go through this entire process, it is important that you should document the hardening process. This will allow you to easily repeat the process for other systems and improve on the process.

For more information, you should check out the following websites:

SANS/FBI Top Twenty list

http://www.sans.org/top20/

HOW TO: Harden the TCP/IP Stack Against Denial of Service Attacks in Windows 2000

http://support.microsoft.com/default.aspx?scid=KB;en-us;315669&

Microsoft Windows 2000 Security Hardening Guide

http://www.microsoft.com/technet/security/prodtech/windows/win2khg/default.asp

Microsoft Solution for Securing Windows 2000 Server—Chapters 6 and 7

http://www.microsoft.com/technet/security/prodtech/windows/secwin2k/default.asp

Windows Server 2003 Security Guide

http://www.microsoft.com/technet/security/prodtech/windows/win2003/w2003hg/sgch00.asp

Microsoft Windows XP Security Guide Overview

http://www.microsoft.com/technet/security/prodtech/winclnt/secwinxp/ default.asp

Help Net Security—Microsoft

http://www.net-security.org/articles_out_cat.php?cat=9

UNIX Security Checklist v2.0

http://www.cert.org/tech_tips/unix_security_checklist2.0.html

The Center for Internet Security (includes information for securing Solaris, Linux, HP-UX, Cisco IOS and Windows)

http://www.cisecurity.com/

National Security Agency Security Recommendation Guides

http://www.nsa.gov/snac/index.html

Help Net Security—Linux

http://www.net-security.org/articles_out_cat.php?cat=12

Help Net Security—Security Checklists

http://www.net-security.org/articles_out_cat.php?cat=8

Titan (Hardening tool for Solaris, FreeBSD, and Linux)

http://www.fish.com/titan

Bastille-Linux (helps administrators lock down a Linux system)

http://www.bastille-linux.org

JASS (Tool used to harden a Solaris system)

http://www.sun.com/blueprints/tools

YASSP (Tool used to harden a Solaris system)

http://www.yassp.org

12.6.3   Application Hardening

Security+ Objective 3.5.3.—Application Hardening

Application hardening is the process of securing applications in use on a network. It can be a major issue simply because there are so many different applications in use on the average network. It's simply difficult to keep track of what's installed where, let alone what the latest security baseline recommendations are for each product. Nevertheless, it's a task that needs to be performed.

A network application is one that communicates with another program across the network. Network applications can be peer-to-peer (in which two computers share resources, as in many popular file-sharing services not relevant to corporate environments) or client/server (where a "client" program, usually on a smaller computer, accesses the functionality of a "service" program, usually on a more powerful computer called a server). As with OS software and networks, it's important to keep up-to-date with the latest fixes and patches for the applications used on your network. And test them before installing in a live environment. See chapter 10 for more information about specific network applications.

12.7   INCIDENT RESPONSE

Security+ Objective 3.4.4—Incident Response

Security+ Objective 5.4.2—Incident Response Policy

As part of the organization's security policy, you should have an **incident response policy,** which should cover how people in your organization are expected to deal with computer or network security incidents including any type of attack. Of course, when this policy is created, remember that your organization must exhibit due care when handling client information. If any incidents get out of control, it can cause problems for you and your organization, especially if you did not take sufficient steps to protect your network and the information on the network and if you did not respond well to the incident.

A **Computer Security Incident Response Plan (CSIRP)** provides guidance and documentation on computer security incident response handling and communication efforts. The CSIRP is activated whenever a computer security incident occurs, and guides the responses to all incidents whose severity is such that they could affect a company's ability to do business, or undermine its reputation.

The inevitability that (possibly successful) attempts will be made to compromise system and network security dictates that every company, from the largest multinationals to the smallest "dot com" startups, should have a formal CSIRP in place. CSIRP development should be the top security budget priority in any company—more important than security services, and more important than security products. When a security incident occurs, reactions and decisions must be made very quickly (often in a matter of minutes). The company has to be prepared to deal with these incidents as soon as they occur; waiting until a new product arrives or a consulting engagement is completed is not an option.

The first step in creating a formal CSIRP is the establishment of a **Computer Security Incident Response Team (CSIRT).** If it is a small company, the team may only be your security office. If it is a larger company, you will need a CSIRT Charter, which is a document that formally establishes the team, and documents its responsibility to respond to computer security incidents. The document should include:

- **CSIRT charter**—Delegates the authority to implement necessary actions and decisions during an incident, usually to the CSIRT leader or manager. Of course the goal of this team should include such tasks as responding to all incidents, minimizing their impact, and collecting data and evidence for prosecution.
- **Organizational structure**—Documents how the CSIRT is organized from a management perspective: how the members of the team are managed, and how the team reports to upper-level management.
- **Information flow**—Describes how information flows before, during, and after an incident. First, this section describes how a potential security incident is reported to the CSIRT, and provides contact information for doing so. Second, it describes how the CSIRT communicates information about an incident to (a) upper-level management, (b) company employees, and (c) the public.

■ **Services provided**—Documents the specific services the CSIRT provides. This is based on the mission statement and may include services such as incident response, policy development, compliance testing, and user education.

A CSIRT usually consists of a manager, a management advisory board, some number of permanent team members, and a larger number of temporary members:

■ **CSIRT manager/leader**—The CSIRT manager (or leader) is responsible for managing the overall response and recovery activities for all security incidents. He or she determines (usually with assistance from others) the severity of each incident, and decides which staff members will perform the actual response and recovery tasks. The CSIRT manager usually has some degree of budget and decision authority to take necessary actions during an incident.

■ **Management advisory board**—The management advisory board is made up of senior managers from the company's IT organizations and other internal business functions. IT organizations represented may include Network Services, Internet Operations, Mainframe Operations, Midrange Operations, Server Operations, Desktop Operations, and Help Desk. Other internal business functions represented may include Corporate Security, Legal, Human Resources, Media Relations, and Disaster Recovery. This group makes decisions and budget requests above the level delegated to the CSIRT manager.

■ **Permanent team members**—Permanent team members are those IT staff whose primary job responsibility is IT security. Usually, these people report to the CSIRT manager. They provide the non-response services (such as user education and policy development), and help the CSIRT manager in the initial response to incidents.

■ **Temporary team members**—Temporary team members report to the IT organizations and other internal business functions represented on the management advisory board. They are the subject matter experts for the particular systems, applications, and business issues involved in the incident. Temporary team members are usually assigned to an incident by their managers (on the advisory board) at the request of the CSIRT manager, and serve for the duration of the incident.

Many security incidents, such as isolated occurrences of computer viruses, are easily handled via well-established procedures (especially in larger companies), and do not justify calling out the entire CSIRT. The CSIRP must describe the criteria used to classify the severity of security incidents, and which severities will result in CSIRP activation. Incidents should usually be grouped into a few different severity levels, with broad sets of criteria for each level. For example:

■ **Severity 1**—Small numbers of system probes or scans detected on internal systems; isolated instances of known computer viruses easily handled by antivirus software.

■ **Severity 2**—Small numbers of system probes or scans detected on external systems; intelligence received concerning threats to which systems may be vulnerable.

■ **Severity 3**—Significant numbers of system probes or scans detected; penetration or denial of service attacks attempted with no impact on operations; widespread instances of known computer viruses easily handled by anti-virus software; isolated instances of a new computer virus not handled by anti-virus software.

■ **Severity 4**—Penetration or Denial-of-Service attacks attempted with limited impact on operations; widespread instances of a new computer virus not handled by anti-virus software; some risk of negative financial or public relations impact.

■ **Severity 5**—Successful penetration or denial of service attacks detected with significant impact on operations; significant risk of negative financial or public relations impact.

In this example, incidents of Severity 3, 4, and 5 would result in CSIRP activation, while incidents of Severity 1 and 2 would be handled without CSIRT involvement.

When an incident requiring CSIRP activation occurs, a formal incident is declared. The CSIRP should document how such a declaration is made and who is responsible for making it. Generally, incident declaration is a procedure by which the CSIRT manager notifies upper-level management that an incident is taking place, and then assembles the other members of the CSIRT.

Response procedures can be described at two levels of detail in the CSIRP. The first level of detail is a set of general guidelines that describes the principle phases of incident response, and what happens during each phase. Every CSIRP should include this level of detail. The second level of detail is a set of step-by-step response procedures, specific to individual incident types (e.g., procedure(s) for handling virus incidents, procedure(s) for handling hacker break-ins, etc.). These procedures will generally be created over time, and can be added to the CSIRP in appendices as they are developed.

The Computer Security Incident Handling Guidelines should include the following six-step process:

1. Preparation—Setting up systems to detect threats and policies for dealing with them, including identifying roles staff will play in incident response, and creating emergency contact lists.
2. Identification—Identifying what the threat is, and/or the effects it is having on your systems/networks, including keeping records of the time/systems involved/what was observed, and making a full system backup as soon after the intrusion was observed, as possible, to preserve as much information about the attack as you can.
3. Containment—Limiting the effects of an incident by confining the problem to as few systems as possible, freezing the scene so that nothing further happens to the compromised system(s) by disconnecting its network connections and possibly console keyboard.
4. Eradication—Getting rid of whatever the attacker might have compromised by deleting files or doing a complete system reinstall.
5. Recovery—Getting back into business, by putting the system back into normal operations, reconnecting it to the network, restoring from backups if necessary, etc.
6. Follow-up—If possible tightening security so that the intrusion cannot happen again, determining the "cost" of the intrusion based on staff time/lost data/lost user work time, considering which, if any, additional tools might have helped handle the incident better than it may have been handled, reflecting on "lessons learned" from both the intrusion and the organization's response to it and tweaking policies as required.

12.8   EVIDENCE, INVESTIGATION, AND FORENSICS

Security+ Objective 5.6—Forensics (Awareness, conceptual knowledge and understanding—know what your role is)

Security+ Objective 5.6.1—Chain of Custody

Security+ Objective 5.6.2—Preservation of Evidence

Security+ Objective 5.6.3—Collection of Evidence

Evidence is information presented in a court of law to confirm or dispel a fact that's under contention. A case cannot be brought to trial without sufficient evidence to support the case. Thus, properly gathering evidence is one of the most important and most difficult tasks of the investigator.

The types of evidence, admissibility of evidence, chain of custody, and evidence life cycle comprise the main elements to be tested in the investigation portion of this domain.

Sources of legal evidence can be presented in a court of law generally fall into one of four major categories:

- **Direct evidence**—Oral testimony or a written statement based on information gathered through the witness's five senses (an eyewitness account) that proves or disproves a specific fact or issue.
- **Real (or physical) evidence**—Tangible objects from the actual crime, such as the tools or weapons used and any stolen or damaged property. May also include visual or audio surveillance tapes generated during or after the event. Physical evidence from a computer crime is rarely available.
- **Documentary evidence**—Includes originals and copies of business records, computer-generated and computer-stored records, manuals, policies, standards, procedures, and log files. Most evidence presented in a computer crime case is documentary evidence.
- **Demonstrative evidence**—Used to aid the court's understanding of a case. Opinions are considered demonstrative evidence and may be either expert (based on personal expertise and facts) or non-expert (based on facts only). Other examples include models, simulations, charts and illustrations.

The best evidence rule, defined in the Federal Rules of Evidence, states that to prove the content of a writing, recording, or photograph, the original writing, recording, or photograph is required. However, an exception to this rule is if data are stored in a computer or similar device, any printout or other output readable by sight, shown to reflect the data accurately, is an original.

Because computer-generated evidence can be easily manipulated, altered, or tampered with, and because it's not easily and commonly understood, this type of evidence is usually considered suspect in a court of law. In order to be admissible, evidence must be relevant and reliable. It must also be obtained through legal means.

Computer forensics is a newly emerged and developing field, which can be described as the study of digital evidence resulting from an incident. It involves collecting and analyzing of digital data within an investigative process that may be used as legal evidence.

When an incident occurs, you should immediately begin to collect evidence. This evidence can help you learn about the intrusion so that you can learn how the intrusion was done and stop future attacks of the same type and it can improve your systems, their operations, and your staff's capabilities. Evidence might be required for the following reasons:

- To locate, educate, reprimand, or terminate negligent or responsible employees.
- To prosecute attackers for computer crimes or misuses.
- To describe your situation and obtain help from your CSIRT or other CSIRTs.

In your incident response policy, you should appoint someone as the point of contact to be responsible for maintaining contact with law enforcement and other CSIRTs. This person should coordinate all activities and disseminate information appropriately to internal and external personnel. This person should also be responsible for coordinating the collection of evidence to ensure that it is done in accordance with all laws and legal regulations.

Before you begin work on a compromised system, remember that you need to concentrate on not altering anything and to document your evidence and all of your actions, as well as gather that evidence. Of course, you might need to disconnect the system from the network to stop the malicious activity because if you don't, you might be held liable for damage to other systems or your organization. If at all possible, analyze a replica of the system instead of the original. For example, make an image of the system's hard disk, or make and restore a backup to another system. This way, you play with the replica to perform your analysis, and you can still use the original system as evidence in court. Of course, you have to make sure that when you do the copying or backup that you don't change the current state of the compromised system.

Many of the tools you need to conduct a forensic investigation are often part of the operating system you are using. However, the built-in operating system tools might not be as effective or easy to use as tools specifically made for forensic investigation. For example, if you go to the following website:

http://www.foundstone.com/knowledge/free_tools.html

you can find free assessment, forensic tools, intrusion detection tools, and scanning tools.

All information concerning the incident must be recorded and securely stored. You need to establish, examine, and preserve an audit trail. An audit trail is a record of who accessed a computer and what operations he or she performed. Some software products create audit trails automatically; sometimes you have to enable the audit trail or manually create one from the logs and any tools that you have access to. In addition, you should:

- Obtain and protect the latest full and partial backups.
- Take a picture or screen shot any messages that can be used as evidence.
- Obtain and protect any security tapes and reports from the time of the incident.
- Recover any deleted encrypted or damaged files related to the intrusion or attack.

A **chain of custody** must be maintained for all evidence. A documented chain of custody shows who collected and had access to each piece of evidence. Failure to maintain this chain of custody might invalidate your evidence. The documentation must be accurate and verifiable, including dates, times, locations, and the verified identities of every person handling evidence. This includes any time evidence is accessed or moved while in storage. Furthermore, anyone accessing stored evidence should provide legitimate, verifiable, and documented purpose for doing so.

When all of this is occurring, you need to coordinate all of your activities with your organization's upper-management and, if available, legal counsel. Legal counsel can advise you of your options, both civil and criminal, in pursuing legal action. If you plan to pursue legal action, you must contact appropriate law enforcement agencies immediately. Their reports and verification are often required to prove that an incident actually occurred. They may also help you collect information and preserve evidence. You should also collaborate with other CSIRTs, which might be able to provide additional experience and guidance.

WHAT YOU NEED TO KNOW

Security+ Objective 1.3—Nonessential Services and Protocols—Disabling unnecessary systems/process/programs.

Security+ Objective 3.5.2.2.1—Enabling and Disabling Services and Protocols

1. The more services and protocols a host has running, the more targets or potential vulnerabilities an attacker can use.
2. You can often reduce your network's vulnerability to both random and specifically targeted attacks, simply by disabling nonessential components and protocols.

Security+ Objective 1.4—Attacks

1. An attacker does not necessarily have to gain access to a system in order to cause significant problems.
2. The majority of the successful attacks on operating systems come from only a few software vulnerabilities.

Security+ Objective 1.4.1—DoS/DDoS

1. Denial of Service (DoS) is a type of attack on a network that is designed to bring the network to its knees either by disabling or crippling a server or by flooding it with useless traffic.
2. Many DoS attacks, such as the ping of death and Teardrop attacks, exploit limitations in the TCP/IP protocols.
3. A DoS attack can also destroy programming and files in a computer system. Although usually intentional and malicious, a DoS attack can sometimes happen accidentally.
4. For all known DoS attacks, there are software fixes that system administrators can install to limit the damage caused by the attacks. But, like viruses, new DoS attacks are constantly being dreamed up by hackers.
5. Distributed Denial-of-Service (DDoS) attacks involve installing programs known as zombies on various computers in advance of the attack. A command is issued to these zombies, which launch the attack on behalf of the attacker, thus hiding their tracks.
6. The real danger from a DDoS attack is that the attacker uses many victim computers as host computers to control other zombies that initiate the attack.

7. When the system that is overwhelmed tries to trace back the attack, it receives a set of spoofed addresses generated by a series of zombies.

Security+ Objective 1.4.12—Software Exploitation

1. Software goes into production while the product has bugs or flaws.
2. While these bugs are unintentional, these bugs can be exploited to gain access to a system or to disable or cripple a system, usually by unusual conditions that it cannot handle well.
3. While the user does not have direct control over these types of exploits, you must check for service packs, patches, and security fixes, and apply them when they become available.

Security+ Objective 1.4.2—Back Door

1. A back door is the name of an illicit server given to a secret access route into the system.
2. The existence of a back door allows anyone unauthorized to penetrate the system with malicious intent.
3. Back door is also the name of several viruses and Trojan horses that attempt to give malicious users access to the computer.

Security+ Objective 1.4.3—Spoofing

1. Spoofing is pretending to be someone else by impersonating, masquerading, or mimicking that person.
2. IP addressing spoofing is forging the IP source address in one or more IP packets to show that the packet came from a source other than the true source of the packet.
3. ARP ache poisoning or spoofing is a method for replacing incorrect information in computers' ARP caches to misroute packets.
4. RIP spoofing uses the Routing Information Protocol (RIP) to update routing tables with bogus information.
5. Web spoofing occurs when an attacker sets up a web page or website that looks like a legitimate website. The attacker then attempts to redirect other systems to this location in the attempt to steal passwords, credit cards, or other potentially valuable information.
6. Email spoofing is the forgery of an email header so that the message appears to have originated from someone or somewhere other than the actual

source. Spam distributors often use spoofing in an attempt to get recipients to open, and possibly even respond to, their solicitations.

7. To prevent address spoofing, you can use a router which will allow you to filter incoming packets on an interface by comparing the source Ethernet address to the permanent ARP entries (or have a table of permitted hosts based on Ethernet and IP address). You can also use an Egress and Ingress Filter.

Security+ Objective 1.4.4—Man in the Middle

1. A man-in-the-middle attack is one in which the attacker intercepts messages in a public key exchange and then retransmits them, substituting their own public key for the requested one, so that the two original parties still appear to be communicating with each other directly.

2. The attacker uses a program that appears to be the server to the client and appears to be the client to the server. The attack may be used simply to gain access to the messages, or enable the attacker to modify them before retransmitting them.

Security+ Objective 1.4.5—Replay

1. Replay attacks involve listening to and repeating data passed on the network.

2. An attacker tries to capture packets containing passwords or digital signatures as they pass between two hosts on the network using a protocol analyzer.

3. The attacker then filters the data and extracts the portion of the packet that contains the password, encryption key, or digital signature.

4. Later, the attacker resends or replays that information in an attempt to gain access to a secured resource.

5. To protect yourself and your organization's network from replay attacks, ensure that the latest security updates are applied to your existing software.

6. Use the latest and most secure encryption techniques for all connections that involve authentication. For example, IPSEC can provide anti-replay services.

Security+ Objective 1.4.6—TCP/IP Hijacking

1. Hijacking is a type of network security attack in which the attacker takes control of a communication between two entities and masquerades as one of them.

2. Hijacking is especially suited to telnet type plaintext connections, where an attacker can watch a TCP session being initiated and data being passed between client and server. If the attacker sees something interesting, he or she can break into the conversation and take control of the user's session for the attacker's own purposes.

Security+ Objective 1.5—Malicious Code

1. Malicious code is software or firmware that is intentionally placed in a system for an unauthorized purpose.

Security+ Objective 1.5.1—Viruses

1. A virus is a program designed to replicate and spread, generally without the knowledge or permission of the user.

2. The characteristics of a virus are a replication mechanism, activation mechanism, and objective.

3. Computer viruses spread by attaching themselves to other programs or to the boot sector of a disk. When an infected file is executed or accessed or the computer is started with an infected disk, the virus spreads into the computer.

4. A boot-sector virus is transmitted by rebooting the machine from an infected diskette.

5. File infector viruses attach themselves to or replace executable files (usually files with the COM or EXE filename extension), but they can also infect SYS, DRV, BIN, OVL, and OVY files.

6. A multipartite virus has the characteristics of both boot-sector viruses and file viruses.

7. A macro, or formula language, used in word processing, spreadsheets, and other application programs, is a set of instructions that a program executes on command.

8. The macro viruses are the newest strain and are currently the most common type of virus.

9. Unlike previous viruses, macro viruses are stored in a data document and spread when the infected documents are accessed or transferred.

10. A polymorphic virus mutates, or changes its code, so that it cannot be as easily detected.

11. Stealth viruses try to hide themselves by monitoring and intercepting a system's call.

12. A virus hoax is a letter or email message warning you about a virus that does not exist. For example, the letter or warning may tell you that certain email messages may harm your computer if you open them. In addition, the letter or message usually tells you to forward the letter or email message to your friends, which creates more network traffic.

13. Some hoaxes will tell you to search for and delete certain files in which it says is a virus. But the file ends up being an important operating system or application file that is needed for the computer to function properly.

14. Antivirus software will detect and remove viruses and help protect the computer against viruses. Whichever software package is chosen, it should include a scanner-disinfector and an interceptor-resident monitor.

15. You should use an updated antivirus software package that constantly detects viruses.

16. Keep your operating system up-to-date with patches.

Security+ Objective 1.5.2—Trojan Horses

1. A Trojan horse is a program that appears to be legitimate software, such as a game or useful utility.
2. Unfortunately, when you run the Trojan horse and the trigger event occurs, the program will do its damage, such as formatting your hard drive.
3. In addition, Trojan horses may have keyboard loggers, backdoor, or remote control programs, or other software that may bypass normal security.

Security+ Objective 1.5.3—Logic Bombs

1. In a computer program, a logic bomb, also known as slag code, is programming code, inserted surreptitiously or intentionally, that is designed to execute (or explode) under circumstances such as the lapse of a certain amount of time or the failure of a program user to respond to a program command. It is in effect a delayed-action computer virus or Trojan horse.
2. A logic bomb, when exploded, may be designed to display or print a spurious message, delete or corrupt data, or have other undesirable effects.
3. Some logic bombs can be detected and eliminated before they execute through a periodic scan of all computer files, including compressed files, with an up-to-date antivirus program.

Security+ Objective 1.5.4—Worms

1. A worm is a self-replicating virus that does not alter files but resides in active memory and duplicates itself.
2. It is common for worms to be noticed only when their uncontrolled replication consumes system resources, slowing or halting other tasks. Typically, a worm enters the computer because of vulnerabilities available in the computer's operating system.
3. Some worms can be detected and removed by using virus checking software.
4. However, since worms function by using operating systems, programs or protocol vulnerabilities, it is important to have the newest service packs, patches, and security fixes installed for your operating system/network operating systems and network applications.

Security+ Objective 1.7—Auditing—Logging, system scanning

Security+ Objective 5.5.4—Auditing (Privilege, Usage, Escalation)

1. Auditing (accounting) is the process of monitoring a system or network, looking for potential security exposures or incidents, and verifying proper operation and configuration.
2. The "system" that you are auditing may be a network, a computer, or your computing environment as a whole (including disaster recovery, physical security, processes, etc.).
3. The two most common approaches to system and network audit today include configuration analysis/log analysis and vulnerability scanning.
4. Audit trails are the auxiliary records that are created that record transactions and other auditable events.
5. The basic component of an audit record should include the date and time of the event, who performed the event, where the event was performed (for example from which computer or terminal) and details about the event.
6. Of course, audit logs must be protected against sabotage and other attacks that would prevent the audit logs from properly recording events.
7. Penetration testing is the process of probing and identifying security vulnerabilities in a network and the extent to which they might be exploited by outside parties.
8. It is a necessary tool for determining the current security posture of your network. Such a test should determine both the existence and extent of any risk.
9. The normal pattern for a malicious user or a person to gain information on a target host or network starts with basic reconnaissance.
10. When a vulnerability is found and the hacker has gained access to a host, he or she will attempt to keep access and cover their tracks.
11. The reconnaissance phase can be done many different ways depending on the goal of the attacker.
12. The fundamental goal of scanning is to identify potential targets for security holes and vulnerabilities of the target host or network.
13. Vulnerability testing is the act of determining which security holes and vulnerabilities may be applicable to the target network or host.
14. The penetration tester or attacker will attempt to identify machines within the target network of all open ports and the operating systems as well as running applications including the operating system, patch level, and service pack applied.

Security+ Objective 2.3.4.3—Buffer Overflows

1. A buffer is a data area that is shared by either hardware devices or program processes.
2. Buffer overflows occur when a program tries to store more data in the buffer than it was designed.
3. The overflowed data can overwrite and corrupt valid data of another program.
4. Buffer overflow attacks is the most common kind of DoS attack is simply to send more traffic to a network address than the programmers who planned its data buffers anticipated someone might send.
5. The best defense against buffer overflow is having software developers follow secure coding practices.
6. You can minimize their effect by running programs as the least privileged account possible (not as administrator).
7. You must constantly check for service packs, patches, and security fixes so that it can fix these types of problems.

Security+ Objective 3.1.1—Firewalls

Security+ Objective 3.1.2—Routers

Security+ Objective 3.1.3—Switches

1. To see what kind of attacks are going through your firewalls and routers, you need to look at the firewall and router logs.
2. A typical firewall and router will generate large amounts of log information. The firewall logs can tell you port scans and unauthorized connection attempts, identify activity from compromised systems and much more.
3. Devices (firewalls, routers and switches) typically ship with a default password used for initial device configuration. Please make sure you change it ASAP.

Security+ Objective 3.1.9—IDS

Security+ Objective 3.4—Intrusion Detection

Security+ Objective 3.4.1—Network-Based

Security+ Objective 3.4.1.1—Active Detection

Security+ Objective 3.4.1.2—Passive Detection

Security+ Objective 3.4.2—Host-Based

Security+ Objective 3.4.2.1—Active Detection

Security+ Objective 3.4.2.2—Passive Detection

1. Trying to detect intruders can be a very daunting task, and it often requires a lot of hard work and a thorough working knowledge of the network operating system and the network as a whole.
2. You should always see what logs (especially the security logs such as those found in Event Viewer) are available with your network operating system (and firewalls/proxy servers too).
3. Sometimes, security logging is enabled by default, other times, it has to be enabled.
4. Intrusion Detection Systems (IDS) are monitoring devices on the network that help security administrators to identify attacks in progress, stop them, and to conduct an analysis after the attack is over.
5. Intrusion detection provides monitoring of network resources to detect intrusion and attacks that were not stopped by preventative techniques. Intrusion detection systems gather their information much like a protocol analyzer, collecting, and reading each packet. Then like virus scanners, intrusion detection systems compare to files of signatures that indicate specific known types of attacks.
6. Any pattern of traffic that deviates from the expected sequence of packets during a session may be suspect and cause a network administrator to be notified. This way, the administrator can look at the traffic pattern and take steps to stop the attack.

7. One of the most important characteristics about IDS is that they must correctly identify intrusions and attacks.
8. True positive occurs when the IDS correctly identifies undesirable traffic.
9. True negative occurs when the IDS correctly identifies normal traffic.
10. False positive occurs when the IDS incorrectly identifies normal traffic as an attack.
11. False negative occurs when the IDS incorrectly identifies an attack as normal traffic.
12. Intrusion detection systems can be categorized is based on their ability to take action when they detect suspicious activity.
13. Passive systems do not take any action to stop or prevent suspicious activity, which could potentially be an attack.
14. Active systems have all the features of a passive IDS, but they also have the additional ability to take action against the offending traffic. Unfortunately, although active systems seem far superior because of their ability to block undesirable traffic, active IDS need to be well tuned so that they don't give too many false positives.
15. Network-based IDS is by far the most commonly employed form of intrusion detection systems.
16. Host-based IDS monitors activity on a host machine. It would be typically used to protect a critical server containing sensitive information since host-based IDS software only protects the hosts on which they are installed.

Security+ Objective 3.4.3—Honey Pots

1. A honey pot is a computer set up as a sacrificial lamb on the network. The system is not locked down and has open ports and services enabled.
2. The honey pot contains no real company information, and thus will not be at risk if and when it is attacked.
3. The administrator can monitor the honey pot so they can see how an attack is occurring without putting your other systems in harm's way, and it may give the administrator an opportunity to track down the attacker.
4. The longer the hacker stays at the honeypot, the more will be disclosed about his or her techniques, methodology, and tools. It may also give early warning that a malicious person has access to the network.

Security+ Objective 3.4.4—Incident Response

Security+ Objective 5.4.2—Incident Response Policy

1. Part of the organization's security policy, you should have an incident response policy, which should cover how people in your organization are expected to deal with computer or network security incidents including any type of attack.

Security+ Objective 3.5—Security Baselines

1. Security baselines are standards that specify a minimum (that is, "baseline") set of security controls that are suitable for most organizations under normal circumstances.
2. The security baselines typically address both technical issues (such as software configuration) and operational issues (such as keeping applications up-to-date with vendor patches).

Security+ Objective 3.5.1—OS/NOS Hardening (concepts and processes)

1. Hardening is the process of identifying and closing vulnerabilities. To make your network more secure, you need to harden your network as a whole, by hardening your network devices, and you need to harden each system or operating system.
2. "Defense in depth" is an important concept that states that you should not rely on a single barrier to protect your sensitive data and system operations. Instead, erect multiple zones of security around your resources, to help ensure that they cannot be compromised if a single security mechanism fails due to a software bug, operator error, etc.
3. Since many data compromises come from within, you should apply the same level of security to your internal systems as you would to your external systems.

Security+ Objective 3.5.1.1—File System

1. You need to also plan the disk partition and file system layout with security in mind and plan the system, user account and group structure.
2. Be sure to use a journaling file system such as NTFS, Ext3 or Reiserfs.

Security+ Objective 3.5.1.2—Updates (Hotfixes, Service Packs, Patches)

1. Keep systems (operating system and applications) updated with the latest security patches.

Security+ Objective 3.5.2—Network Hardening

1. Network hardening involves the steps taken to secure a network and the devices on it.
2. It includes both securing devices which have options set "out of the box" which are generally regarded as insecure, as well as customizing the configuration of the devices to meet the specific security requirements of the organization.
3. OS/NOS products, being software-based with their code stored on server hard disks, are typically updated via software updates on CD or downloaded from the Web.

Security+ Objective 3.5.2.1—Updates (Firmware)

1. With network devices, the program code and data controlling the device is often stored in a form called "firmware."

2. Like OS updates, network device updates are often distributed over the Web.
3. However, rather than being stored on a hard disk, code for network devices is usually written into ROM (read only memory) chips with a special firmware update program.
4. Firmware is a combination of hardware and software, in which network device program code and data is stored.
5. As always, stay on top of the latest versions of firmware available for your networking products. These often address security-related vulnerabilities.
6. To locate updates for your network devices, check the vendors' websites.

Security+ Objective 3.5.2.2—Configuration

1. Configuration deals with setting options on the devices.
2. One key issue to address would be device passwords used to access administrative features of switches, routers, etc.
3. Devices typically ship with a default password used for initial device configuration. Please make sure you change it ASAP.
4. When configuring networking equipment, follow along with the standards already set for your network if possible.

Security+ Objective 3.5.2.2.2—Access Control Lists

1. Access Control Lists (ACLs), sometimes called filters, are used to determine which traffic is permitted to pass through a network interface, in which direction, between which addresses.
2. Routers typically manage access control via a text file of access control rules; operating systems and home networking devices including this functionality generally wrap access control lists in a GUI for ease of use.
3. The network device examines the information in each packet, comparing it to the ACLs, and either lets the packet through or stops it depending on the ACL instructions.

Security+ Objective 3.5.3—Application Hardening

1. Application hardening is the process of securing applications in use on a network.
2. A network application is one that communicates with another program across the network.
3. As with OS software and networks, it's important to keep up-to-date with the latest fixes and patches for the applications used on your network.

Security+ Objective 5.6—Forensics (Awareness, conceptual knowledge and understanding—know what your role is)

Security+ Objective 5.6.1—Chain of Custody

Security+ Objective 5.6.2—Preservation of Evidence

Security+ Objective 5.6.3—Collection of Evidence

1. Evidence is information presented in a court of law to confirm or dispel a fact that's under contention.
2. The types of evidence, admissibility of evidence, chain of custody, and evidence life cycle comprise the main elements to be tested in the investigation portion of this domain.
3. Computer forensics is a newly emerged and developing field which can be described as the study of digital evidence resulting from an incident. It involves collection and analysis of digital data within an investigative process that may be used as legal evidence.
4. When an incident occurs, you should immediately begin to collect evidence.
5. This evidence can help you learn about the intrusion so that you can learn how the intrusion was done and stop future attacks of the same type and it can improve your systems, their operations, and your staff's capabilities.
6. Before you begin work on a compromised system, remember that you need to concentrate on not altering anything and to document your evidence and all of your actions, as well as gathering that evidence.
7. All information concerning the incident must be recorded and securely stored.
8. You need to establish, examine, and preserve an audit trail.
9. An audit trail is a record of who accessed a computer and what operations he or she performed.
10. A chain of custody must be maintained for all evidence.
11. A documented chain of custody shows who collected and had access to each piece of evidence. Failure to maintain this chain of custody might invalidate your evidence.

QUESTIONS

1. When evidence is acquired, a log is started that records who had possession of the evidence for a specific amount of time. This is to avoid allegations that the evidence may have been tampered with when it was unaccounted for, and to keep track of the tasks performed in acquiring evidence from a piece of equipment or materials. What is the term used to describe this process?
   a. Chain of command
   b. Chain of custody
   c. Chain of jurisdiction
   d. Chain of evidence

2. You are the first person to respond to the scene of an incident involving a computer being hacked. After determining the scope of the crime scene and securing it, you attempt to preserve evidence at the scene. Which of the following tasks will you perform to preserve evidence? (Choose all that apply.)
   a. Photograph any information displayed on the monitors of computers involved in the incident.
   b. Document any observation or messages displayed by the computer.
   c. Shut down the computer to prevent further attacks that may modify data.
   d. Gather up manuals, nonfunctioning devices, and other materials and equipment in the area so they are ready for transport.

3. A piece of malicious code that can replicate itself has no productive purpose and exists only to damage computer systems or create further vulnerabilities is called a _____ .
   a. Logic bomb   b. Worm
   c. Trojan horse   d. SYN flood
   e. Virus

4. What statement is most true about viruses and hoaxes?
   a. Hoaxes can create as much damage as a real virus.
   b. Hoaxes are harmless pranks and should be ignored.
   c. Hoaxes can help educate users about a virus.
   d. Hoaxes carry a malicious payload and can be destructive.

5. You have been alerted to the possibility of someone using an application to capture and manipulate packets as they are passing through your network. What type of threat does this represent?
   a. DDoS   b. Back door
   c. Spoofing   d. Man in the middle

6. As the security analyst for your company's network, you become aware that your systems may be under attack. This kind of attack is a DoS attack, and the exploits send more traffic to a node than anticipated. What kind of attack is this?
   a. Ping of death   b. Buffer overflow
   c. Logic bomb   d. Smurf

7. A honey pot is _____ .
   a. A false system or network to attract attacks away from your real network.
   b. A place to store passwords.
   c. A safe haven for your backup media.
   d. Something that exists only in theory.

8. A collection of information that includes login, file access, other various activities, and actual or attempted legitimate and unauthorized violations is a(n):
   a. Audit
   b. ACL (Access Control List)
   c. Audit trail
   d. Syslog

9. Notable security organizations often recommend only essential services be provided by a particular host, and any unnecessary services be disabled. Which of the following does NOT represent a reason supporting this recommendation?
   a. Each additional service increases the risk of compromising the host, the services that run on the host, and potential clients of these services.
   b. Different services may require different hardware, software, or a different discipline of administration.
   c. When fewer services and applications are running on a specific host, fewer log entries and fewer interactions between different services are expected, which simplifies the analysis and maintenance of the system from a security point of view.
   d. If a service is not using a well-known port, firewalls will not be able to disable access to this port, and an administrator will not be able to restrict access to this service.

10. A _____ occurs when a string of data is sent to a buffer that is larger than the buffer was designed to handle.
    a. Brute force attack
    b. Buffer overflow
    c. Man-in-the-middle attack
    d. Blue screen of death
    e. SYN flood
    f. Spoofing attack

11. A program that can infect other programs by modifying them to include a version of itself is a:
    a. Replicator.   b. Virus.
    c. Trojan horse.   d. Logic bomb.

12. Providing false information about the source of an attack is known as:
    a. Aliasing.   b. Spoofing.
    c. Flooding.   d. Redirecting.

13. You are the first to arrive at a crime scene in which a hacker is accessing unauthorized data on a file server from across the network. To secure the scene, which of the followings actions should you perform?
    a. Prevent members of the organization from entering the server room.
    b. Prevent members of the incident response team from entering the server room.
    c. Shut down the server to prevent the user from accessing further data.
    d. Detach the network cable from the server to prevent the user from accessing further data.

14. When a session is initiated between the Transport Control Program (TCP) client and server in a network, a very small buffer space exists to handle the usually rapid "handshaking" exchange of messages that sets up the session. What kind of attack exploits this functionality?
    a. Buffer overflow   b. SYN attack
    c. Smurf   d. Birthday attack

15. An autonomous agent that copies itself into one or more host programs, then propagates when the host is run, is best described as a:
    a. Trojan horse.   b. Back door.
    c. Logic bomb.   d. Virus.

16. You are promoting user awareness in forensics, so users will know what to do when incidents occur with their computers. Which of the following tasks should you instruct users to perform when an incident occurs? (Choose all that apply.)
    a. Shut down the computer.
    b. Contact the incident response team.
    c. Document what they see on the screen.
    d. Log off the network.

17. What kind of attack is a type of security breach to a computer system that does not usually result in the theft of information or other security loss but the lack of legitimate use of that system?
    a. CRL   b. DoS
    c. ACL   d. MD2

18. Active detection IDS systems may perform which of the following when an unauthorized connection attempt is discovered? (Choose all that apply.)
    a. Inform the attacker that he or she is connecting to a protected network.
    b. Shut down the server or service.
    c. Provide the attacker the usernames and passwords for administrative accounts.
    d. Break off suspicious connections.

19. When examining the server's list of protocols that are bound and active on each network interface card, the network administrator notices a relatively large number of protocols. Which actions should be taken to ensure network security?
    a. Unnecessary protocols do not pose a significant risk to the system and should be left intact for compatibility reasons.
    b. There are no unneeded protocols on most systems because protocols are chosen during the installation.
    c. Unnecessary protocols should be disabled on all server and client machines on a network as they pose great risk.
    d. Using port filtering ACLs (Access Control Lists) at firewalls and routers is sufficient to stop malicious attacks on unused protocols.

20. A high-profile company has been receiving a high volume of attacks on their website. The network administrator wants to be able to collect information on the attacker(s) so legal action can be taken. What should be implemented?
    a. A DMZ (Demilitarized Zone)
    b. A honey pot
    c. A firewall
    d. A new subnet

21. A recent audit shows that a user logged into a server with his or her account and executed a program. The user then performed activities only available to an administrator. This is an example of which kind of attack?

a. Trojan horse

b. Privilege escalation

c. Subseven back door

d. Security policy removal

22. Which of the following results in a domain name server resolving the domain name to a different host and thus misdirecting Internet traffic?

   a. DoS (Denial of Service)

   b. Spoofing

   c. Brute force attack

   d. Reverse DNS (Domain Name Service)

23. At what stage of an assessment would an auditor test systems for weaknesses and attempt to defeat existing encryption, passwords, and access lists?

   a. Penetration   b. Control

   c. Audit planning   d. Discovery

24. Computer forensics experts collect and analyze data using which of the following guidelines so as to minimize data loss?

   a. Evidence

   b. Chain of custody

   c. Chain of command

   d. Incident response

25. An application that appears to perform a useful function but instead contains some sort of malicious code is called a _____ .

   a. SYN flood   b. Logic bomb

   c. Virus   d. Worm

   e. Trojan horse

26. As the security analyst for your company's network, you want to trap a hacker attempting to access your systems. From the list below, what is the best solution?

   a. Set up a honey pot to attract hackers.

   b. Close all ports including 21 and 80.

   c. Wait in the parking lot for War Drivers.

   d. Use a firewall that blocks all incoming traffic.

27. As the security analyst for your company's network, you are experiencing problems with your Internet facing devices. They are sluggish in response and one of your NT servers has blue screened. You put up a sniffer and are catching a high volume of ICMP traffic. What could be the cause of the problem?

   a. You are seeing a teardrop attack.

   b. You are seeing a fragmentation attack.

   c. You are seeing a brute force attack.

   d. You are seeing a ping of death attack.

28. Computer viruses are forms of attacks on your company's network. What are computer viruses considered to fall under from the following categories?

   a. Smurf code   b. Malware

   c. Logical bombing   d. RSA

29. As the security analyst for your company's network, you anticipate that a new virus that you just researched may strike your network infrastructure on a specific date. What type of attack is this?

   a. Brute force   b. Logic bomb

   c. Dictionary   d. Smurf

30. In this type of attack, an attacker captures packets from two or more computers and sends out acknowledges, replies, and requests in order to control the communications between these computers.

   a. Ping of death

   b. SYN Flood

   c. Man-in-the-middle attack

   d. TCP flood

   e. IP spoofing

   f. MAC spoofing

   g. Distributed denial of service

   h. DOOM attack

   i. Replay attack

31. By what means can an administrator monitor his or her network for authorized and unauthorized access without any apparent changes to end-users or intruders?

   a. Auditing   b. Authentication

   c. Repudiation   d. Authorization

   e. Handshaking

32. In a _____, an attacker can retransmit packets as desired to a computer, causing it to perform a desired action. (Select the correct answer for the blank.)

   a. Ping of death

   b. SYN flood

   c. Man-in-the-middle attack

   d. TCP flood

   e. IP spoofing

   f. MAC spoofing

   g. Distributed Denial of Service

   h. DOOM attack

   i. Replay attack

33. A _____ attack masks its true source by using the IP information from another network, sometimes even using that of the internal network itself.

   a. Ping of death

   b. SYN flood

   c. Man-in-the-middle attack

   d. TCP flood

   e. IP spoofing

   f. MAC spoofing

   g. Distributed Denial of Service

   h. DOOM attack

   i. Replay attack

34. You are the administrator of a fairly sensitive network. After taking all reasonable and prudent security measures, what should you do to ensure that no unauthorized access is being made to your network without further reducing the capability or usability of your network?

   a. Perform random spot checks of users

   b. Institute a rotating security sweep

   c. Perform auditing of network events that you are interested in monitoring

   d. Install high-security door and window locks

   e. Take your network off the Internet

35. Your network has been prevented from accessing the Internet due to a large amount of malformed incoming traffic. What type of attack are you experiencing?
    a. Replay attack
    b. Spoof attack
    c. Man-in-the-middle attack
    d. Denial of Service attack
    e. KillBot attack
    f. None, the gateway router is malfunctioning and sending malformed packets

36. When an attacker sends a web server a large number of TCP SYN packets, but does not respond to the TCP SYNACK packet from the web server with a TCP ACK packet, what type of attack is occurring?
    a. Ping of death
    b. SYN flood
    c. Loss of SYNACK
    d. TCP flood
    e. IP spoofing
    f. MAC spoofing
    g. Man-in-the-middle attack
    h. Replay attack

37. A _____ attack utilizes the processing power and Internet bandwidth capability of many hosts in order to carry out the attack successfully.
    a. Ping of death
    b. SYN flood
    c. Man-in-the-middle attack
    d. TCP flood
    e. IP spoofing
    f. MAC spoofing
    g. Distributed Denial of Service
    h. DOOM attack
    i. Replay attack

38. A _____ is a condition that can occur when more data is attempted to be put into a program than the programmer designed for. (Select the correct answer for the blank.)
    a. Blue screen of death
    b. STOP error
    c. WEP cracking
    d. Buffer overflow
    e. Frozen application
    f. Service failure

39. What is the main difference between an active detection IDS and a passive detection IDS?
    a. The active detection IDS requires constant monitoring to be effective.
    b. The passive detection IDS is not nearly as capable.
    c. The active detection IDS will actually take steps to terminate the attackers connection.
    d. The passive detection IDS will notify the attacker of the status of their attack.

40. Which denial of service attack exploits the way that the Internet Protocol (IP) requires a packet that is too large for the next router to handle be divided into fragments?
    a. Teardrop attack
    b. Buffer overflow
    c. SYN attack
    d. Birthday attack

41. An intrusion detection system is used for _____ . (Select the correct answer for the blank.)
    a. Preventing unauthorized access to your network
    b. Detecting and monitoring unauthorized access attempts to your network
    c. Detecting and monitoring authorized access attempts to your network
    d. Preventing users with expired passwords from connecting to the network

42. What type of malicious code typically does not cause any apparent damage, but instead quietly produces exact replicas of itself, spreading to all computers and networks that it can?
    a. Worm   b. Virus
    c. Trojan horse   d. ActiveX control
    e. Javascript   f. Logic bomb
    g. Fuzzy logic

43. What is used to maintain a table correlating MAC addresses to IP addresses on a local computer?
    a. DNS cache
    b. ARP cache
    c. Web cache
    d. DHCP cache
    e. FTP cache
    f. IP cache

44. Common security risks present on workstations include all except which of the following? (Choose all that apply.)
    a. Running services that are not required
    b. Opening email containing malicious code
    c. Using IPSec to secure all network traffic
    d. Creating shares of a volume root with no security
    e. Installing a remote access client such as PCAnywhere
    f. Removing the computer from the physical boundary of the building
    g. Allowing coworkers to use their computer
    h. Running updated antivirus software

45. Many intrusion detection systems look for known patterns or _____ to aid in detecting attacks.
    a. Viruses   b. Signatures
    c. Hackers   d. Malware

46. An IDS (intrusion detection system) is sending alerts that attacks are occurring which are not actually taking place. What is the IDS registering?
    a. False positives
    b. False negatives
    c. True negatives
    d. True positives

47. How are honey pots used to collect information? Honey pots collect:
    a. IP addresses and identity of internal users.
    b. Data on the identity, access, and compromise methods used by the intruder.
    c. Data regarding and the identity of servers within the network.
    d. IP addresses and data of firewalls used within the network.

48. Analyzing log files after an attack has started is an example of:
    a. Active detection.
    b. Overt detection.
    c. Covert detection.
    d. Passive detection.

49. An attacker can determine what network services are enabled on a target system by:
    a. Installing a rootkit on the target system.
    b. Checking the services file.
    c. Enabling logging on the target system.
    d. Running a port scan against the target system.

50. NetBus and Back Orifice are each considered an example of a(n):
    a. Virus.
    b. Illicit server.
    c. Spoofing tool.
    d. Allowable server.

51. An email is received alerting the network administrator to the presence of a virus on the system if a specific executable file exists. What should be the first course of action?
    a. Investigate the email as a possible hoax with a reputable anti-virus vendor.
    b. Immediately search for and delete the file if discovered.
    c. Broadcast a message to the entire organization to alert users to the presence of a virus.
    d. Locate and download a patch to repair the file.

52. What is a common type of attack on web servers?
    a. Birthday
    b. Buffer overflow
    c. Spam
    d. Brute force

53. Malicious port scanning is a method of attack to determine which of the following?
    a. Computer name
    b. The fingerprint of the operating system
    c. The physical cabling topology of a network
    d. User IDs and passwords

54. A system administrator discovers suspicious activity that might indicate a computer crime. The administrator should first:
    a. Refer to incident response plan.
    b. Change ownership of any related files to prevent tampering.
    c. Move any related programs and files to non-erasable media.
    d. Set the system time to ensure any logged information is accurate.

55. For system logging to be an effective security measure, an administrator must:
    a. Review the logs on a regular basis.
    b. Implement a circular logging.
    c. Configure the system to shut down when the logs are full.
    d. Configure SNMP traps for logging events.

56. What is the best method of defense against IP spoofing attacks?
    a. Deploy intrusion detection systems
    b. Create a DMZ
    c. Apply Ingress filtering to routers
    d. There is no good defense against IP spoofing

57. Which of the following statements is true about network-based IDSs (intrusion detection system)?
    a. Network-based IDSs are never passive devices that listen on a network wire without interfering with the normal operation of a network.
    b. Network-based IDSs are usually passive devices that listen on a network wire while interfering with the normal operation of a network.
    c. Network-based IDSs are usually intrusive devices that listen on a network wire while interfering with the normal operation of a network.
    d. Network-based IDSs are usually passive devices that listen on a network wire without interfering with the normal operation of a network.

58. A piece of code that appears to do something useful while performing a harmful and unexpected function like stealing passwords is a:
    a. Virus.
    b. Logic bomb.
    c. Worm.
    d. Trojan horse.

59. One of the most effective ways for an administrator to determine what security holes reside on a network is to:
    a. Perform a vulnerability assessment.
    b. Run a port scan.
    c. Run a sniffer.
    d. Install and monitor an IDS.

60. In responding to incidents such as security breaches, one of the most important steps taken is:
    a. Encryption.
    b. Authentication.
    c. Containment.
    d. Intrusion.

61. Missing audit log entries most seriously affect an organization's ability to:
    a. Recover destroyed data.
    b. Legally prosecute an attacker.
    c. Evaluate system vulnerabilities.
    d. Create reliable system backups.

62. Appropriate documentation of a security incident is important for each of the following reasons *except:*
    a. The documentation serves as a lesson learned which may help avoid further exploitation of the same vulnerability.
    b. The documentation will serve as an aid to updating policy and procedures.

c. The documentation will indicate who should be fired for the incident.

d. The documentation will serve as a tool to access the impact and damage for the incident.

63. System administrators and hackers use what technique to review network traffic to determine what services are running?
    a. Sniffer
    b. IDS
    c. Firewall
    d. Router

64. Servers or workstations running programs and utilities for recording probes and attacks are referred to as:
    a. Firewalls
    b. Host-based IDS
    c. Proxies
    d. Active targets

65. A severed T1 line is most likely to be considered in _____ planning.
    a. Data recovery
    b. Off-site storage
    c. Media destruction
    d. Incident response

66. The action of determining which operating system is installed on a system simply by analyzing its response to certain network traffic is called:
    a. OS scanning.
    b. Reverse engineering.
    c. Fingerprinting.
    d. Host hijacking.

67. DDoS is most commonly accomplished by:
    a. Internal host computers simultaneously failing.
    b. Overwhelming and shutting down multiple services on a server.
    c. Multiple servers or routers monopolizing and overwhelming the bandwidth of a particular server or router.
    d. An individual email address list being used to distribute a virus.

68. A team organized for the purpose of handling security crisis is called a(n):
    a. Computer information team.
    b. Security resource team.
    c. Active detection team.
    d. Incident response team.

69. What is the most common goal of operating system logging?
    a. To determine the amount of time employees spend using various applications.
    b. To keep a record of system usage.
    c. To provide details of what systems have been compromised.
    d. To provide details of which systems are interconnected.

70. When hardening a machine against external attacks, what process should be followed when disabling services?
    a. Disable services such as DHCP client and print servers from servers that do not use/serve those functions.
    b. Disable one unnecessary service after another, while reviewing the effects of the previous action.
    c. Research the services and their dependencies before disabling any default services.
    d. Disable services not directly related to financial operations.

71. An effective method of preventing computer viruses from spreading is to:
    a. Require root/administrative access to run programs.
    b. Enable scanning of email attachments.
    c. Prevent the execution of .vbs files.
    d. Install a host-based IDS.

72. The system administrator of the company has terminated employment unexpectedly. When the administrator's user ID is deleted, the system suddenly begins deleting files. This is an example of what type of malicious code?
    a. Logic bomb
    b. Virus
    c. Trojan horse
    d. Worm

73. Of the following, what is the primary attribute associated with email hoaxes?
    a. Email hoaxes create unnecessary email traffic and panic in non-technical users.
    b. Email hoaxes take up large amounts of server disk space.
    c. Email hoaxes can cause buffer overflows on email servers.
    d. Email hoaxes can encourage malicious users.

74. What is a network administrator protecting against by ingress/egress filtering traffic as follows: Any packet coming into the network must not have a source address of the internal network. Any packet coming into the network must have a destination address from the internal network. Any packet leaving the network must have a source address from the internal network. Any packet leaving the network must not have a destination address from the internal network. Any packet coming into the network or leaving the network must not have a source or destination address of a private address or an address listed in RFC1918 reserve space.
    a. SYN flooding
    b. Spoofing
    c. DoS attacks
    d. Dictionary attacks

75. The system administrator has just used a program that highlighted the susceptibility of several servers on the network to various exploits. The program also suggested fixes. What type of program was used?
    a. Intrusion detection
    b. Port scanner
    c. Vulnerability scanner
    d. Trojan scanner

76. TCP/IP hijacking resulted from exploitation of the fact that TCP/IP:
    a. Has no authentication mechanism, thus allowing cleartext password of 16 bytes.
    b. Allows packets to be tunneled to an alternate network.

c. Has no authentication mechanism, and therefore allows connectionless packets from anyone.

d. Allows a packet to be spoofed and inserted into a stream, thereby enabling commands to be executed on the remote host.

77. Performing a security vulnerability assessment on systems that a company relies on demonstrates:

a. That the site *cannot* be hacked.

b. A commitment to protecting data and customer.

c. Insecurity on the part of the organization.

d. A needless fear of attack.

78. Intrusion detection system typically consists of two parts, a console and a:

a. Sensor.   b. Router.

c. Processor.   d. Firewall.

79. As a security administrator, what are the three categories of active responses relating to intrusion detection?

a. Collect additional information, maintain the environment, and take action against the intruder.

b. Collect additional information, change the environment, and alert the manager.

c. Collect additional information, change the environment, and take action against the intruder.

d. Discard any additional information, change the environment, and take action against the intruder.

80. You are the first person to arrive at a crime scene. An investigator and crime scene technician arrive afterwards to take over the investigation. Which of the following tasks will the crime scene technician be responsible for performing?

a. Ensure that any documentation and evidence the technician possessed is handed over to the investigator.

b. Reestablish a perimeter as new evidence presents itself.

c. Establish a chain of command.

d. Tag, bag, and inventory evidence.

HANDS-ON EXERCISES

Exercise 1: Updating and Securing Windows

Run Microsoft Updates

1. Start Internet Explorer.
2. Open the Tools menu and select Windows update.
3. Click on the Scan for Updates link.
4. Click the Review and install updates link.
5. View all of the critical updates and service packs.
6. At the top of the list, click the Install Now button.
7. Follow the instructions on the screen.

Check for Security Fixes with HFNetChk

1. Open the http://www.microsoft.com.
2. Search for and download the Microsoft Network Security Hotfix Checker (HFNetChk).
3. Install the Microsoft Network Security Hotfix checker.
4. Open a command prompt window and execute the hfnetchk command.
5. Study the results.
6. Close the command prompt window.

Run Microsoft Baseline Security Analyzer

1. Open the http://www.microsoft.com.
2. Search for and download the Microsoft Baseline Security Analyzer.
3. Install the Microsoft Baseline Security Analyzer.
4. Click the Scan a Computer link.
5. Click the Start scan link and perform a scan of your computer.
6. When the scan is complete, view the results and look for issues and vulnerabilities and how to correct them.
7. Close the Microsoft Baseline Security Analyzer.

Hardening Certain Settings for Windows

1. Open the registry using the regedit utility.
2. Open the hkey_local_machine\system\currentcontrolset\services\tcpip\parameters\ and create the following values by right-clicking the right pane, selecting New and selecting DWORD. Then create the following values:
    - hkey_local_machine\system\currentcontrolset\services\tcpip\parameters\synattackprotect=1 REG_DWORD
    - hkey_local_machine\system\currentcontrolset\services\tcpip\parameters\tcpmaxconnectresponsere transmissions=2 REG_DWORD
    - hkey_local_machine\system\currentcontrolset\services\tcpip\parameters\tcpmaxdataretransmissions=3 REG_DWORD
    - hkey_local_machine\system\currentcontrolset\services\tcpip\parameters\enablepmtudiscovery=0 REG_DWORD
3. From the http://www.microsoft.com website, find and download the Threats and Countermeasures: Security Settings in Windows Server 2003 and Windows XP.
4. Browse chapter 10.

Exercise 2: Installing Virus Software in Windows

1. Open the http://download.mcafee.com/ website and use the McAfee Freescan to search for viruses on your computer.
2. Install a popular virus-checking software such as McAfee or Norton anti-virus.
3. Connect to the Internet, and update the virus checking software.
4. Scan your computer for viruses.

Exercise 3: Auditing in Windows

Enable Auditing

1. From the Administrative Tools, start the Domain Controller Security Policy console.
2. In the left pane, open Security Policies, open Local Policies and click the Audit Policy options.
3. Double-click the Audit directory service access option in the right pane and enable the Success and Failure options.
4. Double-click the Audit logon events option and enable the Failure options.
5. Close the Domain Console Security Policy console.

Auditing Failed Login Attempts

1. If the Account lockout option has not been set, Use the Domain Security Policy console to enable the Account lockout threshold to 4 invalid logon attempts. If it asks, set the account logout duration to 30 minutes and the reset account lockout counter after 30 minutes.
2. Log out as the Administrator and incorrectly log in as Charlie Brown 5 times.
3. Log in as the Administrator.

Auditing the Access of a File

1. Right-click the C:\DATA folder and select the Properties option.
2. On the Auditing tab, click the Add button.
3. Select Everyone and click on the OK button.
4. Select the following options for Successful and Failed attempts:
    - Create Files/Write Data
    - Create Folders/Append Data
    - Write Attributes
    - Write Extended Attributes
    - Delete Subfolders and Files
    - Delete
5. Select the Apply these auditing entries to objects and/or containers within this container only option, and click on the OK button.
6. Click on the OK button again.
7. Delete the Windows 2000.jpg file from the C:\DATA folder.

Using Event Viewer to View Security Logs

1. Open the Event Viewer from the Administrative Tools.
2. Select the Security Log option in the Left pane.

Exercise 4: Installing and Using NetBus

1. Download, extract and install NetBus from the http://www.nwinternet.com/~pchelp/nb/netbus.htm website. If NetBus is not available from this website, open a search engine and search for NetBus.
2. Open a command prompt window and change to the directory where NetBus is located.
3. Execute the `patch /noadd` command. The /noadd switch keeps NetBus from installing itself each time Windows boots. Note: The trick of using the NetBus utility is to get it loaded on your victim's computer. You either would do this if you have physical access to the computer or trick him or her to load it by pretending it to be a patch or useful utility.
4. To victimize someone's computer, you would execute the `netbus` command and click the Connect! button.
5. Click the Open CD-ROM to open your CD-ROM.
6. Click the Msg Manager button and select the Let the User Answer the Message. For the message type "A virus has been detected. Enter your password to remove the virus." Note: You may need to use the Alt+Tab to switch to the message window.
7. Type a password in and click OK. Note: If a user is not educated in such matters, the user may actually type in the password and send it back to the intruder.
8. Go back to the main screen, and click the Listen button to start keystroke logging.
9. Change back to the command prompt window and type some text. Then back at the Listen window, check the results.
10. If you wish to remove the NetBus, delete the Netbus directory and reboot your computer.

Exercise 5: Checking for Suspicious Ports from Backdoor Programs

1. Open a command in Windows.
2. To list all open TCP ports, at the command prompt, type the following command:

   `netstat -a -p tcp`

3. If you have msn messenger, any other messenger or NetBus running, you should be able to see the ports that they are using.
4. To list all UDP ports, at the command prompt, type the following command:

   `netstat -a -p udp`

5. To show all ports, execute the following command:

   `netstat -a`

6. Download and use GFI LANguard Network Security Scanner (demo software) and execute the software looking for open and unused ports.

Exercise 6: Running Nmap

1. Using a search engine, search for and download nmap and windows.
2. Unpack and install NmapNT.
3. Next, install the winpcap drivers. This can be done by selecting the Start button, selecting Settings, Network and Dial-up Connections and select your network adapter. With your network adapter highlighted, click the Properties button.
4. In the adapter's Properties dialog box, click the Install button.
5. In the Select Network Component Type screen, select Protocol and click Add.
6. In the Select Network Protocol screen, click the Have Disk button.
7. In the Install from Disk screen, click Browse and navigate to the Drivers directory where you installed NmapNT. The directory should be C:\Program Files\NmapNT\DRIVERS. Then choose the directory for your operating system.
8. In the Select Network Protocol screen, select Packet Capture Driver and click OK.
9. When the Files needed screen appears, click OK.
10. Click OK and close.
11. To see some of the options that are available, execute the nmapnt command.

12. To perform a simple scan, execute the `nmapnt 127.0.0.1` command.
13. To check to see if the host is really down instead of just blocking ping probles, use the `nmapnt -P0 127.0.0.1` command. The –P0 option tells Nmap to scan the IP address regardless of whether it allows ICMP traffic to it.
14. To perform a stealth scan, execute the `nmapnt -sS -P0 -p135 127.0.0.1` command. the –sS option performs a SYN scan instead of the default TCP connect scan and the –p option specifies the port to scan.
15. To identify the OS, use the `nmapnt -sT -O 127.0.0.1` command. The –sT option is used for the TCP-connect scan and –O option attemps to perform OS fingerprinting by analyzing the sequence numbers returned form the device.
16. Scan some other ports.

Exercise 7: Using GFI Network Security Scanner

1. Go to the http://www.gfisoftware.com website and download the trial version of the GFI LANguard Network Security Scanner.
2. Install the GFI Language Network Security Scanner program.
3. Type the address of your partner's computer in the Target area and click the start button (first button on the toolbar).
4. After the scan is complete, look at all of the information that is available to you.

Exercise 8: Looking for Security Problem in Linux

1. Login as root.
2. Execute the following command so that Linux can start recording failed logins into the btmp file:

   `touch /var/log/btmp`

3. Change to the second terminal and try to login with the user1 account with the wrong password.
4. Login as user1 with the correct password.
5. Change back to the 1st terminal (root).
6. View the /var/log/messages file. Look for any errors or services being enabled or disabled or any other warnings or notifications of possible security issues. Don't forget you can also use the less command with these logs.
7. View the /var/log/boot.log. Look at times the computer was started or stopped. You should also look in the /var/log directory for other boot.log files (such as boot.log.1).
8. View the contents of the /var/log/secure. Look at when users or groups were added or deleted, programs and services started, passwords changed and other possible security issues. You should also look in the /var/log directory for other secure files (such as secure.1).
9. Execute the `last` command. Look to see when user1 logged on, when user1 logged off and for how long user1 was logged on. Note: You can also use last | less.
10. Execute the `lastb` command.
11. Execute the `lastlog` command.
12. To find out if there are any SETUID or SETGID permissions on files, use the following command:

    `find / -perm +4000 -print`

    Look to see if you were not aware of any of these.
13. View the /home/user1/.bash_history file for User1. Look for suspicious commands that User1 should not be doing.

Exercise 9: Using PAM Configuration Files in Linux

1. Log in as root.
2. Change to the /etc/pam.d directory.
3. Open the login file. Add the following lines at the end of the file.

   ```
   auth      required /lib/security/pam_tally.so onerr=fail no_magic_root
   account   required /lib/security/pam_tally.so deny=5 no_magic_root reset
   ```

4. Save and close the file.
5. Change to the /var/log directory and create an empty file called faillog by using the following command:

   `touch faillog`

6. Change to the 2nd terminal. Try to login as user1 with the wrong password. Do this at least six times.
7. Try to log in with the correct password.
8. Switch back to the 1st terminal (root account).
9. Change to the /sbin directory.
10. Perform the following command:

    ```
    pam_tally
    ```

11. To reset the counter for user1 and reenable the account, use the following command:

    ```
    pam_tally -user user1 -reset
    ```

12. Change to the 2nd terminal.
13. Log in as user1.

Exercise 10: Researching the Internet for Common Security Issues

1. Go the http://www.microsoft.com/security/ website. On the left pane, look at the security bulletins and virus alerts that are available. Click on each link and discover what the security issue is and how to overcome this issue.
2. Go to the http://www.redhat.com/apps/support/errata/index.html website. Look at the last two versions of Linux and look at the security alerts and bugfixes.
3. Go to the http://www.cert.org/ website and look at recent advisories and incidents.
4. Go to the http://www.sans.org/top20/ website and read its contents. View the top vulnerabilities for Windows and UNIX Systems.

CHAPTER **13**

Disaster Recovery and Business Continuity

Topics Covered in this Chapter

Introduction

The last chapter will cover disaster recovery and business continuity. This includes those steps and precautions that you need to keep your network running through a disaster or to minimize the downtime for your network.

Objectives

13.1 PROTECTING BUSINESS CONTINUITY

When a computer has a problem, the user's first response is "Oh no, not now!" I am sure that you will agree that there is no good time for a computer to break down. When a network fails, the failure can affect many people and can literally cost a company thousands of dollars of business or productivity for every hour the network is down.

One of your primary jobs as the administrator is to deal with those disasters and to plan ahead to minimize the frequency of the failures and the degree of the failure. This includes:

1. Establishing a backup plan and performing the backing up of data.
2. Documenting the network so that you and your team can find information quickly about the network.
3. Maintaining a log listing all problems and their solutions to be used for determining trends, planning of network and personnel resources and for easy lookup of solutions for when the same problem occurs again.

The continued survival of a business depends on its continued operation. When a business stops operating for any reason, it loses credibility and income. If the disaster is bad enough, occuring over an extended period of time, it could cause the business never to recover. Business continuity management is a term that has been used to describe the review, planning, and implementation processes that a business must perform to keep operating in the face of any interruption.

The idea behind business continuity management is to have a comprehensive plan worked out in advance that specifies what has to be done to keep the business operational, who will do what when the disaster occurs, and how replacement materials will be obtained.

The process of creating a business continuity plan must be sponsored by individuals at the highest levels of the company and encompass the entire operation, not just the IT department. The primary steps of the continuity should include:

- Identifying the mission-critical processes that the business must perform to continue operating.
- Identifying all the resources required for the mission-critical processes to operate.

■ Rating the relative importance of the mission-critical processes to the continuing operation of the business.

■ Deciding on the course of action to be undertaken for each mission-critical process.

13.2 FAULT TOLERANCE AND DISASTER RECOVERY NEEDS

Security+ Objective 5.2.2—Secure Recovery

Security+ Objective 5.2.2.1—Alternate Sites

When protecting your network, you need to take measures to minimize the impact of computer and network problems. These measures fall into two major categories:

■ **Fault tolerance**—The capability of a computer or network system to respond to a condition automatically, usually resolving it, and thus reducing the impact of the system. If fault-tolerant measures have been implemented, it is unlikely that a user would know that a problem existed.

■ **Disaster recovery**—The ability to get a system functional after a total system failure in the least amount of time.

The cost of server downtime is staggering. For a network of a medium-sized business with 300 employees and 100 million dollars of business going down 24 times a year, 3 hours at a time (less than 1% downtime) can cost more than 3 million dollars per year in lost revenues, user salaries, and server outage costs. In terms of how fault tolerance and disaster recovery are implemented, sites can be described as hot, warm, or cold.

In a **hot site** (or **alternate site**), every computer system and piece of information has a redundant copy. This level of fault tolerance is used when systems must be up 100% of the time. Hot sites are strictly fault-tolerant implementations, not disaster recovery implementations. Of course, you can imagine that these types of systems are costly. To make a system fault-tolerant, you must overcome a failure point as shown in table 13.1.

In a **warm site** (also called a **nearline site**), the network service and data are available most of the time (more than 85% of the time). The data and services are less critical than those in a hot site. With hot-site technologies, all fault-tolerance procedures are automatic and are controlled by the NOS. Warm-site technology requires a little more administrative intervention, but the interventions aren't as expensive as the hot site.

The most cost-effective and most commonly used warm-site technology is a duplicate server. A duplicate server is one currently not being used and is available to replace any server that fails. When the server fails, the administrator installs the new server and restores the data; the network services are

Table 13.1   Common Points of Failures in a Server

Failure Point	Failure Solution
Network hub and network card	Redundant network cards and hubs
Power problems	Uninterruptible power supply (UPS) Redundant power supplies Putting cluster nodes on separate electrical circuits
Disk	Hardware RAID
Other server hardware, such as CPU or memory	Failover clustering
Server software, such as the operating system or specific applications	Failover clustering
Wide area network (WAN) links, such as routers and dedicated lines	Redundant links over the WAN, to provide secondary access to remote connections
Dial-up connection	Multiple modems

available to users with a minimum of downtime. Using a duplicate server is a disaster-recovery method because the entire server is replaced, but in a shorter time than if all the components had to be ordered and configured at the time of the system failure. Note: Corporate networks don't often use duplicate servers, and that's because there are some major disadvantages associated with using them, including keeping a current backup of data on the duplicate server and the fact that you can lose data since the last backup.

A **cold site** does not guarantee server uptime and has little or no fault tolerance. Instead, it relies on efficient disaster-recovery methods to ensure data integrity, especially the backup of the data.

Making backups on a regular basis and storing copies offsite, even with a disaster recovery disks, protects your data, but that doesn't necessarily mean that you can be up and running in a matter of hours if a disaster should strike. Depending on the disaster, you might have to replace a drive, a server, or even the entire office where the server was located. However, there are solutions that can reduce your downtime to a matter of hours, even in the event of a catastrophic disaster. **Secure recovery** refers to an alternate site that contains a replica of all or part of your network. Depending on your budget and the nature of your business, solutions can range from a mirror server running at a site to another site in a completely secure recovery area containing everything you need to keep your business going until you can replace your original equipment. A number of companies specialize in business recovery services. Some are simply hosting services that run mirror servers for you in a protected environment in another city.

13.3   PLANNING DISASTER RECOVERY

Security+ Objective 5.2.3—Disaster-Recovery Plan

A **disaster-recovery plan (DRP)** for a company can be a huge document that contains hundreds of contingencies. When putting together a DRP, there are many items that need to be considered and included. When a disaster occurs, the DRP should specify what actions need to be taken and in what order. Of course, since your organization goes through changes as time goes on, the DRP needs to be constantly reviewed and updated.

To prepare for disaster, you must prepare a disaster-recovery plan. And when developing the disaster-recovery plan, you need to involve stakeholders; all departments need to create recommendations so intelligent choices can be made balancing issues of implementation costs and security. Not involving all departments would result in a flawed disaster recovery plan, which could be worse than no plan at all

The DRP should include a wide range of scenarios including a failure of a single desktop to a failure of a server to an outage of an entire site. It should plan for fire, floods, earthquakes, tornadoes, electrical damage, electrical failure, and terrorist attacks. Depending on the severity of the event, these actions can include:

- Recovery of desktop PCs, servers, network services, LANs, and other systems
- Replacing equipment, furniture, and supplies
- Establishing voice and data communication
- Notifying employees (team leaders and their backups, managers and general employees), clients, customers, suppliers, stockholders, and the news media
- Evacuating a site
- Notifying emergency services
- Establishing a temporary business recovery command center
- Locating temporary facilities to restart your business
- Preliminary and detailed damage assessment
- Recovering or recall of vital records and data
- Handling legal, financial, and insurance issues

A true disaster-recovery plan requires an entire team assembled for each major branch or function of your organization to develop and maintain it. The disaster-recovery team needs to work well together in order to minimize downtime and loss of productivity. If you have a large company, a disaster-recovery plan can take months to prepare.

Creating a DRP requires at least six steps. They are:

1. Exploring the risks
2. Understanding the impact
3. Treating strategies
4. Training for strategy implementation
5. Plan maintenance
6. Documentation

Of course, one of the primary jobs of the administrator is to deal with those disasters and to plan ahead so as to minimize the frequency of the failures and the degree of the failure. To accomplish this, you should always:

1. Establish a backup plan and perform the backing up of data.
2. Document the network so that you and your team can find information quickly about the network.
3. Maintain a log listing all problems and their solutions to be used for determining trends, planning of network and personnel resources, and for easy lookup of solutions when the same problem occurs again.

13.4   RAID

RAID is short for Redundant Array of Inexpensive Disks. It is a category of disk drives that employ two or more drives in combination for fault tolerance and performance. RAID disk drives are used frequently on servers but aren't generally necessary for personal computers. Ideally, you use a RAID system to make sure no data is lost and to recover data from failed disk drivers without shutting your system down.

RAID was originally defined as a memory architecture that uses a subsystem of two or more hard disk drives treated as a single, larger logical drive. The purpose of this proposed architecture was to take advantage of data redundancy inherent in the multiple drive design as well as to capitalize on the lower costs of smaller drives. When RAID was first proposed, it was considerably cheaper to buy five 200 MB hard drives than one 1 GB drive. Of course, today, this is not true anymore, so the current focus for RAID is data integrity and reliability instead of cost saving.

Originally RAID comprised six levels (RAID 0 through RAID 5). See table 13.2. A few more levels have been added to combine the features of other levels. Although RAID 6 follows the general numbering process, most new levels break with the number sequence, usually for marketing reasons. Not all RAID levels are commercially available, and some are supported by only a few products. Only RAID 0, 1, and 5 are supported by Windows Servers, Linux, and NetWare without additional hardware and software from RAID vendors. Those three levels, though, can be supported by a variety of hard disk and controller combinations.

RAID 0 is the base of RAID technology. RAID 0 stripes data across all drives. With striping, all available hard drives are combined into a single large virtual file system, with the file system's blocks arrayed so they are spread evenly across all the drives. For example, if you have three 500 MB hard drives, RAID 0 provides for a 1.5 GB virtual hard drive (sometimes referred to as a volume). When you store files, they are written across all three drives. When a large file, such as a 100 MB multimedia presentation, is saved to the virtual drive, a part of it may be written to the first drive, the next chunk to the second, more to the third, and perhaps more wrapping back to the first drive to start the sequence again. The exact manner in which the chunks of data move from physical drive to physical drive depends on the way the virtual drive has been set up, which includes considering drive capacity and the way in which blocks are allocated on each drive. No parity control is used with RAID 0, therefore, it really is a true form of RAID. RAID 0 does have several advantages, though. Most important is that striping provides some increase in performance through load-balancing.

RAID 1 is known as disk mirroring or disk shadowing. With RAID 1, each hard drive on the system has a duplicate drive that contains an exact copy of the first drive's contents. Since every bit written to the file system is duplicated, data redundancy exists with RAID 1. If one drive in the RAID 1 array fails or develops a problem of any kind (such as a bad sector), the mirror drive can take over and maintain all normal file-system operations while the faulty drive is diagnosed and fixed. RAID 1 also

Table 13.2 Types of RAID

RAID Type	Description
RAID 0—Disk Striping	Data striping is the spreading out of blocks of each file across multiple disks. It offers no fault tolerance, but it increases performance. Level 0 is the fastest and most efficient form of RAID.
RAID 1—Disk Mirroring/Duplexing	Disk mirroring duplicates a partition onto two hard drives. When information is written, it is written to both hard drives simultaneously. It increases performance and provides fault tolerance. Disk duplexing is a form of disk mirroring. Disk mirroring uses two hard drives connected to the same card; disk duplexing uses two controller cards, two cables, and two hard drives.
RAID 2—Disk striping with ECC	Level 2 uses data striping plus ECC to detect errors. It is rarely used today since ECC is embedded in almost all modern disk drives.
RAID 3—ECC stored as parity	Level 3 dedicates one disk to error correction data. It provides good performance and some level of fault tolerance.
RAID 4—Disk striping with large blocks	Level 4 offers no advantages over RAID 5 and does not support multiple simultaneously write operations.
RAID 5—Disk striping with Parity	Raid 5 uses disk striping and includes byte correction on one of the disks. If one disk goes bad, the system will continue to function. After the faulty disk is replaced, the information on the replaced disk can be rebuilt. This system requires at least three drives. It offers excellent performance and good fault tolerance.

includes disk duplexing, which is the same as disk mirroring except the two drives are on different controllers cards so that the drive, controller card, and cable are redundant.

Many RAID 1 disk controllers have software routines that will automatically take a faulty drive offline, run diagnostics on it, and if possible, reformat the drive and copy all data back from the mirror image, all while the file system proceeds as if nothing has happened. Users are usually unaware of faults with RAID 1 controllers. Alert messages can be triggered when a fault occurs.

One big disadvantage of RAID 1 is its use of disks. If you have two 2 GB drives, you can have a total file system of only 2 GB (the other 2 GB is mirrored). You're only getting half the disk space you're paying for, but you do have fully redundant drives. In case of catastrophic failure of a drive, controller, or motherboard, you can remove a mirror drive and boot on another controller or server.

RAID 1 offers an increase in read performance in most implementations, as the controller card allows both drives (primary and mirror) to be read at the same time, resulting in a faster read operation. Write operations are not faster, though, because data must be written to two drives. In many RAID 1 systems that do not use separate drive controllers for the primary and mirror drives, writing can even slow down because the system must perform two complete write operations in sequence.

Implementations of RAID 1 usually require two drives of similar size. If you use a 1.5 GB and a 2 GB drive, for example, the extra 0.5 GB on the second drive is wasted. Some controllers let you combine drives of different sizes, with the extra space used for nonmirrored partitions.

RAID 5 is very similar to RAID 0, but one of the hard drives is used for parity (error-correction) to provide fault tolerance. To increase performance, spread the error-correction drive across all hard drives in the array to avoid the one drive from doing all of the work in calculating the parity bits. RAID 5 is supported by NT 4.0 and most RAID vendors because it is a good compromise between data integrity, speed, and cost. RAID 5 has better performance than RAID 1 (mirroring). RAID 5 usually requires at least three drives, with more drives preferable. Note: The overhead RAID 5 imposes on RAM can be significant, too, so Microsoft recommends at least an additional 16 MB RAM when RAID 5 is used. As with RAID 1, though, drives of disparate capacities may result in a lot of unused disk space because most RAID 5 systems use the smallest drive capacity in the array for all RAID 5 drives. Extra disk space can be used for unstriped partitions, but these are not protected by the RAID system.

Since SCSI drives have command queuing and typically have a higher throughput, SCSI drives are the best choice for RAID systems. According to RAID vendors, SCSI subsystems represent more than 95% of the RAID market. Some RAID systems support hot-swappable drives where a drive can be removed without powering down the system. SCSI controller cards that support RAID through hardware will allow for better performance since they will do many of the calculations that would have been done through the processor as instructed by the software. Lastly, if performance is critical on some systems, I would recommend a system with a RAID controller card that has a relatively large amount of RAM to be used as cache for the controller card.

13.5   REDUNDANT NETWORK CARDS AND HUBS

To make sure that the link that connects to your network has fault tolerance, you have several options. They include:

- Adaptive Load Balancing (ALB)
- Adapter Fault Tolerance (AFT)
- 802.3ad Link Aggregation

Adaptive Load Balancing (ALB) technology can increase server bandwidth up to 800 Mbits/s over Fast Ethernet or 8 Gbits/s over Gigabit Ethernet, by automatically balancing traffic across as many as eight network adapters. Essentially, each additional adapter adds another 100 Mbits/s or 1000 Mbits/s link to the network. Once ALB is configured, all outgoing server traffic will be balanced across the adapter team. Incoming traffic is carried by a single adapter. In most environments, this is a highly effective solution, since server traffic is primarily outbound. Since the distribution of traffic among the adapters is automatic, there is no need to segment or reconfigure the network. The existing IP address of the server is shared by all of the adapters in the server, and traffic is always balanced between them. All of the adapters in a team must be connected to a switch. Note: All adapters in the team should be the same speed. They can be connected to a single switch or hub, or to two or more switches or hubs, as long as they are on the same network segment. In addition, the teamed adapters provide automatic emergency backup links to the network. If one server link goes down, because of a broken cable, a bad switch port, or a failed adapter, the other adapter(s) automatically accept the additional load. There is no interrupt in server operation. Some software and drivers also support a network alert to inform IT staff of the problem.

With two or more adapters installed, Adapter Fault Tolerance (AFT) can be configured to establish an automatic backup link between the server and the network. Should the primary link fail, the secondary link kicks in within milliseconds, in a manner that is transparent to application and users. The redundant link that AFT establishes between the server and the network includes a redundant adapter, a cable, and hub or switch port connection. If there is any problem along the primary link, the secondary link immediately takes over. AFT can also initiate a network alert. When the primary link is fixed, it will automatically revert back to the higher performance link.

Unlike most redundant link technologies, AFT supports mixed-speed teaming using any combination of adapters. With this capability, a relatively inexpensive 100 Mbits/s backup link can be used to safeguard a high-speed Gigabit Ethernet connection. The inexpensive backup may not be able to support the full traffic load as effectively, but it can allow business critical applications to stay online until the higher speed link is fixed.

Link aggregation, also referred to as trunking, is a technique that allows parallel physical links between switches or between a switch and a server to be used simultaneously, multiplying the bandwidth between the devices and to provide fault tolerance. To meet customer requirements for this type of functionality, several companies support proprietary link aggregation schemes. In 2000, IEEE released 802.3ad as an industry standard for link aggregation, which allows for balancing traffic (up to 8 networks cards and 16 Gigabits/s full duplex of bandwidth) among multiple switches from a single server. Different from ALB and AFT, link aggregation requires a switch that supports it.

PCI HotPlug and Active PC developed by Compaq and IBM respectively, allow the adapter to be replaced without interrupting network service. If an adapter fails, AFT automatically moves server traffic onto the redundant link and generates a network alert. Both of these enable you to replace the failed adapter without bringing down the server.

13.6   OVERCOMING POWER PROBLEMS

Security+ Objective 5.3.1—Utilities

When you turn on your PC, you expect the power to be there. Unfortunately, the power that you get from the power company is not always 120-volt AC. The voltage level may drop or increase. While the power supply can handle many of these power fluctuations, other power fluctuations may shut down or damage your computer, corrupt your data, and/or lose any unsaved work.

Studies done by IBM show a typical computer is subject to more than 120 power problems per month. The most common of these are voltage sags. Obvious power problems such as blackouts and lightning make up only 12% of the power problems. American Power Conversion states that data loss caused by power problems occur 45.3% of the time making it the largest cause. Symptoms of bad power can cause frozen computers/keyboards, errors in data transmissions, corrupt or lost data, frequently aborted modem transfers and total failure of a computer or computer component.

13.6.1   Power Irregularities

Power line irregularities can be classified into two categories: **overvoltages** and **undervoltages.** The most dangerous is the overvoltage, which is rated at more than 10% additional voltage than what the power supply is rated. The worst of these is a spike which lasts only a nanosecond but measuring as high as 25,000 volts (normally caused by lightning). A **spike** is sometimes known as a transient. A longer duration overvoltage is called a **surge,** which can stretch into milliseconds. Spikes and surges can visibly damage the electronic components, or cause microdamage, which cannot be seen. Other causes of overvoltage besides lightning is when overburdened power grids switch from one source to another or when a high powered electrical motor tries to grab power. See figure 13.1.

Undervoltages (including total power failure) make up 87% of all power problems. It is when the computer gets less voltage than needed to run properly. Most PCs are designed to withstand prolonged voltage dips of about 20% without shutting down. Power outages and short drops in power typically do not physically damage the computer. Unfortunately, they do result in lost and corrupted data.

Undervoltage can be broken into three categories, sags, brownouts, and blackouts. **Sags,** which usually are not a problem, are very short drops lasting only a few milliseconds. **Brownouts,** on the other hand, last longer than sags and can force the computer to shut down, introduce memory errors and cause unsaved work to be lost. Note: Brownouts or power failures of 200 milliseconds are sufficient to cause power problems with the PC. These can be caused by damaged power lines and equipment which draw massive amounts of power (air conditioners, copy machines, laser printers, and coffee makers). **Blackouts** are total power failures.

13.6.2   Noise

In addition to the overvoltages and the undervoltages on the power lines, the computer may experience electrical noise or radio frequency interference caused by telephones, motors, fluorescent lights, and radio transmitters. Noise can introduce errors into executable programs and files. Note: To limit the change of AC line noise, you should install the computer on its power circuit.

Figure 13.1   Power Irregularities

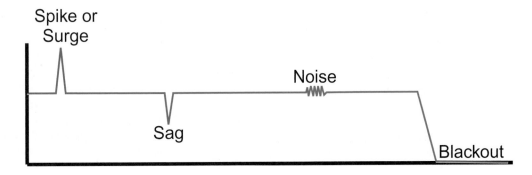

13.6.3   Power Protection Devices

Most of the damage from these voltage fluctuations can be avoided. To protect the computer from overvoltages and undervoltages, several devices can be used. They are surge protectors, line conditioners, standby power supplies, and uninterruptible power supplies.

The most common of these is the **surge protector.** A surge protector is designed to prevent most short duration, high intensity spikes and surges from reaching your PC by absorbing excess voltages.

The most common surge protector uses the metal oxide varistor (MOV). A MOV looks like a brightly-colored plastic-coated disk capacitor. The MOV works by siphoning electricity to ground when the voltage exceeds 200 volts. Consequently, the voltage spike is "clipped." The excess electricity is then converted into heat. Other devices used to suppress overvoltages are gas discharge tubes, pellet arrestors, and coaxial arrestors. The better surge protectors use a combination of these.

When purchasing a surge protector, you should consider the following:

- **Energy absorption**—Surge protectors are rated by the amount of energy that can be absorbed (measured in joules). 200 joules is basic, 400 is good and 600+ is excellent.
- **IEEE 587A voltage let-through**—Underwriters Laboratories has established the UL 1449 standard for surge suppressors. It rates suppressors by the amount of voltage that allows to pass through to the protected equipment. There are three levels of rated protection: 330 V, 400 V, and 500 V. The lower the number, the better the protection.
- **UL listing**—Underwriters Laboratories Inc. is an independent-testing laboratory that certifies electrical equipment specifications. A UL listing indicates that the surge protector meets national electrical code and safety standards.
- **Protection indicator**—An LED indicating if the MOVs are working or not.
- **Circuit breaker or fuse**—Most suppressors will have either a fuse or a resettable circuit breaker, which will blow or trip if there is a short circuit or severe surge that causes excessive current to flow. Breakers are better because fuses, once blown, have to be replaced.
- **Protection guarantee**—Usually an equipment protection guarantee, which says if your equipment is damaged when plugged into the suppressor, the manufacturer will pay to have it repaired or replaced.

Some surge protectors will have site wiring fault lights, which illuminate when there is a wiring fault in the circuit to which the surge protector is connected. This light should be off at all times. In addition, new protectors protect much more than power cables. These may include a RJ-45, RJ-11, or other ports to protect network cards, modems, and the entire system from extremely high surges such as a telephone pole being hit by lightning.

There are several drawbacks to the surge protector. First, it will only protect against overvoltages, not undervoltages. In addition, the life expectancy of a MOV is limited. With every spike, the MOV gets weaker and weaker until it can't protect the PC any more. When buying a surge protector, make sure the surge protector has some kind of indicator (LED light or a beep) to inform you when a surge protector can no longer protect. In addition, you need to be extremely careful when buying a surge protector; make sure its not a device that only gives you extra power connections like an extension cord.

Another type of surge protector is the phone line surge protector. If you have a modem, fax/modem, or fax connection connected in your PC, you should consider getting one. It will prevent surges and spikes, which travel through your telephone lines.

The next level of protection is the **line conditioner.** It uses the inductance of transformers to filter out noise and capacitors (and other circuits) to "fill-in" brownouts. In addition, most line conditioners include surge protection.

The last two forms of protection are based on battery backup systems. They are the **standby power supply (SPS)** and the **uninterruptible power supply (UPS).** See figure 13.2. The standby power supply consists of the battery hooked up parallel to the PC. When the SPS detects a power fluctuation, the system will switch over to the battery. Of course, the SPS requires a small but measurable amount of time to switch over (usually one half of one cycle of the AC current or less than 10 millisecond). Most SPS's will include built-in surge protection devices.

Similar to the standby power supply is the uninterruptible power supply. It differs because the battery is connected in series with the PC. The AC power is connected directly to the battery. Since the battery always provides clean power, the PC is protected against the overvoltages and undervoltages.

Figure 13.2   UPS

For the SPS and UPS, when DC power is sent from the battery, the DC power has to be converted back to AC power before reaching the PC's power supply. Most SPS's and UPS's will generate a sine wave. Note: There are some poorer-quality SPSs and UPSs that generate a square wave instead of a sine wave. These should be avoided.

NOTE: If you do not use a UPS or SPS for long periods of time, you should not discharge the battery. If you do, the battery may lose some of its capacity to store power or may be unable to accept a charge at all. Of course, always check the manufacturer's documentation.

One ideal place in using a UPS is local area networks (LAN) and wide area networks (WAN), which consist of many computers connected together, usually with cable. The computers on the network are divided into servers and workstations. Since the main function of the server is to provide file services (multiple users accessing data files, large databases, and application programs), the servers access disk constantly. If a power disturbance occurs when the file is open or a file is reading or writing, the file can easily become lost or corrupted. If the File Allocation Table is corrupted, it could lead to losing the entire disk. It is probably not cost effective to have UPSs for every PC but it is important that each server has an UPS to help protect against the power-related problems.

Uninterruptible power supplies are usually not designed to keep the PC running for hours without power. Instead, they are usually used to give the user or users enough time to save all files and to properly shut down the PC. In addition, you should not connect laser printers to the UPS since the laser printers have large current demands and can generate line noise.

Most SPSs and UPSs used for servers will have a System Management Port. This is usually a standard serial port or USB port that allows the SPS or UPS to connect to the host computer it is protecting. The host computer runs management software that gathers statistics about the power the SPS or UPS is using and providing. When a power failure occurs, this port is used to signal from the SPS or UPS informing the management software on the host computer that the power to the SPS or UPS has failed. The management software can then initiate a graceful shutdown of the computer including sending out messages to its users to save all of their work and log off the system.

13.6.4   Redundant Power Supplies

One advanced feature available on mission critical computers such as servers is a redundant power supply. The system will have two or more power supplies within the system, each of which is capable of powering the entire system by itself. If for some reason there is a failure in one of the units, the other one will seamlessly take over to prevent the loss of power to the PC. You can usually even replace the damaged unit without taking the machine down. This is called hot swapping, and it is an essential productivity backup for use in servers and other machines used by a number of people. Unfortunately, these types of systems are not cheap.

13.7   CLUSTERING

Clustering is connecting two or more computers, known as nodes, together in such a way that they behave like a single computer. It is used for parallel processing, for load balancing, and for fault tolerance. The computers that form the cluster are physically connected by cable and are logically connected by cluster software. As far as the user is concerned, the cluster appears as a single system to end-users.

Network Load Balancing clusters distribute client connections over multiple servers. Internet clients access the cluster using a single IP address (or a set of addresses for a multihomed host). The clients are unable to distinguish the cluster from a single server. Server programs do not identify that they are running in a cluster. However, a Network Load Balancing cluster differs significantly from a single host running a single server program, because it provides uninterrupted service even if a cluster host fails. The cluster also can respond more quickly to client requests than a single host (for load-balanced ports).

In a fail-over configuration, two or more computers serve as functional backups for each other. If one should fail, the other automatically takes over the processing normally performed by the failed system, thus eliminating downtime. If the server is to share common data, the cluster servers are connected to at least one shared SCSI bus with a storage device connected to both servers, and at least one storage device that is not shared. Of course, fail-over clusters are highly desirable for supporting mission-critical applications.

Storage area network (SAN) is a high-speed subnetwork of shared storage devices. A SAN's architecture works in a way that makes all storage devices available to all servers on a LAN. If an individual application in a server cluster fails (but the node does not), the cluster service will typically try to restart the application on the same node. If that fails, it moves the application's resources and restarts them on another node of the server cluster. This process is called fail-over.

Network-attached storage (NAS) is what many network administrators are using to replace file servers. NAS is a smaller network device with a network card and a large hard disk drive. By removing storage access and its management from the department server, both application programming and files can be served faster because they are not competing for the same processor resources. The network-attached storage device is attached to a local area network (typically, an Ethernet network) and assigned an IP or IPX address. File requests are mapped by the main server to the NAS file server. Network-attached storage consists of hard disk storage, including multi-disk RAID systems, and software for configuring and mapping file locations to the network-attached device. NAS can be part of a SAN. While low cost may be a reason to choose a NAS, NAS devices are not upgradeable.

NAS devices are easy to manage and security and access are easy to configure. It also takes only minutes to set up a Network Attached Storage device, compared to several hours it takes to install and configure a file server.

13.8   TAPE DRIVES

Tape drives read and write to a long magnetic tape. They are relatively inexpensive and offer large storage capacities, making tape backup drives ideal for backing up hard drives on a regular basis. To back up a hard drive, you just insert a tape into the drive, start a backup software package, and select the drive/files you want to backup and it will be done. If a drive or file is lost, the backup software can be used to restore the data from the tape to the hard drive. If the right tape drive and backup software is chosen, the drive could automatically backup the hard drive at night, when it is being used least. The only thing that you would have to remember is to replace the tape each day. Note: Since tapes fail, there have been times when people think they selected a drive or file to be backed up only to find that they have a blank tape when disaster occurs. Therefore, it is important to occasionally test the tapes by choosing a non-important file and restore it back to the hard drive.

The tape player drags a magnetic tape across a head, and the player reads the information from the magnetic tape. The computer may report a tape error if the tape head is dirty. Cleaning the tape drive will normally resolve this problem. If cleaning the tape drive is not effective, then you should try using a new tape. You should replace the tape drive if these troubleshooting attempts fail. If the system reports that no tape drive is present, be sure that the drive is on and plugged in.

13.8.1   The Tape Media

Before the IBM, magnetic tapes were used on older mainframes as a primary storage device and a backup storage device. Eventually the magnetic tape evolved into the floppy disk followed by the hard drive. As the IBM PC was introduced, it included a drive port for a cassette tape storage device.

Floppy disks, which are probably the closest to a tape, consist of a Mylar platter coated with a magnetic substance to hold magnetic fields. In addition, floppy disks are random-access devices. This means that no matter where the data is located on the disk, the read/write heads can move directly to the proper sector and start to read or write.

Instead of using Mylar platters, tapes use a long polyester substrate, which is coated with a layer of magnetic material. Unlike a floppy disk, a tape stores and retrieves data sequentially. Therefore, when a file needs to be retrieved, it has to start at the beginning of the tape and read each area of the tape before it gets to the correct file. Since it takes time to find the appropriate file, tapes are completely inappropriate as a PC's primary storage device.

Tapes come in different sizes and shapes and offer different speeds and capacities. As a result, several standards have been developed including the Quarter-Inch Cartridge (QIC) and the Digital Audio Tape (DAT).

13.8.2   Recording Methods

Tapes are divided into parallel tracks across the tape. The number of tracks vary with the drive and the standard it follows. The data is either recorded parallel, serpentine, or helical scan.

Parallel recording spreads the data throughout the different tracks. An example is if a tape was divided into 9 tracks, a byte of information with parity could be spread out through all 9 tracks (one bit per track). Newer tape systems may lay 18 or 36 tracks across the tape allowing 2 or 4 bytes of information. While the tape offered high transfer rates, data retrieval time was slow because it might have to fast-forward across the entire tape before retrieving the data. In addition, the read/write assembly is quite complicated since it has to consist of several pole and gaps, one for each track. Unfortunately, the complexity also drives the cost of the drive up.

Most PC tape systems use serpentine recording. While the tape is still divided into tracks, it will write the data onto one track, reach the end of the track, move to the next track, and write to the second track. It will keep repeating this process until it runs out of tracks. A serpentine tape can access data quickly by moving its head between the different tracks. Since the read/write assembly requires only one pole/gap, the drives are cheaper.

The newest method of recording is helical scan. Much like a VCR read/write head, tape backup drives with helical scan use read/write heads mounted at an angle on a cylindrical drum. The tape is partially wrapped around the drum. As the tape slides across the drum, the read/write heads rotate. As each head approaches the tape, the heads take swipes at the tape, reading or writing the data. The tape is moved only slightly between swipes allowing data to be packed very tightly. In addition, since each head is skewed slightly from the others, the heads respond well to signals written in the same orientation, but not well to the other signals. Therefore, blank spaces are not needed. Lastly, if two more heads are added to the drum, data can be read immediately after it was written. Therefore, if any errors were detected, the data can be rewritten immediately on the next piece of tape.

13.8.3   Tape Standards

Tapes come in different sizes and shapes and offer different speeds and capacities. As a result, several standards have been developed including the Quarter-Inch Cartridge (QIC) and the Digital Audio Tape (DAT).

In 1972, 3M company introduced the first quarter-inch tape cartridge (QIC) designed for data storage. The cartridge measured $6'' \times 4'' \times 5/8''$. Although the cartridge became the standard, each tape drive manufacturer used different encoding methods, varied the number of tracks and varied the data density on the tape, causing all kind of compatibility problems. See figure 13.3.

As a result, in 1982, a group of manufacturers formed the QIC Committee to standardize tape drive construction and application. The full-size quarter-inch cartridge standardized by the QIC Committee is also referred to as the DC 6000 cartridge. The DC stands for Data Cartridge.

Figure 13.3   A DAT and DC QIC Tape

Table 13.3   QIC Data Cartridges

QIC Standard Number	Capacity Without Compression	Tracks	Interface	Original Adoption Date
QIC-24-DC	45 MB or 60 MB[1]	9	SCSI or QIC-02	4-83
QIC-120-DC	125 MB	15	SCSI or QIC-02	10-85
QIC-150-DC	150 MB or 250 MB[1]	18	SCSI or QIC-02	2-87
QIC-525-DC	320 MB or 525 MB[1]	26	SCSI or SCSI-2	5-89
QIC-1350-DC	1.35 GB	30	SCSI-2	5-89
QIC-1000-DC	1.0 GB	30	SCSI or SCSI-2	10-90
QIC-6000C	6 GB	96	SCSI-2	2-91
QIC-2100-DC	2.1 GB	30	SCSI-2	6-91
QIC-5010-DC	13 GB	144	SCSI-2	2-92
QIC-2GB-DC	2.0 GB	42	SCSI-2	6-92
QIC-5GB-DC	5 GB	44	SCSI-2	12-92
QIC-4GB-DC	4 GB	45	SCSI-2	3-93
QIC-5210-DC	25 GB	144	SCSI-2	8-95

[1]Depending on length of tape.

The first tape that the QIC committee approved was the QIC-24, which used serpentine recording. It had nine tracks and a density of 8,000 bits per inch giving the total storage capacity of 60 MB. It achieved 90 inches per second and offered 720 kilobits per second with the QIC-02 interface.

Throughout the years, the data density was increased and more tracks were added. The last QIC-1000-DC packed 30 tracks across the tape at 36,000 bits per inch allowing up to 1.2 GB per tape cartridge. Its speed was also increased 2.8 megabits per second. Yet, the QIC-1000-DC drives could read previous QIC tapes.

By 1989, the QIC committee revamped the original QIC standard by using 1,7 RRL encoding and higher coercivity. This allowed higher bit density, a high number of tracks, and a faster transfer rates. By 1995, the QIC introduced the QIC-5210-DC, which had 144 tracks and 76,200 bits per inch allowing for 25 GB. See table 13.3.

Table 13.4   QIC Minicartridges

QIC Standard Number	Capacity Without Compression	Tracks	Interface	Original Adoption Date
QIC-40-MC	40 MB or 60 MB[1]	20	Floppy or optional card	6-86
QIC-80-MC	80 MB or 120 MB[1]	28	Floppy or optional card	2-88
QIC-128- MC	86 MB or 128 MB	32	SCSI or QIC	5-89
QIC-3030-MC	555 MB	40	SCSI-2 or QIC	4-91
QIC-3020-MC	500 MB	40	Floppy or IDE	6-91
QIC-3070-MC	4 GB	144	SCSI-2 or QIC	2-92
QIC-3010-MC	255 MB	40	Floppy or IDE	6-93
QIC-3040-MC	840 MB	42/52	SCSI-2 or QIC	12-93
QIC-3080-MC	1.6 GB	60	SCSI-2 or QIC	1-94
QIC-3110-MC	2 GB	48	SCSI-2 or QIC	1-94
QIC-3230-MC	15.5 GB	180	SCSI-2 or QIC	6-95
QIC-3095-MC	4 GB	72	SCSI-2 or QIC	12-95

[1]Depending on length of tape.

Since the full-size QIC is too large to fit into a drive bay, the QIC committee created the mini-cartridge, which was 3.25″ × 2.5″ × 1.59″. The minicartridges are also referred to as the DC 2000 cartridges.

The QIC-40-MC was the first standard adopted. It fit into the 5.25 drive bay, and it connected to the computer by using the floppy drive controller. Since floppy disk drives use MFM encoding, so did the QIC-40-MC. Different from previous tapes, QIC specified the format of the data on the tape, which included how sectors were assigned to files and FAT to list bad sectors. This requires the tapes to be formatted which takes time to complete. Consequently, you could buy tapes formatted or unformatted. Another advantage was the tapes could be accessed randomly. Although the tape had to be moved to the proper sector, it did not have to read each file sequentially although it did have to move the tape. See table 13.4.

In 1995, a number of tape and drive manufacturers, including Conner, Iomega, HP, 3M, and Sony, introduced Travan technology. Instead of using the standard QIC cartridge, the cartridge measured 0.5″ × 3.6″ × 2.8″. The front was smaller, which was inserted into the drive, while the back was larger to contain the tape spools. The different sizes allowed longer tapes and more data capacities. In addition, the Travan drive accepts standard DC2000 cartridges and QIC-Wide cartridges. See table 13.5.

The newest type of tape is the Digital Audio Tape (DAT), which uses the same technology as VCR tapes (helical scan). The 8 mm DAT tapes allow capacities up to 35 GB or larger. The DAT standard has primarily been developed and marketed by Hewlett-Packard. HP chairs the DDS (Digital Data Storage) Manufacturers Group, which led the development of the DDS standards.

Data is not recorded on the tape in the MFM or RLL formats but rather bits of data received by the tape drive are assigned numerical values, or digits. Then these digits are translated into a stream of electronic pulses that are placed on the tape. Later, when information is being restored to a computer system from the tape, the DAT tape drive translates these digits back into binary bits that can be stored on the computer.

Digital Data Storage (DDS) tapes is currently the newest standard of the digital audio tape. DDS-3 can hold 24 GB (or equivalent) of over 40 CD-ROMs) and supports data transfer rates of 2 MBps/sec and some drives can support up to 40 GBs or larger. It is slightly larger than a credit card. In a DDS

Table 13.5   Travan Technology

	TR-1	TR-2	TR-3	TR-4	TR-5
Capacity: Native Compressed	400 MB 800 MB	800 MB 1.6 GB	1.6 GB 3.2 GB	4 GB 8 GB	10 GB 20 GB
DTR: Minimum Maximum	62.5 KBps 125 KBps	62.5 KBps 125 KBps	125 KBps 250 KBps	60 MB/min 70 MB/min	60 MB/min 110 MB/min
Tracks	36	50	50	72	108
Data Density	14,700 ftpi	22,125 ftpi	44,250 ftpi	50,800 ftpi	50,800 ftpi
Compatibility	QIC 80 (R/W) QIC 40 (R only)	QIC 3010 (R/W) QIC 80 (R only)	QIC 3010/ QIC 3020 (R/W) QIC 80 (R only)	QIC 3080/ QIC 3095 (R/W) QIC 3020 (R only)	QIC 3220 (R/W) TR-4 QIC 3095 (R only)

Table 13.6   DDS Drives

Standard	Capacity	Max. DTR
DDS	2 GB	55 KBps
DDS-1	2/4 GB	0.55/1.1 MBps
DDS-2	4/8 GB	0.55/1.1 MBps
DDS-3	12/24 GB	1.1/2.2 MBps
DDS-4	20/40 GB	2.4/4.8 MBps

Table 13.7   DLT Tapes

Standard	Capacity (n/c)	Interface	Maximum DTR
DLT2000	15/30 GB	SCSI	2.5 MBps
DLT4000	20/40 GB	SCSI	3 MBps
DLT7000	35/70 GB	SCSI	20 MBps

drive, the tape barely creeps along, requiring about three seconds to move an inch. The head drum, spins rapidly at 2,000 revolutions per minute, putting down 1,869 tracks across a linear inch of tape which allows 61 kilobits per inch. The main advantage of the DAT is its access speed and capacity. The standard DDS protocols are shown in table 13.6, all of which are backward compatible.

One of the newest tapes is the DLT (Digital Linear Tape). Designed for high-capacity, high-speed and highly reliable backup. DLTs are ½"wide, has capacities of 35 to 70 GB (or more) compressed and data transfer rate of 5 to 10 MBps/sec or more. Unfortunately, the drives are quite expensive and are used primarily for network server backup. See table 13.7.

Table 13.8 SDLT Tapes

	SDLT 220	SDLT 320	SDLT 640	SDLT 1280	SDLT 2400
Native Capacity	110 GB	160 GB	320 GB	640 GB	1.2 TB
Compressed Capacity (2:1 compression)	220 GB	320 GB	640 GB	1.28 TB	2.4 TB
Native DTR	11 MBps	16 MBps	32 MBps	50+ MBps	100+ MBps
Compressed DTR	22 MBps	32 MBps	64 MBps	100+ MBps	200+ MBps
Media	SDLT I Ultra2 SCSI	SDLT I Ultra2 SCSI	SDLT II Ultra 320 SCSI	SDLT III	SDLT IV
Interfaces	LVD HVD	Ultra160 SCSI	Fibre channel	TBD	TBD
Date	Q1 2001	Q1 2002	Q3 2003	Q1 2005	

Table 13.9 8-mm Tapes

Standard	Capacity (n/c)	Interface	Maximum DTR
Standard 8 mm	3.5/7GB	SCSI	32 MB/min
Standard 8 mm	5/10GB	SCSI	60 MB/min
Standard 8 mm	7/14GB	SCSI	60 MB/min
Standard 8 mm	7/14GB	SCSI	120 MB/min
Mammoth	20/40GB	SCSI	360 MB/min

One of the most significant of the new formats is the next generation of Digital Linear Tape (DLT), otherwise known as Super DLT. This is important because developer Quantum accounted for around 80% of the tape drive market by early 1999. Drives based on Super DLT technology will far exceed the 35GB native capacity of the DLT tape IV format—with which it aims to be backwards compatible.

Using a combination of optical and magnetic recording techniques known as Laser Guided Magnetic Recording (LGMR) Super DLT uses lasers to more precisely align the recording heads. At the core of LGMR is an optically assisted servo system referred to as Pivoting Optical Servo (POS). This combines high-density magnetic read/write data recording with laser servo guiding. Designed for high duty cycle applications, the POS has a much lower sensitivity to external influences, which allows a much higher track density than is possible with other tape systems. The POS system decreases manufacturing costs and increases user convenience by eliminating the need for preformatting the tape. Furthermore, 10 to 20% more capacity is gained by deploying the optical servo on the unused backside of the media, making the entire recording surface available for actual data.

As indicated by table 13.8, the ultimate goal is to cram up to 1.2 TB of uncompressed data onto a single cartridge with transfer rates rising to an eventual 100 MBps uncompressed. Initial products, however, offer a more modest 110 GB with sustained data transfer rates of 11 MBps in native mode.

8 mm tape technology was originally designed for the video industry. Its original purpose was to transfer high-quality color images to tape for storage and retrieval. Now 8 mm technology has been adopted by the computer industry as a reliable way to store large amounts of computer data. Similar to DAT but with generally greater capacities, 8 mm also employs helical scan technology. A drawback to the helical scan system is the complicated tape path. Because the tape must be pulled from a cartridge and wrapped tightly round the spinning read/write cylinder, a great deal of stress is placed on the tape. See table 13.9.

There are two major protocols, utilizing different compression algorithms and drive technologies, but the basic function is the same. Exabyte Corporation sponsors standard 8mm and Mammoth while Seagate and Sony represent a new 8mm technology known as Advanced Intelligent Tape (AIT).

Exabyte has been a leader in the tape storage industry for more than a decade, pioneering the use of 8-mm tape for backup, incorporating Sony's camcorder-based mechanisms into over 1.5 million tape drives. While camcorder-based mechanisms are adequate for low duty cycle applications, it is less appropriate for today's demanding server-based applications. Introduced in 1996, Mammoth is a more advanced and reliable technology and represents Exabyte's response to the requirements of this mid-range server market.

Mammoth features an Exabyte-designed and manufactured deck with 40% fewer parts than previous 8-mm drives and specifically designed to improve reliability by reducing tape wear and tension variation. A solid aluminum deck casting provides the extra accuracy and rigidity needed to maintain tight tolerances. The casting shields the internal elements from dust and contamination and directs heat away from the tape path. A three-point shock-mount system isolates the casting from the sheet-metal housing, providing protection from external forces. With seven custom application specific integrated circuits (ASICs), Mammoth calibrates itself regularly, searches for and reports any errors.

The AIT recording technology today offers uncompressed capacities including 25 GB, 35 GB, 50 GB and 100 GB, while showing scalability to a 6th generation product with an uncompressed capacity of up to 800 GB (up to 2 TB compressed), all using the compact 8-mm cartridge form-factor. The higher compression specifications for capacity and performance for the AIT family are achieved through the incorporation of the Adaptive Lossless Data Compression (ALDC) technology, which delivers an average 2.6 to 1 compression ratio—significantly more than some competing products. See table 13.10.

Advanced Intelligent Tape (AIT) was the first multisourced tape standard targeted at the midrange server market, which is typically characterized by systems that support 2 to 129 users in a commercial environment. Several breakthroughs make this possible including stronger, thinner media that is more stable and has better coatings than previously available, new head technologies, higher levels of integration and a unique Memory-In-Cassette (MIC) feature. The result is multi-Gigabyte, high-performance tape drive systems with very low frequencies of error that are perfect for tape libraries and robotic applications associated with midrange systems backup.

The most unique feature of the AIT format remains Sony's innovative Memory-In-Cassette (MIC) drive interface system. In the AIT-2 this consists of a 64-Kbit memory chip built into the data cartridge. The data contained on chip includes the tape's system log, search map, and other user-definable information, allowing data to be accessed immediately no matter what section of the tape is being accessed. The ability of the MIC to support multiple partitions and multiple load points drastically reduces the average time to access data to fewer than 20 seconds, compared to an average of over 100 seconds for conventional, competing technologies.

Table 13.10   AIT Formats

	AIT-1	AIT-2	AIT-3	S-AIT
Native Capacity	35 GB	50 GB	100 GB	500 GB
Compressed Capacity	90 GB	130 GB	26 GB	1.3 TB
Native DTR	4 MBps	6 MBps	12 MBps	30 MBps
Compressed DTR	10 MBps	15.6 MBps	31.2 MBps	78 MBps
Form Factor	3.5 in.	3.5 in.	3.5 in.	5.25 in.
Media Type	8-mm AME	8-mm AME	8-mm AME	1/2-in. AME
MTBF (hours)	300,000	300,000	400,000	500,000

A key factor in the capabilities of AIT technology is the use of the extremely durable and field-proven Advanced Metal Evaporated (AME) tape technology, and AIT-2 uses Sony's latest formulation of AME media providing the patented Diamond Like Carbon (DLC) coating with a higher output metalization layer. The consequent benefits are an extremely long head life and one able to withstand thousands of media uses, in a system capable of providing high density recording in a compact form factor.

In 2001 Sony announced a Write Once Read Many (WORM) variation of its AIT-2 technology format, thereby bringing advanced data security to the 3.5 in. form-factor. The additional security against inadvertent or malicious deletion or alteration of data make the format particularly suited for the archival of financial, securities, government, medical, and insurance data. The following table compares the family of AIT formats, including the S-AIT format which is expected to reach the market by the end of 2002.

13.9   BACKUP

Security+ Objective 5.2.1—Backups

Security+ Objective 5.2.1.1—Off-Site Storage

Security+ Objective 5.3.3—Backups

Data are the raw facts, numbers, letters, or symbols that the computer processes into meaningful information. Examples of data include a letter to a company or a client, a report for your boss, a budget proposal of a large project, or an address book of your friends and business associates. Whatever the data is, it can be saved (or written to disk) so that it can be retrieved at any time, it can be printed on paper, or it can be sent to someone else over the telephone lines.

Data stored on a computer or stored on the network is vital to the users and probably the company. The data represents hours of work and its data is sometimes irreplaceable. Data loss can be caused by many things including hardware failure, viruses, user error, and malicious users. When disaster occurs, the best method to recovery data is back up, back up, back up. When disaster has occurred and the system does not have a backup of its important files, it is often too late to recover the files.

A **backup** of a system is to have an extra copy of data and/or programs. As a technician, consultant, or support person, you need to emphasize at every moment to back up on servers and client systems. In addition, it is recommended that the clients save their data files to a server so that you have a single, central location to back up. This may go as far as selecting and installing the equipment, doing the backup or training other people in doing the backup. When doing all of this, be sure to select the equipment and method that will assure that the backup will be completed on a regular basis. Remember that if you have the best equipment and software but no one completes the backup, the equipment and software are wasted.

NOTE: The best method for data protection is back up, back up, back up.

When developing for a backup, three steps should be followed. They are:

1. Developing a backup plan.
2. Sticking to the backup plan.
3. Testing the backup.

When developing a backup plan, you must consider the following:

1. What equipment will be used?
2. How much data needs to be backed up?
3. How long will it take to do the backup?
4. How often must the data be backed up?
5. When will the backup take place?
6. Who will do that backup?

Whatever equipment, person, and method is chosen, you must make sure that the backup will be done. If you choose the best equipment, the best software, and the brightest person, and the backup is not done for whatever reason, you wasted your resources, and you put your data at risk.

Table 13.11   Types of Backup

Normal/Full	The full backup will back up all files selected and shut off the archive file attribute indicating the file has been backed up.
Incremental	An incremental backup will back up the files selected if the archive file attribute is on (files since the last full or incremental backup). After the file has been backed up, it will shut off the file attribute indicating that the file has been backed up. Note: You should not mix incremental and differential backups.
Differential	A differential backup will back up the files selected if the archive file attribute is on (files since the last full backup). Different from the incremental backup, it does not shut off the archive attribute. Note: You should not mix incremental and differential backups.

Backups can be done with floppy disks, extra hard drives (including network drives), compact disk drives, tape drives, and other forms of removable media. Probably the best method of backing up of files would be tape drives. A tape drive can store 20 or more Gigabytes.

Question:

How often should the backup be done?

Answer:

How often the backup is done depends on the importance of the data. If you have many customers loaded into a database, which is constantly changed or you have files that represent the livelihood of your business, you should back them up everyday. If there are a few letters that get sent throughout the week with nothing vitally important, you can back up once a week.

All types of backups can be broken into the following categories. See table 13.11.

Some vendors also recognize another type of backup called copy. The copy backup is a normal backup but it does not shut off the archive attribute. This is typically used to back up the system before you make a major change to the system. The archive attribute is not shut off so that your normal backup procedures are not affected.

Example 13.1:

You decide to back up the entire hard drive once a week on Friday. You decide to use the full backup method. Therefore, you perform a full backup every Friday. If the hard drive goes bad, you use the last backup to restore the hard drive.

Example 13.2:

You decide to back up the entire hard drive once a week on Friday. You decide to use the incremental method. Therefore, you perform a full backup week 1. This will shut off all of the archive attributes, indicating that all of the files have been backed up. Week 2, week 3, and week 4, you perform incremental backups using different tape or disk. Since the incremental backup turns off the archive attribute, it backs up only new files and changed files. Therefore, all 4 backups make up the entire backup. It is much quicker to back up a drive using an incremental backup than a full backup. Of course, if the hard drive fails, you must restore backup #1, backup #2, backup #3, and backup # 4 to restore the entire hard drive.

Example 13.3:

You decide to back up the entire hard once a week on Friday. You decide to use the differential method. Therefore, you perform a full backup week 1. This will shut off all of the archive attributes, indicating that all of the files have been backed up. Week 2, week 3, and week 4, you perform differential backups using a different tape or disk. Since the differential backup does not turn off the archive attribute, it backs up the new files and the changed files since the last full backup. Therefore, the full backup and the last differential backup make up the entire backup. It is much quicker to back up a drive using a differential backup than a full backup but slower than an incremental backup. If the hard drive fails, you must restore backup #1 and the last differential to restore the entire hard drive.

The worst time to find out if a backup did not work is when your computer crashes and you have to restore your data just to find out that backups are blank or corrupted. Therefore, after the backups are complete, you should check to see if the backups actually worked. This can be done by picking a nonessential file and restoring it to the hard drive. This helps discover if the backups are empty or a backup/restore device is faulty.

You should keep more than one backup. Tapes and disks do fail. One technique is to rotate through three sets of backups. If you perform a full backup once a week, you would then use three sets of backup tapes or disks. During week 1, you would use tape/disk #1. During week 2, you would use tape/disk #2 and during week 3, you would use tape/disk #3. Week four, you start over and use tape/disk #1. If you have to restore a hard drive and the tape or disk fails, you can always go to the tape or disk from the week before. In addition, you would perform monthly backups and store them elsewhere (best place would be offsite). You would be surprised how many times a person loses a file but may not know for several weeks. If the data is important enough, you may consider keeping a backup set in a fireproof safe offsite.

When a system is initially installed and when you make any major changes to the system's configuration, it is always recommended to make two backups before proceeding. This way, if anything goes wrong, you have the ability to restore everything back to the way it was before the changes. The reason for the two backups is tapes have been known to go back on occasion. After the backup is complete, you need to store the backup media in a safe place, and this safe place must be secure.

Offsite storage is important, to protect the organization's data from disasters that affect the immediate area of the network operations center. The purpose of off-site storage is to put a backup of your data in a location that is not likely to be affected by an event in the area in which the servers are located. This way, even if your operations center is rendered inaccessible because flood, etc., you can still get to a copy of your data and business can continue.

Offsite storage can be found in a number of different forms. A trusted backup operator can take home CD-RW or tape. A number of firms offer backup via remote access by either direct dial with a modem or over the Internet. Companies that want media picked up for safe storage can enlist the services of firms specializing in offsite storage.

Some places use the Grandfather, Father, Son (GFS) backup rotation, which requires 21 tapes based on a 5-day rotation. Each month, you create a grandfather backup, which is stored permanently offsite, never to be reused. Each week, you create a full weekly backup (Father) and each day, you create a differential or incremental backup (Son).

After completing a backup, you should properly label the tape or disk before removing the tape or disk and then store the tape and disk to a secure, safe place. In addition, you should keep a log of what backups have been done, especially if you need to rebuild the server, the log will keep track of what was backed up and when it was backed up. It will also let you know if someone is forgetting to do the backup.

13.10   FIRE AND WATER

Security+ Objective 5.1.3.4—Fire Suppression

Although fires don't usually occur with computers, you should know how to put out a fire. There are three major classes of fire extinguishers. Class A is used for wood and paper, Class B is used for flammable liquids, and Class C is used for electrical fires. Since computers are electrical devices, you should use a Class C or an ABC-rated fire extinguisher. Of course, you should not use water to put out an electrical fire. In addition, when you have any kind of computer, you should also look for other hazards that may cause you problems. For example, if you have leaky tiles, which indicate a leaking ceiling, or the room that uses a water sprinkler system.

For large installation, a fire detection and suppression system should be mandatory in the server room. The three main types of fire detection systems are heat-sensing, flame-sensing, and smoke-sensing. The two primary types of fire suppression systems are water sprinkler systems (including wet pipe, dry pipe, deluge, and preaction) and gas discharge systems (carbon dioxide CO_2, soda acid, and Halon).

Since water does not mix well with electricity and electronic components, the fire suppression system should be a gas discharge system. In the event of a fire, these systems flood the room with an inert gas, displacing the oxygen that the fire needs to burn. This puts the fire out quickly and prevents damage to the electronic equipment with water or foam. Of course, these systems also displace the oxygen that people need to breathe, so evacuation alarms and emergency air supplies should also be part of the system. Note: Halon compounds are not a viable option these days because of the damage that it does to the ozone layer. Acceptable replacements include FM-200, CEA-410 or CEA-308, NAF-S-III, FE-13, Argon or Argonite, and Inergen.

13.11   HEAT AND HUMIDITY

One of the biggest enemies of the PC, particularly semiconductor circuits, is heat buildup. Heat is generated by a current flow against electrical resistance and whenever an element of a computer circuit changes logical states. Inside the case, heat cannot escape and builds up, driving up the temperature. Heat causes the circuit's life span to shorten, which will lead to computer failure. Therefore, keeping a system cool means prolonging its life.

In the IBM PC, to keep the PC cool, ventilation holes in the case were added to let the heat out. When setting up a PC, remember to allow good ventilation and not to block or restrict the ventilation holes. The ventilation slots in the case should have at least three feet free space. Additionally, if you run your power supply close to its full capacity or exceed it, the power supply tends to overheat.

Today, most PCs produce heat faster then the heat escaping through the ventilation holes. Therefore, the PC needed some active cooling that will force the heat from the circuits. This was accomplished by adding a fan to the power supply, which circulated the air around the case. Note: To ensure adequate cooling in a computer system, you should always keep the case closed and the card blockoff plates (the plates that cover an expansion card hole in the back of the computer when an expansion slot is not being used) are in place, so that the airflow within the case is maintained.

Heating, ventilation, and air conditioning (HVAC) systems maintain the proper environment for computers and personnel. The ideal temperature range for computer equipment is between 50 and 80°F (10 to 26°C). At temperatures as low as 100°F (38°C), magnetic storage media can be damaged.

The ideal humidity range for computer equipment is between 40–60 percent. Higher humidity causes condensation and corrosion. Lower humidity increases the potential for electrostatic electricity (ESD).

Doors and side panels on computer equipment racks should be kept closed to ensure proper airflow for cooling and ventilation. Heating and cooling systems should be properly maintained and air filters cleaned regularly to reduce dust contamination and fire hazards.

Ideally, HVAC equipment should be dedicated, controlled, and monitored. If the systems aren't dedicated or independently controlled, proper liaison with the building manager is necessary to ensure that escalation procedures are effective and understood. Monitoring systems should alert the appropriate personnel when operating thresholds are exceeded.

WHAT YOU NEED TO KNOW

Security+ Objective 5.1.3.4—Fire Suppression

1. Since computers are electrical devices, you should use a Class C or an ABC-rated fire extinguisher.
2. You should not use water to put out an electrical fire.
3. In addition, when you have any kind of computer, you should also look for other hazards that may cause you problems. For example, if you have leaky tiles, which indicate a leaking ceiling, or the room that uses a water sprinkler system.

4. For large installation, a fire detection and suppression system should be mandatory in the server room.

Security+ Objective 5.2—Disaster Recovery

1. One of your primary jobs as the administrator is to deal with those disasters and to plan ahead as to minimize the frequency of the failures and the degree of the failure.
2. Disaster recovery is the ability to get a system functional after a total system failure in the least amount of time.

Security+ Objective 5.2.1—Backups

Security+ Objective 5.2.1.1—Offsite Storage

Security+ Objective 5.3.3—Backups

1. Tape drives read and write to a long magnetic tape. They are relatively inexpensive and offer large storage capacities making tape backup drives ideal for backing up hard drives on a regular basis.
2. To back up a hard drive, you just insert a tape into the drive, start a backup software package, and select the drive/files you want to back up and it will be done.
3. If a drive or file is lost, the backup software can be used to restore the data from the tape to the hard drive.
4. A backup of a system is to have an extra copy of data and/or programs.
5. The best method for data protection is back up, back up, back up.
6. The three main types of backups are full backup, incremental backup, and differential backup.
7. The worst time to find out if a backup did not work is when your computer crashes and you have to restore your data just to find out that backups are blank or corrupted.
8. After the backups are complete, you should check to see if the backups actually worked. This can be done by picking a nonessential file and restoring it to the hard drive.
9. You should keep more than one backup.
10. One technique is to rotate through three sets of backups.
11. Offsite storage is important, to protect the organization's data from disasters that affect the immediate area of the network operations center.
12. The purpose of offsite storage is to put a backup of your data in a location that is not likely to be affected by an event in the area in which the servers are located.

Security+ Objective 5.2.2—Secure Recovery

1. Secure recovery refers to an alternate site that contains a replica of all or part of your network.

Security+ Objective 5.2.2.1—Alternate Sites

1. In a hot site (or alternate site), every computer system and piece of information has a redundant copy. This level of fault tolerance is used when systems must be up 100% of the time.
2. In a warm site (also called a nearline site), the network service and data are available most of the time (more than 85% of the time). The data and services are less critical than those in a hot site.
3. Warm-site technology requires a little more administrative intervention, but they aren't as expensive as the hot site.
4. The most cost effective and most commonly used warm-site technology is a duplicate server.
5. A cold site does not guarantee server uptime and has little or no fault tolerance. Instead, it relies on efficient disaster recovery methods to ensure data integrity, especially the backup of the data.

Security+ Objective 5.2.3—Disaster Recovery Plan

1. The idea behind business continuity management is to have a comprehensive plan worked out in advance that specifies what has to be done to keep the business operational, who will do what when the disaster occurs, and how replacement materials will be obtained.
2. A disaster recovery plan (DRP) for a company can be a huge document that contains hundreds of contingencies.
3. When a disaster occurs, the DRP should specify what actions need to be taken and in what order. Of course, since your organization goes through changes as time goes on, the DRP needs to be constantly reviewed and updated.
4. A true disaster recover plan requires an entire team assembled for each major branch or function or your organization to develop and maintain it.

Security+ Objective 5.3—Business Continuity

1. The continued survival of a business depends on its continued operation. When a business stops operating for any reason, it loses credibility and income.

Security+ Objective 5.3.1—Utilities

1. When you turn on your PC, you expect the power to be there. Unfortunately, the power that you get from the power company is not always 120 volt AC.
2. While the power supply can handle many of these power fluctuations, other power fluctuations may shut down or damage your computer, corrupt your data and/or loose any unsaved work.
3. To protect the computer from overvoltages and undervoltages, several devices can be used. They are surge protectors, line conditioners, standby power supplies, and uninterruptible power supplies.
4. Most SPS and UPS used for servers will have a Systems Management Port. This is usually a standard serial port or USB port that allows the SPS or UPS to connect to the host computer it is protecting. The host computer runs management software that gathers statistics about the power

the SPS or UPS is using and providing. When a power failure occurs, this port is used to signal from the SPS or UPS informing the management software on the host computer that the power to the SPS or UPS has failed.

5. The management software can then initiate a graceful shutdown of the computer, including sending out messages to its users to save all of their work and log off the system.

Security+ Objective 5.3.2—High Availability/Fault Tolerance

1. Fault tolerance is the capability of a computer or network system to respond to a condition automatically, usually resolving it, and thus reducing the impact of the system. If fault-tolerant measures have been implemented, it is unlikely that a user would know that a problem existed.
2. RAID is short for Redundant Array of Inexpensive Disks. It is a category of disk drives that employ two or more drives in combination for fault tolerance and performance.
3. RAID disk drives are used frequently on servers but aren't generally necessary for personal computers.
4. Ideally, you use a RAID system to make sure no data is lost and to recover data from failed disk drivers without shutting your system down.
5. Originally RAID comprised six levels (RAID 0 through RAID 5). A few more levels have been added to combine the features of other levels.
6. Only RAID 0, 1, and 5 are supported by Windows Servers, Linux, and NetWare without additional hardware and software from RAID vendors.
7. RAID 0 stripes data across all drives. With striping, all available hard drives are combined into a single large virtual file system, with the file system's blocks arrayed so they are spread evenly across all the drives.
8. RAID 1 is known as disk mirroring or disk shadowing. With RAID 1, each hard drive on the system has a duplicate drive that contains an exact copy of the first drive's contents.
9. RAID 5 is very similar to RAID 0, but one of the hard drives is used for parity (error-correction) to provide fault tolerance.
10. To make sure that the link that connects to your network has fault tolerance, you have several options. They include Adaptive Load Balancing (ALB), Adapter Fault Tolerance (AFT), 802.3ad Link Aggregation.
11. Clustering is connecting two or more computers, known as nodes, together in such a way that they behave like a single computer. It is used for parallel processing, for load balancing and for fault tolerance.

QUESTIONS

1. Which of the following is a technical solution that supports high availability?
   a. UDP (User Datagram Protocol)
   b. Anti-virus solution
   c. RAID (Redundant Array of Independent Disks)
   d. Firewall
2. Following a disaster, while returning to the original site from an alternate site, the first process to resume at the original site would be the:
   a. Least critical process.
   b. Most critical process.
   c. Process most expensive to maintain at an alternate site.
   d. Process that has a maximum visibility in the organization.
3. Forensic procedures must be followed exactly to ensure the integrity of data obtained in an investigation. When making copies of data from a machine that us being examined, which of the following tasks should be done to ensure it is an exact duplicate?
   a. Perform a cyclic redundancy check using a checksum or hashing algorithm.
   b. Change the attributes of data to make it read only.
   c. Open files on the original media and compare them to the copied data.
   d. Do nothing. Imaging software always makes an accurate image.
4. Which of the following backup methods copies only modified files since the last full backup?
   a. Full   b. Differential
   c. Incremental   d. Archive
5. A primary drawback to using shared storage clustering for high availability and disaster recovery is:
   a. The creation of a single point of vulnerability.
   b. The increased network latency between the host computers and the RAID (Redundant Array of Independent Disk) subsystem.
   c. The asynchronous writes which must be used to flush the server cache.
   d. The highest storage capacity required by the RAID (Redundant Array of Independent Disks) subsystem.
6. Documenting change levels and revision information is most useful for:
   a. Theft tracking
   b. Security audits
   c. Disaster recovery
   d. License enforcement

7. A well defined business continuity plan must consist of risk and analysis, business impact analysis, strategic planning and mitigation, training and awareness, maintenance and audit, and:
   a. Security labeling and classification.
   b. Budgeting and acceptance.
   c. Documentation and security labeling.
   d. Integration and validation.

8. As the security analyst for your company's network, you need to implement a new plan. From the list below, please indicate which of the following describes how an organization is to deal with potential disasters.
   a. DRP   b. MSP
   c. ADP   d. BCT

9. Keeping backup media offsite provides what benefit to you?
   a. Less costly
   b. Quicker access to in case of an emergency
   c. Decreases recovery time
   d. Protection in case your building is destroyed or rendered unusable

10. A DRP (Disaster Recovery Plan) typically includes which of the following?
    a. Penetration testing
    b. Risk assessment
    c. DoS attack
    d. ACL

11. An alternate site configured with necessary system hardware, supporting infrastructure, and an onsite staff able to respond to an activation of a contingency plan 24 hours a day, 7 days a week is a:
    a. Cold site.   b. Warm site.
    c. Mirrored site.   d. Hot site.

12. Part of a fire protection plan for a computer room should include:
    a. Procedures for an emergency shutdown of equipment.
    b. A sprinkler system that exceeds local code requirements.
    c. The exclusive use of non-flammable materials within the room.
    d. Fireproof doors that can be easily opened if any alarm is sounded.

13. Despite regular system backups a significant risk still exists if:
    a. Recovery procedures are not tested.
    b. All users do not log off while the backup is made.
    c. Backup media is moved to an offsite location.
    d. An administrator notices a failure during the backup process.

14. Which systems should be included in a disaster recovery plan?
    a. All systems
    b. Those identified by the board of directories, president, or owner
    c. Financial systems and human resources systems
    d. Systems identified in a formal risk analysis process

15. Creation of an information inventory is most valuable when:
    a. Localizing license based attacks.
    b. Trying to reconstruct damaged systems.
    c. Determining virus penetration within an enterprise.
    d. Terminating employees for security policy violations.

16. The term cold site refers to:
    a. A low-temperature facility for long term storage of critical data.
    b. A location to begin operations during disaster recovery.
    c. A facility seldom used for high performance equipment.
    d. A location that is transparent to potential attackers.

17. The best reason to perform a business impact analysis as part of the business continuity planning process is to:
    a. Test the veracity of data obtained from risk analysis.
    b. Obtain formal agreement for designing tests to determine efficiency of business continuity plans.
    c. Create the framework for designing tests to determine efficiency of business continuity plans.
    d. Satisfy documentation requirements for insurance companies covering risks of systems and data important for business continuity.

18. The best method for protecting the data is:
    a. RAID.
    b. A surge protector and UPS.
    c. Back up, Back up, Back up.
    d. Antivirus software.

19. Which is ideal for backing up an entire hard drive?
    a. Zip drive   b. RAID
    c. Second hard drive d. Tape drive

20. After backing up a drive, you should occasionally:
    a. Restore a nonessential file to the hard drive.
    b. Reformat the hard drive.
    c. Shut down the system.
    d. Reformat the tape.

21. The archive attribute is the attribute that indicates whether a file is backed up. Which of the following backups does not shut off the archive attribute?
    a. Full
    b. Differential
    c. Incremental
    d. None of the above

22. Which backup method requires you to provide the full backup, and provide a tape for each day you want to go back and restore?
    a. Incremental   b. Full
    c. Differential   d. Daily

23. Which of the following devices provides the highest level of protection for your computer equipment?
    a. A surge protector
    b. A UPS
    c. An SPS
    d. A line conditioner

24. You are the network engineer for a large manufacturing company. Recently, you installed a critical Microsoft SQL Server 7.0 computer on the company's local area network (LAN) in Dallas, Texas. Since you installed the Microsoft SQL Server 7.0 computer, it has stopped responding twice and has spontaneously rebooted several times. You test the Microsoft SQL Server 7.0 computer and determine that it is not causing the problem. You test the power lines and find that fluctuations in the electric power grid are reaching the Microsoft SQL Server 7.0 computer. Which device should you install between the power line and the Microsoft SQL Server 7.0 computer on the LAN in Dallas, to ensure that the computer receives a clean, uninterrupted power signal?
    a. A surge protector
    b. A UPS
    c. A line conditioner
    d. An SPS

25. Which device only provides protection from a power spike or surge?
    a. A UPS
    b. A surge protector
    c. An SPS
    d. A line conditioner

26. You administer a network that is connected to the Internet, and you want to provide your network with the strongest possible virus protection. Where should you install the virus protection software? (Choose two answers.)
    a. On one server
    b. On all servers
    c. On one workstation
    d. On all workstations

27. You want to implement the least expensive form of server fault tolerance. Which method should you choose?
    a. The failover clustering method
    b. The cold site method
    c. The true clustering method
    d. The warm site method

28. You want to implement the most cost-effective fault-tolerance method. Which of the following methods should you use to accomplish this task?
    a. The duplicate server method
    b. The true clustering method
    c. The failover clustering method
    d. The RAID method

29. You want to provide fault tolerance for the servers on your network. Which method should you use?
    a. The failover clustering method
    b. The RAID method

c. The rollover clustering method
d. The two-phase commit method

30. Which Redundant Array of Inexpensive Disks (RAID) level provides disk duplexing?
    a. 0   b. 3
    c. 1   d. 5

31. You want to establish disk striping without parity on a server computer. Which Redundant Array of Inexpensive Disks (RAID) level should you use?
    a. 0   b. 3
    c. 1   d. 5

32. Which of the following are characteristics of disk duplexing? (Choose two answers.)
    a. It uses two hard disks.
    b. It stores parity information on the hard disks in the set.
    c. It stores an exact copy of the primary hard disk in the set.
    d. It uses one hard disk controller.

33. You are completing a full backup of the information stored on a network server. What happens to the archive bit that is associated with each file after the backup is complete?
    a. The archive bit is cleared.
    b. The archive bit is deleted.
    c. The archive bit is incremented by one.
    d. The archive bit is incremented by two.

34. Which type of software should you update most frequently with software patches?
    a. Presentation software
    b. Virus protection software
    c. Spreadsheet software
    d. Word processing software

35. You use a tape drive to back up important data on a server on the local area network (LAN). You start the backup operation, and the computer displays a tape error message. What is the first action that you should perform to resolve this problem?
    a. Use a new tape.
    b. Clean the tape drive.
    c. Ensure that the tape drive is turned on.
    d. Replace the tape drive.

36. What should you do if you are attempting to back up a Windows NT Server 4.0 computer to an external DAT tape drive, and the computer reports that no tape drive is present?
    a. Use a new tape.
    b. Replace the tape drive.
    c. Clean the tape drive.
    d. Ensure that the tape drive is turned on.

37. What are four common tape formats currently in use?
    a. Travan, Linear, TR1, and Audio
    b. QIC, DSS, Travan, and Scotch
    c. QIC, DAT, DLT, and Travan
    d. DAT, DDS, TR3, and TR4

38. Digital Audio Tape (DAT) uses _____ recording method, similar to VCR recording.
    a. Servo scan   b. Reel-to-reel
    c. Helical scan   d. Laser

39. You want to provide a critical file server with the ability to shut down with no power interruption when AC to the building is suddenly cut off. What device do you need to connect to it?
   a. CPS
   b. SPS
   c. VLM
   d. UPS

40. A disk array on your network server has data distributed across several drives providing fast read/write access. You are told by another network admin that if one drive fails, you'll need to restore from backup tape, because the entire volume spanning the disk array would be lost. This array is running what level Raid?
   a. 4
   b. 2
   c. 5
   c. 0

41. Two hard drives are installed in a server, each on their own controller. You've decided to configure disk duplexing, where a disk on one controller automatically copies data to another disk on its own controller. What level Raid do you need to configure?
   a. 4
   b. 1
   c. 5
   d. 0

42. What is the difference between a UPS and an SPS?
   a. An SPS has an external battery.
   b. One uses UTP cable and the other uses STP cable.
   c. A UPS does not have a switching time delay.
   d. There is no significant difference between the two.

43. Your boss wants you to backup all data, applications, and operating systems on a server. Which backup methods could you use? (Choose two answers.)
   a. Full backup
   b. Incremental backup
   c. Differential backup
   d. Copy backup

44. Because of an upcoming driver and/or firmware update to your server's disk array controller, you want to do a full backup of all data first, in case the controller malfunctions after the new drivers are installed. However, you don't want to throw off your current backup schedule. What backup method should you use?
   a. Differential
   b. Incremental
   c. Copy
   d. Full

45. What does RAID level 5 use to implement fault tolerance?

   a. Sequence bit
   b. Security bit
   c. Parallel bit
   d. Parity bit

46. When a network problem occurs, which of the following are not part of your procedures.
   a. Documention
   b. Solving
   c. Performing backups
   d. Troubleshooting

47. You have five hard drives in a RAID 5 array. Approximately how much disk space is available for data?
   a. 75%
   b. 80%
   c. 100%
   d. 50%

48. You have five hard drives in a RAID 5 array. Each drive has a 50-gigabyte capacity. How many gigabytes are available for data storage?
   a. 225 Gig
   b. 200 Gig
   c. 250 Gig
   d. 175 Gig

49. You have two 20-gigabyte hard drives in your server which is running RAID 1. How much disk space is available for data storage?
   a. 60 Gig
   b. 40 Gig
   c. 80 Gig
   d. 20 Gig

50. To ensure security of your company's data, what is the best place(s) to store your backup tapes?
   a. Locked in a file cabinet offsite
   b. Locked in a fireproof safe onsite
   c. Locked in the server room onsite
   d. Locked in a fireproof safe offsite

51. A condition in which voltage quickly increases past normal, then drops back down just as quickly within 1 second (or even within a few milliseconds) is called a what?
   a. Spike
   b. Brownout
   c. Surge
   d. Blackout

52. When voltage quickly rises above normal and stays that way for several seconds, it's called a what?
   a. Spike
   b. Brownout
   c. Surge
   d. Blackout

53. You need to add extra data storage capability to your network and are trying to decide whether to install a Windows 2000 server or an NAS device. What advantage does the NAS device have that might lean you toward deciding on it?
   a. Higher bandwidth
   b. Far greater storage capability
   c. Requires less expensive cabling
   d. Lower cost

HANDS-ON EXERCISES

Exercise 1: Performing a Backup and Restore in Windows

For this lab, you will need a blank formatted floppy disk.

Using the Backup Wizard

1. Log in as the administrator.
2. On your D: drive, create a Data directory.

3. From the C:\WINNT\WEB\WALLPAPER folder, copy all of the files to the D:\DATA folder.

4. To start the Microsoft Backup program, click on the Start button, select the Programs option, select the Accessories option, select the System tools option and select the Backup option.

5. At the Welcome to Windows 2000 Backup and Recovery Tools page, click on the Backup wizard button. Click on the Next button.

6. Select the backup selected files, drives, network data option and click on the Next button.

7. In the Items Back up page, find the DATA folder in the C: drive. Click on the Data drive to show its contents in the box to the right. To select the DATA folder to be backed up, put a checkmark in the box next to the DATA folder. Click on the Next button.

8. In a real-world network, you would typically backup to a tape drive. Since I don't expect many schools to have tape drives for every student, *nor do I expect that a typical user at home will have a tape drive,* we will back up to the floppy drive. Therefore, for the Backup media or file name text box, keep the A:\BACKUP.BKT and click on the Next button.

9. Before clicking on the Finish button, click on the Advanced button.

10. Open the Select the type of backup operation to perform text box and look at the options. When done, choose the Normal option and click on the Next button.

11. Select the Verify data after backup option and click on the Next button.

12. If the archive media already contains a backup, we will replace the data on media with this backup. Therefore select this option and click on the Next button.

13. Accept the default labels and click on the Next button.

14. Keep the default of doing the backup now and click the Next button.

15. Insert the blank floppy disk in drive A.

16. Click on the Finish button.

17. When the backup is complete, click on the Close button.

18. When a backup is done, you would typically remove the tape (or disk) and label the name of the backup. In addition, it is recommended to either log the backup either in a table or notebook or on the disk label. There-fore, remove the disk and Write Backup – Data folder and today's date on the label of the disk.

Using the Restore Wizard

1. Delete the Date folder on the C: drive.

2. Back at the Welcome to the Windows 2000 Backup and Recovery Tools page, click on the Restore Wizard button. Click on the Next button.

3. Notice that because of the catalogs, Windows 2000 remembers the backups that were done. Therefore, click on the + sign next to File, click on the next plus sign and put a check mark for the C drive. Click on the Next button.

4. Before clicking on the Finish button, click on the Advanced button. If you wanted to specify the files to be restored to a different location, there is where it would be done. Click on the Next button.

5. In this case, since we don't have a Data folder anymore, it doesn't matter which option I choose. Therefore, keep the default option and click on the Next button.

6. Since we don't have any system or security information that we are restoring, click on the Next button.

7. Click the Finish button.

8. Click on the OK button to restore from the default file.

9. Click on the Close button.

Using the Backup Program without the Wizards

1. Click on the Backup tab.

2. To backup the entire C: drive, click on the check box next to the C drive.

3. Notice that while the System State (listed after the drives) is on the C drive, it is not considered normal data. Therefore, it was not included. Therefore, select the System State to be backed up.

4. Open the Tools menu and select the Options option. Click the OK button.

5. Click the Backup program

6. At the bottom of the screen, you will find the Backup media or file name text box. Type in M:\Backup.bkf in the text box and click on the Start Backup button.

7. Leave the defaults and click the Start Backup button.

8. After the backup is done, click on the Close button.

9. Click on the Restore tab. Note: The backups that have already been completed as listed by the catalogs on the system. A:\Backup.bkf

10. Double-click the first backup listed in the right pane. Double-click the C drive listed in the right pane. Double-click the Data folder listed in the right pane.

11. On the left pane, deselect the data folder. On the right pane, select the first file listed.
12. Open the Tools menu and select the Options option. On the restore tab, select Always replace the file on my computer. Click the OK button.
13. Click on the Start Restore button.
14. Click on the OK button to confirm.
15. Insert the floppy disk that we used for the original backup. Since we did the backup on the A drive, use the Browse button to find the backup file on the A drive.
16. After the backup file is selected, click on the OK button to close the Enter Backup File Name dialog box.
17. When the restore is done, click on the Close button.

Recreating a Catalog

1. In the Microsoft Backup program, click on the Restore tab.
2. Right-click each of the catalogs listed in the right-pane and select the Delete Catalog option.
3. To recreate the catalog, open the tools menu and select the Catalog a backup file option.
4. Insert the original backup disk in drive A.
5. Use the browse button, to select the backup file in the A drive. Click the OK button to close the Backup File Name dialog box. Remember if this is a large tape, this can take some time.

Exercise 2: Scheduling Backup Jobs

1. Start the Microsoft Backup program and click the Scheduled Jobs tab.
2. To start the Backup wizard, double-click on today's date in the calendar. Click on the Next button.
3. Select the Back up selected files, drives, or network data option and click on the Next button.
4. Select the C:\Data directory. Click on the Next button.
5. Keep the default Backup media or file name of the A:\Backup.bkt and click on the Next button.
6. Keep the default type of backup operation to perform and click on the Next button.
7. On the How to Back Up page, select the Verify data after backup option, click on the Next button.
8. Select the Replace the data on the media with this backup option, and click on the Next button.
9. On the Backup label page, click on the Next button.
10. If it asks the Set Account Information dialog box, provide a user account and password, and click on the OK button. You can use the Administrator account.
11. On the When to Back up page, select the Later option, provide the job name of Test and select the Set Schedule button.
12. On the Scheduled Task option, select the Daily option. Keep the default Start time of 12:00 A.M. and the Scheduled Task Daily every 1 day.
13. Click on the Advanced button. This is where you would specify the start and end dates and how often you want to repeat the task. Click on the Cancel button.
14. Click on the OK button.
15. Back at the When to Back Up page, click on the Next button.
16. Click on the Finish button.
17. Change the time to 11:58 P.M.
18. Wait 3 minutes and see if the backup is performed.
19. Close the Microsoft Backup program.
20. Reset the clock back to its correct time.

Exercise 3: Developing a Disaster Recovery Plan

The Acme Corporation opened a second office building in Miami, Florida. They hired your team to support and maintain all computer systems for your corporation. Occasionally, Miami experiences violent thunderstorms in the summer. Thirty percent (30%) of the business is domestic and 70% is overseas.

The company has 60 computers throughout the building that are connected using an Ethernet-based Microsoft Windows 2000 network. They will be expected to buy 25 new computers within the next year. The cable used to connect the computers is a 10BaseT.

The Windows 2000 network is based on two stand-alone servers (Pentium III processors with 256 MB of RAM). Each server has 10 GB hard drive. Print sharing is when users can share several centrally located printers (3 HP LaserJet 4+ printers, 1 HP LaserJet 5SI and 4 HP DeskJet 860 color printer). The database, which they use to keep track of customers, orders, billing and inventory, is kept on the first server and the payroll software is kept in the second server. With this current setup, they have a single accounting account that can access the payroll/

account receivable/account payable records one at a time for the group of seven. The servers are kept in the accounting office, which is an insecure room.

The other computers are Pentium II and above using Windows 98 or above. Each machine has at least 64 MB of RAM and a minimum of 4 GB hard drive. Most computers use MICROSOFT OFFICE, which includes MS WORD, MS EXCEL and MS POWER POINT. The 10 sales reps also use MS Access. Most people save their information on their local systems.

In the past, hardware repair is done by At Ease Computer Shop. At Ease set up the original network and installs new nodes when someone asks for them. At Ease deals with most service calls in its shop. At Ease fixes the computer and brings it back about a week later. At Ease billed Accounting directly. Last year, At Ease found a virus on one of the computers, but removed it easily.

You and your group form a new IT department. It will be your job to maintain these computers, to insure data integrity and to minimize down time. Your first task would be to develop a DATA RECOVERY PLAN that will make managing of these computers and data easier.

1. The plan must plan for computer/network failure and what can be done to recover from these failures and what could be used to minimize these failures.
2. The plan must include rethinking of employee methods and training if needed.
3. The plan must discuss the security of important data.

Grading

You as students need to breakdown the document. Any information that is not provided, needs to either researched or the information needs to be made up. After you identify what needs to be done for the Acme Corporation, you need to come up with solutions. Again, this may require additional research. Lastly, you will recommend changes and solutions. Whatever is proposed needs to be explained and supported. The final document needs to be a professional looking document done on Microsoft Word or some other word processor.

Recommended Graded:

Identify all stated problems	40%
Supported/Explanations	20%
Proper English/Spelling	20%
Format (readability)	20%

Exercise 4: Updating Your Security Policies

1. Since you have learned a lot since you created the two security policies in chapter 2, you now need to update them.

Glossary

.NET—A Microsoft operating system platform that incorporates distributed applications that bring users into the next generation of the Internet by conquering the deficiencies of the first generation and giving users a more enriched experience in using the Web for both personal and business applications.

10Base2—(Also known as thinnet) is a simplified version of the 10Base5 Ethernet network. The name describes a 10 Mbps baseband network with a maximum cable segment length of approximately 200 m (actually 185 m). Instead of having external transceivers, the transceivers are on the network card, which attaches to the network using a BNC T-connector. The cable used is 50-ohm RG-58 A/U coaxial type cable. Different from the 10Base5 network, the 10Base2 does not use a drop cable.

10Base5—A form of Ethernet that is 10 Mbps baseband network that can have a cable segment up to 500 m long. It used a 50-ohm RG-8 and RG-11 as a backbone cable. 10Base5 uses physical and logical bus topology. It is also known as thicknet.

10BaseT—A form of Ethernet that uses UTP to form a logical bus topology while actually being a physical star topology (network devices connected to a hub or switch).

386 Microprocessor Protection Model—A model used on Intel processor that uses 4 rings to run programs. Each ring has different security levels. The inner ring (ring 0) has the highest security and ring 3 has the lowest security.

802.11 Standards—The wireless standards.

802.11i—A developing IEEE standard for wireless local area networks (WLAN).

A

Access Control—The process by which you restrict access to computing resources. It is a combination of authentication (proving who you claim to be) and authorization (what are you allowed to see, presuming you are whom you claim you are). It defines how users and systems communicate and in what manner.

Access Control List (ACL)—A set of data that informs a computer's operating system which permissions, or access rights, each user or group has to a specific system object, such as a directory or file. Each object has a unique security attribute that identifies which users have access to it, and the ACL is a list of each object and user access privileges such as read, write or execute.

Accounting—Sometimes known as auditing, accounting is when a user accessing a network resource, each resource a user uses or accesses while using a PC or network is recorded.

Acknowledgment (ACK)—A special message that is sent back when a data packet makes it to its destination.

Active Directory—A directory service used on Microsoft Windows or Windows Server 2003 server domains, which uses the "tree" concept for managing resources on a network. It combines domains, X.500 naming services, DNS, X.509 digital certificates and Kerberos authentication. It stores all information about the network resources and services such as user data, printers, servers, databases, groups, computers and security policies. In addition, it identifies all resources on a network and makes them accessible to users and applications.

Active Directory Integrated Zone—A DNS zone defined using the Active Directory, not the zone files.

ActiveX—A loosely defined set of technologies developed by Microsoft. ActiveX is an outgrowth of two other Microsoft technologies called OLE (Object Linking and Embedding) and COM (Component Object Model). As a moniker, ActiveX can be very confusing because it applies to a whole set of COM-based technologies. Most people, however, think only of ActiveX controls, which represent a specific way of implementing ActiveX technologies.

Address Resolution Protocol (ARP)—A TCP/IP protocol that is used to obtain hardware addresses (MAC addresses) of hosts located on the same physical network.

Address Resolution Protocol (ARP) Cache poisoning—When a user puts a false address in the ARP cache, which then causes the packets to be forwarded to the wrong destination.

Addressing—A method used to identify senders and receivers.

Administrative Share—A shared folder typically used for administrative purposes. To make a shared folder or drive into an administrative share, the share name must have a $ at the end of it. Since the share folder or drive cannot be seen during browsing, you would have to use a UNC name, which include the share name (including the $).

Advanced Encryption Standard (AES)—A symmetric 128-bit block data encryption technique developed by Belgian cryptographers Joan Daemen and Vincent Rijmen. The U.S government adopted the algorithm as its encryption technique in October 2000, replacing the DES encryption it used. The National Institute of Standards and Technology (NIST) of the U.S. Department of Commerce selected the algorithm, called Rijndael (pronounced Rhine Dahl or Rain Doll), out of a group of five algorithms under consideration.

Alternate Site—See Hot site.

Anonymous FTP—A FTP server that does not require authentication and instead have users log in as anonymous and then enter their e-mail address as the password.

Anti-virus Policy—Describes the organization's efforts to reduce the exposure to, damage from, and spreading of malicious software. The policy should state requirements of personnel to implement, update, and appropriately utilize antivirus software.

Anycast—Communication between any sender and the nearest of a group of receivers in a network.

Applet—A program designed to be executed from within another application. Unlike an application, applets cannot be executed directly from the operating system. With the growing popularity of OLE (object linking and embedding), applets are becoming more prevalent. A well-designed applet can be invoked from many different applications. Web browsers, which are often equipped with Java virtual machines, can interpret applets from Web servers. Because applets are small in files size, cross-platform compatible, and highly secure (can't be used to access users' hard drives), they are ideal for small Internet applications accessible from a browser.

Application Hardening—Making an application more secure, which includes applying the latest security patches and enforcing user-level security if available.

Application Layer—The highest layer of the OSI reference model, which initiates communication requests. It is responsible for interaction between the operating system and provides an interface to the system. It provides the user interface to a range of network-wide distributed services including file transfer, printer access and electronic mail.

Application-level Gateway—A firewall method and technology that takes requests for Internet services and forwards them to the actual services.

Application Programming Interfaces (APIs)—A set of routines, protocols and tools for building software applications.

Application Server—A server that is similar to a file and print server except the application server also does some of the processing.

ARC Cache Poisoning—Adding bogus entries to the ARP cache on a host computer.

ARP Cache—A portion of system memory dedicated to media access control (MAC) to Internet Protocol address resolution.

ASCII (American Standard Code for Information Interchange) Character Set—An alphanumeric code.

Asymmetrical DSL (ADSL)—DSL that transmits an asymmetrical data stream with much more going downstream to the subscriber and much less coming back.

Asymmetric Algorithm—Encryption algorithm that utilizes two keys. One key is used to encrypt plaintext and another key is used to decrypt the ciphertext.

Asynchronous—Devices that use signals are intermittent signals. They can occur at any time and at irregular intervals. They do not use a clock or timing signal.

Asynchronous Transfer Mode (ATM)—Both a LAN and a WAN technology, which is generally implemented as a backbone technology. It is a cell-switching and multiplexing technology that combines the benefits of circuit switching and packet switching.

Attack—An attempt to bypass security controls on a computer. The attack could alter, release, or deny data.

Attenuation—When the strength of a signal falls off with distance over a transmission medium. This loss of signal strength is caused by several factors such as the signal converted to heat due to the resistance of the cable and as the energy is reflected as the signal encounters impedance changes throughout the cable.

Auditing—To capture security-related events in a log file.

AUI (adapter unit interface) Connector—A female 15-pin D connector used to connect to an Ethernet 10Base5 network. The AUI connector is also known as DIX (Digital-Intel-Xerox) connector.

Authentication—The ability to verify the identity of a user, system, or system element.

Authentication, Authorization, and Accounting (AAA)—A model used to control access to a network and its resources. These combined processes are considered important for effective network management and security.

Authentication Header (AH)—Another name for IP protocol 51, which provides integrity and authenticity for packets, but not confidentiality.

Authentication Policy—Describes the acceptable methods, equipment, and parameters for allowing access to resources.

Authentication Server (AS)—In a Kerberos realm, the AS is the server that registers all valid users (clients) and services in the realm. The AS provides each client a ticket granting ticket (TGT) that is used to request a ticket from a ticket granting server (TGS).

Authenticator—A role in which a LAN port enforces authentication before it allows user access to the services that can be accessed through that port.

Authenticode—Used in Internet Explorer to check for digital signatures before downloading ActiveX components.

Authorization—The process of giving someone permission to do or have something.

Availability—The continuous operation of computer systems. When your system is a target of a denial of service attack, your system may become very slow or may be totally disabled.

B

Backbone Cable—(1) A backbone can be used as a main cable segment such as that found in a bus topology network. (2) A backbone refers to the main network connection through a building, campus, WAN or the Internet.

Backbone Cabling—Provides interconnections between telecommunications closets, equipment rooms, and entrance facilities and includes the backbone cables, intermediate and main cross-connects, terminations, and patch cords for backbone-to-backbone cross-connections.

Backbone Wiring—The system of cables that is often designed to handle a higher bandwidth. It is used to interconnect wiring closets, server rooms and entrance facilities (telephone systems and WAN links from the outside world).

Back Door—The name of an illicit server given to a secret access route into the system. Such routes are usually undocumented and almost certainly were not originally specified. In fact, usually only the original developer would be aware of the back door(s) to their system. Some back doors (such as NetBus, Loki, Masters Paradise, NetCat and Back Orifice) are created because the programmer expects the end users to mess up the system, that normal ID and password routines would not allow access. However, the existence of a back door allows anyone unauthorized to penetrate the system with malicious intent. It is reasonable to assume that a programmer with sufficient skill to build the system in the first place will also have the skills necessary to penetrate the system and withdraw again without leaving any evidence of the incursion.

Backup—To have an extra copy of data and/or programs. As a technician, consultant or support person, you need to emphasize at every moment to backup on servers and client systems.

Backup Domain Controllers—A server that contains duplicate copies of the domain database on Windows NT networks.

Band—A contiguous group of frequencies, that are used for a single purpose.

Bandwidth—The amount of data that can be carried on a given transmission media.

Baseband Systems—A system that uses the transmission medium's entire capacity for a single channel.

Basic Rate Interface (BRI)—A form of ISDN that defines a digital communications line consisting of three independent channels, two Bearer (or B) channels, each carrying 64 Kbps per second and one Data (or D) channel at 16 Kbps. For this reason, the ISDN Basic Rate Interface is often referred to as 2B+D.

Basic Service Set (BSS)—A portion of the wireless network that acts as a single Ethernet collision domain. When using a BSS, wireless devices can communicate with each other directly or through a single access point.

Bastion Host—A host computer that is exposed to the Internet by a three-pronged firewall or because it is placed between the firewall and the external network. This host should have a secure configuration.

Baud Rate—The modulation rate or the number of times per second that a line changes state.

Bearer Channels (B-channels)—A channel used in ISDN lines to transfer data at a bandwidth of 64 Kbps for each channel.

Binary Digits (bits)—A piece of information that can represent the status of an on/off switch. When several bits are combined together, they can signify a letter, a digit, a punctuation mark, a special graphical character or a computer instruction.

Bindery—A flat database that keeps track of users and groups on Novell NetWare server 3.2 or earlier, and it is administered with a menu-based DOS utility known as SYSCON.

Biometric Authentication—Automated method of identifying a person based on a physical characteristic, such as thumbprint or the retina of his or her eye.

Birthday Attack—A translation of the birthday paradox into an attack that involves creating multiple versions of two opposing documents in hopes of getting two copies that have the same digital signature or hash. The two documents can then be switched as a form of attack against people agreeing to the first, but not the second.

Blackouts—Total power failures.

Blind FTP—Servers or directories that allow write access, but not file listings (read access).

Blue Screen of Death (BSOD)—An error that can appear on computers running in a Windows environment. Jokingly called the blue screen of death because when the error occurs, the screen turns blue, and the computer almost always freezes and requires rebooting.

Bluetooth—A form of short-range radio technology aimed at simplifying communications among devices and the Internet. It also aims to simplify data synchronization between Net devices and other computers.

BNC Barrel—Connector that allows connecting two coax cables together.

BNC Connector—Short for British Naval Connector, Bayonet Nut Connector or Bayonet Neill Concelman. It is a type of connector used with coaxial cables. The basic BNC connector is a male type mounted at each end of a cable. This connector has a center pin connected to the center cable conductor and a metal tube connected to the outer cable shield. A rotating ring outside the tube locks the cable to any female connector.

BNC T-connectors—Used with the 10Base-2 system. They are female devices for connecting two cables to a network interface card (NIC).

Bootstrap Protocol (BOOTP)—A TCP/IP protocol that enables a booting host to configure itself dynamically.

Bridge—A device that works at the Data Link OSI layer, is a device that connects two LANs and makes them appear as one or is used to connect two segments of the same LAN. The two LANs being connected can be alike or dissimilar such as an Ethernet LAN connected to a Token Ring LAN.

Bridge CA—A certification authority that connects mesh and hierarchical architecture together. This allows different companies to have their own trust architecture, and then have a single connection using a bridge CA.

Broadband System—A system that uses the transmission medium's capacity to provide multiple channels by using frequency-division multiplexing (FDM).

Broadcast Domain—A segment, subnet, or virtual local area network (VLAN) that doesn't filter broadcast traffic. Each host on a broadcast domain can broadcast packets to all other hosts on the broadcast domain.

Broadcasting—A method that sends unaddressed packets to everyone on the network.

Brouter—Short for bridge router, a device that functions as both a router and a bridge. A brouter understands how to route specific types of packets (routable protocols), such as TCP/IP packets. For other specified packets (non-routable protocols), it acts as a bridge, which simply forwards the packets to the other networks.

Brownouts—Drops in power that can force the computer to shut down, introduce memory errors and cause unsaved work to be lost.

Brute Force—An attack that attempts to crack the password by trying every possible value. They tend to proceed from A to Z. If the system includes digits and uses both upper and lower case combinations, it will also have to include those combinations.

Brute Force Attack—Attacks that use mathematical algorithms to break encryption keys, passwords, or other logical security measures with brute force; trying every combination available.

Buffer—A buffer is a data area that is shared by either hardware devices or program processes. Buffer overflows occur when a program tries to store more data in the buffer than was designed. The data that does not fit into the designated buffer can overflow into an adjacent buffer. The overflowed data can overwrite and corrupt valid data of another program.

Buffer Overflow Attack—The most common kind of DoS attack is simply to send more traffic to a network address than the programmers who planned its data buffers anticipated someone might send. The attacker may be aware that the target system has a weakness that can be exploited or the attacker may simply try the attack in case it might work.

Bus Topology—A topology that looks like a line, where data is sent along the single cable. The two ends of the cable do not meet and the two ends do not form a ring or loop.

Byte—8 bits of data. One byte of information can represent one character.

C

Cable Modems—A device that is located in subscriber homes to create a virtual local area network (LAN) connection over a cable system.

Cables—A physical transmission medium that has a central conductor of wire or fiber surrounded by a plastic jacket, used to carry electrical or light signals between computers and networks.

Cable System—A system that delivers broadcast television signals efficiently to subscribers' homes using a sealed coaxial cable line.

Cabling System—The veins of the network that connect all of the computers together and allows them to communicate with each other.

CDFS—Short for CD-ROM File System, is the read-only file system used to access resources on a CD-ROM disk. Windows supports CDFS so as to allow CD-ROM file sharing. Because a CD-ROM is read-only, you cannot assign specific permissions to files through CDFS.

Cell Relay—A form of packet switching network that uses relatively small, fixed-size packets called cells.

Cells—A relatively small, fixed-size packets.

Cellular Topology—A topology used in wireless technology whereas an area is divided into cells. A broadcast device is located at the center and broadcasting in all directions to form an invisible circle (cell). All network devices located within the cell communicate with the network through the central station or hub, which are interconnected with rest of the network infrastructure. If the cells are overlapped, devices may roam from cell to cell while maintaining connection to the network as the devices.

Centralized Computing—When the processing is done for many people by a central computer.

Centralized Management—A security model where a network uses one security database.

Certificate—A digital representation of information that identifies you and is used by a Certificate Authority (CA), which is often a trusted third party (TTP).

Certificate Authority (CA)—A trusted third-party organization or company that issues digital certificates used to create digital signatures and public-private key pairs. The role of the CA in this process is to guarantee that the individual granted the unique certificate is, in fact, who he or she claims to be. Usually, this means that the CA has an arrangement with a financial institution, such as a credit card company, which provides it with information to confirm an individual's claimed identity. CAs are a critical component in data security and electronic commerce because they guarantee that the two parties exchanging information are really who they claim to be.

Certificate Policy (CP)—A very broad, high-level security policy that provides the basis for trust between organizations.

Certificate Revocation List (CRL)—A signed, time-stamped list of server serial numbers of CA public key certificates that have been revoked. The CRL is necessary to allow CAs to accept and reject certificates that were issued by a different CA.

Certificate Trust List (CTL)—A signed list of root certification authority certificates that an administrator considers reputable for designated purposes, such as client authentication or secure email.

Certification Practice Statement (CPS)—A statement or document that provides the process through which certificates are issued, maintained, and revoked by a Certification Authority.

Chain of Custody—Procedures and documentation to ensure the integrity of the information collected by tracking its handling and storage from point of collection to final disposition of the evidence.

Challenge Handshake Authentication Protocol (CHAP)—An authentication protocol that is the most common dial-up authentication protocol used, which uses an industry Message Digest 5 (MD5) hashing scheme to encrypt authentication.

Channel Service Unit (CSU)—The CSU is a device that connects a terminal to a digital line that provides the LAN/WAN connection.

Checksum—A form of error control where a computation is applied to a file that results in a string that can be used to check the integrity of a downloaded file.

C-I-A Triad—A security model based on confidentiality, integrity and availability.

Ciphertext—Information that is encrypted.

Circuit-level Gateways—A method used in firewalls to validate TCP and UOP sessions before opening a connection.

Circuit Switching—A technique that connects the sender and the receiver by a single path for the duration of a conversation. Once a connection is established, a dedicated path exists between both ends, that is always consuming network capacity, even when there is no active transmission taking place (such as when a caller is put on hold). Once the connection has been made the destination device acknowledges that it is ready to carry on a transfer. When the conversation is complete, the connection is terminated.

Clear Text—In cryptography, clear text refers to any message that is not encrypted.

Client—A computer that requests services.

Client for Microsoft Networks—Provides the redirector (VREDIR.VXD) to support all Microsoft networking products that use the Server Message Block (SMB) protocol.

Client for NetWare Networks—A program that runs with the IPX protocol, is used to process login scripts, support all NetWare 3.XX command-line utilities and some 4.X/5.X command-line utilities, connects and browses to NetWare servers, access printers on the NetWare server and process login scripts on the NetWare server.

Client/Server Network—A network that is made of servers and clients, which is typically used on medium or large network.

Client Software—Software that allows a workstation attached to the network to communicate.

Cloud—Represents a logical network with multiple pathways as a black box. The subscribers that connect to the cloud, don't worry about the details inside the cloud. Instead, the only thing that the subscriber needs to know is that they connect at one edge of the cloud and the data is received at the other edge of the cloud.

Clustering—Software and services that enable two or more servers to work together to keep server-based applications available (fault tolerance). It is used for parallel processing, for load balancing and for fault tolerance. The computers that form the cluster are physically connected by cable and are logically connected by cluster software. As far as the user is concerned, the cluster appears as a single-system to end-users.

Coaxial Cable—Sometimes referred to as Coax, is a cable that has a center wire surrounded by insulation and then a grounded shield of braided wire (mesh shielding). The copper core carries the electromagnetic signal, and the braided metal shielding acts as both a shield against noise and a ground for the signal. The shield minimizes electrical and radio frequency interference and provides a connection to ground.

Cold Site—A site that does not guarantee server uptime and has little or no fault tolerance. Instead, it relies on efficient disaster recovery methods to ensure data integrity, especially the backup of the data.

Commercial CA—Operated by a certificate-issuing company; provides certificates to the general public, or for use when communicating with other entities.

Common Criteria—Created by a joint effort between security organizations from the United States, Canada, France, Germany, the Netherlands and the U.K. The Common Criteria replace the previous standard of C2 or orange book certification. Unlike the ISO17799 Standard, the Common Criteria defines the features of computer systems and products which offer support and control security.

Common Gateway Interface (CGI)—Programs that are commonly used on Web servers to produce dynamic content. CGI is a specification for transferring information between an application for transferring information between an application and a Web server. For example, CGIs are frequently used to perform data input, search, and retrieval functions on databases.

Common Internet File System (CIFS)—A public or open variation of the Server Message Block Protocol used by Microsoft Windows and is currently used by Linux with Samba, Novell Netware 6.0 and AppleTalkIP.

Communication Server—A remote access server.

Complex Passwords—Also known as strong passwords, are passwords that have mixed case, alphanumeric, and multiple characters. Such passwords are difficult to guess or crack with a password-cracking program.

Computer Emergency Response Team Coordination Center (CERT/CC)—CERT was started in December 1988 by the Defense Advanced Research Projects Agency, which was part of the U.S. Department of Defense, after the Morris Worm disabled about 10% of all computers connected to the Internet. CERT/CC is located at the Software Engineering Institute, a federally funded research center operated by Carnegie Mellon University. Cert/CC studies Internet security vulnerabilities, provides services to websites that have been attacked and publishes security alerts. CERT/CC's research activities include the area of WAN computing and developing improved Internet security. The organization also provides training to incident response professionals.

Computer Forensics—The investigation and analysis of computer security incidents in the interest of gathering and preserving potential legal evidence.

Computer Security Incident—An actual, suspected, or attempted compromise of any information technology system. Any activity that threatens a computer system or violates a security policy can lead to an incident.

Computer Security Incident Response Plan (CSIRP)—A plan that provides guidance and documentation on computer security incident response handling and communication efforts. The CSIRP is activated whenever a computer security incident occurs, and guides the responses to all incidents whose severity is such that they could affect a company's ability to do business, or undermine its reputation.

Computer Security Incident Response Team (CSIRT)—A team of people assembled to respond to computer security incidents.

Confidentiality—The protection of data from unauthorized disclosure to a third party.

Connectionless—A type of protocol that does not require an exchange of messages with the destination host before data transfer begins, nor do they make a dedicated connection, or virtual circuit, with a destination host. Instead, connectionless protocols rely upon upper-level, not lower-level protocols for safe delivery and error handling.

Connection-Oriented Network—A network that you must establish a connection using an exchange of messages or must have a preestablished pathway between a source point and a destination point before you can transmit packets.

Container—In directory services, an object that can hold other objects.

Cookie—A small amount of data that a Web server stores about a user on the user's own computer.

Countermeasures—Actions or measures deployed to counteract threats and vulnerabilities, therefore reducing the risk in your environment.

Cracker—Someone who breaks security on an automated information system or network. Crackers are typically doing something mischievous or malicious, and although they might be trying to break into a system for what they consider a good and higher cause, they are still breaking into a system.

Crossover Cable—A cable that can be used to connect from one network card to another network card or a hub to a hub, reverses the transmit and receive wires.

Crosstalk—When signals induct (law of induction) or transfer from one wire to the other.

Cryptography—The art of protecting information by transforming it (encrypting it) into cipher text. In data and telecommunications, cryptography is necessary when communicating over any untrusted medium. Cryptography not only protects data from theft or alteration (integrity), but can also be used for user authentication.

Cyclic Redundancy Check (CRC)—A form of error control that provides a bit-level integrity check for the packet. Also known as the frame check sequence (FCS).

D

Daemon—A background process or service that monitors and performs many critical system functions and services.

Data—The raw facts, numbers, letters, or symbols that the computer processes into meaningful information.

Database—A collection of information organized in such a way that a computer program can quickly select desired pieces of data. You can think of a database as an electronic filing system.

Database Management System (DBMS)—A collection of programs that enables you to enter, organize, and select data in a database. There are many different types of DBMSs, ranging from small systems that run on personal computers to huge systems that run on mainframes. Some examples include computerized library systems, automated teller machines, flight reservation systems and computerized parts inventory systems.

Data Channel (D-channel)—A channel used in ISDN lines used for transmitting control information.

Data Circuit-Terminating Equipment (DCE)—Special communication devices that provide the interface between the DTE and the network. Examples include modems and adapters. The purpose of the DCE is to provide clocking and switching services in a network and they actually transmit data through the WAN. Therefore, the DCE controls data flowing to or from a computer.

Data Encryption Standard (DES)—A popular symmetric-key encryption method developed in 1975 and standardized by ANSI in 1981 as ANSI X.3.92. DES uses a 56-bit key and is illegal to export out of the U.S. or Canada if you don't meet the BXA requirements.

Datagram—A packet on an IP network.

Data Link Layer—The OSI layer that is responsible for providing error-free data transmission and establishes local connections between two computers or hosts. It divides data it receives from the Network layer into distinct frames that can then be transmitted by the physical layer and it packages raw bits from the physical layer into blocks of data called frames.

Data Service Unit (DSU)—The DSU is a device that performs all error correction, handshaking, protective, and diagnostic functions for a telecommunications line.

Data Terminal Equipment (DTE)—A devices used on end systems that communicate across the WAN. They control data flowing to or from a computer. They are usually terminals, PCs, network hosts, which are located on the premises of individual subscribers.

De jure Standard—By law standard is a standard that has been dictated by an appointed committee.

Decentralized Management—A security model in which every computer contains its own security database.

Decimal Number System—The most commonly used numbering system where each position contains 10 different possible digits. Since there are 10 different possible digits, the decimal number system are numbers with base 10. These digits are 0, 1, 2, 3, 4, 5, 6, 7, 8 and 9.

Decryption—The process of converting data from encrypted format back to its original format.

Default Gateway—A TCP/IP setting for a host that specifies the local address of a router.

Defense-in-breadth—Multiple security devices at multiple levels of the network infrastructure.

Demarcation Point (demarc)—The point where the local loop ends at the customer's premises.

Demilitarized Zone (DMZ)—An area that is used by a company that wants to host its own Internet services without sacrificing unauthorized access to its private network. The DMZ sits between the Internet and an internal network's line of defense, usually some combination of firewalls and bastion hosts. Typically, the DMZ contains devices accessible to Internet traffic, such as Web (HTTP) servers, FTP servers, SMTP (e-mail) servers and DNS servers.

Demultiplexing—The technique that occurs when the destination computer receives the data stream and separates and rejoins the application's segments. See multiplexing.

Denial of Service (DoS)—A type of attack on a network that is designed to bring the network to its knees by flooding it with useless traffic.

DHCP—Short for **Dynamic Host Configuration Protocol,** is an extension of BOOTP. It is used to automatically configure a host during boot up on a TCP/IP network and to change settings while the host is attached. There are many parameters that you can automatically set with the DHCP server including IP addresses, subnet masks, DNS servers, WINS servers, and domain names.

Dial-up Networking—A method used when a remote access client makes a nonpermanent, dial-up connection to a physical port on a remote access server by using the service of a telecommunications provider such as analog phone, ISDN, or X.25.

Dictionary Attack—Using words from a database (dictionary) to test against passwords until a match is found.

Diffused IR—Infrared that spread the light over an area to create a cell, limited to individual rooms.

Digital Certificate—An attachment to an electronic message used for security purposes, such as for authentication and to verify that a user sending a message is who he or she claims to be, and to provide the receiver with a means to encode a reply.

Digital Envelope—A type of security that encrypts the message using symmetric encryption and encrypts key to decode the message using public-key encryption.

Digital Signals—A system that is based on a binary signal system produced by pulses of light or electric voltages. The site of the pulse is either on/high or off/low to represent 1s and 0s. Digital signals is the language of computers.

Digital Signature—A digital code that can be attached to an electronically transmitted message that uniquely identifies the sender. Like a written signature, the purpose of a digital signature is to guarantee that the individual sending the message really is who he or she claims to be.

Digital Subscriber Line (DSL)—A special communication line that uses sophisticated modulation technology to maximize the amount of data that can be sent over plain twisted pair copper wiring, which is already carrying phone service to subscribers homes.

Directed IR—Infrared that uses line of sight or point-to-point technology.

Directory Number (DN)—The 10-digit phone number the telephone company assigns to any analog line.

Directory Services—A network service that identifies all resources on a network and makes those resources accessible to users and applications. Resources can include e-mail addresses, computers and peripheral devices (such as printers).

Directory Services Servers—A server used to locate information about the network such as domains (logical divisions of the network) and other servers.

Direct-Sequence Spread-Spectrum (DSSS)—A technique that generates a redundant bit pattern for each bit to be transmitted. This bit pattern is called a chip (or chipping code). The intended receiver knows which specific frequencies are valid and deciphers the signal by collecting valid signals and ignoring the spurious signals. The valid signals are then used to reassemble the data.

Disaster Recovery Plan (DRP)—A plan that contains contingencies when problems occur. When putting together a DRP, there are many items that need to be considered and included. When a disaster occurs, the DRP should specify what actions need to be taken and in what order. Of course, since your organization goes through changes as time goes on, the DRP needs to be constantly reviewed and updated.

Discretionary Access Control (DAC)—Permits the owner of an object (such as a process, file, or folder) to manage access control at their own discretion.

Diskless Workstation—A computer that does not have its own disk drive. Instead the computer stores files on a network file server.

Distance Bector–based Routing—A routing protocol that to periodically advertise or broadcast the routes in their routing tables, but they only send it to their neighboring routers.

Distributed Denial of Service (DDos)—A denial of service attack that involves installing programs known as zombies on various computers in advance of the attack. A command is issued to these zombies, which launch the attack on behalf of the attacker, thus hiding their tracks. The zombies themselves are often installed using worms. The real danger from a DDos attack is that the attacker uses many victim computers as host computers to control other zombies that initiate the attack. When the system that is overwhelmed tries to trace back the attack, it receives a set of spoofed addresses generated by a series of zombies.

Distribution System (DS)—Forms the spine of the wireless LAN, making the decisions whether to forward traffic from one Basic Service Set (BSS) to the wired network or back out to another access point or BSS.

DIX Connector—Short for Digital-Intel-Xerox, is a female 15-pin D connector used to connect to an Ethernet 10Base5 network. The DIX connector is also known as an AUI connector.

DNS Cache Poisoning—When attackers exploit flaws in a DNS server by placing bogus entries in the DNS cache.

DNS Name Space—The hierarchical structure of the DNS database as an inverted logical tree structure. Each node on the tree is a partition of the name space called a domain. Domains can be further partitioned at node points within the domain into subdomains.

DNS Zone—A portion of the DNS namespace whose database records exist and are managed in a particular DNS database file.

Domain—A logical unit of computers and network resources that define a security boundary. It is typically found on medium or large size networks or networks that require a secure environment. Different from a workgroup, a domain uses one database to share its common security and user account information for all computers within the domain. Therefore, it allows centralized network administration of all users, groups and resources on the network.

Domain Controller—A Windows server that contains the domain database.

Domain Local Group—A group used in Windows NT family domains that is usually used to assign rights and permissions to network resource that are in the domain of the local group. Different from a domain local group, it can list user accounts, universal groups and global groups from any domain and local groups from the same domain.

Domain Name Service (DNS)—A service that provides mappings between names and IP addresses, along with distributing network information (i.e., mail servers).

Domain User Account—In Windows NT family domains, an account that can log onto a domain to gain access to the network resources.

DS0 Channel—A channel that can carry a 64-Kbps of data, sufficient to carry voice communication.

Due Care—A minimum or customary practice of reasonable protecting assets.

Dumb Terminal—A display monitor and keyboard that has no processing capabilities. A dumb terminal is simply an output device that accepts data from another computer such as a main frame.

Duplex Cables—A cable that has two optical fibers inside a single jacket. The most popular use for duplex use for duplex fiber optic cable is as a fiber optic LAN backbone cable. Duplex cables are perfect because all LAN connections need a transmission fiber and a reception fiber.

Dynamic Host Configuration Protocol (DHCP)—A TCP/IP server that is used to automatically assign TCP/IP addresses and other related information to clients.

Dynamic IP Addresses—An IP address that is automatically configured on a host by a DHCP server.

E

E1 Line—A digital line with 32 64-Kbps channels for a bandwidth of 2.048 Mbps.

E3 Line—A digital line with 512 64-Kbps channel for a bandwidth of 34.368 Mbps.

EAP-Transport Level Security (EAP-TLS)—An EAP type that is used in certificate-based security environments. The EAP-TLS exchange of messages provides mutual authentication, negotiation of the encryption method, and secured private key exchange between the remote access client and the authenticating server.

Eavesdropping—The act of capturing and decoding network transmissions.

E-carrier Systems—An entire digital system that consist of permanent dedicated point-to-point connections. It is typically used in Europe.

Electromagnetic Interference (EMI)—Signals caused by large electromagnets used in industrial machinery, motors, fluorescent lighting and power lines that cause interference to other signals.

Electronic Mail (email)—A sophisticated tool that allows you to send text messages and file attachments (documents, pictures, sound, and movies) to anyone with an email address.

Electrostatic Discharge (ESD)—Electricity generated by friction such as when your arm slides on a tabletop or when you walk across a carpet. Electronic devices including network cards and computer components can be damaged by electrostatic discharge.

Elliptical Curve Cryptography (ECC)—A type of public key system that requires a shorter key length than many other systems and requires less computing power. It is based on elliptic curve theory.

Email Spoofing—The forgery of an email header so that the message appears to have originated from someone or somewhere other than the actual source.

Encapsulating Security Payload (ESP)—Another name for IPSec protocol ID 50, which provides confidentiality, authenticity and integrity.

Encapsulation—The concept of placing data behind headers (and before trailers) for each layer.

Encoding—The process of changing a signal to represent data.

Encryption—The process of disguising a message or data in what appears to be meaningless data (cipher text) to hide and protect the sensitive data from unauthorized access.

Enrolling—A setup procedure for biometric authentication in which an administrator stores the user's biological feature that will be used later to verify the user's identity. This is typically acquired by using a sensor (hardware device) that can record the particular feature, such as a thumbprint scanner.

Enterprise—Any large organization that utilizes computers, usually consisting of multiple LANs.

Enterprise WAN—A WAN that is owned by one company or organization.

Entity—It identifies the hardware and software, which fulfills a role or service of a server.

Equipment Room—The area in a building where telecommunications equipment is located and the cabling system terminates.

Error Control—Refers to the notification of lost or damaged data frames.

Ethernet—The most widely used LAN technology in use today that uses a logical bus topology.

Event Viewer—In Windows NT family, a very useful utility used to view and manage logs of system, program, and security events on your computer. Event viewer gathers information about hardware and software problems, and monitor Windows security events.

Exchange—The service that provides email on Microsoft Windows NT, Windows 2000 or Windows .NET server.

Exploit—A type of attack on a resource that is accessed by a threat that makes use of a vulnerability in your environment.

Extended Network Prefix—Part of an IP address which consists of the network prefix and the subnet number.

Extended Service Set (ESS)—A wireless networking implementation that has more than one basic service set (BSS) available. This allows user to voice between multiple infrastructure BSSs. In an ESS, the access points talk amongst themselves, forwarding traffic from one BSS to another, as well as switch the roaming devices from one BSS to another.

Extensible Authentication Protocol (EAP)—An authentication protocol that allows new authentication schemes to be plugged in as needed. Therefore, EAP allows third-party vendors to develop custom authentication schemes such as retina scans, voice recognition, finger print identification, smart card, Kerberos and digital certificates.

Extensible Markup Language (XML)—A specification developed by the W3C. XML is a pared-down version of SGML, designed especially for Web documents. It allows designers to create their own customized tags, enabling the definition, transmission, validation, and interpretation of data between applications and between organizations.

External IPX Address—An 8-digit (4-byte) hexadecimal number used to identify the network on an IPX network.

Extranet—An intranet that is partially accessible to authorized outsiders.

F

False Acceptance Rate (FAR)—The percentage of unauthorized users who are incorrectly identified as valid users during biologic authentication. Also known as type 2 errors.

False Rejection Rate (FRR)—The percentage of authorized users who are incorrectly rejected during biological authentication. Also known as type 1 errors.

Fast Ethernet—An extension of the 10BaseT Ethernet standard that transports data at 100 Mbps yet still keeps using the CSMA/CD protocol used by 10 Mbps Ethernet.

FAT32—A file system that is an enhancement of the FAT/VFAT file system, which uses 32-bit FAT entries. It supports hard drives up to two terabytes.

Fault Tolerance—The ability of a system to respond gracefully to an unexpected hardware or software failure. There are many levels of fault tolerance, the lowest being the ability to continue operation in the event of a power failure. Many fault-tolerant computer systems mirror all operations—that is, every operation is performed on two or more duplicate systems, so if one fails the other can take over.

Fax Server—A server that manages fax messages sent into and out of the network through a fax modem.

Federal Information Processing Standards (FIPS)—A set of standards that describe document processing, provide standard algorithms for searching, and provide other information processing standards for use within government agencies.

Fiber Distributed Data Interface (FDDI)—A MAN protocol that provides data transport at 100 Mbps and can support up to 500 stations on a single network.

Fiber Optic—Cable consists of a bundle of glass or plastic threads, each of which is capable of carrying data signals in the form of modulated pulses of light.

File Allocation Table (FAT)—A simple and reliable file system, which uses minimal memory. It supports file names of 11 characters, which include the 8 characters for the file name and 3 characters for the file extension.

File Attribute—A characteristic about each file. Attributes can be either on or off. The most common attributes include Read-only, Hidden, System, and Archive.

File Server—A server that manages user access to files stored on a server. When a file is accessed on a file server, the file is downloaded to the client's RAM. For example, if you are working on a report using a word processor, the word processor files will be executed from your client computer and the report will be stored on the server. As the report is accessed from the server, it would be downloaded or copied to the RAM of the client computer. Note: All of the processing done on the report is done by the client's microprocessors.

File Sharing—A network server that allows you to access files, which are on another computer, without using a floppy disk or other forms of removable media. To ensure that the files are secure, most networks can limit the access to a directory or file and what kind of access (permissions or rights) that a person or a group of people have.

File Transfer Protocol (FTP)—A TCP/IP protocol that allows a user to transfer files between local and remote host computers.

Firewall—A system designed to prevent unauthorized access to or from a private network. Firewalls can be implemented in both hardware and software, or a combination of both. Firewalls are frequently used to prevent unauthorized Internet users from accessing private networks connected to the Internet, especially intranets. All messages entering or leaving the intranet pass through the firewall, which examines each message and blocks those that do not meet the specified security criteria.

Firewall Policy—Describes the type of network traffic and data that is and is not allowed to traverse the firewall.

Flow Control—The process of controlling the rate at which a computer sends data.

Forensics—The investigation and analysis of a computer for the purpose of gathering and preserving evidence.

Forest—In Active Directory, a grouping of one or more trees that are connected by two-way, transitive trust relationships, which allow users to access resources in the other domain/tree.

Frame—A structured package for moving data that includes not only the raw data, or "payload," but also the sender's and receiver's network addresses and error checking and control information.

Frame Relay—A packet-switching protocol designed to use high-speed digital backbone links to support modern protocols that provide for error handling and flow control for connecting devices on a WAN.

Frequency—Indicates the number of times that a single wave will repeat over any period. It is measured in hertz (Hz) or cycles per second.

Frequency-Division Multiplexing (FDM)—A method that uses its transmission medium's capacity to provide multiple channels. Each channel uses a carrier signal, which runs at a different frequency than the other carrier signals used by the other channels.

Frequency Hopping—A technique that quickly switches between predetermined frequencies, many times each second. Both the transmitter and receiver must follow the same pattern and maintain complex timing intervals to be able to receive and interpret the data being sent.

FTP Bounce—An exploit in which attackers run scans against other computers through an FTP server.

Full-Duplex Dialog—A form of dialog allows every device to transmit and receive simultaneously.

Fully Qualified Domain Names (FQDN)—Sometimes referred to as just domain names, are used to identify computers on a TCP/IP network. Examples include MICROSOFT.COM and EDUCATION.NOVELL. COM.

G

Gateway—A hardware and/or software that links two different types of networks by repackaging and converting data from one network to another network or from one network operating system to another.

Geosynchronous (GEO) Orbits—Orbits used by satellites that are positioned 22,300 miles (35,800 km) above the earth's equator.

Gigabit Ethernet—A form of Ethernet that has a bandwidth of a Gigabit throughput.

Global Catalog—In Active directory, a database that holds a replica of every object. But instead of storing the entire object, it stores those attributes most frequently used in search operations (such as a user's first and last names).

Global Group—A group used in Windows NT family domains that usually used to group people within its own domain. Therefore, they can list user accounts and global groups from the same domain. The global group can be assigned access to resources in any domain.

Global WAN—A WAN, which is not owned by any one company and could cross national boundaries. The best known example of a global WAN is the Internet, which connects millions of computers.

Grandfather, Father, Son Backup Rotation—A backup rotation system that requires 21 tapes based on a 5-day rotation. Each month, you create a grandfather backup, which is stored permanently offsite, never to be reused. Each week, you create a full weekly backup (Father) and each day, you create a differential or incremental backup (Son).

Group—A collection of user accounts. Groups are not containers. They list members but they do not contain the members.

H

Hacker—Someone who can write code to provide a solution to a problem, the code is not always writing eloquently, but does provide a solution to a difficult problem and is created quickly.

Half-Duplex Dialog—A form of dialog that allows each device to both transmit and receive, but not at the same time. Therefore, only one device can transmit at a time.

Handshaking—The process that communication devices use to negotiate a common data rate and other transmission parameters.

Hardware Abstraction Layer (HAL)—In Windows NT family, a library of hardware manipulating routines that hides the hardware interface details. It contains the hardware-specific code that handles I/O interfaces, interrupt controllers and multiprocessor operations so that it can act as the translator between specific hardware architectures and rest of the Windows software.

Hash—One-way mathematically function that creates a fixed-size value (known as a hash or message digest) based on a variable-sized unit of data. A hashing algorithm will always produce the same hash value base on the same input data and never have two different data units produce the same hash value.

Hash Encryption—Also known as message digests, a one-way encryption that uses algorithms that don't really use a key. Instead, it converts data from a variable length to a fixed length piece of data called a hash value. This shorter hashed key is faster to retrieve and use. Hashing is always a one-way operation. There's no need to "reverse engineer" the hash function by analyzing the hashed values. In fact, the ideal hash function cannot be derived by such analysis.

Hashing Scheme—An encrypting method that scrambles information in such a way that it's unique and can't be reversed back to the original format.

Hexadecimal Number System—A number system based on sixteen digits (1, 2, 3, 4, 5, 6, 7, 8, 9, A, B, C, D, E and F). One hexadecimal digit is equivalent to a four digit binary number (4 bits or a nibble) and two hexadecimal digits are used to represent a byte (8 bits).

High-Level Data-Link Control (HDLC) Protocol—The protocol used with PPP protocols that encapsulate its data during transmission.

Hijacking—A type of network security attack in which the attacker takes control of a communication, just as an airplane hijacker takes control of a flight, between two entities and masquerades as one of them.

HKEY—Short for Handle to a key, HKEY is a subtree for the Windows registry.

Hoax—A false virus warning that people believe is real. These hoaxes are typically spread through email messages.

Home Directory—A folder used to hold or store a user's personal documents.

HomeRF SWAP—SWAP is short for Shared Wireless Access Protocol. A form of Bluetooth that is designed specifically for wireless networks in homes.

Honey Pots—Systems that have no production value and are designed to be targets for attackers. They help administrators learn about attacks and attack methods.

Hop—The trip a data packet takes from one router to another router or a router to another intermediate point to another in the network.

Hop Count—The number or routers that a data packet takes to its destination.

Horizontal Cabling—The cabling system covers from the work area receptacle to the horizontal cross-connect in the telecommunications closet. It includes the receptacle and optional transition connector (such as under-carpet cable connecting to round cable).

Horizontal Wiring System—The system of cables that extend from wall outlets throughout the building to the wiring closet or server room.

Host—Computer or device that connects to the network and is the source or final destination of data.

HOSTS File—A text file that lists the IP address followed by the host name used to resolve host names to IP addresses.

Hot Site—Also known as alternate site. A site that includes a redundant copy of every computer system and piece of information. This level of fault tolerance is used when systems must be up 100 percent of the time. Hot sites are strictly fault-tolerant implementations, not disaster recovery implementations.

Hub—A device, also known as a concentrator, which works at the physical OSI layer. It is a multiported connection point used to connect network devices via a cable segment.

Hybrid Fiber Coaxial (HFC) Network—A telecommunication technology in which optical fiber cable and coaxial cable are used in different portions of a network to carry broadband content (such as video, data, and voice).

Hybrid Topology—A topology scheme that combines two of the traditional topologies, usually to create a larger topology. In addition, the hybrid topology allows you to use the strengths of the various topologies to maximize the effectiveness of the network.

Hyperlink—An element in an electronic document that links to another place in the same document or to an entirely different document. Typically, you click on the hyperlink to follow the link. Hyperlinks are the most essential ingredient of all hypertext systems, including the World Wide Web.

HyperText Markup Language (HTML)—The authoring language used to create documents on the World Wide Web.

Hypertext Transfer Protocol (HTTP)—A TCP/IP protocol that is the basis for exchange over the World Wide Web (WWW).

I

ICMP Flood—A DoS attack that attempts to overwhelm the target with ICMP packets so that it cannot service them and become unresponsive.

IEEE 802.11—A set of standards that covers wireless networking.

IEEE 802.1x—A standard for port-based network access control that provides authenticated network access to 802.11 wireless networks and wired Ethernet networks.

IMAP-4—A standards-based message access protocols. It follows the online model of message access, although it does support offline and disconnected modes. IMAP-4 offers an array of up-to-date features, including support for the creation and management of remote folders and folder hierarchies, message status flags, new mail notification, retrieval of individual MIME body parts, and server-based searches to minimize the amount of data that must be transferred over the connection.

Incident Response Policy—Part of the organization's security policy. A policy that covers how people in your organization are expected to deal with computer or network security incidents including any type of attack. Of course, when this policy is created, remember that your organization must exhibit due care when handling client information. If any incidents get out of control, it can cause problems for you and your organization, especially if you did not take sufficient steps to protect your network and the information on the network and if you did not respond well to the incident.

Independent Computing Architecture (ICA)—A protocol that allows multiple computers to take control of a virtual computer and use it as if it were their desktop (thin client).

Indirect IR—See diffused infrared technology.

Infrared (IR)—Light that is just below the visible light in the electromagnetic spectrum.

Infrastructure Mode—A wireless mode used when wireless devices communicate with a wireless access point.

Instant Messaging (IM)—A popular method by which people communicate today. IM allows people to send pop-up messages, files, audio, and video between computers.

Integrated Services Digital Network (ISDN)—A planned replacement for POTS so that it can provide voice and data communications worldwide using circuit switching while using the same wiring that is currently being used in homes and businesses. Because ISDN is a digital signal from end to end, it is faster and much more dependable with no line noise. ISDN has the ability to deliver multiple simultaneous connections, in any combination of data, voice, video or fax, over a single line and allows for multiple devices to be attached to the line.

Integrity—Refers to the assurance that data is not altered or destroyed in an unauthorized manner.

Interference—When undesirable electromagnetic waves affect the desired signal.

International Organization for Standardization (ISO)—An international standard organization for communications and information exchange.

Internet—A global network connecting millions of computers.

Internet Connection Sharing (ICS)—A program/server that allow a single dial-up connection to be shared across the network. Typically found on newer Microsoft OSs.

Internet Control Message Protocol (ICMP)—A TCP/IP protocol that sends messages and reports errors regarding the delivery of a packet.

Internet Group Management Protocol (IGMP)—A TCP/IP protocol that is used by IP hosts to report host group membership to local multicast routers.

Internet Information Server (IIS)—The service that provides Web services (HTTP and FTP) on a Microsoft Windows NT, Windows 2000, or Windows .NET server.

Internet Protocol (IP)—Connectionless protocol primarily responsible for addressing and routing packets between hosts.

Internetwork—A network that is internal to a company and is private. It is often a network consisting of several LANs, which are linked together. The smaller LANs are known as subnetworks or subnets.

Intranet—A network based on the TCP/IP protocol, the same protocol that the Internet uses. Unlike the Internet, the Intranet belongs to a single organization, accessible only by the organization's members. An intranet's websites look and act just like any other web sites, but they are isolated by a firewall to stop illegal access. Note: an Intranet could have access to the Internet, but does not require it.

Intrusion—Any compromise of your organization's C-I-A triad.

Intrusion Detection—A process of monitoring and evaluating computer events and network traffic for signs of intrusion.

Intrusion Detection System (IDS)—A hardware device with software that is used to detect unauthorized activity on your network.

Inverse Query—A DNS query provides the IP address and requests a FQDN.

IP Address—A logical address used to uniquely identify a connection on a TCP/IP address (logical address).

IPSec Transport Mode—IPSec mode that secures an existing IP packet from source to destination.

IPSec Tunnel Mode—IPSec mode that puts an existing IP packet inside a new IP packet that is sent to a tunnel end point in the IPSec format.

IP Security (IPSec)—A set of protocols developed by the IETF to support secure exchange of packets at the IP layer. IPSec has been deployed widely to implement Virtual Private Networks (VPNs). IPSec supports two encryption modes: Transport and Tunnel. Transport mode encrypts only the data portion (payload) of each packet, but leaves the header untouched. The more secure Tunnel mode encrypts both the header and the payload. On the receiving side, an IPSec-compliant device decrypts each packet. For IPsec to work, the sending and receiving devices must share a public key. This is accomplished through a protocol known as Internet Security Association and Key Management Protocol/Oakley (ISAKMP/Oakley), which allows the receiver to obtain a public key and authenticate the sender using digital certificates.

IP Spoofing—A situation in which an attacker use the IP address of another system to attack that system or to hide his or her identity.

IPv6—Also known as IPng is a new version of the Internet Protocol (IP) currently being reviewed in IETF standards committees. It is designed to allow the Internet to grow steadily, both in terms of the number of hosts connected and the total amount of data traffic transmitted.

IPX—Short for Internetwork Packet Exchange, a networking protocol used by the Novell NetWare operating systems. Like UDP/IP, IPX is a datagram protocol used for connectionless communications. Higher-level protocols, such as SPX and NCP, are used for additional error recovery services.

ISP—Short for Internet Service Provider, a company that provides access to the Internet.

Iterative Query—A DNS query that gives the best answer it currently has back as a response. The best answer will be the address being sought or an address of a server that would have a better idea of its address.

J

Jabber—An error in which a faulty device (usually a NIC) continuously transmits corrupted or meaningless data onto a network. This may halt the entire network from transmitting data because other devices will perceive the network as busy.

Java—A programming language created by Sun Microsystems.

Java Applet—An applet is a small Internet-based program written in Java, a programming language for the Web, which can be downloaded by any computer. The applet is also able to run in HTML. The applet is usually embedded in an HTML page on a website and can be executed from within a browser.

JavaScript—Netscape's object-based scripting language, which is commonly used to communicate with other components or to accept user input.

Java Virtual Machine (VM)—A software component that takes the plain-text Java code and translates it to native instruction on the client system.

Jitter—A term used to describe instability in a signal wave. It is caused by signal interference.

Journaling Filesystems—A file system that can either keep track of the changes to a file's "metadata" (information such as ownership, creation dates, and so on), or to the data blocks associated with a file, or to both so that the filesystem becomes more resistant against corruption or damage.

K

Kerberos—An authentication system designed to enable two parties to exchange private information across an otherwise open network. It works by assigning a unique key, called a ticket, to each user that logs on to the network. The ticket is then embedded in messages to identify the sender of the message.

Kernel—The central module of an operating system. It is the part of the operating system that loads first and it remains in RAM. Because it stays in memory, it is important for the kernel to be as small as possible while still providing all the essential services required by other parts of the operating system and applications. Typically, the kernel is responsible for memory management, process and task management and disk management.

Key—A string of bits used to map text into a code and a code back to text. You can think the key as a super-decoder ring used to translate text messages to a code and back to text. There are two types of keys, public keys and private keys.

Key Distribution Center (KDC)—Contains the information that allows Kerberos clients to authenticate.

Key Escrow—The procedure of keeping a copy of a user's private key in a centralized location that is only accessible to security administrators, or of implementing a mechanism whereby the private key can be recovered without having to be physically stored. Escrow allows for the future recovery of the key, should it be lost due to disaster or by its owner, or needed by someone authorized to view the information encrypted by it, such as in certain regulatory environments or situations in which law enforcement is involved.

Key Life Cycle—There are five stages in the key life cycle: certificate enrollment, certificate distribution, certificate revocation, certificate renewal, and certificate auditing.

L

Land—A flaw exploitation attack where an attacker sends a forged packet with the same destination and source address and port.

Last Mile—The telephone line that runs from your home or office to the telephone company's central office (CO) or neighborhood switching station (often a small building with no windows). Also known as local loop and last mile.

Layer 3 Switch—A device that combines a router and a switch. It has been optimized for high-performance LAN support and is not meant to service wide area connections.

Layer 2 Tunneling Protocol (LT2P)—An extension to the PPP protocol that enables ISPs to operate Virtual Private Networks (VPNs). L2TP merges the best features of two other tunneling protocols: PPTP from Microsoft and L2F from Cisco Systems. Like PPTP, L2TP requires that the ISP's routers support the protocol.

Layered Defense—A layered approach to building a defense that includes security the network infrastructure, communication protocols, servers, application that run on the servers, and the file system. It should also include some form of user authentication.

Lightweight Directory Access Protocol (LDAP)—A set of protocols for accessing information directories. LDAP is based on the standards contained within the X.500 standard, but is significantly simpler.

Line Conditioner—A device that uses the inductance of transformers to filter out noise and capacitors (and other circuits) to "fill-in" brownouts. In addition, most line conditioners include surge protection.

Line Printer Daemon (LPD)—A TCP/IP protocol that provides printing.

Link-State Algorithms—Also known as shortest-path-first algorithms. A routing protocol that sends updates directly (or by using multicast traffic) to all routers within the network. Each router, however, sends only the portion of the routing table that describes the state of its own links. In essence, link-state algorithms send small updates everywhere.

Linux—Pronounced LIH-nuhks with a short "I", is a UNIX-like operating system that was designed to provide personal computer users a free or very low-cost operating system comparable to traditional and usually more expensive UNIX systems.

LMHOSTS File—A text file similar to a HOSTS file used to resolve computer names to IP addresses.

Load Sharing—See Round-robin.

Local Area Nnetwork (LAN)—A network that has computers that are connected within a geographical close network, such as a room, a building or a group of adjacent buildings.

Local Loop—The telephone line that runs from your home or office to the telephone company's central office (CO) or neighborhood switching station (often a small building with no windows). Also known as subscriber loop and last mile.

Local User Accounts—In Windows NT family domains, an account that allow users to log on at and gain resources on only the computer where you create the local user account. The local user account is stored in the local security database. When using a local user account, you will not be able to access any of the network resources. In addition, for security reasons, you cannot log on as a local user account on a domain/domain controller.

Logical Link Control (LLC)—The sublayer of the data link layer (OSI model) that manages the data link between two computers within the same subnet.

Logic Bomb—A destructive program that goes off when a predetermined event takes place, such as the user typing a certain series of keystrokes, changing a file, or at a certain time and date.

Logical Topology—Part of the Data Link Layer, describes how the data flows through the physical topology or the actual pathway of the data.

Long File Name (LFN)—A file name that can be up to 255 characters.

M

Mail Server—A server that manages electronic messages (email) between users.

Main-in-the-Middle—An attack where an attacker's computer captures the communications between two computers and impersonates them both.

Management Information Bases (MIB)—A database.

Mandatory Access Control (MAC)—A model that uses nondiscretionary control based on multilevel security. In the MAC model, you classify all users and resources to a security label or level. If the user has the same level or higher as the resource that they are trying to access, they are granted access. If not, they are denied access.

Man in the Middle Attack—A DOS attack which the attacker intercepts messages in a public key exchange and then retransmits them, substituting their own public key for the requested one, so that the two original parties still appear to be communicating with each other directly. The attacker uses a program that appears to be the server to the client and appears to be the client to the server. The attack may be used simply to gain access to the messages, or enable the attacker to modify them before retransmitting them.

Mathematical Attacks—An attack that is based on the fact that a key is generally easier to break, the shorter it is, and the less the variety in characters used in the key, than those that somehow "break" an encryption algorithm by finding a way to reverse it without discovering the original key. A long key is better than a short key because longer keys have more possible combinations that you need to try before you find the correct key value using brute force. But with the key length, you also need to look at it mathematically.

MD5—A message digest and algorithm that is used to verify data integrity through the creation of a 128-bit message digest from data input (which may be a message of any length) that is claimed to be as unique to that specific data as a fingerprint is to the specific individual. MD5, which was developed by Professor Ronald L. Rivest of MIT, is intended for use with digital signature applications, which require that large files must be compressed by a secure method before being encrypted with a secret key, under a public key cryptosystem. MD5 is currently a standard, Internet Engineering Task Force (IETF) Request for Comments (RFC) 1321.

Media Access Control (MAC) Address—A hardware address (physical address) identifying a node on the network. It is a unique hardware address (unique on the LAN/subnet) burned onto a ROM chip assigned by the hardware vendors or selected with jumpers or DIP switches.

Media Access Control (MAC) Sublayer—The lower sublayer of the Data Link layer (OSI model) that communicates directly with the network adapter card. It defines the network logical topology, which is the actual pathway (ring or bus) of the data signals being sent. In addition, it allows multiple devices to use the same media and it determines how the network card gets access or control of the network media so that two devices don't trample over each other.

Member Server—A server that is not a domain controller and does not have a copy of the domain database).

Mesh Topology—A topology whereas every computer is linked to every other computer.

Message Digests—Also known as hash encryption, a one-way encryption that uses algorithms that don't really use a key. Instead, it converts data from a variable length to a fixed length piece of data called a hash value. This shorter hashed key is faster to retrieve and use. Hashing is always a one-way operation. There's no need to "reverse engineer" the hash function by analyzing the hashed values. In fact, the ideal hash function cannot be derived by such analysis.

Message Transfer Agent (MTA)—The program responsible for receiving incoming emails and delivering the messages to individual users. The MTA transfers messages between computers. Hidden from the average user, it is responsible for routing messages to their proper destinations. MTAs receive messages from both MUAs and other MTAs, although single-user machines more often retrieve mail messages using POP. The MTA is commonly referred to as the mail server program. UNIX sendmail and Microsoft Exchange Server are two examples of MTAs.

Metric—A standard of measurement, such as hop count, that is used by routing algorithms to determine the optimal path to a destination.

Metropolitan Area Network (MAN)—A network designed for a town or city, usually using high-speed connections such as fiber optics.

MIB—Short for Management Information Base, a database of objects that can be monitored by a network management system. Both SNMP and RMON use standardized MIB formats that allow any SNMP and RMON tools to monitor any device defined by a MIB.

Microsoft Baseline Security Analyzer (MBSA)—A software utility for vulnerability scanning.

Microsoft Challenge Handshake Authentication Protocol (MS-CHAP)—An authentication protocol that is Microsoft's proprietary version of CHAP. Unlike PAP and SPAP, it lets you encrypt data that is sent using the Point-to-Point Protocol (PPP) or PPTP connections using Microsoft Point-to-Point Encryption (MPPE).

Microwave—A form of electromagnetic energy that operates at a higher frequency (low GHZ frequency range) than radio wave communications. Since it provides higher bandwidths than those available using radio waves, it is currently one of the most popular long distance transmission technologies.

Modem (modulator-demodulator)—A device that enables a computer to transmit data over telephone lines. Since the computer information is stored and processed digitally, and the telephone lines transmit data using analog waves, the modem converts digital signals to analog signals (modulates) and analog signals to digital signals (demodulates).

Modulation—The process of changing a signal to represent data.

M of N Control—A policy of dividing up a task among multiple entities so that no one person acting alone can perform the entire task. It is used to help minimize an organization's exposure to the risk of one person misusing a privilege, and performing a sensitive action like key recovery without authorization.

MT-RJ Connector—A fiber optic connect that uses a connected that is similar to a RJ-45 connector. It offers a new small form factor two-fiber connector that is lower in cost and smaller than the duplex SC interface.

Multicast—Communication between a single sender and multiple receivers.

Multi-Factor Authentication—A system that uses two or more authentication methods to authenticate someone.

Multifiber Cable—A cable that has anywhere from three to several hundred optical fibers in them, typically in a multiple of two.

Multimode Fiber (MMF)—Fiber-optic cable that is capable of transmitting multiple modes (independent light paths) at various wavelengths or phases.

Multiplexer (mux)—A device that sends and receives several data signals at different frequencies.

Multiplexing—The technique that allows data from different applications to share a single data stream.

Multipoint—A connection that links three or more devices together through a single communication medium.

Multipurpose Internet Mail Extensions (MIME)—A specification for formatting non-ASCII messages so that they can be sent over the Internet. Many email clients now support MIME, which enables them to send and receive graphics, audio, and video files via the Internet mail system. In addition, MIME supports messages in character sets other than ASCII.

Multistation Access Unit (MAU or MSAU)—A physical layer device unique to Token Ring networks that acts as a hub. While a hub defines a logical bus, the MAU defines a logical ring.

Mutual Authentication—A situation in which both the server and client must authenticate with one another. Named pipes and mailslots are high-level Interprocess Communication mechanism used by network computers. Different from the other mechanism, both are written as file system drivers.

N

Name Servers—A server or program that translates names from one form to another. Name servers are often associated with Domain Name Services (NDS) that translates host and domain names to IP addresses.

Namespace—The set of names in a naming system.

Narrowband Radio System—A radio system that transmits and receives user information on a specific radio frequency. Narrowband radio keeps the radio signal frequency as narrow as possible just to pass the information.

NDIS—Short for network device interface specification (developed by Microsoft) that allow multiple protocols to use a single network adapter card at the same time.

Nearline Site—See warm site.

Need to Know—A basic security concept that holds that information should be limited to only those individuals who require it.

NetBEUI—Short for NetBIOS Enhanced User Interface, which provides the transport and network layers for the NetBIOS protocol, usually found on Microsoft networks. NetBEUI is a protocol used to transport data packets between two nodes. While NetBEUI is smaller than TCP/IP or IPX and is extremely quick, it will only send packets within the same network. Unfortunately, NetBEUI is not a routable protocol, which means that it cannot send a packet to computer on another network.

NetWare—A popular local-area network (LAN) operating system developed by Novell Corporation. NetWare is a software product that runs on a variety of different types of LANs, from Ethernets to IBM token-ring networks. It provides users and programmers with a consistent interface that is independent of the actual hardware used to transmit messages.

NetWare Directory Services (NDS)—A global, distributed, replicated database that keeps track of users and resources and provides controlled access to network resources. It is typically found on Novell NetWare networks.

NetWare Loadable Module (NLM)—Software that enhances or provides additional functions in a NetWare 3.x or higher server. Support for database engines, workstations, network protocols, fax and print servers are examples.

Network—Two or more computers connected together to share resources such as files or a printer. For a network to function, it requires a network service to share or access a common media or pathway to connect the computers. To bring it all together, protocols give the entire system common communication rules.

Network Access Server—See Remote access server.

Network Address—An address that uniquely identifies a network.

Network Address Translation (NAT)—A method of connecting multiple computers to the Internet (or any other IP network) using one IP address. With a NAT gateway running on this single computer, it is possible to share that single address between multiple local computers and connect them all at the same time. The outside world is unaware of this division and thinks that only one computer is connected.

Network Analyzer—See protocol analyzer.

Network-Attached Storage (NAS)—Hard disk storage that is set up with its own network address rather than being attached to the department computer that is serving applications to a network's workstation users.

Network Basic Input/Output System (NetBIOS)—A common program that runs on most Microsoft networks. It is used by applications to communicate with NetBIOS-compliant transports such as NetBEUI, IPX or TCP/IP. It is responsible for establishing logical names (computer names) on the network, establishing a logical connection between the two computers and supporting reliable data transfer between computers that have established a session.

Network File System (NFS)—A TCP/IP protocol that provides transparent remote access to shared files across networks.

Network Information Service (NIS)—A centralized database that client machines refer to for authentication, typically used in UNIX networks. If you are familiar with Microsoft networks, this is similar to Microsoft's domain controller.

Network Interface Card (NIC)—A device used to connect computers to the network by using a special expansion card (or built into the motherboard). The network card will then communicate by sending signals through a cable (twisted-pair, coaxial and fiber optics) or by using wireless technology (infrared or radio waves). The role of the network card is to prepare and send data to another computer, receive data from another computer and control the flow of data between the computer and the cabling system.

Network Layer—The OSI model layer that is concerned with addressing and routing necessary to move data (known as packets or datagrams) from one network (or subnet) to another. This includes establishing, maintaining and terminating connections between networks, making routing decisions and relaying data from one network to another.

Network Operating System (NOS)—An operating system that includes special functions for connecting computers and devices into a local-area network (LAN), to manage the resources and services of the network and to provide network security for multiple users.

Network Time Protocol (NTP)—An Internet standard protocol that assures accurate synchronization to the millisecond of computer clock times in a network of computers.

Nodes—Devices connected to the computer including networked computers, routers and network printers

Noise—Interference or static that destroys the integrity of signals. Noise can come from a variety of sources, including radio waves, nearby electrical wires, lightning and other power fluctuations, and bad connections.

Nonrepudiation—Prevents an individual or process from denying that he, she, or it performed a task or sent data.

Novell Directory Services (NDS)—A directory service based primarily on the X.500 Internet directory standard used on Novell NetWare servers 4.0 and higher. All of the network resources are represented as objects and placed into a hierarchical structure, called an **NDS Tree.**

NTFS—A file system for the Windows NT Family OSs designed for both the server and workstation. It provides a combination of performance, reliability, security and compatibility.

NTLM Authentication—The client selects a string of bytes, uses the password to perform a one-way encryption of the string, and sends both the original string and the encrypted one to the server. The server receives the original string and uses the password from the account database to perform the same one-way encryption. If the result matches the encrypted string sent by the client, the server concludes that the client knows the username/password pair.

NWLink—Microsoft's NDIS-compliant, 32-bit implementation of the Internetwork Packet Exchange (IPX), Sequenced Packet Exchange (SPX), and NetBIOS protocols used in Novell networks. NWLink is a standard network protocol that supports routing and can support NetWare client/server applications, where NetWare-aware Sockets-based applications communicate with IPX/SPX Sockets-based applications.

O

Object—A distinct, named set of attributes or characteristics that represent a network resource, including computers, people, group and printers.

One-Time Pad (OTP)—A system in which a private key generated randomly is used only once to encrypt a message that is then decrypted by the receiver using a matching one-time pad and key. It is considered a perfect encryption scheme because it is unbreakable and each pad is used exactly once.

One-Time Password—A password that is used only once for a very limited period of time and then is no longer valid. If someone intercepts the password at any point, the password is useless because it has already expired. One-time passwords are typically counter-based or clock-based tokens.

Open Architecture—Specification of the system or standard is public.

Open Shortest Path First (OSPF)—A Link State Route Discovery protocol where each router periodically advertises itself to other routers.

Open Systems Interconnection (OSI) Reference Model—The world's prominent networking architecture model.

Optical Time Domain Reflectometer (OTDR)—The fiber-optic equivalent of the TDR that is used to test copper cables. The OTDR transmits a calibrated signal pulse over the cable to be tested and monitors the signal that returns back to the unit. Instead of measuring signal reflections caused by electrical impedance as a TDR does, however, the OTDR measures the signal returned by backscatter, a phenomenon that affects all fiber optic cables.

Organization Units (OU)—In directory services, a container that is used to hold and organize objects including users, groups, computers and other organization units. See figure 10.5.

Overvoltages—When power is rated at more than 10% additional voltage than what the power is supposed to be.

P

Packet—A piece of a message transmitted over a packet-switching network. One of the key features of a packet is that it contains the destination address in addition to the data.

Packet Switching—A technique which messages are broken into smaller parts called packets. Each packet is tagged with source, destination, and intermediary node addresses as appropriate. Packets can have a defined maximum length and can be stored in RAM instead of hard disk. Packets can take a variety of possible paths through the network in an attempt to keep the network connections filled at time.

Password—A combination of text used to validate the person's identity when that person logs on.

Password Authentication Protocol (PAP)—An authentication protocol that has Passwords sent across the link as unencrypted plaintext.

Password Guessing—An attack that involves guessing a user name and password in an attempt to gain access to a network or system. These are password programs available that attempt to break a password using a brute force technique, and others that try passwords against a dictionary.

Patch—A temporary fix to a program bug. A patch is an actual piece of object code that is inserted into (patched into) an executable program.

Patch Panels—A panel with numerous RJ-45 ports. The wall jacks are connected to the back of the patch panel to the individual RJ-45 ports. You can then use patch cables to connect the port in the front of the patch panel to a computer or a hub. As a result, you can connect multiple computers with a hub located in the wiring closet or server room.

Peer-to-Peer Network—A network that has no dedicated servers. Instead, all computers are equal. Therefore, they provide services and request services. Since a person's resources are kept on his or her own machine, a user manages his or her own shared resources. A peer-to-peer network is sometimes referred to as a workgroup.

Penetration Testing—The process of probing and identifying security vulnerabilities in a network and the extent to which they might be exploited by outside parties. It is a necessary tool for determining the current security posture of your network. Such a test should determine both the existence and extent of any risk.

Perimeter Network—A separate network segment and set of resource between an internal and external network. The purpose of the perimeter network is to provide services to the public without compromising the security of the private network. Also known as DMZ.

Perimeter Security—Security that controlls access to critical network applications, data, and services. Perimeter security is often controlled with routers and firewalls.

Permanent Virtual Circuits (PVCs)—A permanently established virtual circuit that consists of one mode, data transfer. PVCs are used in situations in which data transfer between devices is constant.

Permission—Defines the type of access granted to an object or object attribute. The permissions available for an object depend on the type of object.

Personal Computer (PC)—A computer meant to be used by one person. The first personal computer produced by IBM was called the PC, and increasingly the term PC came to mean IBM or IBM-compatible personal computers, to the exclusion of other types of personal computers, such as Macintoshes. In recent years, the term PC applies to any personal computer based on an Intel microprocessor or an Intel-compatible microprocessor.

Personal Identification Number (PIN)—A code made of numbers. PINs are commonly assigned to bank customers for use with automatic cash dispensers and they are also used, sometimes with a security token, for individual access to computer networks or other secure systems.

Physical Layer—The OSI model that is responsible for the actual transmission of the bits sent across a physical media. It allows signals, such as electrical signals, optical signals, or radio signals, to be exchanged among communicating machines. Therefore, it defines the electrical, physical and procedural characteristics required to establish, maintain and deactivate physical links.

Physical Topology—Part of the Physical Layer, describes how the network actually appears.

Ping—A utility to determine whether a specific IP address is accessible. It works by sending a packet to the specified address and waiting for a reply. Ping is used primarily to troubleshoot Internet connections.

Ping of Death (POD)—A flaw exploitation attack in which the attacker sends an ICMP echo request that is larger than 65,536 bytes as multiple fragmented packets to the target host.

Plain Old Telephone Service (POTS)—The PSTN/ standard telephone service that most homes use.

Plaintext—Information that is not encrypted.

Pluggable Authentication Modules (PAM)—Modules used in Linux that allow you to change your authentication methods and requirements on the fly, and encapsulate all local authentication methods without recompiling any of your programs.

Point-to-Point Protocol (PPP)—The predominant protocol for modem-based access to the Internet that provides full-duplex, bidirectional operations between hosts and can encapsulate multiple network-layer LAN protocols to connect to private networks.

Point-to-Point Tunneling Protocol (PPTP)—A new technology for creating Virtual Private Networks (VPNs), developed jointly by Microsoft Corporation, U.S. Robotics, and several remote access vendor companies, known collectively as the PPTP Forum. A VPN is a private network of computers that uses the public Internet to connect some nodes. Because the Internet is essentially an open network, the Point-to-Point Tunneling Protocol (PPTP) is used to ensure that messages transmitted from one VPN node to another are secure. With PPTP, users can dial in to their corporate network via the Internet.

Policies—(1) A document that makes a specific statement requiring that a rule must be met. (2) In Windows NT family networks, a tool used by administrators to define and control how programs, network resources and the operating system behave for users and computers in a domain or Active Directory structure.

Polling—An access method that has a single device (sometimes referred to as a channel-access administrator) designated as the primary device, which polls or asks each of the secondary devices known as slaves if they have information to be transmitted.

POP-3—The newest version of the Post Office Protocol, which can be used with or without SMTP.

Port—An address on a host where an application makes itself available to incoming data.

Portal—In wireless networks, the logical integration or connection between wired LANs and 802.II wireless LANs.

POSIX—A set of IEEE and ISO standards that define an interface between programs and UNIX. By following the POSIX standard, developers have some assurance that their software can be easily ported or translated to a POSIX-compliant operating system.

Postal, Telegraph and Telephone (PTT)—The European organization that is responsible for providing combined postal, telegraph, and telephone services.

Post Office Protocol (POP)—A TCP/IP protocol that defines a simple interface between a user's mail client software and email server. It is used to download mail from server to the client and allows the user to manage their mailboxes.

PPPoE (PPP over Ethernet)—A protocol that was designed to bring the security and metering benefits of PPP to Ethernet connections such as those used in DSL.

Preemptive Multitasking—The operating system parcels out CPU time slices to each program.

Presentation Layer—The OSI model layer that ensures that information sent by an application layer protocol of one system will be readable by the application layer protocol on the remote system. It also provides encryption/decryption, compression/decompression of data and network redirectors.

Pretty Good Privacy (PGP)—A technique for encrypting messages, which is based on the public-key method. To encrypt a message using PGP, you need the PGP encryption package, which is available for free from a number of sources.

Primary Domain Controller (PDC)—The server that contains the master copy of the domain database on Windows NT networks.

Primary Name Server—A DNS name server that stores and maintains the zone file locally. Changes to a zone, such as adding domains or hosts, are done by changing files at the primary name server.

Primary Rate Interface (PRI)—A form of ISDN that includes 23 B-channels (30 in Europe) and one 64-KB D-Channel. PRI service is generally transmitted through a T-1 line (or an E1 line in Europe).

Print Server—A server that manages user access to printer resources connected to the network, allowing one printer to be used by many people.

Print Sharing—A network service that allows several people to send documents to a centrally located printer in the office.

Privacy Policy—Explains reasonable expectations of privacy for clients, customers, and partners. This policy should detail such issues as monitoring of email, maintaining logs of websites visited, and restrictions and exceptions for accessing users' files.

Private Branch Exchange (PBX)—A telephone system within an enterprise that switches calls between enterprise users on local lines while allowing all users to share a certain number of external phone lines.

Private-Key Encryption—The most basic form of encryption that requires that each individual must possess a copy of the key. Of course, for this work as intended, you must have a secure way to transport the key to other people. You must keep multiple single keys per person, which can get very cumbersome. Private-key algorithms are generally very fast and easily implemented in hardware. Therefore, they are commonly used for bulk data encryption.

Private Network—A network that is not connected to the Internet.

Process—An executing program.

Project 802—A set of standards that have several areas of responsibility including the network card, the wide area network components and the media components.

Promiscuous Mode—A condition that a network adapter can be placed in to gather all passing information.

Proprietary System—A system or architecture that is privately owned and controlled by a company and has not divulged specifications that would allow other companies to duplicate the product.

Protocol Analyzer—Also known as a network analyzer, is software or a hardware/software device that allows you to capture or receive every packet on your media, stores it in a trace buffer, and then shows a breakdown of each of the packets by protocol in the order that they appeared. Therefore, it can help you analyze all levels of the OSI model to determine the cause of the problem.

Protocols—The rules or standards that allow the computers to connect to one another and enable computers and peripheral devices to exchange information with as little error as possible.

Protocol Suite—A set of protocols that work together.

Proxy—Any device that acts on behalf of another.

Proxy Server—A server that performs a function on behalf of other computers. It is typically used to provide local intranet clients with access to the Internet while keeping the local intranet free from intruders.

Public Key—Provided to many people and used to validate that a message came from the private key holder or to encrypt data to send the private key holder.

Public Key Cryptography Standards (PKCS)—A set of unofficial standards that is used in public key cryptography.

Public Key Encryption—The nonsecret key that is available to anyone you choose, or made available to everyone by posting them in a public place. It is often made available through a digital certificate. The private key is kept in a secure location, which is used only by you. When data needs to be sent, it is protected with a secret key encryption that was encrypted with the public key of the recipient of the data. The encrypted secret key is then transmitted to the recipient along with the encrypted data. The recipient will use the private key to decrypt the secret key. The secret key will then be used to decrypt the message itself.

Public Key Infrastructure (PKI)—Security infrastructure that uses asymmetric key pairs and combines software, encryption technologies, and services to provide a means of protecting the security of communications and business transactions.

Public Network—A network that allows everyone connected to have access to the data on the network. Typically, it is a network that is connected directly to the Internet.

Public Switched Telephone Network (PSTN)—The international telephone system based on copper wires (UTP cabling) carrying analog voice data.

Pull Partner—A WINS server that requests new database entries from its partner. The pull occurs at configured time intervals or in response to an update notification from a push partner.

Punch-Down Block—A device used to connect several cable runs to each other without going through a hub.

Push Partner—A WINS server that sends update notification messages. The update notification occurs after a configurable number of changes to the WINS database.

Q

Quality of Service (QoS)—Guaranteed bandwidth on a connection-oriented network that provides sufficient bandwidth for audio and video without the jitters or pauses and the transfer of important data within a timely manner.

Query—A request for information from a database.

R

Rackmount Cabinet—A cabinet designed to hold several servers.

Radio Frequency (RF)—Signals that reside between 10 KHz to 1 GHz of the electromagnetic spectrum. It can be used to transmit data through the air.

Radio Frequency Interference (RFI)—Signals caused by transmission sources such as a radio station, which may cause interference with other signals.

Realm—An organization boundary that is formed to provide authentication boundaries. Each realm has an authentication server (AS) and a ticket granting service. Also known as Kerberos realm.

Recursive Query—A query that asks the DNS server to respond with the requested data or with an error stating that the requested data doesn't exist or that the domain name specified doesn't exist.

Redirectors—Intercepts file input/output requests and directs them to a drive or resource on another computer.

Redundant Array of Independent (or Inexpensive) Disks (RAID)—A category of disk drives that employ two or more drives in combination for fault tolerance and performance. RAID disk drives are used frequently on servers but aren't generally necessary for personal computers.

Reflective IR—See diffused infrared technology.

Registration Authority (RA)—An entity that is designed to verify certificate contents for the CA. When a person requests a certificate, the CA verifies that individual's identity, constructs the certificate, signs it, delivers it to the requester, and maintains the certificate over its lifetime. When another person wants to communicate with this person, the CA will vouch for that person's identity.

Registry—A central, secure database in which windows store all hardware configuration information, software configuration information and system security policy.

Registry Editor (REGEDIT. EXE)—A windows utility that allows you to view or edit the registry.

Remote Access Server—A server that hosts modems for inbound requests to connect to the network.

Remote Access Service (RAS)—A service that allows users to connect remotely using various protocols and connection types.

Remote Authentication Dial-In User Service (RADIUS)—An industry standard client/server protocol and software that enables remote access servers to communicate with a central server to authenticate dial-in users and authorize their access to the requested system or service for authenticating remote users.

Repeater—A device that works at the physical OSI layer, which is a network device used to regenerate or replicate a signal or to move packets from one physical media to another.

Replay Attack—A DoS attack that involves listening to and repeating data passed on the network. An attacker tries to capture packets containing passwords or digital signatures as they pass between two hosts on the network using a protocol analyzer. The attacker then filters the data and extracts the portion of the packet that contains the password, encryption key, or digital signature. Later, the attacker resends or replays that information in an attempt to gain access to a secured resource.

Requesters—A program or part of a program that requests services.

Request for Comments (RFC)—The series of documents that specify the TCP/IP standards.

Resolver—A client that uses a name server.

Reverse Address Resolution (RARP) Protocol—A TCP/IP protocol that permits a physical address, such as an Ethernet address, to be translated into an IP address.

Reverse Query—A DNS query is used by a resolver that knows an IP address and wants to know the host name.

Right—(1) Authorizes a user to access a file or directory on a network server. (2) Authorizes a user to perform certain actions on a computer, such as logging on to a system interactively/log on locally to the computer, backing up files and directories, performing a system shutdown, or adding/removing a device driver.

Ring Topology—A topology that has all devices connected to one another in a closed loop. Each device is connected directly to two other devices.

RIP Spoofing—Forging the Routing Information Protocol (RIP) packets to tell the router to send packets to an unauthorized network.

Riser Cable—Cable intended for use in vertical shafts that run between floors.

Risers—Vertical connections between floors.

Risk—Exposure to loss or possible injury. With information security, the risk is that your company's information will fall prey to outside forces and cause your company losses in time, money, and reputation.

Risk Assessment—The evaluation of threats, vulnerabilities, and potential impact on assets.

Risk Management—The complete process used to identify, control, and mitigate the impact of uncertain events.

RJ-45—A connector that supports 10Base-T/100Base-TX (UTP) cabling.

Role—A special type of group defined by job roles or duties.

Role-Based Access Control (RBAC)—Access is based on the role a user plays in the organization. For instance a human resources manager would need access to information that a department manager would not need access to, and both would need access to some common information.

Root CA—A certification authority (CA) at the top of a CA hierarchy that issues certificates to subordinate CAs. Those CAs can then issue certificates to other CAs, and so on. The CAs at each level can issue certificates to subordinate CAs or users.

Root Domain—The top of the DNS tree. It is sometimes shown as a period (.) or as empty quotation marks (""), indicating a null value.

Round-Robin—Rotates the order of resource records data returned in a query answer in which multiple resource records exist of the same resource record type for a queried DNS domain name. Since the client is required to try the first IP address listed, a DNS server configured to perform round-robin rotates the order of the A resource records when answering client requests. Also known as load sharing.

Router—A device that works at the network OSI layer. It connects two or more LANs. In addition, it can break a large network into smaller, more manageable subnets. As multiple LANs are connected together, multiple routes are created to get from one LAN to another. Routers then share status and routing information to other routers so that they can provide better traffic management and bypass slow connections.

Router Information Protocol (RIP)—A distance vector route discovery protocol where the entire routing table is periodically sent to the other routers.

RSA Standard—A public-key encryption technology based on the fact that there is no efficient way to factor very large numbers. Deducing an RSA key, therefore, requires an extraordinary amount of computer processing power and time. The RSA algorithm has become the de facto standard for industrial-strength encryption, especially for data sent over the Internet. It is built into many software products, including Netscape Navigator and Microsoft Internet Explorer.

Rule of Least Privilege—When you give a person or group only the required amount of access and nothing more.

S

Sags—Which usually are not a problem, are very short drops in power lasting only a few milliseconds.

Samba—Software used on a Linux computer that provides file and print sharing like a Windows NT server using the CIFS protocol.

Sandbox—A security measure in the Java development environment. The sandbox is a set of rules that are used when creating an applet that prevents certain functions when the applet is sent as part of a Web page.

Satellite Systems—A microwave system that provides far bigger areas of coverage than can be achieved using other technologies. The microwave dishes are aligned to geostationary satellites that can either relay signals between sites directly or via another satellite. The huge distances covered by the signal result in propagation delays of up to 5 seconds.

Schema—Pronounced *skee-ma,* the structure of a database system, described in a formal language supported by the database management system (DBMS). In a relational database, the schema defines the tables, the fields in each table, and the relationships between fields and tables. Schemas are generally stored in a data dictionary. Although a schema is defined in text database language, the term is often used to refer to a graphical depiction of the database structure.

Search Engine—A program that searches documents for specified keywords and returns a list of the documents where the keywords were found.

Secondary Name Server—A DNS name server that gets the data from its zone from another name server, either a primary name server or another secondary name server. The process of obtaining this zone information across the network is referred to as a zone transfer.

Second Extended File System (ext2)—The native Linux filesystem. It is very similar to other modern UNIX filesystems but most closely resembles the Berkeley Fast Filesystem used by BSD systems. The maximum size of an ext2 filesystem is 4 TB, while the maximum file size is currently limited to 2 GB by the Linux kernel.

Second-Level Domain Names—Part of the DNS system, they are variable-length names registered to an individual or organization for use on the Internet.

Secure Electronic Transaction (SET)—An open encryption and security specification designed to protect credit card transactions on the Internet. It was supported initially by Mastercard, Visa, Microsoft, Netscape, and others. With SET, a user is given an electronic wallet (digital certificate) and a transaction is conducted and verified using a combination of digital certificates and digital signatures among the purchaser, a merchant, and the purchaser's bank in a way that ensures privacy and confidentiality. SET makes use of Netscape's Secure Sockets Layer (SSL), Microsoft's Secure Transaction Technology (STT), and Terisa System's Secure Hypertext Transfer Protocol (S-HTTP). SET uses some but not all aspects of a public key infrastructure (PKI).

Secure FTP (S-FTP)—Secure FTP (S-FTP) is a program that uses SSH to transfer files or you need to transfer them over an encrypted pathway. Unlike standard FTP, it encrypts both commands and data, preventing passwords and sensitive information from being transmitted in the clear over the network. It is functionally similar to FTP, but because it uses a different protocol, you cannot use a standard FTP client to talk to an SFTP server, nor can you connect to an FTP server with a client that supports only SFTP.

Secure Hash Algorithm (SHA)—The algorithm specified in the Secure Hash Standard (SHS, FIPS 180), was developed by NIST. Its design is very similar to the MD4 family of hash functions developed by Rivest. SHA-1 is also described in the ANSI X9.30 standard. The algorithm takes a message of less than 2^{64} bits in length and produces a 160-bit message digest. The algorithm is slightly slower than MD5, but the larger message digest makes it more secure against brute-force collision and inversion attacks.

Secure Hypertext Transfer Protocol (S-HTTP)—Also referred to as HTTP/S, an extension to HTTP to support sending data securely over the Word Wide Web.

Secure Multipurpose Internet Mail Extensions (S/MIME)—This specification is similar to PGP in that it seeks to enable the encryption and digital signing of email messages. S/MIME is designed and marketed for integration into email and messaging products.

Secure Recovery—A term that refers to an alternate site that contains a replica of all or part of your network. Depending on your budget and the nature of your business, solutions can range from a mirror server running at a site in another site in a complete secure recovery area containing everything you need to keep your business going until you can replace your original equipment. A number of companies specialize in business recovery services. Some are simply hosting services that run mirror servers for you in a protected environment in another city.

Secure Shell (SSH)—A protocol and software package developed at the Helsinki University of Technology and is a secure, low-level Transport protocol. SSH allows users to log on to a remote computer over the network, execute commands on it, and move files from one computer to another while providing strong authentication and secure communications over unsecure channels.

Secure Sockets Layer (SSL)—A protocol developed by Netscape for transmitting private documents via the Internet. SSL works by using a public key to encrypt data that's transferred over the SSL connection. Both Netscape Navigator and Internet Explorer support SSL, and many websites use the protocol to obtain confidential user information, such as credit card numbers. By convention, URLs that require an SSL connection start with https: instead of http:.

Security—The process and techniques by which digital information assets are protected. The goals of network security are to maintain integrity, protect confidentiality and assure availability.

Security Accounts Manager (SAM)—The database used in Windows NT machine that contains information about all the users and groups within a domain.

Security Administrator Tool for Analyzing Networks (SATAN)—A software utility for vulnerability scanning.

Security Association (SA)—A contract laying out the rules of the connection for the duration of the SA. It is used with IPSec.

Security Baseline—Standards that specify a minimum (that is, "baseline") set of security controls that are suitable for most organizations under normal circumstances. They typically address both technical issues (such as software configuration) and operational issues (such as keeping applications up to date with vendor patches).

Security Policy—Set of rules regarding access and use of an organization's technology and information assets. Security policy is often created using a series of subordinate policies.

Segment—A segment could be a single cable such as a backbone cable, or a cable that connects a hub and a computer.

Sendmail—The most widely used Mail Transfer Agent (MTA).

Serial Line Interface Protocol (SLIP)—A simple protocol, in which you send packets down a serial link delimited with special END characters.

Server—A service provider that provides access to network resources.

Server Message Block (SMB)—The SMB protocol, which was jointly developed by Microsoft, Intel and IBM, defines a series of commands used to pass information between networked computers. Clients connected to a network using NetBIOS over TCP/IP, NetBEUI or IPX/SPX can send SMB commands. Note: Microsoft refers to NetBIOS over TCP/IP as NBT.

Server Rack—A rack designed specifically to hold multiple computers.

Service—A program, routine, or process that performs a specific system function to support other programs.

Service Access Point (SAP)—Used by the LLC to identify which protocol it is.

Service Advertising Potocol (SAP)—An IPX protocol used to advertise the services of all known servers on the network, including file servers, print server and so on. Servers periodically broadcast their service information while listening for SAPs on the network and storing the service information. Clients then access service information table when it needs to access a network service.

Service Level Agreement (SLA)—A contract that defines business or technical support parameters that an IT outsourcing firm aggress to provide its clients.

Service Profile Identifier (SPID)—A directory number and additional identifier used to identify the ISDN device to the telephone network.

Service Set Identifier (SSID)—A 32-character identifier that is attached to each packet, identifying the wireless LAN to which the traffic belongs, so that multiple wireless LANs can exist in the same physical area.

Session—A reliable dialog between two computers.

Session Hijacking—An attack that occurs after a source and destination computer have established a communications link or session. The attack occurs when a third computer disables the ability of one of the computers to communicate, and then imitates that computer (takes over the connection/session).

Session Layer—The OSI-model layer that allows remote users to establish, manage and terminate a connection (sessions).

Share-Level Security Model—A model that a network administrator assigns passwords to network resources.

Sharing—The process of making a drive, directory or printer available to users on the network.

Shell—Shell is a term for the interactive user interface with an operating system. The shell is the layer of programming that understands and executes the commands a user enters. In some systems, the shell is called a command interpreter. A shell usually implies an interface with a command syntax (think of the DOS operating system and its "C:>" prompts and user commands such as "dir" and "edit").

Shielded Twisted Pair (STP)—Similar to Unshielded Twisted Pair except that is usually surrounded by a braided shield that serves to reduce both EMI sensitivity and radio emissions.

Shiva Password Authentication Protocol (SPAP)—An authentication protocol that sends password across link in reversibly encrypted form. It is typically used when connecting to a Shiva LanRover, or when a Shiva client connects to a Windows 2000-based remote access server.

S-HTTP—An extension to the HTTP protocol to support sending data securely over the World Wide Web.

Signaling—The method for using electrical, light energy or radio waves to communicate.

Simple Mail Transfer Protocol (SMTP)—A TCP/IP protocol for the exchange of electronic mail over the Internet. It is used between email servers on the Internet or to allow an email client to send mail to a server.

Simple Network Management Protocol (SNMP)—A TCP/IP protocol that defines procedures and management information databases for managing TCP/IP-based network devices.

Simplex Dialog—A form of dialog that allows communications on the transmission channel to occur in only one direction. Essentially, one device is allowed to transmit and all of the other devices receive.

Simplex Fiber-Optic Cable—A type of cable that has only one optical fiber inside the cable jacket. Since simplex cables only have one fiber inside them, there is usually a larger buffer and a thicker jacket to make the cable easier to handle.

Single-Mode Fiber (SMF)—Fiber-optic cable that can transmit light in only one mode, but the narrower diameter yields less dispersion, resulting in longer transmission distances.

Single Sign-On—A user only has to log on once to be granted access to all the resources that they have access to.

Small Office/Home Office (SOHO)—Small networks used primarily in home offices that might be part of a larger corporation but yet remain apart from it. SOHO networks are usually peer-to-peer networks.

Smurf Attack—A specific type of ICMP flood DoS attack that involves sending spoofed ICMP echo packets to a subnet. The spoofed address is the target of the attack and all hosts on the subnet reply to the target.

SNMP Agent—A client or device that returns the appropriate information to an SNMP manager.

SNMP Community—A collection of hosts grouped together for administrative purposes. Deciding what computers should belong to the same community is generally, but not always, determined by the physical proximity of the computers. Communities are identified by the names you assign to them.

SNMP Manager—The console through the network administrator performs network management functions.

Social Engineering—A term used to describe the process of circumventing security barriers by persuading authorized users to provide passwords, or other sensitive information.

Socket—A logical address assigned to a specific process running on a host computer. It forms a virtual connection between the host and client and it identifies a specific upper-layer software process or protocol.

SONET—Short for Synchronous Optical Network, is the North America equivalent of SDH that specifies synchronous data transmission over fiber optic cables.

Source-Route Bridging (SRB)—A bridging method used on Token ring networks that is responsibility of determining the path to the destination node.

Spam—Electronic junk mail or junk newsgroup postings. Some people define spam even more generally as any unsolicited email. Typically, spam consists of emails advertising for some product sent to a mailing list or newsgroup. In addition to wasting people's time with unwanted email, spam also eats up a lot of network bandwidth.

Spanning Tree Algorithm (STA)—A method used with Ethernet bridges that designates a loop-free subset of the network's topology by placing those bridge ports that, if active would create loops into a standby (blocking condition) mode.

Spike—Sometimes known as a transient, a spike is a overvoltage that occurs that may damage the computer.

Spoofing—Pretending to be someone else by impersonating, masquerading, or mimicking that person.

Spread-Spectrum Signals—Signals that are distributed over a wide range of frequencies and then collected onto their original frequency at the receiver. Different from narrowband signals, spread spectrum signals use wider bands, which transmit at a much lower spectral power density (measured in Watts per Hertz).

SPX—Short for Sequenced Packet Exchange, a transport layer protocol (layer 4 of the OSI Model) used in Novell NetWare networks. The SPX layer sits on top of the IPX layer (layer 3) and provides connection-oriented services between two nodes on the network. SPX is used primarily by client/server applications.

SQL Server—A server that is a database management system (DBMS) that can respond to queries from client machines formatted in the SQL language, a database language.

Standards—A dictated specifications that a PC, hardware or software follow or a PC, hardware or software that has become popular.

Standby Power Supply—A device consists of the battery hooked up parallel to the PC. When the SPS detects a power fluctuation, the system will switch over to the battery to power the PC. Of course, the SPS requires a small but measurable amount of time to switch over (usually one-half of one cycle of the AC current or less than 10 millisecond). Most SPSs will include built-in surge protection devices.

Star Topology—The most popular topology in use. It has each network device connect to a central point such as a hub, which acts as a multipoint connector.

Stateful Inspection—A packet filtering method that monitors the state of active connections and use this information to determine which network packets to allow through a firewall.

Static IP Addresses—An IP address that is manually configured on a host.

Static Routing—A method that uses table mappings established by the network administrator prior to the beginning of routing. These mappings do not change unless the network administrator alters them.

Statistical Time-Division Multiplexing (SDTM)—A modified method of Time-division multiplexing that analyzes the amount of data that each device needs to transmit and determines on-the-fly how much time each device should be allocated for data transmission on the cable or line. As a result, the SDTM uses the bandwidth more efficiently.

Storage Area Networks (SAN)—A high-speed subnetwork of shared storage devices. A SAN's architecture works in a way that makes all storage devices available to all servers on a LAN. If an individual application in a server cluster fails (but the node does not), the cluster service will typically try to restart the application on the same node. If that fails, it moves the application's resources and restarts them on another node of the server cluster. This process is called fail-over.

Straight-Through Cable—A cable that can be used to connect a network card to a hub has the same sequence of colored wires at both ends of the cable.

Straight Tip (ST) Connector—Probably the most widely used fiber-optic connector. It uses a BNC attachment mechanism similar to the Thinnet connector mechanism.

Stranded Cable—Cable that is typically used as patch cables between patch panels and hubs and between the computers and wall jacks. Since the stranded wire isn't as firm as solid wire, it is a little easier to work with.

Strong Password—Also known as complex passwords, are passwords that have mixed case, alphanumeric, and multiple characters. Such passwords are difficult to guess or crack with a password-cracking program.

Structured Query Language (SQL)—A standardized query language for requesting information from a database. Historically, SQL has been the favorite query language for database management systems running on minicomputers and mainframes. Increasingly, however, SQL is being supported by PC database systems because it supports distributed databases (databases that are spread out over several computer systems). This enables several users on a local-area network to access the same database simultaneously.

Subdomain Names—Part of the DNS system, additional names that an organization can create that are derived from the registered second-level domain name. The subdomain allows an organization to divide a domain into a department or geographical location, allowing the partitions of the domain name space to be more manageable. A subdomain must have a contiguous domain name space. This means that the domain name of a zone (child domain) is the name of that zone added to the name of the domain or parent domain.

Subkey—A subdivision or folder in the Windows registry.

Subnet—A simple network or smaller network which is used to form a larger network.

Subnet Mask—Numbers used to define which bits represent the network address (including the subnet number) and which bits represent the host address.

Subscriber (SC) Connectors—Sometimes known as the square connector, are typically latched connectors. This makes it impossible for the connector to be pulled out without releasing the connector's latch (usually by pressing some kind of button or release).

Subscriber Loop—The telephone line that runs from your home or office to the telephone company's central office (CO) or neighborhood switching station (often a small building with no windows). Also known as local loop and last mile.

Subtree—A subdivision of the Windows registry. Subtrees have names that begin with the string HKEY, which stands for Handle to a Key.

Supernetting—The process of combining multiple multiple IP address ranges into a single IP network such as combining several Class C networks.

Surge—An overvoltage that can stretch into milliseconds and that may damage the computer.

Surge Protector—A device designed to prevent most short-duration, high-intensity spikes and surges from reaching your PC by absorbing excess voltages.

SVC—See Temporary Virtual Circuit (SVC).

Switch—See Switching hub.

Switched Multimegabit Data Service (SMDS)—A high-speed, cell-relay, wide area network (WAN) service designed for LAN interconnection through the public telephone network.

Switching Hub—Sometimes referred to as switch or a layer 2 switch, is a fast multi-ported bridge, which builds a table of the MAC addresses of all the connected stations. It then reads the destination address of each packet and then forwards the packet to the correct port.

Symmetric Algorithms—Encryption algorithms that use the same key for encrypting and decrypting data, and everyone that is allowed to encrypt and decrypt the data has a copy of the key. This is also known as a shared secret.

Symmetric Encryption—The most basic form of encryption that uses a single key (secret key) for both encryption and decryption. It requires that each individual must possess a copy of a private key. Of course, for this work as intended, you must have a secure way to transport the key to other people.

Symmetric MultiProcessing (SMP)—A computer that uses two or more microprocessors that share the same memory. If software is written to use the multiple microprocessors, several programs can be executed at the same time or multithreaded applications can be executed faster.

SYN Attack—DoS attack in which an attacker attempts to send TCP connection request packets to a specific TCP port or ports faster than the target server can expire them. A successful SYN flood consumes all of the target's available TCP connection resources so that it is unable to service new client requests.

SYN Segment—The first segment of the three-way handshake. The information sent by computer includes source and destination port, starting sequence number, the receive buffer size, maximum TCP segment size, and the supported TCP options.

Synchronous—Devices that use a timing or clock signal to coordinate communications between the two devices.

Synchronous Digital Hierarchy (SDH)—An international standard that specifies synchronous data transmission over fiber optic cables.

SYS Volume—The primary volume on a NetWare server.

System Hardening—Making a system more secure. This includes removing unused services, ensuring that the latest security patches and service packs are installed, and limited the number of people with administrative permissions.

T

T-1 line—A digital line that has 24 64-Kbps channels for a bandwidth of 1.544 Mbps.

T-3 line—A digital line that has 672 64-Kbps channels for a bandwidth of 44.736 Mbps.

Tape Drives—A device that reads from and writes to a long magnetic tape. They are relatively inexpensive and offer large storage capacities making tape backup drives ideal for backing up hard drives on a regular basis.

T-Carrier System—The first successful system that converted the analog voice signal to a digital bit stream. While the T-carrier system was originally designed to carry voice calls between telephone company central offices, today it is used to transfer voice, data and video signals between different sites and to connect to the Internet.

Teardrop Attack—A fragmentation attack that involves two or more IP fragments that cannot be properly configured fragment offset numbers.

Telecommunication Network (TELNET)—A virtual terminal protocol (terminal emulation) allowing a user to log on to another TCP/IP host to access network resources. (RFC 854)

Telecommunications Closet—The floor serving facilities for horizontal cable distribution and can be used for intermediate and main cross-connects.

Telephony Server—A server that functions as an intelligent answering machine for the network. It can also perform call center and call-routing functions.

Temporal Key Integrity Protocol (TKIP, pronounced tee-kip)—A protocol that fixes the key reuse problem of WEP, that is, periodically using the same key to encrypt data. The TKIP process begins with a 128-bit "temporal key" shared among clients and access points. TKIP combines the temporal key with the client's MAC address and then adds a relatively large 16-octet initialization vector to produce the key that will encrypt the data. This procedure ensures that each station uses different key streams to encrypt the data. TKIP uses RC4 to perform the encryption, which is the same as WEP. A major difference from WEP, however, is that TKIP changes temporal keys every 10,000 packets. This provides a dynamic distribution method that significantly enhances the security of the network. TKIP also includes a message integrity check.

Temporary Virtual Circuit (SVC)—Virtual circuits that are dynamically established on demand and terminated when transmission is complete. Communication over an SVC consists of three phases: circuit establishment, data transfer, and circuit termination. Also known as a switched virtual circuit.

Terminal Access Controller Access Contol System Plus (TACACS+)—An authentication protocol that allows a remote access server to communicate with an authentication server. The system is used to determine whether a dial-in user should be allowed to access the network.

Terminal Emulation—A program for TCP/IP networks such as the Internet. The Telnet program runs on your computer and connects your PC to server on the network. You can then enter commands through the Telnet program and they will be exceuted as if you were entering them directly on the server console. This enables you to control the server and communicate with other servers on the network. See also Telecommunication Network.

Terrestrial Systems—A microwave system that uses relay towers to provide an unobstructed path over an extended distance. These line-of-sight systems use unidirectional parabolic dishes that must be aligned carefully.

Thicknet—See 10Base5.

Thin Client—A computer that is between a dumb terminal and a PC. A thin client is a client designed to be especially small so that the bulk of the data processing occurs on the server.

Thread—In programming, a part of a program that can execute independently of other parts. Operating systems that support multithreading enable programmers to design programs whose threaded parts can execute concurrently.

Threat—A person, place, or thing that has the potential to cause harm to a network or network resource.

Three-Way Handshake—The process that two computers use when establishing TCP communication sessions. This process involves the passing of three packets (SYN, SYN-ACK, and ACK), hence the name three-way handshake.

Ticket—A block of data that allows a user to prove their identity to a service. Each ticket is stored in a ticket cache on the user's local computer and is time stamped.

Ticket Granting Server (TGS)—A Kerberos-enabled server that grants the session tickets used by clients to start a session with a service.

Ticket Granting Ticket (TGT)—A ticket that is granted as part of the Kerberos authentication process and is stored in the ticket cache. The TGT is used to get other tickets that specific to a service.

Time-Division Multiplexing (TDM)—A method that divides the single channel into short time slots, allowing multiple devices to be assigned a time slot.

Time Domain Reflectometer (TDR)—The primary tool used to determine the length of a copper cable and to locate the impedance variations that are caused by opens, shorts, damaged cables, and interference with other systems. The TDR works much like radar, by transmitting a signal on a cable with the opposite end left open and measuring the amount of time that it takes for the signal's reflection to return to the transmitter. When you have this elapsed time measure, called the nominal velocity of propagation (NVP), and you know the speed at which electrons move through the cable, you can determine the length of the cable.

Token—A packet that is passed around the network in an orderly fashion from one device to the next to inform devices they can transmit data.

Token Passing—An access method that specifies that a network device only communicates over the network when it has the token (a special data packet that is generated by the first computer that comes online in a Token Ring network. The token is passed from one station to another around a ring. When a station gets a free token and transmits a packet, it travels in one direction around the ring, passing all of the other stations along the way.

Token Ring—A network technology that is a ring logical topology. For computers to access the network, they use a token.

Tone Generator and Probe—Sometimes called a "fox and hound" wire tracer, this type of device consists of a unit that you connect to a cable with a standard jack or an individual wire with alligator clips, which transmits a signal over the cable or wire. The other unit is a penlike probe that emits an audible tone when touched to the other end of the cable or wire or even its insulating sheath.

Top-Level Domains—Immediately below the root domain found on the top of the NDS tree. They indicate a country, region or type of organization. Three letter codes indicate the type of organization. For example, COM indicates Commercial (business) and EDU stands for educational institution.

Topology—Describes the appearance or layout of the network. Depending on how you look at the network, there is the physical topology and the logical topology.

Traceroute—A utility that traces a packet from your computer to an Internet host, showing how many hops the packet requires to reach the host and how long each hop takes. If you're visiting a website and pages are appearing slowly, you can use traceroute to figure out where the longest delays are occurring.

Transceivers—Devices that both transmit and receive analog or digital signals.

Transition State—A digital signal that represents data by how the signal transitions from high to low or low to high. A transition indicates a binary 1 while the absence of a transition represents a binary 0.

Transmission Control Protocol (TCP)—A protocol that provides connection-oriented, reliable communications for applications that typically transfer large amounts of data at one time or that require an acknowledgement for data received.

Transport Layer—An OSI-model layer that can be described as the middle layer that connects the lower and upper layers together. In addition, it is responsible for reliable transparent transfer of data (known as segments) between two end points. Since it provides end-to-end recovery of lost and corrupted packets and flow control, it deals with end-to-end error handling, dividing messages into smaller packets, numbers of the messages and the repackaging of messages.

Transport Layer Security (TLS)—The successor to the Secure Sockets Layer (SSL), TLS is composed of two layers: the TLS Record Protocol and the TLS Handshake Protocol. The TLS Record Protocol provides connection security with some encryption method such as the Data Encryption Standard (DES). The TLS Record Protocol can also be used without encryption. The TLS Handshake Protocol allows the server and client to authenticate each other and to negotiate an encryption algorithm and cryptographic keys before data is exchanged.

Trap—An unsolicited message sent by an SNMP agent to a SNMP management system when the agent detects that a certain type of event has occurred locally on the managed host. The SNMP management console receives a trap message is known as a trap destination. For example, a trap message might be sent when a system restarts or when a router link goes down.

Trivial File Transfer Protocol (TFTP)—A simple form of the File Transfer Protocol (FTP). TFTP uses the User Datagram Protocol (UDP) and provides no security features. It is often used by servers to boot diskless workstations, X-terminals, and routers.

Trojan Horse—A seemingly useful or benign program that when activated performs malicious or illicit action, such as destroying files.

Trunk—The single cable usually designed to carry the bulk of the network traffic to other sites or to connect multiple network or buildings at a site.

Trust—A relationship that allows a CA to trust a certificate issued by another CA.

Trust Path—A logical path that links several certification authorities together so that the trust relationship can extend beyond two certification authorities that have formed a trust.

Trust Relationship—A relationship between domains that makes it possible for users in one domain to access resources in another domain. The domain that grants access to its resources is known as the trusting domain. The domain that accesses the resources is known as the trusting domain.

Tunnel—The logical connection through which the packets travel in a virtual private network (VPN).

Tunneling—The method for transferring data packets over the Internet or other public network, providing the security and features formerly available only on private networks. A tunneling protocol encapsulates the data packet in a header that provides routing information to enable the encapsulated payload to securely traverse the network.

Twisted Pair—Consists of two insulated copper wires twisted around each other. While each pair acts as a single communication link, twisted pair are usually bundled together into a cable and wrapped in a protective sheath.

Two-Factor Authentication—A system that uses two authentication methods such as smart cards and a password.

U

Undervoltages—When the computer gets less voltage than needed to run properly.

Unicast—Communication that occurs when a single sender communicates with a single receiver over the network.

Uniform Naming Convention (UNC)—See Universal Naming Convention (UNC).

Uninterruptible Power Supply—A device that has a battery connected in series with the PC. The AC power is connected directly to the battery. Since the battery always provides clean power, the PC is protected against the overvoltages and undervoltages.

Universal Asynchronous Receiver/Transmitter (UART)—A single IC chip that is the translator between the serial device and the system bus and is the component that processes, transmits, and receives data.

Universal Naming Convention (UNC)—Also known as Universal Naming Convention is a PC format for specifying the location of resources on a local-area network (LAN). UNC uses the \\server-name\shared-resource- pathname format.

Universal Security Group—A Windows NT family group that is only available in native mode. It can contain users, universal groups and global groups from any domain and it can be assigned rights and permissions to any network resource in any domain in the domain tree or forest.

UNIX—A multiuser, multitasking operating, is the grandfather of network operating systems, which was developed at Bell Labs in the early 1970s.

Unshielded Twisted Pair (UTP)—The same type of cable that is used with telephones and is the most common cable used in networks. UTP cable consists of two pairs or four pairs of twisted wires.

User—A person that logs onto a computer or accesses a network resource.

User Account—An account that represents the user and enables a user to log on to a network.

User Datagram Protocol (UDP)—A TCP/IP protocol that provides connectionless communications and does not guarantee that packets will be delivered. Applications that use UDP typically transfer small amounts of data at one. Reliable delivery is the responsibility of the application.

User Mode—A Windows NT family mode that run in Ring 3 of the Intel 386 microprocessor protection model, which are protected by the operating system. It is a less privileged processor mode that has no direct access to hardware and can only access its own address space. Since programs running in Ring 3 have very little privilege to programs running in Ring 0 (Kernel mode), the programs in User mode should not be able to cause problems with components in Kernel mode.

Username—A name used to identify a user account, so that it can keep track of the user.

User Profile—In Windows, a collection of folders and data that stores the user's current desktop environment and application settings.

User-Level Security Model—A model that a user has a user account that includes a user name and password. The user account is provided with an Access Control List (ACL) each time the user logs on to the network. A user can only access a network resource if that resource is on the ACL. A user cannot access a network resource if a resource is not on the ACL. The user-level security model allows a network administrator to manage network security from a central network location.

An administrator would normally assign users to group accounts and then grant the group accounts permissions to resources on the network.

V

VFAT—An enhanced version of the FAT structure, which allows Windows to support long file names (LFN) up to 255 characters. If someone refers to FAT, they probably mean VFAT.

Vi—A text editor used on Linux machines.

Virtual Circuit—A logical circuit created to ensure reliable communications between two network devices. To provide this, it provides a bi-directional communications path from one device to another and is uniquely identified by some type of identifier. A number of virtual circuits can be multiplexed into a single physical circuit for transmission across the network.

Virtual File System (VFS)—A kernel software layer used on Linux machines that handles all system calls related to the Linux file system.

Virtual Local Area Networks (VLANs)—A collection of nodes that are grouped together in a single broadcast domain that is based on something other than physical location. A VLAN is a switched network that is logically segmented on an organizational basis, by functions, project teams, or applications rather than on a physical or geographical basis.

Virtual Private Network (VPN)—A protocol that uses a public or shared network (such as the Internet or a campus intranet) to create a secure, private network connection between a client and a server. The VPN client cloaks each packet in a wrapper that allows it to sneak (or tunnel) unnoticed through the shared network. When the packet gets to its destination, the VPN server removes the wrapper, deciphers the packet inside and processes the data.

Virus—A program designed to replicate and spread, generally without the knowledge or permission of the user.

Virus Hoax—A letter or email message warning you about a virus that does not exist.

Voltmeter—A device that measures voltage output or voltage signal.

Volume—A fixed amount of storage on a disk or tape. The term volume is often used as a synonym for the storage medium itself, but it is possible for a single disk to contain more than one volume or for a volume to span more than one disk.

Vulnerability—A point where a resource is susceptible to attack. It can be thought of as a weakness.

W

WAP (Wireless Application Protocol)—A specification for a set of communication protocols to standardize the way that wireless devices with limited capability, such as cellular telephones and radio transceivers, can be used for Internet access, including email, the World Wide Web, newsgroups, and Internet Relay Chat (IRC).

War Dialing—A technique used to dial all of the telephone numbers in a specified range, and then record those that have a modem connected. Once the phone numbers that have modems are identified, an attacker can redial the system and attempt to break into the computer system.

War Driving—A technique in which a person with a portable device drives around attempting to locate wireless access points.

Warm Site—A site that the network service and data are available most of the time (more than 85 percent of the time). The data and services are less critical than those in a hot site. With hot-site technologies, all fault tolerance procedures are automatic and are controlled by the NOS. Warm-site technology requires a little more administrative intervention, but they aren't as expensive as the hot site.

Web Browser—The client program/software that you run on your local machine to gain access to a web server. It receives the HTML commands, interprets the HTML and displays the results.

Web Pages—A document on the World Wide Web. Every Web page is identified by a unique URL (Uniform Resource Locator).

Web Server—A server that runs WWW and FTP services for access by uses of the intranet or the Internet.

Web Spoofing—When an attacker sets up a Web page or website that looks like a legitimate website. The attacker then attempts to redirect other systems in an attempt to steal passwords, credit cards, or gather other potentially valuable information.

Wide Area Network (WAN)—A network uses long-range telecommunication links to connect the network computers over long distances and often consists of two or more smaller LANs. Typically, the LANs are connected through public networks, such as the public telephone system.

Wi-Fi—Short for wireless fidelity and is another name for IEEE 802.11b. Wi-Fi is used in place of 802.11b in the same way that "Ethernet" is used in place of IEEE 802.3.

Windows 2000—A newer operating system based on the Windows NT architecture.

Windows Driver Model (WDM)—A driver technology developed by Microsoft to create drivers that are source-code compatible for Windows 98, 2000, Me, and XP. WDM works by channeling some of the work of the device driver into portions of the code that are integrated into the operating system. These portions of code handle all of the low-level buffer management, including DMA and Plug and Play device enumeration. The WDM device driver becomes more streamlined with less code and works at greater efficiency.

Windows Internet Naming Service (WINS)—A system that contains a database of IP addresses and NetBIOS (computer names) that update dynamically. It is used to resolve IP addresses from the computer names.

Windows NT—An operating system that can act as a high-performance network operating system, which is robust in features and services, security, performance and upgradeability. While NT stands for New Technology, it is several years old.

Windows NT Directory Service (NTDS)—The system of domains and trusts for a Windows NT Server network. To manage the users and groups of a domain and to setup trust with other domains (trusts allow users to access resources in other domains), you use the User Manager for Domains program.

WINS Proxy Agent—A WINS-enabled computer configured to act on behalf of other host computer that cannot directly use WINS. WINS proxies help resolve NetBIOS name queries for computers located on a subnet where there is not a WINS server by hearing broadcast on the subnet of the proxy agent and forward those responses directly to a WINS server. This keeps the broadcast local, yet get responses from a WINS server without using the P-node.

WINS Replication Partner—A computer that duplicates WINS databases to other WINS servers.

WinNuke—A Windows program that sends special TCP/IP packets with an invalid TCP header. Windows will crash when it receive one of the packets because of the way Windows TCP/IP stack handles bad data in the TCP header. Instead of returning an error code or rejecting the bad data, it sends the computer to the **"blue screen of death"**.

Winsock—A programming interface and supporting program that handles input/output requests for Internet applications in a Windows operating system. It's called Winsock because it's an adaptation for Windows of the Berkeley UNIX sockets interface.

Wire Map Tester—A device that uses a wire map testing, which transmits signals through each wire in a copper twisted-pair cable to determine if it is connected to the correct pin at the other end.

Wired Equivalent Privacy (WEP)—A form of encryption used by wireless communication.

Wireless Application Protocol (WAP)—Provides a suite of protocols used for security communications in layers 3 through 7. The Communications model can be compared to the seven-layer OSI model.

Wireless LAN (WLAN)—A local area network without wires that transfer data through the air using radio frequencies.

Wireless Spectrum—A continuum of electromagnetic waves, with varying frequencies and wavelengths, that are used for telecommunications.

Wireless Transport Layer Security (WTLS)—The security level for Wireless Application Protocol (WAP) applications. Based on Transport Layer Security (TLS) v1.0 (a security layer used in the Internet, equivalent to Secure Socket Layer 3.1), WTLS was developed to address the problematic issues surrounding mobile network devices—such as limited processing power and memory capacity, and low bandwidth—and to provide adequate authentication, data integrity, and privacy protection mechanisms.

Work Area—The area that includes the station equipment, patch cable, and adapters (such as a media filter).

Workgroup—(1) A peer-to-peer network (2). A logical subgroup of computers, typically used in peer-to-peer networks. In a workgroup, each computer has its own user and group account information. The user information is not shared wtih other workgroup computers.

Workstation—(1) In networking, workstation refers to any computer connected to a local-area network. It could be a workstation or a personal computer. (2) A type of computer used for engineering applications (CAD/CAM), desktop publishing, software development, and other types of applications that require a moderate amount of computing power and relatively high-quality graphics capabilities.

Word Wide Web (WWW)—A system of Internet servers that support specially formatted documents.

Worm—A program or algorithm that replicates itself over a computer network and usually performs malicious actions, such as using up the computer's resources and possibly shutting the system down. Typically, a worm enters the computer because of vulnerabilities available in the computer's operating system.

X

X.500—A directory service which uses a hierarchical approach, where objects are organized similar to the files and folders on a hard drive.

X.509 Certificates—The most widely used digital certificates.

Index

Boldface page numbers indicate the primary pages for an entry.